Appraisal, Market Analysis, and Public Policy in Real Estate

Essays in Honor of James A. Graaskamp

Appraisal, Market Analysis, and Public Policy in Real Estate

Essays in Honor of James A. Graaskamp

edited by

James R. DeLisle
Equitable Real Estate Investment Management, Inc.

and

J. Sa-Aadu
University of Iowa

The American Real Estate Society

Kluwer Academic Publishers

Boston / Dordrecht / London

Distributors for North America:
Kluwer Academic Publishers
101 Philip Drive
Assinippi Park
Norwell, Massachusetts 02061 USA

Distributors for all other countries:
Kluwer Academic Publishers Group
Distribution Centre
Post Office Box 322
3300 AH Dordrecht, THE NETHERLANDS

Library of Congress Cataloging-in-Publication Data

Appraisal, market analysis, and public policy in real estate: essays
 in honor of James A. Graaskamp / edited by James DeLisle and
 J. Sa-Aadu.
  p. cm.
 ISBN 0-7923-9344-9
 1. Real estate business. 2. Real property—Valuation. 3. Real
 estate development. 4. Graaskamp, James A.—Contributions in
 real estate business. I. DeLisle, James R. II. Sa-Aadu, Jarjisu.
 III. Graaskamp, James A.
 HD1375.A66 1933
 333.33'2—dc20   93–16953
                                                                      CIP

Copyright © 1994 by American Real Estate Society

All rights reserved. No part ot this publication may be reproduced,
stored in a retrieval system or transmitted in any form or by any means,
mechanical, photo-copying, recording, or otherwise, without the prior
written permission of the published, Kluwer Academic Publishers, 101
Philip Drive, Assinippi Park, Norwell, Massachusetts 02061

Printed on acid-free paper.

Printed in the United States of America

AMERICAN REAL ESTATE SOCIETY
1993 INSTITUTIONAL SPONSORS

AEtna Realty Investors*
Alex Brown Kleinwort Benson Realty Advisors*
Appraisal Institute
Building and Office Managers Institute*
Business One Irwin*
CIGNA Investments
Counselors of Real Estate
Dryden Press
Equitable Real Estate Investment Management
Industrial Development Research Council
Institute of Real Estate Management
Institutional Real Estate
International Association of Corporate Real Estate Executives
International Council of Shopping Centers
JMB Institutional Realty
MIG Realty Advisors*
National Association of Industrial and Office Parks
National Association of REALTORs*
Pension Real Estate Association*
Price Waterhouse*
Prudential Realty Group
Real Estate Research Corporation*
Real Estate Consulting Group of Deloitte & Touche
The Roulac Group
The RREEF Funds
Society of Industrial and Office REALTORS^R
Urban Land Institute

*New for 1993

1993 INSTITUTIONAL MEMBERS

AMB Institutional Realty Advisors
Ameritech Applied Technology
Austin Valuation Consultants
Charles M. Ritley Associates
Citadel Realty
CN Real Estate
CNL Institutional Advisors
Columbia Union College
Coopers & Lybrand
CRM, Inc.
Crosson Dannis, Inc.
Dearborn Financial Publishing, Inc.
Great-West Life
Gruen & Gruen Associates
Howell-Viggers Corporation
The Institutional Real Estate Letter
Investment Corporation of Saskatchewan
IRE Data Group
John Wiley & Sons, Inc.
Karsten Realty Advisors
Lincoln Graduate Center
Lincoln Institute of Land Policy
Merrill Lynch Hubbard
National Association of Independent Fee Appraisers
National Association of Master Appraisers
National Association of Real Estate Appraisers
National Association of Review Appraisers and Mortgage Underwriters
Principle Financial Group
Prentice-Hall, Inc.
Richard D. Irwin, Inc.
Real Estate Center at Texas A&M University
The Real Estate Department of Georgia State University
South-Western Publishing Company, College Division
Summa Corporation
Stefano and Associates
The Townsend Group
University of Hong Kong
University of Quebec at Montreal
US F&G Realty Advisors
West Educational Publishing

1993 SUSTAINING MEMBERS OF THE AMERICAN REAL ESTATE SOCIETY

Joseph D. Albert
James Madison University

Dennis H. Anderson
L.W. Ellwood & Co.

John S. Baen
University of North Texas

Stan Banton
Banton Associates

John D. Benjamin
American University

J. Thomas Black
Urban Land Institute

Waldo L. Born
Eastern Illinois University

Terrence M. Clauretie
University of Nevada at Las Vegas

Donald W. Conley
American Institute of Real Estate Appraisers

James R. Cooper
Georgia State University

Charles G. Dannis
Crosson Dannis, Inc.

James R. DeLisle
Equitable Real Estate Investment Management

Joseph B. Diehl
NCREIF

Mark G. Dotzour
Wichita State University

Donald R. Epley
Mississippi State University

John L. Glascock
Louisiana State University

William C. Goolsby
Washington State University

G. Hayden Green
University of Alaska at Anchorage

D. Wylie Greig
The RREEF Funds

Karl L. Guntermann
Arizona State University

Richard L. Haney
Texas A&M University

Patricia Hart
American University

Forrest E. Huffman
Temple University

Jerome R. Jakubovitz
MAI

G. Donald Jud
University of North Carolina at Greensboro

Steven D. Kapplin
University of South Florida

George R. Karvel
St. Cloud State University

James B. Kau
University of Georgia

William N. Kinnard, Jr.
Real Estate Counseling Group of Connecticut

Ed G. Lane
Lane Consultants

Donald R. Levi
Wichita State University

Joseph Lipscomb
Texas Christian University

Christopher A. Manning
Loyola Marymount University

Thomas E. McCue
Duquesne University

Willard McIntosh
MIG Realty Advisors

John McMahan
McMahan Real Estate Advisors

Ivan J. Miestchovich Jr.
University of New Orleans

Philip S. Mitchell
Mitchell & Associates

Glenn R. Mueller
Alex, Brown, Kleinwort, Benson Realty Advisors

F.C. Neil Myer
Cleveland State University

Theron R. Nelson
University of North Dakota

Hugh O. Nourse
University of Georgia

Thomas D. Pearson
Thomas D. Pearson & Associates

Stephen A. Pyhrr
Davis & Associates

Stephen E. Roulac
The Roulac Group

(continued)

Jack H. Rubens
Bryant College

Jay Sa-Aadu
University of Iowa

Arthur L. Schwartz, Jr.
University of South Florida

C. F. Sirmans
University of Connecticut

Almon R. "Bud" Smith
Ohio Association of REALTORS

C. Ray Smith
University of Virginia

Halbert C. Smith
University of Florida

Rocky Tarantello
Tarantello & Company

Wayne A. Tenenbaum
Tenenbaum Hill Associates

James R. Webb
Cleveland State University

Larry E. Wofford
C&L Systems Corporation

Elaine M. Worzala
Colorado State University

Charles H. Wurtzebach
JMB Institutional Realty

Alan J. Ziobrowski
Lander College

CONTENTS

Editorial Board — v
About the Editors — xiii
James A. Graaskamp Award — xvi
Introduction — 1

Section I: Philosophical Issues

1
The Evolution of Real Estate Decisions — 15
Stephen E. Roulac

2
The Search for a Discipline: The Philosophy and the Paradigms — 65
Terry V. Grissom and Crocker H. Liu

3
Crisis in Methodology: Paradigms vs. Practice in Real Estate Research — 107
John M. Clapp, Michael A. Goldberg, and Dowell Myers

4
Is There a Body of Knowledge in Real Estate?: Some Mutterings about Mattering — 133
Austin J. Jaffe

Section II: Appraisal, Feasibility, and Special Use Analysis

5
The Price of Wilderness and Scenic Beauty: A Methodology for the Inventory and Appraisal of Wilderness and Scenic Land — 149
Michael L. Robbins and Sean C. Ahearn

6
Using Prior Information to Improve Estimation Efficiency and Predictive Performance for Mass Appraisal 183
Otis W. Gilley and R. Kelley Pace

7
PHYS-FI: A Physical-Financial Model for Design Economy Trade-Offs 203
M. Atef Sharkawy

8
An Insight into the Ideas of Professor James A. Graaskamp on Practice and Reform in Appraisal 237
R. R. Fraser and E. M. Worzala

Section III: Market Analysis and Trade Area Delineation

9
A Four-Square Design for Relating the Two Essential Dimensions of Real Estate Market Studies 259
Dowell Myers and Kenneth Beck

10
Refining Empirical Procedures for Market Area Delineation 289
Kim Peterson

11
An Investigation into the Competition Between the Downtown Shopping Area and the Suburban Shopping Mall 307
Donald H. Bleich

12
Multiple Store Trade Area Relationships and Logistic Response Function Estimation 325
Craig E. Stanley

Section IV: Public Policy Issues

13
Transfer of Ownership Rights via Rent Control 347
William N. Kinnard, Jr.

14
Interpreting Monte Carlo Simulation with Generalized Sensitivity Analysis: The Case of Historic Rehabilitation 381
George A. Overstreet, Jr. and Geoffrey M. Rubin

15
Toward Socially Efficient Broker Behavior in Factual Representations 413
Donald R. Levi, Curtis D. Terflinger, and Samuel C. Webb

CONTENTS

**16
The Price of Owner-Occupied Housing Services: 1973–1989**   425
David C. Ling

**17
The Measurement of Effective Rent**   463
Cynthia A. Kroll and Sam Taff

About the Editors

James R. De Lisle

James R. DeLisle is Senior Vice President in charge of Equitable Real Estate's Investment Research Department. He oversees all research activities and provides portfolio managers with strategic and tactical information in support of portfolio planning and investment decision-making. He also serves on several key committees, including the Investment Committee, New Products Committee, and Retail Coordination Committee. Additionally, he is a member of the Strategic Information Steering Committee, which is charged with making the most effective usage of the company's data resources through implementation of a unified system in the home and field offices.

DeLisle began his real estate career in 1972, after spending two years in the National Football League. He has had a wide array of real estate experience including consulting and development, and has worked for over five years in institutional investment research and portfolio management. He has published more than twenty-five articles on real estate in academic and industry journals, as well as a number of proprietary publications on behalf of Equitable Real Estate. He is an active member of numerous major real estate industry groups and serves on the Board of Directors of the American Real Estate Society. He is an active public speaker on institutional real estate investment, portfolio management, and industry trends and outlook.

DeLisle holds a Ph.D. in real estate and urban land economics, an M.S. in marketing research, and a BBA in real estate from the University of Wisconsin—Madison. He is a protege of the late James A. Graaskamp, a Wisconsin professor and the leading proponent of extending theoretical and applied academic research concepts to real estate decision making. DeLisle taught at the university level for more than ten years, while pursuing selective consulting activities. He was a tenured associate professor of real estate at the University of Texas—El Paso and at Florida State University. At Florida State, he established and directed the university's real estate research center. He also has been a visiting professor and lecturer at the University of Wisconsin.

J. Sa-Aadu

Dr. J. Sa-Aadu is currently Associate Professor and Chairman, Department of Finance, University of Iowa, Iowa City, Iowa. Dr. Sa-Aadu obtained his Ph.D. from the University of Wisconsin and has also held faculty positions at the University of Florida and Louisiana State University.

Professor Sa-Aadu's articles have appeared in journals such as *Land Economics*, *Journal of the American Real Estate and Urban Economics Association*, *Journal of Real Estate Finance and Economics*, *Public Finance Quarterly*, *Journal of Urban Economics*, and *Journal of Property Finance*. He currently serves on the editorial boards of the *Journal of Real Estate Research*, the *Journal of the American Real Estate and Urban Economics Association*, and *the Journal of Real Estate Finance and Economics*, and he is also on the Board of Directors of the American Real Estate and Urban Economics Association.

THE AMERICAN REAL ESTATE SOCIETY

Proudly Presents the

James A. Graaskamp Award

ESSAYS IN HONOR OF JAMES A GRAASKAMP

EDITORIAL BOARD

CO-EDITORS

James R. DeLisle
Equitable Real Estate Investment Management, Inc.
Atlanta, GA 30326

J. Sa-Aadu
University of Iowa
Iowa City, IA 52242

ASSOCIATE EDITORS

Richard B. Andrews†
University of Wisconsin-Madison

Crocker Liu
New York University

Austin Jaffe
Pennsyvania State University

David Hartzel
University of North Carolina

Terry V. Grissom
Price Waterhouse

Kerry Vandell
University of Wisconsin-Madison

Norm Miller
University of Cincinnati

James D. Shilling
University of Wisconsin-Madison

Rick Peiser
University of Southern California

The Co-Editors acknowledge the assistance of (alphabetically)

Roger Cannady
Peter F. Colwell
Jack Corgel
David Geltner
Donald Jud
William Kinnard
David Ling
Kenneth M. Lusht

Isaac Megbolugbe
Kim Paterson
Dowell Myers
Atef Sharkawy
G. Stacy Sirmans
Marc Smith
Thomas G. Thibodeau
James R. Webb

THE JAMES A. GRAASKAMP AWARD

The James A. Graaskamp award was established in 1990 by the American Real Estate Society to honor and eulogize this great real estate academician and practicing professional. Each year nominations are solicited by mail from the members of the American Real Estate Society (ARES) with the following letter.

Call for Nominations:

This award is in honor of James A. Graaskamp. He was an avid supporter of ARES but, more importantly, he was a pioneer of iconoclastic thought and action in the development of a multidisciplinary philosophy of real estate. Jim was aptly described by Richard U. Ratcliff as "*a man of broad talent, unobtrusive generosity, unshakable courage, and a true and cherished friend.*" This award is to be made as often as annually, but may be given on an occasional basis. If possible, a monetary stipend and/or other considerations will accompany the plaque that is given with the award. The recipient must have exhibited both imagination and bold leadership toward developing new thought and insights in real estate research and practice. Although a distinguished record of achievements may be associated with a candidate, the Grasskamp Award should not be considered an achievement award.

The recipient of the James A. Grasskamp Award shall be determined by a committee of the following five people:

Immediate Past President of ARES, Chairperson (_____).

President of ARES (_____).

President Elect of ARES (_____).

Editor, *The Journal of Real Estate Research* (_____).

Executive Director of ARES (_____).

Nominations should be made to the chairperson of the committee (_____) at the address below by January 15. The nomination should be in a letter that makes the case for the person being nominated. A complete and current resume of the person being nominated must accompany the nomination. A person may not nominate him/her self.

The results of the process will announced at the general membership meeting held during the annual ARES Conference. In addition, one page of *The Journal of Real Estate Research* well be used to announce the results for all issues during the year.

Thus far there have been only two winners of this award. They are

1990	**JAMES R. WEBB**, "In recognition of his contribution to significantly changing the model of real estate professional organizations, the role they play, and the service they provide through his effforts to develop the American Real Estate Society."
1991	**NO WINNER**
1992	**HUGH O. NOURSE**, "In recognition of his contribution to academic and professional real estate through his leadership, scholarship, and perseverance in making the management of corporate real estate assets a viable, important, and fruitful area of research and teaching."
1993	**NO WINNER**

INTRODUCTION

The real estate discipline is at a crossroads affecting both the industry and the academic spheres. In the industry, there is an attempt to make the transition back from asset-based demand analysis that created the current glut to spatial demand analysis that focuses on tenant needs. Recently, however, movements to prolong the asset-based side of the spectrum, reflected by securitization of the asset class and changes in ownership structure, have emerged. In the academic community, the discipline has continued to move from its urban land economics foundation toward a more contemporary financial analysis model. It is not clear how these issues will be resolved in the short term. However, in the long term, if the discipline is to survive, focus must be turned to the underlying fundamentals that determine the success or failure of participants who invest in the asset class. Dr. James A. Graaskamp was one of the leading proponents of the balanced industry and academic view of the world necessary to implement such a program.

The purpose of this monograph is twofold: first, to recognize the contribution that Graaskamp made to the real estate discipline, both on the industry and academic side, and, second, to advance the discipline. Jim Graaskamp was a multidimensional man who built his reputation on applied research and decision making, but based many of his positions on a solid theoretical framework. This theoretical framework was multidisciplinary in nature, drawing from the strong urban land economics tradition that developed at Wisconsin in the 1930s. The theoretical foundation also included the behavioral theories Richard U. Ratcliff extended to real estate appraisal. Graaskamp was also intrigued by organizational theory and information processing.

Before the articles in this monograph are discussed, it may be useful to review some of Graaskamp's positions on the various issues that face the discipline in industry and academia. On the academic side, Graaskamp prided himself on establishing a program at the University of Wisconsin that was "at the cutting edge of education and land ethics, analytical technique, and improved definition of concepts, business opportunities and social rules for the real estate industry." He saw the mission of the university curriculum to have several dimensions, including: training real estate enterprise managers who have synthesized the multiple disciplines, instilling an ethic in decision makers that recognizes land as a limited resource, recruiting and motivation talent for careers in real estate related enterprise, and, finally, providing students with the foundation necessary to make them productive contributors to both public and private sector real estate decisions.

In terms of the real estate process, Graaskamp saw it as a dynamic system charged with balancing the spatial and economic needs of three constituencies: space users, space producers, and public representatives. Even though the various participants in the real estate process had different levels of economic motivation, he saw each entity as operating as a cash cycle enterprise with different goals, objectives, and bottom lines. Instead of maximizing the position of any one member of this triad, he saw the challenge of real estate to train students on how to balance the competing positions to achieve a socially desirable equilibrium.

Graaskamp employed three basic approaches to develop the Wisconsin real estate program so that it could produce the quantity and quality of students who could achieve the social and economic balance that he espoused. First, he assembled a multidisciplinary pool of faculty members, each of whom had expertise in a specific discipline ranging from demography to civil engineering. Second, he forced his business students to take courses outside of the business school in areas that would "round them out" so that they could understand the broader context within which real estate decisions should be made. Finally, he solicited non-business students for his courses so that he could establish a dialogue between the producers and regulators of space that would affect the future decisions.

INTRODUCTION

Graaskamp was a believer in the importance of objectivity in the academic environment, and was a strong proponent of independent support for research and teaching that could remove university and/or industry biases that might affect the output of faculty members. He stated, "Real estate educators must remain independent of the politics involved in the industry... the choosing of instructors, text, and subject matter should rest wholly with an independent body of real estate educators." Despite this strong call for objectivity, Graaskamp also argued that academic research should be socially and pragmatically relevant. He recognized that if academicians did not respond to industry issues, then the industry could bypass these barriers and move outside of the context of a traditional business school environment.

With respect to his industry contributions, Graaskamp pursued four avenues to achieve his goals and objectives. First, he was an active participant in academic and professional associations, ranging from The American Real Estate Society to PREA (Pension Real Estate Association). Within each of the organizations to which he belonged, he was an active participant and a spokesperson. Second, he was a forceful speaker at trade associations and other national forums. Third, he maintained an active consulting operation, which helped him maintain contact with real world decisions and provided a laboratory in which he could develop and refine his case approach to teaching. Finally, he was an active participant in litigation, whereby he sought to further the industry by establishing precedents that could help set the legal environment within which real estate decisions would be made. This involvement ranged from expert witness in individual cases to testifying before congress on the appraisal reform movement.

This monograph is organized into the four functional areas that are reflective of the multidisciplinary philosophy of Graaskamp. The first section focuses on theoretical or philosophical issues. The second section explores real estate appraisal, feasibility, and special use analysis: The third section explores market analysis and trade area delineation, which are critical to spatial analysis of real estate. The final section explores public policy issues.

Section I: Theoretical and Philosophical Issues

The first paper in the series, "The Evolution of Real Estate Decisions" by Roulac, presents a review of the evolution of real estate decision making. The author takes a long-term historical view of changes in real estate decisions from 1950 to 1990, and then provides an outlook that carries into the twenty-first century. Over the same time period, he traces the evolution of real estate enterprise concerns, addressing such issues as geographic scope, organizational focus, developmental emphasis, sources of capital, financial control, and housing finance. He expands his discussion of real estate capital markets and provides a framework within which the major structural changes can be evaluated. Finally, the author traces the evolution of decision tools and information requirements, thereby establishing a foundation against which current real estate decision and academic programs can be positioned. He concludes that Graaskamp's decision style that involved conceptual thinking and creativity is the appropriate and necessary perspective from which real estate should be approached.

"The Search for a Discipline: The Philosophy and the Paradigms," by Grissom and Liu, provides an exhaustive review of the struggle that the real estate discipline has undergone in its attempt to evolve a theoretical structure. The authors begin the discussion with a review of the debate that evolved as to whether or not real estate can qualify as a discipline. The basic question the authors address is whether the field of study is an academic discipline, a functional area of study, or simply a collection of trade preparation courses. Although they recognize the importance of the financial dimension to real estate, they argue that the spatial dimension must be integrated into the financial perspective to fully understand the underlying market fundamentals. The authors discuss various paradigms that link spatial and capital issues. The first paradigm builds on some of Graaskamp's work regarding the space/time, money/time equation of real estate investment analysis. The authors then attempt to integrate urban land economics and urban economics theories into contemporary decision making. They conclude that real estate can be an organized discipline, although it does not do so by embracing a unified field theory, but by integrating a variety of approaches.

In the "Crisis in Methodology: Paradigms vs. Practice in Real Estate Research," Clapp, Goldberg, and Myers explore the real estate discipline in terms of scientific thought. The authors pay particular attention to the perceived gap between industry and academia, explore how this gap evolved, and discuss the efforts that have been made and must be made to close it. The authors conclude that the existing paradigms that are used in real estate are inappropriate in that they do not satisfy the decision support needs of the industry. They review alternative modes of thought that would help strengthen the discipline and call for new research initiatives

INTRODUCTION 5

that would develop and refine new paradigms that focus on problem solving in a real world context.

Jaffe provides a wrap-up to the discussion of the theoretical side of the discipline in his paper entitled "Is There a Body of Knowledge in Real Estate: Some Mutterings About Mattering." In this article, Jaffe explores the evolution of real estate as a discipline within the broader academic environment. The purpose of his essay is to provide some food for thought on the topic of how real estate is postured within the broader university community. He notes that, relative to other disciplines, real estate is rather young, with the current faculty leaders constituting the second generation of full time academicians in the field. Despite the progress that has been made in the evolution of real estate as a distinct discipline, the author raises the warning flag that structural changes that define the political environment within universities would become increasingly hostile toward real estate curricula. Although he does not offer answers to the various issues that the trend raises, he attempts to serve as a catalyst toward discussion that would lead to further refinement of the role of the discipline.

Section II: Appraisal, Feasibility, and Special Use Analysis

One of Graaskamp's major contributions to real estate was his work in the appraisal area. The papers presented in this section provide some insights into how Graaskamp approached the appraisal process in specific, as well as how he approached the problem solving process surrounding valuation in general. In the article entitled "The Price of Wilderness and Scenic Beauty: A Methodology for the Inventory and Appraisal of Wilderness and Scenic Land," Robbins and Ahearn attempt to articulate the Graaskamp philosophy toward real estate problem solving with regard to appraisal. The authors present the appraisal of a 22,000 acre wilderness tract in the Alpine Lakes area in the state of Washington. The article is particularly appropriate for this monograph in that James A. Graaskamp was the lead researcher on the special use appraisal assignment. The article is noteworthy in that it establishes several precedents, including (1) highest and best use of the subject property was wilderness, vs. timber, (2) pricing of the property under the wilderness scenario could be quantified, and (3) by utilizing spatial models the subject could be appraised using traditional market comparison analysis. As a result of the appraisal assignment, the value of the parcel was concluded to be in excess of 2.5 times the value based on the raw timber itself.

One of Graaskamp's major contributions to the appraisal practice was the MKTCOMP model, he developed with some University of Wisconsin colleagues in the latter 1960s and early 1970s. The paper by Gilley and Pace entitled "Using Prior Information to Improve Estimation Efficiency and Predictive Performance for Mass Appraisal" provides an extension of some of Graaskamp's work to mass appraisal type assignments. The authors recognize the use of statistical models in mass appraisal but note that there are several limitations to their application. Despite high levels of R-square, the authors find the failure to explain "out of sample" performance and the failure to satisfy the intuitive filter regarding parameter estimates to render them invalid. They also recognize that the models that are currently used that exhibit high R-squares may do so due to the inclusion of models with a large number of correlated variables that invalidate them from a statistical perspective. The authors employ Monte Carlo simulations to test the parameters generated by IRLS (inequality-restricted least squares) vs. OLS (ordinary least squares) models. The authors concluded that IRLS could produce a lower mean absolute error, thus supporting the potential value added by prior information.

One of Graaskamp's major philosophical points regarding real estate appraisal was that it is a subset of a larger problem labeled *real estate feasibility analysis*. He noted that many of the problems that the industry faced were the result of separating the risks and reward of real estate through structured arrangements in which the success of a particular position could be insulated from the success of the underlying spatial asset relative to tenant demand. In "PHYS-FI: A Physical-Financial Model for Design Economy Trade-Offs," Sharkawy provides a conceptual framework within which developers and investors can evaluate the design economy trade-off decisions that invariably must be made. The author recognizes that real estate is a cash cycle enterprise. He notes that to support the production of real estate the producer group must attract capital over the entire investment life cycle. He notes that design or physical models are inductive and include a synthesis of individual decisions that are made within the framework of a broader choice set. On the other hand, financial decisions are deductive and operate within the framework of utility theory. The model integrates that investment cycle stage with the inherent decisions that must be made during the design stage. He concludes that the PHYS-FI framework provides a useful tool for identifying and improving planning, development, or rehab repositioning decisions that must be made at various stages of the investment life cycle.

Frazier and Worzala, in their paper "An Insight into the Ideas of Professor James A. Graaskamp on Practice and Reform in Appraisal," attempt to summarize and extend the contribution that Graaskamp made to real estate appraisal. The authors begin with a brief review of Graaskamp's views on appraisal practice and theory. They note Graaskamp's awareness of the dilemma facing the appraiser, that of being paid by entities that benefitted from doing deals vs. rejecting deals. The authors begin with a review of the historical evolution of the three approaches to value and conclude that the three approaches place successive emphasis on the form of the appraisal rather than on the content and relevance to the appraisal assignment. They review the evolution of behavioralism and the extension of Ratcliff's notion of most probable price. The authors offer a Graaskamp quote that helps explain his disdain for the appraisal profession, namely, "Institutional customers subvert appraisal sophistry to create the appearance of independent objectivity for subjective, self-serving decisions." The authors then provide a brief overview of the Barnard Report and the call for appraisal reform contained therein. Although the report triggered the R-41 series of regulations, they note that the replacement of the series in favor of a regulatory mode that focused on regulation of insured institutions was an unacceptable replacement. They concluded that Graaskamp was correct in his position that federal control of the appraisal industry, as well as the uses to which appraisals are placed, would be necessary to unify the industry.

Section III: Market Analysis and Trade Area Delineation

Meyers and Beck, in their paper "A Four-Square Design for Relating the Two Essential Dimensions of Real Estate Market Studies," struggle with the need for making quantitative decisions that are based on limited data, and qualitative decision making that is usually applied to such data. They argue that the lack of methodology for dealing with sparse data that may also suffer from inconsistent sources leads to an underutilization of available data and distracts researchers from efforts to collect more meaningful data. The authors contend that sound logic requires researchers to first determine how to span the gap between current historic market data and the future and, second, to fill the linkage between market level macro data and micro level property decisions. The authors offer a four-square design that addresses these two issues. They then apply their model to a case study in which two apartment complexes are compared for acquisition. The authors present six steps in the process: (1) identify the property and the target use, (2) collect available forecast information, (3) evaluate the subject property in terms of the forecast data, (4) establish the capture ratios and positioning of the subject property in terms of micro and macro variables, (5) project the future, and (6) estimate the implications of the future for the subject property. The authors conclude that the four-square design can make a significant contribution to investment decision making and by applying such quantitative methods, investors can exploit the inefficiencies inherent in the real estate market and achieve superior returns.

In "Refining Empirical Procedures for Market Area Delineation," Peterson extends the discussion of spatially based real estate and feasibility analysis. The author compares two empirical methods for delineating market trade areas. These methods include a customer-spotting or analog approach, and a consumer survey approach. The author begins his paper with recognition of the critical role that market analysis should play in real estate decision making. He notes that for enterprises that draw on limited trade areas, gravity models, regression models, and various forms of time/distance boundary establishment can often be employed. However, he contends that when the trade area is extended to large geographic areas such methods are problematic.

The author presents two basic alternatives for estimating trade areas for large area enterprises, as well as empirically testing or qualitative approaches in smaller area enterprises. The author spends some time exploring the traditional customer-spotting approach and concludes that, while the data may provide some insights into the customers who support the given enterprise, they give no insights into the larger population that does not patronize the establishment. He argues that this unrepresented population is of most interest to the analyst in that it represents an untapped population that may have a significant impact on the profitability of the enterprise itself.

In his article entitled "An Investigation into the Competition Between the Downtown Shopping Area and the Suburban Shopping Mall," Bleich explores methods for delineating trade area boundaries. The author begins with the premise that retail centers will locate where they can serve the largest proportion of the market in the most efficient way. Thus, with the trend toward suburbanization of the population, retail centers also followed the move away from center cities. The author posits that in order for the downtown shopping centers to regain their competitive edge, planners must first understand consumer choice models. The author

INTRODUCTION

presents a probablistic model try to explain the process by which consumers choose between downtown and suburban shopping centers. This probablistic model is then compared to Huff's model, which adds the importance of center and distance measures to Reilly's Law of Retail Gravitation, which focused on sheer size of center and tenant mix. The author posits that a variety of factors influence consumer choice, including attributes of store location such as access, motor transit, parking, attributes of consumer perceptions of location, and finally, a combination of shopping center attributes, and nonshopping amenities. The author tests the model with a consumer survey of shoppers and finds that the extended model provides a superior prediction of customer choice.

Stanley, in "Multiple Store Trade Area Relationships and Logistic Response Function Estimation," further explores trade area estimation for retail investment. The author builds on prior research in travel modeling and Central Place Theory, utilizing a logit response function to estimate the coefficients. The author begins his paper with a discussion of Central Place Theory and introduces the advances that have been made to the basic model to account for variations in such attributes as population density, transportation, competition, and a variety of demand-related variables. The author attempts to expand and improve procedures that can be used to estimate the probability of visitation at retail stores, treating a dependent variable as the discrete value rather than the continuous scale used in other research. The model is then extended to case study, which focuses on retail patronage patterns for a sample of supermarkets in the Midwest. The author concludes that the logit function provided statistically reliable estimates of the parameters.

Section IV: Public Policy Issues

Kinnard, in "Transfer of Ownership Rights Via Rent Control," presents a case study of the impact of rent control on sales prices of mobile homes. The research problem stems from problems associated with the California Mobile Home Residency Law. In effect, the law creates a tenancy of indefinite duration that may be transferable to another party of the tenant's choosing, subject to limited acceptance or concurrence approvals of the landlord. Thus, the law vests the right of occupancy or use, as well as the right of disposition or transfer that are normally held by the fee owner of real estate, with the tenant. The author contends that the impact of these provisions results in a substantive transfer of real property rights from the landlord or owner to the tenant, producing an uncompensated transfer of ownership rights. He hypothesizes that (1) there is indeed a discernable, identifiable, and measurable impact on sales prices in mobile home parks effected by the rent stabilization or rent control legislation and (2) such sales prices are significantly higher than in similar mobile home parks. The author concludes that the impact of such regulations on transfer of economic interests depends on the particular regulations in the county or community in which the property is located. Furthermore, the author concludes that rent control does indeed "monetize" the rights transferred to the tenant via the California law.

Overstreet and Rubin, in their article "Interpreting Monte Carlo Simulation with Generalized Sensitivity Analysis: The Case of Historic Rehabilitation," explore the indeterminate effect of tax code on historic rehab. Because of the lack of historical data, the authors argue that traditional empirical analysis cannot correctly quantify the linkage between changes in tax code and levels of investment to rehab. As an alternative, the authors turn to an investment simulation model to establish the relationships between the tax code and rehab levels. In the absence of statistical techniques in traditional business literature, Monte Carlo simulation, borrowed by the authors from the physical sciences literature, is extended to the issue. The authors conclude that Generalized Sensitivity Analysis (GSA) is an appropriate methodology for analyzing or exploring financial systems that are clouded by sparse data. The authors also note that macroeconomic forces surrounding real estate markets constrain the ability of policy markers to influence levels of historic rehab through the tax code vehicle. The authors conclude that the GSA methodology provides important insights into the impact of structural change on investment behavior in terms of parameter estimation and parameter interaction.

In their article entitled "Toward Socially Efficient Broker Behavior in Factual Representations," Levi, Terflinger, and Webb provide an overview of the interaction of law and economics in the area of real estate broker liability for misrepresentation. The authors review recent liability cases to establish trends in judicial thought, as well as the application of legal remedies as influenced by the dual goals of equity and efficiency. The authors also note the significant difference in the legal principle underlying such cases that resides in negligence or strict liability theory. They content that, although strict liability is the most socially efficient theoretical foundation, the majority of states have adopted negligence as a primary liability rule. In exploring the case history, the authors note that the majority of liability problems facing real estate licensees revolve on factual misrepresentation and/or nondisclosure, with few instances of outright fraud. They recognize that in such cases strict liability is the more economically efficient solution, since it internalizes all costs to all parties. However, the authors conclude that negligence and strict liability theories both provide economic incentives to licensees not to misrepresent material facts. Since the majority of states have adopted negligence as the preferred legal standard to apply to such cases, the authors deduce that equity is of paramount importance to most court systems, rather than economic efficiency.

In "The Price of Owner-Occupied Housing Services: 1973–1989," Ling explores the decision process for households regarding two fundamental questions: whether to own or rent and how much housing to acquire. The author assumes that such decisions are made in an economic context, but that they implicitly include recognition of the household as an investment as well as an economic good. The author attempts to estimate the real price of owner-occupied housing services for a variety of income classes and household types. The conceptual framework adopted by the author assumes that households will purchase sufficient housing such that the present value of after-tax cash flows, including implicit rent generated by the last dollar of housing expenditure, equals the cash the household invests to obtain that level of housing. The author calculates tax rates and user costs for owner-occupied housing services for 57 income/household type cohorts over a 68-quarter period. He concludes that the index of housing affordability published by National Association of Realtors was negatively correlated with real economic cost of housing during the 1980s. In particular, the NAR index displayed little correlation with changes in real user costs, in spite of lowered volatility and inflation, interest rates, and housing prices. The author recognizes that the cost of capital model employed in the paper is consistent, but that a better-developed model of the role of uncertainty in housing decisions could be developed with special emphasis on expectations of future tax environment.

The real estate glut of the latter 1980s cut across property types and markets, but was most severe for office investments. Much of the overbuilding of office investments can be explained by the excesses of capital that were allocated to the property type when compared to the spatial requirement of the underlying tenant base. Part of this oversupply was a function of the inefficiency of the market and the inability of investors and lenders to correctly model cash flown. Kroll and Taff, in "The Measurement of Effective Rent," explore the role that effective rent can play in assessing the strength of a particular market. The authors posit that rent is a driving factor in determining additions to the supply of space, as well as the absorption of that space. The authors correctly recognize that contract rent provides incorrect signals to potential investors as to the relative health of the market. The authors explore some of the different terminology applied to rent and conclude that valid effective rent measures for office investments have not been produced through traditional sources. In an attempt to better understand the differences among various types of rent, the authors explore the lease arrangements for R&D space in Santa Clara, California. The authors concentrate on the differences between effective rent that stem in part from differences in such factors as rental abatement or free rent, rental escalation, lease term, and tenant improvements. The authors empirically show that contract rents clearly do not provide sufficient insights into the strength and direction of a market. Furthermore, on an intramarket basis, failure to understand such differences may result in an understating of the value of real estate fundamentals in terms of property and submarket characteristics.

I PHILOSOPHICAL ISSUES

1 THE EVOLUTION OF REAL ESTATE DECISIONS
Stephen E. Roulac

Dr. James A. Graaskamp observed, in his seminal monograph for the American Council of Life Insurance, that real estate was created by an early caveman's decision to push a rock in front of a cave.[1] While that decision can be considered straightforward and noncomplex, as the political-economic system has evolved to reflect more variability, specialization, sophistication, complexity, and discontinuity, the evolution of real estate decisions, which today are anything but simple and straightforward, has been concurrently influenced by these change forces.

Among those aspects of real estate decisions considered in this paper are:

- How decisions concerning real estate have evolved
- The forces that have influenced the evolution of real estate decisions
- The quality of those real estate decisions
- How real estate decisions, in turn, have influenced the built environment

---

* This paper is an extract from a book of the same title to be published in 1994.

- The primary decision-making priorities in the last decade of the twentieth century
- The possible direction of real estate decisions in the first quarter of the twenty-first century

The character, scope, complexity, parameters, information employed in, and tools utilized for real estate decision making have changed dramatically over time, and especially so in modern society.

Despite the changes in the world that redefine real estate decisions, many decision makers approach real estate decisions with a style more reminiscent of the caveman's narrow and primitive view of the world, with strength of personality, if not brute force per se, subjugating strategic thinking, calculation, and acumen. For evidence of this Neanderthal style,[2] the casual observer has to look no further than the popular press, which chronicles the latest consequences of miscalculations. Further evidence can be gathered by strolling down the main street of virtually any community to observe the plethora of dysfunctional structures and neighborhoods whose inner workings are more negative than positive, as well as evidence of excess space and plummeting prices reflected by the proliferation of "Sale," "For Sale," and "Space Available" signs that dominate the early and mid-1990s urban scene.

Extraordinary financial losses and market disruption in the late 1980s and early 1990s are eloquent, if damning, testimony to the proposition that the quality of many real estate decisions is less than distinguished. Despite extraordinary advances in databases and analytical tools, the quality of real estate decisions made in the 1980s is not readily distinguishable from those of earlier times. Whereas real estate decisions made as recently as a decade ago could be described as primitive, some assert that real estate decision makers are now smarter than they were previously, but casual empiricism does not lead to a conclusion of superior contemporary real estate decision making. Today, the discontinuity in space using patterns, early 1990s markets plagued by an intractable oversupply of space and a daunting capital shortfall, and extraordinary instability in organization relationships conspire to create a complicating context for real estate decisions that materially compromises their probable quality.

The consequences of deficient real estate decisions for households, business enterprises, public agencies, and society as a whole are disquieting, since no enterprise, whatever its scale, can hope to achieve its full potential if it makes suboptimal decisions with one of its most important resources—real estate. As Winston Churchill insightfully observed, "We first design our structures, then they design our lives."

THE EVOLUTION OF REAL ESTATE DECISIONS

James Graaskamp's less than sanguine assessment of "decisions in regard to real estate" is as timely today as it was when written two decades ago:

> ... gravely mismanaged by a majority of investors due to the emotional mystique that surrounds real property ownership and the difficulty of obtaining and analyzing the mass of information necessary to make a sound investment decision. Much of the risk in real estate investment is created by inadequate research and organization of factual data so that expectations are unknown rather than unpredictable and the surprise potential inherent in planning for the future is unnecessarily magnified.[3]

Beyond the dubious quality of the design and physical parameters of many current real estate structures, the gross misappropriation and misallocation of resources (land, labor, and capital) imposes a burden on society overall, impairing its ability to achieve its full potential. Unfortunately, all too many of those responsible for real estate decisions are doubly flawed, manifesting both a scant sense of history, therefore repeatedly validating the veracity of George Santayana's dictum that ". . . those who cannot remember the past are condemned to fulfill it," and a bereft sense of the future, therefore persistently proving the wisdom of Edmund Burke's admonition, "You can never plan the future by the past." Simultaneously disregarding history's lessons and failing to plan, the real estate sector, in aggregate, is a system that is more often dysfunctional than functional, exemplifying many of the attributes of a perpetually dysfunctional family.[4]

The thesis of this paper is that the state-of-the-art and science of real estate decisions is driven by the problems and choices faced by organizations involved in the real estate markets and is influenced by a multitude of forces that define the environment in which such decisions are made. The context for real estate analysis is established as much by specific organizational needs and considerations as it is by overall environmental factors, human needs, and particular client objectives. Not only has the environment in which real estate decisions are made changed significantly over time, but the types of organizations confronting real estate decisions and the questions they are asking have changed markedly as well.

Graaskamp strongly believed in the importance of the "client" context on real estate decisions,[5] the influence of which is profound as new patterns of industry, structure, and organization bring new real estate decisions. Whether the dominant organizations and their leaders define these decisions by their initiatives or whether broader forces make such decisions inevitable is a variant on a classic debate in history: Do the masses act in their own interests or do heroes[6] make history? This question is most germane to the subject inquiry, since understanding how real estate decisions have evolved requires both a comprehension of the environment and the forces that define it, as well as an understanding of the nature and motivations of the organizations that make real estate decisions.

The forces that define the environment of real estate decision making embrace the political economy of the time, social patterns, primary visible "actors," organization patterns, and technology. Understanding the nature, direction, and implications of these forces and how they relate to real estate decisions is a requisite precondition for effective decisions. By examining the multiple forces that influence the theory and practice of the real estate decision-making process generally, and in an historic context specifically, insights can be derived to

- Improve the actions and preferences of consumers of real estate resources
- Enhance the quality of decisions by real estate practitioners and the organizations in which they work
- Stimulate more appropriate and valuable research by academics
- Contribute ultimately to a superior built environment and also a more responsible interaction with the natural environment

Such an orientation is certainly consistent with the values and interdisciplinary orientation to real estate decisions espoused by Graaskamp.

Decision Process and Components

Historically, real estate decisions have been driven by a transaction emphasis, reflective of the "do a deal" style of those who initiated, orchestrated, and consummated real estate transactions. These transactions were primarily funded by capital whose commitment was on nonrecourse terms, meaning that the primary decision maker simultaneously controlled all of the upside and was exposed to a very limited downside. As a consequence of the institutionalization of real estate markets, the control of assets is moving from entrepreneurial developers and promoters to fiduciaries who, in their capacities as trustees for pension and other institutional funds to whom they have primary accountability and the obligation to proceed with "due diligence," necessarily place more emphasis on the process of how the decision is made. This process emphasis is distinguished from the historic transactions emphasis.

THE EVOLUTION OF REAL ESTATE DECISIONS

The real estate decisions process is common to entrepreneurs who emphasize transactions as well as to fiduciaries. Indeed, the process is inherently generic to any decision involving major capital commitments, and thus has close parallels to the corporate capital budgeting process. Fundamental to the components of the real estate decision process is consideration of the sequence of the critical phases of a decision:

1. *Decision structure*—Specification of the decision process, if not explicitly articulated, is implicit, as is so often the case, which can lead to ambiguity and suboptimal decisions.
2. *Opportunity initiation*—The opportunity to be considered may result from initiative taken by the organization to identify that opportunity, or, alternatively, a third party may present the opportunity to the organization.
3. *Opportunity assessment*—How the opportunity is to be evaluated—what information is to be considered, in what degree of detail, who will be involved, in what format will the results of the evaluation be presented to which audience(s)—is largely influenced by the motivations, requirements, constraints, and expectations of those involved in the opportunity initiation and who controls the investment decision.
4. *Decision implementation*—Who participates in, has veto power over, and ultimate authority to approve the decision has a material impact on the decision process.

The deal-making transaction orientation combines the phases of initiation, assessment, and decision into one entity. Some organizations may involve multiple individuals and/or departments in these three phases, with some degree of "separation of powers" varying over time, depending upon shifting leadership, priorities, and staff composition.

In the institutional setting, which emphasizes process, the initiation, assessment, and decision sequence are separated rather than combined, and are performed by three distinct parties. The investment management organization essentially goes through its own internal sequence of origination, assessment, and decision *prior* to presenting the opportunity to the institutional investor. Essentially, the manager recommends that the investor proceed with the proposed investment. Then the investor undertakes its own independent assessment, usually led by its staff and often involving third-party professionals. This assessment involves consideration of economic, market, appraisal, financial, legal, political, regulatory, environmental, and engineering issues. At the conclusion of the assessment process, the staff makes a decision to recommend acceptance or appropriate equivalent decision-making body, rejection, or consideration on modified terms. The Board of Trustees would then determine whether or not to proceed with the investment, based on consideration of the manager's proposal, consultants' evaluations and staff's recommendations.

The four phases of the real estate decision—structure, opportunity, assessment, and decision—can be expanded into ten components. Of these components, the first two reflect the structure, the third relates to the opportunity, the next six components embrace the assessment, and the tenth subsumes the decision. The specific components include:

Structure
1. *Decision formulation*—The statement of the decision to be made, usually either a problem to be resolved, an opportunity to be accepted or rejected, or a choice to be made from multiple options.
2. *Objectives*—The objectives may be basic to the explicit and implicit primary objectives of the organization and/or individual on whose behalf the decision is to be made. Further, the objectives may embrace as well situational objectives that complement and/or modify the basic objectives, or perhaps, replace them.

Opportunity
3. *Alternative identification*—In the instance of a packaged investment, such as a security interest in a venture or an enterprise organized specifically for that particular investment, the decision choices are yes, how much, and no. In the instance of an opportunity whose terms are susceptible to negotiation, the choices turn on different permutations of the variables inherent in the structure of arrangements amongst multiple parties.[7] To the extent a decision concerns multiple opportunities that might be elected in different forms and combinations, the number and attributes of alternatives increase accordingly.

Assessment
4. *Decision criteria*—Most decisions are evaluated against multiple criteria, which can include profit maximization, risk minimization, adherence to specified guidelines, and the like.
5. *Environmental context*—Understanding the external environment in which a decision is to be made is fundamental. The relative degree of optimism and pessimism, confidence and uncertainty can be of meaningful concern.

6. *Organizational context*—The attributes, resources, constraints, circumstances, culture, structure, and personalities of the organization making the decision necessarily exert a major influence on the decision process.
7. *Competitive context*—Whether the decision involves the real or possible involvement of other organizations that are concurrently competing to acquire the same asset or might seek to acquire that asset should the subject organization elect not to proceed, as contrasted to a decision that is uninfluenced by competitive considerations, defines the factors influencing the decision and the motivations of the parties involved in the decision.
8. *Analysis*—Competent quantitative and qualitative analysis, embracing financial, economic, market, accounting, tax, legal, merchandising, political, regulatory, and management considerations, are preconditions to effective decision making. Included within quantitative analysis is specification of the model/decision system, specification of the desired data, determination of data that could realistically be available and can be afforded within the resource budget, selection of the preferred strategy to gain access to and collect data, identification of the software to be employed to implement the model, and accessibility to the hardware on which the analysis will be implemented.

    Emphases of qualitative analysis include the property's relative competitive position in its cohort of "peer properties"; a critique of pertinent contractual documents, especially sharing arrangements; and an assessment of management's capability, commitment, and motivation to perform. Necessarily, multiple disciplines may be involved in the analysis, with each professional pursuing a particular approach appropriate to that discipline.
9. *Synthesis*—Given the plethora of information generated and the multiple parties involved in the decision process, it is necessary to organize the findings in a coherent manner that facilitates the decision making process. This synthesis involves distillation, summarization, organization and highlighting:

    - the critical numbers resulting from the analysis
    - the compatibility of the indicated parameters and attributes of the opportunity to decisions criteria
    - the risks, their likelihood, and possible consequences as well as mitigating options, relative to comparable alternative opportunities
    - the critical success factors

Depending upon various considerations, the synthesis may or may not include a recommendation, with or without rationale for such recommendation.

Decision

10. *Decision*—Depending upon the nature of the decision, the result of the decision making process can take multiple forms including yes unconditionally, yes conditionally, yes subject to, defer or no.

As noted, all ten steps are implicitly involved in every decision, even though the decision maker may not explicitly address any one step incrementally.

The decision process in operation is materially different in those instances where objective third-party professional firms are involved than when the decision is self-contained (without outside influence). Further, the narrower the number and range of perspectives brought to bear on the decision, the greater the likelihood the decision may be premised upon a less informed rather than a broader set of perspectives. Committee considerations, however, can yield the insidious consequences of "group think."[8] Further, it is a fundamental truism that "blinding insights" are considerably less likely to be generated by a group process than the focused passion and intensity of a brilliant innovator.

While the ten components of the decision process can be considered a classic timeless statement of the decision sequence, the evolving conditions and circumstances concerning those forces that influence real estate markets and the players within those markets necessarily cause changes in the decisions that are made, the pressures upon those decisions, the scope of options considered, the scale and complexity of the real property interests, the sophistication of the models, the breadth and depth of databases, and the technology employed. The influence of such factors as geopolitics, technology, and the state of the economy impact the decision process in numerous ways, including:

1. *Decision formulation*—What might in previous times have been of critical concern is now either of lesser concern or irrelevant, where forces of change may introduce new decision priorities.
2. *Alternatives*—Advances in geopolitics, technology, and industry structure have vast impacts on the geographic breadth, diversity, and complexity of the array and attributes of available alternatives to be considered.
3. *Objectives*—The evolving and dynamic structures of organizations and the concerns of the constituencies to which they must answer influence the objectives to be considered.

4. *Decision criteria*—The particulars of certain criteria and the relative priority of different criteria are defined by the factors that influence the decisions.
5. *Environmental context*—The transformation of society through globalization, geopolitical revolution, technological innovation, economic expansion, and relative prosperity have transformed the scale and range of real estate decisions.
6. *Organizational context*—As new organizational structures emerge and existing organizational patterns recede in prominence, the types of decisions faced, and the relative priorities of factors influencing those decisions, change apace.
7. *Competitive context*—Globalization forces dramatically expand the competition and thereby profoundly affect decisions.
8. *Assessment*—The expanding sophistication of decision systems, the burgeoning data available to employ in making decisions, and the economy and power of software and computers are directly stimulated by technological advances.
9. *Synthesis*—The greater the dynamism and complexity associated with the decision, the more critical the synthesis function becomes. Further, to the extent the implications and issues are more subtle and strategic than they have been in times past, how the synthesis function is implemented and the particular "spin" that is given to implications of findings loom large.
10. *Decision*—The quality of decisions is influenced by multiple forces. The nonrational is often less readily articulated, if it is even acknowledged. As those with ultimate authority are less likely to be either principals investing on their own account or investment professionals, nonrational factors expand in importance.

A continuing challenge to those responsible for real estate decisions is balancing the timeless structure of rationality with the dynamics of forces of discontinuity that determine the critical variables of real estate decisions.

Real Estate in the Twentieth Century

Real estate markets in the twentieth century reflect the evolution of economics as a dominant theme in planning and executing real estate transactions. Appreciation of the full implications of this evolution is best gained by considering the attributes of the economy as well as those of the real estate markets in an historic context.[9] Consideration of the historic forces that have created the current real estate market provides a useful frame of reference for making future real estate decisions. Although many real estate decision makers currently manifest disdain for historic patterns and influences, essentially dismissing their relevance to today's decisions, such a cavalier approach is, at best, naive.

Over the last half century, the forces that determine the conditions of real estate markets have changed markedly. In the years preceding the stock market crash of 1929 and the resulting Great Depression of the 1930s, there was an extraordinary amount of speculative building, largely financed by mortgage bonds — a financing instrument not dissimilar from the securitized mortgage interests so popular in the 1980s. Although not generally understood, the development excesses and overbuilding of the Roaring Twenties era directly contributed to imbalances in the economy, including debacles within the stock market.

Following the stock market crash of 1929 and the Depression, there was only limited building activity. Supply was substantially greater than what could be justified by any extrapolation of the precrash level of economic activity, and certainly was much in excess of what was needed to meet the largely depressed levels of demand during the 1930s. Then, in the 1940s the nation's economic priorities and energies were devoted to the military effort. Further, the need for space was substantially reduced because a large number of demand units (people) were domiciled offshore.

As the country returned to a peacetime economy at the conclusion of the Second World War, there had been no significant new construction for approximately two decades. During this time, the population had increased and the excesses of the 1920s had been wrung out of the system through the Depression and World War II. Substantial demand had been created through curtailed consumption, forced savings, and the deprivation of wartime economic conditions.

As a result, demand for business and residential space dwarfed the available supply. During the 1950s demand so outstripped supply that the concept of economic feasibility was given scant consideration. Priority was placed on the construction of new buildings, with little consideration given to their economic viability. This rapid pace of development continued through the 1960s, when supply and demand became more balanced.[10] On occasion, supply exceeded demand during this period. However, through the 1970s, new development continued to be fueled by various tax incentives and, increasingly, by inflation, as double-digit changes in the cost of living pushed prices ever higher.[11]

In the mid-1970s the real estate markets were adversely impacted by a demand shortfall resulting from recessionary conditions, which exacerbated overbuilding. A daunting capital crisis added a further element of challenge to real estate decisions in a fluid, highly uncertain environment. The resulting building slowdown combined with a recovering economy set the stage for a robust, expansionary 1980s real estate market.[12]

By the mid-1980s, inflation had been reduced to single digit levels, but the 1981 Tax Reform Act provided extraordinary development incentives. Such incentives were not really needed, since the expanding economy absorbed the surplus supply of the mid-1970s, and thereby motivated new development. Aggressive lenders replaced discriminating underwriting with pliant loan approvals, generously, almost indiscriminately, providing funds for new projects. These forces triggered a wave of building activity, which led to a substantial oversupply of space for many property types in multiple markets. Even when market forces suggested it was inappropriate, this building volume was sustained by strong capital flows from individuals investing in various retail real estate securities products, aggressive savings and loan joint ventures, accommodating bank lending, growing pension real estate involvement, and avaricious foreign purchases. The combined effect of these many investors voraciously competing for properties was to subjugate basic economic rationale to speculative motivation.[13]

Although the last two decades have been characterized by accelerating discontinuities in technology, globalization, pluralistic social and political structures, and knowledge, in Peter Drucker's view the half-century prior to 1968 was characterized by remarkable continuity in the basic structure of the economy.[14] Given the relative stability and continuity in the general economy, that real estate markets and enterprises were perceived as manifesting stability and continuity is not surprising. Indeed, the first-year property course in law schools was very similar to medieval English history, dealing with long-established traditions, precedents, and principles. The real estate field was appealing because one could, in a relatively short period, "master" the discipline, and then, like the medieval master craftsmen, practice the discipline, honing and improving over time, but not really venturing into new territories or confronting new technologies.[15]

However, by the early 1970s it was clear many of the discontinuities in the economy were spilling over to the real estate markets. A subject that had been static became dynamic. Every course in the law school curriculum, from securities to future interests to environment to bankruptcy to corporations to taxation and more, became relevant, even integral, to real estate decision making. But not many of those responsible for making or advising on real estate decisions perceived the implications of these discontinuities.

Real estate decision makers' lack of historical perspective was aptly captured in the lead to a 1977 *Business Week* cover story:

> A short 18 months ago, U.S. real estate men were talking little else but disasters—distressed properties, foreclosures, forced sales, losses. The industry had just gone through its worst crunch in 40 years... Today, the talk—and it is heard everywhere—is all about big deals, properties bought and sold, new projects just launched or about to be launched, and especially the unprecedented flood of investment dollars chasing U.S. real estate.
>
> Today prime U.S. real estate is probably the most sought-after investment target in the industrial world.
>
> U.S. real estate has achieved this enviable position because investors, domestic and foreign, are convinced that it can only appreciate in value.[16]

Looking back, however, it seems that the conviction that property could only appreciate in value was founded less on hard analysis than self-serving optimism.

Indicative of the propensity of those responsible for real estate decisions to miscalculate is the introductory statement to a 1990 *Wall Street Journal* feature on the real estate markets:

> It wasn't that long ago that people talked about real estate as a "sure thing"—an investment that couldn't lose. What's happened? Too much money, too much greed, too much optimism—and bad government policy. What is ahead? More hard times.[17]

The current status of real estate markets reflects both a lack of appreciation of the consequences of discontinuities in the structure of the economy, and also an undisciplined approach to capital commitments, irrespective of changes in the structure of the economy.

The veracity of Drucker's prediction two decades ago of prospective discontinuities is reflected by a political-economic environment characterized by extraordinary change. The combined effect of domestic politics, the demise of communism and the Soviet Union and the rise of democracy, international interdependency, industry consolidation, organizational downsizing, pervasive government deficits, escalating debt levels, restructuring of ownership arrangements, market turmoil, deregulation, environmental issues, technology transformations, racial tension, and the wealth–poverty dichotomy is a system characterized more by volatility, instability, and uncertainty than by stability, predictability, and permanence.

At the same time that Drucker addressed systemic discontinuity, Graaskamp warned of the inadequacy of real estate decisions generally, independent of daunting circumstances that place a primacy on superior decisions. Graaskamp warned against the risks deriving from:

> exposure to the dynamics of a changing society to which the real estate cannot readily adapt due to its immobility, inflexibility, ability, and complexity. Constant adaptation to changing outside circumstances requires ever-constant management attention, and the ability of real estate investments to glide through economic adversity can be likened to the helicopter which, in the absence of power and pilot control, has a natural glide angle of a falling brick.[18]

The performance of many properties in the late 1980s and early 1990s provides compelling testimony to the validity of Graaskamp's "falling brick" metaphor.

The property markets are increasingly globalized, with major segments of space use demand and capital supply being largely fungible, rather than restricted to a specific geographic region. Global interdependence reinforces the import of diversity to reduce the dependency on any one segment of business activity. Consequently, properties located in markets supported by a diverse economic base will inherently be characterized by less risk than those situated in more narrow, vertical economic regions. Given the increased dominance of institutional investors in the real estate markets, such risk disparities may be anticipated to be reflected in property pricing.

In the contemporary global economy, the proverbial "shot heard around the world" has profound regional and national economic ramifications, since many regions within the United States are ever more dependent upon what happens in countries that were heretofore far distant, if not remote and alien. Given the globalization of real estate space demand and capital markets, major events in significant segments of the world economy reverberate locally. As the context in which real estate decisions evolves, so also do the considerations governing such decisions change.

Real Estate Environment

Since real estate decisions both influence and are influenced by the economic environment, it is helpful to consider the context of real estate decisions over the last half of the twentieth century and the first quarter of the twenty-first century. Such an overview of the real estate environment from 1950 through 2025 is provided in Table 1, by ten-year intervals for the 1950s and 1960s, then five-year increments for the decades of the

Table 1. Overview of the Real Estate Environment: 1950–2025

Time period	Economic & investment environment	Commercial property markets	Real estate capital markets	Real estate financial services	Regulatory priority
1950–1960	Stable growth	Balanced	Uncomplicated	Traditional	Pro-development
1961–1970	Rapid growth	Balanced	Expansion	Innovation	Housing production incentives
1971–1975	Recession	Overbuilt	Diversification	Expansion	Capital formation
1976–1980	Rapid growth	Balanced to tight	Creativity	Sophistication	Land use controls
1981–1985	Dramatic changes	Tight to seriously overbuilt	Excess	Integration	Tax incentives
1986–1990	Sustained growth as economy restructures	Seriously overbuilt	Excess	Refinement	Environmental liability
1991–1995	Downturn & uncertainty	Seriously overbuilt	Contraction	Consolidation	Lending restraint
1996–2000	Consolidation	Overbuilt	Return to fundamentals	Stability	Housing subsidy
2001–2010	Strong growth	Moderately overbuilt to balanced	Expansion	Creativity	Fiscal impacts of new projects
2011–2025	Stable growth	Balanced	Continued diversification	Efficient implementation	Transit impacts

© Stephen E. Roulac, 1991. May not be reproduced, cited, or used in any manner without express written authorization.

1970s, 1980s, and 1990s, and periods of 2000–2010 and 2010–2025. The primary elements of the real estate environment considered include:

- **Economic and Investment Environment**—The inherent momentum and pace of change in the economy influences current demand and perceptions of future demand by defining value and simulating or constraining new building prospects.
- **Commercial Property Markets**—The responses of the organizations involved in real estate development to the economic environment determine the degree to which commercial property markets are balanced, constrained, or overbuilt.
- **Real Estate Capital Market**—The structure and function of the real estate capital market have exerted a profound impact on real estate decisions, as capital for real estate ventures moved from a residual status prior to the 1970s to being accessible on a direct basis over the last two decades. This change, when coupled with lack of appreciation of the changing structure of the economy overall and undisciplined assessment of the aggregate demand for space, led to severe overbuilding, as capital was made available for projects whose feasibility was not justified by identifiable demand.
- **Real Estate Financial Services**—The nature of financial services required to serve the participants in the real estate capital markets is necessarily influenced by the structure of those markets as well as the technology available to support such services. Over time, as the real estate sector has gained direct access to the capital markets, the sophistication of real estate financial services has expanded exponentially.
- **Regulatory Priority**—The relative priority of the regulatory process has reflected shifting emphases on economic expansion, housing policy, capital access, controlling land uses approvals and associated approvals, stimulating development through tax incentives, accounting for environmental consequences, constraining an out-of-control financial system, and incorporating fiscal impacts of new projects. To be sure, many of these themes are concurrent; what is presented is the dominant new emphasis of the particular period.

In contrast to the relative stability and growth that characterized the 1950s and 1960s, the 1970s and 1980s were characterized by substantial transition, dislocation, and excess. In the 1990s the environment of real estate decisions reflects restructuring, consolidation, and retraction. The impact of these forces is to shift the decision focus from the opportunity

Table 2. Evolution of Real Estate Enterprise Concerns: 1950–2025

Time period	Geographic scope	Organizational focus	Developmental emphasis	Source of equity for development	Financial control	Housing finance
1950–1960	Concentration on local market; primarily local; few multimarket involvements	Few service organizations; mostly project centered arrangements; home building companies expand	Suburbs, tract housing; regional shopping centers emerge	Demand exceeds supply	Builder	FHA organized; standard mortgages dominant
1961–1970	Regional orientation	Enterprises w/going concern character more prevalent; emerging public ownership of developers & brokers	Urban renewal; strip retail; new communities; large shopping malls proliferate	Demand exceeds supply	Builder financial institutions	S&L's active regarding housing mortgages; FHA programs subsidize apartment mortgage interest
1971–1975	Emerging national awareness	Separate investment vehicles: REIT, RELP, CREF	Suburban office development	Tax shelter	Corporate executive	Decent home; 26M hsg. units needed in 10 years; Nat'l Hsg. Partnership created
1976–1980	Multimarket involvement dominant	Expansion of service organizations to cover multiple markets; combination of multiple profit centers	Rejuvenation of major downtown office & hotel development	Tax shelter and inflation expectation	Entrepreneurial developers; bank workout specialists	Tax-exempt mortgage revenue bonds become major source of housing finance
1981–1985	Primarily national market	Multimarket developers & investment managers emerge as large organizations	Extensive suburban apartment, office & industrial development	Tax shelter and inflation expectation	Financial promoters specializing in tax shelter structuring; Wall Street bankers	Mortgage backed securities dominate housing finance

1986–1990	Strong national focus; regional specialization emerges	Life companies move to profit center structures; master limited partnership provides single tax entity for operating businesses	Concentration on large-scale, city-center high-rise projects	Investor demand: anticipated gain from sale	Entrepreneurial investment managers; fee oriented bankers; aggressive international investors developers	Proliferation of specialized mortgage instruments: variable interest rates, higher loan to value
1991–1995	Global orientation	Downsizing, restructuring & reorganization; style emphasized over entrepreneurial	Limited to selected infill	Cash investment	Bank workout executives; pension trustees (often those with limited knowledge of real estate)	Home equity credit lines
1996–2000	Global orientation	Consolidation, specialization, unbundling of services	Strong emphasis on project flexibility	Cash investment	Fiduciaries of major institutions	More efficient loan processing
2001–2010	Global	Dominance by major institutions and specialized entrepreneurs extensively utilizing professionals and contractors	Infrastructure	Revenue streams linked to privately-financed infrastructure	Fiduciaries of major institutions	Mortgage pools of global portfolios of housing mortgages
2011–2025	Global	Specialized securities	Public-private relationships	Project-specific securities	Global enterprises	Innovative instruments linking housing equity to multiple financial management and investment purposes

© Stephen E. Roulac, 1991. May not be reproduced, cited, or used in any manner without express written authorization.

exploitation that dominates concerns in an expansionary era to a resource preserving emphasis in a period of risk control.

The concerns of real estate enterprises in terms of geography, organization, development, and finance have evolved over the last half century in ways not dissimilar from those that applied to the real estate environment. The evolution of real estate enterprise concerns from 1950 to 2025 is shown in Table 2, with time periods similar to those in Table 1. The primary concerns of real estate enterprises include:

- **Geographic Scope**—The evolution of the economy generally, in combination with technological advances in communications and transportation, has dramatically extended the geographic scope of real estate decisions from the local orientation of the 1950s to the global focus of the 1980s.
- **Organizational Focus**—Just as the economy has matured and expanded, so also has the structure of real estate organizations evolved from a project orientation to larger, more sophisticated organizations involved in multiple markets and multiple businesses. Real estate investment management companies responsible for major institutional portfolios as well as real estate securities owned by individual investors have emerged. In the restructuring of the real estate industries of the 1990s following the excesses and dislocation of the 1980s, downsizing, consolidation, specialization, and unbundling of services are emphasized, with corporate and fiduciary styles replacing the entrepreneurial orientation dominant in the years leading up to and through the 1980s.
- **Development Emphasis**—The emphasis of development activity, logically and appropriately, has mirrored that of the economy overall, with housing and economic expansion being the primary orientation through the midyears of the century.
- **Sources of Equity for Development**—A series of favorable circumstances—embracing demand imbalance, tax shelter subsidy, inflation expectations, and investor demand for investment—allowed development to proceed with minimal if any actual equity investments for much of the latter half of the twentieth century. Now, however, in sharp contrast to previous practice, actual cash equity investment is required to initiate new development projects.
- **Financial Control**—Over time the financial control of real estate ventures and portfolios has reflected the structure of the economy, the condition of the property markets, and the nature of the capital markets. During periods of rampant growth, with market conditions

favoring those engaged in the development process, the builders/developers were in a dominant position. This dominance was disrupted in the early 1970s when corporations made a brief and abortive attempt to penetrate the real estate markets, motivated by desires to introduce modern management to an industry which has perceived to be lacking in these disiplines.

During periods of market reversal, such as the mid 1970s and the late 1980s and early 1990s, financial institutions and specialists dominate. Through the 1990s the institutional investor perspective with a strong fiduciary orientation are in the dominant position.

- **Housing Finance**—Similar to the development emphasis over time, housing finance reflects the nature of the markets as well as government policies and priorities. In the 1950s, 1960s, and 1970s, housing was a critical government priority, with substantial emphasis being placed on both facilitating and subsidizing the housing process. In the 1980s the federal government substantially deemphasized housing finance at the same time that the Wall Street community placed a major emphasis on integrating mortgage-backed securities, which activity emerged to be both a primary source of housing capital and Wall Street revenues and profits. In recent years, specialized mortgage instruments have proliferated, offering homeowners both more choices and more creativity in electing financial arrangements, with higher loan to value ratios.

The evolving emphasis of geography, organization, development, and finance manifests parallel developments of the overall real estate environment, particularly extended horizons and complexity in organizations and finance.

Real Estate Markets

The real estate markets have been transformed dramatically in the last two decades in terms of geographic orientation, relative priority of different disciplines, complexity, nature of participants, and related considerations.[19] Among some of the primary forces redefining the real estate markets are the following:

- **Geographic Orientation**—Whereas earlier real estate participants focused on more local or regional levels, today the orientation is very much national and international. The firms that develop, invest, finance, broker, and provide professional services have offices in multiple regions. A growing part of the real estate markets is dominated by firms with national and international service delivery.

- **Securitization**—Increasingly, real estate transactions are dominated by financial structures in the form of securities, where the deals are presented as prepackaged securities rather than as generalized investment opportunities whose structures, price and terms are subject to refinement, open to negotiation, and susceptible to customization. The securities orientation introduces a layer of intermediate participants, processes, and structure between the investor and the real estate, allowing arrangements and opportunities that would not otherwise be possible, but also bringing a plethora of new issues, potential pitfalls, and management considerations.
- **Institutionalization**—Concurrent with the change in geographic scope and securities orientation, the business has become institutionalized. Larger players, many of whom have strong connections to financial institutions and Wall Street firms, exert an ever-more dominant role. The financial wherewithal required to take on megasize transactions and to "carry" a project for a sustained period means that the minimally capitalized enterprise must bring extraordinary special qualities to the market to gain effective penetration.
- **Sophistication**—The decision makers in all aspects of the real estate markets are more knowledgeable, more discriminating, and more demanding than in earlier times. A greater proportion of real estate executives have considerable experience and/or advanced professional training. Contemporary management techniques and systems, coupled with modern business machinery, bring the potential for more informed business decisions. Those providing professional services in the real estate markets are increasingly held to higher standards.
- **Fiduciary Asset Management**—A growing proportion of real estate involvements embrace considerations of fiduciary asset management rather than a "one-time" deal orientation, as was previously prevalent. The emphasis on a fiduciary obligation represents a transfer of responsibility and a relocation of risk, a development with profound implications for the nature of services desired and the types of transaction arrangement that might be structured.

The interplay of the many facets of the real estate system means that professionals and their firms must be aware more than ever of what is going on, not only in other parts of the country, but also in other countries, with other property types, and in other segments and services.

Since contemporary real estate decisions are made in the context of an uncertain economic environment and shifting basic market structures, the strategies for effective involvement must build upon these changes, for if they do not, failure is much more likely than success. Knowledge of the current conditions and future directions of the real estate markets is fundamental to formulating successful deal making strategies in the new era.

Changing Capital Access

One critical force that has revolutionized the real estate decision making process is capital access. A one hundred year perspective of the real estate capital markets is presented in Table 3 and highlights the key evolutionary events in the real estate capital market. Such a historic perspective is pivotal to understanding the forces that have led to a transformation of the structure of the real estate markets.

Historically, real estate gained access to development capital on a residual rather than primary basis. Rather than directly appealing to individual or major institutional investors to lend money on real estate projects or to acquire real estate equities, the real estate industry relied on access to capital through intermediaries, such as life insurance companies. Thus, capital availability was often more a function of how much was available to the intermediary and the portfolio investment allocation decisions made by the intermediary than by an explicit judgement of how much to invest in real estate.

Access to capital on a residual basis tended to serve as a form of a financial governor, limiting the level of investment made available to real estate, especially in light of decision processes by these institutions that tended to be more conservative than aggressive. Over the last two decades, however, access to capital and the real estate financing process have been dramatically transformed. As access to capital for real estate activity has become more direct than indirect, the amount of capital available to real estate activities has increased exponentially. This additional capital has funded a plethora of development ventures, transforming the landscape of America's cities and suburbs. Forces that have shaped the transformation of the real estate capital access process include securitization, financial deregulation, financial engineering, tax reform, inflationary expectations, and a legitimization of real estate as a primary institutional investment.

In earlier days, real estate developers were largely known as investment builders, creating projects for their own portfolios that they would expect to hold for an extended time. In the 1970s, however, new investors

Table 3 The Real Estate Capital Market: A One Hundred Year Perspective

1920–1929	1930–1939	1940–1949	1950–1960	1961–1970	1971–1975	1976–1980
$10 billion of mortgage bond financings speculative excesses—and subsequent losses—parallel stock market experiences of the 1920s	Institutions become owners of many properties through mortgage foreclosures	Production devoted to World War II armament	Great pen-up demand justifies 100+% development financing	Tax law rx eform creates real estate investment trust vehicle	SEC public syndication emerges	Capital shortfall slows financing activity
Excessive overbuilding contributes to financial instability	New construction limited during Depression, mostly public works	Many demand units domiciled overseas	Emergence of New York-based syndication	Urban crisis and Kaiser Commission report focuses attention on need for 26 milxlion housing units	REIT's gain substantial size but experience heavy construction and development loan losses	Invasion of foreign capital
		Limited effective demand, some remaining surplus supply		Corporate involvement in real estate and housing through acquisitions	Corporations experience heavy losses in many direct corporate real estate subsidiaries	Mid 1970s downturn described as "worst" since Depression—major loan losses
				California land syndications invest in real estate as tax shelter	Major life insurance companies stress developer joint ventures	ERISA establishes pension diversification requirement
					Beginning of pension involvement	
					Tremendous expansion of "Sunbelt" markets	

© Stephen E. Roulac, 1991. May not be reproduced, cited, or used in any manner without express written authorization.

1981–1985	1986–1990	1991–1995	1996–2000	2001–2010	2011–2025
Inflation-wracked capital markets lead to demise of long-term fixed-rate mortgages	Economic expansion tax incentives, and easy money following financial deregulation sitmulate aggressive development of office, retail and hotel	Financial services contraction plunges Northeast into recession	Financial institution consolidation accelerates	Real estate perceived as competitive institutional asset, with broad spectrum of risk attributes	Proliferation of securities of both major properties and portfolios of specialized regions/property types
Equity investment dominant		Transaction incidence slows	National markets continue to be largely overbuilt	Special tax incentives implemented to encourage privately financed infrastructure development and enhancement	Global investing fully recognized
Real estate becomes legitimate institutional investment after housing price explosion, market softens, prices decline	Banks provide extraordinary capital for development, often without permanent commitments	Major cutbacks and extensive business failures of real estate enterprises	Divergent timing of market recoveries exacerbate portfolio performance variability		Investing in South America and Africa recognized as the "last frontier" of global institutional real estate
		Real estate oversupply and high vacancy persists, real rents plummet	Pricing reflects cash flow reality rather than appreciation expectation	Global investing gradually gains acceptance: major emphasis on investing in Eastern Europe	
1981 tax law creates extraordinary incentives through rehab credits, 15-year depreciation, and opens up new IRA/Keogh funding source	S&Ls provide 100+% development joint venture deals	S&L debacle leads to large losses	Emergence of new financing sources to replace demise of many traditional institutions		Price for special housing continues to outpace other investment assets
		Financial institutions face mounting losses, restrict credit access		Real estate prices overall closely linked to management of both political unit and property	Emergence of treaties between major political units and fiduciaries controlling substantial property portfolios and capital goods
Real estate syndication dominated market—$20 billion capital raised in 1984	Japanese emerge as major players, provide $96 billion by 1989, active in high profile properties	Foreign investors reduce pace of involvements		Prices for monopoly assets explode	
		Speculative building is curtailed		Capital impact analysis introduced by International Finance Authority as a precondition to gaining access to capital for projects larger than minimal size	Building expansion
1986 tax law removes favored tax status, triggers demise of syndication as primary force	Housing prices surge in later years of decade				Core portfolio defined as primary business properties located in North America, Asia, Western Europe, Eastern Europe

emerged whose desire to acquire real estate created the market for merchant builders, whose business was to build products for quick sale to investors, rather than to keep properties they had built in their own portfolio. The primary buyers of these "made to sell" real estate development projects were investors in various forms of securitized investment products, including partnerships, real estate investment trusts, and comingled funds organized for pension investors and offshore investors.

A multitude of factors, including favorable trade balances, advantageous relative purchasing power of currencies, global diversification motives, and comparably unattractive host country opportunities stimulated a wave of offshore capital flowing into the U.S. markets in the initial years of the 1980s from Canada, Europe, and South America, and then in the latter years, primarily from Japan. Although the amount of offshore investment capital falls far short of what the business press headlines suggest, their aggressive publicity about acquisitions at top-of-the market sales prices led to overall higher prices generally, and also created "two tier" markets whereby certain favored so-called trophy properties commanded premium prices on terms that were not reflective of the overall market.

In addition to the aggressive involvement of foreign investors, individual investors, and domestic institutional investors, especially pension funds, committed vast sums of capital to real estate. During the last two decades real estate limited partnerships emerged as a major supplier of funds to the real estate market, reaching a zenith of some $20 billion in 1985. However, the true impact of real estate securities on the market was much more profound, because such ventures often employed a high degree of leverage, at least 80%, and on occasion approaching or even exceeding 100%, so that each dollar of equity might support four or five dollars of mortgage debt. But more important was the extensive publicity directed to the popularity and apparent strong investment results achieved by real estate securities. This media message was broadly perceived as largely representative of the real estate markets overall and inevitably influenced those responsible for portfolio allocations, investment policy, and review of specific capital commitment decisions. The pervasive perception was that "real estate was on a roll," which no doubt motivated many to commit more dollars with less discernment than otherwise might have been the case.

Significantly, the advent and expansion of real estate securitization had the effect of separating the decision to commit dollars to real estate from the decision about which specific deals or ventures to invest in. Investors seeking real estate investment through a securitized product selected a manager and/or a specific fund, through a decision process that often involved a blind, yet-to-be-specified portfolio. In the instance where the portfolio was specified, the investor, lacking the sophistication or resources to be discriminating in investment selection, largely relied on "faith" that the manager of the securitized product would do a proper job.

At the same time that individual investors were romanced by the appeal of retail real estate securities and financial institution executives were confidently committing major amounts of capital to real estate investment, Wall Street firms became aggressively involved in marketing real estate. Several of the prominent investment banks created real estate financing functions, selling various forms of real estate securities, direct transactions, and an array of "financially engineered" products. Soon, real estate transactions were primary sources of revenue and profit for major Wall Street houses.

The last two decades, and the decade of the 1980s particularly, witnessed a radical transformation of the structure of the real estate financing process. With direct access to capital markets, the constraints of the formerly "governing" phenomenon of controlled access to capital were removed. As real estate became accepted as a legitimate investment, investors and those making decisions concerning capital allocation became more aggressive in seeking real estate investments and less concerned about the terms of such investments. Deregulation, competitive pressures, motivations to book apparently "easy, high profit" new business, and perceptions of lower risk all contributed to dramatic increases in the amount of capital made available to real estate ventures.

Decisions: Priorities, Tools, Process

The real estate environment and the concerns of real estate enterprises have in turn influenced the critical questions, decision emphases, and decision making processes over the last half-decade, as depicted in Real Estate Decision Priorities: 1950–2025 shown in Table 4. Highlights of the evolving emphasis, presented in time intervals similar to those in Table 1, include:

- **Critical Questions**—The critical questions for real estate decision makers have reflected the underlying conditions of the economy, demand, government priorities and incentives, capital flow priorities, and market conditions. The orientation at midcentury on

Table 4. Real Estate Decision Priorities: 1950–2025

Time period	Critical questions	Decision emphasis	Real estate decision making
1950–1960	Where are resources?	Emphasis on property-related transaction and basic organizational issues	Limited client or consulting sophistication
1961–1970	Where is growth potential?	Private and government property investment grows	Steady growth in property-specific consulting; management consultant and real estate investment analysis techniques improve as property size and complexity increase
1971–1975	How to get access to capital?	Client decisions grow more complicated as financial services expand and capital markets diversify	Non-property-specific consulting market grows dramatically
1976–1980	How to get land use approved?	Property markets boom, financing increases in complexity, and financial services potential is recognized	Rapid growth in property and non-property-specific consulting
1981–1985	Which tax structure? Which project? Which managers?	Institutionalization of markets, record levels of construction securitization and economic uncertainty	Strong non-property-specific demand; property analysis demand also up
1986–1990	Which domestic market?	As building declines, workouts, legal economics, systems analysis, and mergers and acquisitions continue	Non-property-specific consulting remains strong as property-specific consulting growth slows

1991–1995	What is the value? How much risk?	Steady growth in valuation and problem resolution; risk management, performance of existing portfolios	Strong demand for portfolio valuations and risk management systems
1996–2000	What is a viable strategy? What is value? How to manage risk?	Business direction, internal systems, diversification of business interests	Growth in strategic management and market selection services; great demand for sophisticated valuations
2001–2010	Which country?	Strategic location, investment policy, due diligence	Complexity mandates emphasis on sophistication and credibility
2011–2025	How will real estate fare as location becomes less critical? Which real estate security?	Advanced marketing and financial management	Strategic insight plus "rocket science" applications

© Stephen E. Roulac, 1991. May not be reproduced, cited, or used in any manner without express written authorization.

growth and gaining access to resources has been supplanted by concerns regarding value, risk, and strategy in the recent more daunting market conditions.
- **Decision Emphasis**—Similar to the evolution of critical questions, the decision emphasis has evolved in a manner reflecting the priorities and concerns of the time. The evolution from fundamental property questions to more complex financial services and capital access issues of the 1950s to the early 1980s period reflected the relative priorities of those periods. The emphasis in the latter years of the 1980s and into the 1990s parallels that of the critical questions, having to do with consolidation, problem resolution, risk management, valuation, systems and reporting, and basic business direction.
- **Real Estate Decision Making**—Real estate decision making in the 1950s and 1960s reflected limited sophistication and a primary emphasis on property specific issues. The change in the structures of the economy and industry, as well as the capital market access in the 1970s, placed a greater priority on non-property-specific consulting. The expansionary 1980s continued these trends while also simulating strong demand for property analysis. In the 1990s portfolio level issues, risk management systems, market selection, sophisticated valuations, and strategic management emerged as priorities for real estate decision makers.

The interdependency of the economy, the real estate markets, the orientations of those involved in real estate decisions, and the primary concerns of real estate decision makers are highlighted by the parallel waves of emphasis shown in Tables 1–4.

It used to be that the most important factors driving real estate decisions and values were "location, location, location." In the early 1990s, the critical factors are demand, location, information, management, and financing. The traditional view of location primacy was premised on several critical primary considerations. In a market where demand outstripped supply, the relative desirability of the site as determined by access, physical attributes, and relationship to surrounding sites ruled the day. Information and transportation technologies traditionally dictated that workers traveled to where the work was to be done. Similarly, those wanting to buy retail goods traveled to the location of the merchandise. Those wanting to engage in a transaction went to the decision makers.

In a less sophisticated time, the "location, location, location" concept implicitly incorporated many elements that impacted a property's value.

It was understood that when one talked about location, much more than just the physical site was being discussed. Also implied was the site's relationship to other sites, the demand for the type of space provided at that site, and multiple related factors, such as rent levels and operating economics. No longer can it be assumed that if you begin with good dirt and do a good job, good results will be achieved. Today, and increasingly in the future, one must have actual demand for the space to be provided, information for those who will make financial commitments to the property, and management to ensure that the promise of the property's prospects are realized.

The long-prevalent "sellers' market" favoring landlords, in which tenants exceeded space available, has been reversed. The imperative of real estate has shifted to the other side of the equation—now demand rules the day. Without demand, there is no value. If demand is deferred in time, value is proportionally diminished and must be discounted accordingly. Location continues to be important, but in a different way. With a surplus of space, tenants can be more selective, so quality commands a premium, putting secondary and inferior sites at an even greater discount than might be the case in a more balanced market equilibrium.

In the early 1990s many corporations occupy substantially more space than they are likely to occupy once their leases expire and they have disposed of properties no longer needed. Real vacancy rates are most likely substantially greater than the published figures, inasmuch as many organizations have not bothered to put sublease space on the market, discouraged by the remote prospects of leasing it in the near future. As a consequence, statistics on office vacancy may not decline as quickly as a simple analysis of statistics on job growth might suggest. Any enhanced demand for space resulting from a recovering economy will first absorb the substantial excess space that many companies control, but do not use. Further increases in demand would then motivate other companies to make available space for subleasing that they previously had not tried to market. When existing leases are up for renewal, many corporations will be signing on for less space.

Perhaps more significant than the reduced amount of space that will be demanded in the future by current users is the consideration that space use patterns are changing dramatically. Many organizations are moving space-intensive functions, particularly those having to do with back office activities, out of the central business district to suburban locations. This "grey collar" information and paper processing work that formerly was located in a downtown central business district high-rise office building is now performed in a lower cost structure located in an industrial park setting that is the information economy's equivalent to the manufacturing plant. Since these paper-processing activities do not require immediate proximity, locations in distant communities, including even foreign countries, is increasingly prevalent due to significantly lower costs.

Other organizations are dispensing with offices entirely, recognizing that much of the time workers are not actually working in offices, but "on the road" visiting customers and potential customers. Consequently, corporations who employ a strategic, rather than a custodial, approach to their real estate decisions are increasingly liberating their employees from fixed office-based work stations and employing technology to give workers more autonomy and flexibility (i.e., providing them with car phones and laptop computers rather than offices). All of this means fewer workers in offices and therefore less demand for office space. The traditional linkage of white collar employment being a proxy for office space demand has been severed. Going forward, more attention will need to be paid to the micro components of the demand for space, especially office space.

A combination of increasing concentration of population and a transportation system that lags society's needs has led to location choices in the suburbs to escape central city congestion. These patterns of locational decisions are facilitated by advances in information technology where it is now possible to move information to the decision maker's site. Thus, the point of sale can be shifted from the showroom to the living room. Work is electronically transported from the workplace to the worker's place. Similarly, advances in information technology have transformed how organizations are structured, how work is performed, and the equipment that is employed. All of these factors impact the work setting and, therefore, the needs for various types of real estate and ultimately the value of real estate.

Up until the last decade or so, real estate firms had long resisted the separation of managerial decisions from equity ownership benefits. Those who made the decisions and provided the essential managerial and professional services to real estate enterprises more often than not were those at financial risk and who stood to reap the gains from real estate activities. Consequently, there was little need to communicate to third parties, document decisions, or address many of the critical elements of real estate in an explicit manner.

Although a declining core group of old-line real estate barons still controls massive portfolios, real estate is increasingly controlled by major institutions and individuals, many participating in securitized forms. This ownership and control shift brings with it a concurrent change from managerial and professional services being offered largely in an entrepreneurial, contingent, deferred-compensation mode to noncontingent compensation arrangements for professional services and salaried managerial structures. Consequently, decisions about the property's management are made by persons who do not have an equity stake. Thus, communicating the important points of real estate investment to those who are putting capital at risk in a passive, as contrasted to an active, investor role is very important, but also very difficult.

Communicating the important aspects of real estate investment extends to the design and packaging of securities involving multiple specialized interests with distinct priorities, attributes, and sharing arrangements. Increasingly, the investor is not buying the ultimate fee simple title to property, as broadly presumed in the "location, location, location" era, but rather a specialized, fractionalized interest in property whose valuation requires initial consideration of the property's economics and then the multiple facets of the security interest itself.[20]

Those entities seeking to exploit the opportunities inherent in a globalizing economy are finding that access to real estate for those businesses is among the more significant challenges to resolve. The significant strategic locational decisions are often dwarfed by operational considerations of identifying available space and then implementing the transaction, which is made even more difficult when the country's underlying economy is being transformed from statistic to market principles.[21]

The discordant pace of technological progress, relative to organizational patterns, represents a major challenge to implementing real estate decisions. What is possible physically can be much more difficult to implement politically. The physical globalization of markets may be in direct conflict with political considerations. Indeed, "the financial services market place resembles a 21st century global electronic village; the political market place is still rooted in eighteenth century ideas of the nation-state."[22] The view many have of the real estate decision process is accurately depicted by substituting "location decision" for "political market place." Too many still view location decisions as rooted in thinking that can only charitably be described as obsolete. Continuing to employ primitive styles and models premised upon circumstances that are obsolete, rather than contemporary, is dangerous.

Much of the housing stock and business space created in the last four decades is highly deficient and is failing to meet people's expectations of "a building not only to function, to be structurally solid, and to fit into their surroundings, but also to conform to what is proper and fitting."[23] Among the deficiencies of the business and housing stock are failings in quality, responsiveness to user needs, compatibility to contemporary

Table 5. Evolution of Real Estate Decision Tools & Information Resources

Time period	Personal analytic tools	Decision systems	Investment & valuation methodology	Economic & demographic data	Scope of property market coverage	Source of property market data	Capital markets data
1950–1960	Hand calculations, abacus, slide rule	Financial tables and files	Simple, static one-year setups; recapture to reflect expected change in property performance and value over holding term	Chamber of Commerce reports	Local	Anecdotal sources, impressionistic	Impressionistic, descriptive
1961–1970	Large desktop calculator	Financial tables and formulas	Mortage-equity analysis to reflect financing terms; primitive profitability measures	Regional economic profiles by banks	Local	Local and regional brokerage estimates	Aggregate totals of capital resources for major institutions
1971–1975	Smaller desktop calculator	Card sort batch processing	Recognition of present value; sensitivity/probability	Census books, local planning department studies	Some regional	Regional brokerage surveys	Anecdotal "reports" on segments
1976–1980	Portable multifunction calculator	Mainframe computers, early analytic software applications	More sophisticated market comparisons	Emergence of proprietary economic consulting services	Regional	Informed brokerage surveys	Estimates of segments
1981–1985	Portable programmable calculator	Customized investment analysis software	After-tax IRR analysis	Advanced disaggregated analysis of census data survey resources	Mostly regional, some national	Published national brokerage firm surveys	Measurement of select segments

Period	Hardware	Software	Analysis	Database access	Geographic scope	Database extent	Measurement
1986–1990	Personal computer	Proliferation of real estate software; financial functions within calculators; geographic information systems	Broad acceptance of DCF and financial modeling	Readily accessible online databases	Mostly regional, some national	Limited databases	Measurement of more segments
1991–1995	Laptop computer	Flexible spreadsheets readily accessible	More finite analysis, including lease-by-lease	Sophisticated databases	National	Extensive databases	Quantification of real estate capital flow components and composite
1996–2000	Computers accommodate direct data entry via character recognition	Expert systems	Probabilistic models incorporating explicit risk measures	More refined & focused databases	Multiple countries within continent	Expanding database coverage and sophistication	More discrete information on capital market components
2001–2010	Voice-activated computers	Property specific variants of virtual reality	Sophisticated online real-time market comparisons and reproduction cost models	Broadened coverage—multiple countries	Global	Online databases	On-line information on financing transactions
2011–2025	Smaller, ever more powerful computers	Highly sophisticated quantitative methods with graphic display	Chaos theory application	Global online databases	Global	Online databases	Online databases

© Stephen E. Roulac, 1991. May not be reproduced, cited, or used in any manner without express written authorization.

work content and organizational patterns, and technological function. The reasons for these multitudinous shortcomings include the following:

- Supply-driven markets of the 1950s stimulated construction at the expense of design aesthetics.
- Speculative tract housing, which is an ever greater proportion of the nation's housing stock, does not incorporate the same standards as housing that was initiated by the occupant or that was to be owned for the long term.
- Projects are built for sale to purchasers acting as agents for tax shelter syndication investors seeking creative structures of tax deductions rather than building structures of substance and longevity.
- Office buildings designed for an American economy dominated by middle management and lower-skilled white collar administrative functions located in central business districts are no longer compatible with an information era.

Although some of the real estate development in recent years represents superb planning and design, many additions to the built inventory manifest attributes far short of excellence.

The Evolution of Real Estate Decision Tools and Information Resources depicted in Table 5 presents parallel considerations for the means to make real estate decisions over time periods consistent with the economic changes shown in Tables 1, 2, and 4. Key real estate decision issues and information resources include:

- **Personal Analytic Tools**—The analytic tool kit has evolved from hand calculations and the slide rules of the 1950s through the steady progress of more sophisticated computational machines to the laptop computer of the 1990s.
- **Decision Systems**—The systems and resources that facilitate real estate decisions have evolved from rigid, precalculated financial tables to a proliferation of customized software, readily accessible spreadsheets, and expert systems.
- **Investment and Valuation Technology**—The orientation of financial analyses for real estate has moved from one year, simple static "setups" to comprehensive, integrated, after-tax discounted analyses, including finite consideration of all pertinent economic variables at the level of individual leases.
- **Economic and Demographic Data**—Whereas economic data in the 1950s were largely derived from Chamber of Commerce reports, the

breadth, depth, and sophistication of economic and demographic information have progressed significantly, to where meaningful disaggregated data are readily accessible on sophisticated on-line databases.
- **Scope of Property Market Coverage**—Concurrent with the local orientation of the 1950s, property market information was largely local throughout the 1950s and 1960s, leading to a regional emphasis in the 1970s and early 1980s, then national in the 1980s and global in the 1990s.
- **Source of Property Market Data**—Property market data initially were anecdotal and impressionistic in the 1950s, replaced by brokerage estimates in the 1960s, and then surveys in the 1970s. Property market data bases published on a national basis with explicit and control quality are primary for the 1990s.
- **Capital Markets Data**— Capital market data in the 1950s were impressionistic and descriptive, then in the 1960s they were available on an aggregate basis for major institutions. In the 1970s segment reporting on such key elements as real estate securities, pensions, and offshore began to become of concern, with more specific measurements available in the 1980s. In the 1990s quantification of real estate capital for components and composites, and assessment of ramifications, were of particular emphasis.

Over the last half-century real estate decision tools and information resources have evolved in sophistication, reflecting parallel changes in the economy, information technology, and user expectations, yet results achieved from the application of more powerful decision tools compare unfavorably to what was accomplished with more primitive decision tools.

Although the sophistication of decision tools and information resources have evolved markedly over the last 15 years, the problems plaguing real estate markets in the early 1990s were very similar to conditions in the mid 1970s. At that time this author introduced an assessment of real estate decisions with the following statement:

> Disappointing investment results should prompt those involved to examine how their bad decisions were made. Such an examination leads almost inescapably to deficiencies in the economic analysis behind the decisions:
>
> 1) Too little economic analysis was done.
> 2) That which was done was misfocused.
> 3) The presentation of the economic analysis was inadequate.

Much of what passes for "economic analysis" is actually a superficial presentation of a "best case" optimistic outcome, an advocate's assertion not supported by adequate evidence. Much more is grossly misfocused.

There are a number of reasons for this. The methodologies relied on by many for measuring investment performance are primitive. Their techniques for communicating financial data do not provide useful information because existing general prohibitions against projections deny the investment community the information fundamental to decision making. Very few of those providing real estate economic analysis services have a sufficient breadth of background and expertise, combined with the multiperson, multidisciplinary organizational structure essential to superior economic analysis. Finally, many real estate participants have a false impression of their abilities as investment economists. As a consequence, they decline to commit sufficient resources to perform useful analysis of probable investment results, and some do not bother to utilize any analytic services at all.[24]

In the last fifteen years, similar deficiencies continue, as advances in decision tools and information resources have outpaced their application.

Indicative of the plethora of real estate decision tools now available is a listing of some 1000 commercially available real estate software models[25] and over twenty providers of mapping capabilities, geographic information systems, and regional database management systems allowing analysis and display of geographic data through modern computing technology.[26] Despite quantum advances in the technology available to support real estate decisions, the progress in adapting such technology has been less than impressive. Simplicity still dominates sophistication, even though simplistic approaches may lead to suboptimal decisions. Too often, those making real estate decisions employed a deal making, rather than a strategic orientation. Lacking a context, decisions at the margin will often be marginal. As Maury Seldin has cogently observed, "Relying on 'bottom up' alone may bring 'belly up'."[27]

Advances in word processing technology generally, and the personal computer specifically, have had profound implications on analysis and documentation for real estate decisions. Prior to the advent of word processing, the documentation aspects of real estate decisions, reflected both by analyses and contracts, were necessarily circumspect. The requirement to re-keyboard[28] every revision of written communications meant that fewer issues were addressed, those issues that were addressed were done more in summary than in detail, and that subtleties, nuances, and special situations were seldom emphasized. Whereas, in the 1960s contractual documents for major transactions were often no more than twenty or so pages and seldom much longer than forty pages, by the late 1980s documents for a standard transaction might run scores of pages, and for major transactions, hundreds of pages.

With professionals having the ability to access word processing technology directly through their own personal computer, the temptation to fine tune, modify, and/or embellish is nearly irresistible. Further, the facility with which changes and modifications can be made has led to a lower standard of first drafts, since all involved know that changes can be readily made and multiple revisions of documents are expected.[29] In major transactions today, the attorney who will be reviewing, as contrasted to initiating, the draft of the document, asks not for the hard copy but the disk, if for no other reason than to save time in retyping the document.

Inevitably, with the ease in modification of writing and the temptation to engage in more writing, the time required to prepare a document expands exponentially, given that more issues are addressed, the issues are addressed in greater detail, and the refinements and nuances concerning such issues are massaged more extensively.[30] Although the basic process of producing documents moves much more expeditiously, as a consequence of technological advances, the technological advances in turn have stimulated the pattern of much more extensive, but not necessarily useful, professional documentation.

Beyond facilitating the dubious extension of legal documents, the personal computer has dramatically enhanced the economy and power of analytic work to support real estate decisions, but with certain insidious consequences. Financial analyses presented in spreadsheet formats on computer paper assumed an unwarranted legitimacy unsupported by the validity of the assumptions, sophistication of the analytic model itself, and the probable confidence of the analyst preparing such analyses, an insidious, but not necessarily useful, phenomenon known as the "black box effect." But the very availability of a "new toy" attracted considerable interest and attention from academics and researchers who devoted their energies to writing cash-flow models, at the expense of more significant and important strategic and conceptual issues.[31]

To date, no usable decision rules have emerged from this "computer play." Indeed, the record is uncontested that such computer play contributed to extraordinary financial losses, prior to consideration of the significant opportunity cost of what might have been accomplished had the creativity and intellectual energies of engaging in "computer play" been devoted to promoting the efficient use of society's resources and to creating knowledge.[32]

The precomputer analysis to support real estate decisions had been largely a simplistic, single-period, deterministic approach. The number of the revenue and expense line items considered were constrained rather than detailed and comprehensive. Few time periods were covered and the analysis was limited to an initial or "stabilized" year. Full holding period or life cycle analyses were seldom provided. Adjustments for changes in operating results and values over time were made implicitly rather than explicitly. As such, the numbers employed for particular revenue and expense items were mainly based on assertion, rather than derived from a critical assessment of historic experience adjusted for diverging future expectations, comparison to competitive properties, or source influences on the probable future magnitude of key variables.

Although the rationale, methodology, and tools to undertake more insightful analyses have clearly been available over the last two decades, less sophisticated deterministic analyses have dominated. Such single-point deterministic numbers were often more self-serving than objective, more advocacy-based than independent, and best case more often than reasonable. Probabilistic approaches as well as ranges of outcomes, best case–worst case scenarios, and break-even analyses, although often discussed in academia, were disregarded. Assumptions of future results were essentially treated as certain outcomes.

Even in 1989, some 60% of broker-dealers indicated that the due diligence assessment they undertook did not examine the economics of a transaction.[33] This observation is particularly significant, since broker-dealers represent to their prospective investors that they have, in fact, examined the economics of the transaction, at least implicitly. Such a misplaced emphasis is troubling, especially due to the track record of real estate limited partnership offerings in recent years that have resulted in results generally far short of expectations, if not substantial losses.

Real estate decision makers essentially discounted the possibility of any variance from the representations made by sellers, promoters, and developers. This conduct amounted to a denial of the concept of risk, which was identified by Graaskamp as the difference between assumptions and their realization.[34] Notably, Graaskamp observed that real estate decisions ultimately turn on the credibility of the assumptions of the respective parties to the transaction.[35] Since the advocates' assumptions were largely accepted without question, the decision makers committing capital to real estate ventures were functionally operating with tacit denial of the applicability of risk, having assigned unchallenged credibility to the other side's representations.

While the concept of risk in corporate securities investing was introduced in the early 1950s[36] and only gained acceptance in the later years of the 1960s and in the 1970s,[37] real estate decision makers tended to adopt a mistakenly stable rather than dynamic view of real estate. Significantly, Graaskamp early on recognized the inherent uncertainties of real estate decision making in his election of doctoral work emphasis on risk management and real estate.

During the 1980s the decisions of many were suboptimal, if not dysfunctional. On the capital budgeting front, beyond the specific deficiencies of project analysis addressed above, there were fundamental shortcomings in recognizing the consequences of an inefficient market. The variability of prospective outcomes from an expected value or norm and the associated implications for due diligence in transaction implementation were ignored.[38]

Material shortcomings were evident in the strategic approach to market selection and portfolio construction. By concentrating a disproportionate amount of the portfolio into a single element of risk — property type, geographic region, type of transaction, developer/manager/lender — those involved in real estate capital commitments consistently validated the dictum that owning a good property in a weak market was insufficient, for if a property generated negative cash flow, even after achieving rents and occupancy above the competition, the investor still lost money.

Evidence of decision deficiency during the 1980s by the various market participants include:

- **Space Users** — Lacking a perspective on the persistent patterns of excess in the real estate markets and tending to get caught up in the conviction of ever higher real estate prices, tenants became speculators in leasehold commitments, taking down more space than was needed immediately, to ensure that space would be available for future expansion and to sublet to other tenants who somehow would not be equally prescient in their own planning. Further, beyond this optimistic market momentum mentality, many tenants presumed that unsustainable levels of fundamental growth in their businesses would continue. As a consequence, tenants committed to more space at higher rates than they needed. Then, when both their own growth and expected sublease demand failed to materialize, such tenants found themselves paying space costs disproportionate to both their revenues and the market, at the very time the business space market was viewed to offer great bargains.
- **Developers** — The excesses of developers are legendary, broadly recognized, and well documented. Developers' miscalculations have caused the creation of perhaps a decade excess inventory of business

space, at current absorption levels and record vacancy levels during a decade of unprecedented economic demand for the product.[39]
- **Investors**—The consequences of investors' miscalculations in committing disproportionate capital without sufficient strategic insight, underwriting discipline, and third party due diligence have been extraordinary financial losses.[40]
- **Service Providers**—Service providers were implicit contributors to certain decisions by other lead players—and selectively "aiders and abettors" of the most egregious decisions. At the same time, in some instances the chasm between what those providing services advocated in support of significant real estate decisions and what the market willingly bought was a replay of the classic economic conflict between substantial perceived need and lack of effective demand. With real estate decisions, however, the perceived need was real and valid; the paucity of demand, the symptom of the quality shortfall of real estate decisions.
- **Public Sector**—Regulatory initiative, interpretation, expansion, and retraction by the public sector have created an environment of complexity, uncertainty, and a destabilizing lack of continuity in the "rules of the game." Wave after wave of changing tax laws stimulated, redirected, restricted, and frustrated real estate participants. Often redundant, sometimes conflicting, always difficult, land use approval and growth controls administered by multiple government agencies complicated the development process and increased building costs. Overlapping state and federal regulation of the capital formation process posed daunting burdens to those making financing and investment decisions. A deteriorating infrastructure and shortage of such crucial resources as water were legitimate sources of concern regarding the leadership, or lack thereof, in dealing with critical issues defining the built environment.

As suggested previously, since the decisions a market participant confronts are interdependent with and greatly impacted by the quality of others' decisions, an empathetic approach offers a greater prospect for superior outcomes.

The rationale for a more considered approach to real estate decisions was clearly implied by both the social foment of the 1960s and 1970s as well as Drucker's explicit identification of emerging discontinuities.[41] This author concluded a mid 1970s assessment of the "state-of-the-art" of real estate decisions as follows:

Real estate investment experience in this century is characterized by extreme miscalculations and is unarguably the most persuasive reason for a greater commitment of resources to economic analysis for decision making purposes. For most in the business such a commitment will represent the highest return on investment expenditure they can possibly make.[42]

The methodology and desirability of employing probabilistic approaches to real estate investment analysis was advocated by academics, including Stephen Phyrr[43] and Peter Pellatt.[44] An initial contribution to developing a body of literature of empirical analyses of realized invested returns was advanced by Bruce Ricks.[45] Harris Friedman introduced portfolio theory applications to real estate decisions.[46] The computer dramatically enhanced the means to implement such progressive and meritorious analyses, yet as Jim DeLisle has insightfully observed, the unfortunate outcome was a disproportionate emphasis on manipulating deterministic project-specific numbers with insufficient consideration of their reliability or the insights that could be derived regarding the factors crucial to project success.

Unfortunately, the 1970s critique of the "state-of-the-art" of real estate analysis is still valid today:

> Such analysis as is done is too often characterized by questionable assumptions, incorrect data, conceptually illegitimate models, dubious motives, perverse ethics, and fraudulent representations.[47]

To some degree, the quest to upgrade the quality of real estate decisions is perhaps a classic exposition of the aphorism: "You can lead a horse to water, but you can't make him drink."

Future Priorities

In making real estate decisions, the choice seems to be between explicit insight or implicit myopia.[48] The complexity, economic discontinuity, space surplus, technological change, securitization of property interests, and greater complexity and sophistication of the business require that real estate decisions be explicit, rather than the all-too-prevalent, unreliable implicit approach. Since implicit approaches run the risk of misreading a key element or missing the measure of the market, analyses should be explicitly built on disciplined consideration of each relevant variable.

Those who astutely execute the explicit approach to decision making should eventually be able to realize an extraordinary competitive advantage, for too many market participants are clinging to tried and proven untrue practices. This approach, which promises extraordinary rewards, is not novel. It integrates contemporary models, old-fashioned hard work, and the organizational and information resources necessary for effective participation in today's challenging markets. The explicit approach is more demanding, more resource-intensive, more daunting. But that is the real estate business today, if long-term success is the goal.

Effective participation in the real estate market comes from understanding the prime decisions that the different segments will face. The interdependency of the decisions made by, and the prospective fortunes of, space users, capital suppliers, service providers, and builder-developers, as well as the public sector, requires that each of these players be sensitive to the ramifications of their counterparts' strategic decisions. Consequently, considerations of the major issues these major players face should guide one's own planning.

New strategic management initiatives to cope with the changing environment and new "rules of the game" are needed. Too many real estate participants pursue the business in a manner that has striking parallels to the former business conduct of many Detroit auto executives: insular patterns of decision making unrelated to customers' changing needs and competitors' more aggressive initiatives. Critical decisions that each major segment of the real estate market must confront in the 1990s include:

- **Capital**
  - Which geographic markets and property types to commit capital to, in what amounts, and with what diversity?
  - How to ensure that acquisitions/disposition/lending decisions at the property level are responsibly executed.
  - Monitoring of the portfolio to have requisite information to make informed decisions to ensure investment objectives are met, with particular attention to valuation that serves both decision making and financial reporting.
- **Space Users**
  - Selecting sites and business locations that respond to the enterprise's economics and support its strategy. If the role of real estate has not been explicitly assessed in a strategic context, the enterprise's real estate decisions will probably be suboptimizing, if not inconsistent with its strategy. Thus, a precondition for effective space use decisions is determining what the enterprise's real estate strategy should be and using that statement as a frame of reference to assess particular real estate decisions.

- Acquiring/financing/negotiating particular space-use arrangements on terms that provide the proper balance of economics, timing, flexibility, support for customer relations, and employee productivity and morale.
- Putting in place a meaningful portfolio-management system to track the status of all real estate commitments and to ensure that they are responsibly managed and that surplus properties are disposed of on a timely and, hopefully, profitable basis.

- **Services**
  - Making the strategic decisions to have the right combination of skills, pricing, and market outreach. Just as the business environment overall, and the real estate markets in particular, have changed radically, so must the approaches by companies serving those markets change. Service companies responsive to changing conditions and client needs are rapidly gaining major market share, whereas those that are static are incurring significant erosions of their markets.
  - Supporting clients' primary decisions, encompassing both marketing and implementation issues.

- **Builder-Developers**
  - Putting in place the strategic management systems to ensure effective oversight of the enterprise's direction. Those builder-developers who are close to their markets, intimately knowledgeable of space users' circumstances and needs, and employ contemporary management technologies to deal with dynamic conditions in today's real estate business are thriving. Their success stands in stark contrast to the "we'll do it the way we have always done it because that's what we like, and we just know it will work out over time" attitude.
  - Selecting proper markets in which to build and confirming that the projects meet both consumer needs and are financially feasible.
  - Establishing capital access arrangements to support the development program to ensure that the requisite resources are available.

- **Public Sector**
  - Putting in place effective planning and control systems to manage their substantial holdings properly. Just as real estate is corporate America's most important undermanaged asset, so is real estate an important public resource.
  - Determining appropriate bases for regulating property use and for other decisions concerning property.

Strategic insight is of critical priority in the contemporary discontinuous real estate markets, for as noted investor Warren Buffett observed, "Superior management records are more determined by which boat you are in than by how effectively you row."

For the 1990s, the real estate labor market enjoys an imbalance of would-be decision makers, relative to the demand for their services. In fact, the condition of the labor market for real estate professional and managerial services mirrors the business space markets: excess supply relative to demand. Notably, however, many of the would-be decision makers are ill-equipped for the challenges they face in the 1990s. The crisis in real estate management was identified in the mid 1980s:

> The gap between the need for and supply of management capabilities for the real estate sector is growing at an alarming rate.[49]

Given this assessment, that the experiences in the second half of the 1980s were so disappointing is not surprising, in light of the warning of prospective "pitfalls for rapidly expanding and newly involved organizations active in real estate."[50]

The management crisis was identified as posing a grave threat:

> The number of qualified individuals in the real estate business is grossly inadequate. The result of this managerial crisis has been excessive personnel turnover, organizational disruption, and strategic malaise, if not misdirection. Integrating a business which is entrepreneurial in nature with the large organizational context of the financial services firm, and doing this during a period of dramatic economic and technological change, requires an effort which should not be underestimated. Those managers and professional advisors who have the ability to address these issues in a responsible manner are at a premium.[51]

At the same time,

> ... it also represents great opportunities for those executives and organizations that can cope effectively with it. Thus, strategic planning should be a great priority for real estate enterprises and for the entrepreneurially-driven financial institutions that will be increasing their real estate involvements.[52]

However, in practice strategic thinking has been an alien concept for many real estate decision makers.

Guidelines this author offered a decade ago for real estate decisions[53] aptly apply to real estate decisions in the 1990s:

- A multidisciplinary approach, complemented by multiple perspectives, offers a greater prospect for successful solutions to complex problems than does a more narrow and singular orientation.

THE EVOLUTION OF REAL ESTATE DECISIONS 59

- Whereas one must guard against the creativity-stifling tendency of certain group processes, generally the constructive contribution of critical peer review and professional dialogue enhances the quality of the problem solution over what it would be were a single analyst to work alone.
- An explicit approach with full disclosure and clear documentation of the analytic processes and information utilized enhances the reliability of, and therefore the confidence in, the solution to a complex problem.
- A suitably detailed forecast of anticipated future benefits, based on imaginative generation of original source data and the careful use of secondary data sources, together with appropriate analytic techniques to develop the relevant figures, is fundamental to solving the complex problem.
- The relevant information should be incorporated in an economic model that employs analytic techniques appropriate in sophistication and complexity to the problem, being sufficiently powerful to reflect the nuances and character of the data, yet not so sophisticated as to overwhelm the reliability of the underlying information.
- In the valuation analysis, realistic discount rates derived from capital markets and realized historical return on investment data should be employed, with appropriate adjustments to differentiate between nominal and real monetary values, as well as different levels of risk.
- Consideration should be directed to the behavioral pattern involving relationships between parties who can influence the property's performance and hence its value, with particular attention given to goal congruency between managers and investors.
- All factors influencing a property's value should be considered, including, but not limited to, the legal form in which it is held, the tax posture of the owners, the regulatory setting, and the like.
- Care should be taken that allowances are made for the relative differences in efficiency of various real estate markets, recognizing that the more inefficient market gives rise to and, indeed, is characterized by the prospect of greater variance of outcome, hence the larger the chance of error in the appraisal process.

Ultimately, superior real estate decisions depend upon requisite human capital, organization context, decision systems, information resources, decision tools, up-to-date machinery, and strategic insight. Effective real estate decisions in the twenty-first century require the analyst to embrace simultaneously the scientific as well as the artistic approaches.[54]

The pace and direction of the evolution of real estate decisions is determined by the interaction of numerous forces, including:

- Fiduciary imperatives of decision makers
- Regulatory requirements and legal precedents
- Community desires and political considerations
- Client's demand for real estate space and services
- Requirements of capital providers
- Opportunity for enhanced results from superior decisions
- Perception of downside risk associated with inferior decisions
- Availability of superior decision tools and databases
- Competitive pressures
- Education and training of decision makers
- Advancement of knowledge supporting real estate decision making.

Certainly, real estate decision making is concurrently subject to the broad array of forces that influence decision making generally.

The holistic, multiperspective, interdisciplinary orientation described in this writing parallels Graaskamp's advocacy that real estate decisions be made from a concurrent micro view and appreciation of the systems context while embracing consideration of "any factor influencing communication, persuasion, or recognition of needs and motivation in the transactional interface of enterprises in the real estate network."[55]

Graaskamp's work reflected a blending of creative approaches involving conceptual thinking[56] and what he described as "extrasensory perceptions" that represented "convictions, which may be difficult to document statistically or to accept as foregone conclusions, may suggest certain strategic priorities"[57] with structured decision models.[58] Thus, Graaskamp's real estate decisions style reflected the artist's creativity, which continually evolved to depict a contemporary evolving society, and the scientist's rigor, which persistently sought new technologies and tools.[59]

Notes

1. Graaskamp, James A. "The Role of Investment Real Estate in Portfolio Management" Monograph. Bryn Mawr, PA: The American Council of Life Underwriters, 1972, p. 1.
2. Ibid.
3. Ibid., p.1.
4. Bradshaw, John. *Bradshaw On: The Family*. Deerfield Beach, FL: Health Communications, 1988.

5. Personal conversation with author.

6. Most prominent of the recent aniculation of the masses make history theory is Mikhail Gorbachev, *Perestroika: New Thinking for Our Country in the World* (Harper & Row, New York, 1987). A parallel perspective is the contral theme of the classic novel by Leo Tolstoy, *War and Peace* (Penguin Books, London. 1957), first published in 1869. Among those who argued that heroes make history is, Ivin Torgenev, *Rudin* (Penguin Books, New York, 1982), published in 1865; *On The Eve* (Penguin Books, New York, 1957), published in 1860; *Fathers and Sons* (Penguin Books, New York, 1986), published in 1862.

7. Stephen E. Roulac, "Structuring the Joint Venture," *Mergers & Acquisitions* (Spring 1980), 4.

8. Janis, Irving L. and Leon Mana. *Decision Making—A Psychological Analysis of Conflict, Choice and Commiment.* New York: The Free Press, 1977.

9. For an historic perspective on the real estate markets see Mark A. Weiss, *The Rise of the Community Builders: The American Real Estate Industry and Urban Land Planning.* New York: Columbia University Press, 1987.

10. For a history of real estate finance in the twentieth century through the mid-1960s, see Graaskamp, James A. "Development and Structure of Mortgage Loan Guarantee Insurance in the United States." *Journal of Risk and Insurance* (March 1967), 47.

11. Roulac, Stephen E. "Valuation Decisions in a Turbulent Economy: Challenge to Tradition, Opportunity for Distinction." *The Appraisal Journal* (October 1982), 564.

12. These forces are addressed in Roulac, Stephen E. "New Economic Conditions Create New Investment Opportunities." *The Appraisal Journal* (July 1975), 337, and Roulac, Stephen E. "Changing Economic Imply New Real Property Investment Relationships." *California Management Review* (Spring 1976), 57.

13. Roulac, Stephen E. *Real Estate Capital Flows 1989* Report prepared for Equitable Real Estate Investment Management, Inc. by The Roulac Group.

14. Drucker, Peter. *The Age of Discontinuity—Guidelines to Our Changing Society.* New York: Harper & Row, 1969, p. 3.

15. Indicative of the formerly staid status of property law is the observation of Charles Goldstein, prominent New York attorney, who related to the author in a conversation in New York in 1972 that he elected real estate law as a profession because of his impression from the state of law in law school that he could readily master the discipline, and thereafter apply that mastery throughout his professional career.

16. "The New Money Target: Profitable Real Estate." *Business Week* (August 1, 1977), 52–53.

17. "Real Estate." *The Wall Street Journal Reports* (August 10, 1990), 1.

18. Supra note 1, p. 3.

19. The commentary on changing real estate markets is adapted from Roulac, Stephen E. and Loren D. Volk. "Deal-Making Strategies in the New Era." *Real Estate Finance* (Winter 1989), 13–22.

20. One perspctive on the multiple forces impacting the complexity of real estate decisions is provided in Graaskamp, James. "Book Reviews." *The Financial Review* (1973), 81.

21. Martin, Fred. "Heard the One About the Copy Shop in Budapest?" *The New York Times* (December 16, 1990), 42.

22. Hale, David D. "Global Finance and the Retreat to Managed Trade." *Harvard Business Review* (January-February 1990), 150, 151.

23. Rybczynski, Witold. *The Most Beautiful House in the World.* New York: Viking, 1989 p. 153.

24. Roulac, Stephen E. "Real Estate Investment Analysis, and Valuation: Economic Analysis, Disclosure and Risk." *Real Estate Issues* (Winter 1977), p. 8.

25. Publication Number 337. College Station, Texas: Real Estate Center at Texas A&M University

26. Twenty providers are listed in the *Best 100 Sources for Marketing Information—Who's Who for American Demographics*, published by *American Demographics*, 1989.

27. Seldin Maury, "A Reclassification of Real Estate and Market Analysis: Toward Improving the Line of Reasoning." *Real Estate Issues* (Spring/Summer 1984), 44, 47.

28. Re-keyboard means to enter all elements of the documents again, as contrasted to accessing pre-entered characters and numbers from memory.

29. This section benefitted from a January 1990 discussion with Phil Adler, partner in the Los Angeles law firm of Loeb & Loeb.

30. James Webb, Professor at Cleveland State University, observed in a conversation with the author, "Machines can do it, but humans love to read, reread and reread all this stuff which increases time and cost."

31. As James DeLisle, head of Investment Research for Equitable Real Estate Investment Management, observed in a convensation with the author. "In the early 1970s as a discipline we were making significant progress in the application of simulation in Monte Carlo approaches to real estate decision making, yet the attention of academics and researchers has been directed away from those types of issues and towards playing with their computers."

32. "Monte Carlo is playing with a computer and has resulted in no usable decisions rules to date!", Webb, supra note 30.

33. Survey by The Roulac Group of Broker-Dealers active in considering underwriting real estate securities offerings.

34. Graaskamp, James A. "An Approach to Real Estate Finance Education by Analogy to Risk Management Principles." *Real Estate Issues* (Summer 1977), 53.

35. Graaskamp, James A. "Don't Buy Real Estate, Buy a Set of Assumptions." Class notes reproduced in Jarchow, Stephen P. editor. *Graaskamp on Real Estate*. Washington, D.C.: Urban Land Institute, 1991, p. 376.

36. Markowitz, Harry, "Portfolio Selection." *Journal of Finance* (March 1952), 77.

37. Bernstein, Peter L. *Capital Ideas—The Improbable Origins of Modern Wall Street*. New York: The Free Press, 1992.

38. Roulac, Stephen E. "Games the Stock Market Didn't Teach You." *Real Estate Investing*, monograph published by The Institute of Chartered Financial Analysts and Dow Jones-Irwin, 1985, p. 36.

39. Roulac, Stephen E. *Capital Flows 1990: Real Estate Alternatives for Institutional Investors*. Report prepared for Equitable Real Estate Investment Management, Inc. by The Roulac Group of Deloitte & Touche.

40. Supra note 13.

41. Supra note 14.

42. Supra note 24.

43. Phyrr, Stephen A. "A Computer Simulation Model to Measure the Risk in Real Estate Investment." *American Real Estate and Urban Economic Association Journal* (June 1973), 57.

44. Pellatt, Peter G. K. "A Normative Approach to the Analysis of Real Estate Investment Opportunities under Uncertainty and the Measurement of Real Estate Investment Portfolios." Ph.D. Dissertation, Univ. of California, Berkely, 1970.

45. Ricks, R. Bruce. "Imputed Equity Returns on Real Estate Financed with Life Insurance Company Loans." *The Journal of Finance* (December 1969), 921.
46. Friedman, Harris C. "Real Estate Investment and Portfolio Theory." *Journal of Financial and Quantitative Analysis* (April 1970), 861.
47. Supra note 24.
48. The commentary that follows on the critical real estate decisions is adapted from Roulac, Stephen E. "Reevaluating Real Estate Captial Commitments." *Real Estate Finance Journal* (Summer 1988), 6–15.
49. Roulac, Stephen E. "Management Challenges in an Era of Institutional Transformation." *Real Estate Issues* (Spring-Summer 1984), 37.
50. Ibid.
51. Ibid., pp. 42, 43.
52. Ibid., p. 43.
53. These decision guildelines are adapted from Roulac, Stephen E. "Balancing Right Brain Creativity and Left Brain Discipline to Value Complex Real Estate Interests." *The Real Estate Appraiser and Analyst* (Summer 1982), 49; (Fall 1987), 50, 56, 57.
54. Ibid.
55. Graaskamp, James A. "Identification and Delineation of Real Estate Market Research." *Real Estate Issues* (Spring-Summer 1985), 6.
56. Ibid.
57. Graaskamp, James A. "Strategic Planning Approach to Major Real Estate Decisions." Unpublished essay appearing in Jarchow, Stephen P. (editor). *Graaskamp on Real Estate*. Washington, D.C.; Urban Land Institute 1991, p. 378.
58. Supra note 55.
59. For a critical, more complete assessment of the Graaskamp philosophy of real estate decision making see Roulac, Stephen E. "Linking James Graaskamp's Work to Mainstream Thought," and related papers to be published in a volume sponsored by the University of Wisconsin, Madison, in collaboration with the American Real Estate and Urban Economics Association.

2 THE SEARCH FOR A DISCIPLINE:
The Philosophy and the Paradigms
Terry V. Grissom and Crocker H. Liu

Decades of debates have addressed whether or not academic real estate can qualify as a discipline. The perspectives of whether the field of study is an academic discipline, a functional area of study (either as a separate area of study or as a concentration in finance), or simply a collection of trade preparation courses can be identified in the literature on real estate education and curriculum. Research by Brown (1978, 1979, 1981), Cook (1971, 1974), Grissom, et al. (1982), Miller and Gardner (1982), and Pearson (1985) identify courses and course content that industry surveys show is important to students in finding jobs.

This literature can be considered either as the basis for viewing real estate as a functional area of study or an area of trade training. It does not establish the premises required for a discipline.

The literature and mindset of the trade training approach runs contrary to the course of investigation in this paper. The trade approach represents a utilitarian philosophy of real estate education that is in place in most real estate programs [see Garrigan and Wardrop's (1981) NAR survey of colleges and universities]. Although this utilitarian approach is lacking in the more rigid academic parameters of a discipline, it is consistent with the philosophic educational bases that resulted in the founding of the nation's land grant universities. Wofford and Preddy (1980) illustrate the economic importance of a utilitarian perspective. They identify a dichotomy of the low prestige of careers in real estate but the high level of compensation expected by students. Though comparative pay levels is a weak basis to proclaim a discipline, it asserts a strong argument that the market places value on people trained in specific real estate skills.

Unfortunately the idea of defining real estate by course topics designates real estate study as a trade-oriented training program. This limits real estate to a functional area of study that will ebb and flow with geographic economic cycles. However, as economic trends in the Southwest illustrate, the down period is when trained real estate skills are needed. Atkinson (1972) emphasizes the mix of specialized training with capital and realty assets required in cyclical economic patterns.[1] In general the ebb and flow of graduates in a major is a function of the market and technical advancement. It cannot be the prime determinant of a discipline.

The impression of academic real estate as a trade training program is what Gordan and Howell (1959) attacked in their study of higher education in business. The premise developed from their survey concludes that specialized training in specific business areas is not necessary for employment. Review of their study shows that the survey structure, design, and specification of the approach can be attacked with limited difficulty. The Wofford and Preddy (1980) findings, using a more representative sample and more sophisticated survey and statistical analysis, offsets Gordon and Howell's sample, which shows non-real-estate majors are hired for real estate jobs. The Wofford and Preddy study illustrated the demand and superior compensation levels for real estate graduates.

In part the difference in the findings of the two studies has occurred because industries and the overall economic environment have changed in the term between the timing of the studies. Currently, greater levels of specialized technical expertise are required. Also, as Grissom (1989a) and Jaffe (1988) have indicated, the structure of real estate markets and the organization of industry professionals have changed in the last two decades. This is significant given that Gordon and Howell's study only addressed corporate employment. Their study did not consider any aspects of entrepreneurial or small business training. This later delineation of business activities would be most descriptive of the real estate industry.[2]

The Gordon and Howell study did point out the lack of a cohesive approach to problem analysis in real estate curriculum and other specialized areas. Kinnard (1968) reinforces this concern by inferring that the trade-oriented approach communicates detached facts and avoids the development of general principles. An agreement on general principles and relevant paradigms is identified by Kuhn (1970) as central to disciplinary status.

The failure to achieve this academic coherence is what is lacking in many real estate programs. In part an underlying philosophy is needed to achieve the desired level of coherence.

Philosophical Basis

Works by Graaskamp (1976a,b), Dasso and Woodward (1980), and Weimer (1956) identify alternative philosophical bases for the study of real estate and propose the status of a discipline. The essence of a philosophical basis is that it provides the context to develop general principles relating facts and enables the powers of abstraction necessary to eliminate the mundane and emphasize the relevant.

A philosophical investigation of premises for the study of real estate can be built on the chronological links in land economic philosophies, as illustrated by Weimer (1984). His investigation identifies the strong tradition emphasized in the works of Ely, Fisher, Ratcliff, Andrews, and Graaskamp.

An investigation of the literature, university curriculums, and a taxonomy of issues researched over the years is used to indicate the topical areas that constitute a study of real estate. A key reference is the work by Garrigan and Wardrop (1981) prepared for the National Association of Realtors in 1981. Supportive work over time is from Andrews (1978), Grebler (1959), Ely (1898), Wendt (1949, 1987), Sa-Aadu and Shilling (1988), Isakson and Ordway (1987), Jaffe (1988), and Smith and Greenwade (1987). The cited works identify the aggregated areas of study involved in real estate analysis, policy, and decisions.

A synthesis of this prior research enables a systematic approach to the knowledge base required for an academic pursuit of real estate. The systematic synthesis of disciplines, areas of study, and subject matter comprising real estate are illustrated in Figure 1.

Synithesis of Disciplines and Issues

Wendt (1974) identified real estate as an eclectic area of study. As such it comprises information, questions, and concerns that can be identified in the disciplines and studies of law, engineering, geography, sociology/

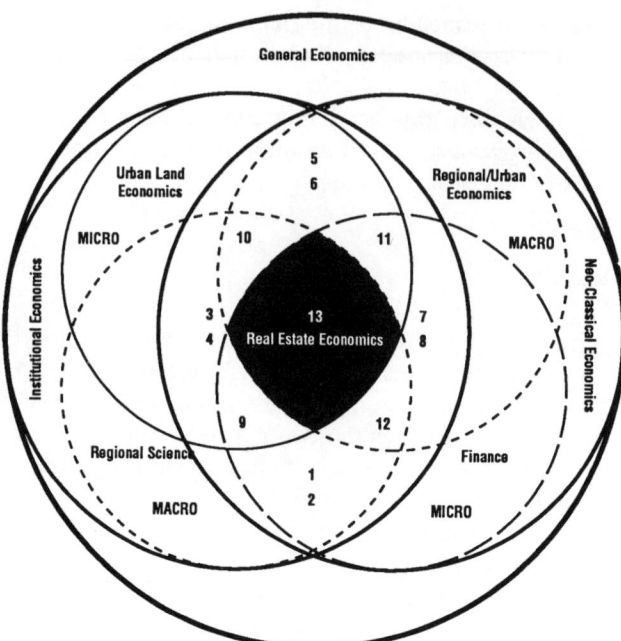

Figure 1. Integrative Philosophical Basis for a Real Estate Discipline: The Concerns of Real Estate Economics or Fixed Asset Management. The following are examples of the areas of study that occur in the disciplinary overlap. This list of topics is not exhaustive or mutually exclusive. Any topic can logically appear in other areas of research. The black area might be delineated as the study of Real Estate Economics or Fixed Asset Management. Examples of the topics and their interdisciplinary origins as numbered are (1) Public Utility Economics, (2) Regional Accounting, (3) Land Use Allocation, (4) Urban Growth Theory, (5) Industry Location Theory, (6) Urban Structure Theory, (7) Public Finance Policy, (8) Transportation Economics, (9) Local Finance and Tax Policy, (10) Location Economics, (11) Spatial Capital Markets, (12) Share-Shift Analysis, and (13) Real Estate Management: and the property, the project, the deal.

demography, history, psychology, political science, urban planning, economics, finance, marketing, management, and general business. Andrews (1978) identified subareas within this array of academic groups illustrating the eclectic interests of real estate and showing its interdisciplinary nature. The potential for overlapping issues and problem situations is characteristic of most academics. For example, the classical Hawthorne study has been taught in management, sociology, psychology, and economic courses. To delineate a discipline is difficult without encroaching on the paradigms of other academic endeavors.

The process of encroachment can be one perspective of viewing Figure 1. However, a broader perspective is that of a tool to help delineate the topical/information set that is real estate or fixed asset management.

As Figure 1 illustrates the universe for disciplinary activity for real estate is the study of economics. At this level, the concern is economics in the broad sense, the traditional perspective of political economy or socioeconomics. This initial context was established in the writings of Ely and Morehouse (1922), Ratcliff (1976), Andrews (1978), and Graaskamp (1973). Chryst and Back (1966) placed the study of real estate/land economics within the scope of the rational allocation of resources. The essence of the allocation process is choice. The processes of rational choices links the study of real estate to the other areas of business and economic study.

Despite this common foundation in the economic science, a dialect has evolved in the approach to making decisions in the different disciplines depicted in Figure 1. This dialectic is based on the philosophical perspectives of neo-classical and institutional economics (Chryst and Back, 1966).[3] The neo-classic approach has been the dominate perspective in academic literature since the 1930s. It forms the basis of positive economics and is favored by its capacity for the development of formal theory (Langlois, 1989) concerning the free or impaired flow and structure of markets. It is founded on the Marshallian Synthesis of Classical Economics with the Austrian marginalist's theories.

Langlois (1989) identified the institutional prospective as characterized by appreciative theory. It perceives economic decisions as derivative of social institutions. The central paradigm requires a historical perspective in which economic activities are best understood in an evolutionary process heavily influenced by cultural preferences. As economic decisions are made institutions are formed; as institutions evolve, decision processes are influenced.

The significance of delineating these economic philosophies is that they are the soils of the study of the disciplines of regional/urban economics, finance, urban land economics, and regional science. Thompson (1968), Mills (1972), Heilbrun (1974), and Segal (1977) have identified the roots of urban economics as neo-classical. Martin et al. (1988) established a direct relationship of finance to neo-classical economics.

Chryst and Back (1966), Weimer (1984), and Ely and Morehouse (1922) established the basis for the study of land economics from an institutional perspective. Ratcliff (1976) offered an entire paper on the linkage of urban land economics to institutionalism.

Figure 1 symbolically illustrates the disciplinary areas (topics) of overlap in the subdivision of economics. The subdivisions identified in Figure 1 are not consistent with the economic fields identified by Ward (1972). This lack of consistency may in part be attributed to the fact that finance, urban economics, regional science, and urban land economics (as well as land economics and real estate) are covered in schools of business, planning, and agriculture, as opposed to departments of economics (with given exceptions). This would suggest that real estate is not isolated in a lacking of academic recognition. All of these areas have roots in economic theory and originally evolved as applied areas. The applied character, in part, is the results of distinct institutional characteristics influencing the perception of unique market structures. This creates sets of issues not significant to the concerns of main-line economist.

However, as Figure 1 illustrates, these various fields of study contain areas of topical (issue) overlap that all relate to real estate concerns. The common topics are all delineated in the central vertical ellipse of Figure 1. A list is presented at the bottom of Figure 1, with examples of problem areas or issues that are offered and addressed in the literature or classes of the various fields of study and topics discussed. All of the topics are a concern and often are taught and researched by real estate academics. The central ellipse, while depicting an academic concern with numerous issues and topics, supports the contention of real estate as a multidisciplinary area of study. This is both a blessing and curse. As a blessing the multiple areas of study presents a broad array of topics for investigations. As a curse, however, it prevents (as per Kuhn, 1970) the development of an orthodox theoretical framework of problem-solving activity that is unique to the discipline. The sociology of a disciplinary foundation is that the "profession" must agree on the relevant topics and the appropriate paradigm with which to investigate the pertinent issues.

The heterodoxy of real estate academics has prevented this disciplinary advancement. However, as Figure 1 symbolically illustrates, there is a conceptual area of topical and paradigm overlap that can be defined as real estate or real (fixed) asset economics. The black area revealed in Figure 1 conceptually contains the unique or pertinent topics and paradigms that are the real estate discipline. Around this core are the extended areas of investigation depicted by the central ellipse of the Venn diagrams. These are the related or extended areas of real estate research (education). This notion of extended areas of interest is not uncommon in all disciplines.

Real Estate as a Business School Discipline

Taxonomy on the philosophic origins of various economic disciplines is directly related to the status of real estate as a discipline offered in business schools. This is premised on the functional areas and the factors of production. The institutional perspective has retained the original classification of four factors of production: labor, land, capital, and entrepreneurship. The neo-classical school is divided between three, two and one factor of production premises (with varying attributes; 1981–82, 1984–89). See Palmquist (1989) for further insights into this issue. In the three-factor perspective, the entrepreneurial effort is simply another form of labor. In the two-factor perspective, land is another form of capital. In the one-factor perspective, given the research description of human capital, labor is a capital issue also; therefore, it is argued that all factors collapse to capital. The most predominant view appears to be the concern for two factors, labor and capital, with the Austrian branch of classical economics still insisting on the power of entrepreneurial innovation to stimulate economic activity.

Given these economic premises, business schools are often established along functional areas as management, financial, and marketing departments. Therefore, if land is simply another form of capital, then real estate is definitely a subsection in the study of finance. However, if land is a distinct factor of production as per Palmquist (1989), it merits the functional equivalence of labor (management) and capital (finance).

As Ratcliff (1949) pointed out, real estate is characterized by two factors of production in dispute of residual claims: land and entrepreneurship. This is important to curriculum since the link between these two factors is key to teaching real estate development. Also, the link has lead to a plethora of books relating personalities to real estate, see Zeckendroff and McCreary (1971), Thomas (1977), Powell (1986), Stevens (1984), Trump (1989), and others.

This cult of personality that often characterizes the "popular" notion of real estate study has probably interfered with its acceptance as a serious area of academic study.[4] The influence of the entrepreneur along with the perception of a lack of formal theory (especially independent of general economics) has subordinated the study of real estate in many business schools.

The low regard for real estate, in part, is because of the failure to integrate institutional and neo-classical perspectives. Witness the typical real estate principles course. It is taught as a survey course, offering some discussion of the physical and legal attributes of real estate and then a sequence of related institutional and functional areas (i.e., brokerage, appraisal, management, public and planning impacts) with the conclusive segment of the course addressing investment parameters. Contrast this to finance or even management and marketing, which do the same but also present the theoretical constructs of the discipline.

What is needed is to address the relationship between the eclectic dimensions of real estate within a traditional economic perspective. The institutionalist would approach this as an economic process. Graaskamp builds on this basis and uses appreciative theory to construct a real estate process. The process relates business activity to location in the context of the city. Recognizing the needed link in the process of business analysis to the urban environment, Ratcliff (1976) encouraged urban land economics theory as the undergraduate emphasis of real estate.

Basic of a Real Estate Discipline

Considering real estate as a process, the Venn diagrams of Figure 1, illustrate an area of overlap that can be identified as a set of topical issues that can be called real estate economics. Whether land or capital, the real estate asset is unique in that it must be addressed in a spatial dimension. Whether viewed in the institutional framework of urban land economics as per Ratcliff (1976), Andrews (1978), and Ely and Morehouse (1922) or in the neo-classical context of urban economics via Mills (1972), Segal (1977), and Heilbrun (1974), or in the spatial economics of Vickerman (1980), Losch (1954), or Marshall (1979), the study of the locus of economic activity and its relationship to other economic activities and externalities does not exist in the current stream of finance literature. Only in international finance is a spatial dimension introduced. This in part is because capital is assumed to be spatially ubiquitous and fungible, and readily transferable given the general equilibrium assumptions of arbitrage and capital-asset pricing models. These paradigms are not sufficient to address a major portion of real estate market issues. However, they offer a needed dimension to some very relevant concerns.

Specific research in real estate investment and finance has indicated the importance of the spatial dimension to decision makers. For example, mortgage market analysis by Winger (1969) and Jones (1985) has illustrated variations in spatial markets. Overall investment returns have also been illustrated to be spatially dispersed in the works of Miles and McCue (1982), Hartzell et al. (1987), Grissom et al. (1987b), and Grissom et al. (1987a).[5]

The failure outside of real estate academics to recognize the spatial significance in investment is observed in current industry problems. The extremes are characterized by the positions of David Shulman, of Solomon Brothers, and Harold Ellis, Jr. of Grubb & Ellis. Shulman reveals the financial market perspective of real estate investment when he states "just show me the numbers." He continues that "dealers don't really need to know everything about the properties they peddle. . . ." Ellis, on the other hand, has criticized Wall Street promoters for lacking an understanding of the underlying concepts that motivate property decisions, development, and investment.[6] Ellis's concern is for the specific product and market perspective.

The academic research has revealed the need to integrate both perspectives. Given the current market environment, the projection of the financial returns over time for real estate as a separate investment or even in a portfolio context was not sufficient. The failure to understand the nature of the real estate product and its market shows a need for fundamental analysis based upon a process of linking the physical, legal, and location attributes of real estate to urban and market structure. This linkage is necessary to further delineate the level of returns and to evaluate appropriately levels.[7]

Urban land economics and finance theory is needed to appropriately address current real estate problems. The real estate discipline lies in relating urban land economic and finance paradigms, premises, constructs, and tools to these problems. The discipline must also further define the relevant problems to address. The portfolio context and concerns with adequate measurement of risk and return illustrate the contention of this integration. The growing internationalization of capital markets further requires this integration.[8]

For example, as national policies and influences diminish in their impact on international capital flows, an understanding of the hierarchy of cities and their market areas must be emphasized. As Hamilton (1986) illustrates, the financial links between London, Toyko, and New York cannot be denied. In turn, these cities are linked to financial submarkets throughout the world.

The changing structure of financial relationships throughout the world will alter economic interaction. The nature of financial enterprise requires educated and technically astute employees, whose activities are characterized by interpersonal communication. The theoretical constructs for an understanding of both financial and fixed capital investment can be linked to Haig's (1926) "packet of functions." This concept enables the analysis of enterprises in an urban setting. Haig states that enterprises are influenced by the surrounding socio-economic activities, with the packet of functions premise suggesting that, although a corporate enterprise may be vertically integrated, specific functions within the firm are located in areas compatible with a particular firm function. If this is the case, then real estate research must address the conflict of ubiquitous international capital flows with the uneven development of the built environment.[9] Harvey (1989) and Smith (1984) have investigated this topic in a nontraditional perspective. However, it is a general issue that can be approached by the integration of urban land economics and finance.

Economic, social, and political issues in a spatial context will be the source of problems and concerns into the next century. Therefore a primary emphasize of real estate as a discipline is the development of a basis of knowledge investigating capital formulation and how it relates to the built environment (the urban place) in a spatial context. However, to develop this line of investigation further, it is necessary to identify the constructive paradigms of real estate, urban land economics, and finance that can be integrated.

The systematic identification of topical areas and related disciplines of real estate study establish the context of the paradigms that support or derive from general principles of academic real estate. As the synthesis process in Figure 1 illustrates, the philosophical basis of real estate is a study of eclectic issues but from the perspective of economic thought. Economic thought, for example, reduces the study of land, land use, resource, and capital components to issues of choices under the constraints of limited resources.[10] Many of the paradigms unique to real estate are decision methods concerning real capital under constraints and states of uncertainty. Choices under resource constraints are a conceptual link to land economics (in the broad sense). Choices under uncertainty are a conceptual link to finance.

Paradigms

The emphasis of real estate study in the context of spatial and capital issues identifies the array of paradigms unique or linked to the study of real estate. The introduction and discussion of these paradigms also identify the gaps in the discipline that must be investigated in order to achieve the level of general and integrated principles.

Instructional Paradigms

There are a series of paradigms that set the context for an analysis of real estate problems and help decision making. The following general models have been offered in real estate instruction. Each of the following paradigms establish an analytical framework for the study of real estate.

The Space–Time to Money–Time Equation of Real Estate Analysis

Following the abstraction process of neo-classical economics, Graaskamp reduced the essence of the real estate product to space available for use over time. He delineated the constraints on space–time choices in the format of a process. The capital components of time via Fisher (1954) and Markusen (1979) are introduced into the process with Graaskamp's formulation of the space–time to money–time equation. With this simple abstraction, Graaskamp reduced the study of real estate from a highly institutionalized procedure to one of converting space available for use over time into money or capital measures subject to the constraints of interacting parties. Graaskamp asserted that these interacting parties often have diverse goals. Despite the varying objectives of the parties, the ultimate goal is the cash cycle conversion represented by the space–time to money–time equation.

The paradigms of the space–time to money–time equation and the real estate process enable a philosophical shift of the study of land economics and real estate from a traditionally institutional economic framework (see Ratcliff, 1976 and Gibson et al., 1966) to a neo-classical format of abstract analysis (as specified by Jaffe, 1988).

This paradigm shift enables a central philosophical basis for real estate study. Russell (1962) identified the importance of abstraction in scientific method by suggesting that scientific thought is power thought. He suggest that as irrelevant details are omitted from the analysis more powerful links of the relevant variables can be identified. As such, urban real estate as space–time has a foundation in the philosophy of Hume (1972), in which he identifies the causal premise of most activities as spatio-temporal occurrences. Marshall (1979) via the neo-classical synthesis built on Hume's premise by linking urban value to relative situation over time. These themes continue in the conceptual developments of the neo-classical works of Von Thunen (1966), Weber et al (1964), Losch (1954), and Hotelling (1929).

The conceptual relationship of spatio-temporal elements to probability analysis is a key concern of Institutional Economics. Heiner (1988) established a direct link between economic behavior and decisions under uncertainty based on probabilities of outcomes. Ratcliff (1953, 1965) has linked this institutional concern to spatial choices, land use mixes, and the behavioral perspective of valuation. Ely and Morehouse (1922), Commons (1934), and Andrews (1971) illustrated the institutional approach to space–time issues.

The abstraction of the space–time to money–time equation is the root paradigm for expanding real estate research into spatial economic investigation as well as the domain of financial economics. The equation as the base paradigm supports the financial management–land economic education philosophy promulgated by Dasso and Woodward. Also, the paradigm shows to an extent that the financial management-land economic premise is the same as the multidisciplinary approach suggested by Graaskamp.[11]

Space–Time Models and Definitions

DeLisle (1985) offered a key tool in linking the spatial to financial dimension on a micro level with the presentation of the maximum building envelope in his Interactive Design/Marketing Model (IDM). For an example of the use of the building envelope as a direct link of the space–time dimension of real estate to the monetary projection over time see Grissom (1990). Greenhut's (1974) theories support this link with his analysis of the spatial impact to revenue trends over time.

The space–time dimension of the equation establishes the essence of realty's economic function (Greenhut, 1974). This function establishes the uniqueness of real estate from other forms of capital, (Grissom, 1990). Space is a physical, social, economic, legal, and political element. This multiple characterization of space then requires an extensive level of investigation that requires a knowledge base beyond a superficial identification of the land and everything attached to it. Graaskamp (1976a) expanded the definition of real estate to allow for a learned investigation of the space–time product and its unique problems by defining real estate as

> Artificially delineated space with a fourth dimension time, referenced to a fixed point on the surface of the earth; created to house an economic activity and subject to the cultural preference as it is constrained by the public infrastructure.

As linked to financial theory, the space–time to money–time equation forms the basis for fundamental analysis of real estate. Not only does it afford the basis for the level and duration of the real estate returns, it also enables a more thorough delineation of the risk parameters of real estate. There is an obvious need for this analytical capacity, given the place of real estate within the current national economy. The failure to appropriately forecast real estate returns and to account for risk emphasizes the need for an expertise other than the unadjusted application of financial techniques to real estate.

The studious investigation of the space–time elements of real estate can be formulated using the productivity analysis proposed by Ratcliff (1965, 1972). Productivity analysis entails the investigation of the physical, legal, and locational components of real estate and the basis for projecting net operating income into the future. The productivity analysis as the construct of fundamental return potential and risk exposure is influenced by the literature on the property rights paradigm and urban land economics theory as related to land use models. Both of these areas of investigation sufficiently merit separate discussions as paradigms.

The establishment of the space–time/money–time equation as the central issue concerned with land use decisions can relate financial concerns to an array of land use models. This relationship, along with the issues of property rights and their impact on economic decisions (such as value and solvency), is key to the acceptance of real estate as a discipline. Each of these issues, in turn, can be identified as paradigms in and of themselves. Along with the IDM model, an understanding of the space–time/money–time equation can be gained through the paradigm of the Real Estate Process.

The Real Estate Process.

The modeling of real estate as a process is found in the educational approach promulgated by Graaskamp (1976a). Its foundation is the Institutional Economic perspective that economic phenomena should not be analyzed solely in terms of static equilibria but as processes with a history and a future (see Langlois, 1989). This perspective is observed in the land economics of Andrews (1977), Ratcliff (1953), Ely and Morehouse (1922), Barlow (1986), Chryst and Back (1966), and Dovring (1987), on which Graaskamp's process is built.

Langlois (1989) suggested that an economic process can be identified as a causal and sequential evolution taking place in real time. This is in contrast to neo-classical analysis, which is normally concerned with an equilibrium situation. Unfortunately, this equilibrium is not defined as the end result or rest state of a process, but as the condition of logical consistency among a group of mathematical relations. As per Walras (1954), equilibrium is the logical consistency of relations. However, logic

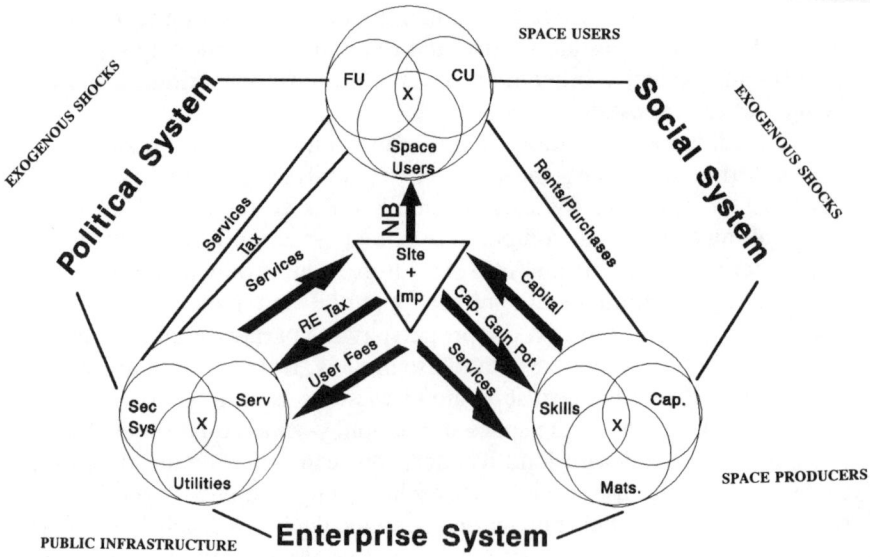

Figure 2. The Real Estate Process.
Source: Wurtzebach and Miles; Modern Real Estate

alone may miss the existence of relationships and the causal nature of those relationships. Hayek (1948), as an alternative to Walras, offered a process approach in which economic agents develop plans and strategies in which equilibrium occurs when those plans come into mutual consistency after a process of learning.

This philosophy is evident in Graaskamp's real estate process on both a macro and micro level. As depicted in Figure 2, the macro level is contingent upon the interfacing of a space consumer group, a space producer group, and the public infrastructure group. All the groups are concerned with a common nemesis of land use (as depicted in the center of Figure 2). Each of the groups is characterized by a set of objectives, policies, and institutional constraints of operations. The cost and benefits of the interaction are demonstrated by the labeled flows between the groups (Figure 2). These procedures and objectives per group often lead to conflicts between the groups. The producer group, as private developers with profit-maximizing objectives, is often diametrically opposed to the environmental objectives of the planning groups.

Figure 2 shows Wurtzebach's (1981) extension of Graaskamp's macro

THE SEARCH FOR A DISCIPLINE 79

model to the site-specific level by illustrating the interaction of the participants in the development process of a specific site. The actions of the developers, lender, and public agencies as producers of space are subject to the needs and wants of the consumer groups, with all activities being regulated by public agencies and informal community groups.

Steps in Process

Graaskamp relates the micro level analysis of the process to the feasibility process. The real estate process itself is composed of three general stages. Ratcliff (1965), Graaskamp (1972b), DeLisle (1985), and Grissom (1984) have identified these steps as productivity analysis, market analysis, and investment analysis. Productivity analysis is unique to real estate as opposed to other assets (especially financial assets, which are often a matter of contractual agreement and, hence, investment analysis). Productivity analysis can be equated to fundamental analysis in investment and corporate valuation. It is important in real estate because land and capital within the built environment is economically flexible; it can be converted or placed in alternative uses. Therefore much of the analysis in real estate is to identify the use or purpose of the property: to define the product. This requires an understanding of the physical, legal, and locational dimensions of the property. A sophisticated analysis of the locational parameters necessitates a knowledge of the building blocks of urban land economics.

With the appropriate delineation of the product, the competitive supply and potential demand can be identified. For real estate the market interaction is considered in a spatial context. The tools of situs, structure, and succession (as well as the impact of institutions) must be used to interpret and delineate market thresholds. Market analysis for real estate uses general marketing theory; however, out of necessity it must consider the geographical concerns of spatial concentrations of supply and diffused demand. Therefore in real estate, market analysis must incorporate urban and urban land economics. The tools of these disciplines often enable the comparison of heterogeneous assets, which are often assumed homogeneous in general marketing theory.

Another aspect of real estate analysis often ignored in the literature is market structure. Because of the spatial implications of real estate and the physical and hence economic constraints it imposes, real estate markets are often not perfectly competitive. Graaskamp addressed this issue with the strategy of seeking natural monopolies in the development and investment of real estate. Greenhut (1974) has approached the issue by proposing that spatial markets are best understood by oligopolistic models. Hotelling (1929) identified a duopoly. Losch (1954), Huff (1962), and Berry (1964) have proposed models of monopolistic competition. The end result is that many forecasts and appraisals may result in inappropriate conclusions because they assume a perfectly competitive market structure.

The final phase of the process is investment analysis. At this point a direct link to financial investment paradigms is possible. The productivity analysis and market analysis of the process is useful in the investment context to evaluate elements of unsystematic and systematic risk. The sequential dynamics of the process relates the real estate product to the constraints and options possible in the market. The final decision then collapses to the comparisons of rates of return and risk levels.

The real estate process is a paradigm that qualifies the space–time to money–time equation by integrating the eclectic dimensions of real estate. It supports the contention of a unique discipline that synthesizes the issues and fields of study depicted in Figure 1.

Risk Management

Graaskamp (1976b) promulgated the use of a risk management paradigm in the study of real estate. He suggested that risk analysis and management is the philosophical premise guiding the feasibility process. This proposal is consistent to the analysis of economic phenomena as a process and can be fully integrated into the Real Estate Process identified above. See Grissom (1989b) for the link between these two perspectives and the benefits of land economic analysis.

The risk management procedure is concerned with the identification of possible variation from expectations. The management component incorporates the general skills of overall business administration concerns, but with an emphasis on risk issues. The management of risk involves the identification of the possibilities of variation in expectations as modified by the potential severity and frequency of the deviations. With the identification and analysis of risk exposures, management techniques are employed to minimize, absorb, or transfer the cost of alternative occurrences. The risk management perspective enables a procedure that links the probabilistic analysis of land economics to the uncertainty concerns in finance.

Risk management functions as a paradigm in the real estate context because of the complex character of real assets. The analytical concern with deviation from expectations can be identified within the sequences of the real estate process. The identifications of potential deviations within the physical, legal, and locational dimensions of the property can significantly alter the final decision on any given site. This concern can also be carried out in the market and investment levels of the process. As Grissom (1989b) and Grissom and Wang (1988) have shown, the measure of space–time and money–time issues are much improved by the added dimension of risk within spatial markets.

Risk management offers a paradigm that links the Real Estate Process directly to the topical issues and paradigms of finance studies. Graaskamp (1972a) further illustrated this potential within the context of institutional investors. Overall risk management can be used as a context to link the financial management/land economics approach of Dasso and Woodward (1980) to the business administration approach to real estate study proposed by Weimer (1956).

Business Administration Approach

Business administration as a paradigm for the instruction of real estate is linked to the impact of the Gordon and Howell study. In fact the designation of real estate as urban land economics and insurance as risk management can be tied to the generalist move in education in the later 1950s and early 1960s.

A major proponent of the administrative approach to real estate education was Weimer (1956). Weimer stated that the administrative viewpoint differed from that of the physical or social scientist. Administration was concerned with the accomplishment of desired results through human effort. The format was a problem-solving orientation, involving selection among alternative courses of action. The techniques used included processes of planning, organizing, motivating, and controlling operations to achieve desired results. The end objective was to achieve a purpose. The emphasis involved informed, rational, and deliberate action.

The business administration approach is limited as a philosophy for the development of a discipline. However, it offers three main tools for professional analysis—the formulation of goals, the choice of ways and means, and the direction of people in some group purpose. These elements are key components in a problem-solving process and, as per Kuhn, an agreement on the relevant problems is the crux of the sociology of a discipline.

If allowance is made for the expansion of knowledge (training) as possible within the multidisciplinary concerns, then business administration's problem-solving matrix is the glue that can pull the plethora of issues, attributes, and institutions that comprise real estate together in an active process. As a paradigm the Real Estate Process can be neatly placed within the administrative umbrella. Therefore, like the previous paradigms (Space–time/Money–time, Real Estate Process, and Risk Management), the administrative approach is logically integrated with the interdisciplinary philosophy depicted in Figure 1. See the example of urban resource and asset management located in the Venn diagrams.

The problem-solving orientation of the administrative approach can be linked to the hypothesis that institutions are created and evolve to address economic problems.

Property Rights Paradigm

Many of the institutions characteristic of real estate (land economics) are legal in nature (Barlow, 1986; Ely, 1898; Andrews, 1978). In fact, many principal texts in real estate are concerned with the delineation of real estate, realty, and property rights. Many of the problems in real estate are linked directly to contractual relations, market behavior, and land use controls. Jaffe (1987) identified the "property rights paradigm as the foundation for the analysis of many problems in finance, markets and public and private claims on real property."[12]

Given the legal foundations of this paradigm, concerns with alternative institutional arrangements often confront different individuals in a variety of ways based on the myriad range of property rights possible. De Alessi (1980) suggested that by taking these differences into account, the theory of consumer choice can be extended to cover the behavior of a large number of previously unexplained events. The issue of allocation of resources or market choices is important because, as Coase (1937) pointed out, they are linked to transaction cost and thus to the bargaining and exchange process. Therefore the right of control will ultimately rest with the party who values it most highly. Demsetz (1967) supported the economy of property rights by stating that the emergence of new property rights take place in response to the desires of interacting persons for adjustments to new benefit–cost possibilities. The paradigm of property indicates the dynamics of a process.

The relationship of the process to property rights is observed in the works of Jaffe (1987), Ratcliff (1949), and Graaskamp (1967). Jaffe (1987) allowed an overview of the link between finance, market, and product decisions. This is right in line with the links of productivity, market analysis, and investment analysis promulgated by Ratcliff. Graaskamp (1973) supplied a practical format for the application of the process via feasibility analysis and established its theoretical basis in the definition he promulgated for real estate.

The property rights paradigm not only offers great opportunities for research in general economics, but lies at the essence of real estate, which is potentially the ultimate source of conflict between social and property conflict (Bonbright, 1965).

Financial Theory Paradigms

Martin et al. (1988) identified several prominent contributions to the theory of finance, some of which are linked to property rights. They identified the significance of Coase (1937) and Alchian and Demsetz (1973) to Jensen and Meckling's (1976) investigation of agency cost and attendant property rights in finance instruments. Although limited to property issues and transfer cost of financial contracts, these issues can be expanded to the more general property concerns of realty as it relates to financial issues. This is in essence Graaskamp's money–time dimension. The classical works of Fisher (1954) and Hirshleifer (1970) on intertemporal consumption/saving and investment, Hicks (1939) work on rate structure and Williams' (1938) formulation of the principle of the conservation of investment, Miller and Modigliani's (1961) treatment of financing choices, are all extensions of the complex issue of money over time.

The time element as a concern of finance and investment injects the need for the consideration of risk and more specifically uncertainty. The works of Knight (1971), Markowitz (1952), Sharpe (1964), and Ross (1976) simply integrated risk issues into the money–time component as it relates individual investment contracts to overall markets. Sharpe, Litner (1965), Fama (1970), and Black and Scholes (1973) and Ross illustrated the importance of information and market structure on the risk levels and valuation of the money–time contracts.

The financial literature is well established and respected in academia. Its understanding is essential to individuals interested in real estate academics, not only because most real estate jobs are available in finance departments, but also because financial issues are as essential to the understanding of real estate as legal and locational factors.

However, the money–time component represented by the classical literature cited is only a portion of the total real estate equation. The space–time dimension must be fully comprehended to understand the nature of real estate products, markets, and problems. In a financial context the failure to grasp the space–time component will result in inappropriate analysis of the risk dimension of real estate.

Summary of Instructional Paradigms

The preceding paradigms are offered as the context by which to study academic real estate. An investigation of the paradigms indicate an overlap between the techniques and the philosophies of the overviews. The space–time/money–time equation supports the essence of the investigation of real estate as an area of study. The latter component of the equation links real estate directly into the study of finance. Many of the issues, property rights, and techniques that will be developed as money–time concerns will be addressed in the future development of finance literature. The link of these issues to real estate will come from economists, people trained in finance and real estate academicians. The evolution of the discipline will result from a consensus of these diverse groups as to the relevant issues to investigate and the appropriate paradigms to employ.

The former component (space–time) relates real estate to spatial economic studies. This is an area of investigation influenced by a more eclectic group of academicians, including economists, geographers, regional scientists, planners, sociologists, and real estate academicians.

Despite the eclectic combination of academic contributors, a distinct area of topical concerned can be delineated as the study of real estate.

This area of investigation is depicted in the blackened region of the Venn diagrams in Figure 1. The conceptual/issue area symbolized in the diagram by the black area is the specific analysis of the space–time to money–time equation. The investigation of the components of this equation has lead to the development of paradigms often associated with the specific study of real estate.

Paradigms Unique to Real Estate/Land Economics

Land Use Paradigms

As Dasso and Woodward (1980) suggested, a central point to the evolution of a discipline in real estate is the development of techniques to assist in the efficient distribution of land uses. The land use diatribe can be generally categorized as both spatial and capital issues, involving both production and distribution problems. None of general issues have been appropriately integrated in the models and/or paradigms to form general equilibrium theories. Therefore much of the real estate research is classified as ad hoc or case studies. This perception applies to many land use decisions, which must originate from the perspective of a specific use.

Land use problems are identified in the literature of urban economics, general economics, urban land economics, planning, geography, finance, and real estate appraisal and finance. The extent and nature of the problems and the models consider various levels of constraints and abstraction. In general the land use models and processes each suffer from potential inefficiencies and issues that need to be addressed in further research to achieve a single integrated paradigm as the basis for general theory of land use and markets. This general equilibrium model (if possible) may be what is needed to develop the credibility of the study of real estate.

As noted above, the origins of land use models come from various areas of study. The following models are specifically associated with the appraisal literature and typically address site-specific issues, with relative location often being a given or fixed constraint. At best the appraisal models only implicitly address surrounding land uses and their impact. The specific nature of the models are observed in their definitional construction.

Highest and Best Use

Highest and Best Use (HBU) is a concept enforced by law to enable a comparative standard for making real estate value decisions. Vandell (1982) pointed out the relationships between the concepts of market value and HBU. Its importance to the valuation of a property is repeated throughout the appraisal literature. The concept is applied in practice as a process. The process is concerned with identifying the legal, physical, and market (?) constraints on the property as interpreted by the appraiser's experience and judgment.

Although HBU is touted as the central concept to valuation, it has been an ambiguously defined concept premised on an appraiser's judgment. This has led to the proposal of alternative models that emphasize different constraints than those of HBU. Another concern identified by Colwell (1988) is whether HBU is appropriately considered on a macro or micro level. This dichotomy in part can be attributed to the origins of research in land use problems—urban land economics or appraisal. For an insight into the theoretical dichotomy behind the HBU concept and a survey of the literature, see Dotzour et al. (1990).

Several efforts have been made to formalize a quantifiable HBU model. The most recent attempts have been made by Grissom (1983), Pearson (1985), and Dotzour et al. (1990). The inability to evolve an applicable general equilibrium model has resulted in Most Fitting Use and Most Probable Use Models as alternatives to HBU.

Most Fitting Use and Most Probable Use

Numerous modifications and explanations of the HBU process, have been proposed over time (see the articles in AIREA's Highest and Best Use Readings; AIREA, 1981) However, analytical concerns have lead to more than just modifications and quantitative models of HBU. Two distinctive alternatives were suggested by Kinnard (1966) and Graaskamp (1979).

Understanding of the relationship of Kinnard's most probable use model (MPU) and Graaskamp's most fitting use model (MFU), is helped by the micro vs. macro issues delineated by Colwell. Graaskamp identified MFU as a macro-level land use concept, which was the optimal reconciliation of the goals and objectives involving effective consumer demand, the cost of production, and the fiscal and environmental impact of third parties. The conflicting objectives of these groups must operate within the physical and financial constraints of the property.

The end result of this reconciliation of objectives and constraints is a range of possible uses, as opposed to the point-specific use analysis derived in the concept of HBU. This is reflective of the Real Estate Process, which identifies that real estate is economically flexible and subject to risk ranges in terms of physical, legal, locational, and economic potential.

This characterization of real estate necessitates a specialized analytical capability, for, unlike many assets, the asset of real estate can have alternative uses and different economic functions. This requires that a given site be considered in the context of different markets with an array of probable buyers in each segment. This results in the consideration of uncertainty in the analysis of both land uses and land markets. The recognition of uncertainty makes real estate more consistent with financial markets and less consistent with traditionally defined competitive markets. The paradigms of land use models may suggest the linkage point of real estate modeling to urban and financial issues.

Graaskamp (1973), in developing his MFU model for feasibility, also developed an operational definitions for Kinnard's MPU paradigm. He identified MPU as a micro-level land use analysis concerned with topical constraints imposed by current political factors, the state of current real estate technology, and the short-term solvency pressures on consumers, producers, and/or public agencies.

Being site specific, MPU imposes more rigid restraints on the potential of land use options than MFU. To an extent this enables a more quantifiable analysis of use, reducing the decision from one under uncertainty to one with measurable risk. For a summary of the MFU, MPU, and HBU concepts and an analytical depiction, see Grissom (1983).

Urban Land Economic Land Use Paradigms

As an area of study land economics encompasses the issues of land in production, the land market, the role of land in distribution, and the relationship of land use to the claims on output arising out of the control of land.

Land economics emphasizes the well-being of groups. A reason for this orientation is the spatial context of land markets in which decisions external to the individual often impact the choices of the persons controlling a given site. Therefore, land economics must recognize the interest of those other than the direct users of land (Chryst and Back, 1966).

This orientation is important to the process of real estate market analysis. For those with a strict financial orientation, this perspective can identify elements of risk–return trade-offs. The current trend of identifying the need to get back to the "basic economics" of the project is not just a concentration on before-tax analysis. Analytically, there must be a tie between the market components of supply and demand, and the use potentials of the site (within a spatial context).

Situs

The paradigm of situs is a vehicle that enables a tie between the market and a site's use potential. The general model of Situs from an extreme micro viewpoint is the set of relations between a specific land use on a specific land parcel and the total urban environment (as they function in time).[13] As Andrews (1977) illustrates, the theory of situs is the building block to allow the analysis of intra-urban land use location. It can be envisioned as the micro structure that supports ecological relations comprising an urban system and its economy. As a paradigm, it is at the heart of the basis for a general (aggregating) model of the urban structure.

Viewed as a process, situs can be applied as the steps needed to identify economic activities within a spatial context. The situs paradigm, as it has currently evolved, qualifies the associations between economic activities, the accessibility or spatial flows between activities, and the eclectic environments of externalities that influence land use allocation and returns. The extent of the environmental issues can be political, physical, psychological, economic, social, and institutional.

Situs is a central paradigm (along with the space–time/money–time equation) to the application of the Real Estate Process. It enables the conceptualization and practical application of the ties between the various groups involved in land use decisions. It enables a qualification (and in some cases, a quantification) of land use relationships and an understanding of urban structure and land markets. Real estate market analysis cannot be appropriately performed without the employment of the situs concept.

Urban Structure

The disciplines that have created a substantial literature in urban structure are geography, history, sociology, planning, and economics. Real estate as applied economics has only contributed to structure theory with the pioneering works of Hurd (1970) and Hoyt (1964). Their work alone indicates the importance of an aggregative spatial paradigm to the analysis of values, returns, and risk in real estate markets.[14]

The spatial form is clearly one of the most fundamental of the urban characteristics. The structure is a primary expression of the dynamic relationship between groups. The spatial structure is a constraint on political, economic, and social activities and a result of these systems. Whitehead (1977), and Rogers (1967) emphasized that structure theory is mainly influenced by the mediums of rents and prices as vehicles to promote greater efficiency in the arrangement of activities in urban space. While the literature characterized by Whitehead and Rogers has emphasized the land market as a primary determinant of structural form, others have emphasized physical and social issues; see Walters (1976) for a survey of these topics.

The dichotomy of the emphasises establish the premises for two distinct schools of structuralists. They are the rent theorist and the social ecologist. The rent theorist can be linked directly to Von Thunen's works and characterizes the first and second generation works (see Anas and Dendrino, 1976, for explanations of these classifications) of Alonso (1964), Haig (1926), Beckman (1972), Muth (1969), Mills (1972), Solow and Vickrey (1971), and others. The first generation models illustrated that income expended for location is allocated between site rents and transportation cost. The second generation models extended this base work to a general equilibrium approach to land use.

The ecologist group has developed descriptive and/or historical or "genetic"[15] models. Examples are the models of Burgess (1925), Hurd (1970), Hoyt (1964), and Harris and Ullman (1945). In these models land use is grouped within the context of an overall urban system. These models identify land use changes over time and the potential direction of city growth. They further define land use ecology patterns. The patterns help delineate the influence of surrounding activities on individual sites and offer descriptive suggestions of possible land use changes.

The structural schools are linked by empirical studies identifying parameters impacting real estate values in delineated areas of a city. The study of urban structure and its dynamics are important given the significance of externalities to real property performance, function, and value.

Land Use Succession

The dynamics of both structure and situs theory is addressed in the theory of land use succession. Succession as applied to urban land use is a direct transfer from the field of physical ecology.[16] Urban real estate, both land and buildings or land alone, is subject to land use change. Therefore, the phenomena of change can take place in individual properties and on a neighborhood or multiproperty level. However, given the spatial relationships defining real estate (such as neighborhood homogeneity, land use patterns, and examples of zoning), the idea of changes in a single property alone are relatively isolated events. Changes tend to accumulate in fairly concentrated areas. This is reflected in the appraisal process addressing land use succession in the context of the "life cycle of the neighborhood."

Whether the concern is of an individual property or for an area, the information flow from spatial analysis to markets, to the real estate investment sector, could be much improved. These issues involve the externalities that are definitely relevant to the analysis of risk and return. Furthermore, as Andrews (1980–82) points out, there is a logical (causal) connection between the shifting conditions that illustrate succession and the qualitative locational ties that characterize situs. In turn, both situs and succession are vital theoretical components of urban structure from its physical and land use points of view.

Therefore land use changes can be linked to the broad forces that impact on structure, such as the market (supply and demand), technology, societal changes, and institutional change. In relating these broad forces to specific neighborhoods or individual properties, the issues of external and internal forces that can alter real estate returns and values can be identified. Examples are the changes in cultural norms and technology. Obsolescences are almost exclusively a human cultural concept involving technology and design. However, it may be expected with normal physical aging and deterioration and/or the phases of economic life.

Examples of the theoretical works on the economics of succession are Andrews (1971, 1980–82), Ratcliff (1949), Heibrun (1974), and Ordway and Harris (1981). Empirical research is available from Bourne (1973), Phillips (1981), and Brueckner (1977).

The further development of the three urban land economic theories and their integration or synthesis into a unified field theory may hold the essence of a disciplinary development. An understanding of these theories is also key to a linkage of real estate investment analysis to the research in spatial market structure.

Spatial Market Structure and Real Estate Market Analysis

Little work has been done in directly linking spatial market studies directly to real estate analysis. Much of the spatial market research has been in the field of urban economics (or related areas) on a macro level. Vickerman (1980) has offered an analysis of spatial economic behavior on a micro level, but it essentially addresses the trade-off issues of site vs. transportation cost, which are the key issues of the rent theorist. Andrews (1980–83, 1971) offered links between sites and users that is effective in identifying parameters for future modeling, much of which is incorporated into Graaskamp's feasibility process (1972b, 1973). However, there still remain several gaps between theoretical development and models available for spatial market analysis.

The real estate market analysis work of Graaskamp (1985), Clapp and Messner (1988), and Rabianski, et al. (1989) all offer techniques that help in the analysis of macro-level data and the descriptive application of those data to specific sites. However, the missing component in the market analysis process is the linkage of the quantitative techniques between the city level and the site level. Huff (1962) offered some linkage with the behavioral adjustments made to traditional gravity models. However, the theoretical support to justify some of the links has not been forthcoming. Also very little research has been found to link valuation or investment analysis to spatial market studies.

Greenhut (1974) has suggested the theory of the firm in economic space as an oligopoly. This description of market structure holds some promise for valuation in a spatially defined context. This context is supported by the monopolistic competition assumed to underlie Huff's model (and the theories of Losch, 1954; Christaller, 1966; and others). However, the monopolistic competition and the oligopolistic structure are totally contrary to the competitive markets assumed by the traditional appraisal process and much investment theory. Perhaps further research in the area of spatial market structure could result in improvement in valuation/investment analysis.

A initial model establishing a research process in the direction of the spatial investment analysis of an individual project is offered by Robbins (1989). Robbins' work integrating geographic information systems with cash-flow projections may set the pattern for this element of needed real estate investigation in the future.

The deficiency in the linking of spatial market research to the valuation/investment analysis of real estate delineate a remaining area of paradigms that are unique to real estate study. These paradigms address issues of value theory.

The Value Paradigms

Another key area of concern with the study of real estate deals is the overall need to make economic decisions relative to land or land-related financial products and real assets. The paradigms that have evolved over time are directly related to concerns in land economics and finance. Traditionally issue of value theory were addressed in the alternative schools of economics that have developed over time. However, as Wendt (1974) pointed out, since the 1950s economic concepts of value have been limited to price determination considered by models. Value has taken on a subjective connotation to many researchers that is inappropriate, given the scientific status of economic research. It appears only the institutional branch, as defined by Gordon (1980)[17] and some of the radical economic groups, still address value concepts.[18]

The study of finance has followed the general economic field of limiting value theory to price determination. The concepts of efficient markets and the free flow of information are emphasized over value estimation and policy impacts. An efficient and active market of homogeneous assets fully fits the price-determination paradigm. Even technical analysis, with its expectation of cycles and trends based on historical patterns, omits the value theory paradigms that justify much of the analysis.

The one area of finance retaining a value concern is fundamental analysis. It assumes that a difference between price and value exist, and that specific analysis of value determinants can enable the capture of above-market returns. The concept of intrinsic value has links to value procedures available in appraisal analysis

Babcock's work (1932) during the 1930s has influenced much of the current appraisal literature and the key assumption that there is a difference between price and value (at least in real estate markets and assets). The potential for this difference, in part, is because of the heterogeneous nature of the real estate asset, the uncertainty due to infrequent asset trading, the spatial structure of the market, and various potential uses possible on any given site. Babcock (1932) identified this problem by observing that a two-tiered market existed for real estate composed of both competitive uses and competitive users. Liu et al. (1990) have addressed these problems with the formation of an overall capital market model allowing for the impact of asset "lumpiness" and omitted assets as they influence market structure.

The significance of the nature of real estate and its market structure on the development of decision models is that there is a need for ad hoc decision tools. The appraisal process being the traditional ad hoc decision tool employed for many real estate problems. Grissom (1990) made an extensive argument for the promulgation of the appraisal process in real estate and the inadequacy of general models because of the lack of available data, the infrequent trading, and the physical, locational, and legal dimensions of real estate.

The limitations of the real estate market as compared to an efficient market, as pointed out by Gau (1987), have resulted in legislation and litigation defining normative value concepts. Grissom (1985) showed that much of the value debate is a conflict of emphasizing the role of institutional constraints over direct market activity. The incongruency of the market vs. institutional policy often influences the level of risk or uncertainty identified in the various value definitions used by decision makers. The perception of the market structure, its level of certainty, and the employment of the emphasis on institutional policy has resulted in an array of value paradigms available in the real estate field.

Ratcliff (1972) identified that a major purpose of a value estimation is to reach a decision; the decision is needed to solve a problem. This could imply that as problems change the concept of value may change. This, however, can lead to several sophomoric debates that can mislead or further confuse the issue, as witnessed in the valuation confusion that existed with the dissolution of the bankrupt railroads in the latter 1970s and early 1980s (see Grissom, 1986, for insights to these value conflicts).

Regardless of the value definition often employed to address specific problems, these definitions often end up being a mutation or an extension of a market value definition. It is difficult to avoid the comparative basis afforded by the concept of a value in exchange.

This preference for exchange value is tied to the basics of value theory, which is concerned with the sources or bases of the worth of an asset. The process that identifies why an asset has worth can result in a different quantitative measure than the dollar amount indicated by a transaction price. Therefore a standardizing concept as a basis for comparison can be useful to decision makers. This is important in an area such as real estate where the objects of comparison are not *perfect substitutes*. The need for this comparative standard has given rise to a reliance on the concept of market value.

Market Value

The practice of using market value as a comparative standard has it roots in law as much or more so than straight economic concerns. Market value is encouraged in condemnation via the enforcement of constitutional law. Because condemnation is a contrived market with unequal bargaining positions as defined by Commons (1934), it is necessary to assume standards of a fair competitive market that in the context of spatial markets may not actually exist.

Ratcliff (1965) suggested that these assumed standards result in an allocation model that has equity components as well as a concern for market efficiency. He went further to infer that often the concept's consideration for equity often distorted the efficiency of land use allocation. Ratcliff stated that the equity component of the value definition was so predominant that it should be symbolized as V_e. Grissom (1985) extended this argument, suggesting that variations of the standard value definitions are not concerned with emphasizing the measurement of pricing efficiency, but with the implementation of policy issues. He further showed that the policy issues are consistent with the long-term normative value concept promulgated by Smith (1980).

Most Probable Selling Price

Though many value definitions are simply modifications of a general market value model, reflecting policy implications (Grissom, 1985), one conceptually distinct value alternative was initially offered in the 1960s. The proponents of the most probable selling price concept, Kinnard (1966) and Ratcliff (1965), suggested that the concept of a probable selling price was devoid of the normative assumptions of market value (except for the need to identify a normal time on the market, as later pointed out by Graaskamp, 1979).

Most probable selling price (V_p) is more consistent with a process concept of real estate and fits the probabilistic perspective of economic behavior promulgated by institutional economist Ratcliff's (1965) arguments for employing V_p were that the market players often have limited information on which to act. The limitations are the result of variances in expectations and economic means and a lack of parity in bargaining positions in most transactions. Hence he argued the forecast of a conclusive price of most transactions has a probabilistic range of outcomes, the outcome being a price rather than a value indication. Therefore he promulgated that the function of analysis is not to estimate a value but to predict the probable price of a future hypothetical transaction. To represent the price and probabilistic nature of the prediction, Ratcliff suggested that the concept be symbolized as V_p.

The concept of most probable selling price was identified by Grissom (1986) to be consistent with Smith's and Marshall's short-term transaction price concept. Therefore, the most probable selling price is a useful tool for short term decisions (such as current marketing and negotiating decisions). Market value is more appropriate for longer term problems (such as permanent financing decisions). The risk concerns of V_p may be more consistent with real estate decisions in a portfolio context and the finance concern of value addivitity. The value addivitity issues of finance may fit the property economics of plattage and plottage, identified by Colwell and Sirmans (1978).

Alternative Methods to Value

As the previous paradigms have illustrated, value is a conceptual premise to help decision making in real estate. It is appropriate in some situations but not all. Alternative decision tools are available. Many adopted from finance are appropriate for investment analysis. The investment literature tends to emphasize rate criteria. The real estate literature has developed three distinct models of its own, the Ellwood model (1977), the financial management rate of return (Messner and Findley, 1975), and the modified internal rate of return (Graaskamp, 1972a). Each of these models incorporates specific modifications of traditional return models that address issues of concern to real estate decision makers. Cannaday and Colwell (1981) have proposed a heroic premise for a unified field theory linking the conceptual issues of these and other income models. This direction of research has not received the full attention it deserves.

Solvency

Given the context of his Real Estate Process, which identified the interaction of various interest groups, Graaskamp (1976a) argued for solvency as a decision alternative to value as a central premise. Graaskamp's concept of solvency continues the dynamic dimension of institutional economics as process. Traditional finance defines solvency as the excess of assets over liabilities. Solvency in the context of a process links to Ratcliff definition of real estate productivity (based on the space–time dimensions).

Solvency as a process is concerned with the excess of money coming in over cash outflows. The outflows are basically liabilities arising from debt and periodic operating expenses. The inflows are linked to the asset's productivity (not just the measure of asset value as in the traditional definition).

The basis for solvency (money in) is linked to the traditional finance concept of intrinsic value (contract rents, property specific) but is augmented by the behavioral influences of interdependent market decisions. In this context, solvency is a flow concept rather than the traditional fund premise. As a flow concept, it is a tool applicable in viewing individual but interdependent real estate projects in a dynamic process. As a dynamic measurement tool, solvency as a flow is flexible to enable the periodic impact of internal and external economic activities on a given property enterprise.

Summary

The contention of this research is that a discipline is an organized course of study. The philosophical approaches presented in this paper illustrate that real estate is not only an organized course of study but has alternatives approaches available. However, it can be promulgated with a logical investigation that they all reduce to a similar approach. This seems consistent with Kuhn's definition of a discipline (science).

On the other hand, the study of real estate is an eclectic endeavor. Multiple disciplines are involved in an academic investigation of realty and land use. This array of coexistent fields currently limits real estate's recognition as a distinct area of study, even though it has sufficient paradigms and philosophies to justify such a status. In part this independent status has not been claimed because of the economic advantage of being housed and marketed as finance professors. This is sufficient rationale (currently) to not claim the property right of a discipline. However, long-term survival and risk management suggest that revealing the significant set of real estate issues to be more than an extension of the financial paradigms (although highly related) will significantly advance the disciplinary status and broaden the career opportunities.

The attempt to achieve decision and policy formulation to help in the options available to real estate asset decision makers has resulted in several paradigms that are unique to the field. The evolution of paradigms and the extent to which these paradigms can be discussed and debated is evidence of the development of general principles of real estate economics and the basis for verification as a discipline.[19]

Notes

1. An example is an incident recorded by Atkinson in an attempt to get appraisal courses installed at Yale University. The college president felt trade courses should not be taught at the university level. After the courses were turned down, the president of Yale asked questions concerning real estate problems of the university. After the discussion the

courses were approved. The president recognized the need for specialized training. The time period Atkinson addresses (1922–1938) was a term in which several real estate/land economic classics were published (for example, Babcock, 1932, and Bonbright, 1965).

2. Discussions with R.K Brown at a corporate real estate seminar in 1986 indicated that corporate real estate has changed over the years since the Gordon and Howell study. The corporate real estate or fixed asset departments continue to grow as other departments are reduced. The new employees are real estate trained.

3. Friedman (1966) identifies the difference between neo-classical (positive) and institutional (normative) economics to the emphasis placed on policy. The delineation of neo-classical-institutional economics is defined by Keynes. See Chryst and Back (1966) for a detailed discussion.

4. Although corporate takeovers and LBOs are characterized by personalities in the financial area.

5. Graaskamp was an early proponent of real estate portfolio analysis for institutional investors doing research on insurance company portfolios (Graaskamp, 1966, 1967).

6. The debate is an extension of the dichotomy of land as capital or a separate resource. It also extends the analytical conflict of fundamental analysis or market behavior as the focus of prediction, from finance to real estate.

7. The failure to understand the nature of the real estate product and its market shows a need for fundamental analysis based upon a process of linking the physical, legal, and location attributes of real estate to urban and market structure. This linkage is necessary to delineate further the level of returns and to evaluate appropriately risk levels.

8. The relationship between real estate and other functional areas is illustrated by the growing emphasis on international business studies. Many may view international business study as an indication of the demise of real estate's position as the fifth functional area. However, an international interest can only serve to strengthen real estate's position as a needed area of study within a business school. This expectation is based on the spatial economic dimension of real estate and the importance of urban complexes, and hence urban land economics, to international markets. This perspective of real estate and international studies is the result of a discussion with Jack Friedman.

9. This is a major concern of Marxist theory, but is at the heart of capitalistic location decisions. However, a traditional approach has not addressed this issue.

10. This context is established by Blaug (1983) as the procedure of economists to explain economic phenomena. However, the bulk of these issues are not the problematic concern of economists or financiers, and thus establish the problem set for real estate study.

11. It is important to point out this link because if an area of study is termed *interdisciplinary*, it is often not considered a discipline. Institutional economics, hence land economics, is a multidisciplinary area of study. Witte (1954) stated that institutional economics involved the use of noneconomic factors in economic decisions. As such this would involve a broad range of socio-political-spatial topics in the study of real estate. In this regard it does not differ from professional curriculums, such as architecture and urban planning, which combine various social sciences, management, engineering, and design, nor does it vary from more aged social sciences, such as geography, psychology, anthropology, or philosophy. Given these analogies, how can it then be less of a discipline than marketing and management, which call upon economics, psychology, geography, sociology, and statistics? Unlike these areas, as the synthesis illustrates in Figure 1, real estate is heavily rooted in economic analysis.

However, as delineated in Figure 1, the land economic–financial management relationship misses the broader issues important to real estate decisions that are offered in an institutional context, such as that offered by regional science or even the macroeconomic perspective of neo-classical regional and urban economics. Despite the source of the tools employed in analysis, the foundation of the analytical roots, or the origination of the problem, the common concern is an economic decision, the need to make a choice under limiting constraints. The space–time to money–time equation enables the instructor or researcher to focus the real estate problem. The nature of real estate problems can be generally separated into a spatial (land) or capital (monetary) related issue or a combination of both. The focus on spatial or capital issues enables an expansion to a more general economic dimension.

12. The property rights paradigm is of interest because it has a link in both neo-classical and institutional economics. The neo-classical link is via the public choice economics of Buchanan.

13. This is the micro-level definition of situs proposed by Andrews (1980–83).

14. Both developed their structure models to ultimately help with the mortgage underwriting process.

15. This is a term used by Andrews, representing the institutional models with philosophical foundations in the German Historical School of economics.

16. Andrews (1980–82) pointed out this relationship in his investigation of land use succession.

17. Gordon's delineation of institutional economics carried on the tradition of John Commons, who devised the concept of reasonable value as an appropriate concept in law.

18. The radical economic groups primarily view value in the Marxist concept. This concept is labor based rather than capital (or land) based.

19. One empirical basis for the verification of real estate as a discipline as defined by Ward (1972) is the increase of scholarly articles and professional journals concerned with real estate (Sa-Adu and Shilling, 1988; Smith and Greenwade, 1987) as opposed to the emphasis on books observed from the 1920s to 1960s as the major medium of transferring information.

References

Alchian, A. and H. Demsetz. "Production, Information Costs, and Economics Organization." *American Economic Review* (1972), 777–95.

Alchin, A. and H. Demsetz. "The Property Rights Paradigm." *Journal of Economic History* 33 (March, 1973), 16–27.

Alonso, William. *Location and Land Use*. Cambridge, MA: Harvard University Press, 1964.

American Institute of Real Estate Appraisers (AIREA). *Readings in Highest and Best Use*. Chicago: AIREA, 1981.

Anas, Alex and Dimitrios Dendrino. "The New Urban Economics: A Brief Survey." *Mathematical Land Use*. Lexington, MA, Lexington Books, D.C. Heath: 1976, pp. 23–52.

Andrews, Richard B. *Urban Land Economics and Public Policy*. New York: Free Press, 1971.

Andrews, Richard B. "Urban Land Use Succession Theory Parts I, II, and III," Center for Urban Land Economics Research Theory Discussion Papers,

Graduate School of Business, University Of Wisconsin—Madison, 1980, 1981, and 1982, respectively.

Andrews, Richard B. *The Urban System.* Center for Urban Land Economics Research Theory Discussion Papers, Graduate School of Business, University Of Wisconsin–Madison, 1977.

Andrews, Richard B. "The Nature of Urban Land Economics and its Relation to Urban Land Use" Center for Urban Land Economics Research Theory Discussion Papers, Graduate School of Business, University Of Wisconsin—Madison, 1978.

Andrews, Richard B. "Situs Theory Parts I, II, III and IV." Center for Urban Land Economics Research Theory Discussion Papers, Graduate School of Business, University Of Wisconsin—Madison, 1980, 1981, 1982 and 1983, respectively.

Andrews, Richard B. "Urban Structure Theory Parts I, II, III, IV and V." Center for Urban Land Economics Research Theory Discussion Papers, Graduate School of Business, University Of Wisconsin–Madison, 1984, 1985, 1986, 1987 and 1989, respectively.

Atkinson, Harry Grant. "Recollections of the Founding of AIREA." *The Appraisal Journal* 40:4 (October, 1972), 491–507.

Babcock, Frederick M. *The Valuation of Real Estate.* New York: McGraw-Hill, 1932.

Barlowe, Raliegh. *Land Resource Economics*, 4th ed. Englewood Cliffs, NJ: Prentice-Hall, 1986.

Beckmann, M.J. "Von Thunen Revisited: A Neoclassical Land Use Model." *The Swedish Journal of Economics* 74, (1972), 1–7.

Berry, Brian J.L. "Approaches to Regional Analysis: A Synthesis." *Annals of the Association of American Geographers* 54 (1964), 2–11.

Black, F. and M. Scholes. "The Pricing of Options and Corporate Liabilities." *Journal of Political Economy.* (May/June 1973), 637–59.

Blaug, Mark. *The Methodology of Economics: or How Economist Explain.* Cambridge, England: Cambridge University Press, 1983.

Bonbright, James C. *The Valuation of Property*, 1 & 2. Charlottesville, VA: The Michie Co., 1965, reprint.

Bourne, L.S., R.D. MacKinnon, and J.W. Simmons, eds. *The Form of Cities in Central Canada: Selected Papers.* Toronto: University of Toronto, 1973.

Brown, James R. Determining the Relative Importance of Real Estate Topics in Undergraduate Real Estate. Unpublished dissertation, University of Georgia, 1978.

Brown, James R. "Real Estate Education: A Curriculum Guideline." *Appraisal Journal* 47:4 (October 1979), 574–586.

Brown, James R. "Is There a Utopian Undergraduate Real Estate Program?" *The Real Estate Appraiser and Analyst* 47:3 (Fall Quarter 1981), 53–58.

Brueckner, J. "The Determinants of Residential Succession." *Journal of Urban Economic*, 4 (1977), 45–59.

Burgess, E.W. "The Growth of the City." in *The City*. Chicago: University of Chicago Press, 1925.

Cannaday, R.E. and P.F. Colwell. "A Unified Theory of the Income Approach to Appraisal-Parts 1, 2 and 3." *The Real Estate Appraisal and Analyst* 47:1,2,3 (1981), 5–18, 29–43.

Christaller, Walter. *Central Places in Southern Germany*, translated by C. W. Baskin. Englewood Cliffs, NJ: Prentice-Hall, 1966.

Chryst, Walter E. and W. B. Back. "Perspectives on the Content and Methodology of Land Economics." *Methods for Land Economic Research*. Lincoln, NE: University of Nebraska Press, 1966, 1–17.

Clapp, John M. and Stephen D. Messner. *Real Estate Market Analysis*. New York: Praeger, 1988.

Coase, Ronald H. "The Nature of the Firm." *Economica* 4 (November 1937), 386–405.

Commons, John R. *Institutional Economics*. New York: Macmillan, 1934 sect 2, chapt 2.

Cook, Edgar D. "The Professionals Approach to Education and Licensing." *The Real Estate Appraiser and Analyst* 38:2 (1971), 25–31.

Cook, Edgar D. "Toward Professionalism: Developing a Real Estate Discipline." *The Appraisal Journal* 42:2 (April 1974), 222–34.

Cowell, Peter. "Highest and Best Use: Is it a Micro or a Macro Concept?" *ORER Letter*, a publication of the Office Real Estate Research, University of Illinois (Fall 1988), 1–3.

Colwell, Peter and C.F. Sirmans. "Area, Time, Centrality and the Value of Urban Land." *Land Economics* 54:4 (November 1978), 514–19.

Dasso, Jerome and Lynn Woodward. "Real Estate Education: Past, Present and Future—The Search for a Discipline." *Journal of American Real Estate and Urban Economics Association* 8:4 (Winter 1980). 404–16.

De Alessi, Louis. "The Economics of Property Rights: A Review of the Evidence." *Research in Law and Economics* 2 (1980), 1–47.

DeLisle, James. "The Interactive Design/Marketing Model Determining Highest and Best Use." *The Appraisal Journal* 53:3 (July 1985), 145–57.

Demsetz, Harold. "Toward a Theory of Property Rights." *American Economic Review* (1967, Papers and Proceedings), 347.

Dotzour, Mark, Terry Grissom, Crocker Liu, and Thomas Pearson. "Highest and Best Use: The Evolving Paradigm." *Journal of Real Estate Research*, forthcoming, Fall 1990.

Dovring, Folke. *Land Economics*. Boston: Breton Publishers, 1987.

Ellwood, L.W. *The Ellwood Tables*. Cambridge, MA: Ballinger Publishing, 1977.

Ely, Richard T. *The Distribution of Wealth*. New York, MacGraw-Hill: 1898.

Ely, Richard T. and A.M. Morehouse. *Elements of Land Economics*. New York: McGraw-Hill, 1922.

Fama, E. "Efficient Capital Markets: A Review of Theory and Empirical Work." *Jornal of Finance* (May 1970), 383–417.

Fisher, Ernest McKinley. *Advanced Principles of Real Estate Practice.* New York: MacMillan, 1930, 148–49.
Fisher, Irving. *The Theory of Interest.* New York, Kelley and Millman, 1954.
Friedman, Milton *Essays in Positive Economics.* Chicago, University of Chicago Press: 1966, p. 7.
Garrigan, Richard T. and Robert L. Wardrop. *Real Estate Programs at Business Schools Accredited by the American Assembly of Collegiate Schools of Business.* Chicago: NAR, 1981.
Gau, George W. "Efficient Real Estate Markets. Paradox or Paradigm?" *Journal of American Real Estate and Urban Economics Association* 15:2 (Summer 1987), 1–12.
Gibson, W.L. R.J. Hildreth, and Gene Wunderlich. *Methods for Land Economics Research.* Lincoln, NE: University of Nebraska Press, 1966.
Gordon, Robert A. and James E. Howell. *Higher Education for Business.* New York, Columbia University Press: 1959, pp. 90–91, 216.
Gordon, Wendall. *Institutional Economics: The Changing System.* Austin: University of Texas Press, 1980.
Graaskamp, James A. "Development and Structure of Mortgage Loan Guaranty Insurance in the United States." *Journal of Risk and Insurance* (1966) 47–67.
Graaskamp, James A. "Implications of Vested Benefits in Private Pension Plans: Comment." *Journal of Risk and Insurance* (1967), 489–94.
Graaskamp, James A. *The Role of Investment Real Estate in Portfolio Management.* Bryn Mawr, PA: The American College of Life Underwriters, 1972a.
Graaskamp, James A. "A Rational Approach to Feasibility Analysis." *The Appraisal Journal* 40:4 (October 1972b), 513–21.
Graaskamp, James A. *A Guide to Feasibility Analysis.* Chicago: Society of Real Estate Appraisers, 1973.
Graaskamp, James A. "Redefining the Role of University Education in Real Estate and Urban Land Economics." *The Real Estate Appraiser* 42:2 and 42:3 (March–April and May–June 1976a) 23–8 and 17–8.
Graaskamp, James A. "An Approach to Real Estate Finance Education by Analogy to Risk Management Principles." In *Recent Perspectives in Urban Land Economics.* Vancouver, BC: University of British Columbia: 1976b), pp. 180–95. This article also appeared in *Real Estate Issues* 2:1 (Summer 1977), 53–70.
Graaskamp, James A. *Appraisal of 25 N. Pinckey St.* Madison, WI: Landmark Research, 1979.
Graaskamp, James A. "Identification and Delineation of Real Estate Market Research." *Real Estate Issues* 10:1 (Spring/Summer 1985), 6–13.
Grebler, Leo. "The Role of the University in Real Estate Research." *The Appraisal Journal* 27:3 (January 1959), 353–58.
Greenhut, Melvin L. *A Theory of the Firm in Economic Space.* Austin, Austin Press, 1974.
Grissom, Terry V. "The Semantics Debate: Highest and Best Use vs. Most Probable Use." *Appraisal Journal* 51:1 (January 1983), 45–57.

Grissom, Terry V. "A Feasibility Process: The Benefits of Land Economics and Risk Management." *Appraisal Journal* 52:3 (July 1984), 356–74.

Grissom, Terry V. "Value Definition: Its Place in the Appraisal Process." *Appraisal Journal* 53:2 (April 1985), 217–25.

Grissom, Terry V. "Argument Forms and Market Structure." *Appraisal Journal* 54:1 (January 1986), 124–35.

Grissom, Terry V. *Appraising Without Comparables: An Expanded Concept of Appraisal Practice.* Real Estate Center publication 674. 1988.

Grissom Terry V. "Solvency: Key to Risk Management." *Real Estate Center Journal* 695. (1989a).

Grissom, Terry V. *Investment Returns and Risk in Metropolitan Texas.* Real Estate Center publication 739. (1989b).

Grissom, Terry V. *Alternative Cash Flow Returns and Related Mathematics.* Real Estate Center publication 636. (1990).

Grissom, Terry V. and Ko Wang. *Market Segmentation Using Capitalization Rates.* Real Estate Center publication 604. (1988).

Grissom, Terry V. David Hartzell, and Crocker Liu. "An Approach to Industrial Real Estate Market Segmentation and Valuation Using the Arbitrage Pricing Paradigm." *AREUEA Journal* 15:3 (Fall 1987a), 199–219.

Grissom, Terry V. James L. Kuhle, and Carl H. Walther. "Diversification Works in Real Estate, Too." *The Journal of Portfolio Management* 13:2 (Winter 1987b), 66–71.

Grissom, Terry V. James Kuhle, and John Ramzy. "A Statistical Analysis of Curriculum Development in Real Estate Programs: A Professional and Academic Perspective." Working Paper 81/82-2-56, Department of Finance, University of Texas, Austin. (1982).

Murray Haig, Robert. "Toward an Understanding of the Metropolis." *The Quarterly Journal of Economics* (Febuary 1926), 179–208 and (May 1926), 402–34.

Hamilton, Adrian. *The Financial Revolution.* New York: Free Press, 1986.

Harris, C.D. and E.L. Ullman, "The Nature of Cities." *The Annals of the American Academy of Political and Social Science*, 5 (1945).

Hartzell, David J., David G. Shulman, and Charles H. Wurztebach. "Refining the Analysis of Regional Diversification for Income-Producing Real Estate." *The Journal of Real Estate Research* 2:2 (Winter 1987), 85–96.

Harvey, David. *The Urban Experience.* Baltimore: John Hopkins University Press, 1989.

Hayek, F.A. *Individualism and Economic Order.* Chicago: University of Chicago Press, 1948.

Heilbrun, James. *Urban Economics and Public Policy.* New York: St. Martin Press, 1974.

Heiner, Ronald A. "Uncertainty, Signal-Dectection Experiments, and Modeling Behavior." in *Economics as a Process*, Richard N. Langlois, ed. Cambridge, England: Cambridge University Press, 1989, 59–116.

Hicks, J.R. *Value and Capital.* Oxford: Oxford University Press, 1939.

Hirshleifer, J. *Investment, Interest and Capital.* Englewood Cliffs, NJ: Prentice-Hall, 1970.

Hotelling H. "Stability in Competition." *Economic Journal* 29 (1929), 41–57.

Hoyt, Homer. "Recent Distortions of the Classical Models of Urban Structure." *Land Economics* 40:2 (May 1964), 199–211.

Huff, David L. "A Probabilistic Analysis of Consumer Spatial Behavior." *Emerging Concepts in Marketing.* American Marketing Association, (December 1962).

Hume, David. "An Enquiry Concerning Human Understanding," in *Probability and Evidence*, A.J. Ayer, ed. London: MacMillan Press, 1972, 3–26.

Hurd, Richard M. *Principles of City Land Values.* New York: Arno Press & The New York Times, 1970.

Isakson, Hans R. and Nicholas Ordway. "Real Estate Programs: A Note on Publication Performance." *The Journal of Real Estate Research* 2:1 (Fall 1987), 99–111.

Jaffe, Austin J. ed. "The Economics of Property Rights." *Research in Law and Economics*, Vol. 10. Greenwich, CT.: JAI Press, 1987.

Jaffe, Austin J. "Toward an Evolutionary Theory of Trade Associations: The Case of Real Estate Appraisers." *Journal of American Real Estate and Urban Economics Association* 16:3 (Fall 1988) 230–56.

Jensen, M. and W. Meckling. "Theory of the Firm: Managerial Behavior, Agency Costs and Ownership Structure." *Journal of Financial Economics* (October 1976), 305–60.

Jones, Ted C. "Systematic Differences in Interest Rates for Conventional Fixed-Rate Residential Mortgage Loans Across Select U.S. Cities 1980–83." Dissertation, Texas A&M University, July 1985.

Kinnard, William. "New Thinking in Appraisal Theory." *The Real Estate Appraiser* 32 (August 1966), 8.

Kinnard, William N. "An Approaching Crisis in Appraisal Education." *The Appriaisal Journal* 36:2 (April 1968), 166–74.

Knight, Frank H. *Risk, Uncertainty, and Profit.* Chicago: University of Chicago Press, 1971 (original 1921).

Kuhn, T.S. *The Structure of Scientific Revolutions*, 2nd ed. Chicago: University of Chicago Press, 1970.

Langlois, Richard N. "The New Institutional Economics: An Introductory Essay," in *Economics as a Process*, Richard N. Langlois ed. Cambridge, England: Cambridge University Press, 1989, pp. 1–26.

Lintner J. "Security Prices, Risk and Maximal Gains from Diversification." *Journal of Finance* (December 1965), 587–615.

Liu, Crocker, Terry Grissom, and David Hartzell. "Market Imperfections, Omitted Asset Markets, and Abnormal Real Estate Returns: A Theoretical Investigation." *AREUEA Journal* (1990).

Losch, August. *The Economics of Location.* New Haven, CT: Yale University Press, 1954.

Markowitz, H. "Portfolio Selection." *Journal of Finance.* (March 1952), 77–91.

Markusen, James R. "Elements of Real Asset Pricing: A Theoretical Analysis with Special Reference to Urban Land Prices." *Land Economics* 55:2 (May 1979) 152–66.

Marshall, Alfred. *Principles of Economics*, 8th ed. London: MacMillan Press, 1979. Specifically Chapter XI of Book V.

Martin, John, Samuel Cox, and Richard MacMinn. *The Theory of Finance*. Chicago: Dryden Press, 1988.

Messner, Stephen D. and M. Chapman Findley, III. "Real Estate Investment Analysis: IRR Versus FMRR." *The Real Estate Appraiser* (July-August 1975), 5–20.

Miles, Mike and Tom McCue. "Historic Returns and Institutional Real Estate Portfolios." *AREUEA Journal* 10:2 (Summer 1982), 184–99.

Miller, Norman G. and Gregory P. Gardner. "Graduate Level Needs and Opportunities in Real Estate." *Real Estate Issues* (Fall/Winter 1982), 47–50.

Miller, M. and F. Modigliani. "Dividend Policy, Growth and the Valuation of Shares." *Journal of Business* (October 1961), 411–33.

Mills, E.S. "Markets and Efficient Resource Allocation in Urban Areas." *The Swedish Journal of Economics* 74 (1972), 100–13.

Muth, R.F. *Cities and Housing*. University of Chicago Press: Chicago, 1969.

Ordway, Nicholas, and Jack Harris. "The Dynamic Nature of Highest and Best Use." *The Appraisal Journal*, 69 (April 1981), 325–34.

Palmquist, Raymond B. "Land as a Factor of Production." *Land Economics* 65:1 (Feburary 1989), 23–8.

Pearson, Thomas. "A Microeconomic Framework for the Analysis of Highest and Best Use." Presented at the American Real Estate Society Meetings, October 1985, Denver, Co.

Pearson, Thomas D. "Education for Professionalism: A Common Body of Knowledge for Appraisers, Part I: Background and Historical Trends." *Appraisal Journal* 56:4 (October 1988), 435–50.

Phillips, R. S. "A Note on the Determinants of Residential Succession." *Journal of Urban Economics* 9 (1981), 49–55.

Powell, Jim. *Risk, Ruin and Riches*. New York: MacMillan, 1986.

Rabianski, Joseph, Neal Carn, Ronald Racster and Maury Seldin. *Real Estate Market Analysis*. Englewood Cliffs, NJ: Prentice-Hall, 1989.

Ratcliff, Richard U. "The Price and Rewards of Professionalization." *The Real Estate Appraiser* 33:8 (1967), 3–11.

Ratcliff, Richard U. "Institutionalism and Urban Land Economics." *Recent Perspectives in Urban Land Economics*. Vancouver, BC: University of British Columbia 1976, pp. 3–9.

Ratcliff, Richard U. *Valuatiion for Real Estate Decisions*. Santa Cruz: Democrat Press, 1972.

Ratcliff, Richard U. *The Madison Central Business Area*. Madison, WI: Bureau of Business Reseach and Service, 1953.

Ratcliff, Richard U. *Modern Real Estate Valuation*. Madison, WI: Democrat Press, 1965.

Ratcliff, Richard U. *Urban Land Economics*. New York: MacGrawHill, 1949.
Robbins, Michael. "Forecasting Retail Sales with Geographical Information Systems: A Preliminary Methodology." *Forecasting: Market Determinants Affecting Cash Flows and Reversions* 4 (Chicago: AIREA Research Series, 1989).
Rogers, Andrei. "Theories of Intra-Urban Spatial Structure: A Dissenting View." *Land Economics* 43:1 (1967) 108.
Ross, Stephen. "The Arbitrage Theory of Capital Asset Pricing." *Journal of Economic Theory* (December 1976), 343–62.
Russell, Bertrand. *The Scientific Outlook*. New York: W.W. Norton, 1962.
Sa-Aadu, J. and James D. Shilling. "Ranking of Contributing Authors to the *AREUEA Journal* by Doctorai Origin and Employer: 1973–1987." *Journal of American Real Estate and Urban Economics Association* 16:3 (Fall 1988), 257–70.
Segal, David. *Urban Economics*. Homewood, IL: Richard Irwin, Inc., 1977.
Sharpe, W. "Capital Asset Prices: A Theory of Market Equilibrium under Conditions of Risk." *Journal of Finance* (September 1964), 425–42.
Smith, Adam. "An Inquiry into the Nature and Causes of the Wealth of Nations." In *Classics of Economics*, Charles W. Needy, ed. Oak Park, IL: Moore Publishing, 1980.
Smith, Charles A. and George D. Greenwade. "The Rankings of Real Estate Publications and Tenure Requirements at AACSB Versus Non-AACSB School." *The Journal of Real Estate Research* 2:2 (Fall 1987), 105–112.
Smith, Neil. *Uneven Development: Nature, Capital and the Production of Space*. Oxford: Basil Blackwell, 1984.
Solow, R. M. and W. S. Vickrey. "Land Use in a Long Narrow City." *Journal of Economic Theory* 3 (December 1971), 430–47.
Mark, Stevens. *Land Rush*. New York: McGraw-Hill, 1984.
Dana, Thomas. *Lords of the Land*. New York: McGraw-Hill, 1977.
Thompson, Wibur R. *A Preface to Urban Economics*. Baltimore: John Hophins Press, 1968.
Trump, Donald. *The Art of the Deal*. New York: Random House, 1987.
Vandell, Kerry D. "Toward Analytically Precise Definitions of Market Value and Highest and Best Use." *The Appraisal Journal* 50, 2 (April 1982), 253–68.
Vickerman, R. W. *Spatial Economic Behaviour*. New York: St. Martin's Press, 1980.
Von Thunen, Johann H. Der Isolierte Staat in Beziehung auf Landwirtschaft und Nationalekonomie, (1st Vol. Hamburg, 1826; translation by Carla M. Wartenberg as the *Isolated State*. New York: Pergamon Press, 1966.
Walras, Leon. *Elements of Pure Economics or the Theory of Social Wealth*. Homewood, IL: Richard Irwin, Inc. 1954.
Walters, G. R. "Urban Land and the Environment: The Physical and Social Dimensions," in *Recent Perspectives in Urban Land Economics*. University of British Columbia: Vancouver, 1976, pp. 28–41.
Ward, Benjamin. *What's Wrong with Economics*. New York: Basic Books, 1972.
Weber, Melvin W., John Dyckman, Donald Foley, Albert Guttenberg, William

Wheaton, and Catherine Bauer Wurster. *Explorations into Urban Structure*. Philadelphia: University of Pennsylvania Press, 1964.

Weimer, A. M. "A Note on the Early History of Land Economics." *Journal of American Real Estate and Urban Economics Association* 12:3 (Fall 1984), 408–17.

Weimer, A. M. "The Teaching of Real Estate and Business Administration." *Land Economics* 32:1 (1956), 92–4.

Wendt, Paul F. "The University and Real Estate Research." *Appraisal Journal* 1949 17, 1 (93–5).

Wendt, Paul F. Wendt, "Theory of Urban Land Values." *Land Economics* 33, 3 (1957), 228–40.

Wendt, Paul F. "Recent Developments in Appraisal Theory." *Appraisal Journal* 37:4 (October 1969), 485–500.

Wendt, Paul F. *Real Estate Appraisal: Review and Outlook*. Athens, GA.: University of Georgia Press, 1974.

Whitehead, J. "Basis for a Historical Geographic Theory of Urban Form." *Institute of British Geographers*, Transactions, 2, 3 (1977), 400.

Williams, J. B. *Theory of Investments Value*. Cambridge, MA: Harvard University Press, 1938.

Winger, Alan R. "Regional Growth Disparities and the Mortgage Market." *Journal of Finance* (1969), 659–62.

Witte, Edwin. "Institutional Economics." *Southern Economics Journal* 21 (October 1954), 131–140.

Wofford, Larry E. and R. Keith Preddy. "Assessing Student Perceptions of Real Estate Careers." *Journal of American Real Estate and Urban Economics Association* 8, 4 (Winter 1980), 417–27.

Wurtzebach, C. H. "Real Estate Feasibility Analysis and the Emerging Public-Private Partnership in Land Use Decisions." 6, 2 (Fall/Winter) 1981, 12–6.

Wurtzebach C. H. and Mike Miles. *Modern Real Estate*. New York: Wiley, 1987.

Zeckendroff, William and Edward McCreary. *Autobiography of William Zeckendroff*. New York: Holt, Rinehart and Winston, 1971.

3 CRISIS IN METHODOLOGY:
Paradigms vs. Practice in Real Estate Research
John M. Clapp, Michael A. Goldberg, and Dowell Myers

Introduction

Kuhn (1970) defines a paradigm in part as a scientific achievement that is

> Sufficiently unprecedented to attract an enduring group of adherents away from competing modes of scientific activity. Simultaneously, it is sufficiently open-ended to leave all sorts of problems for the redefined group of practitioners to resolve. (p. 10)

Kuhn points out that a paradigm narrows the scope of scientific activity by excluding alternative modes of thought. On the other hand, Kuhn argues that a paradigm allows scientists to assume a common body of knowledge and to probe deeply into their subject.[1]

The most important paradigms in real estate and urban economics research (REUER) are derived from finance (the efficient markets hypothesis, the capital asset pricing model, and the options pricing model) and from economics (the new urban economics and hedonic regression methodology).[2]

The crisis in REUER derives primarily from the narrowness of its paradigms and their consequent failure to account for important aspects of the practice of real estate. Secondarily, there are a number of empirical anomolies, notably departures from the efficient markets hypothesis, that cannot be adequately explained by existing theory.[3]

As an example of the crisis, it is extremely unlikely that leading REUER journals would publish well-done descriptive studies[4] of the institutional particulars relating to such urban issues as the barriers to higher density and low cost housing or to the actual decision processes of mortgage lenders or urban planners. Similarly, urban economic models assume rational behavior by real estate developers and landholders. However, there have been very few careful studies of these centrally important actors in the urban development process and of their risk taking, information gathering, and decision making behavior. We will argue that we need such studies in order to develop a basic understanding of the details surrounding the real estate markets that we are attempting to model.

Real estate academia has always been susceptible to intellectual currents emanating from the university and broader society. In the 1960s, real estate departments attempted to elevate themselves above trade school status by forming a professional association (the American Real Estate and Urban Economics Association, AREUEA) independent of trade associations; prior to 1965 real estate academics had met with the National Association of Real Estate Boards (now, NAR).[5] More importantly, many real estate researchers began adopting the new deductive and quantitative mode of analysis sweeping the social sciences. Today, philosophies of science are evolving beyond that earlier positivist stance. In addition, there is newfound interest in linking the academy to the needs of industry and society. This changing climate is contributing to a crisis in methodology for real estate academia.

The purpose of this paper is to evaluate the nature and extent of the crisis in real estate research. The following pages elaborate on the gap between industry and academia, briefly tracing the historical development of this gap. We explore a number of recent efforts to bridge the gap.

We discuss facts that are difficult to explain with existing paradigms, or outside the boundaries of those paradigms (anomolies). Recent evidence challenging the efficient markets hypothesis poses a serious threat to a major paradigm used in real estate research. We use the office market literature to illustrate important facts that are beyond the scope of existing paradigms. Given this need for alternative approaches, we then review alternative modes of thought that would strengthen REUER research. Finally, there is a need for research designed to synthesize new paradigms.

Special attention is given to the contributions of James Graaskamp. For two decades he was one of the guiding lights of real estate thought for sizeable segments of industry and academia.[6] He maintained an often lonely position, advocating an open-ended, problem-solving methodology for real estate. The Wisconsin school was viewed with great favor by the industry, but there were many doubters within academia. The question of how academia should relate to industry continues to be a concern for real estate educators. This paper explores how real estate research paradigms might be expanded to serve broader academic and applied purposes.

A number of questions arise from our sense of crisis. For example, should scholarly real estate and urban economic research start with institutional and actual problem description? Should a major goal of this work be to set up hypotheses that can be examined using structured empirical and theoretical models? Should the accretion of evidence on institutional realities and market behavior be a part of the formal process of theoretical model development and testing? In turn, should there be greater attention paid to data collection efforts (including survey research methods) and to describing empirically specific urban phenomena and testing specific urban models in given urban settings?

The Industry–Academia Gap

In some minds evidence of a crisis is provided by the gap between industry and academia.[7] The importance of bridging this gap has been widely recognized for some time; recent emphasis has been given by Bok (1990) and Boyer (1990). Some methodological approaches have been more effective than others.

Responsibilities of Real Estate Academics

In this section we will argue that educators in professional schools have a unique role to play. Unlike their social science or humanities colleagues, who may investigate knowledge for knowledge's sake, in any shape or form that seems interesting to the academic mind, real estate educators should have a close relationship to knowledge used in the real world. They sit on the bridge between academia and real world practice, a position with important responsibilities as well as advantages.

Real estate academics have a clear responsibility to equip students with skills and knowledge for real world practice. Presumably, this set of skills and knowledge is drawn from the body of accumulated research conducted in real estate. Of course, this training may also draw upon a more generalized academic base, helping to infuse the real estate profession with a sounder academic foundation.

Academics may help to improve the level of practice in real estate in other ways. In addition to the direct education of young professionals, real estate researchers help to solve problems in the industry and to elevate the level of analytic techniques used there. Researchers in private practice do not contribute to industrywide advances because their work is proprietary. Their methods are not presented for critical peer review, as is the academic and scientific custom, nor are their methods and findings shared with other researchers. Many proprietary researchers, working in isolation, are likely reinventing the proverbial wheel, and the wheels produced are likely of lower quality than if they were influenced by peer review.

Academics who tap into current practices (and databases) used in industry research may serve to bring general features of these research methods into public view. Academic writing and discussion at conferences disseminate ideas through the industry, and critical review of the academics' formulation helps to improve concepts and methods. This academic review process may serve as a reflected critique of industry practices, affording a backdoor conduit of professional criticism not directly available to proprietary practices.

Limited Successes in Bridging the Gap

The ideal model cited above has been reflected in reality in only a few instances. We will discuss the successful case of real estate finance, a recent trend in pension fund portfolio management, and the development of the Homer Hoyt Institute and The American Real Estate Society.

Finance. Real estate finance has seen the most successful recent marriage of academia and practice. Finance has successfully used the methodology and assumptions of economics to study organized markets in financial instruments and to apply the computer to real estate investment. In the finance literature, economics is applied to markets that approximate the assumptions of decentralized competition. Thus opportunities abound for using the deductive model to test the assumptions of efficient and competitive market theory in finance.

Research applied to real estate finance has benefitted from a remarkably rich and well-organized database distributed through the CRISP tapes. This has facilitated the development and testing of elaborate statistical models. The richness of data and the utility of complex models stands in sharp contrast to other sectors of real estate research. Outside the Census or other government surveys, and local MLS data on residential properties, there is a general poverty of data, which handicaps real estate research. Thus, theory is partly dependent on data.

The finance literature not only begins with these scientific and data assets, it has also has geared itself toward practical questions of industry significance. The literature generally starts with practical issues of relevance to the financial manager, such as those pertaining to risk management, investments, institutional structures, instrument pricing, and dividend policy.[8] While addressing these issues the finance literature has found detailed institutional knowledge highly relevant. For example, the empirical literature in finance has investigated the relevance of corporate structure, insider positions in common stock, and legal clauses in financial contracts.

For present purposes, the financial literature illustrates the following:

1. The value of scholarly research that begins with practical issues of importance to professionals in the field.
2. The value of seriously studying institutional realities and using these institutional characteristics as part of model building.
3. The unique advantages of ready access to a richly structured database.

In other words, descriptions of reality can be a vital part of the model building process, and they can be extremely useful. The data available for making those descriptions often serves to direct the nature of the analytical technique employed as much as theory.

Portfolio Research for Pension Funds. A second example of relatively successful bridging of the gap has emerged more recently. Pension funds began to allocate higher fractions of their capital to real estate in the 1980s, calling for the need to hire talent skilled in real estate portfolio research. The move toward greater real estate investment was directed in part by the concept of the efficient frontier drawn from finance theory, which states that risk can be reduced, holding the expected rate of return constant, by combining investments into a portfolio.

The pension funds and advisory firms hired M.B.A.- and sometimes

Ph.D.-trained real estate researchers, who brought knowledge of both portfolio theory and urban economics. These researchers have built macro databases recording the current and projected economic characteristics of metropolitan and county real estate markets. These macro databases are being linked to micro databases describing the characteristics and performance of each property in the portfolio (Malizia, 1990). The research is intended to yield the optimal diversification of property holdings according to locational and property-type dimensions.

Private-sector researchers have been leading the portfolio research because the databases are proprietary. Hopefully, some of the lessons from this proprietary research will funnel back into academia so that the academic knowledge base can be enriched and so that peer review can be applied.

Emergence of the American Real Estate Society. Dissatisfied with the perceived domination by urban economists in the American Real Estate and Urban Economics Association (AREUEA), a group of real estate professors, James Graaskamp prominent among them, founded the American Real Estate Society (ARES) as a breakaway group in 1985. The new organization has the avowed goal of building stronger linkages to the real estate industry. The general research goal is to emphasize micro aspects of business decision making related to real estate.

Substantial success has been achieved in a short time, as measured by the number of institutional members and the financial support garnered from industry sources for conferences and publications. Within four years ARES membership equaled that of AREUEA, indicating sizable dissatisfaction with the other academic model. To date, however, the new organization has not substituted a substantially different paradigm, except to emphasize research that is relevant to business decision making rather than government policy or theory. Change is proceeding slowly as researchers explore incremental adjustments in methodology that are credible and valuable in light of the organization's philosophy.

The formation of the ARES group has accentuated the continuing crisis in real estate methodology rather than offering a resolution to that crisis. However, promising steps have been taken. To the organization's credit, not only has it encouraged links between academia and industry, but it also has sponsored debates and forums on the methodology crisis in an effort to expedite the search for resolution.

A referee has pointed out that ARES is to AREUEA as the Financial Management Association (FMA) is to the American Finance Association (AFA). Both are narrow in different ways, e.g., ARES and FMA stimulate little theoretical research so ARES and AREUEA complement each other; they are likely to coexist, just as FMA and AFA do.

The Urban Land Institute and Homer Hoyt Institute. The gap between academia and industry has also drawn the attention of a number of research organizations. Most notable among these is the Urban Land Institute (ULI), which began to strengthen its education mission in two ways in the mid 1980s. A series of short courses was initiated, taught in a multidisciplinary fashion. The lead instructor for the first series was James A. Graaskamp, who encouraged the formation of the workshop series and guided the curriculum development. Following this guidance, ULI has allocated funds for curriclum development, targeting these to encourage the growth of multidisciplinary real estate programs.

Another organization coming to the fore in recent years is the Homer Hoyt Institute, named after one of the great figures of urban land economics and funded by investments Hoyt made in Florida. The institute has a purely research mission and is not allied with any industry group. Nevertheless, under the direction of Maury Seldin, who has long been active in both academia and the practice of market research, the institute has moved to coordinate academics in a campaign to produce methodologies and databases of practical value.

The combined effect of funding programs from the two institutes is to provide a directional beacon guiding academic research toward industry-relevant research. These initiatives reflect the crisis in methodology and escalate the crisis still further.

Unexplained Empirical Results

The gap between academia and industry is only one dimension of the current methodological crisis. Academic paradigms suffer their own internal contradictions and omissions that are creating growing tensions on scientific grounds.

There are numerous examples of empirical results that conflict with paradigms established in the REUER literature or are unexplained by those paradigms. According to Kuhn (1970), these are the conditions that stimulate the development of alternative paradigms (see our discussion in the introduction), so we explore this aspect of the current crisis in methodology.[9] Two major examples will be discussed here. The first deals with the literature on efficient markets as applied to real estate, and the second is drawn from the literature on office markets.

The Efficient Markets Hypothesis (EMH) Applied to Real Estate

There are several reasons why real estate markets should not be as efficient as stock markets. Most importantly, participants in a real estate transaction have invested substantial amounts of time and money that are "sunk" in the sense rigorously defined by Baumol and Willig (1981). These costs arise from information that must be collected on differences across neighborhoods and properties; monopolistic markets develop whenever sunk costs are important.

There are two implications of monopolistic markets. One is thin markets, where prices reflect the information obtained by a few participants in the transaction who have paid the sunk costs. Secondly, there are high transactions costs that have to be paid to the real estate professionals facilitating the sale. Both of these factors stem from the very reason for the existence of real estate and urban economics as separate disciplines, namely, the frictions associated with space. Both limit the ability of real estate prices to reflect information available to all market participants, not just those who have incurred transaction costs.

In view of this institutional context, early studies of real estate market efficiency (Gau, 1984, 1985; Linneman, 1986) are puzzling because they support weak-form efficiency in real estate markets. Similarly, a study of the mortgage market treats EMH as a maintained hypothesis (Malatesta, 1986). Edmister and Merriken (1988) conclude that mortgage markets are weak-form efficient.

We maintain that the efficients markets hypothesis should have been viewed as conflicting with the fundamental structure of real estate markets. From this point of view, the studies supporting EMH, and those treating EMH as a maintained hypothesis, require considerable explanation and justification. In fact, these studies were generally accepted without question, even though the real estate journals were at the same time entertaining a literature emphasizing transactions costs and frictions (Shilling et al. 1987). This was undoubtedly due to the strong allegiance to EMH as a central paradigm in economics and finance. The institutional structure of real estate markets was ignored and conflicting evidence was dismissed (Edmister and Merriken, 1988) in favor of the received paradigm.

An important exception to the uncritical acceptance of EMH applied to real estate is the article by Gau (1987). He squarely faces the "paradox" of real estate institutions and information gaps vs. EMH assumptions. Gau points out that real estate markets are undoubtedly less efficient than financial markets, but his intuition and his review of empirical work supports EMH (both weak and semistrong forms) as a reasonable approximation. He concludes that acceptance of EMH allows scientific analysis of real estate finance and public policy issues.

Recent studies in finance and economics have presented important evidence opposed to EMH (see LeRoy, 1939, for a review). Similarly, evidence that real estate markets are not efficient is beginning to accumulate (Case and Shiller, 1989, 1990; Scott, 1989). From the point of view of the received paradigm, these findings are anomalous. They require a rethinking of much of the literature on spatial economics and mortgage markets. If financial markets are not efficient, then mortgage pricing need not follow the options model. Lack of efficiency in spatial markets invalidates a basic premise of the hedonic pricing model. A large percentage of the REUER literature deals with options pricing or hedonic pricing models. Therefore, questions about the efficiency of real estate and financial markets pose a serious crisis to real estate research.

The Office Market Literature

The office market literature presents a very different situation. Here we find failure to explain or predict in a satisfying manner due to disregard for alternative approaches to the same problem. Better explanation would follow from linking complementary lines of research.

We will focus on two important, and largely separate, branches of the office markets literature. The first seeks to forecast cycles and trends for office space demand and supply. Several forecasting methodologies, including a small simultaneous equation econometric model, have been tested. These methodologies for model specification are largely inductive and pragmatic (Kelly, 1983; Kroll, 1984; Wheaton, 1987; Wheaton and Torto, 1988). However, they draw heavily on macroeconomic paradigms for their overall structure.

A second branch of the office literature, largely based on contributions from British geographers, examines spatial patterns of office and service sector employment (Daniels, 1979, 1980, 1982; Marshall, 1982, 1983; Cowan et al., 1969; Pye, 1977; Clapp, 1980; Goddard, 1973, 1975). The methodology in this literature uses survey research, including contact diaries and secondary data sources, to develop inductive empirical generalizations. Moreover, Americans have also made important contributions to this approach (Armstrong and Pushkarev, 1972; Lichtenberg, 1960; Hamer, 1974).

The part of the office literature in REUER journals needs the part in geography journals. For example, spatial contact patterns (understood through contact diaries and other survey research) influence the location of employment. Furthermore, the location of employees involved in routine contacts is clearly suburbanizing faster than the location of other office employees. Thus, predictive theory needs to draw on the survey research published in geography journals.

The time-series literature on office markets fails to explain important cross-sectional patterns. If these patterns are unexplained, how can we expect these models to predict cycles and trends? In particular, predictions for the future of downtown office markets appear to depend on the role of telecommunications technology and suburbanization of office activities. This implies that predictive power requires broader models using survey research as well as concepts from other disciplines. Development of models (i.e., new paradigms) are discouraged by the exclusivity of the received paradigms; this is at the heart of the crisis.

Exclusivity of Methodology

Gatekeepers of quality control in academia are the editors and reviewers of articles published in (or rejected from) the leading journals in the field. If the review process judges articles as substandard based on their nonconforming methodology, and therefore screens them out, alternative approaches to knowledge building will be excluded from academic audiences. Earnest efforts to bridge the gap between academia and the industry are often casualties in the process because these do not conform to the dominant, deductive mode of inquiry. Through this gatekeeping system, untenured faculty who pursue nonconforming methodologies are eliminated from academia.

This section discusses four general issues embodied in the exclusivity problem. First, we review some of what is known about the evolution of paradigms in science. Second, we address the notion of paradigm transition in real estate, focusing on the rapidly changing context of real estate problems. Finally, we address the classic contrast between inductive and deductive research models, arguing that the choice between them need not be exclusive.

Efficiency and Exclusion in Paradigms

Kuhn's (1970) seminal work on paradigm evolution in the sciences holds important insights on our current predicament. In the preparadigm stage of a field, knowledge is fairly disorganized so that each author has to restate assumptions and to introduce his audience to basic concepts. As a paradigm is formalized it becomes more efficient at knowledge production. An accumulated body of work provides a common reference point, concepts are well understood, and a special language evolves. Within this established framework scholars can focus their energies most productively. With no further need for external justification, paradigms grow introverted and researchers concentrate narrowly on key research questions within the paradigm. Kuhn judges that the progress of scientific knowledge is swiftest at this stage.

There is a negative side effect to the growing efficiency of paradigms. As Kuhn notes, they grow increasingly exclusive and closed to outsiders. The special language, assumptions, and techniques are only accessible to initiates who are trained to work inside the paradigm. Extraneous information is purged because it is irrelevant and distracts from the efficient structure of the paradigm.

At some point in a paradigm's history, diminishing returns set in. Kuhn notes that normal science consists of "mopping up operations." The big conceptual breakthroughs are rare; these are followed up by extensive testing of paradigm implications. The exclusive structure of the paradigm keeps scholars focused on these chores, to the betterment of science in Kuhn's view. Exclusion also keeps fresh ideas at bay.

Problems of Scientific Progress in a Changing World

It bears emphasis that the classic model of scientific progress poses special problems in a profession that addresses real world concerns, because changing events in the world pose new problems at a rapid rate. The context for research in real estate and urban economics is constantly changing, unlike the more stable context for hard sciences, such as biology, geology, or astronomy. An efficiently structured, but slowly changing, paradigm in real estate may quickly fall out of step with reality, leading to growing opportunity costs, if not diminishing returns.

It is not so much that earlier paradigms are being falsified through scientific progress, rather that the context of real estate problems keeps shifting more quickly than real estate paradigms can evolve. This volatile environment has led to rapid switching *between* paradigms. John Weicher observes that urban economics received great impetus in the 1960s from the urban crisis at the time (Kinnard et al., 1988). Similarly, he notes that the effects of high inflation in the early 1980s fueled the increased prominence of finance in real estate. Today we have a context that calls for much stronger attention to markets than before. Obviously, our field requires a rich array of methodologies and paradigms if it is to cope with an ever-changing environment.[10]

Deductive Research vs. Inductive Models for Problem Solving

The classic scientific model, dating from the sixteenth and seventeenth centuries, is deductive. Beginning with a theory, hypotheses are deduced. These are then tested with data to see if they can be falsified. If so, then the theory requires revision. The whole process is negatively structured. Knowledge gains credibility as it withstands repeated criticism.

The stock in trade for deductive thought is the logical syllogism, beginning with a set of assumptions (behavioral, limiting, and/or simplifying) and drawing their logical implications. Deductive logic is timeless (ahistorical), reproducible, and analytical. As an analytical mode of thought, the organic whole of actual economics behavior is broken down into its component parts.

Karl Popper has made famous the notion that truth is elusive (Burke, 1983; Popper, 1959). When we have disconfirming evidence we can recognize a generalization that is incorrect; that is we can falsify general statements but never prove them. Thus, the best that science can ever hope to do is narrow the range of the possible, and thus reduce the number of propositions that are acceptable.

Milton Friedman preached the tenets of the deductive paradigm in his 1953 essay, and he added a proposition: A theory should not be tested by the truth or falsity of its assumptions. Friedman's (1953) argument for this proposition is twofold:

1. Simplifying assumptions (in physics, the assumption of a perfect vacuum) might be ignored in some situations (e.g., predicting the acceleration of a dense object in the atmosphere).
2. Theory might predict accurately despite the falsity of assumptions (e.g., economic agents behave *as if* they were utility or profit maximizing).

Neither argument necessarily holds in all situations. For example, if one tries to predict the speed at which decision makers respond to a change in price (e.g., the adjustment of regional exports and imports to changes in the terms of trade), then the validity of maximizing behavior might be crucial. Unfortunately, zealous followers of Friedman have taken his propositions as gospel. Unrealistic assumptions, such as the Law of the Single Price (for an analysis of this law, see Stiglitz, 1987, p. 8) have been made in the belief that realism is unimportant.

Friedman's argument effectively protected the assumption of profit maximization (as well as other assumptions) from tests based on direct observation of what managers do. It significantly discouraged survey research that might ask economic agents about their actual decision behavior.

The alternative approach is inductive. Researchers begin with data and try to find some order in it. From this order they may then derive generalizations, which can grow into a theory that can be tested deductively. Thus, the inductive and deductive modes of research may complement one another.

The inductive mode is more conducive to problem solving. The early founder of urban land economics, Richard T. Ely, held the motto: "Look and see." Given a real world problem, the researcher would collect data around the problem and then provide a diagnosis. The major fault here is simple: How do we know what data to collect or how to interpret it? Some problem inquiries may be obvious (such as the characteristics of borrowers, loan terms, and markets for explaining defaulted mortgages). Other problems may be much harder to define, and no two researchers may approach inquiries in the same way. The inductive approach has the danger of being ad hoc and unsystematic.

Despite their official methodology, economists do learn inductively from empirical research. A famous example is the Phillips curve, initially an empirical observation that caught the attention of, and was subsequently sanctioned by, leading economists. It has had a major impact on theories designed to explain the trade-off between inflation and unemployment. The Cobb–Douglas production function is another case in point.

Recently, Popper has qualified his theory of falsification. He states that "it is never possible to prove conclusively that an empirical scientific theory is false." (Burke, 1983, p. xxii). He goes on to say that it is always possible to protect theories from disproof by postulating that crucial variables were not held constant or that observations are inaccurate. Falsification is difficult because "anything like conclusive proof to settle an empirical question does not exist." (Burke, 1983, p. xxii). This is remarkable because Popper is discussing physics and related natural sciences. Living urban and regional systems grow and develop over time so they are considerably more difficult to study empirically.

Alternative Paths Toward Paradigm Development

Given the crisis in existing methodology, how is a new body of theory to be formed? The deductive approach begins with a reality in the mind of the model builder, but where do the assumptions of deductive logic come from? In particular, what role is played by observed empirical patterns? Is not the new theory developed so as to fit the available data? If so, it would appear that some metascience must be operating in the building of the new theoretical model.

Exploratory research is a prescientific activity that discovers new relationships and uses these to create new paradigms. Exploratory research synthesizes diverse empirical observations and theoretical generalizations into a coherent whole. Synthesis is the creative act of seeing a relationship, the great "aha" associated with a new discovery. In short, exploratory research is the missing link in REUER and a much ignored and undervalued skill in traditional analytic science and social science (Koestler, 1967).

In this section, we review methods for finding new relationships between observed facts and theory, that is, for building new paradigms. A good knowledge of both theory and fact is thus required. The factual end of the bridge is given relatively short shrift in the urban economics and real estate literature. Insufficient attention is paid to careful data collection, verification, and analysis, especially when the purpose of the research is to describe and analyze institutional realities. Over-reliance on existing research paradigms constrains our ability to develop new theory.

This section does *not* attempt to create a new paradigm: As Kuhn points out, this can only be done by research on a specific problem. Instead, this section outlines alternative approaches that might be used in the search for new paradigms.

Urban Land Economics (ULE)

Perhaps the time is right to reach back to the methodology of ULE as developed by Ely, Andrews, Ratcliff, and Graskamp. As summarized by Ratcliff (1984), this is an inductive approach that is strongly oriented towards institutional characteristics and other details of the problem to be solved; that is, a comprehensive, careful definition of the problem is considered an appropriate starting point for ULE. In pursuit of the problem as found in practice, ULE is explicitly interdisciplinary, appropriating whatever tools or data seem suited to the problem. The weakness of this approach is the ad hoc decisions about appropriateness; the strengths are the openness to alternatives and the focus on real world problems.

An Inductive Approach Used in Regional Science

The umbrella of regional science covers many disciplines, including REUER, geography, demography, and planning; these disciplines span the methodological approaches discussed here. The descriptive inductive tradition is well represented in regional science by the work of Tornqvist (1970) and Thorngren (1970).

Tornqvist (1977) emphasizes the need to base models on the limited information available to decision makers, and on their limited ability to process it. He cites the profound influence of physical and socio-political environments on the perception and processing of information. He strongly endorses inferences from detailed study of individual cases:

> All kinds of aggregation and average figures involve putting distance between oneself and reality. On the other hand, the problem that micro-studies run into is the frequent necessity of waiving the demand for general applicability and completeness. It is to be hoped, however, that *repeated* studies of separate chains of events and situations will, *in the long run*, lead to insights. (Tornqvist, 1977, p. 30, emphasis in original)

Therefore, the regional science literature nicely illustrates the fact that a substantial following can be obtained by drawing upon and being tolerant of a diversity of methodologies. Furthermore, by embracing different methodologies, one is able to deal with a broad array of research issues that may not be tractable using any single approach.

An Alternative: Strong Inference

Platt's (1964) theory of strong inference cleverly extends deductive logic to the investigation and description of physical reality. He begins with alternative hypotheses; these need *not* be derived deductively from assumptions. Then he advocates devising experiments that will exclude one or more of the hypotheses, just as in the deductive model. His approach requires "intellectual inventions which must be cleverly chosen so that hypotheses, experiment, outcome and exclusion will be related in a logical syllogism." (Platt, 1964, p. 347). Platt provides examples of strong inference in which scientists describe physical realities, such as X-rays and DNA molecules, providing identifying information.

It is surprising that the official methodology of REUER lacks the powerful descriptive methodology suggested by Platt. In the REUER literature, any attempt to apply strong inference would likely be labelled as "ad hocery" or "mere data grubbing," because an attempt was made to describe rather than test deductive hypotheses. But Platt's approach provides a rigorous basis for descriptive empirical research.

Strong inference can be applied to REUER by emphasizing unusual situations that are analogous to a laboratory experiment. Changes in public policy provide a rich source of before and after experiments. For example, the housing allowance supply experiment (HASE) revealed important information about the way the housing market adjusts to exogenous shifts in demand and regulations. The importance of noncash transactions in housing markets was revealed by HASE. Although HASE has been well documented in the REUER literature, it has not had the impact that it deserves; for example, one might have expected a flood of literature that used the speed of inventory adjustment revealed by HASE. A methodology that deemphasizes the deductive paradigm and emphasizes alternatives such as strong inference would allow REUER to build rapidly on the information revealed by policy experiments.

Systems Thinking and Descriptive Studies

REUER deals with living urban systems and highly diversified individuals and behaviors. Inherent in the field is great complexity. There are so many variables influencing the urban economic system that it is impossible to account for all of them. Of course, many of these variables have relatively small influence, and a large number of small variables tend to cancel each other out at any time. However, any local economy is a living system that changes over time; the relative influences of different variables can change in turn.

Daniel Bell (1980) argues that changing technology, new institutions, and new social arrangements and customs cause the subjects of economics to change over time, calling deductive modes of thought into question. "There is no intrinsic order, there are no 'economic laws' constituting the 'structure' of *the* economy; there are only different patterns of historical behavior" (p. 77). This argument is particularly compelling for REUER, where local political institutions play such a large role.

In an evolving, living system, any variable that is in the background at any one point in time can assume a prominent position at a later point in time. Thus, a model that assumes that a given variable is in the background may be proved incorrect later on (i.e., give incorrect predictions) when that variable assumes a foreground position. This is a necessary part of the complexity of living systems; many casual conditions may operate simultaneously. Leibenstein (1976) has argued that this situation is particularly likely at turning points in the growth of real gross product (national, regional, and state), when the many variables that influence growth are roughly cancelling each other out. Thus, the failure to predict turning points is caused partly by the inappropriate application of deductive thought to living economic systems. The relevance of this becomes clear when one considers the importance of real estate cycles to issues addressed by REUER.

Since REUER deals with complex living systems, there is a need to describe all of its parts and the way they fit together, just as medical science describes the human body. Therefore, we turn to descriptive studies as practiced in another field (biology) and to systems analysis.

Descriptive Studies as Used in Ecological Biology

Biological ecologists, dealing as they do with the behavior of ecological systems, are faced with problems of complexity and change over time that are similar to the problems faced in the social sciences. Consequently, biological ecologists have debated the merits of using intuition and direct observation to supplement deductive and "strong inference" models of thought (Roughgarden, 1983; Quinn and Dunham, 1983; Simberloff, 1983).

The biological ecologists point out that complex biological systems are unique, evolving, and grounded in history. Some think that this disables the falsification test; even strong inference (as well as deductive modes of thought) may be inapplicable. This group (represented by Quinn and Dunham, and by Roughgarden) argues that biological scientists should make sense out of complex systems by finding regular patterns of behavior, a point also may be Roth (1986, pp. 269–271) concerning experimental economics. If these patterns can be applied to other systems and in other times, then useful predictions have been obtained. If not, some new variable(s) or new sets of hypotheses have to be introduced. Note the similarity between this view and that of the regional science.

Simberloff (1983) stresses the need for bold predictions and falsification tests. However, he points out that it is important to be tolerant of budding research programs; complexity and history should make one cautious about rejecting research because it is "poorly done" as defined by deductive or strong inference methods. Similarly, Platt stresses the need to use a wide array of methodologies (1964, p. 351). Thus, tolerance for inductive thinking is the most important lesson to be learned from ecological biology.

Like Simberloff and Platt, deductive methodology is an important part of rigorous problem solving. The deductive approach, complete with mathematics and statistical analysis, is a powerful tool for testing and refining an existing paradigm. On the other hand, we do not wish to glorify the deductive approach or to give it an exclusive claim on "rigor."

Using Simulations

After describing a living system, either a local ecology or a local real estate market, it is desirable to fit the pieces together. The systems thinking necessary at this point is facilitated by simulation analysis. Simulations allow the analyst to explore possible (and even probable) relationships among parts of the system, As McCloskey points out: This is why simulation is important in economics and related fields. Simulation is affirmative, not falsifying, asking whether one can make a case for such and such, not whether one can prove it wrong. It tests systems, not isolated hypotheses, and affirms a framework in which to test them (McCloskey, 1985, p. 14).

Alternative Empirical Methods

The current economics literature is filled with discussions of empirical methodology (McAleer et al., 1985; Leamer, 1983; McCloskey, 1983, 1985). Much of this literature questions the value of significance tests because

1. Regression estimates are often discarded without reporting that they have been performed
2. Reported results are often explained by appeal to collinearity, to omitted variables, or to vagaries of the available data

Most proposals for reforming empirical research suggest loosening the rigid paradigm that requires that models first be specified (assumed to be given with certainty by theory) followed by empirical estimate of model parameters. Thus, Leamer suggests extreme bounds analysis (EBA), where a subset of variables is classified as important based on economic theory, to be included in every regression model. Then another set of "doubtful" variables can be systematically searched with alternative regressions. Extreme bounds on the parameters of the important variables should be reported together with statistical tests that relate the bounds to sampling variability.

Implicit in EBA is the discovery of inductive conclusions from the "doubtful" group of variables. There is enough ambiguity in economic theory that any variable of interest can be classified as "doubtful." By addressing the coefficients of the doubtful variables, it is possible to discover and to report inductive inferences.

An extreme reaction to the received paradigm for empirical research is found in the vector auto-regressive regression (VAR) approach to time-series analysis. This approach is based on the notion that a priori model restrictions are often not informative when examining cause-and-effect relationships among a group of variables. Therefore, detailed specification of structural equations is pointless. Instead, the researcher simply searches distributed lagged relationships by regressing each variable on lagged values of all variables.

Common to these approaches, and to the emerging field of experimental economics (Roth, 1986), is the notion that theoretical and empirical studies are mutually supportive. Good theory needs to be built upon sound empirical observation. Raising the stature of strong empirical work in REUER, independent of the methodology employed, cannot but help the development of better theory.

Rhetoric as the Currency for Knowledge Exchange

A major alternative methodology has recently entered economics from the humanities. The argument of Donald McCloskey (1983) for the importance of rhetoric in economic analysis has been widely influential. In brief, the assertion is that truth is unknowable by numbers alone. Research evidence must be packaged and communicated through verbal or written argument. The ancient skill of rhetoric plays a vital role in shaping scientific knowledge.

McCloskey emphasizes that rhetoric is not flowery language, but logical persuasion. He claims that the human requirements for persuasion are the fundamental criteria for advancing scientific knowledge. Rhetoric does not replace hypotheses or quantitative evidence. Rather, it provides a meta-framework within which the truthfulness of those matters is argued, substantiated, or rejected. For example, rhetoric is required to justify simplifying assumptions, to validate choice of one statistical test over another, or to substantiate a particular problem definition.

Rhetoric is the currency used to transact exchanges of knowledge in a broader marketplace of ideas. In contrast, paradigms dictate boundaries, prescribe behavior, and generally restrict the free commerce of knowledge. McCloskey's argument for the primacy of rhetoric is especially significant in a world of multiple paradigms.

Conclusions and the Challenge for Continuing Research

The crisis in methodology is deeply rooted, both in its historical context and in the conflicting goals we hold as scholars in the real estate profession. On the one hand, we wish to be respected as scholars within academia; on the other hand, we seek relevance to solving interesting and important problems in the industry and society at large. For a period, real estate academicians have followed the social sciences in their positivist focus and emphasis on deductive science. Now we find the social sciences shifting from this single-minded course, and there is new demand for greater problem relevance.

Among university leadership, former Harvard University President Derek Bok's call for greater academic attention to problem solving has been influential (Bok, 1990). Indeed, the president of the Carnegie Foundation for the Advancement of Learning has amplified Bok's theme, arguing that "What's needed on America's campuses today is a recognition that the application of knowledge is scholarly work that flows out of serious inquiry and, in turn, leads to new knowledge and new insights" (Boyer, 1990). That this statement should emanate from the Carnegie Foundation is a shock to the very foundation of real estate academia, because a late 1950s report from the Carnegie Foundation that criticized the teaching of real estate is often cited as a prime motivation for shaping a more scientific, and less problem-oriented, profile for our field (Kinnard et al., 1988).

Much has been achieved in the deductive and quantitative revolutions dating from the 1960s. We should not surrender those gains, but closing the gap between industry and academia may require re-evaluation of some past changes. We should examine again the lost virtues of the old urban land economics, paying particular heed to its inductive problem-solving orientation and its comprehensive scope. This reconsideration should not be judged as an unscientific retreat: Kuhn observes that recycling of old themes (such as the urban economists did with Losch) and doubling back is common in the progress of science. Moreover, it is important to note that real estate academia is not alone in this re-evaluation of the positivist revolution.

Foremost, we must develop a disciplined mode of inquiry that is inclusive of alternative research strategies. One source of our current crisis is that we do not know how to codify the choice process in research other than by following the less flexible deductive model. The art of problem formulation must be made part of our method, one more adaptive to the variety of problems found in the industry and elsewhere. The question is, how do we build a flexible research method that allows application of diverse tools and that informs us when to use which tool?

With the pendulum swinging toward greater problem relevance, real estate academics face a major challenge. Our objectives of rigor and scholarship must not be abandoned. But how can we act as scholars in a professional world? In the words of the Carnegie Foundation's Boyer (1990), our work "at the core, is disciplined inquiry and critical thought . . . ," and should remain so. The challenge is to bring this disciplined inquiry to the task of problem solving. A variety of disciplined approaches may contribute to our field. Quality will need to be judged less on conformity to restrictive patterns of analysis and more on problem relevance, logical coherence, thoroughness, and clarity of presentation. The search proceeds for an exemplar that demonstrates excellence of scholarship in a new, more inclusive paradigm focused on problem solving in real estate.

Notes

1. One critic has argued that we put too much emphasis on Kuhn's philosophy at the expense of later developments. While our thinking incorporates some later philosophy, notably by McCloskey (1983), we choose to emphasize the application of Kuhn's influential thesis to real estate research.

2. This list is not intended to be exhaustive or to span the fields associated with REUER, but it is intended to cover the most important paradigms.

3. Kuhn argues that paradigm change occurs when a competing theory offers better explanation of anomalies and/or covers a range of phenomenon excluded from existing paradigms.

4. One referee argued that the phrase "well-done descriptive studies" is an oxymoron since the "best institutional studies are analytical rather than descriptive." We think that this view is excessively narrow. See our discussion of "strong inference" (Platt, 1964) and descriptive studies in biology.

5. For details of the emergence of AREUEA, see the panel discussion by Kinnard et al. (1988).

6. Several of Graaskamp's intellectual achievements can be noted, many of which date from the 1960s and 1970s. He pioneered the application of discounted cash flow analysis in academia and the profession, and in the early 1970s he sponsored the pioneer computer time-sharing service for real estate analysts, EDUCARE. Graaskamp's prominence is illustrated in later sections of the paper that describe his influence on the development of the Urban Land Institute's education programs and his leadership in the formation of the American Real Estate Society. Indeed, that organization's highest award, presented only in special instances—not annually—is named the James A. Graaskamp award. The prominence and lasting impact of his leadership was signified after his death by the uncommon number of retrospectives and edited journals initiated in his honor (three at this writing). Newer academics in real estate may not acknowledge his leadership, but clearly he has been a source of inspiration to many.

7. Financial support from the real estate industry is jeopardized by leaders' perception of this gap. For example, a confidential 1990 internal memorandum circulated within a major real estate trade organization expressed doubt about the wisdom of investing substantial funds in academic research:

> I must tell you that my personal feeling, based on having interacted with the academic community for some years, I have strong hesitations to a commitment to dissertation grants as an ongoing activity. Academic research, from my vantage point as a researcher, has been the place to demonstrate not an interest in strategic solutions to the problems of [the industry] but where merit is acquired on the basis of use of sophisticated techniques—and the more sophisticated the better!! That is how one makes one's name in the academic world.
>
> The result is a paucity of much transfer of knowledge from academic to practitioner. This is particularly true of younger academics.

8. Note that practical issues motivated major theoretical developments by Markowitz, Sharpe, Linter, and Black.

9. As we point out in the introduction, the narrowness of REUER paradigms is also their strength, making them effective and efficient. But Kuhn argues that narrowness leads to the need to develop new paradigms. We will argue in this section that the time has arrived for new REUER paradigms.

10. We are not advocating "anything goes"; instead, we want careful evaluation of each research effort. We should allow research to persuade us rather than judging it by conformity with received paradigms (McCloskey, 1983).

References

Armstrong, Regina Belz and Boris Pushkarev. The Office Industry: *Patterns of Growth and Location.* Cambridge, MA: MIT Press, 1972.

Baumol, W. J. and R. D. Willig. "Fixed Costs, Sunk Costs, Entry Barriers, and Sustainability of Monopoly." *Quarterly Journal of Economics* 95 (1981), 405–431.

Bell, Daniel. "Models and Reality in Economic Discourse." *The Public Interest* (Special Issue, 1980).

Bok, Derek Curtis. *Universities and the Future of America*. Durham, NC: Duke University Press, 1990.
Boyer, Ernest L. "Ivory Tower Has Grown Too Tall." *Los Angeles Times* (September 6, 1990), B7.
Burke, T. E. *The Philosophy of Popper*. Manchester University Press, 1983.
Case, Karl E. and Robert J. Shiller. "Efficiency of the Market for Single-Family Homes." *American Economic Review* 79, 1 (March 1989), 125–137.
Case, Karl E. and Robert J. Shiller. "Forecasting Prices and Excess Returns in the Housing Market." Draft Paper, August, 1990.
Clapp, John M. "The Intrametropolitan Location of Office Activities." *Journal of Regional Science* 20, 3 (1980), 387–99.
Cowan, Peter, et al. *The Office: A Facet of Urban Growth*. London: Heinemann Publishers, 1969.
Daniels, Peter W. "Office Location and the Journey to Work." Grower, 1980.
Daniels, Peter W. *Service Industries: Growth and Location*. Cambridge, UK: Cambridge University Press, 1982, p. 100.
Daniels, Peter W., ed. *Spatial Patterns of Office Growth and Location*. London: John Wiley & Sons, 1979, p. 414.
Edminster, Robert O. and Harry E. Merriken. "Pricing Efficiency in the Mortgage Market." *AREUEA Journal* 16, 1 (Spring 1988), 50–62.
Friedman, Milton. "The Methodology of Positive Economics," in *Essays on Positive Economics*. Chicago: University of Chicago Press, 1953.
Gau, George W. "Weak Form Tests of the Efficiency of Real Estate Investment Markets." *Financial Review* 19 (November 1984), 301–20.
Gau, George W. "Public Information and Abnormal Returns in Real Estate Investment." *AREUEA Journal* 13 (1985), 15–31.
Gau, George W. "Efficient Real Estate Markets: Paradox or Paradigm?" *AREUEA Journal* 15, 2 (1987), pp. 1–12.
Goddard, John B. *Office Linkages and Location*. Oxford: Pergamon Press, 1973.
Goddard, John B. *Office Location in Urban and Regional Development*. London: Oxford University Press, 1975.
Hamer, Andrew M. "Metropolitan Planning and the Location Behavior of Basic Office Firms: A Case Study." *The Review of Regional Studies* 4, (Supplement, 1974), 34–45.
Kelly, Hugh F. "Forecasting Office Space Demand in Urban Areas." *Real Estate Review* 13, 3, (fall 1983).
Kinnard, William N., Jr., Herman G. Berkman, Hugh O. Nourse, and John C. Weicher. "The First Twenty Years of AREUEA." *AREUEA Journal* 16, 2 (1980), pp. 199–205.
Koestler, A. *The Ghost in the Machine*. London: Pan Books, 1967.
Kroll, Cynthia. "Employment Growth and Office Space Along the 680 Corridor: Booming Supply and Potential Demand in a Suburban Area." Working Paper 84-75, Center for Real Estate and Urban Economics, February 1984.
Kuhn, Thomas S. *The Structure of Scientific Revolutions*, 2nd ed. Chicogo: University of Chicago Press, 1970.

Lakatos, Imre and Alan Musgrave. *Criticism and the Growth of Knowledge*. Cambridge, England: Cambridge University Press, 1970.

Leamer, Edward E. "Lets Take the 'Con' Out of Econometrics," *The American Economic Review* 73, 1 (March 1983), 31–43.

LeRoy, Stephen F. "Efficient Capital Markets and Martingales." *Journal of Economic Literature* (December 1989), 1583–621.

Lichtenberg, Robert M. *One-Tenth of a Nation*. Cambridge, MA: Harvard University Press, 1960.

Linneman, Peter. "An Empirical Test of the Efficiency of the Housing Market." *Journal of Urban Economics* 20, 2 (September 1986), 140–54.

Malatesta, Paul H. "Discount Mortgage Financing and House Prices." *Housing Finance Review* 5, 1 (Summer 1986).

Malizia, Emil E. "Competition for Investment Spurs Innovative Real Estate Market Research." *Urban Land* (January 1990), 26–27.

Marshall, J. N. "Linkages between Manufacturing Industry and Business Services." *Environment and Planning, A* 14, 11 (November 1982), 1523–40.

Marshall, J. N. "Business Service Activities in British Provincial Conurbations." *Environment and Planning, A* 15, 10 (October 1983), 1343–59.

McAleer, Michael, Adrian R. Pagan, and Paul A. Volker. "What Will Take the Con Out of Econometrics?" *The American Economic Review* 75, 3 (June 1985), 293–307.

McCloskey, Donald N. "The Rhetoric of Economics." *Journal of Economic Literature* 21, 2 (June 1983), 481–517.

McCloskey, Donald N. "The Loss Function Has Been Mislaid: The Rhetoric of Significance Tests." *The American Economic Review: Papers and Proceedings* 75, 2 (May 1985), 201–05.

Platt, John R. "Strong Inference." *Science* 146, 3642 (October 16, 1964).

Popper, Karl. *Logic of Scientific Discovery*. New York: Basic Book, 1959.

Pye, R. "Office Location and the Cost of Maintaining Contact," *Environment and Planning, A* 9, 2 (February 1977), 149–68.

Quinn, James F. and Arthur E. Dunham. "On Hypothesis Testing in Ecology and Evolution." *The American Naturalist* 122, 5 (Novermber 1983).

Ratcliff, Richard U. "Foreword to Goldberg, Michael and Peter Chinloy," in *Urban Land Economics*. New York: John Wiley and Sons, 1984.

Roth, Alvin E. "Laboratory Experimentation in Economics." *Economics and Philosophy* 2 (1986), 245–273.

Roughgarden, Jonathan. "Competition and Theory in Community Ecology." *The American Naturalist* 122, 5 (November 1983).

Scott, Louis O. "Do Prices Reflect Market Fundamentals in Real Estate Markets?" *The Journal of Real Estate Finance and Economics* 3, 1 (March 1990).

Shilling, James D., C. F. Sirmans, and John D. Benjamin. "On Option-Pricing Models in Real Estate: A Critique." *AREUEA Journal* 15, 1 (Spring 1987).

Simberloff, Daniel. "Competition Theory, Hypothesis-Testing, and Other Community Ecological Buzzwords." *The American Naturalist* 122, 5 (November 1983).

Stiglitz, Joseph S. "The Causes and Consequences of the Dependence of Quality on Price." *The Journal of Economic Literature* 25, 1 (1987) 1–48.
Strong, Donald R., Jr. "Natural Variability and the Mainfold Mechanisms of Ecological Communities." *The American Naturalist* 122, 5 (November 1983).
Thorngren, B. "How Do Contact Systems Affect Regional Development?" *Environment and Planning* 2 (1970), 409–27.
Tornqvist, Gunnar. "Contact Systems and Regional Development." *Lund Studies in Geography*, Series B 35, The Royal University of Lund, Sweden, 1970.
Tornqvist, Gunnar. "The Geography of Economic Activihes: Some Critical Viewpoints on Theory and Application." *Economic Geography* 53, 2 (April 1977).
Wheaton, William C. "The Cyclic Behavior of the National Office Market." *AREUEA Journal* 15, 4 (1987).
Wheaton, William C. and Raymond G. Torto. "Vacancy Rates and the Future of Office Rents." *AREUEA Journal.* 16, 4 (Winter 1988), 430–36.

4 IS THERE A BODY OF KNOWLEDGE IN REAL ESTATE?:
*Some Mutterings about Mattering**

Austin J. Jaffe

Introduction

The growth and development of real estate as a field of study within the academy is a topic of continuing interest to many in this field.[1] In addition, it is also a topic with a historical path with various twists and turns.[2] One of the challenges the current generation of academicians faces is the current posture of real estate within the university community.[3] It is this important charge that serves as the motivating force behind the present essay.

Jim Graaskamp was an academician who loved this type of debate. Many of his thoughts on these matters are spread throughout his papers, speeches, and class notes.[4] His belief was that real estate as a field was

---

* An earlier version of this paper was presented at the American Real Estate Society meetings in Sarasota, Florida, April 10–13, 1991. Other versions of this manuscript were entitled "What Real Estate Academicians Do: Some Mutterings about Mattering and Other Stories." The author wishes to thank J. Sa-Aadu and an anonymous referee for their helpful comments and suggestions. The usual caveat applies.

underappreciated, its complexity was underestimated, and its advocates undermanned when facing hostile clienteles within the university community. His sense was that institutional incentives and constraints made it so for real estate academicians, many of whom he would often, perhaps purposefully, infuriate. His multidisciplinary approach to the subject is germane to this discussion and we miss his contributions to the debate.

Real estate academicians are relatively new members of the university team. If one were to exclude part-time players, as the evidence suggests has been occurring throughout the country in response to the Ford and Carnegie Commissions' recommendations 30 years ago, the starting, modern real estate line-ups are now the second-generation of full-time professionals. The first modern generation of real estate faculty are still well-represented throughout the university community. Most of them would no doubt agree that academic real estate and the university environment in which real estate is located has changed tremendously over the past several years.[5]

There exists a small set of essays that attempts to deal with developmental issues facing faculty and their constituents. Issues such as theory vs. practice, analytical modeling vs. intuitive common sense, the body of literature assessment, and the proper place for experience in the classroom are bantered around in the discussion. In addition, some treatment is afforded the issue of the academicians' proper role in society, what the contributions of scholars are, and how valuable academic research is to society. In effect, these essays might caustically be termed the "mutterings about mattering" literature.[6]

Overview of the Paper

This paper contemplates the status of real estate as an academic subject, the notion of the existence of a separable body of literature in real estate, and the status of real estate academicians within universities. The future of the field may well lie in the balance. The status of real estate academicians is arguably the most serious matter for the next generation of academicians. Nonetheless, most observers would doubtlessly agree with the observation that "probably most . . . professional colleagues want very much to matter more than they do."[7] Real estate faculty are likely to be little different in this regard.

The general thesis of this essay is that, despite the gains in achieving success made over the past thirty years towards the promotion of real estate as one of the legitimate fields of study within universities,[8] there are several danger signals about. This suggests that current and future political environments within universities are likely to be increasingly hostile toward real estate as a field should current trends continue. This claim is not based upon any crystal-ball predictions. Rather, the thesis stems from several observations about trends in the field and perceived changes in competing fields within universities extending over the next several years.

These comments are intended to raise more issues than provide answers to questions about some of the alarming trends. It is also hoped that this essay can serve as further impetus to help evaluate the fragile state of real estate scholarship.

Assessment of the State of Academic Real Estate

Real estate education has been surveyed extensively over the past several years. Real estate courses are offered at various levels and by different types of institutions throughout the country. In addition, new graduate programs in real estate have been widely reported at some of the nations' leading universities.[9] However, real estate retains a "second class" citizen status in many parts of the academic community.

The Revolution in Finance

Over the past two decades, academic research and scholarship in "financial economics" has revolutionized the way in which courses are taught, the type of preparation students receive for professional employment, and the manner in which the discipline is conceived. Not surprisingly, the focus of research has changed from prescriptive decision rules to descriptive modelling with empirical support. In fact, empirical finance has arguably become the only game in town (read "leading paradigm"), much to the quite proper chagrin of many in and out of the field.

While there are methodological implications for this shift and development, it is also important to note that the "rise of finance" within colleges of business has occurred whether implicitly or by design, with the adoption of social science as the appropriate methodological paradigm. Following economics rather than sociology, finance has become *the* leading discipline in business schools by following the traditional academic route: the production of a *scientific* common body of knowledge, complete with general but elegant formulations. These logical and conceptual structures define what is relevant and irrelevant within the field. The expansive and rigorous body of empirical research is a predictable conclusion. Finance as a social science is now a reality.[10]

What Has Happened in Real Estate?

The example of finance can be contrasted to what has concurrently occurred in academic real estate, the latter of which is now often separable, if not separate, from the former. Nonetheless, real estate has *not* gone its own way, perhaps because many of the current real estate faculty have finance interests, background, or pedigrees.[11] However, a major thrust of what is going on in real estate differs from the primary thrust that has occurred in finance.

It is sometimes argued with considerable merit that finance evolved with substantive immigration from other fields as well. Prior to the developments in various aspects of the field, traditional financial management was a far cry from modern financial economics.[12] Academic finance in the 1960s, and to some extent in the 1970s, was no less descriptive, normative, or vocational than most real estate treatments in the 1980s. The concern here is twofold. First, the pace of adding to the body of knowledge in real estate seems very, very incremental. Second, opportunities for success as a real estate researcher seem very large, but few seem ready or willing to step up to the plate. Academic revolutions don't just happen; they are almost always forced upon the establishment, usually by young bucks, despite various institutional barriers erected by the not-so-young bucks.

While it is probably indisputable that real estate as a field has changed dramatically over the same period finance has developed, the changes in real estate as a field seem less pronounced. Some of the changes have not been toward scientific inquiry with the same force. Moreover, real estate has not had the *revolution* that seems so apparent in finance, holding constant factors such as the maturity of the body of knowledge. Some possible hypotheses are offered below.

The Lack of Theoretical Work. Consider the fact that few real estate theories scarcely seem farther along than they did many years ago. To be sure, a general theory of real estate is presently nowhere on the horizon. It seems real estate analysis in 1963 was much the same as it is thirty years later; it is only now more technically competent, rigorous in calculating force, and modern in approach and presentation. Real estate education remains indistinguishable from undergraduate courses to graduate programs for the most part.[13] Successful doctoral programs in real estate are based upon the real estate faculty members' acumen for getting students enrolled in rigorous non-real estate fields. It may be that too many graduate real estate courses in one's doctoral program are inversely related to one's successful academic career.[14] Empirical work in real estate has made truly solid advances, but this process adds knowledge at a very slow pace for the field as a whole.[15] While the future looks brighter for empirical knowledge, the theoretical field appears somewhat barren at the moment.[16]

Some Political Battles. Perhaps the most troublesome development stems from institutional forces. Many real estate faculty seem to believe that the future lies in separating themselves from the rest of the university.[17] This strategy often manifests itself in attempts to get political support to require that real estate courses be mandated for all students in colleges of business administration or management.[18] However, the movement toward differentiating real estate as a stand-alone discipline cannot succeed without solid scholarship within the field.[19] As is the case with many fields in addition to real estate, but especially in newer ones, scholarship is in very short supply. Real estate as a relatively new and applied field, at least within business schools, does not have excess academic scholarship to waste.

The Continuing Quest for External Funding. Financial support for academic research in real estate has never been very strong. Numerous observers have berated the funding organizations for their alleged benign neglect.[20] Small grants have traditionally been available to some faculty who wanted to do related work of interest to real estate trade associations. Some organizations continue to employ faculty to create educational material for their constituents and, to be fair, for the field in general. These developments have not proven to be very problematic, which is perhaps somewhat surprising since it is often difficult, if not impossible, to differentiate between "basic" and "applied" real estate research.[21]

Some Curricular Issues. Course material in real estate and many real estate curricula as a whole retain the reputation of being less rigorous and more descriptive than other similar courses and programs.[22] The response from real estate faculty has often been defensive in nature; for example, "empirical data are lacking for us to test our theories," or "real estate courses are more applied by design," or "our students are taught know how to do ——— as a preview of what their initial positions will be like" and so on.[23] These observations are not intended to be indictments. On the contrary, they are indicative of the sorry state of real estate education. As recently noted, they are symptoms of the "crisis in real estate and urban economics research methodology."[24]

The Troubled State of Doctoral Education in Real Estate. Productive doctoral programs in real estate are relatively few in number. Production also tends to be lumpy. More importantly, the evidence in recent years suggests that some of the production is drawn off to private and governmental institutions or to consulting practices. Also, some teaching positions in real estate have very low research expectations or responsibilities. Recent fiscal problems at public universities at the beginning of the 1990s will certainly reduce the supply of real estate positions, at least in the short run.[25] It may be that if a crisis exists in academic real estate, it will be in the external assessment of the research contributions of real estate faculty.[26]

What Do Real Estate Academicians Do?

Real estate academicians probably do what most other academicians do.[27] The problem for many of us is to be able to separate productive from nonproductive activities. Everyone would like to think that their efforts make a substantive difference. Hard work is simply too painful to endure if it does not result in some noticeable achievements, at least every once in a while.

Real estate educators have historically been closely bound to the professional trade associations that guide professional practice. In the United States, the association with the closest ties to universities currently rests with the leading real estate appraisal organization.[28] In the future, we may see corporate asset managers, real estate portfolio managers, or land use commentators who move closer to university faculty and begin to exert an influence on university curricula.[29]

Real estate coursework often seems overly descriptive and professionally oriented, given the developments that *have* taken place in recent decades. In addition, given the scant support by the professions, it is surprising that the relationship between real estate practice and real estate scholarship is even as close as it is. At the risk of oversimplification, it is surprising that real estate education is *so* descriptive in method, and where not descriptive, *so* demonstrative. The charge that business school education is dominated by the "how to" method remains alive and well in many American business schools, if not everywhere, certainly in real estate courses.[30]

What is Real Estate Education?

One might ask: What is being learned by the students? Practitioners wonder why more of the material from their professional training programs is not taught. Such individuals tend to attribute courses in the standard curriculum as teaching "theory rather than practice." Alternatively, universities may be viewed as "boot camps" for future business professionals rather than as institutions of higher learning (or even, less ambitiously, as training grounds in areas useful to the field).[31] Roberts has suggested that decision makers are more easily convinced by concrete examples than by competent statistical analysis.[32] It seems the slow development of real estate theory and the current rage in the development of case studies supports Roberts' suspicions.[33]

Unlike other areas in business, but perhaps not so different from undergraduate accounting, the demanders of baccalaureate and graduate real estate students seem to remain interested in *technical training*, including computerized financial analysis, mortgage-equity analysis, and a strong familiarity with various reports, procedures, and methods used in standard real estate practice. While other markets for students, especially at the masters level, have reacted against "students as technicians," the real estate market is far from saturated with technical expertise for making real estate decisions. Indeed, successfully completing a single real estate course with an appropriate technical (or academically rigorous) background is often sufficient to land a competitive position ahead of numerous real estate students with far more institutional coursework.[34]

Real estate students rarely are viewed as "friends and guides to the public.[35] Nor for that matter, are most real estate faculty. In effect, the public may be unsure what happens within universities regarding real estate, but if anything, there is a belief that technical training in real estate financial analysis (i.e., where "the numbers make a difference") is worthwhile.[36]

Of course, in many parts of the "real world" real estate community, the numbers *do* count, but perhaps not everywhere. The epitome of this characterization is in the area of real estate development. As indicated previously, a number of institutions have moved to embrace real estate development into their curricula. These shifts may be due to the rise of graduate programs in the area, to the perception that real estate developers are good sources for external support, or to the decline of traditional urban planning with a public sector focus and its rejuvenation as a public–private partnership operation, especially in the market for office buildings. Historically, however, the real estate development community has rarely cared about the typical university outputs: educated students, academic research, or faculty expertise. As is well known and often taught, most traditional real estate developers do not want to analyze their projects; they simply want to develop them. The numbers may or may not confirm their predilections. Developers often see themselves as visionaries of the future. Historically, developers have found little use for real estate at universities, either for themselves, their projects, or their employees.[37]

Do Real Estate Academicians Matter?

The general answer to this question is largely moot since mattering can always be defined to fit the purpose. Real estate academicians seem to have a place in many schools, but the future remains less assured. Without a solid body of knowledge in real estate, the field will never be more than a stepchild to the other disciplines. Without economic and social incentives for top researchers to come to real estate and stay in the field, real estate scholarship cannot hope to achieve a better position in the future. External funding for real estate will likely remain a problem. Perhaps the most serious institutional development is the attempt to separate real estate from related fields of finance and economics. Even if a "multidisciplinary" model is followed, real estate would have a tough path to blaze.[38]

The good news is that real estate research appears to be growing in magnitude and, more importantly, in quality. But the more relevant question is whether this growth is high relative to competing fields in business. In this sense, it is highly uncertain what the condition of the state of real estate research is. There may, indeed, be a crisis in real estate research for which we are presently unprepared.

The real test for the current generation of real estate academicians is whether or not we have added to our academic legacy, handed to us by previous generations of scholars. This test is the ultimate evaluation of the health of any field. We should be prepared to meet this test head on.

In the end, real estate academicians ought to be more like most other academicians: inquisitive, scholarly, and reverent to the established literature that constitutes the given knowledge in the field. However, none of these prescriptions implies an oath of poverty for all members of the club. Nor is there an explicit requirement that practice needs to be differentiated sharply from scholarship. One fear is that real estate academicians tend to view their world differently than do other academics. My suspicion is that thinking in the future may move in this direction and we may not fulfill the hopes and expectations of the early real estate scholars on whose shoulders we stand and whose trust we carry.

Conclusions

In 1976, Gordon Donaldson, as President of the Financial Management Association, likened academicians to surfers.

> Most academicians are like surfers who, with their shiny new doctoral surfboards tucked under them, paddle out in search of an intellectual wave created by a force outside themselves and who, with a host of others, will proceed to mount and ride the crest until the wave loses its energy and breaks as a gentle ripple on the shore of established thought. It is a sobering question to ask: How many of us ride more than one major wave in our academic lifetime?[39]

Newly minted real estate academicians also seem to take their doctoral surfboards out in search of an intellectual wave. In many cases, their rides are very short; their surfboards prove to be unexpectedly small and poorly constructed. Thus, it is not surprising that the tougher waves are often passed up and left for other surfers with relatively high-tech boards. Most troublesome is the observation that many real estate academicians do not seem to care about the lack of competitiveness of surfers in real estate. After all, you can still get a pretty good suntan lying on the beach.

Notes

1. For recent examples, see Diaz III, Julian. "Science, Engineering and the Discipline of Real Estate." *Journal of Real Estate Literature* (forthcoming, July 1993); Nourse, Hugh O. "The Role of Real Estate in a College of Business Administration." Unpublished working paper, University of Georgia, 1989; Lahey, Karen E. and James R. Webb. "An Overview of Real Estate Higher Education and Research." *The Real Estate Appraiser and Analyst* 53 (Spring 1987), 54–61; and Carn, Neil G. and Joseph S. Rabianski. "Real Estate and the AACSB's Common Body of Knowledge." *Real Estate Issues* 11 (Fall/Winter 1986), 42–8. See also Brown, Jr., James R. "Is There a Utopian Undergraduate Real Estate Program?" *The Real Estate Appraiser and Analyst* 47 (Fall 1981), 53–9; Dasso, Jerome and Lynn Woodward. "Real Estate Education: Past, Present, and Future: The Search for a Discipline. *American Real Estate and Urban Economics Association Journal* 8 (Winter 1980), 404–16.

2. For example, see Boykin, James H. "Review and Prospects for Real Estate Appraisal Education." *The Appraisal Journal* 53 (July 1985), 347–53; Ordway, Nicholas and Donald W. Bell. "Can We Teach Appraisal Better or Can We Teach Better Appraisal?" *The Appraisal Journal* 52 (July 1984), 436–42; Brown, Jr., James R. "Real Estate Education: A Curriculum Guideline." *Appraisal Journal* 47 (October 1979), 574–86; Graaskamp, James A. "Redefining the Role of University Education in Real Estate and Urban Land Economics." *The Real Estate Appraiser* 42 (March–April 1976), 23–8, as corrected; Ferguson, Jerry T. "How Should the Professional View College Real Estate Education." *The Real Estate Appraiser* 41 (March–April 1975), 42–4; and others.

3. For a recent study of real estate education, see Jaffe, Austin J., John D. Benjamin, and Shiawee X. Yang. "An Assessment of University Real Estate Education." (Paper presented at the American Real Estate Society meetings in Sarasota, Florida, April, 1991). There is also an unpublished survey of graduate education in real estate by the Urban Land Institute.

4. A recent compilation contains several examples in addition to the Graaskamp paper cited above. See Jarchow, Stephen P. ed. *Graaskamp on Real Estate.* Washington, DC: ULI—The Urban Land Institute, 1991.

5. It is noteworthy that the recent assessment of business school education more than a quarter-century after the Ford and Carnegie Commissions made their findings known in 1959 (which came out strongly against "practical" fields without full-time faculty, including real estate) failed to designate real estate as an illegitimate or immature area taught within business schools. However, fields such as transportation and insurance remain so noted. See Porter, Lyman W. and Lawrence E. McKibbin. *Management Education and Development: Drift or Thrust into the 21st Century?* New York: McGraw Hill, 1988.

6. The term is taken from a 1976 journal comment. See Bronfenbrenner, Martin. "Mutterings about Mattering." *Southern Economic Journal* 42 (January 1976), 355–63. The comment was in response to Stigler, George J. "Do Economists Matter?" *Southern Economic Journal* 42 (January 1976), 347–54. The author has also been able to locate the equivalent discussion amongst statisticians. See Roberts, Harry V. "Statisticians Can Matter." *The American Statistician* 32 (May 1978), 45–51; and two comments and a rejoinder. No doubt other fields have introspectively played this game as well.

7. Bronfenbrenner, op. cit., p. 358.

8. One trend is the development of specialized, interdisciplinary, graduate-level programs outside graduate schools of business. Another trend is the growth of real estate programs within architecture or urban planning departments. These two trends are also not mutually exclusive.

9. For example, new programs have been created as Massachusetts Institute of Technology, New York University, and Columbia University. Others may be in the developmental stages at some comparable institutions. For example, the University of Chicago and Stanford University are beginning to offer courses in real estate finance as MBA electives.

10. For a different and opposing view of finance as it compares to real estate, see Clapp, John M., Michael A. Goldberg, and Dowell Myers. "Crisis in Methodology: Paradigms vs. Practice in Real Estate Research." This volume.

11. An alternative view is that real estate faculty with backgrounds in finance and/or economics behave as methodological gatekeepers for measures of academic success: journal editorships, editorial review boards, external peer review committees, etc. This proposition tends often to be asserted rather than tested in practice. Also, to steal a Kuhnian notion, leading paradigms are defeated in science by discovering and presenting superior paradigms.

Competing notions about the nature and structure of real estate's body of knowledge cannot avoid the market tests of suitability and acceptability. There may soon come a time when academic real estate distances itself from finance and economics, but it will not likely occur unless and until something better comes along.

12. For an overview of the major thrusts in modern financial economics and some of the real estate applications that have been made using these developments, see Jaffe, Austin J. "Recent Developments in Techniques of Investment Analysis." *Proceedings of the Fourth AIREA Research Forum* (May 2, 1989), 43–57.

13. Most graduate courses in real estate involve either additional material compared to their undergraduate equivalents or rigorous, methodological material taken from *outside* the field. For a discussion of differences, see Jaffe et al., op. cit.

14. Some programs certainly appear to be designed as if this proposition held fast.

15. Consider that the replication of empirical studies found in finance with "real estate data" (e.g., REITs) is viewed as a *basic* contribution to what might be called *real estate science*. In the author's opinion, given the current state of the body of knowledge in real estate, it would be proper to do so.

16. An anonymous reviewer suggested that the rise of accounting in American business schools parallels but also can be differentiated from real estate by their evolutionary paths. Indeed, it is surprising that changes in academic accounting and real estate are similar in some respects. Accounting seems to be wrestling with the same fundamental issues. For example, what constitutes the field called *accounting* which is distinguishable from finance (as in financial accounting), psychology (as in behavioral accounting), or economics (as in information economics and accounting systems)? I am also aware, as a veteran of political battles with these types, that this classification of accounting has now become obsolete; a new scheme is being proposed. This is one more sign of turbulence in the world of accounting. Or, what kind of human capital do accounting doctoral students build that is distinctive from finance, psychology, or economics? There may be good answers to these questions from within the accounting faculty, but real estate faculty often debate well, too.

On the other hand, accounting as a field has some distinctive characteristics compared to real estate. It is a large and almost mandatory group in virtually all business schools with baccalaureate programs. It has a longer and richer academic tradition than real estate. It has been able to garner substantial levels of industry support (and even market power within some business schools) compared with real estate faculties. Finally, accounting's alleged crisis is probably nonexistent at the undergraduate level. Since real estate courses often overlap heavily between undergraduate and graduate offerings, there is likely to be a greater crisis in real estate, or at least, the crisis is probably more pervasive.

17. The intent here is to suggest that such faculty would rather *not* fight it out using academic ground rules. For some individuals in real estate, an affiliation with a university may, indeed, serve a legitimization function, as a helpful reviewer notes. The point here is that for the profession as a whole, the ability of real estate faculty to use academic positions as legitimizing devices is the precise problem, and this strategy is also often understood by others within the department, college, and university environments.

18. See Carn and Rabianski, op. cit.

19. One can view the creation of specialized masters' programs in "real estate development" in the 1980s (and just plain "real estate" in the 1990s) as pedagogical experiments in professional education. Will these programs succeed at first-rate universities without full-time academic faculty? (i.e., can success come to programs who trade a reduction in scholarship for monetary and public relations enhancements?) For the record, the author's pre-

diction is that such experiments are likely to remain unstable as currently structured. In addition to the comments later in the essay, in the future we expect that the administrators of these programs, or perhaps more likely, the administrators of the programs' administrators, will find scholars to take over both administrative as well as teaching obligations. If not, it may be that these programs will be short lived, much to the chagrin of their financial supporters, their newly created alumni, and other stakeholders who seek rents by arguing about favorable spillovers from real estate at the nation's best academic institutions.

20. See, for example, Lahey and Webb, op. cit.

21. Some fields seem to wrestle with this distinction within colleges of business. Of course, academicians outside professional schools seem to live by this distinction every day. An important question for the future may be whether basic real estate research can or will be produced, and if not, can the body of knowledge ever be sufficient to support the claim that real estate is a legitimate field of study? These queries are gladly left for future commentators.

22. The notion is that the absence of theoretical constructs leaves even motivated instructors with a range of unattractive options. At one end, some programs have developed detailed descriptions of real estate institutions (the so-called institutionalists). At the other end of the spectrum, only analytical models, devoid of any institutional elements, are trotted out for exposition (the so-called neo-classicists). In between rests combinations of these extremes. The claim here is that the absence of theory causes the curriculum to be subject to criticism at any point along the continuum.

23. Or consider a slightly different version of the same claim. According to a recent paper, real estate as a field is "well adapted to the needs of practice, [although] it fails at the demands of academia." See Clapp et al., op. cit., p. 9.

24. Ibid.

25. A confidential estimate of the size of the reduction made recently to the author is as much as 10% of the research-oriented positions throughout the United States may be lost to real estate during the early 1990s.

26. One interesting observation is the proliferation of new real estate journals in an era when the conventional wisdom is that an absence of high-quality real estate manuscripts exists for the current supply of journal space, even without any new vehicles. While this essay is part of an ongoing internal assessment of the field, it remains to be seen what the external assessment will be like based upon a dramatically increased supply of journal space in a field that wants to lay claim to enhanced quality in research and scholarship.

27. Similar discussion can be found in Gordon, Paul J. "What Do Professors Do?" *Business Horizons* 29 (May–June 1986). Coincidentally, of course, the same language is used in this earlier paper.

28. The newly merged real estate appraisal associations into the Appraisal Institute has replaced real estate brokerage and mortgage lending associations from earlier eras in the competition. It should also be noted that some other professional associations (e.g., the Urban Land Institute), are genuinely interested in improving relations with academicians.

29. This is not intended to imply that this action is improper or inappropriate. In fact, the body of knowledge may be substantively enhanced via these affiliations. This is a comparative study that needs to be done.

30. It should be noted, however, that relative to British courses at universities and, more likely, polytechnics, American programs tend to follow professional syllabi to a much lesser degree than their British counterparts. The Royal Institute of Chartered Surveyors virtually mandates content for all programs from their lofty offices within the shadows of Buckingham Palace in London.

31. Of course, this raises substantive questions not only about the "mattering" of real estate courses, but also about the value of real estate faculty as well.

32. Roberts, op. cit., p. 45.

33. Among other evidence, the Urban Land Institute has begun a process of developing a series of case studies in the area of real estate development. The American Real Estate Society has also devoted a session during its annual meetings to new and original real estate cases, perhaps in the hope that such sessions will assist academicians in their teaching of "relevant" material.

34. In the area of real estate development, this has always been the case. However, currently, there is no demand for *additional* developers in any event!

35. Roberts, op. cit., p. 45.

36. My speculation is that the value added from acquiring modern, applied computer skills (i.e., spreadsheet experience and practice) for real estate students exceeds that for any other student population as a whole in business schools. This claim is based more on the relatively low, technical skills employed in many real estate product markets rather than as a criticism of the low, technical endowments that students who declare themselves to be real estate majors bring to the classroom. But alternative hypotheses might also be supported by the evidence.

37. It is noted, in passing, that in recent months, MIT's Center for Real Estate Development (CRED) has now become the Center for Real Estate (CRE).

38. Perhaps this is the point where future discussions of the topic should begin. When baby sparrows leave their mother's nests, it is a major step toward the next generation of the species. It is a risky and dangerous step, but it is also an important one. If fundamental skills have not been learned carefully by the young birds, there will be substantive costs to pay. But perhaps most importantly, the baby sparrows cannot return to the warmth of the nest. The harsh reality of the outside world is the new environment now and survival in such a world is the top priority. But causal empiricism suggests that the species of sparrows somehow manages to survive from generation to generation. But what happened to the dodo bird?

39. Donaldson, Gordon. "Making Intellectual Waves." *Financial Management* 6 (Winter 1977), 9.

References

Boykin, James H. "Review and Prospects for Real Estate Appraisal Education." *The Appraisal Journal* 53 (July 1985), 347–53.

Bronfenbrenner, Martin. "Mutterings about Mattering." *Southern Economic Journal* 42 (January 1976), 355–63.

Brown, James R., Jr., "Real Estate Education: A Curriculum Guideline." *The Appraisal Journal* 47 (October 1979), 574–86.

Brown, James R., Jr. "Is There a Utopian Undergraduate Real Estate Program?" *The Real Estate Appraiser and Analyst* 47 (Fall 1981), 53–59.

Carn, Neil G. and Joseph S. Rabianski. "Real Estate and the AACSB's Common Body of Knowledge," *Real Estate Issues* 11 (Fall/Winter 1986), 42–8.

Clapp, John M, Michael A. Goldberg, and Dowell Myers. "Crisis in Methodol-

ogy: Paradigms vs. Practice in Real Estate Research." This volume.
Dasso, Jerome and Lynn Woodward. "Real Estate Education: Past, Present, and Future: The Search for a Discipline." *American Real Estate and Urban Economics Association Journal* 8 (Winter 1980), 404–16.
Diaz, III, Julian. "Science, Engineering and the Discipline of Real Estate." *Journal of Real Estate Literature* (forthcoming, July 1993).
Donaldson, Gordon. "Making Intellectual Waves." *Financial Management* 6 (Winter 1977), 7–10.
Ferguson, Jerry T. "How Should the Professional View College Real Estate Education." *The Real Estate Appraiser* 41 (March–April 1975), 42–44.
Gordon, Paul J. "What Do Professors Do?" *Business Horizons* 29 (May–June 1986), 38–43.
Graaskamp, James A. "Redefining the Role of University Education in Real Estate and Urban Land Economics." *The Real Estate Appraiser* 42 (March–April 1976), 23–8 as corrected.
Jaffe, Austin J. "Recent Developments in Techniques of Investment Analysis." *Proceedings of the Fourth AIREA Research Forum*, (May 2, 1989), pp. 43–57.
Jaffe, Austin J., John D. Benjamin, and Shiawee X. Yang. "An Assessment of University Real Estate Education." Paper presented at American Real Estate Society meetings in Sarasota, FL, April, 1991.
Jarchow, Stephen P., ed. *Graaskamp on Real Estate*. Washington, D.C.: ULI— The Urban Land Institute, 1991.
Lahey, Karen E. and James R. Webb. "An Overview of Real Estate Higher Education and Research." *The Real Estate Appraiser* 53 (Spring 1987), 54–61.
Nourse, Hugh O. "The Role of Real Estate in a College of Business Administration." Unpublished working paper, University of Georgia, 1989.
Ordway, Nicholas and Donald W. Bell. "Can We Teach Appraisal Better or Can We Teach Better Appraisal?" *The Appraisal Journal* 52 (July 1984), 436–42.
Porter, Lyman W. and Lawrence E. McKibbin. *Management Education and Development: Drift or Thrust into the 21st Century?* New York: McGraw Hill, 1988.
Roberts, Harry V. "Statisticians Can Matter." *The American Statistician* 32 (May 1978), 45–51.
Stigler, George J. "Do Economists Matter?" *Southern Economic Journal* 42 (January 1976), 347–54.

II APPRAISAL, FEASIBILITY, AND SPECIAL USE ANALYSIS

5 THE PRICE OF WILDERNESS AND SCENIC BEAUTY:
A Methodology for the Inventory and Appraisal of Wilderness and Scenic Land

Michael L. Robbins and Sean C. Ahearn

Dedication

Professor James A. Graaskamp stressed the view of appraisal as a generalized form of real estate feasibility. As such, appraisal is not only a necessary core component for anyone wishing to understand the essence of real estate decision making, appraisal is first and foremost a systematic application of behavioral research in which the appraiser strives to fit the attributes of the subject property into a market context driven by decisions of market participants.

Following the pathway of appraisal analysis opened up at the University of Wisconsin—Madison by Richard U. Ratcliff and building on the urban land economic concepts of Richard B. Andrews, Graaskamp forged a philosophy of real estate education that recognized real estate first as an economic commodity, then as a conduit for financial transactions (on both the equity and lender sides), and lastly as an asset for wealth enhancement. In his monograph *The Fundamentals Of Real Estate Development*, published by the Urban Land Institute, Graaskamp's discussion of "solvency" first, "minimum yield" second, and "profit maximum" last are clear statements of this position.

Graaskamp strongly believed in the need to understand the financial structure of the real estate (be it individuals, pension funds, corporations, or public sector units). However, his concept of real estate Solvency (the view of real estate as an economic commodity) extended beyond simple deal structuring; in his teachings he stressed the need to understand the behavior and motivations of the participants impacting on the decision process in order to assess financial viability. In his appraisal text *The Appraisal Of 25 N. Pinckney: A Demonstration Case for Contemporary Appraisal Methods*, Jim Graaskamp left a legacy, and a challenge, for those of us who were fortunate to study and work with him.

The appraisal process discussed in this paper is an articulation, by the authors, of how Graaskamp approached real estate problem solving. He believed in the multidisciplinary approach in order to be adequately sensitive to the context and participants involved in the problem.

The appraisal discussed in this paper was produced by a multidisciplinary team of experts from business, landscape architecture, and civil and environmental engineering, who together gave substance to the solution of the problem statement. The final settlement price (without recourse of trial) was within the predicted after-tax value range of the appraised value. The American Society Of Landscape Architects awarded the 85th National Honor Award to the faculty working on the visitor employed photography component of the appraisal (reported in the 1985, September/October issue of *Landscape Architecture*), and since its completion the appraisal methodology presented has been successfully applied by the authors on several large natural landscapes, the last being 100,000 acres in the Gates Of The Arctic National Park, located in the Brooks Range in the State of Alaska.

Foreword

The Pack River Appraisal Project

The Alpine Lakes Region of the Eastern Cascades is a unique wilderness tract and a scenic resource which everyone agrees should be preserved. Growing public sensitivity to the need for preservation has paralleled declining government financial resources for acquisition so that demand for wilderness tracts is manifested by private funding for acquisition through collective groups such as Nature Conservancy, The Trust for Public Lands, and many other state and national groups. There is a market for large scale landscapes where price reflects scenic quality and there is a measurable consensus on combinations of land forms and features which coalesce to create scenic quality. Placing a price tag on scenic and wilderness quality is necessary to efficiently allocate available dollars from the marketplace, prioritize the sequence of the purchases, and compensate equitably the private property owner for not exploiting resource values. This project combines the efficiency of data processing for small scale sensitivity of data for large land areas, the measurement of user aesthetic evaluations of landform combinations, and contemporary appraisal methods for selection, adjustment, and ranking of comparable sales with which to price a property for acquisition under federal rules of fair market value.

James A. Graaskamp
August, 1982

Introduction

The impetus for the research presented in this paper was a Congressional act, the Alpine Lakes Management Act (ALMA) of July 12, 1976, that mandated the establishment of the Alpine Lakes Wilderness Area.[1] ALMA specified that all private lands within the designated wilderness boundaries would be purchased at fair market value. At the time of the Act, the Pack River Management Company (PRMC) owned more than 22,000 acres of land within the boundary. The U.S. Forest Service offered PRMC $13,500,000 for the property, based on timber value. While the value of the timber was not in dispute, an offering price based on timber value seemed inconsistent with the physical setting of the land.[2]

It was at this juncture that an interdisciplinary team of scientists from the University of Wisconsin—Madison was engaged to appraise the PRMC subject property. The team, lead by the late Professor James A. Graaskamp, Department of Real Estate and Urban Land Economics, University of Wisconsin—Madison, developed an approach to valuation based on contemporary real estate appraisal theory. The marriage of contemporary real estate appraisal theory with wilderness assessment, in the context of a spatial database that relied on remotely sensed data as a data source, formed the basis for the appraisal.

The functional issues of this research included:

- An underlying primes that the market (both buyers and sellers) recognized that wilderness consisted (at least in part) of tangible attributes that were capable of interacting with people in a way as to make them desirable and in demand.
- Since the subject was unimproved raw land, legal precedent indicated that a methodology that enabled the sales comparison

approach to be applied in pricing the subject property would yield the most supportable estimate of market value.
- The sales comparison valuation approach prefers to compare the subject property in terms of specific, physically ascertained attributes to broadly similar properties that have been sold to a class of buyers with similar motivation. The valuation methodology had to be adaptable to comparison of scale, physical diversity, ruggedness, and quality of the property. Nevertheless. the diverse distinctions between subject property and comparables had to be retained if pricing inference was to be equitable.
- The most general and difficult problem in the application of the sales comparison method is the determination of the comparability of individual sales. The general issue was how a scoring system for wilderness attributes could be developed that provided for a relevant unit for comparison. Determination of comparability based on a most probable use of wilderness had two major problems: (1) Wilderness is a condition that is not defined by a single set of attributes but one that is a result of the synergism of various combinations of attributes, and (2) there was no established methodology to inventory the wilderness attributes once they were identified.
- Following the development of a unit of comparison, dual objectives of needing to maintain consistency in the application of the pricing methodology while remaining sensitive to the diversity within and among the comparables and the subject property, led the appraisal team to determine that a geographic information system (GIS) would be necessary to manage the data. In addition, it was determined that the automated data management function of the GIS would need to be tied directly to the automated pricing process so that individual components of the subject could be priced with selected units from comparable properties.

The Valuation Process

Establishing the most probable use of the subject property is a pivotal step in the contemporary valuation process. In this process (Table 1), the analysis moves inductively from what is known about the property to be appraised toward identification of alternative uses. The alternative uses are then ranked in terms of economic benefit, physical suitability, political acceptability, effective demand, and financial viability at a particular point in time. The resulting matrix of choices suggest scenarios of possible

Table 1. Contemporary Appraisal Outline

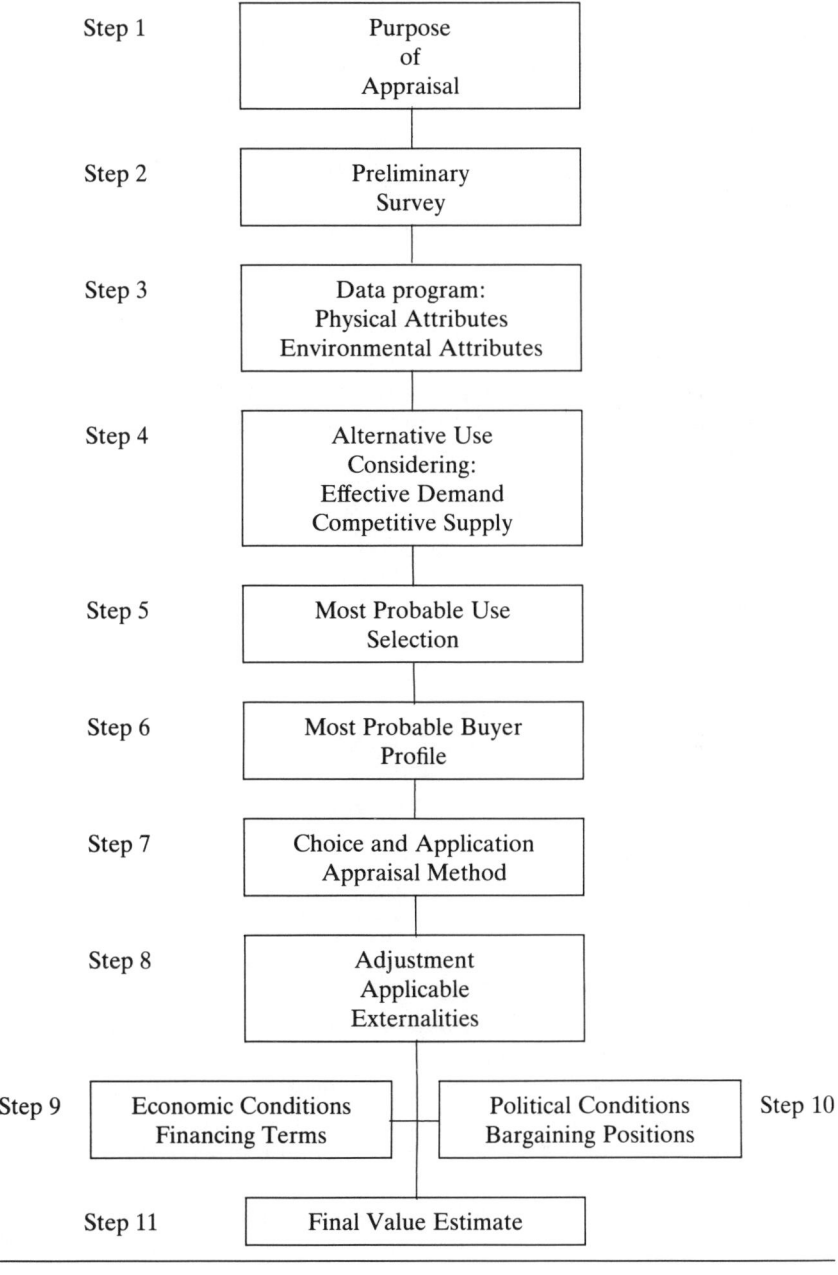

use for the parcel. The determination of most probable use, in turn, suggests the nature of the most probable buyer.

To estimate what the most probable buyer would pay in terms of market value, or most probable price, the appraiser must either find direct cash equivalent sales of comparable property between fully informed parties, or in the absence of current market information, simulate the economic logic and pricing calculus of the most probable buyer, given political constraints and available market alternatives. After determination of wilderness as the most probable use for the subject property, transactions between informed buyers and sellers were structured so that the sales comparison approach (market inference) could be employed to price the subject property.

The contemporary appraisal process (Table 1) generally is divided into eleven steps; however, the principal focus of this paper will be Step 7, Choice and Application of Appraisal Method. Steps 1–6 are briefly described to provide the context for the research.

Step 1: The Appraisal Issue

The issue for which fair market value was required stemmed from the Alpine Lakes Management Act of 1976, Section 4 (Land Acquisition and Exchange),[3] which authorized and directed the Secretary of Agriculture to acquire more than 41,000 acres of nonfederal lands in the Alpine Lakes Wilderness and the "intended wilderness".[4]

While ALMA used the term *just compensation*, there was no condemnation action at the time of the appraisal (nor any condemnation action up to the time of arms-length acquisition by the Federal Government).

Step 2: Preliminary Survey

An initial survey of the unique physical attributes of the subject property suggested to the appraisal team that the most probable use could be wilderness, with a significant component for scenic quality conservation. The initial survey also suggested that this traditional public use concept (wilderness preservation) could be identified as a private market phenomenon in which there was an organized market acquiring land without right of eminent domain, for the specific purpose of wilderness and scenic preservation. (The initial five state transaction survey found over 100 sales in which private individuals, private groups, quasi-public groups,

THE PRICE OF WILDERNESS AND SCENIC BEAUTY   155

and various units of government were purchasing land for preservation purposes.)

Step 3: Data Program

To be sensitive to the attributes affecting economic value, it is important to analyze the economic land unit by collecting relevant data according to five categories:

1. *Physical attributes* such as size, shape, soils, geology, slope, water, flora and fauna, etc.
2. *Legal and political attributes* affecting use and degree of decision making within the private sector, including federal, state, county, and private land use control relevant to the parcel.
3. *Linkage attributes* that tie the site to infrastructure systems, such as roads and trails, or to peripheral activities and establishments that may generate demand for the parcel.
4. *Dynamic attributes* related to how people perceive a site — prestigious, dangerous, attractive, enjoyable, beautiful, etc.
5. *Environmental attributes* related to off-site effects of the subject property, for example, storm water runoff, or destruction of a view shed.

Step 4: Alternative Use Determination

The detailed property analysis resulted in two sets of uses being identified for PRMC land: (1) logging, recreation, and recreation lot development and (2) wilderness and recreation. These are conflicting uses in that logging or development precludes the use of the land as wilderness.[5] Appraisal theory suggests that the use of the land that yields the highest present value within the practical constraints of public policy, market demand, physical resource base, and financial viability when sold on the open market, in a negotiated purchase, by a knowledgeable buyer and seller, neither acting under duress, and given a reasonable time for sale, will determine the most probable use of the land.[6] While the economic ranking of PRMC land had been established for its timber value, the economic ranking of the land for its use as wilderness and recreation had to be established in order to determine the most probable use.

Table 2 is a chart from the appraisal that illustrates some of the

Table 2. Alternative Use Comparisons by Property Cluster for PRMC Properties

	Timber potential	Lot potential	Park potential	Damage potential to other alpine areas views & ecosystems	Wilderness/ public access route potential	Acres allocated to trailhead corridor	Acres allocated to wilderness
Public benefits	Long-term damage	Permanent damage	Long-term damage		Long-term benefits		
Cluster 1*	Modest	Insignificant	Good	Serious	Established	640	1,909
Cluster 2*	Insignificant	None	Modest	Modest	Firmly established	1,028	00
Cluster 3*	Fair	Modest	Excellent lakes, mt. peaks, high scenic quality scores	Serious	Established	640	3,057
Cluster 4*	Good east half only	Good	Excellent west half, lakes, mt. peaks, high scenic quality scores, good east half	Serious	Potential alternative to overcrowded Enchanted area; less hiker pressure currently	1,280	13,903
Total Subject Property Acres							22,457

*As part of a strategic ploy by the appraisal team (in anticipation of possible court rulings), the subject property was organized into four separate clusters.

James A. Graaskamp, and Michael L. Robbins. The Appraisal of the Pack River Lands, Madison, WI: Landmark Research, Inc, p. III-17.

THE PRICE OF WILDERNESS AND SCENIC BEAUTY   157

alternative uses evaluated by the appraisal team, as well as some of the logic applied to those uses. (It should be noted that Table 2 is for illustration purposes only and does not represent the analysis applied to each alternative use).

Step 5: Most Probable Use Determination

While the appreciation and preservation of wilderness and scenic lands has been well accepted, the market valuation of such lands has received little attention.[7] Wilderness and scenically beautiful lands are bought and sold every day, but the valuation process has yet to recognize the attributes associated with wilderness lands as economic commodities.[8] When valuing a single-family house, the appraiser is able to assign adjustments to differences between attributes of the house (number of bathrooms, square footage, etc.) and a comparable because the motivation and behavior of buyers indicate that such attributes have economic importance to them. Wilderness and scenic beauty attributes had been considered intangibles that could not be priced in the marketplace, in part, because the tie between buyer motivation and the physical attributes had not been established. Recall that the underlying primes of this research is that the market (both buyers and sellers) recognized that wilderness consisted (at least in part) of tangible attributes that were capable of interacting in a way as to make them desirable and in demand.

Step 6: Most Probable Buyer Determination

The selection of the most probable use of the subject property by the appraiser leads to identification of the most probable buyer. Most probable buyer identification then enables the appraiser to begin the search for sales with a most probable use similar to that of the subject property. Wilderness land purchases, or comparables, could then be used to determine the fair market value of the subject property based on the application of the sales comparison approach to value.[9]

After careful matching of the attributes making up the subject property with previous buyer history of similar attributes, it was determined that the most probable use of the subject property was for wilderness and the most probable buyer would be buyers motivated to protect the unique condition of the subject property.

The appraiser has determined in his opinion that highest and best use of each cluster shall be allocated between certain acres appropriate as trailhead and public corridor to the back country and certain acres shall be allocated as wilderness for public purposes as these uses have not only immediate and higher present value than alternatives but are in addition most compatible with community environment and development goals. *These uses presume a probable buyer or buyers motivated to preserve high priority wilderness tracts and representing collective private citizens financing.* (emphasis added)[10]

Step 7: Choice and Application of Appraisal Method

Once the most probable use has been determined, the best approach to valuation is to estimate value from what the most probable buyers have done in prior transactions of similar properties (inference). This method of determining most probable price involves inferring future market behavior from recently completed market transactions. The method implies that a prudent person will not pay more for a property than a comparable substitute property would cost.

The Sales Comparison Approach To Value. Land appraisal depends primarily on the sales comparison approach, as opposed to an income capitalization or cost approach to valuation.[11] The sales comparison valuation approach compares the subject property in terms of specific, physically ascertained attributes to broadly similar properties that have been sold to a class of buyers with similar motivation. Therefore, it is necessary to describe the physical attributes of the subject property that may be significantly related to alternative uses for the selection of the best use. In the case of the Alpine Lakes Wilderness, where the subject property was owned in a checkerboard pattern adjoining both government and privately owned properties, it was also necessary to place the subject property within the context of a regional pattern and subenvironmental systems (Figure 1). Comparison of scale, physical diversity, ruggedness, and quality of the property in question created a data problem of unusual proportions (Figure 2). Nevertheless, the diverse distinctions between subject property and comparables had to be retained if pricing inferences were to be equitable.

The automated selection and pricing process of this research fit the basic strategy of the sales comparison approach, which is to search for properties that might have served the same uses as the indicated most probable use for the subject property, on the principle that buyers' top price will be only as much as they would pay for reasonable substitutes.

THE PRICE OF WILDERNESS AND SCENIC BEAUTY

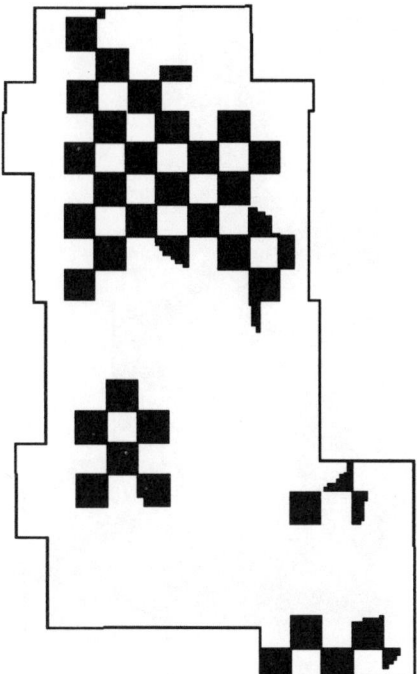

Figure 1. Ownership map.
Map legend: ──── Boundary of extents of spatial data base (13 mi × 22 mi).
■ Owned sections or partial sections (subject properties).

In general, there are three major conditions for executing the sales comparison approach (even for wilderness land)[13]:

1. There is an orderly market for parcels of wilderness and scenic attributes in which arms-length transactions occurred without recourse to eminent domain.
2. Adequate information is available to adjust sale prices of transactions meeting the first condition for external factors, such as time of sale, financial terms, and custom conditions, short of a cash sale in fee simple. The appraiser must have enough information to make reasonable adjustments for differences in location, or for imbalances in the market, to the degree that these differences are unique to only some of the comparables.
3. The subject property and the comparables need to have some

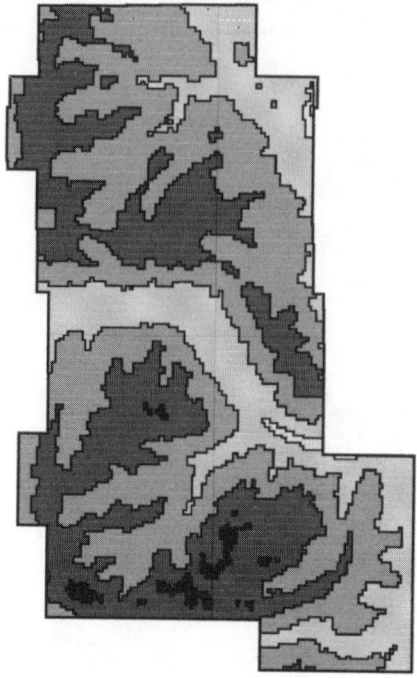

Figure 2. Elevation.
Map legend: Relative elevation. Light = low el. (~1,200 ft.). Dark = high el. (~8,000 ft. above sea level).

common denominator with respect to both size and quality or suitability, for the presumed use, for comparison of the subject property and the comparables.

Attributes for Sales Comparison — The Common Denominator. The concept of comparable substitute (see 3 above) infers that buyers attach personal values to combinations of specific attributes. Then, through a process of evaluation and elimination, they match attributes from one property to another, to decide which property (if any) provides the greatest amount of satisfaction relative to its cost. Thus, application of the sales comparison approach requires the collection and analysis of pertinent data describing the attributes of both the comparable and subject properties. Through these analyses a transaction range for the subject property can be estimated.

Comparability Determination. Each parcel of real estate is distinctive relative to the unique position on the earth on which it is situated. Land may vary in its locational features, topography, views, soil conditions, etc. Consequently, the appraiser employing the sales comparison approach must consider all these factors in using market sales of differing parcels to estimate the value of the subject property.

Establishing Comparative Wilderness Scores. Following the preliminary survey (Step 2) indicating wilderness as a potential most probable use, an assessment of the attributes associated with wilderness began. The attributes most pertinent to wilderness (Step 3) as a most probable use are the physical, dynamic, and environmental attributes. Of the three, definition of the dynamic attributes for wilderness posed the most difficult problem. The two problems confronted were how to identify wilderness attributes and, once identified, how they could be inventoried. The more general issue, however, was how a scoring system for wilderness attributes could be developed that provided for a relevant unit for comparison — a unit that measures the kinds of utility buyers think they are purchasing when they buy wilderness lands.

In the search for wilderness and scenic attributes that could be used for the valuation of the PRMC lands, two systems were identified that attempted to categorize lands based on their wilderness and scenic beauty quality: the Wilderness Attribute Rating System (WARS)[14] and the Variety Class Assessment System (VCAS).[15] Both systems were developed by the U.S. Forest Service to rank lands for their wilderness and scenic quality by identifying the attributes that described these phenomena. These two systems provided a point of departure for the geographically based information system developed for the appraisal described in this paper.

Wilderness Components

Origins of the Wilderness Concept

Wilderness, as a concept, has evolved over the years from a phenomena that had to be conquered by man in the eighteenth and nineteenth centuries, to one in which it is seen as a national treasure needing protection in the twentieth century. Various definitions of wilderness were promulgated in the early twentieth century. Aldo Leopold described wilderness as "a continuous stretch of country preserved in its natural state, open to lawful hunting and fishing, big enough to absorb a 2 weeks' pack trip, and kept devoid of roads, artificial trails, cottages or other works of man" (1921).[16] It was not until the Wilderness Act of 1964, that a legal definition of wilderness was established. In the act, wilderness was described as "an area which 1) generally appears to have been affected primarily by forces of nature with the imprint of man's work substantially unnoticeable; 2) has outstanding opportunities for solitude or a primitive and unconfined type of recreation; 3) has at least five thousand acres of land or is of sufficient size to make practicable its preservation and use in an unimpaired condition; and 4) may also contain ecological, geological, or other features of scientific, educational, scenic, or historical value."[17]

Wilderness Evaluation

The U.S. Forest Service was mandated to review all roadless areas in the National Forest System in accordance with the Wilderness Act. Given this task, a process was initiated called Roadless Area Review and Evaluation (RARE).[18] Part of this process was the creation of the Wilderness Attribute Rating System (WARS), which derived many of its major attributes from the language of the Wilderness Act.[19] WARS is a programmatic system that is intended to be used to inventory and evaluate wilderness areas throughout the United States. It has four components: (1) natural integrity/apparent naturalness, (2) opportunity for solitude, (3) opportunity for a primitive recreation experience, and (4) supplementary attributes: geologic, scenic, and cultural features. Problems have arisen with the system due to its rather subjective evaluation procedures where repeatability is questionable.[20] This, in part, is caused by an inventory procedure that treats the study site as an aggregate. Analyzing the site as an aggregate leads to a lack of sensitivity to site-specific variability, yields no spatial understanding of the resource, provides no means for a retest, and does not provide for a uniform unit for comparison to comparable lands (necessary not only for valuation but also for prioritization).

Visual Quality Assessment

Visual quality is one of four "supplementary attributes" defined in the fourth component of WARS. Determination of visual quality for WARS is done using the Variety Class Assessment System (VCAS). The system was designed by the U.S. Forest Service as a guide for management and evaluation of the nation's scenic resources. VCAS uses a diversity index

THE PRICE OF WILDERNESS AND SCENIC BEAUTY 163

to rate the variety or diversity of five landscape elements: landform, rockform, vegetation, waterform (lakes), and waterform (streams). This system also treats the site as an aggregate, which leads to many of the same problems inherent in the WARS approach.

Enhancements to Wilderness Components

Visitor Employed Photography

The Wilderness Attribute Rating System and the Variety Class Assessment System provided the departure point for the creation of the GIS based valuation system created as part of this project. To augment the information provided by these two systems, it was determined that site-specific information was needed to assist in linking the attributes of the subject property with the inventory process via user input. To provide the link between the users of the site (aggregate buyers) and the attributes being inventoried, a survey of users was initiated.

Visitor employed photography (VEP)[21] was the survey technique employed on the subject property. Hikers were asked to take photographs of various scenes encountered during their travels though the property and to supply corresponding survey data. The primary feature in a photograph was rated on the survey as to whether it adds to or detracts from the scenic beauty of the scene, and each scene was given an overall rating for its scenic beauty. The survey included questions that asked for comparisons to other wilderness areas, as well as user biographical information. VEP is an extremely powerful tool because it yields both a visual (photographic) and a ranked description of what features are deemed to be scenically beautiful or those deemed to be detractors of scenic beauty by the users of the wilderness.

The Wilderness Evaluation System (WES)

The term assigned to the process of combining GIS based wilderness evaluation with automated sales comparison price estimating was the *Wilderness Evaluation System* (WES). WES was designed to extract the best aspects of WARS and VCAS for use in a spatial approach to wilderness evaluation (Table 3). WES augments the systems discussed above by using the additional tools provided in a spatial database and the information gleaned from VEP. WES was designed to provide a mechanism for a

Table 3. The Wilderness Evaluation System (WES)

I. *Natural integrity—Apparent naturalness** is damaged by presence of
   1. Paved road
   2. Clear cut, logging operation
   3. Buildings
   4. Trails, fences

II. *Opportunity for solitude* is aided and abetted by data factors reflecting:
   1. View from
   2. View to
   3. Vegetative screening (stocking class)
   4. Distance perimeter to core

III. *Opportunity for a primitive recreation experience* is increased by each additional element in diversity reflected in data factors that impute challenge or diversity
   1. Challenge
      a. Rockform present
         1. Avalanche chute (snow or rock)
         2. Talus slope or boulder field
         3. Rock outcrop
         4. Cliff
         5. Pinnacle
         6. Cirque
         7. Permanent snow field
         8. Glacier
      b. Vegetative overstory
      c. Percent slope
   2. Diversity
      a. Physiography
      b. Rockform
      c. Vegetation
      d. Waterform

---

*These two elements are separate categories in RARE II; given the fact that comparables were presumed to be wilderness candidates, a perfect wilderness score of 10 is presumed and adjusted downward for items listed. Apparent naturalness is recognized indirectly in the descending penalty score, which reflects curability and observability from a distance. All areas were subject to fire control and fire histories were not available, so this factor in apparent naturalness was ignored.

Graaskamp, James A. and Michael L. Robbins. *The Appraisal of the Pack River Lands.* Madison, WI: Landmark Research, 1982, p. II–20.

site-specific comparison of the subject property's wilderness/scenic attributes with comparable properties' attributes in accordance with the sales comparison approach to value.

WES has several features that distinguish it from other approaches to wilderness evaluation: (1) evaluation is done on a site-specific basis; (2) it provides an understanding of the spatial relationships and attribute variability within a wilderness area; (3) it uses a standardized unit of evaluation, enabling retesting and comparative analysis to be performed; and (4) it is a programmatic approach that is specific in application.

System Structure

WES contains the four major components of wilderness (Table 3): (1) natural integrity/apparent naturalness, (2) opportunity for solitude, (3) opportunity for primitive recreation experience, and (4) scenic beauty (Table 4).

Natural integrity is defined as the extent to which physical development has affected long-term ecological processes. The ratings are based on the same physical impacts used in WARS but are geared toward impacts on the natural processes as perceived by the non-expert typical user. Rating was done on individual cells (spatial unit of analysis) starting with 10 points. The value of any physical impacts contained within the cell's boundary was added. Values range from -10 (paved road) to 0 (no impact). A weighting factor was applied to each cell to account for physical impact occurring on surrounding cells. Therefore, the final natural integrity score for each cell reflected both internal and external physical development.

Opportunity for solitude was rated for each cell using four attributes: (1) distance from the perimeter to the core, (2) view from the cell, (3) view to the cell (both from the same selected viewing platforms), and (4) vegetative screening. The first attribute is generated using a simple distance function in the GIS, and the second and third attributes are generated using viewshed algorithms (Figure 3). The last attribute is derived from the density information collected in the landscape attribute inventory (Table 4). A rating system was devised that combined the four components into a single solitude score.

Opportunity for primitive recreation experience was made up of three attributes: (1) challenge, (2) diversity of terrain, and (3) diversity of landscape. Challenge is scored on the basis of several environmental attributes, such as the presence of various types of rock forms (Table 3)

Table 4. The Scenic Quality System (SQS)*

I. Physiography
   1. Sharp dissected uneven slopes
   2. Moderately dissected slopes
   3. Irregular landscape
   4. Ridged landscape
   5. Peak
II. Rockform
   1. Avalanche chute (rock)
   2. Avalanche chute (snow)
   3. Talus slope or boulder field
   4. Rock outcrop <2 acres
   5. Rock outcrop 2–5 acres
   6. Rock outcrop 5+ acres
   7. Cliff
   8. Pinnacle
   9. Cirque
   10. Permanent snow field
   11. Glacier
   12. Rock dome
III. Vegetation
   1. Stocking 10–39%
   2. Stocking 49–69%
   3. Stocking 70%+
   4. Large old-growth timber
   5. West meadow
IV. Waterform
   1. Unusual shoreline configuration (lakes)
   2. Falls
   3. Rapids
   4. Meander

*These factors reflect elements of diversity revealed by VEP study to be prominent in scenic quality ratings of people who make the effort to enter the area on foot and selected for the fact that data could be gathered from air photos. Each data point implies smaller subsystems, such as flowers in the dry meadow, color patterns in rock outcrops, or distant views that include a mountain peak.

A. Graaskamp, James and Michael L. Robbins. *The Appraisal of the Pack River Lands.* Madison, WI: Landmark Research, 1982, p. II–22.

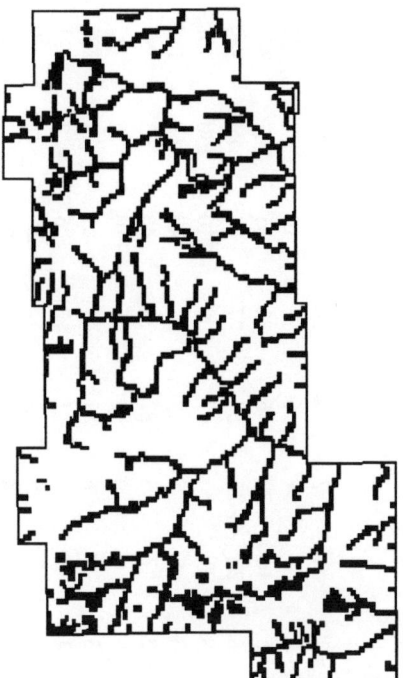

Figure 3. Waterforms.
Map legend: ■ Water feature. Water feature is present within 10 acre cell.

and the density of vegetation (Table 4). Diversity of terrain uses the percent slope as a measure of challenge (more elaborate measures could be made, i.e., fractal dimension). Diversity of landscape is a measure of the number of different landscape features contained within a single cell (physiography, vegetative, rockform, waterform; (Table 4). Each cell was scored with respect to this component.

Scenic quality system (SQS) is based on many of the attributes described in the variety class assessment system. The primary difference is that SQS uses an inventory procedure based on individual cells using color vertical photographs for the inventory procedure and a visual interpretive key for each of the environmental attributes.[22] In addition, SQS relies on the VEP study to augment those environmental attributes identified by users which were not delineated by wilderness and scenic experts. Scoring of each cell was done using the number of landscape attributes found in each cell (diversity) and the exposure of the cell to viewing platforms (as determined by a viewshed analysis).

Table 5. Scenic Beauty Diversity Score

Dynamic attribute	1	2	3	4	5	6	7	8	9	10	Total
1. Sharply dissected slopes	0	0	0	4	10	9	25	58	56	78	240
2. Moderately dissected slopes	0	0	2	3	8	6	14	31	30	31	125
3. Irregular slopes	1	0	1	4	4	20	33	48	42	48	201
4. Ridged lands	0	0	1	0	1	0	2	2	4	8	18
5. Peaks	0	0	0	1	6	7	22	37	48	74	195
6. Avalanche chute—rock	0	0	0	1	2	2	4	16	9	25	59
7. Avalanche chute—snow	0	0	0	0	0	1	6	7	10	8	32
8. Talus or Boulder lands	0	2	3	5	16	28	46	82	95	107	384
9. Rock outcrop—foreground (FG)	0	1	3	8	22	26	54	77	74	84	349
10. Rock outcrop—midground (MG)	1	0	4	8	21	30	57	100	110	130	461
11. Cliff	0	0	0	3	6	8	19	38	43	68	185
12. Pinnacle	0	0	0	3	7	6	22	38	46	63	185
13. Cirque	0	0	0	0	0	0	1	5	10	6	22
14. Snow field	0	0	0	3	9	8	11	41	61	74	207
15. Glacier	0	0	0	1	3	2	1	2	5	7	21
16. Stocking 0–10% FG	0	1	1	5	7	9	11	12	30	13	79
17. Stocking 0–10% MG	0	0	2	0	5	4	7	21	16	32	87
18. Stocking 10–39% FG	0	1	0	3	8	16	29	40	35	51	183
19. Stocking 10–39% MG	0	1	1	2	10	13	29	43	47	39	185
20. Stocking 40–70% FG	0	0	5	6	16	10	32	29	41	20	159
21. Stocking 40–70% MG	1	0	3	4	7	10	18	34	21	30	128
22. Stocking 70%+—FG	0	1	3	3	4	10	31	41	38	30	161
23. Stocking 70%+—MG	0	0	0	0	1	1	4	8	15	12	41
24. Large old growth	0	0	1	0	1	0	7	3	9	4	25

Scenic beauty ratings

25. Bushes	0	2	5	8	15	30	63	88	77	70	358
26. Dry meadow	0	1	1	3	4	11	20	30	23	44	137
27. Valley—wet meadow	0	0	0	1	2	8	12	13	25	24	85
28. Slope—wet meadow	0	0	0	0	0	4	7	14	5	22	52
29. Unusual shoreline	0	0	0	0	1	3	6	8	10	9	37
30. Water falls	0	0	0	2	3	5	6	12	12	17	47
31. Rapids	0	1	2	2	6	6	16	25	17	16	91
32. Stream meander	0	0	0	0	0	0	1	1	7	6	15
33. Lake or pond	1	1	2	1	6	17	25	45	49	59	206
34. Stream	0	0	2	2	0	4	14	11	10	7	50
35. Column total	4	12	40	84	211	310	641	1049	1110	1299	4760
36. Recond count	1	3	11	18	43	61	133	179	184	178	811

The diversity measure was derived by correlating the scenic score that users gave to scenes they photographed with an inventory of the WES landscape attributes that occurred in each picture. Correlations had an r^2 of 94% using 800+ samples (Table 5). The rational behind using view from as the other component of the scenic score is that a scenically beautiful region is even more valuable if it is visible from a variety of vantage points.

As stated previously, a complicating factor in the assessment of wilderness lands is that no one set of environmental attributes (those relating to the physical characteristics of the land) constitutes wilderness. WES addresses this problem (as does WARS) by defining four components of the system whose subattributes are constant regardless of the region or landscape on which the analysis is performed. It is the identification and interpretation of the environmental attributes used to score those components that will vary from region to region. For example, the attribute challenge in a mountainous region may have a high score (indicating a significant challenge) in the regions with steep slopes because of the difficulty in traversing such terrain, whereas in a relatively flat terrain with no visible mountains, the score could be high due to orientation problems. This consistency of the wilderness components and their attributes in WES allows for comparison of wilderness areas, regardless of their geographic region or characteristics. Site-specific information for each new study area is obtained from the environmental attributes for each of the components. The environmental attributes are identified and interpreted on a case-by-case basis. Thus, WES is simultaneously programmatic and site specific in application.

The other key feature of WES is its spatial approach to wilderness evaluation. Wilderness scores are calculated for each of the four components in a defined spatial unit (for the PRMC appraisal a 10 acre cell was used). This unit forms the basis for comparison of the subject and comparable properties. This unit is, however, not evaluated in isolation. The viewshed analysis in the GIS permits including off-site effects that influence the wilderness score of a cell. This spatial approach to wilderness evaluation has the advantages of site specificity, repeatability, context (visual exposure), and comparability (comparisons with other wilderness areas).

Data Sources

The WES component attributes were scored using environmental attributes obtained from map and photographic data and using the spatial operations of a GIS. The map data source (7.5 minute U.S. Geological

Survey Quadrangles) yielded information on physical development, human impact (roads and buildings), topographic data, and surface water. The photographic data (1:11,000 vertical color aerial photographs) were used to derive the landscape attributes defined in WES. Derived data sets were generated using the spatial operations of the geographic information system and the U.S. Forest Service's View-It program.[23] The derived data included view from and view to each cell (from the same selected viewing platforms), distance perimeter to core, and slope for each cell.

Attribute Weighting

WES consists of 10 attributes scored on an ordinal basis, each attribute having a minimum possible score of 0 and a maximum possible score of 10 (Table 6). The 10 attributes were grouped into the four components of

Table 6. Comparable Summary Sheet

I. Wilderness (.25)			
.25	1. Natural integrity (apparent naturalness)	x.xxx	x.xxx
II. Solitude (.25)			
.0625	1. Distance to perimeter	x.xxx	
.0625	2. View FROM cell (rev.)	x.xxx	
.0625	3. View TO cell (rev.)	x.xxx	
.0625	4. Vegetation screening	x.xxx	x.xxx
III. Primitive recreation experience (.25)			
.083	1. Challenge (physical feature)	x.xxx	
.083	2. diversity—% slope	x.xxx	
.083	3. Diversity—terrain	x.xxx	x.xxx
IV. Scenic quality (.25)			
.20	1. Scenic quality	x.xxx	
.05	2. View from cell	x.xxx	x.xxx
Average attribute score per cell			x.xxx
Adjusted Purchase price		xxx,xxx.	
Total cells in comp		xx.xx	
Total acres in comp		xx.xx	
Total attribute points		xxx.xx	
Average price per point per cell		xxx.xx	

wildernesss. Each attribute was weighted equally, relative to the component in which it was assigned, and each component was weighted equally. The Wilderness Act of 1964 identified the three primary wilderness components—wilderness quality, solitude, and primitive recreation experience. The act also permitted any of four supplemental attributes, including scenic quality, if present to a significant degree. Neither the Wilderness Act, the Alpine Lakes Management Act, nor the RARE-II analysis suggest that one component is more important than another; therefore an equally weighted model was implemented. The Wilderness Attribute Score (WAS) was derived by summing the resultant weighted attributes constituting the WES. Estimates for each of the attributes and components were derived and combined to establish a WAS for each 10 acre cell making up the subject property, as well as the individual comparable properties.

Model Output

The output of the WES is a systematic inventory of the site and each comparable property, structured as follows:

1. The spatial unit of analysis was 10 acres.
2. For each spatial unit, 10 ordinally ranked scores were derived.
3. Each score was based on the physical components existing within the spatial unit.
4. The 10 scores represented recognized characteristics of wilderness.

These databases (one for the subject property and another for the comparable properties) became the basis for pricing the subject property with the attribute matching methodology built into the Market Comp program.

Application of Wilderness Appraisal Method

Selection of Market Transactions

In selecting market transactions, location, physical attributes, and motivation of buyer and seller were considered for comparability. The general search for sales transactions was first constrained by the determination of most probable use, in this instance, mountainous wilderness tracts featuring lake and stream waterforms, some commercial forest cover of the type found in generally dry, noncoastal altitudes, and relatively similar opportunities for challenging wilderness recreation. Coastal rainfalls ruled out properties in the Western Cascades of Washington and Oregon and northern California. Snowcapped mountain ranges were considered in Colorado, Wyoming, Washington, Idaho, and western Montana. The search was further narrowed to emphasize the northern and eastern Cascades in Chelan, Skagit, and Snohomish Counties in Washington; the Idaho Primitive Areas in the general vicinity of the Salmon, Big Creek, Monumental Creek districts; and in the Spanish Peaks Primitive Areas of Gallatin and Lewis and Clark Counties of Montana. The latter two areas were somewhat drier but more similar in elevation and terrain than lands to the south.

Within these broad parameters, the methods of sale transaction search reflected the emphasis placed on proximity to the eastern Cascades, similarity of terrain, latitude, altitude, and, as far as possible, a motivation on the part of the buyer to conserve the property in its natural state.

A title company searched Chelan County for land transactions. Contact with Washington appraisers uncovered additional sales in Skagit and Snohomish counties, and correspondence with appraisers in other states, government agencies, conservancy groups, as well as review of various public reports on acquisition programs identified many other candidates in the five state area. Ultimately, a list of forty sales became the focus of analysis. The list was reduced to fifteen when sites for home construction, acreage for timber cutting, recreational development, and commercial outfitting were eliminated, or conversations with federal officials or the grantor indicated that buyer motivation and economic purpose were not compatible with the concept of best use established for PRMC properties.

Many properties that seemed appropriate in terms of purpose of acquisition and locale were determined to be inappropriate after visual inspection by helicopter by the appraiser. At this point the transactions had been selected because of their size, representative character of a mountain region or high country, buyer motivation, and broad visual similarity but prior to detailed analysis.

Equalization Of Market Forces

To equalize the fifteen comparative sales for terms of sale, regional locale, improvements included with the land, differences in development or market pressures, and price change over time due to dollar devaluation, it was necessary to establish rules for adjusting sales prices to a common date, a common bundle of rights, terms of sale, and market context.[24] The fifteen sale prices, adjusted for time and other externalities, became the basis on which the subject property was appraised. The fifteen adjusted sales represent prices paid for wilderness properties, generally purchased with the buyer's explicit objective or implicit recognition that the property would largely remain wilderness, and meet the second condition of the sales comparison approach (adequate information to adjust sale prices for external factors).

Determination of average price paid per WES attribute

The adjusted purchase price represented the value of the physical characteristics of the total parcel. Through the application of WES to the comparable properties, it was possible to estimate the total wilderness attributes within the property's boundary. With this information, the average price paid per WES attribute could be estimated. For example, for one of the comparable properties, the adjusted purchase price of the 357 acre property was $287,000. When the site inventory information was processed, the analysis indicated that the total number of wilderness attribute points scored was 265.66 (WAS). By dividing the adjusted purchase price of $287,000 by the total attribute score of 265.66, the average attribute price per point per cell was determined to be $1080.31. This indicates that the buyer paid $1080.31 for each wilderness attribute point inventoried in this comparable.

Distribution of price paid

Having determined the average price paid for each wilderness attribute, the next step was to use this information to indicate the price paid for individual cells of the comparable. The price for each cell in the comparable was determined by multiplying the number of attributes within the cell times the average price paid for each attribute. For the example comparable, the average attribute score per cell was 6.325; however, evaluation of individual cells indicate that the attribute scores ranged from a high of 6.592 to a low of 2.946. Redistributing the adjusted purchase price by the number of attributes present within the cell indicated that the price paid for the maximum attribute cell was 6.592 times $1080.31, or $7121.40, and the lowest cell was 2.946 times $1080.31, or $3182.59. The sum of all the cells' assigned prices was equal to the adjusted purchase price for the entire comparable ($287,000). The important point is that the better quality cells (those with the greater number of attributes) received a greater portion of the purchase price.

This process of allocating price to the cells with the greater number of attributes was modeled after the process frequently used in the appraisal of timberland.[25] This procedure, usually referred to as the *allocation method*, requires the appraiser to identify the major types of land making up the subject, and then distribute a portion of the price to each of the landscape units. The appraiser must evaluate the market of timber sales and develop an evaluation procedure for valuing each of the composite parts to derive an overall price estimate.

WES operated on the same premise, except that the spatial unit was fixed at 10 acres (for the PRMC appraisal), and the number of attributes evaluated was fixed at 10.

Attribute Matching — The Pricing Process

The implementation of the attribute-matching process utilized a data processing technique designed specifically for automated market comparison, MKTCOMP.[26] Over the years, MKTCOMP has been used intensively by such federal agencies as the National Park Service in the acquisition of the southwest Everglades in Florida, the National Wildlife Service in the evaluation of border waters in Minnesota, and the Bureau of Indian Affairs for pricing agricultural land. Private appraisers have used it for ranchlands, single-family homes, and rental comparisons, as well as automated community tax assessment.[27]

The MKTCOMP process permits selection of an initial subset of sales using Euclidian distance in terms of the sum of the squared dollar adjustments, to rank a preliminary subset of user specified number. A second refinement ranks the selected comparables in order of "closeness" to the subject parcel. (For the PRMC appraisal the parameters of the program were set to select the most similar unit from each of the fifteen comparables. The second step then selected the most similar seven comparables to use as the basis for pricing the subject.) In identifying the degree of difference between each wilderness attribute, by subtracting the attribute score of the comparable from that of the subject, two important steps have occurred — the indication of difference and the implicit indication of the degree of similarity. For example, if the scores for apparent naturalness were 10.00 for the subject and 8.30 for the comparable, this would indicate that the two parcels were different by 1.7 units, but also would show that they were similar by 8.3 units. This implicit recognition of the

Table 7. Comparable Adjustment Matrix

Factor	Subject score	Comp-1 score	Adjusted amount	Comp-2 score	Adjusted amount
Sale-ID	0.00	30.00	0	22.00	0
Price	0.00	69250.00	69250	84785.00	84785
Apparent natural	10.00	9.15	2063	8.30	4126
Distance	0.00	0.00	0	2.50	−1518
View from rev.	2.46	0.55	1159	1.00	886
View to rev.	2.31	0.55	1068	1.50	492
Vegetation screen	1.58	1.88	−182	0.83	455
Challenge	1.25	1.25	0	0.55	566
Diversity—slope	0.75	1.74	−801	2.21	−1181
Diversity—terrain	1.66	1.33	267	1.77	−89
View to normal	0.05	1.56	−732	1.20	−558
Scenic quality	3.20	2.80	777	3.73	−1029
Adjusted amount			72869		86936
Selection index			2937		4864

level of similarity is an important component of the attribute-matching method of price estimating.

In the attribute-matching method, *an adjustment is applied only to the difference between attributes*; thus, for the units of similarity between the subject and the comparable, no adjustment is made.[28] To account for the market price difference between attribute scores, the difference is multiplied by an adjustment factor (generally determined by the appraiser through analysis of the comparables). The adjustments are then combined and added to the selling price of the comparable (Table 7). If the net adjustments are negative (indicating that the comparable is superior to the subject), the comparable's selling price is reduced; if the net adjustments are positive (indicating that the comparable is inferior to the subject), the selling price of the comparable is increased. In this way, the attributes of the comparable are made similar to the subject, and any difference is used to adjust the selling price of the comparable.

Comparable Ranking

The Euclidian distance model is used to rank comparables. Euclidian distance operates on the premise that the total distance (measure of difference) in multidimensional space (multiple attribute measures) is equal to

Table 8. Euclidian Distance Comparable Ranking Model

Factor	Subject score	Comp score	Adjusted amount	Adjusted sqrd.
Sale-ID	0.00	30.00	0	
Price	0.00	69250.00	69250	
Apparent natural	10.00	9.15	2063	4,255,969
Distance	0.00	0.00	0	0
View from rev.	2.46	0.55	1159	1,343,281
View to rev.	2.31	0.55	1068	1,140,624
Vegetation screen	1.58	1.88	−182	33,124
Challenge	1.25	1.25	0	0
Diversity—slope	0.75	1.74	−801	641,601
Diversity—terrain	1.66	1.33	267	71,289
View to normal	0.05	1.56	−732	535,824
Scenic quality	3.20	2.80	777	603,729
Adjusted amount			72869	8,625,729
Selection index			2937	2,937

the square root of the sum of the squares of the individual attributes. In appraisal this means that an index for selection can be determined for each comparable by summing the squares of the adjustments made for differences between the subject and the comparable, and then taking the square root of the sum (Table 8).

The resulting number (Euclidian distance) is referred to in the MKTCOMP program as the selection index and is the basis for determining the level of similarity between the subject and comparable, measured in absolute dollars.[29]

Conclusions

Contemporary appraisal theory recognizes that an appraisal is an opinion of value for an adequately described property, as of a specific date, supported by the analysis of relevant data. It further recognizes that the appraisal opinion is founded on acceptable evidence, but with less than perfect knowledge. Thus, the determined value estimate will be subject to variance, leading to determination of the most probable price.

This research did not attempt to remove any decision-making or rule-setting controls from the appraiser. The goal was to address the issue of adequately describing the subject and comparable properties, and providing the property descriptions to the appraiser in a usable and easily understood format. The latter is important in facilitating the appraiser's simulation of the reactions of users in the market in response to particular combinations of attributes, and to the net benefits these attributes are capable of generating.

The implementation of a sales-comparison pricing model, driven by procedures for selecting similar comparable subsales explicitly, recognizes that buyers and sellers weigh similar attributes differently, even when the intended use is the same. By selecting the single most similar subsale from individual comparable properties, the price or weight difference within individual comparable properties is recognized and utilized in ascertaining the price estimate of individual subject subunits.

Significance Of Research

This article shows that spatial database concepts can be used to value individual appraisal units, explicitly recognizing the unique combinations of ascertainable facts present in each appraisal unit. Rather than assigning average values for only limited amounts of the total site (valuing the site for timber or recreational lot development by either the aggregate or multiple regression methods), the techniques utilized in this project allowed valuing each individual appraisal unit making up the subject property.

The development of the Wilderness Evaluation System (WES) enabled the use of physical attributes and user attitudes in establishing proxies for recognized wilderness characteristics. Having established the wilderness proxies, the wilderness scores were evaluated and processed using an attribute-matching methodology, which was not dependent on inferential statistical reliability for accuracy. In addition, the attribute-matching pricing methodology provided for testing of alternative pricing models, allowing internal consistency and appraisal goals to be evaluated and maintained. Finally, the derived price estimate was provided in a format that is easy to follow and explain, thus greatly enhancing the defensibility of the price estimate.

This research demonstrated that there is an active and informed market for natural landscapes that contain significant concentrations of attributes associated with wilderness. By bringing together acceptable market transactions between knowledgeable buyers and knowledgeable sellers, where wilderness was recognized as a significant component of the transaction, with systematic and detailed inventory of the subject and comparable properties, market inference could be employed to estimate the value of the subject, under a wilderness use scenario.

The research concluded:

1. The highest and best use of the Pack River Alpine Lakes Area Lands was wilderness.
2. The complex issue of Wilderness Evaluation could be addressed by building on a foundation of knowledge and guidelines laid out by the U.S. Forest Service in the years since the conception of the Wilderness Act of 1964.
3. A comprehensive Wilderness Evaluation System necessitated modification of the U.S. Forest Service Systems of Wilderness and Scenic Beauty Evaluation, for inclusion into a GIS, to provide an effective data structure for site-specific analysis
4. A Fair Market Valuation of the Pack River Alpine Lakes Property could be attained by building on well-established Wilderness evaluation and real estate appraisal techniques.

Notes

1. Public Law 94–357, 94th Congress, H.R. 7792, July 12, 1976.

2. The fact that the subject property was located within the boundary of designated wilderness area had no direct bearing on the determination of the "highest and best use" of the subject property being wilderness. Wilderness was one of several land use options tested by the appraisal team. The economic analysis developed by the appraisal team determined that wilderness use was the best fit of the lands characteristics to the context of the problem (determination of market value) and as such was determined to be the most probable use for the subject.

While the terms *highest and best use* and *most probable use* are used interchangeably in this paper (and in the original appraisal), the reader is cautioned to note that in actual application highest and best use and most probable use are derived under very different formats. To minimize any confusion within the appraisal (or in any following court application), the appraisal team employed the contemporary appraisal format to determine most probable use and then called it *highest and best use*.

3. It was the hope of Congress and the intent of ALMA that compensation agreements could be negotiated that included exchange of other federally owned property or donations. Timber trades for national forest lands were considered probable; however, when PRMC sold its saw mill operations in the Wenatchee, Washington area of the intended wilderness, the Forest Service fount it expedient to withdraw any trade offers from PRMC. (See Section 4 (c) (2) of ALMA and Alternatives B1, B2, and E Final Environmental Statement, Alpine Lakes Area Acquisition, USDA-FS-FES (Adm) 78–06, pp. 50–9.

4. One of the unique features of ALMA was that it gave the owners within the intended wilderness special rights that modify the appraisal rules affecting condemnation. For exam-

ple, since ALMA provided three years for negotiated purchase, the Forest Service saw one of their alternatives to be no action at all (referred to as Plan D) in order to prompt land owners to force a purchase by court action. Final Environmental Statement, Alpine Lakes Area Acquisitions, op. cit., see Alternative D—No Action, p. iv.

5. Public Law 88-577, Wilderness Act, 88th Congress, September 3, 1964 (78 Stat. 890: 16 U.S.C. pp. 1131-36).

6. Interagency Land Acquisition Conference. *Uniform Appraisal Standards for Federal Land Acquisition*. Washington, D.C.: U.S. Government Printing Office, 1973, pp. 25-8.

7. Robbins, Michael L. "Methodology for Evaluating, Ranking, and Pricing Mountainous Wilderness Lands," Ph.D. dissertation, University of Wisconsin, 1983, pp. 3-7.

8. At a meeting between Bureau of Land Management (BLM) personnel and State of New Mexico representatives regarding the exchange of three million acres, BLM representatives indicated a value based solely on grazing rights, yet both parties agreed that the "highest and best use" of the land was wilderness. (Interview with Mr. Craig Hungerford, President, Real Estate Dynamics, Inc., Madison, WI.)

9. Graaskamp, James A. *The Appraisal of 25 N. Pinckney: A Demonstration Case for Contemporary Appraisal Methods*. Madison, WI: Landmark Research, 1985, pp. 7-8.

10. Graaskamp, James A. and Michael L. Robbins. *The Appraisal of the Pack River Lands*. Madison, WI: Landmark Research, 1982, p. III-21.

11. Graaskamp, p. 9.

12. A Geographic Information System is a computerized data management system combines information retrieval technology with locational identifiers to display analysis in an image format.

13. Robbins, Michael L. "The Valuation Of Large Scale Natural Landscapes using Contemporary Appraisal Theory." *The Appraisal Journal* (April 1987), 232.

14. U.S.D.A. Forest Service. *Rare II Wilderness Attribute Rating System: A User Manual*. Developed by the Wilderness Attribute Rating System Task Force. Washington, D.C.: U.S.D.A., Nov/Dec 1977, p. 1.

15. U.S.D.A. Forest Service. The Visual Management System," *National Forest Landscape Management*, Volume 2. Washington, D.C.: U.S. Government Printing Office, 1977, p. 13.

16. Hendee, J. C., G. H. Stankey and R. C. Lucas. *Wilderness Management*. U.S.D.A. Forest Service, publication no. 1365, 1977.

17. Wilderness Act, op. cit.

18. U.S.D.A. Forest Service. *Rare II Wilderness Attribute Rating System: A User's Manual*. Developed by the Wilderness Attribute Rating System Task Force. Washington, DC: U.S.D.A., Nov/Dec 1977, p. 1.

19. RARE II, p. 34.

20. California vs. Bergland, nos. 79-523, January 8, 1980.

21. Chenoweth, Richard and Benard Niemann. "Alpine Lakes Area User VEP Survey Study." *The Appraisal of the Pack River Lands*. Madison, WI: Landmark Research, 1982, Appendix D.

22. Ahearn, Sean C. "The Dynamic Attributes Used In The Appraisal Of Pack River Lands." *The Appraisal of the Pack River Lands*. Madison, WI: Landmark Research, 1982, Appendix B.

23. U.S.D.A. Forest Service VIEWIT: Computation of Seen Areas, Slope and Aspect for Landscape Planning, PSW-11/1975. Pacific Southwest Forest and Range Experiment Station, 1975.

24. Graaskamp and Robbins, op. cit., pp. III 18-21.

25. *The Appraisal of Rural Property*. Chicago, IL: 1983, *American Institute of Real Estate Appraisers*, pp. 332–35.

26. MKTCOMP is an automated market comparison program specifically designed to implement the sales comparison approach. The system was developed at the University of Wisconsin by H. Robert Knitter, James A. Graaskamp, and Michael L. Robbins, with the cooperation of EDUCARE, The Educational Foundation for Computer Applications to Real Estate.

27. The MKTCOMP program has gone through several sets of changes since its use on this project. Its current form is written in TRUE Basic as a interactive program for the typical desktop computer. In this form the program is a regular part of both the introductory and advanced appraisal courses taught in the Real Estate Department at the University of Wisconsin — Madison.

28. In most automated sales comparison programs a statistically derived weighting factor is applied directly to the attributes of the subject, thus reducing the subject to a statistical average that results in losing the uniqueness of the subject.

29. An extended discussion of the selection and weighting process of the MKTCOMP program can be found in Robbins, Michael L. "The Valuation of Large Scale Natural Landscapes," op. cit., pp. 236–242.

6 USING PRIOR INFORMATION TO IMPROVE ESTIMATION EFFICIENCY AND PREDICTIVE PERFORMANCE FOR MASS APPRAISAL*

Otis W. Gilley and R. Kelley Pace

Introduction

Statistical mass appraisal models often have difficulty achieving the dual goals of good predictive performance and reasonable parameter estimates. Frequently models achieve good predictive performance — within the sample — as documented by high levels of R^2. However, rarely do researchers present evidence on out-of-sample performance, the more relevant criterion for appraisal purposes. Also, models predicting better in terms of in-sample R^2 do not necessarily produce plausible parameter estimates. Indeed, models with the highest levels of R^2 frequently achieve their good in-sample fit through inclusion of a relatively large number of correlated variables. Consequently, such models often pay the price of higher levels of multicollinearity, which decreases the precision of parameter estimation, and thus raises the likelihood of implausible estimates. Such estimates may appear in the form of negative coefficients for hous-

---

* Financial support for this research from a Louisiana Tech Faculty Development Grant and from the Louisiana Tech Center for Real Estate Research is gratefully acknowledged by Otis Gilley. The views expressed in this paper are strictly those of the authors.

ing characteristics clearly of value, such as a garage, bathroom, or living area. Alternatively, an estimated parameter's value may exceed the cost of adding the characteristic via a home improvement. For example, the regression might yield an estimate of $7500 for fireplace value. Most individuals would find it difficult to accept this estimate if it costs only $2500 to add one to an existing house. Unfortunately, unreasonable estimates reduce the model's value for mass appraisal due to problems in convincing taxpayers (and sometimes the courts) of the model's validity. For other discussions of the effects of multicollinearity in appraisal models see Vandell and Zerbst (1984), Reichert and Moore (1986), and Kang and Moore (1987).

The goal of this paper is to define an estimation procedure that will by construction yield reasonable coefficient estimates and to demonstrate the consequent of out-of-sample prediction error. We will show the use of a procedure yielding reasonable coefficients actually increases the out-of-sample predictive performance.

What determines reasonable coefficient estimates? Clearly, estimates for characteristics representing goods such as a swimming pool must exceed zero. Also, rational consumers will not pay more for a characteristic than the cost, properly defined, of adding the characteristic via a post construction improvement.[1] Note many housing characteristics, such as bathrooms, bedrooms, fireplaces, garages, and so forth, do trade in the home improvement market. The positive value of goods and the upper bound upon their value determined by this market constitutes a wealth of inequality prior information. By construction, estimates that satisfy this prior information will seem more reasonable.

A variety of procedures can incorporate inequality prior information. However, for those familiar with OLS, inequality restricted least squares (IRLS) represents the most straightforward way to estimate with prior information. Like OLS, IRLS minimizes the sum of squared errors, but subject to inequality constraints on the parameters. With correct inequality information, IRLS dominates OLS in terms of the mean squared error measured relative to β (Judge et al., 1985, p. 69). Given correct information, the improvement proves greatest for situations where OLS has difficulty providing good estimates. This situation can arise when either the model goodness of fit is poor or if a considerable degree of multicollinearity is present. To provide an estimate of the amount of improvement possible using IRLS, a Monte Carlo experiment appears below that measures the improvement offered by IRLS over OLS as a function of goodness of fit (as measured by R^2) and of multicollinearity (as measured by the condition number). Also, the improvement of IRLS over OLS depends upon the location of β. To avoid biasing the experiment against OLS, we randomly select β out of the subspace determined by the inequality prior information for each iteration. To ensure accurate results, each of the 20 cases examined uses 10,000 iterations for a total of 400,000 OLS and IRLS regressions. The experiment documents the great potential of prior information to assist in parameter estimation.

The IRLS estimator employing both zero and upper bounds also has an interesting and intuitively appealing interpretation. If, for a particular variable, the restriction of zero binds, the variable essentially vanishes. If the upper bound from submarket restrictions binds, the model yields an estimate for the variable based solely upon cost data. If neither restriction binds, the model yields an estimate for the variable based upon market data and upon nonsample data (providing any of the other variables bind). Hence, the IRLS estimator hybridizes market and cost approaches to value.

As alluded to earlier, the relevant criteria for appraisal is out-of-sample prediction error. Unfortunately, the only prediction statistic usually available is R^2, which measures in-sample error. Generally this does not correctly measure the out-of-sample error. As Effron (1986, p. 461) says, ". . . the apparent error rate usually underestimates the true error rate. The reason is simple: the model is selected to lie near the observed points, which is what *fitting* means, so these points give a falsely optimistic picture of the model's true accuracy." To provide a better estimate of out-of-sample error we will use cross-validation. The simplest example of cross-validation is data splitting, whereby a researcher splits the sample into two parts—the sample and the hold-out sample. The researcher fits the model on the sample and assesses its accuracy on the hold-out sample. This technique dates from the 1930s in the psychometric literature (see Linhart and Zucchini, 1986, p. 23). A more recent version of the cross-validation technique (Geisser, 1975) performs the data splitting and assessment stages above but does so repeatedly. Each iteration consists of randomly splitting the data, fitting the model on the sample, and assessing its accuracy on the hold-out sample. A single data split between the sample and hold-out sample could yield misleading results due to sampling error. Repetitive data splitting (in this paper, 5000 iterations) avoids this possibility.

The cross-validation technique described above enables us to evaluate the predictive accuracy of IRLS vs. OLS in an appraisal environment. Note by construction, OLS always dominates IRLS within the sample. Both minimize the sum of squared errors, but IRLS must obey constraints and thus can at best match the OLS R^2. If any constraint binds,

IRLS must produce a lower R^2 compared to OLS. However, by evaluating IRLS and OLS via cross-validation we will show that IRLS can offer less error out of sample.

The ability to measure out-of-sample errors allows us to deal with concerns over the correctness of prior information. Of course, one can never know whether prior information is totally correct; however, one can determine whether prior information is useful. Since using the prior information allows IRLS to outperform OLS in terms of out-of-sample error, prior information appears useful, especially given the presence of a wealth of such information in appraisal contexts.

In what follows, the mechanics and the properties of IRLS are discussed first, followed by a discussion of the model, the sample, and the nonsample information. Then the Monte Carlo experiment, which details the improvement offered by IRLS over OLS as a function of R^2 and multicollinearity, is outlined. Next OLS and IRLS are cross-validated and the improvement in prediction error of IRLS over OLS is presented. Finally, the key points are summarized.

The Inequality Restricted Least Squares Estimator

The IRLS estimator minimizes the sum of squared errors subject to a set of linear inequality constraints

$$\text{Minimize } y'y - 2\beta'X'y + \beta'(X'X)\beta \text{ subject to } R\beta \geq r,$$

where y is the N by 1 dependent variable vector, X is the N by K matrix of independent variable data, β is the K by 1 vector of coefficients, R is a J by K matrix, and r is a J by 1 vector. There are J hypotheses, N observations, and K independent variables. The term $y'y$ does not depend upon the coefficients and hence remains constant. Similarly, multiplying the sum of squared errors by 1/2 also leaves the minimum unchanged. Therefore, an equivalent problem is

$$\text{Minimize } -\beta'X'y + \left(\frac{1}{2}\right)\beta'(X'X)\beta \text{ subject to } R\beta \geq r.$$

Transposing the scalar term $-\beta'X'y$ yields

$$\text{Minimize } (-X'y)'\beta + \left(\frac{1}{2}\right)\beta'(X'X)\beta \text{ subject to } R\beta \geq r.$$

By letting $x = \beta, H = X'X, g = (-X'y), A = R,$ and $b = r$, this problem has the form of the quadratic programming problem stated by Goldfarb and Idnani (1983):

INFORMATION TO IMPROVE ESTIMATION EFFICIENCY

$$\text{Minimize } g'x = \left(\frac{1}{2}\right)x'Hx \text{ subject to } Ax \geq b.$$

Fortunately, this statement of the problem leads to an easy and efficient implementation via IMSL Fortran subroutines.[2]

Alternatively, the IRLS estimate could be obtained from running the restricted least squares regressions stemming from all possible combinations of the J hypotheses and choosing the one with the highest R^2. This intuitive computational method is easy to implement when only a few restrictions exist.

Indeed, Geweke (1986) suggests many practitioners essentially apply a form of IRLS by searching for OLS regressions with the highest R^2 that simultaneously satisfy intuitive inequality priors. They accomplish this, however, by examining many different specifications. Unfortunately, this pretesting means the significance levels given by typical OLS regression packages overestimate the true, unconditional significance levels. Rather than altering specifications to avoid coefficients incompatible with priors, the use of IRLS, with its desirable properties, seems preferable.

The works of Geweke (1986), Judge and Yancey (1986), and Judge et al. (1985) discuss in detail the properties of IRLS and reference a comprehensive set of papers on the subject. IRLS is a biased estimator. However, as mentioned earlier, if the a priori restrictions embody correct information, IRLS dominates OLS under squared error loss. In this case the reduction in the variance of IRLS outweighs its bias relative to OLS.

Naturally, it is difficult to know much concerning the accuracy of prior information. The approach taken here, as outlined later, is to assess the out-of-sample prediction error for IRLS and OLS. Since the data show IRLS can predict better than OLS, the prior information appears valuable.

The Model, Sample, and Nonsample Information

We now discuss the model, sample, and nonsample information used in the succeeding development. We begin by postulating a simple model compatible with the incorporation of nonsample information and follow this with a discussion of both the sample and the nonsample information.

An Illustrative Model

Using cost data as the *a priori* bounds implies a natural means to model value by decomposing a house into fundamental units differing by cost such as different functional areas.[3] Typically, bathroom area costs the most per square foot, followed by kitchen area, followed by bedroom area, and so on. Since individual features or rooms such as fireplaces, garages, and bathrooms also vary by cost, these too may serve as variables. Therefore, we estimate the following[4]:

Price = $\beta_0 + \beta_1$(lot area) + β_2(bedroom area) + β_3(kitchen area)

$+ \beta_4$(other area) $+ \beta_5$(number of bathrooms)

$+ \beta_6$(number of fireplaces) $+ \beta_7$(number of garage spaces).

Sample Information

The data used to estimate the above illustrative model comes from the Memphis Multiple Listing Service's *Multiple Listing Book*, published by the Memphis Board of Realtors for January 1987. Properties were selected randomly until 100 observations passed a screening procedure. We restricted the data to observations on single family dwellings located in Memphis with complete information on each characteristic.

Nonsample Information

The nonsample data (*a priori* information) come from three sources. First, under this model specification, all variables represent goods; hence, their coefficients should exceed zero. Second, both the upper and lower bounds for the lot area variable derive from the highest and lowest priced lot (per square foot) in the Memphis MLS residential lot sales section. Third, data from the *Means Home Improvement Cost Guide* (1985), adjusted to 1987 Memphis prices, enables the formulation of upper bound cost estimates for each submarket component of housing. These figures appear in Table 1 in the column labeled Submarket Cost. The use of remodeling addition costs ensures that these estimates serve as legitimate upper bounds.[5]

Effects of *A Priori* Information

The relative performance of the OLS and IRLS estimators depends upon many factors. For example, the multicollinearity of the data affects the variability of the estimates and hence the associated probability of violating restrictions. In addition, the variability of the true error term affects both the goodness of fit, commonly estimated by R^2, and the relative performance of IRLS and OLS. For example, in the absence of true errors, both OLS and IRLS would yield an R^2 of 1 and identical estimates, assuming a correct model specification and restrictions. Also, the exact location of β relative to the *a priori* bounds can affect the relative results. For example, when the true β is close to a boundary value, the probability of a bounds violation rises for any given estimation attempt under OLS. In such a situation, IRLS has an advantage over OLS. Finally, the number of observations affects the variability of the estimates, and hence the probability of bound violations.

To gauge the two estimators' relative performance, we controlled for multicollinearity, model goodness of fit, the location of β within the restricted parameter space, prior information, and sample size. The latter two factors were held constant while the first three factors were systematically varied.

Specifically, to examine the effect of the first two factors, we generated twenty cases. These twenty cases include all combinations stemming from five different, multicollinear data matrices and four different levels of R^2. To examine the effect of the third factor, we randomly varied β over the restricted parameter space. Thus, each regression in the Monte Carlo experiment involved a different β in addition to a different error vector. Hence, the comparisons reported below result from an average across all β satisfying the *a priori* restrictions. Given these two sources of variation for each regression, the experiment involves 10,000 OLS and 10,000 IRLS regressions for each of the twenty cases to ensure representative results. Consequently, the Monte Carlo experiment employs 400,000 OLS and IRLS regressions.[6] The subsections below detail the data generation and discuss the results of the experiment.

Generation of Data

To control for multicollinearity, we simulated data rather than directly employing the actual MLS data. Accordingly, following Belsley et al. (1980, p. 104), five independent variable data matrices were simulated, each with a different degree of multicollinearity as measured by the condition number.[7] According to Belsley et al., condition numbers higher than 30 imply the potential of disruptive ill conditioning, while values over 100 suggest very serious problems. What condition numbers and R^2s typify statistical appraisal studies? Unfortunately, we know of none that report condition numbers. Because of the emphasis on prediction, statistical appraisal models usually have high R^2s and probably have high condition numbers, given the large number of regressors and the use of highly correlated variables such as number of rooms and total area. While we do not have condition number data on statistical appraisal models, we do have some on the closely related hedonic pricing models. Relative to statistical appraisal models, hedonic pricing models tend to have fewer variables, lower R^2s, and presumably smaller condition numbers. Belsley et al. discuss a hedonic pricing study on housing values and pollution by Harrison and Rubinfeld (1978) with an R^2 of .80 and a condition number of 66. Given these considerations, we elected to use condition numbers of 30, 45, 60, 75, and 100 for the simulated matrices to span the set of likely conditions. We will refer to the case of an R^2 of .80 and a condition number of 60 as "typical," since it comes closest to the Harrison and Rubinfeld study.

To retain some features of the original data set, we required each of the five simulated independent variable data sets varying by multicollinearity to have the same minimums, medians, and maximums as the Memphis MLS data set. These summary measures appear in Table 1. In addition, we screened the simulated data to avoid implausible observations by discarding observations whenever (1) the lot size was less than 25% larger than the total area of the house or (2) the kitchen area exceeded the bedroom area. After screening we rescaled the data to ensure the data sets possessed the same minimums, medians, and maximums as the Memphis MLS data set. Each data set uses 401 observations, which seems typical of many mass appraisal and hedonic pricing data sets.

Table 1. Summary of Data and Submarket Costs

Variable	Mean	Minimum	Median	Maximum	Submarket Cost
Price	92062.02	36500	73250	197500	
Lost area	26324.73	4125	11070	77000	1.95
Bedroom area	486.96	242	446	1053	58.50
Kitchen area	209.81	72	144	435	121.00
Other area	1257.02	383	966	2919	58.50
Bathrooms	2.17	1	2	4	9316.00
Fireplaces	1.26	0	1	3	3700.00
Garage spaces	1.25	0	1	3	5400.00

For each regression, the relation $Y = X\beta + e$ determines the dependent variable vector, Y, where β denotes the vector of true parameter values, X denotes an independent variable data matrix, and e denotes an error vector. To ensure an impartial treatment of the estimators, each trial of the Monte Carlo experiment uses a β selected randomly from the restricted parameter space, determined by the region between the upper and lower bounds on the restricted parameters. Since we did not restrict the intercept, we arbitrarily set its value at 1000. The error vector follows a normal distribution with mean 0 and standard deviation σ. The value of σ was selected to produce average R^2s of .99, .90, .80, and .70 across each group of 10,000 OLS regressions for each of the five independent variable data matrices varying by condition number. For all cases in the Monte Carlo experiment, J, the number of hypotheses, is 14.

Monte Carlo Results

The results for the typical case of an R^2 of .80 and a condition number of 60, similar to the Harrison and Rubinfeld study, follow. To gain a comprehensive understanding of the performance differences between the estimators, the results on each of the seven restricted variables are first presented. Since the estimators' performance on the unrestricted variable is particularly interesting, a histogram of the estimates for the unrestricted coefficient are included in the next section.

Then the results over all the 20 cases differing by four levels of R^2 and five levels of multicollinearity are presented. To show the performance of IRLS relative to OLS as a function of R^2 and multicollinearity, the overall error for each estimator and case across both the restricted and unrestricted variables are described. To determine whether IRLS significantly outperforms OLS, each estimators' performance is tested nonparametrically across both the unrestricted and the restricted variables for each case.

In the results below, each estimators' performance is measured relative to the true parameter values, β, though three statistics—the scaled bias, the scaled standard error, and the scaled mean absolute error. The term *scaled*—for the restricted variables means normalization of the results by the interval defined by the inequality information. For example, the kitchen area variable has a lower bound of 0 and an upper bound of 121. Accordingly, we scaled the kitchen area statistics—bias, standard error, and mean absolute error—by 1/121. This scaling does provide some benefits. First, it removes units. Second, it expresses all statistics in terms of a unit of prior information. Hence, the results will show the benefits of IRLS over OLS as a percentage of the prior information employed. We also note normalizing the statistics by β would prove problematical because of the possibility of an individual β close to zero for a restricted variable. For the unrestricted variable, the intercept, the term *scaled* means normalization by β (1000). Since all the statistics quoted are in scaled terms, this will be understood in the subsequent discussion.

Per-Variable Results for the Typical Case. These statistics on each variable appear in Table 2 for the single case of a condition number of 60 and an R^2 of .80. For each restricted variable, OLS has lower bias, higher standard error, and higher mean absolute error than IRLS. These results, as well as subsequent ones, prove highly significant.[8] In addition, we performed a sign test for differences in the absolute error relative to β on each variable for the two estimators. The lowest proportion for the sign tests was .63 while the highest was .80.[9]

To examine the results across the restricted variables, we took the average of the restricted variable statistics for OLS and IRLS. The bias across all seven relevant OLS coefficients was 0.10%. The standard error was 0.62% for OLS. These bias and standard errors attest to the proper functioning of the Monte Carlo experiment.

We then computed the ratio of the aggregated OLS statistics to the aggregated IRLS statistics. Across the restricted variables, OLS had, relative to IRLS (1) 4.5% of the bias (2) 58% higher standard error, and (3) 51% higher mean absolute error. Hence, while OLS will come closer to the true parameter than IRLS in a repeated sampling context, IRLS will typically come much closer to the true parameter in any single regression.

Unrestricted Variable Results for the Typical Case. The intercept under IRLS was not restricted in any way. Yet relative to IRLS, the OLS intercept had (1) 23% of the bias (2) 21% higher standard error and (3) 20% higher mean absolute error. The same effect occurs with IRLS as with Bayesian estimators—prior information on any variable affects the estimation efficiency on all the variables (Judge et al., p. 109). Figure 1 depicts the histogram of the intercept estimates for both OLS and IRLS. Note the IRLS estimates fall more frequently into the class containing the true value relative to the OLS estimates. The large reduction in dispersion of the IRLS estimates relative to the corresponding OLS estimates reveals the benefits of using prior information on variables other than those of main interest. For mass appraisal models this reduced coefficient

Table 2. Results for Single Case with Condition Number of 60 and R^2 of .80

Variable	Scaled bias	Scaled standard error	Scaled mean absolute error
Averages Across Regressions for OLS By Variable			
Lot Area	−0.0326	0.1030	7.9050
Bedroom area	0.0007	0.0080	0.6134
Kitchen area	0.0124	0.0117	0.8987
Other area	−0.0041	0.0049	0.3753
Bathrooms	0.0011	0.0025	0.1946
Fireplaces	−0.0018	0.0020	0.1518
Garage spaces	−0.0024	0.0078	0.5925
Constant	−0.0127	0.0113	0.8624
Mean	0.0010	0.0062	0.4717
Averages Across Regressions for IRLS By Variable			
Lot Area	−0.1415	0.0849	6.5670
Bedroom area	0.0196	0.0048	0.3873
Kitchen area	0.0617	0.0057	0.4759
Other area	0.0248	0.0038	0.3019
Bathrooms	−0.0223	0.0022	0.1677
Fireplaces	−0.0139	0.0018	0.1344
Garage spaces	0.0597	0.0050	0.4043
Constant	0.0891	0.0158	0.4829
Mean	0.0216	0.0039	0.3119
Averages Across Regressions for OLS Relative to IRLS By Variable			
Lot Area	0.2304	1.2136	1.2040
Bedroom area	0.0339	1.6561	1.5840
Kitchen area	0.2004	2.0407	1.8880
Other area	−0.1653	1.2750	1.2430
Bathrooms	−0.0491	1.1701	1.1600
Fireplaces	0.1290	1.1285	1.1290
Garage spaces	−0.0402	1.5664	1.4750
Constant	−0.1430	1.9392	1.7860
Ratio of aggregated means	0.0450	1.5830	1.5120

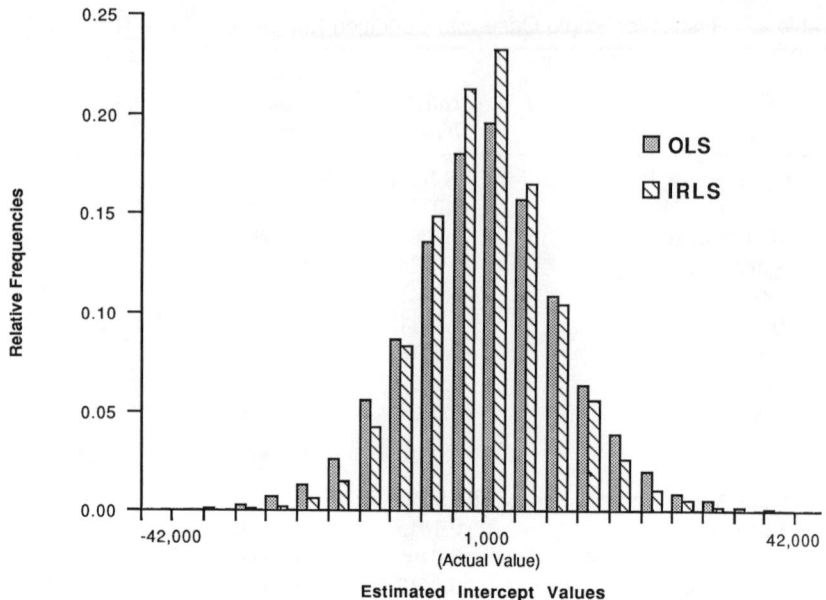

Figure 1. Histogram for Unrestricted Estimates.

Table 3. Scaled Mean Absolute Errors (OLS Relative to IRLS)

Condition Number	R^2 levels			
	0.70	0.80	0.90	0.99
30	1.395	1.273	1.154	1.035
45	1.554	1.388	1.221	1.047
60	1.721	1.512	1.298	1.060
75	1.911	1.656	1.393	1.078
100	2.239	1.910	1.561	1.114

dispersion could translate into differences in the sign, significance, or magnitude of the unrestricted coefficients.

Overall Improvements of IRLS Over OLS. Table 3 gives the relative (OLS/IRLS) mean absolute error across all restricted variables for each of the twenty cases. OLS had from 4% to 124% more error than IRLS. Across all cases OLS had 43% higher mean absolute error than IRLS. Fig-

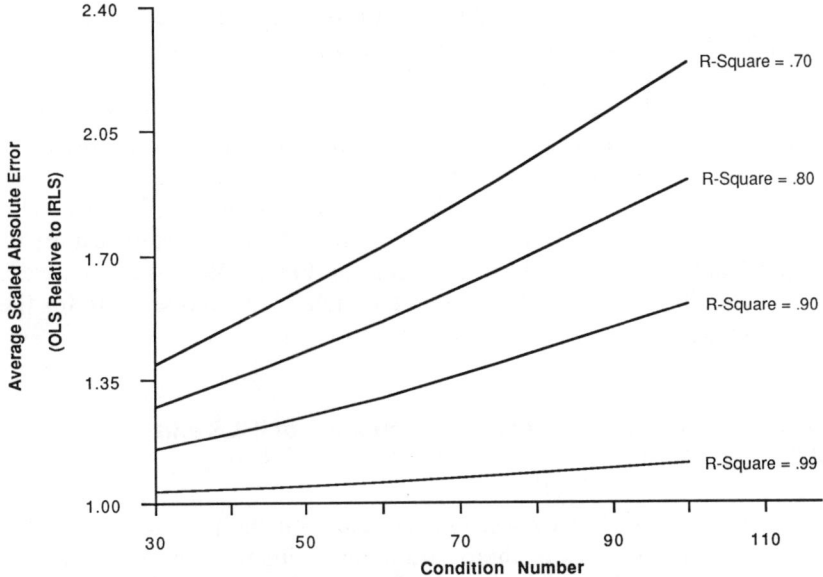

Figure 2. Relative Improvements vs. Condition Numbers.

ure 2 depicts this relative error vs. the condition number for each of the four levels of R^2. The figure not only illustrates how IRLS improves upon OLS as R^2 decreases and as the condition number increases, but also illustrates how these effects are reinforcing. Finally, the mean absolute error seems to respond almost linearly to individual changes in the condition number and R^2.

Tests for Overall Significance. As an additional test of whether IRLS significantly improves over OLS in terms of the mean absolute error, we computed separate sign tests for the intercept and the restricted variables by comparing the proportion of regressions, where IRLS improved over OLS (with ties discarded). This was done for each of the 10,000 regressions and for each of the twenty cases. For the restricted variables, the lowest proportion among the twenty cases was .69, while the highest proportion was .99. The proportions on the restricted variables' sign test rose relative to the ones for individual variables, since averaging across the variables reduced the noise, thereby increasing the sensitivity of the test. For the unrestricted intercept variable, the lowest proportion among the twenty cases was .36, while the highest proportion was .72. Examining these results further we find the sign test proportions for all the cases with R^2s of .70, .80, and .90 exceeded .50. For the cases with R^2 of .99 the sign test proportions were .36, .37. .37, .39, and .42. These rose with increasing condition number. To see whether these low sign test proportions really measured significance or not for these cases, we also computed paired t tests on the absolute errors. These t statistics ranged from 12.6 to 16.7. Furthermore, the ratio of the OLS to the IRLS mean absolute error ranged from 1.022 to 1.036, while the ratio of standard errors ranged from 1.026 to 1.031. In all cases the lower valued statistics were for the condition number of 30, while the higher valued ones were for the condition number of 100.

The Out-of-Sample Prediction Performance of IRLS and OLS

In the previous section we were concerned with the performance of the two estimators in terms of their parameter estimation efficiency. This is important to appraisers since unreasonable coefficients are difficult to justify to the tax-paying public. However, the central goal of appraisal is accurate prediction, especially out of sample. We now estimate the out-of-sample predictive performance of OLS and IRLS. We will show, contrary to the results within the sample, IRLS outperforms OLS in out-of-sample error. While we cannot test the correctness of the prior information, the superior performance of IRLS relative to OLS suggests the prior information has value.[10]

As mentioned earlier, the within sample sum of squared errors for OLS is smaller than that of IRLS by construction. However, this relation does not necessarily extend to out-of-sample errors. First, due to prior information's ability to limit the influence of potentially erroneous observations, IRLS could outperform OLS on out-of-sample error (Belsley et al., 1980, pp. 204–12). Second, the estimated error within sample is not necessarily an unbiased estimate of out-of-sample error. The use of observations both to fit a model and to measure the goodness of its fit usually results in overly optimistic error estimates (Effron, 1986; Picard and Cook, 1984). Researchers traditionally solved this "overfitting" problem by dividing the sample into two parts—the sample observations and the out-of-sample observations (or hold-out sample). Fitting a model to the sample observations and testing the model's goodness of fit on the out-of-sample observations can lead to a better estimate of the out-of-sample error, the most relevant criterion for appraisal applications.

The elementary procedure discussed above is an example of cross-validation. However, other and more general forms of the cross-validation procedure exist. Following Geisser (1975), one could form a sample of $n - o$ observations, where o represents the number of out-of-sample observations. After fitting a model to the sample of $n - o$ observations, the resulting estimates enable calculation of the o out-of-sample errors. Repeating this for all possible ways of drawing $n - o$ observations out of n produces the error distribution. Partitioning the total sample in all possible ways usually requires an infeasible number of iterations. Accordingly, most researchers randomly partition the total sample for a fixed number of iterations. The use of this form of cross-validation eliminates the dependency of the results upon a single, random partition. Accordingly, this technique yields a better picture of the out-of-sample error than a single data partition.

Prior to implementing this procedure, we augmented the sample of 100 Memphis MLS observations, as described before, with an additional 300 observations collected in the same way. This allows us to study the prediction error on 300 out-of-sample observations based upon calibration on 100 sample observations. Specifically, each of the 5000 iterations of the cross-validation procedure randomly partitions the data set into 100 sample observations and 300 out-of-sample observations.

Before presenting the cross-validation results, it might prove instructive to see how IRLS and OLS behave on an actual data set. Table 4 provides the results for the two estimators on the combined data set of 400

Table 4. Actual OLS and IRLS Estimates

Variable	OLS estimates	IRLS estimates	Submarket costs
Price			
Lot area	0.38	0.40	1.95
Bedroom area	62.07	58.50	58.50
Kitchen area	46.49	59.72	121.00
Other area	45.91	50.92	58.50
Bathrooms	13631.91	9316.00	9316.00
Fireplaces	1544.41	2387.99	3700.00
Garage spaces	7407.30	5400.00	5400.00
Constant	−39247.42	−35767.31	
R^2	.820	.818	
Sample size	400	400	

observations along with the home improvement costs. Note the IRLS estimator uses the restrictions for the bedroom area, bathroom, and garage coefficients. As a consequence of these binding restrictions, all the estimates for IRLS are different from OLS. The loss in in-sample R^2 caused by these restrictions is very small—.002 (.82 vs. .818). Note the IRLS intercept is smaller in absolute value than the OLS intercept. Also for IRLS, kitchen area has a higher value than bedroom area, a result more plausible than the contrary relation, which holds for OLS. Naturally, a single comparison of regressions can only illustrate but not prove any advantage for one estimator over the other. Hence, in addition to the Monte Carlo evidence on the superiority of IRLS over OLS in terms of parameter estimation efficiency, we now discuss the results from the cross-validation of the estimators that will show the predictive superiority of IRLS.

To examine the predictive performance of each estimator, we computed the absolute deviation between the prediction and the true value of the out-of-sample observation. We selected absolute deviation as an error measure due to its straightforward interpretability. We computed the mean of the absolute deviations across all out-of-sample observations for each iteration. Across all iterations we computed the mean, the standard deviation, and some order statistics on the averaged absolute errors. These statistics and the ratio between the OLS and IRLS statistics appear in Table 5.

Note IRLS outperformed OLS on all out-of-sample error statistics. Figure 3 presents a histogram of the OLS and IRLS out-of-sample absolute

Table 5. Cross-Validation Results Based on 5000 Iterations, with 100 In-Sample and 300 Out-of-Sample Observations

	Mean	Standard deviation
OLS absolute errors	16572.405	16.0244
IRLS absolute errors	15912.402	13.1345
Ratio (OLS/IRLS)	1.041	1.220

	Order statistics				
	Minimum	25%	50%	75%	Maximum
OLS absolute errors	13859.515	15771.741	16362.220	17172.650	23287.568
IRLS absolute errors	13527.687	15301.777	15752.079	16300.452	21075.236
Ratio (OLS/IRLS)	1.025	1.031	1.039	1.054	1.105

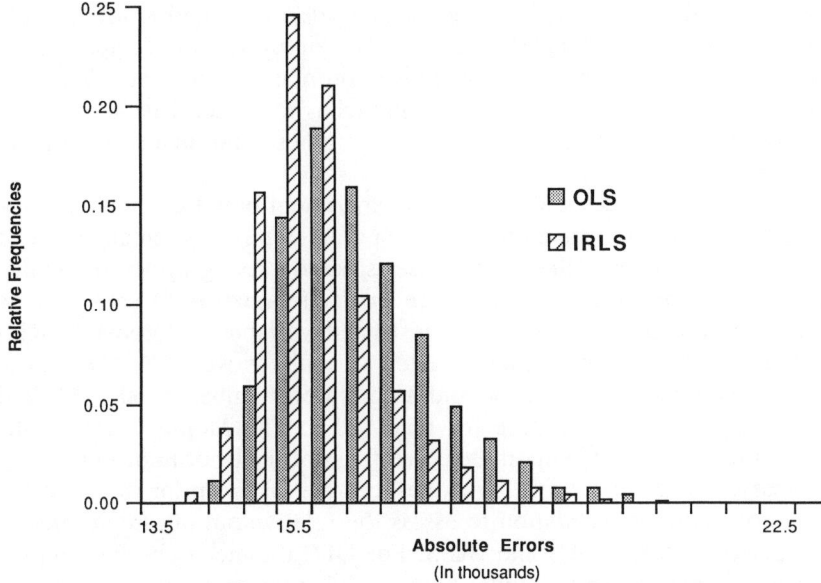

Figure 3. Histogram of OLS and IRLS Out-of-Sample Absolute Errors.

errors for the 5000 trials. Note the frequency of the IRLS errors is always higher than the OLS ones for values below the modal OLS error. The converse is true for errors above the modal OLS error. Also IRLS had about $660 less error on an average property. Moreover, the variability of this error for OLS was 22% greater than for IRLS. Also, across the 5000 trials the maximum average error was 10.5% greater for OLS than for IRLS. The other order statistics corroborate the superiority of IRLS. Finally, we also computed the proportion of times the absolute error of OLS exceeded its IRLS equivalent across all of the 5000 trials. In 84% of the trials IRLS did better than OLS.

Conclusions

Appraisers have a wealth of inequality *a priori* information on the sign and magnitude of regression coefficients. For example, characteristics of value should have positive coefficients, while characteristics obtainable in the home improvement market should have coefficients less than the cost, properly defined, of adding these after construction. Statistically, the

IRLS estimator optimally combines such *a priori* information with sample information. Since the *a priori* information employed depends upon costs, while the sample information depends upon market data, the IRLS estimator hybridizes cost and market approaches to value. This allows it to provide plausible estimated characteristic values while maintaining good predictive powers.

The paper provides a Monte Carlo experiment based upon 400,000 regressions designed to assess the relative parameter estimation efficiency of IRLS and OLS. Over the twenty cases studied varying by R^2 and multicollinearity, the OLS mean absolute error (relative to β) exceeded its IRLS equivalent by 43% for the restricted variables. Moreover, IRLS outperformed OLS on the unrestricted variable as well. For the typical case studied with an R^2 of .80 and a condition number of 60, OLS had 20% higher mean absolute error than IRLS. The Monte Carlo results were in part conditional upon the correctness of the prior information. To address the natural concern over the accuracy of the prior information, we employed cross-validation to assess the relative out-of-sample predictive performance of OLS and IRLS. For OLS the mean absolute out-of-sample prediction error, standard error, and maximum error were 4.1%, 22%, and 10.5% higher than for IRLS. In addition, in 84% of the iterations (ties excluded) IRLS outperformed OLS. Naturally, the superior predictive performance of IRLS over OLS does not necessarily imply the prior information's accuracy. However, it does illustrate the potential utility of prior information for appraisal.

Notes

1. Naturally, a proper definition of the costs must include a valuation for the potential disutility associated with remodeling. The utility of actually tailoring the addition to specific tastes and the higher initial service flow from the new addition may outweigh this potential disutility. In particular, the time necessary for the addition's completion could have an effect. For some additions, such as landscaping, this time could prove considerable and should factor into the upper bounds. In any case, some multiple of the home improvement market cost could always determine a reasonable upper bound.

2. This formulation is exactly the same as required by the IMSL subroutine DQPROG as detailed on pp. 892–4 of the Math/Library manual. Note the IRLS computations do not prove especially costly. For example, the cross-validation used here employs 5000 pairs of OLS and IRLS regressions on 400 observations with 8 variables. This takes 314 seconds on a VAX 8800.

3. Construction costs and resale prices tend to vary with the total heated living area and the fixtures associated with bathrooms, kitchens, fireplaces, and other features. Unheated areas, such as porches, some greenhouses, and garages, may yet vary by the type and quality of construction. Accordingly, the cost data described later reflect the differences in fixtures and construction type.

4. In reality this model with only eight variables would probably not predict well enough for mass appraisal needs. Such a model could, however, incorporate design, quality, and neighborhood variables to capture qualitative effects. Restrictions could also apply to these variables. For example, measures indicative of higher quality, positive externalities, or better design should have positive signs. In addition, appraisers could use their knowledge to rank neighborhood values or the value of other characteristics. These rankings lead naturally to restrictions on the coefficients. Finally, other sources of prior information can improve predictive performance. Pace and Gilley (1989a) demonstrate such an improvement by using data in one assessment jurisdiction as prior information for a jurisdiction in a contiguous state. While the prior information was not strictly correct, its use improved predictive performance for sample sizes of 200 observations or less.

5. Specifically, the costs for "deluxe" additions from the Means Guide were used to formulate the cost per square foot of each of the functional areas, including all finishings and fixtures. The "deluxe" additions were chosen to provide the least restrictive cost bounds consistent with each functional area.

6. We adopted two means to maintain a reasonably high level of experimental precision. The first, most obvious means was to use many random numbers. Every case employs 10,000 different error vectors, each with 401 elements. Thus each case employs 4,010,000 random numbers. The second means was to employ the Monte Carlo variance reduction technique of "correlated sampling," which refers to using a common set of random numbers for each case. See Rubinstein (1981, pp. 124–6) for a discussion of this and other variance reduction techniques.

7. The condition index of the normalized data matrix is a vector composed of the ratio of the individual singular values to the minimum element. This index summarizes the ill-conditioning of the matrix. The largest element in the condition index, the condition number, measures the ill-conditioning for the variable with the smallest contribution of independent information. Hence, the condition number proves a convenient scalar measure of multicollinearity. For a complete and detailed discussion of this point, see Chapter 3 in Belsley et al. (1980).

8. All of the results herein are significant at extremely high levels. The lowest significant t statistic on the bias of IRLS is 1.66, the lowest F statistic on the test for differences in variance between the two estimators is 1.27, and the lowest proportion on a sign test for differences in the mean absolute error between the two estimators is .63. We will not take space discussing significance of the results individually since significance levels are so uniformly high given the 10,000 iterations employed for each case.

9. The sign test for the mean absolute error is identical to the sign test on the root mean squared error, since squared errors are a monotonic transformation of absolute errors.

10. Indeed, Pace and Gilley (1989b) have shown in a Monte Carlo experiment with a fixed β but with varying prior information that IRLS can improve over OLS in the presence of some incorrect information. Consequently, any improvement by IRLS over OLS could result from only some of the prior information being correct.

References

Belsley, David A., Edwin Kuh, and Roy E. Welsch. *Regression Diagnostics, Identifying Influential Data and Sources of Collinearity.* New York: Wiley, 1980.

Effron, B. "How Biased is the Apparent Error Rate of a Prediction Rule?" *Journal of the American Statistical Association* 71 (June 1986), 461–70.

Geisser, Seymour. "The Predictive Sample Reuse Method with Applications." *Journal of the American Statistical Association* 70 (June 1975), 320–28.

Geweke, John. "Exact Inference in the Inequality Constrained Normal Linear Regression Model." *Journal of Applied Econometrics* 1 (January 1986) 127–41.

Goldfarb, D. and A. Idnani. "A Numerically Stable Dual Method for Solving Strictly Convex Quadratic Programs." *Mathematical Programming* 27 (1983): 1–33.

Harrison, D. and D. Rubinfeld. "Hedonic Prices and the Demand for Clean Air." *Journal of Environmental Economics and Management* 5 (1978), 81–102.

Judge, George G. and T. A. Yancey. *Improved Methods of Inference in Econometrics.* New York: North Holland, 1986.

Judge, George G., W. E. Griffiths, R. Carter Hill, Helmut Lutkepohl, and Tsoung-Chao Lee. *The Theory and Practice of Econometrics*, 2nd ed. New York: Wiley, 1985.

Kang, Han Bin and Alan K. Reichert. "An Evaluation of Alternative Estimation Techniques and Functional Forms in Developing Statistical Appraisal Models." *Journal of Real Estate Research* 2 (Fall 1987), 1–29.

Linhart, H. and W. Zucchini. *Model Selection.* New York: Wiley, 1986.

Math Library. International Mathematical & Statistical Library, January 1989.

Means Home Improvement Cost Guide. Kingston, MA: R.S. Means Co., 1985.

Multiple Listing Book. Memphis, TN: Memphis Board of Realtors. Vol. 2, January 23, 1987.

Pace, R. Kelley and Otis W. Gilley. "Appraisal Across Jurisdictions Using Bayesian Estimation with Bootstrapped Priors for Secondary Mortgage Market Applications." *Property Tax Journal* 8 (March 1989a), 27–42.

Pace, R. Kelley and Otis W. Gilley. "Estimation Employing A Priori Information within Mass Appraisal and Hedonic Pricing Models." *Journal of Real Estate Finance and Economics*, (August 1989b).

Picard, Richard R. and R. Dennis Cook. "Cross-Validation of Regression Models." *Journal of the American Statistical Association* 79 (September 1984), 575–83.

Reichert, Alan K. and James S. Moore. "Using Latent Root Regression to Identify Nonpredictive Collinearity in Statistical Appraisal Models." *AREUEA* 14 (Spring 1986), 136–52.

Rubinstein, Reuben V. *Simulation and the Monte Carlo Method.* New York: Wiley, 1981.

Vandell, K. D. and R. H. Zerbst. "Estimates of the Effect of School Desegregation Plans on Housing Values Over Time." *AREUEA* 2 (Summer 1984), 109–35.

7 PHYS-FI:
A Physical-Financial Model for Design Economy Trade-Offs
M. Atef Sharkawy

Introduction

The mainstream of research on the subject of trade-offs between the physical and financial dimensions of real estate is well presented by Kerry Vandell's concluding statement to his deductive statistical analysis, "Economics of Architecture and Urban Design" (Vandell, 1987). He wrote, "Ultimately these exercises may lead us not only to better respond to the question: Does 'good' design pay?, but beyond, to the more enigmatic question of: What is 'good' design?"

This research addresses the enigmatic question first by accounting, with deductive inference, for the pattern of cost-income-value trade-offs; then by tracing identified patterns of trade-offs in successful developments, seeking, by inductive reasoning, to formalize "expert" knowledge into concepts.

Both tasks call for a brief overview of the real estate development process, to identify those participating in the trade-offs, and the stages during which trade-offs take place during the development cycle. They also require an overview of the development planning process, to identify the sequence of decision making by the participants and the context for trade-offs among them.

The Real Estate Development Process

In presenting "Fundamentals of Real Estate Development," James Graaskamp described real estate as a cash cycle: cash—to raw materials—to goods in process—to inventory—to accounts receivable—to cash (Graaskamp, 1981). He defines the business goal of the "production group" as recapture of capital and a profit appropriate to both risk and capital. Capital involves both equity and construction debt obtained in periodic disbursements until completion, at which time capital involves equity and a permanent mortgage. The key players of the production group are accordingly the developer, the equity investor(s), and the lenders. Development stages are, in turn, keyed to funding decisions by construction period equity investors, construction lenders, long-term equity investors, and permanent lenders. Figure 1 shows the players and their roles during the different stages of development: predevelopment, document development, and product development.

Working with the production group to devise the physical and financial shape of the venture, starting gradually in the predevelopment stage, is a group of professionals. The design team, responsible for the physical dimension, involves the architectural/engineering and possibly construction management professionals. They develop a schematic design and a rough cost estimate during the predevelopment stage; then develop preliminary designs and related estimates and schedules; and later complete construction documents, budgets, and schedules during the document development stage. The business team, responsible for the financial dimension, involves those professionals preparing market and marketability studies, feasibility analysis, financial modeling for investment analysis, and later real estate appraisal.

The two teams follow different sets of models in their tasks, reminiscent of the differences between design and planning schools, on the one hand, and business schools on the other. Typical design (physical) models are inductive reasoning based and can be epitomized as Platonic—what exists is form: a synthesis of particulars, achieved by successive composition, within a framework of choice theory. The typical business (financial) models, on the other hand, are deductive inference centered and can be epitomized as Aristotelian—what exists is: particular objects and fixed attributes, identified by successive partition, within a framework of utility

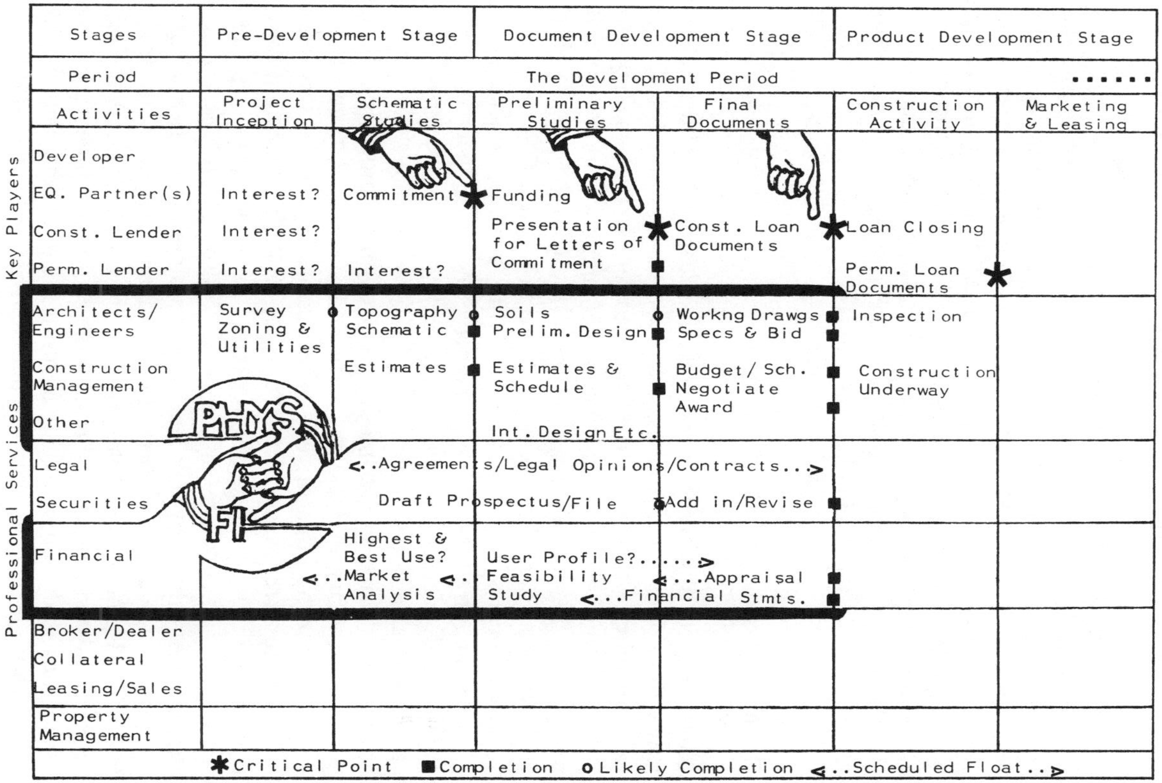

Figure 1. The Real Estate Development Process.

theory. Yet, it is the responsibility of the two teams to help the developer, investors, and lenders attain their goal of recapturing capital, namely, a return of equity and payoff of mortgage debt, together with earning a return on equity.

The obvious need to integrate the efforts of the two teams, to interface their different deductive inference and inductive reasoning approaches, and to mesh the physical and financial dimensions of real estate, throughout the development process, led the author and James Graaskamp to work together in the late 1960s to early 1970s to develop a multidisciplinary development planning model (MDPM). The work was done under a grant from the Great Lakes Regional Commission, which made it possible to also apply the model to a 3000 acre recreational development in Wisconsin (Graaskamp and Sharkawy, 1971).

The Graaskamp–Sharkawy MDP Model

Separating deductive inference from inductive reasoning, objective from subjective procedures, and analytic from synthesis-oriented sequences, the multidisciplinary model is structured into ten decision-making processes. Table 1 outlines a breakdown of the major components of the ten functionally linked processes in the Graaskamp–Sharkawy MDP Model, with the sequence and linkages shown in Figure 2.

The model begins by identification of the strategic objectives and priorities of the production group, namely, the developer, the equity investors, the lenders, and the public enterprise, to narrow down acceptable tactical alternatives.

The "financial" side of the model involves three processes: market analysis, marketability analysis, and financial modeling. Recognizing that it is market absorption that drives the real estate cash cycle, this deductive inference-centered segment of the MDP Model is structured to first define market trends in the aggregate, then to narrow down opportunity areas through market segmentation. Next, consumer profiles and merchandising targets are identified; and product differentials, price specifications, effective demand, and preferred merchandising methods are defined. The third process, financial modeling, involves establishing a timeline for financial assumptions, estimating the required capital budget, and identifying financial resources and terms for equity and debt. It also projects operating budgets and revenue sources, evaluates direct cash profit expectations, and pinpoints indirect profit centers and returns.

Table 1. Elements of the Graaskamp-Sharkawy Multidisciplinary Development-Planning Model

1. Goals and objectives
2. Market analysis
   2.1 Trends
   2.2 Segmentation
   2.3 Supply & occupancy
   2.4 Demand & absorption
3. Marketing analysis
   3.1 Consumer profiles
   3.2 Market standards
   3.3 Market differentials
   3.4 Merchandising strategy
4. Site analysis
   4.1 Zoning & utilities
   4.2 Access & linkages
5. Environmental analysis
   5.1 Suitability analysis
       (geology, soils, topo, & water)
   5.2 Vegetation
6. Facilities program development
   6.1 Product mix
   6.2 Space requirements
   6.3 Functional analysis
   6.4 Phasing
7. Synthesis concept development
   7.1 Thematic frameworks
   7.2 Cultural schemata
   7.3 Relational schemata
   7.4 Form schema
8. Schematic design/plan
   8.1 Functional categories definition
   8.2 Problem structure—Diagram
   8.3 Partial solutions
   8.4 Composite solution
   8.5 Rough cost estimate
9. Financial modeling
   9.1 Capital cost components
   9.2 Equity–debt Plan
   9.3 Income & expense elements
   9.4 Timeline and rates
10. Preliminary design/plan
    10.1 Material & detail files
    10.2 Other A/E input
    10.3 Preliminary plans & elevations
    10.4 Detailed cost/capital budget estimate

Sources: Graaskamp, James A. and M. Atef Sharkawy. *The Lily Lake Forest Recreation Environ*. Madison, WI: Foster Printing, 1971.

Sharkawy, M. Atef. "Economic Programmatic Ecological Analysis for Planning/Design in Land Development." Ph.D. Thesis, University of Wisconsin School of Business, 1975.

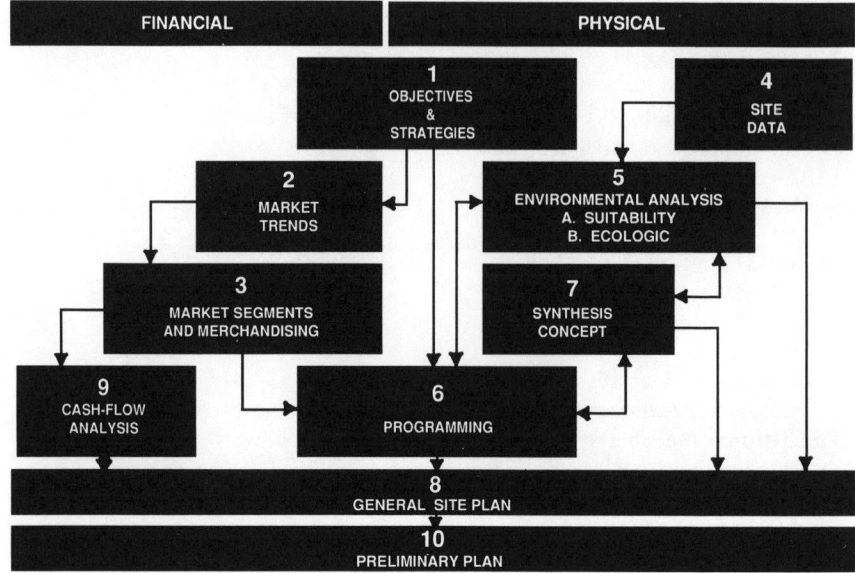

Figure 2. The Graaskamp–Sharkawy Multidisciplinary Development Planning Model (MDPM).

Source: James Graaskamp and M. Atef Sharkawy. *The Lily Lake Forest Recreation Environment.* Madison, Wisconsin: Foster Printing, 1971.

Measurement of risks and yields is accomplished by computerized discounted cash-flow modeling.

The physical side of the MDP Model involves five inductive reasoning-based processes dealing with the site's environment, the development's facilities program, a framework of synthesis concepts for design, then schematic and preliminary design plans. The environmental aspect of the model inventories the site's biota and abiota (Sharkawy, 1969) and utilizes a suitability analysis technique to enable the planner to avoid limitations imposed, and to capitalize on opportunities offered by, the natural environment. Facilities program development involves identifying the project's basic components based on product mix and merchandising cycles, selecting amenities based on use cycles and participation rates, and providing the related service components. The model then formalizes the synthesis process by outlining the needed framework of concepts, ideas, and partial solutions in order to generate alternative concept plans.

While the Multi-Disciplinary Development Planning Model provided an organization for multidisciplinary decision making by identifying functional processes and sequences, it became clear from subsequent applications of the model that a detailed clinical model of trade-offs in design economy was still needed to integrate financial logic in design decisions, to interface business goals of the production group into design concepts, to enforce consideration of the cost–income–value continuum, and to bridge the development–operations–disposition stages. Such a clinical model is the focus of this study.

Developing the PHYS-FI Model

Design Economy Research

Recent research addressing design economy has typically focused on financial implications of individual attributes of the physical dimension of real estate.[1] Most research seemed to focus on a single or very few attributes, on a single stage of the real estate investment cycle, and/or on a single financial goal. In addition, most research followed deductive inference procedures in addressing design economy. The lack of inductive reasoning led to forced use of numerical operations on subjective issues, for example, mean design quality, optimal aesthetic ratio, leading back to the question, What is "good" design?

A literature review reveals the following concerning recent research:

1. Its focus on a single or a few attributes ignored the need for a theoretical framework for trade-offs in design economy.
2. Its focus on isolated stages of development as independent periods for study and analysis ignored the need to consider the development–operations–disposition linkages.
3. Its focus on a single financial goal ignored the need to account for the cost–income–value continuum.
4. Most importantly, deductive research procedures seem to be inadequate to address both the financial and physical aspects of design economy.

The PHYS-FI model presented in this study addresses all four areas. It offers an integrative framework for design economy concepts that encompasses the cost–income–value continuum and bridges the development–operations–disposition stages in the real estate investment cycle.

Research Procedures

In developing the PHYS-FI clinical model presented in this study, a deductive-inductive procedure evolved as follows:

First: A framework of classes of trade-offs was identified, using deductive inference, based on a review of recognized real estate financial models.

Second: Categories in each of the defined classes for trade-offs were identified, again using deductive inference, based on a review of both financial and design models.

Third: A series of observations was generated from the Urban Land Institute's Project Reference Files for the previously defined classes of trade-offs. The observations were then arranged into subgroup nodes, using inductive reasoning, based on similarity rating and matrix analysis.

Fourth: Inductive reasoning was again used to interpret the observations in each node into a generalized concept of trade-offs in design economy. The concepts were then arranged to fit the categories identified earlier, based on relevance rating and matrix analysis.

Fifth: Classes, categories, and concepts of trade-offs were finally organized in a hierarchial semilattice structure, and were grouped in the PHYS-FI model.

Briefly, these five steps, listed in outline format, and described in detail in the following segment of this study, are

1. Defining classes of trade-offs
2. Identifying categories of trade-offs
3. Generating and grouping observations
4. Generating and grouping concepts
5. Grouping classes, categories, and concepts.

Defining Classes of Trade-Offs

Recent research addressing the financial dimension of real estate development[2] has provided us with excellent financial models, together with certain premises concerning trade-offs with the physical dimension, namely,

1. That a change in development capital cost generates financial changes in equity funding, and in required debt during the development stages, which in turn impact debt service, cash flow from operations, return on equity, and proceeds from sale at the end of the holding period.
2. That a change in real estate value of the completed project generates financial changes in available mortgage debt, in construction debt, and in required equity during development stages, which in turn impact annual debt service and the income stream from operations, and most importantly, proceeds from reversion upon disposition.
3. That a change impacting net operating income during the holding period, as rental rates, vacancies, and operating expenses change, will in turn impact real estate value and related proceeds from refinancing or from sale at end of the development holding period.

It could be deduced from these premises that financial decisions involve three classes of trade-offs between the physical and financial dimensions of real estate to encompass the cost–income–value continuum during the real estate development–operations–disposition cycle. These are

Class 1: Optimizing capital cost

Class 2: Creating real estate value

Class 3: Maximizing net operating income

Identifying Categories of Trade-Offs

Categories of Trade-Offs for Optimizing Capital Cost

The cash inflows and cash outflows of capital during project development can be expressed as:

$$DC = EQ_d + CL$$
$$DC = HC + SC + LC,$$

where DC is total development cost, EQ_d is equity during development stages, CL is construction loan, HC is construction hard cost, SC is development soft cost, and LC is land cost.

It is evident that optimizing development cost is a direct function of optimizing hard, soft, and land costs. Thus concepts pertaining to optimizing capital cost will be organized in three categories: hard cost, soft cost, and land cost.

Categories of Trade-Offs for Creating Real Estate Value

The basic goal of the real estate developer is to create a real estate market value far in excess of development cost to generate higher proceeds from refinancing and from eventual sale of the property. This also reduces equity requirements[3] and increases debt funds, since financing is tied to value[4] and not to cost, expressed as

$$EQ_o = DC - (LVR \times AV_m),$$

where EQ_o is equity during operations stage, DC is total development cost, value at completion time m, LVR is loan-to-value ratio, and AV_m is appraised market value.

Creating real estate value is the most powerful tool in real estate development to maximize returns on investment by reducing equity, as well as by increasing returns from refinancing and from sales proceeds. To identify qualitative classifications pertaining to creating real estate value, a review of established design theories about the creative process was completed. Three groups of theories emerged and can be classified as environmental, glass box, and black box. The environmental category includes McHarg's design with nature (McHarg, 1969) and Lewis' environmental corridors (Lewis, 1964). They espouse avoiding limitations of the natural environment and capitalizing on the opportunities it offers to create the most desirable environments.

The second group includes such established design theories as Jones' (1966) systematic design, Archer's (1963) technical innovation, and Alexander's (1968) pattern language. They adopt the view that creative design is systematic, proceeding from defining requirements and criteria, to different versions of functional categories/structure, to partial solutions, to a composite solution, all in a visible sequence like in a glass box.

The third group includes Osborn's (1957) applied imagination; Gordon's synectics (1961) Halprin's (1969) RSVP cycles and Norberg-Schulz's (1965) schematization. They believe that phenomena are perceived with form, that perceptions differ between individuals because of different phenomenal contexts, and that creative leaps in design differ with designers' phenomenal schematizations, all in an invisible sequence, as if in a black box.

Thus concepts pertaining to creating real estate value will be organized in three categories: the environment, product synergy (as a proxy for glass-box sequences), and design differentials (as a proxy for black-box sequences).

Categories of Trade-Offs for Maximizing Net Operating Income

A project's income and expenses can be expressed as

$$NOI_t = EGI_t - OE_t, \text{ where}$$
$$EGI_t = (R_t Q + O_t)(1 - v_t), \text{ and}$$
$$OE_t = \alpha + \beta_t (1 - v) Q,$$

where NOI_t is net operating income in stabilized year t, EGI_t is effective gross income in stabilized year t, OE_t is operating expenses in stabilized year t, R_t is average effective rental rate per income unit, Q is quantity of income units (square feet, apartments, etc.), O_t is other income in year t, v_t is vacancy rate in year t, α is total fixed cost, and β_t is variable cost per occupied income unit in year t.

It follows that change in net operating income is a function of the following variables that pertain to the physical dimension:

$$\Delta NOI = \Delta Q (R - \beta)(1 - v).$$

Thus, concepts pertaining to maximizing net income during the operating period will be organized into three categories: increasing product efficiency, increasing rates/decreasing vacancy, and reducing operating expenses.

Generating and Grouping Observations

Proceeding from deductive inference of the financial dimension to structure a framework of classes and categories of trade-offs between the physical and financial dimensions of real estate, inductive reasoning was utilized to seek specific concepts of trade-offs, in order to develop the identified framework of classes and categories into a complete clinical model.

The research procedure involved first generating a series of observations of actual trade-offs in projects considered successful by the industry, grouped for each of the three defined classes as temporary enumeration, then clustered into nodes for elucidation of the structure or pattern of trade-offs.

The observations were obtained from the Urban Land Institute's Project Files for 1978–1989. A total of 148 observations were deduced from 126 projects. The inductive methodology used to proceed from individual observations to concepts of trade-offs parallels Jones' (1960) synthesis of random factors into partial solutions, then into combined solutions; Alexander's (1968) synthesis of misfits into component diagrams, then into composite diagrams, Archer's (1963) synthesis of crucial issues into subproblems/solutions, then into overall solutions; and Nadler's (1967) work system design leading to the ideal concept.

Systematic ranking, a ranking scale (Nijkamp et al., 1985) based on similarities between the observations, and a matrix (cluster) analysis were used to group the observations within each of the three defined classes of trade-offs into nodes, later deduced into concepts of trade-offs. Following is an example of such a node, with a listing of some of its constituent observations:

Representative Observations from Node #131

Observation. Developers of the Cascades, an 80,000 square foot specialty shopping center in Ocala, Florida, acquired an old limestone quarry in a highly developed area. The developer created an inward-oriented project, focused on a series of ponds and waterfalls, surrounded by the center's first level, inside the depression. The developer created an environment that contrasted with the surrounding streetscape and a building with a low profile to blend with the architecture of the neighborhood. While saving money on land cost, he managed to create a project with a distinct identity, higher leasing rates, lower vacancy, and increased value.

Observation. The developers of the Watergrove apartment community in Memphis, Tennessee purchased a wetland site inexpensively. They invested the savings in amenities, which included six swimming pools, six tennis courts, racquetball courts, spa and saunas, and a $1 million clubhouse. The wetlands were made into an environmental reserve. The additional hard cost from land cost savings enabled the developer to build a project with a higher cash-flow stream and an increased value.

Observation. Cimmarron is a 255-unit, 38-acre, planned unit development in Phoenix, Arizona, targeted to first-time home buyers, with a product mix of townhouses and zero-lot-line homes. The developer acquired the land at a low cost due to its limited road frontage. The developer then used highly intensive landscaping for an attractive pronounced entrance, which made the project competitive with others with more frontage. The lower land cost combined with the extra landscaping totaled less than the cost of acquiring and landscaping a site with more frontage.

Generating and Grouping Concepts

Continuing with inductive reasoning, a generalized concept for trade-offs in design economy was developed for each of the identified nodes. Following is a concept description derived from the previously detailed node.

Concept: Opportunity Sites

Site selection should include thorough consideration of those sites that appear to be problem sites, instead of only seeking standard sites. Occasionally a less expensive site, due to limitations to development, can provide an opportunity to create a unique project, with land cost savings that can be used to reduce the capital budget or to improve project amenities.

Similarly, a total of nine concepts of trade-offs were derived in the class of optimizing capital cost, nine concepts in the class of creating real estate value, and six concepts in the class of maximizing cash flow from operations.

Systematic ranking, a ranking scale, and matrix analysis were again applied to group the concepts in each of the categories of the PHYS-FI model. Following is an example of one category, its constituent concepts of trade-offs, and the related concept descriptions.

Concepts Involving Optimizing Hard Cost

Concept: Cost Intensity. It is not cost alone or quality alone that ensures a project's success; but the combination of both, concentrating quality design and materials in those facets of the project that would result in increased overall value and returns with such quality-dollar expenditures.

Concept: Cost Transfer. A creative deal structure focusing on imaginative facility programming and on symbiotic associations with other private or public enterprises can provide access to amenities for little or no cost in order to reduce hard cost and required equity and/or debt.

Concept: Functional Efficiency. Design decisions should be made prudently with thorough consideration of alternatives as it pertains to cost relative to projected income. Functional efficiency can be achieved by layouts with higher efficiency ratios, by configurations with less exterior surface, or by optimizing a project's critical mass.

Concept: Cost Efficiency. Construction and engineering decisions should be made after thorough cost engineering studies of alternatives relative to both initial and future operating costs, and to construction schedules. Design decisions should consider alternatives, evaluate related value assessments of hard cost, and examine benefit analysis of early completion. Prime attention should focus on the more expensive building components, namely, the superstructure (15% to 29% of HC), and HVAC and electric systems (17.5% to 24.5% of HC) (Canestaro, 1989).

Grouping Classes, Categories, and Concepts

Proceeding from deductive inference with successive partition of the financial dimension into classes and categories, to inductive reasoning with successive composition of the physical dimension from observations into nodes and concepts, a physical-financial model for trade-offs finally emerged. Figure 3 presents a diagram of the PHYS-FI model, and Table 2 provides an outline of the classes, categories, and concepts in the model.

Categories and concepts of trade-offs in design economy involving creating real estate values are then presented in the concept—the war stories format that James Graaskamp mastered—with observations from the ULI project files presented in a narrative format to explain the concepts.

Creating Real Estate Values with the Environment

Concept: Topographic Fit

Nature is process and value, exhibiting both opportunities and limitations to human use. The shape and configuration of a site offer a multitude of opportunities, even with slopes and characteristics that seem like unsurmountable limitations at the outset. Topographic fit offers opportunities for creating real estate values with signature features, for increasing both income and value by unique and visually appealing settings, for value en-

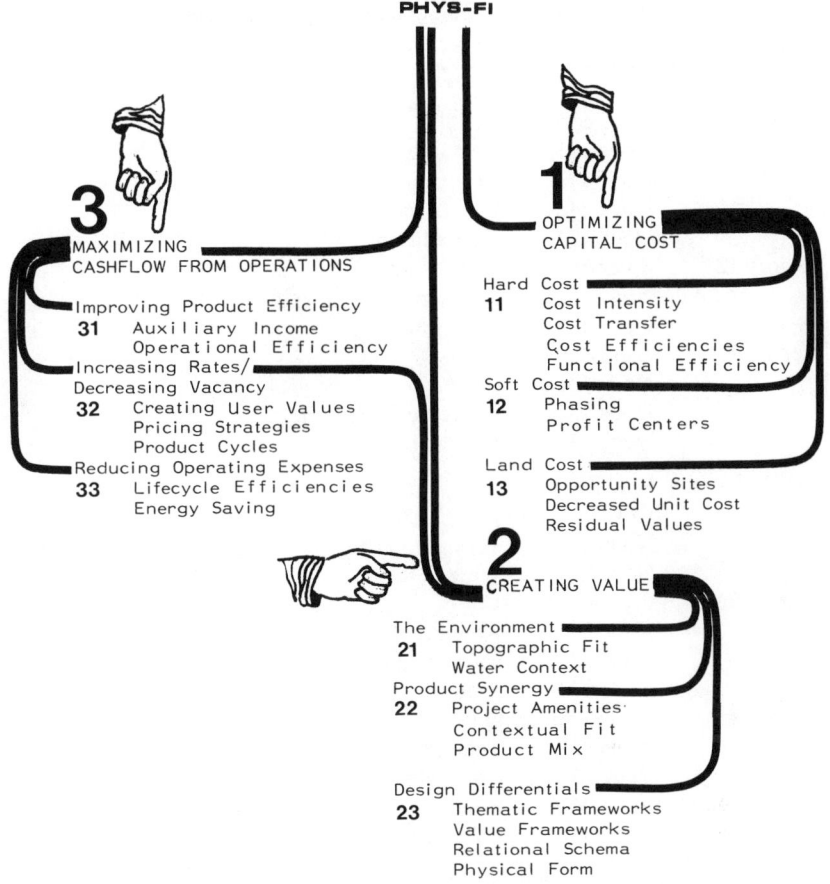

Figure 3. PHYS-FI: A Physical-Financial Model For Design Economy Trade-Offs.

hancement by facilitating traffic, and for reducing cost by adhering to natural slopes.

Exemplifying unsurmountable topographic limitations turned into opportunities is the 375-acre Coldspring phased housing development in Baltimore, Maryland, with grades frequently exceeding 36% slope and a 7-acre 180-feet-deep trap rock quarry. The developer achieved topographic fit by building deckhouses with walkout basements leading to cantilevered decks, bridgehouses with elevated walkways leading from street level to upper level of units, and maisonnette horizontal duplexes on slopes allowing for ground-level entrances from both the top and base of

Table 2. PHYS-FI: Classes, Categories, and Concepts of Design Economy Trade-Offs

Class 1: Optimizing Capital Cost
Category 11:   Hard cost
                  Node 111,   Cost intensity
                  Node 112,   Cost transfer
                  Node 113,   Functional efficiency
                  Node 114,   Cost efficiencies
Category 12:   Soft cost
                  Node 121,   Phasing
                  Node 122,   Profit centers
Category 13:   Land cost
                  Node 131,   Opportunity sites
                  Node 132,   Decreased unit cost
                  Node 133,   Residual values

Class 2: Creating Real Estate Value
Category 21:   Environment
                  Node 211,   Topographic fit
                  Node 212,   Water context
Category 22:   Product synergy
                  Node 221,   Amenity dollars
                  Node 222,   contextual fit
                  Node 223,   Product mix
Category 23:   Design differentials
                  Node 231,   Thematic frameworks
                  Node 232,   Cultural schemata
                  Node 233,   Relational schemata
                  Node 234,   Form schemata

Class 3: Increasing Cash Flow from Operations
Category 31:   Increasing product efficiency
                  Node 311,   Auxiliary income
                  Node 312,   Operational efficiency
Category 32:   Increasing rates/decreasing vacancy
                  Node 321,   Creating user values
                  Node 322,   Pricing strategies
                  Node 323,   Product cycles
Category 33:   Decreasing operating expenses
                  Node 331,   Life-cycle efficiencies
                  Node 332,   Energy saving

the slope. The developer utilized the 7-acre trap quarry to erect 20-story apartment buildings, with entrance lobbies at the top, and enclosed bridges leading to parking at the same level at the quarry's rim.

Likewise, topographic limitations of an old quarry were turned into signature quality for the 1200-acre low-density Black Diamond Ranch residential golf course community in Lecanto, California. The center attraction in the phased development is five signature fairways, in the project's first 18-hole golf course, which pass over, down into, or dogleg around ponds and rock formations created in the two abandoned limestone quarries. Home prices in the development ranged from $180,000 to $250,000; and cottage homes from $295,000 to $575,000, as compared to a $60,000 to $100,000 range recommended by the market study, which failed to account for topographic fit and instead considered the limestone quarry a negative factor.

Topographic fit similarly increased home values in the 1700-unit, 409-acre Big Canyon residential development in Newport Beach, California. The developer capitalized on the extreme variations in terrain to create a unique and visually appealing setting for high-value homes, and to provide maximum privacy and security for the more expensive homes. The canyon floor was used for most of the single fairway, 18-hole golf course, while maintaining the predominant natural contours to maximize the view from and market value of each lot or home.

Capitalizing on topographic fit to increase income, developers of the 925,000 square foot, 53-acre regional shopping center, Coquitham Centre, in Vancouver utilized the site's natural slopes with a gradual drop of 17 feet to accommodate a two-level mall concept. Providing each mall level direct access to on-grade parking ensured equal traffic on both levels. Increasing traffic increased sales, income for tenants, percentage income for developer, and market value of the mall for investors.

Reducing capital cost by adhering to topographic fit, developers of the Beach waterpark in Mason, Ohio utilized the steeper gradients of the natural slopes to build the water slides. This decreased construction costs, utilized relatively unuseable land, and achieved the needed design fit of the waterpark in the surrounding natural environment.

Concept: Water Context

Properties surrounding the relatively limited supply of natural and man-made water features usually attain substantially higher market values. Careful design and planning should add water features whenever possible, maximize opportunities for waterview, and capitalize on the overall ambience around waterfronts, beaches, and other water features. The water context includes limitations of floodplains and storm drainage requirements, which can often be turned into opportunities by creating lakes, ponds, waterfalls, and similar features, and by using land subject to floods for golf courses, equestrian facilities, and other amenities.

Exemplifying this concept is the 890-acre Horseshoe Bend residential development in Georgia, which occupies a long tract of land, with a narrow river frontage on the backside. It is divided into nine neighborhoods with different price ranges and/or architectural styles. Overlooking the river, a golf course was built to utilize the floodplain, and was surrounded by the more expensive and the higher density neighborhood homes. To add value to the long site, two dams were built on the creek that runs through the site to create two lakes. The lakes absorb the runoff from the development, saving the cost of a below-grade storm drainage system, while providing views for the surrounding homes, thereby increasing the in-land real estate values and adding to the overall ambience of the development.

Another example of a development master planned to enhance real estate values by emphasizing the relationship between the various residential products and the site's natural and manmade amenities is Florida's Longboat Key Club. High density clusters are located on the golf courses, beaches, and waterfronts, with waterviews opened or created whenever possible to accentuate the water context as the development's key marketing differential.

The best opportunities for developing a water context are occasionally offered by problem sites, as in Riverchase planned community in Birmingham, Alabama. Its 2700-acre site was acquired at a very inexpensive price tag because it included flood-plains, ravines with 40% slopes, and an old coal strip mine. The development's water context involves floodplains, which are utilized for the golf course and open play fields; creeks and ravines, which are incorporated in a greenbelt system; and ponds, created in the old mine, to be used as a storm drainage system, as a source for golf course irrigation, and as a real estate value enhancer.

Emphasis on the water context in design increases as the density increases and provides a distinct market advantage in the urban setting. The high density Embarcadero Cove is a 3.14-acre, 23-unit patio condominium home development in Stockton, California. Its homes are clustered around a small private cove, connected to a manmade lake by a channel inlet, with most of the one- and two-story, zero-lot-line homes having direct views of the water. Price differentials between units with the best waterviews, units with secondary waterviews, and units without waterviews were in excess of 35% and 20%, respectively.

Emphasis on the water context further increases with urban high-rise structures, as with Rowes Wharf, which occupies 5.4 acres on Boston Harbor in the financial district, with 330,000 square feet of office space, a 230-room hotel, 100 residential condominiums, and 12,500 square feet of retail space. The developer capitalized on the waterfront location and views with a project design that includes a large waterfront building, two water-surrounded wharf buildings, thirty-eight marina slips, docking space for eight commercial vessels, and a ferryboat terminal. The project is exemplary in its contextual design, the quality of its water promenades, and the siting of its buildings to benefit from waterfronts, waterviews, and water access. Office leases and hotel room rates are among the highest in Boston, and condominium prices have set new records in that market.

Creating Real Estate Values with Product Synergy

Concept: Amenity Dollars

Success or failure of a project in the marketplace depends on both meeting the market demand with a particular product mix and on exceeding standards of market supply with project amenities that would differentiate the development from competition. Allocating amenity dollars to provide unique market differentials and phasing to provide adequate up-front critical mass are most central to a developer's ability to create real estate values in excess of cost.

Selection of project amenities involves a market analysis of supply to identify the standard amenities and a marketability analysis to identify the consumer profiles and the potential differential amenities that would appeal to such consumers. A developer can then use amenity dollars on those differential amenities that would generate the highest return.

Selecting accessibility as one of their key differentials, developers of the 1,400,000 square foot, 130-acre, Chesterbrook office development near Philadelphia, Pennsylvania spent $1,700,000 from their amenity dollars on an interchange on Route 202. Easy and convenient access changed the project's perception and market share to ensure its success, as its land value increased by 30%.

Amenity dollars in the 70-acre Village Homes development in California, planned in the 1970s for first-time home buyers with strong interest in community living and in energy conservation, were spent on common agricultural land, bicycle and pedestrian trails, a coop kindergarten, a coop store, and energy-conserving passive and active solar systems in both homes and common buildings. The developer selected an amenity package that reflected the values and interests of the target customer group and benefitted from sales at faster absorption rates, and at prices above competing products in the market.

Allocating amenity dollars to security, developers of the Martin Luther King shopping center built an on-site station manned by a two-officer beat unit of the Los Angeles Police Department and by the center's own private security officers, complete with a holding tank and a patrol room. The immediate presence of the police and the related facilities added a sense of security to the mall, thus increasing traffic and reducing shoplifting. This, combined with other security measures, have resulted in increased traffic, more sales, and higher profits for tenants, leading to a stable tenant mix, and lower turnover and vacancy rates, and to higher rental and percentage incomes for the developer and the investors.

A yet different allocation of amenity dollars involves University and Technology Center, an industrial park in a campus-like setting in Minneapolis that targets new upstart technology companies with modular cost-effective space. Its project amenities are business services that young companies often cannot provide for themselves. These include a central receptionist; conference rooms copy center; and secretarial, bookkeeping, accounting, and payroll services.

Developers of the 720-acre, 976-unit Mariner Sands planned recreational community in Florida spent their amenity dollars on 36 holes of golf, a tennis and pool center, and an extensive open space with trails and nature reserves, to complement a housing product mix of single-family detached homes, zero-lot-line homes, four-plexes, and condominium apartments. The developers also addressed the critical mass issue, recognizing that the viability of a large-scale phased recreational development required establishing a critical mass as quickly as possible. They accomplished this goal by building adequate upfront amenities, placing a building time restriction on all lots, and seeding the development by selectively locating spec homes. The allocation of amenity dollars, coupled with the phasing of a critical mass, enabled the project to attain the desired positioning in the market and to achieve targeted absorption rates at projected sales prices.

Concept: Contextual Fit

Contextual fit involves an understanding of the attitudes and concerns of the neighborhood, on the one hand, and the architectural and environmental texture and scale of the project's surrounds, on the other hand. While it requires extra effort to achieve a functional fit and a compatible architectural style, form, and feeling with the surrounds, the results could include cost savings from an accelerated project schedule and increased income from faster absorption due to market acceptance heightened with positive media coverage.

Exemplifying contextual fit in the cityscape is the $110 million, 11-acre multi-use Levi's Plaza development in San Francisco, with 773,000 square feet of office space, 60,000 square feet of retail space, and 370 luxury condominiums. It was developed in a multiple building, low-rise, informal campus setting, with buildings in a stepped-back architecture that accentuates and blends with the residential scale and urban feeling of surrounding Telegraph Hill. The developer was able to gain strong support from the city and the neighborhood by proposing an open park to front the project, and renovating and incorporating two historic buildings in the development to further blend with the cityscape. This contextual fit created a signature quality to the building, resulting in higher rates, lower vacancies, and an exceptionally higher market value due to lower required capitalization rates by investors because of the signature quality of the project.

Contextual fit with the scale of the neighborhood is well represented by the Cascades specialty shopping center, where the developer enlarged the site's lime rock depression to accommodate one story of the two-story project, resulting in a lower profile from the street. The north facade facing the residential area was integrated further in the scale of the neighborhood by use of landscaped berms with a matching slope to the wood-shingled roofs. The neighborhood acceptance resulted in more repeat consumers, more retail sales, more tenants, and a higher real estate value with the increased net operating income.

Another elaborate example of contextual fit with the scale of architecture, and with the fabric of the project's surrounds involves the Wilshire Courtyard low-rise 8.2-acre, 1,000,000 square foot office development in Los Angeles, with accessory retail, health club, and restaurant uses. After meeting with representatives of local resident associations, the development team decided against the use of high rise and instead arrived at the concept of placing two opposing C-shaped, terraced, low-rise buildings on the site to satisfy the neighborhood concerns. The building scale was further reduced by use of an alternating red granite and bronze solar glass finish, and an angular architectural form. Simultaneously, the human scale was enhanced by an entry arcade with sidewalk cafés and shops, and a grand entry plaza and courtyards. The developer's attention to contextual fit was rewarded by community acceptance, reflected in an entrenched prestige image, stable qualified tenants, and a higher real estate value with the ensuing reduced risk.

Concept: Product Mix

Value can be added by creatively mixing income-producing units in a development, such as units with different shared facilities, with different lease rates or prices, with different styles, or units of different zoning classes or of different product cycles. A successful product mix optimizes income with a higher market share and/or rates, lowers vacancy with reduced tenant turnovers and increased tenant trade-ups, and maximizes real estate market values.

Providing a broad stratified product mix to gain a higher market share, and tenant trades between different price ranges, the PGA National in Florida, offers single-family detached homes, zero-lot-line homes, townhouses, patio homes, and condominium apartments. These are arranged in neighborhoods, segmented by price level and by architectural style. The various neighborhoods, with styles ranging from the rustic and California Contemporary to the French Provincial, Spanish, and Mediterranean, are bound by natural features, golf course fairways, or waterways to separate the different price levels, as well as any discordant architectural styles.

A unique product mix of traditional retail space with indoor pushcarts and antique trucks is utilized by the Rouse Company in the Underground Atlanta specialty shopping center. The carts add to the constantly changing festive atmosphere, while offering local would-be retailers an outlet for their merchandise with cart rentals by the week, and providing the developer with a leasing pool as tenants trade-up from carts to trucks to stores. The tenants and the developer benefit from mixing the carts with retail space, with increased traffic, increased sales, lower turnover, and increased percentage rents. The investors, too, benefit from higher rental income with a diverse tenant mix, and from refinancing or reversion with higher property values.

Introducing price leaders in the product mix of Presidential Towers in Chicago, developers created eight corner units out of the thirteen apartments on each floor of the four towers in the project. Corner units typically obtain higher rental rates than noncorner units and drive rent levels of adjacent units upward, increasing both net operating incomes and real estate market values.

Utilizing an unconventional product mix of units and shared facilities, the Sara Frances in San Diego, a new four-story, 160-unit, single-room-occupancy (SRO) residential hotel, offers units with an average size of 125 square feet, each equipped with a sink and most with small private bathrooms with showers. Common areas include a lobby, a central landscaped courtyard, a television room, a vending machine area, and two laundry rooms. Shared facilities on each floor include a kitchen, dining/card room, two bathrooms, and two shower rooms. With this product mix, the developer was able to provide low-income affordable housing at half the average monthly rent of a studio apartment in the city. The low rentals and the available broad market segment create enough demand to keep the building almost 100% occupied, resulting in higher income and a higher market value for the project.

Providing examples of product mix by price stratification, and by product cycle, is Treetop Village in Lake Ozark, Missouri, a 30-acre, 110-unit resort development with a product mix priced from $5000 to $250,000, with luxury homes at $250,000+, villas at $90,000 to $140,000, quarter-shares at $30,000 to $45,000, and time-shares at $5000 to $15,000. The developer designed a luxury product mix stratified for the broadest possible market share, differentiated by unit size, location uniqueness, waterfront views, and the percentage of time-shared ownership. Further, the phased project was planned for two product cycles by offering two different design products in two overlapping phases, in order to capitalize on higher absorption rates for new products; to avoid price stagnation on the market, aggravated by competition from resales; and to escape gradually escalating merchandising costs with a longer product cycle.

Creating Real Estate Values with Design Differentials

Concept: Thematic Frameworks

In our Western culture, we distinguish strictly between living and inanimate objects, as we intend the more invariant properties of things. Physiognomic perception, on the other hand, intends the expression of things, as feelings come to dominate perception. In describing differing responses to architecture, Norberg-Schulz (1965) states: "To perceive is to interpret; that is to choose between the 'intentional' possibilities." Perception is anything but passive reception of impressions, and no perception is in reality completely free from an emotional content.

Thematic frameworks in design offer strong stimuli for intentional possibilities involving emotional content and generate higher order response patterns. Thematic frameworks could capitalize on the contextual architecture of its urban surrounds or capitalize on the local history of a particular structure. Thematic frameworks could also be value based, as with nature-related themes, or activity based.

Successfully implemented thematic frameworks could establish a higher quality image, higher market acceptance, and faster absorption rates, leading to higher occupancies and rentals. Thematic frameworks are also most complimentary in achieving signature quality for the project, thereby creating higher demand by investors, reducing developers' and lenders' risk, and occasionally lowering return rate expectations, especially with foreign investors.

Rowes Wharf successfully utilized a thematic framework that capitalized on both Boston's harbor contextual architecture and the wharf's local history. Brick and granite pavement were used throughout the site to blend with surrounding buildings, together with brick pavement and wood decking to blend with adjacent cityscape. The moderately scaled fifteen-story towers are characterized by a series of setbacks stepping down over six stories to respond to the historic scale of older buildings near the waterfront. The six- and seven-story pier buildings are related to Boston's traditional wharf structures in scale and gradually step down to only three stories at the water's edge. The thematic framework is further established by such architectural elements as fenestration patterns, curved building corners, highly detailed precast concrete with the density and effect of carved limestone, slate and copper roofs, and painted wood accents.

To capitalize on local history in establishing the needed thematic framework for the Trapper's Alley adaptive use specialty shopping center in Detroit, developers focused on the history of the old fur tannery. They retained the name, identity, and architectural appearance, and used artifacts and machinery from the original processing operation to enhance the project theme and its uniqueness.

To create a value-based thematic framework, with a focus on nature, for the Wilderness Gulf Coast second home development in Naples, Florida, the developers adopted wetland development restrictions, built a golf course on open pasture land while maintaining the forested areas, and added 12 manmade lakes. The value-based natural theme resulted in a rapid sellout, at higher prices, and in owner satisfaction, exemplified by both a lower resale activity and a better performing receivable portfolio of company financed sales.

Using food for an activity-based thematic framework, the developer of Gourmet Fair created a 32,000 square foot food center within the 775,000 square foot Sherway Gardens shopping center in Toronto. The fair serves foods of the world by eighteen 200 to 1700 square foot shops and kiosks; includes two wine stores, fruit store, florist, and delicatessen; and has its own separate management, merchant's association, common area maintenance, and distinct design. The activity-based theme was so successful that Gourmet Fair's successor, the food court, has become a traffic-generating anchor in almost every regional shopping center.

Concept: Cultural Schemata

Schemata are typical stereotyped reactions to situations, that is, habits of perception.[5] Schemata are formed during socialization and mirror our cultural value system and are clustered in formalized coherence systems, which encompass both tangibles and intangibles. Market research seeks to segment a market and its constituent consumer profiles, and to define those tangible product differentials that should be included in a project's facilities program. Design synthesis, on the other hand, seeks to identify relevant formalized coherence systems for the specific consumer profile(s), to define intangible qualities, and to identify related design elements that could provide evidence that tangibilizes the intangibles in the daily experiences of the consumers. Property management should, then, seek to manage the evidence in order for the designated cultural intangible qualities to continually dominate consumers' perceptions during the life span of the real estate product.

Successfully implemented, the use of cultural schemata could bridge the gap between market research and design synthesis by focusing attention on both tangible and intangible qualities for product differentiation. Cultural schemata could also provide for continuity between development and property management, centered around those elements of evidence in the project.

Combined differently in formalized coherence systems, schemata include, among others, exclusivity, sense of community, security, and sense of arrival. For example, in the 22-acre, 125-unit Eagle Bay condominium project in New York, the developers created a sense of arrival and sense of security for tenants and owners, and more importantly for would-be tenants and buyers. This was tangibilized by a formalized design sequence, which started by an attractively landscaped entrance and signage to set the tone for the project; followed by a security gate at the beginning of a divided driveway curving in a high impact zone with a concentration of vistas, waterscape, and landscape features. The sequence typically leads to a clubhouse with distinct architecture and visible amenities, such as a pool, decks, jacuzzi, etc., together with the leasing-sales office. This sequence has become almost a standard in resort communities, multifamily residential projects, and prestige single-family developments.

Expanding the previous coherence system, developers of the 135-unit McMillan Place luxury apartment complex in Charlotte added a sense of tradition to the schemata used in Eagle Bay to generate an even higher market response. The sense of tradition was tangibilized by historic renovation of an old mansion on the 11-acre old estate, appropriately furnished for use as a clubhouse by tenants and guests. The developer's success in tangibilizing a selected cultural schemata stimulated high response and resulted in higher rental rates, below average vacancy rates, and higher market value.

The 900-acre Amelia Island Plantation second-home resort development on the Atlantic Coast in Northern Florida capitalizes on another cultural coherence system—naturalism, that is, preserving and living with nature. Related tangible elements in the master plan include the protection of sand dunes, tangibilized by providing boardwalks for passage through the fragile dunes, and protection of marsh areas from intrusion or change, tangibilized by elevated walkways and wildlife lookout decks. Interior drainage is handled by an interconnected canal system for minimizing drainage impact on the marshland, tangibilized by incorporating water hazards in the golf courses. The effort and expense of addressing both the tangibles and the intangibles of naturalism were well rewarded by the response of the marketplace.

Selection of multiple coherence systems for design synthesis should carefully resolve conflicts between schemata in selected systems, as with conflict between speed, accessibility, and route efficiency for cars, on the one hand, and serenity, pedestrian safety, and children domains on the other. The Opus 2, an industrial and office park in Minneapolis, adopted both coherence systems and resolved the conflict by providing two circulation systems: a primary system for vehicular traffic and a secondary system for pedestrian and bicycles. The secondary system is physically separated from the primary roadways, tangibilized by a series of bridges and underpasses, and carefully integrated in the landscape for evidence of serenity. The developer was successful in capitalizing on cultural schemata in creating a safe human domain for children's play, adult's movement, and socialization, resulting in a higher market share and faster absorption for the project.

Concept: Relational Schemata

Elementary schemata 6 are the result of such concrete operations during childhood as puttings things close to each other, into each other, or after each other. Relational schemata start to develop on a sensomotoric basis from birth on and evolve with coherence systems based on proximity, separation, succession, closure, and continuity. Individual coherence systems are formed by combining more schemata such as cluster, order, and movement, among many others. Schemata eventually accommodate intellectual abstraction; interpretation, and symbolization, as with inward or outward orientation, centralization, and dispersion, among others.

Successfully implemented, the use of relational schemata could provide the link between market research and site planning by focusing attention on schemata-based alternative strategies for site plans.

Focusing on the movement dynamics of relational schemata, developers of the 155,000 square foot 1600 Parkwood mid-rise, Class A office building in Atlanta, tailored the project design to the view from the road. The depression in the foreground of the building was made into a water feature with fountains and waterfalls, surrounded with extensive landscape to draw the zone of vision of an approaching tenant or visitor to the building base. The building was finished in rich marble and polished granite in that same focal visual zone, with the remainder in the secondary visual zone beyond the second floor, finished with less expensive materials. The developer's understanding of the dynamics of movement enabled him to cut hard cost to $16.2 million, with total development cost to only $18 million, while achieving an aesthetic quality that made it possible to attain full lease-up within one year, in a highly competitive overbuilt market. The project was sold two years later for $23.6 million.

Working with both centralization and dispersion, developers of the 1600-unit Horseshoe Bend planned community in suburban Atlanta grouped different types of residential units and different price ranges in eight separate neighborhoods. The developer elected to centralize the golf course, country club, and swim and tennis club amenities together, and to disperse the more expensive and the higher density neighborhoods around the centralized amenities. The topography of the site and an extensive floodplain area dictated the centralization relational schema, vs. dispersion of amenities, to maximize real estate values of lots and homes in the project.

Inward orientation to a mall and dispersal of anchor stores are routinely used in shopping center design. In addition, to ensure adequate traffic throughout, developers of Vancouver's Coquitham regional shopping center dispersed centralized food operations in a food court to the upper level, while developers of Perimeter Mall in Atlanta placed the food court at the mall's lowest level. Both were successful in increasing overall traffic, generating higher sales volume for tenants and a higher percentage income to the investors and developer. Lower vacancy rates with improved traffic pattern meant even more rental income and higher real estate value.

Another example of using an inward orientation relational schema applied to a real estate asset redevelopment is provided by the 214,000 square foot Merchantile Wharf in Boston, built in 1857 for shipping-related business, and under conversion into 122 apartments, and 13,400 square feet of retail space. The developer opened up a seven-story skylighted atrium in the center of the building, with an emphasis on the aesthetic qualities of the original building materials, with brick, stone, and timber surfaces exposed and sandblasted to accentuate their natural qualities. The inward orientation to the atrium made it possible to avoid dark, deep units on a double-loaded corridor, to include multilevel duplexes and triplexes with lofts and atrium views, and to give the project an identity, and its tenants a sense of community with atrium-centered activities.

In contrast, developers of the 105-unit, 16-story La Mer luxury condominium complex on the shoreline of the Gulf of Mexico opted to use outward orientation as the primary relational schema. The single-loaded, U-shaped design provides every luxury residence with views of the beach and the Gulf of Mexico. The use of outward orientation as a relational schema resulted in 20% preconstruction sales, 50% within six months, and 100% sellout before construction completion.

Outward orientation is combined with the relational schemata of group, cluster, and buffer in the case of the 7.7-acre, 62-unit, Stoney Creek Villas second-home condominium development in Hilton Head. The two- and three-bedroom townhouses, designed in Caribbean-inspired wood and stucco architecture, are grouped in individual buildings with three to seven units each, and are clustered in groups of two to five buildings on two cul-de-sacs. The clusters are complemented by buffers between the units to provide privacy and are arranged with an outward orientation to overlook a marsh area, a lagoon, and the forest surrounds. The relational schemata accentuated the natural setting and provided the project's key marketing differential in a very competitive market.

Concept: Form Schemata

Christian Norberg-Schulz (1965) has probably provided the most complete account of the interface between psychology, sociology, and design with his concepts relating perception schematization and architectural form. He views the later as elements (Gestalten) and relations that determine a formal totality,[7] with decisive impact by spatial order[8] at times, and by architectural treatment[9] of boundaries at other times.

The process of selecting individual form schemata and combining them in coherence systems in design synthesis remains intuitive. However, identifying form schemata and their coherence systems in real estate projects with exceptional market values could certainly help in setting form schemata for a new project.

An example of a coherence system with key form schemata of division, style, and scale is provided by the York Green office complex in Lutherville, Maryland. Its site was originally zoned for a single building and is bordered by an upper-income residential neighborhood. To blend the project in the neighborhood, instead of a tower, the developer built Williamsburg-styled residential-like two- and three-story office buildings, connected together with covered walkways to meet the one building requirement. By selecting to build at a residential scale, the developer gained the goodwill of the surrounding neighbors/potential tenants while creating an office complex with a unique character.

A contrary approach with addition and mass was taken in the Stoney Brook luxury residential complex in Denver, Colorado, where individual units are grouped in freestanding triplex and four-plex buildings, designed and sited to give the mass of single-family large detached homes. The buildings are designed in the French country style to enchance the single-family dwelling perception, while contrasting the predominantly contemporary architecture in the Denver market. By opting for mass in the design of the individual units, the developer created a differential that set the image and the demand for the development apart from equivalent townhouse projects in the market.

Focused on architectural treatment schemata with texture and contradiction is the ocean-front 3-acre, 51-unit seascape planned unit development on Solana Beach in California. It derives its identity and success from its architectural treatment. The two-story townhouses and apartment-condominiums are designed with emphasis on repetitive use of sharp angles, with contrasting tall slender chimney cylinders and curved patio walls, all covered in wood shingles for a highly textured look.

Concentrating on mass and style form schemata, developers of the 1,100,000 square foot IBM Tower in Atlanta were able to build a signature building with superb quality and a dramatic identifiable image. They opted for a Post-Modernistic style in the tradition of the 1920s and 1930s skyscrapers, wish granite exteriors and high marble arches, and a distinctive pyramidal top. They also selected a square tower mass for maximum impact on the Atlanta skyline. The financial success of the design is reflected in leasing rates of $25 to $28 per square foot, compared to market rates of $18 to $22 per square foot, and the addition of six more floors to the original plans to meet market demand. Furthermore, the developers and investors made windfall profits from the sale of the building within 3 years to a Japanese life insurance company for $300 million, as the signature quality generated an exceptional net operating income and justified below-market returns for the new investors.

Summary and Conclusions

By using deductive-inductive analysis, this study developed PHYS-FI: a classification system for trade-offs between the physical and financial dimensions of real estate. The model offers an integrative framework that encompasses the cost–income–value continuum during the development–operations–disposition stages of the investment cycle and presents a coherent set of concepts of trade-offs in design economy.

PHYS-FI is useful for real estate professionals in identifying and improving trade-off decisions for design economy during planning real estate development or rehabilitation; in evaluating cost, value, and returns in real estate investment qualitative analysis; and in rehabilitation and repositioning decisions in real estate asset management.

PHYS-FI is also useful for market analysts and appraisers in identifying comparable properties based on similarities of both physical attributes and the equally important underlying design concepts that create the real estate value at hand. Future research with PHYS-FI utilizing the deductive–inductive procedure of this study is needed to focus on identifying similarities in attributes and concepts to open the way for a new generation of studies in multidimensional classifications of variables in value decisions and to narrow the gap between quality of input and sophistication of procedures in appraisal and market research.

Notes

1. These studies include Kain and Quigley on housing quality (1970), Pollard on views, topographic amenities, and building heights (1980), design trade-offs by Grimm (1976), design configurations by Steyert (1972), masonry and glass building enclosures by Grimm (1976), artistic qualities by Singer (1978), "good" architecture by Hough and Kratz (1983), visual preferences by Im (1984), landscape preferences by Lyons (1983), urban amenities by

Diamond and Tolley (1982), and architecture and urban design by Vandell (1987) among others.

2. Prominent among these studies are such models as Wurtzebach and Kim's "Investment Analysis and Decision Making Framework for Real Estate Development" (1979); Miles and Wurtzebach's "Conceptual Framework and Computer Simulation Model for Risk Analysis in Real Estate Development" (1977); Peiser's "Risk Analysis in Land Development" (1984); DeLisle's "Interactive Design/Marketing Model" (1985); and Canestaro's "Refining Project Feasibility" (1989).

3. In a separate study by the author (Sharkawy, 1990), over 50% of all loans in a 38-construction-development loan sample were found to have less than 5% net equity.

4. Appraised property value and estimates of income are entwined:

$$\text{Value} = \frac{\text{NOI}_{n+1}}{\text{CR}}$$

where NOI_{n+1} is estimated net operating income in year of sale at the end of period n and CR is the assumed market capitalization rate at the time of sale.

5. According to Gestalt psychologists, we assimilate experiences through the schemata, and these come to life when we have an experience that fits.

6. Jéan Piaget has provided us a basic understanding of schematization in that the first schema acquired by a child are proximity, enclosure, continuity, and related relational schema.

7. Formal totality involves such form schemata as mass, scale, and style, and accommodates intellectual abstraction by other form schemata, such as symbolization and contradiction, among others.

8. Spatial order involves such form schemata as division, modularity, addition, terracing, cascading, and many more such detailed schemata, such as axiality, symmetry, rhythm, proportion, etc.

9. Architectural treatment involves many form schemata, such as texture, angularity, pattern, transparency, reflectivity, etc.

References

Alexander, Christopher. *Notes on the Synthesis of Form*. Cambridge, MA: Harvard University Press, 1967.

Alexander, Christopher. *A Pattern Language which Generates Multi Service Centers*. California: Center for Environmental Structures, 1968.

Archer, Bruce. "Systematic Method for Designers." *Design* (April 1963), 172–88.

Canestaro, James. *Refining Project Feasibility*. Blacksburg, VA: Refine Group, 1989, pp. 1.1–1.30, and 9.2–9.5.

Chermayeff, Sergé and Christopher Alexander. *Community & Privacy*. Garden City, NY: Anchor Books, 1965, p. 149.

DeLisle, James. "The Interactive Design/Marketing Model in Determining Highest and Best Use." *The Appraisal Journal* (July 1985), 325–39.

Diamond, D. and G. Tolley. *The Economics of Urban Amenities*. New York: Academic Press, 1982.

Halprin, Lawrence. *The RSVP Cycles: Creative Processes in the Human Environment*. New York: George Braziller, 1969.
Graaskamp, James A. *Fundamentals of Real Estate*. ULI Development Series. Washington, DC: Urban Land Institute, 1981.
Graaskamp, James A. and M. Atef Sharkawy. *The Lily Lake Forest Recreation Environ*. Madison, WI: Foster Printing, 1971.
Grimm, Clayford. "Building Design Trade-Offs: Initial Cost versus Operating Cost versus Rental Income." *The Appraisal Journal* (April 1976), 247–57.
Grimm, Clayford. *Relative Thermal and Economic Performance of Masonry and Glass Building Enclosures*. Austin, TX: Texas Building Materials and Systems Testing Laboratory, 1975.
Hough, D. E. and Kratz, C. G. "Can 'Good' Architecture Meet the Market Test?" *Journal of Urban Economics* 14 (1983), 40–54.
Im, Seung-Bin. "Visual Preferences in Urban Spaces: An Exploration of a Scientific Approach to Environmental Design." *Environment and Behavior* 16:2 (March 1984), 235–62.
Jones, J. C. *The Design Method: Design Methods Reviewed*. New York: Plenum Press, 1966.
Kain, J. and J. Quigley. "Measuring the Value of Housing Quality." *Journal of American Statistical Association* 65 (June 1970), 532–48.
Lewis, Philip. "Quality Corridors for Wisconsin." *Landscape Architecture Quarterly* (January 1964).
Lyons, Elizabeth. "Demographic Correlates of Landscape Preferences." *Environment and Behavior* 15:4 (July 1983), 487–511.
McHarg, Ian. *Design with Nature*. Garden City, NY: Doubleday/The Natural History Press, 1969, p. 104.
Michalski, R. and R. Stepp. "Conceptual Clustering of Structured Objects: A Goal-Oriented Approach." *Artificial Intelligence* 28 (1986), 43–69.
Miles, M. and C. Wurtzebach. "Risk Analysis in Real Property Development Process: A Conceptual Framework and a Computer Simulation Model." *Journal of Business Research* 5 (December 1977), 325–57.
Nadler, Gerald. *Work System Design: The Ideals Concept*. Homewood, ILL: Richard Irwin, 1967, pp. 4, 50.
Nijkamp, P., H. Leitner, and N. Wrigley. *Measuring the Unmeasurable*. NATO ASI Series. Boston: Martinus Nijhoff Publishers, 1985, pp. 1–28.
Norberg-Schulz, Christian. *Intentions in Architecture*. Cambridge, MA: MIT Press, 1965.
Osborn, A. F. *Applied Imagination: Principles and Procedures of Creative Problem Solving*. New York: Scribners Publishing, 1957.
Peiser, Richard. "Risk Analysis in Land Development." *AREUEA Journal* 12:1 (1984), 12–29.
Pollard, Robert. "Topographic Amenities, Building Height, and the Supply of Urban Housing." *Regional Science and Urban Economics* 10 (1980), 181–99.
Sharkawy, M. Atef. *Rationalization in Environmental Design*. Madison, WI: Foster Printing, 1969.

Sharkawy, M. Atef. "Exploring Cost Ratios as Underwriting Criteria for Acquisition-Development-Construction Loans." Presented at the American Real Estate Society Annual Conference, Lake Tahoe, Nevada, March 1990.

Singer, Leslie. "Micro-Economics of the Art Market." *Journal of Cultural Economics* (June 1978), 21–40.

Steyert, Richard. "The Economics of High-Rise Apartment Buildings of Alternate Design Configurations." *American Society of Civil Engineers* (July 1972), 1.

ULI PRF Editors. *ULI—The Urban Land Institute Project Reference File*. Washington, D.C. The Urban Land Institute (January–March 1979 to January–March 1989), 9–19.

Vandell, Kerry. "The Economics of Architecture and Urban Design." Presented at the Allied Social Sciences Association Meeting, Chicago, Illinois, December 1987.

Vandell, Kerry. "Preliminary Findings, The Economics or Architecture and Urban Design." Presented at the Lincoln Land Institute Meeting, Cambridge, Massachusetts, September 1988.

Wurtzebach, C. H. and K. S. Kim. "An Investment Analysis and Decision Making Framework for Real Estate Development." *Journal of the American Real Estate and Urban Economics Association* 7, 3 (Fall 1979), 410–26.

8 AN INSIGHT INTO THE IDEAS OF PROFESSOR JAMES A. GRAASKAMP ON PRACTICE AND REFORM IN APPRAISAL

R. R. Fraser and E. M. Worzala

Introduction

Professor James A. Graaskamp[1] built the University of Wisconsin–Madison Real Estate Department into what many in the industry considered the finest in the United States (Bolan and Hovde, 1983). Employers from the length and breadth of the country sought Graaskamp's students. Starting salaries for graduates were high, in 1986 the highest in the University of Wisconsin's School of Business. The cooperative spirit built amongst students in the program spilled over to make the alumni group a powerful voice (Eisen, 1987). In 1985 43% of all graduates came to the biennial reunion, in 1987 350 attended (Kerch, 1987), and in 1989 there were 400. Few alumni associations attract such a consistently high proportion of graduates (Curtis, 1985).

Over the Graaskamp years the university produced about 900 real estate graduates, mostly at the master's level. The program grew to be the fourth largest in the School of Business (Kerch, 1987). Recent surveys indicate 25% employed in consulting and appraisal—many are presidents, CEOs, or principals of firms—20% work for banks, insurance companies, and other providers of capital with job titles of manager, CEO, director, investments officer, vice-president, and president in companies such as Prudential, Equitable, Metropolitan, Wells Fargo, and Pacific Mutual. Development and management careers accounted for 24% of graduates with careers as project managers, principals, and partners in large and small companies. Wall Street and the law accounted for an additional 20% of graduates. Academic careers for alumni see them in prominent real estate departments and centers at places such as Georgia State University, Texas A&M, New York University, and Denver University. As further evidence of the capability of graduates, in a recent survey of large real estate development firms, the Wisconsin program was ranked first for MBAs in real estate by 87% of the respondents (Kroll and Smith, 1988). In another survey of business schools and real estate departments, the Wisconsin program was ranked number two behind University of Pennsylvania and was the only University of Wisconsin—Madison business school department to appear (US News, 1990). Base starting salaries for new graduates were an average of $35,000 in 1991 and for all graduates an average of $48,000 in 1981 (Real Estate Alumni, 1982, 1991). Judged by the success of his graduates, Graaskamp was a powerful voice in U.S. real estate education.

During his tenure at the University of Wisconsin—Madison Graaskamp also made important contributions to real estate theory and practice through his work on feasibility analysis, appraisal theory, development of computer cash-flow simulation models, and a general view of the real estate process. He disseminated his thinking, primarily by way of lectures, workshops, consulting, courtroom testimony, and activism on public policy issues.

The object of this paper is to analyze the Graaskamp philosophy of the genesis and development of (1) a definition of value in real estate, (2) some related key elements in the way appraisal is practiced, and (3) the need and prospects for appraisal reform.

Appraisal Practice and Lenders

Graaskamp's views on appraisal were rooted in the work of his predecessor at Wisconsin, Richard U. Ratcliff. Both were convinced that an appraisal profession could not rely only on a professional society credential. Such a credential could never command the respect needed to carry out the vital social function as a guardian of informed judgement in virtually every type of real estate decision. Graaskamp claimed that the appraiser must aim to be "an advocate of the public interest as a check and balance on a lending system which is anti-appraisal, protransaction and biased towards credit enhancement."[2]

However, mainstream appraisers, he claimed, were trapped by customers who wanted certainty instead of truth, by procedures learned parrot fashion, and by practice preserved in mystique rather than empirical observation (Graaskamp, 1976b). A decade later his ideas on the subject had crystallized to

> ... the appraisal process is evolving into one of the following: (1) The art of disinformation... where the appraiser is implicitly part of a conspiracy with his client [the lender] to provide documents that satisfy regulators, provide cover against future charges of negligence... etc. (2) The discipline of rigid format and language for purposes of standardisation at the expense of relevance... (3) A counseling assignment wherein the appraiser must select and match the basic elements of the appraisal assignment to the requirements of the decision for which the appraisal is sought as a bench-mark (Graaskamp, 1985a).

These points represent the manifestation of the problem (1 and 2) and the ideal (3). Graaskamp transmitted these ideas to at least two decades of students and practitioners, and they formed the basis for his motivation to change the way appraisers worked.

Approach to Value — Historical Perspective

In the 1930s, following the Great Depression, collapsed and moribund appraisal and banking industries were reorganized. Appraisal politics were dominated by three power groups. The rationale of the three approaches to value is indelibly stamped with their authority (Graaskamp, 1986, and Graaskamp and Dilmore (date unknown). The compromise decision of the collective minds produced the substance of what was needed for a "proper appraisal" report. What purported to be scholarship rested on political compromise.

The Marshallian economic theory of competitive prices, wherein value is equal to the cost of replacement or reproduction at a given point in time, provides the first method (Graaskamp, 1978b). Since replacement cost sets the upper limit to value, cost to reproduce or replace, as an appraisal technique (Bonbright, 1937), is enhanced. Advocates of this so-called cost approach were the major consumers of appraisals — insurance companies and banks. Their interest in value carried the ulterior motive of asset protection in case liquidation of property assets was necessary. Furthermore, appraisal in general helped prove and ensure that the owner had a stake in the property—another way to protect the lender's interests. Lender's lives were much simpler then because high loan-to-value ratios (80–90%), now commonplace, were out of the question.

Graaskamp (ever skeptical of economists' counterfactual simplifying assumptions) hammered the idea that in a world of imperfect information, actors whose profit centers were unrelated to ultimate project success, and inescapable risks, frequently made mistakes in the allocation of capital. In plain English, stuff gets built that nobody wants to buy—it may cost a lot but the actors in the market make their own decision on whether to transact. In the short run, cost has a tenuous relationship to sales price; thus the cost approach is flawed because the foundation (cost) is not directly linked with the edifice (sale price).

Appraisal based on income, the second method, represents a medium-term viewpoint of the market. With a five- or ten-year time horizon, income-based appraisal contains thought and investment patterns for the holding period of a typical investor. Net present value of expected benefits less costs drives the value. A leading proponent of this group was F. M. Babcock (1927, 1932), along with the Federal Housing Authority. Babcock (and other academics) perceived a certain theoretical rationalization and elegance in the time value of money and capitalization techniques, and were among the few who could understand the mathematics. Value theory based on income was a natural outgrowth.

Even so, cash-flow projections and market supply and demand analysis were originally considered far less important than an accurate appraisal of cost to replace. Only with the advent of low-cost computers has the income approach moved to the forefront. Unfortunately, the ease of "cooking" models to give the desired answers by the use of unrealistic input assumptions means that the use of such models may have paved the way to disaster more often than it has improved decision making. It is all in how science is used, the scientists would say. By basing cash-flow model inputs on unrealistic estimates of the market for space/time products through projecting overly optimistic rates of growth in rents, absorption rates, or resale values, the appraiser can make cash-flow models bark, whistle, sing "Dixie," and justify ski resorts anywhere! Graaskamp always insisted that appraisal and feasibility study clients should not simply examine the value conclusion, internal rate of return, payback period, capitalization rate, or other bottom-line measure of worth, but should critically examine the assumptions leading to the conclusions. If assumptions were unrealistic, the conclusion would be affected likewise (Graaskamp,

1972). Computer buffs use the hackneyed phrase "garbage in means garbage out"; the appraisal process, like the computer, can process garbage and unreal assumptions and still produce, to the uninitiated, a perfectly plausible conclusion.

Finally, the market approach using comparable property transactions takes a short-term perspective; it analyzes the market today with current buyers and sellers. Brokers were the proponents of this approach, since they were privy to all of the market data.

Many view this approach as the most important, but also the most difficult and subjective, since no two properties are identical. Historically, adjustments for different attributes are made and the appraiser often uses "market experience" or "gut feeling" to make adjustments. Two alternative approaches, Quality Pointscore or QP (also called RATGRAM and price-quality regression in earlier versions) and MKTCOMP, have been advocated by Ratcliff (1972), Graaskamp (1978), and Robbins (1987). The techniques attempt to replace the ad hoc adjustment of the traditional sales comparison approach with systematic analysis of comparables and their similarities and differences from the subject property.

The income, cost, and market comparison approaches were in evidence in the early part of the century. However, following the upheaval of financial systems and real estate markets in the 1930s, all three were "deified... enthroned" (Ratcliff, 1963, p. 5) and set in concrete. It then became obligatory to include each in every appraisal. So, today the typical appraisal seems to be more concerned with form, and inclusion of all three approaches to value, rather than content and relevance to the property being appraised.

Dogma and Most-Probable Price

Graaskamp was a disciple of Richard U. Ratcliff, first as a student and then as a life-long colleague. Ratcliff (1972), following the academic lead provided by F. M. Babcock in the 1920s and 1930s, rejected the long-held professional canon that "market value" was something arrived at by bargaining between knowledgeable adversaries, each of whom was willing and able to trade but neither under compulsion or prepared to take an imprudent step. "Bargaining," by that definition of "market value," Graaskamp would say, leads to "value" with (apparent) empirical justification in a real world where idealized assumptions do not hold true. Thus the principle was ineffective and inappropriate. He conceded, however, that market value may be satisfactory as a basis for real estate taxing, where mass appraisal could not be expected to achieve the accuracy of single property appraisals; in condemnation, Graaskamp asserted, it had a place too. Ballard encapsulated Graaskamp's viewpoint as follows (1989):

> In the first instance "market value" was ineffective because of the unreal assumption that both parties get to a bargaining position. In ordinary circumstances the property would be advertised for sale. However, it wouldn't be if the seller wasn't keen on a sale; but let's assume there comes a meeting and one says to the other "so you want to sell." The other says "yes, but I don't care if I do and I don't care if I don't"—this comment equates with "willing but not anxious." The first retorts "I too want to buy but, I don't care if I do and I don't care if I don't"—the buyer displays too that he is willing but not anxious. The first quickly observes little enthusiasm for a transaction and suggests "let's have a cup of coffee" and the second agrees. They proceed to discuss anything but the property. The result is social discourse but no sale.

A definition that produces a circumstance not resulting in a sale is of little use and, as Graaskamp would have it, fatally flawed. As any sales person will attest, the market doesn't work this way. One party, at least, must be motivated strongly enough to cause the transaction to take place. In land transactions the ideals are seldom approached of "buyer and seller each acting prudently, knowledgeably, . . . , and assuming that neither is under undue duress," the basis of a widely accepted definition espoused in *The Appraisal of Real Estate* and the well-known text of the American Institute of Real Estate Appraisers (1987). Some of the required assumptions or conditions may prevail, for either the seller or the buyer, but usually not in equal proportion to each party.

The contemporary approach to value follows a specific logic that examines the property in its surroundings to determine its most probable use. The most probable use then dictates the most probable buyer, which in turn will directly impact the most probable price for the property.

Graaskamp identified with Ratcliff's definition: "The most probable price is that selling price which is most likely to emerge from a transaction involving the subject property if it were to be exposed for sale, in the current market, for a reasonable time, at terms of sale which are currently predominant for properties of the subject type."[3] Graaskamp and his disciples tried valiantly to adjust the thinking of the appraisal profession in the United States to adopt most probable price, a definition that takes the realities of a marketplace into account.

The widespread favor accorded the original market value definition attracted notable detractors, including Ratcliff, in the 1960s (1963). Even more appeared in the 70s and 80s but the original definition could not be replaced. The best that could be achieved was acceptance by the American Institute of Real Estate Appraisers of a definition that employed the words *most probable price* but gave only lip service to its primary provisions. In the eighth edition of their *Appraisal of Real Estate* (American Institute of Real Estate Appraisers, 1983), some reliance was placed on the Ratcliffian definition, from whence the words *most probable price* arose. Although Graaskamp tolerated this new definition,[4] he was riled by what he saw as "a travesty on the work of modern theorists and a deliberate attempt to confuse or negate the implied criticism of traditional ways by contemporary analysis." In the ninth edition of the *Appraisal of Real Estate*, the probable price idea remained mixed with some of the incongruities of the original definition (1987). Rumour has it that Graaskamp, who prior to its publication had reason to believe the battle won, was sufficiently disgusted to give thought to driving his wheelchair and 250 pound frame back and forth on it like a smoker pirouetting on a spent cigarette.[5]

In spite of his failure to succeed entirely, Graaskamp's contemporaries regard the inroads (as an advocate of Ratcliff's most probable price idea) on the appraisal profession, as monumental (Ballard, 1989). Universal acceptance may soon prevail to the point where most probable price will be accorded the same dignity as its predecessor because, according to Ballard (1989), even the courts are attracted to the logic of the definition. An emerging wave of credibility has come in the form of support by recent writers in *The Appraisal Journal*, such as Thair (1988) and Pearson (1988), both of whom discussed and applauded the work of Ratcliff and (to a lesser extent) Graaskamp in their grapplings with differentiation of contemporary and traditional methods of appraisal. The contemporary process assumes the use of most probable price.

Graaskamp was, in our view, the dean of a chorus of intellectuals pursuing substantial change in the definition and practice of assessing "market value." The Wisconsin school under Ratcliff invented the contemporary approach that Graaskamp articulated and practiced. An example of its use is provided by Robbins (1987). Wendt and Kinnard Jr. have gone down the same path, and their role in the process is discussed by Pearson (1988).

Problems with the Appraisal Industry

One of the strengths of real estate education under Graaskamp was his passion to make students aware of what was logical and proper in appraisal practice. He expected high standards of report presentation, and his

1978 publication *The Appraisal of 25 North Pinckney Street* was a demonstration of what he thought was appropriate (Graaskamp, 1978). To make the case of good vs. bad practice he often referred to examples of failure by appraisers in practice gained from his experience in the consulting firm he established, Landmark Research. A classic of these examples is as follows:

> Citing poor appraisal practice as one of the reasons for a spectacular failure of a real estate securitization enterprise, he wryly alluded, in the following terms, to the "very modern um method"[6] of appraisal employed. The investment banker who had a vested interest in getting the highest price estimation did the initial income projections while an accounting firm did a careful audit of expense projections. The two reports were given to an appraiser with a cover note to the effect that "if the income and expenses are what is projected in the reports, what is the value?" Subsequently, a credit rating agency enquired as to possible bias but was countered with: "the appraisal was independent because the appraiser could have said he didn't like either of the projections, but he didn't. Therefore, the appraisal is independent." The appraiser, later informed of this exchange, retorted "hey, wait a minute. I don't remember it being presented that way but even if it had been and I had raised my voice I would have been fired and another appraiser would have been appointed in my place. To make matters worse, I wouldn't have got any more work from that firm. Besides, my report did outline the limitations of where the income and expenses came from. Under the circumstances, I did all I could."

About four years prior to this episode Graaskamp, apparently well versed in other examples of this practice, wrote that "institutional customers subvert appraisal sophistry to create the appearance of independent objectivity for subjective, self-serving decisions" (Graaskamp and Dilmore, 1983). He knew what was happening and tried valiantly to fix it.

Why, asked Graaskamp, will a lender pay 1% of value to protect a property from fire damage but will not pay 1% to ensure the property will be sufficiently leased-up to reach rental levels required to make the investment profitable? He then concluded something must be awry and asserted that lenders were more concerned about obtaining a fee for making a loan than in ensuring the long-term viability of the project and ultimate payback of the loan. This view is understandable, for the payback is usually 15 to 30 years into the future and out of mind for current lenders. Let someone else worry about repayment seems to be a commonplace attitude. To quote Graaskamp (1988b) again: "The appraisal process has become . . . subverted by the investment industry that is protecting the fees of the loan officer rather than the funds of the saver"!

Graaskamp continually mixed and engaged in discourse with appraisal and real estate practitioners. In the 1970s and 1980s by way of lectures to students (and others), he predicted doom for the appraisal industry unless they cleaned up their act.[7] The doom was manifested when a government-appointed subcommittee, headed by Congressman Barnard, reported (the Barnard Report) that 10% to 40% of the $420 million loss (in 1985) from the Veterans Administration loan guarantee program was due to inaccurate or dishonest appraisals. Appraisal abuses were detected as well in all major financial markets, including saving and loans, banks, credit unions, the Federal Housing Authority, private mortgage insurers, Fannie Mae, Freddie Mac, and mortgage-backed securities. For example, collateral overvaluations of $3 billion were found in 25% of the loans made by federally insured saving and loans. Furthermore, the Federal Deposit Insurance Corporation (FDIC) found evidence of appraisal malpractice in thirty institutions in the early 1980s that resulted in court actions. In addition, losses of between $750 million and $1 billion were found to be due to appraisal malpractice when in-depth investigations were made of four separate financial institutions (Barnard Report, 1986). Empirical evidence for Graaskamp's point of view continues to mount as the savings and loan debacle unfolds.

Where the Blame Lies

The Barnard Report hit hard. Part of the problem it outlined could be attributed to "client advocacy appraising," requiring the production of figures to "make the deal work." Pliable appraisers stayed in business by virtue of a compliant lending industry prepared to lend on the nod of an appraiser, who typically was a member of a fragmented and undisciplined profession. Only one third of the 200,000 appraisers nationwide had affiliations with highly regarded professional groups. Even within these groups disciplinary proceedings against 1600 in one year resulted in just 40 suspensions (Barnard Report, 1986).

Graaskamp believed that users of appraisals were major culprits in the demise of the industry. Conflict of interest between the lender's desire to make a profit from loan origination fees and a need to protect against the long-term prospect of a defaulting loan drives the need for outside regulation. As Graaskamp describes in his testimony for the 1987 Appraisal Reform Act:

> "They [appraisers] are encouraged to do that [hide behind hypothetical assumptions] by a lending fraternity that is antiappraisal. An appraisal can cool

the deal as far as the lending officer is concerned and there is considerable bias against the appraiser unless he is a controllable appraiser. That is a word the major bank lending institutions use all the time . . . an appraiser should be controllable. It is exactly the opposite of the function that he is supposed to perform" (Graaskamp, 1988a).

Graaskamp repeated the point in 1988 (Scott, 1988). The lender can control by "shopping the appraisal" to find an appraiser willing to provide the desired value, or the lender can threaten to withhold payment for a lowball appraisal. Or, as small appraisal shops fear, the lender can threaten to cut off future business if a value is not high enough to make a given loan.

The appraisal process itself is also at fault. To illustrate, let's turn to some of the Graaskamp maxims. An appraisal is a "highly stylized report which answers nobody's question."[8] In written work he preferred to call it a fictional feasibility.[9] An appraisal has to satisfy the most probable buyer concept represented by a class of persons. Feasibility is, by contrast, to satisfy an individual. A statement about value (the result of an appraisal) is only one part of the decision making process concerning real estate. Appraised value is unlikely to be the only answer or piece of information required in a question about real estate. The question is more likely to be at what price the property will attract buyers. Even at its simplest, such a question has much more substance than can be answered by a mere quotation of an expected price. An appraisal is done by "a generalist and his product perhaps establishes the parameters within which a project could work, but it needs confirmation by a specialist in order to determine if it *will* work" (Graaskamp, 1976a).

Thus, for Graaskamp an appraisal was of little use in its own right. Appraisal was just one part of a process to answer a question about real estate. Depending on its purpose, the bottom-line figure can vary widely. At its best, appraisal is a blunt tool in the process of judging whether to lend money on a real estate project.

Finally, outright fraud, mismanagement, and political corruption were also major causes of the losses in many savings and loan institutions and banks. In a "network of experienced swindlers," losses were exacerbated by "hyperaggressive developers and dealmakers who saw thrifts as giant cash cows ready to be milked" (Adams, 1990). Some of the "appraisers who jacked up their estimates of land values to accommodate land flips" (Pilzer and Dietz, 1989) have been prosecuted. Their culpability as partner/consultants in the "row upon row of empty office buildings and shopping centres" (Pilzer and Dietz, 1989) at least carries with it a suspicion of poor appraisal practice.

Bearing in mind these findings, it is easy to understand why, aside from his passion to have appraisal organizations adopt a rigorous (yet pragmatic) definition of value, Graaskamp was possessed with a desire to strengthen the system under which appraisers worked. He was unforgiving in his quest to prevent blatant collusion, bias, and malfeasance in appraisal practice.

Support in his quest has surfaced in other parts of the world. Whipple (1990), for example, cites examples of malpractice from the United States, England, Canada, and Australia. Whipple implies that misunderstanding of the client's position and incompetence in application of professional principles (leading to an undermining of appraiser credibility) was the biggest problem in Australia; and, in the several countries he took examples from, the problems were remarkably similar to those outlined by Graaskamp for the United States.

Recommendations for Reform

Notwithstanding the effect investigations and subsequent revelations might have on some colleagues who relied on the industry for campaign funds, the Barnard committee proclaimed that regulation of the appraisal and lending institutions was essential. Federally backed loans must be based on true market values, they asserted. Their concerns spawned the Real Estate Appraisal Reform Act of 1987 to regulate the appraisal industry (H.R. 365, 1987).

Earlier federal attempts at solving the problems with appraisal were contained in Federal Home Loan Bank Board (FHLBB) Memorandums R41a, R41b, and R41c.[10] The memorandums required lenders to be more responsible for hiring and supervising the appraisal process, and to be partly culpable for faulty appraisals. Care in choosing appraisers and analyzing the reports, it was supposed, would improve standards. Scuttling of speculative projects and concomitant control of some overbuilding, as a result, was seen by Graaskamp (1987b) as one of the major advantages of this sort of legislation.

Intense lobbying by the real estate appraisal and brokerage industry resulted in the original R41 regulations being replaced by a system requiring "management of insured institutions... to develop and implement prudent appraisal policies and procedure" (Federal Home Loan Bank Board, 1987). Graaskamp saw the system as a poor substitute for federal legislation. The chagrin and frustration endured by Graaskamp (and others) when the campaign for making lenders and their boards of directors responsible for actions about appraisal practice slipped away (when R41c was rescinded in 1987) did not deter his efforts. He continued with his advocacy for a system wherein lenders, as fiduciaries, would be held responsible (in part) for acting on appraisals. He vented at least some of his invective on the chairman of the FHLBB for rescinding of R41c.[11]

Graaskamp and the Aftermath of R41

With the R41 series gone, Barnard, Graaskamp, and others began a crusade attempting to right some of the structural problems causing the appraisal profession to go astray. Graaskamp criticized appraisal organizations. "Indeed, the status quo of the members in the short run is an underlying cause in the appraisal organizational reluctance to research or advocate significant redefinition, refinement or endorsement of newer methods. Without heavy pressure from important customer groups to adapt alternative methods, there is a natural inertia of appraisers" (1986, p. 30). Graaskamp went on to explain a number of factors that made the appraisal fraternity outmoded. Firstly, the financial cost of changing the existing status quo, as well as fear that the effort to reeducate the public would detract from the mystique and status of the appraisal designation. The professional MAI certification does not explicitly define what a "certified MAI is certified to do." The frequency of the use of the expressions "professional judgment" and "gut feeling" within the appraisal fraternity should at the very least engender a fear that technical skills are subverted by jumping to conclusions without search and analysis of supporting information. The client suffers under the illusion that the credential itself allows for such a conclusion.

Secondly, change usually shifts expertise and earning power from old to young. Many appraisers are older and do not have the skills needed to carry out a contemporary analysis. Younger appraisers are computer literate and have the ability to run sensitivity analysis and projections to play the "what if" game necessary to accurately come to grips with probable value. Older members, who hold the most influential positions with the major professional organizations, seem to be content with Marshall and Swift cost analyses and direct capitalization.

Thirdly, marketing of services becomes much more difficult and expensive if rules are changed. New valuation methods and techniques rule out the possibility of reliance on the old-boy network. Many established firms would have to take on specialities and differentiate themselves in the competitive marketplace. This change would impinge directly on the price of appraisal services.

Fourthly, Graaskamp cites the rising costs of insurance and therefore costs of running the appraisal business as the analyses becomes more complex. Finally, he delivers a heavy broadside at the appraisal organization administrators who, he claimed, are not committed to change the industry or lack the understanding necessary to change the appraisal process.

Dealing with client advocacy appraisals is clearly difficult; appraisers need to stay solvent and some care more or less about ethics (just like any other professional). Those who put ethics above everything will hear, or more likely will have heard already, what Graaskamp has declared. Others will be partially receptive or ignore it all. Righting the wrongs of the latter group should be the concern of professional organizations. However, all of the reasons for slow reform of the whole process that Graaskamp articulated are probably less important in the system than the client's vested interest—client pressures corrupt and in some cases work without overt appraiser malfeasance. Appraisers simply apply consistent methods that give high or low results. Optimists are hired by developers, pessimists by banks. Reform to fix fiery optimists and frigid pessimists and make them all lukewarm is a supreme challenge.

A possible compromise might be a change in the appraiser's role or context in real estate analysis. Joint employment by all parties to a transaction, together with a contract to shift loss for faulty appraisals directly to the party at fault, without too much opportunity for lengthy litigation, may help. The system must also go high on ethics and technical competence—the Graaskamp path. Changing methods or employment context will be insufficient by themselves.

Need for Appraisal Reform

In lectures on appraisal reform, Graaskamp argued for federal legislation. State legislation and appraisal supervision of the kind presently in progress (FIRREA of 1989) would be unsuccessful in changing the appraisal industry, he asserted. Fragmentation of the industry would mitigate against agreement on standards, sanctions, and the means of financing reforms. The weakness of the industry could (and would) be exploited by organizations with a vested interest in preserving the status quo of fragmentation and disarray. In particular, the National Association of Realtors want no appraiser to be in a position to "kill the deal with a lowball appraisal." Furthermore, with each state responsible for their own programs, the solutions are bound to be different.

The merger of the Society of Real Estate Appraisers and the American Institute of Real Estate Appraisers (including the separation of the latter from the National Association of Realtors) would have pleased Graaskamp. He was frustrated with those who advocated maintenance of the ties between the Institute (appraisers) and the National Association of Realtors (dealmakers), and saw this relationship as a major conflict of interest.

The federal government, through its agencies (Federal Deposit Insurance Corporation and Federal Savings and Loan Insurance Corporation), provides guarantees for the loans. Graaskamp reasoned that he who pays the piper should call the tune and thus the federal government has good grounds for an interest in appraisal regulation. Vickory (1990) is clearly worried about the mechanics of control where the federal government has a role but not as sole proprietor and, like Graaskamp, sees pitfalls in fragmentation of the industry and the prospect of state level certification.

Conclusions

Taking the lead provided by R. U. Ratcliff, Professor James A. Graaskamp advocated the use of most probable price in place of market value. We think that the apparent reversion to the old market value definition is only a hiccup in the process of widespread acceptance of most probable price as the foundation for appraisal. Graaskamp was one of its unrelenting advocates. It's one thing to outline an idea; it's another to put it into practice. He was a champion of the cause.

The subject matter of appraisal reform suited his notion of a social conscience. That an appraiser should be even partially "controllable" by the loan origination officer was an anathema. However, if Graaskamp was right in that an appraisal is a highly stylized report that answers nobody's question, and thus at best a blunt tool for judging whether to lend money on a project, who can blame the lending industry for placing small importance on the notion. Acceptance of this concept by the profession would have had a cathartic effect on the whole industry. That this acceptance was not to be, nor anything like it, was sufficient motivation for Graaskamp's advocacy of a major reformation. Reform was to be achieved by federal legislation to control appraisers, on the one hand, and to control the way in which appraisal information is employed by the lending industry, on the other hand. The concept would make directors of financial institutions liable for the excesses of loan officers.

Graaskamp was aware that changes would have substantial effects on existing appraisal businesses—retraining, costs of insurance, etc. The extra costs the lending industry incurred would, he implied, be more than offset by savings on bad debts. However, in the absence of motivation to use other techniques, appraisers have tried to stay in business by keeping appraisal costs low enough so that people would buy their services. Attempts by innovators to provide better services that some enlightened clients wanted has become a tug of war between providing useful additional information and satisfying a demand for services at the lowest cost. Historically, lower costs seem to have won.

Graaskamp, in Wisconsin, where social issues seem more important than in other places, seemed like a solitary voice. He was among the few who made the first move in the appraisal reform battle. While appraisers were in no position to do him great harm, they managed to ignore a very loud voice. Some did listen, however. One only had to count the number of days he spent on lecture tours to realize that he had a large and enthusiastic audience. That he was, and continues to be, hard to ignore is momentum enough for the Graaskamp/Ratcliff contemporary appraisal analysis to prevail.

Graaskamp saw everything in rational terms. "That doesn't make sense" or "that doesn't compute" were favorite expressions. He thought logic and maximizing social benefits should prevail over self-interest, greed, laziness, and ignorance. He thought truth would win in the end. But vested interests and politics do often overcome truth and justice. Thus for Graaskamp's ideas to prevail, the battle must go far beyond a mere clash of ideas and become a clash of money, power, organization, and economic interests. Graaskamp needs a Franklin Delano Roosevelt who will organize natural constituencies of appraisal reform (for example, lenders hurt by bad appraisals, government agencies, Congress, and others) into a force powerful enough to overcome organized interests favoring the made-as-instructed philosophy.

On the other hand, given the epistemological difficulties involved, a possible rather gloomy scenario is that the Graaskamp method may not yet be a great practical improvement on the three-approach cookie cutter. Maybe we need to rely less on appraisals. Perhaps appraisals will come to be more widely recognized as inherently unreliable and paid for accordingly (dimestore appraisals may command dimestore prices). In recognition of this problem, appraisers may out of self-interest begin to insist on standards and quality, and become serious about punishing malfeasance. If such a scenario happens, proper reform is way down the track, and the Graaskamp momentum halts.

More likely, Graaskamp's vision of the key role of the appraiser as a defender of social capital by means of information incorporating expertise, logic, and integrity will win respect for a revitalized profession. In that case, his was step one—delineating problems and designing technical solutions. Step two will be organizing and implementing his ideas. What Graaskamp thought of as a technical, intellectual problem may be more successfully attacked as a political, institutional change problem. Graaskamp seems to have recognized this dichotomy towards the end of his life in his involvement with Barnard and the appraisal reform movement.

Graaskamp's professional life was filled with trying to change the way the real estate industry viewed the appraisal and valuation component of the real estate process. With new legislation based on state certification and fragmentation of control (somewhat less than the ideal Graaskampian solution) just taking effect, the future is cloudy. Complete federal control, Graaskamp asserted, was the far superior approach.

Acknowledgments

We wish thank Professor Tom Whipple, Professor Kerry Vandell, Max Kummerow, and anonymous reviewers for their intellectual critique, and Genny Mittnatch for editorial assistance. Jean Davis, Graaskamp's longtime partner, deserves a special mention. She provided incisive comments on an early manuscript and access to Landmark Research documents, essential in the preparation of this paper.

Notes

1. Graaskamp, James Arnold—born Milwaukee, Wisconsin, 1933—died Madison, Wisconsin, 1988. Acute poliomyelitis at age 17 confined him to life in a wheelchair. Studied literature at Rollins College, finance at Marquette, gained a Ph.D. in risk management and urban land economics at the University of Wisconsin—Madison. Over twenty years as Chairman of the Department of Real Estate and Urban Land Economics, University of Wisconsin—Madison. He was stoic (moving without use of limbs was "a materials handling problem"), sharp witted, excelled as a raconteur (his father's advice—"never take a house with a back yard bigger than a wife can mow"), and a captivating speaker. He had a deep love and concern for the natural and built environment, and was excited by the challenge of real estate development. His trademark was that man first created space-time product (real estate) by rolling a rock in front of a cave. He wrestled tirelessly with analytical techniques

in real estate and was a constant advocate for improvement in the appraisal process. Aptly known as "Chief," the size of his tribe is his legion of success.

2. Graaskamp, J. A. in Scott (1988).

3. The definition given was an "unpublished" version used by Graaskamp in a lecture entitled "Pension Fund Real Estate Valuation Issues," given in San Fransisco on 11/11/85, which was originally provided by Richard U. Ratcliff in a speech about his book *Valuation for Real Estate Decisions* (the book, long since out of print as a separate volume, is included in Graaskamp, J. A. ed. *Ratcliff Readings on Real Estate and its Economic Foundations*. Madison, WI: Landmark Research, ca. 1980).

4. Evidence that Graaskamp accepted the definition is provided in a paper he presented to the Urban Land Institute (October 22, 1986) entitled "Forces Working to Revitalize Appraisal Techniques," wherein he displays the eighth edition definition as Exhibit 2.

5. If Graaskamp's reaction to the language on Market Value seems inapropriate, the reader is invited to look at the pages in question (16–24) in the *Appraisal of Real Estate* (ninth edition). A reviewer mentioned that upon first reading of our paper thought it an over-reaction. However, on contemplation (and re-reading), the section in question he described it as a "waffling invitation to abuse" and came to regard Graaskamp's reaction as rather mild.

6. From an audio tape (Graaskamp, 1987a). The words *very modern, um method* is a verbatim quote—actually there was long pause between the words *modern* and *method*, indicating that he was trying to find a more appropriate way of describing it.

7. While the emphasis in this paper is on appraisal, at least some of the problem is associated with the structure of the finance industry. As one of the reviewers pointed out, Graaskamp taught real estate lending as a risk management process where each decision maker had to set up pleasure (satisfaction of the borrower for possession of the property, for example), pain (sanctions for default), and bail-out (protection of capital where default leads to the sale) options (Graaskamp, 1976c). With the advent of private mortgage insurers and securitization, the lenders have mitigated their risk and still kept a portion of the return to obtain almost a "free lunch." The reviewer goes on (paraphrased) . . . part of the problem with the lending fraternity is that the ultimate risk bearer, the mortgage insurance company, is not choosing or compensating the appraiser. This leads to moral hazard problems where the lender, developer, or investment banker dictates the value but bears little risk associated with making the loan.

8. M. Eppli. Personal recollection of the Graaskamp philosophy in 1989. Since 1987 a Ph.D. student and teaching assistant in the real estate program at the University of Wisconsin–Madison.

9. There are many examples of his use of this expression, one of which is in Graaskamp (1976a).

10. FHLBB Memorandum #R41-b "Appraisal Policy and Procedure of Insured Associations and Service Corporations" (March 12, 1982); #R41-c "Revised Memorandum" (September 1986). January 7, 1988, R41-c was rescinded and replaced by revised appraisal standards that were mandated by the Competitive Equality Banking Act. The Real Estate Reform Act of 1987 was eventually modified and turned into the Financial Institutions Reform and Recovery Act of 1989 (FIRREA).

11. J. A. Graaskamp. Letter to Mr. M. Danny Wall, Chairman FHLBB (December 14, 1987) and D. W. Dochow. Letter to Dr James A. Graaskamp, Chairman, Real Estate and Urban Land Economics (January 13, 1987). Copy can be found in The James A. Graaskamp Collection of Teaching Materials, University of Wisconsin Archives.

12. At the time, Bolan was vice president of Real Estate Research Corporation and Hovde was awaiting confirmation as a member of the Federal Home Loan Bank Board.

References

Adams, J. R. *The Big Fix: Inside the S&L Scandal*. New York: John Wiley and Sons, 1990, pp. 40–1.
American Institute of Real Estate Appraisers. *The Appraisal of Real Estate*, 9th ed. Chicago: American Institute of Real Estate Appraisers, 1987, p. 19.
American Institute of Real Estate Appraisers. *Appraisal of Real Estate*, 8th ed., 1983.
Babcock, F. M. *The Appraisal of Real Estate*. New York: Macmillan Company, 1927.
Babcock, F. M. *The Valuation of Real Estate*. New York: McGraw Hill, 1932.
Ballard, C. Speech to the University of Wisconsin—Madison Real Estate Alumni, Concourse Hotel, Madison, Wisconsin, October 14, 1989.
Barnard Report. "Impact of Appraisal Problems on Real Estate Lending, Mortgage Insurance, and Investment in the Secondary Market." *48th Report by the Committee on Government Operations*, 1986.
Bolan, Lewis and Donald Hovde, in C. Blaine "He's teacher, master of real estate's bottom line." *USA Today* (May 31, 1983).[12]
Bonbright, J. C. *The Valuation of Property*, Vol 1. Charlottesville, VA: The Michie Company, 1937 (1965 reprint), pp. 153–7.
Curtis, Alvin L. "Chief Graaskamp at the center of a national real estate network." *Milwaukee Sentinel* (November 12, 1985).
Eisen, Marc. "Graaskamp's graduates fly high." *The Capital Times* (Madison, WI; July 25, 1987).
Federal Home Loan Bank Board. "Appraisal Policies and Practices of Insured Institutions and Service Corporations." *Final Rule* (December 21, 1987).
Financial Institutions Reform, Recovery, and Enforcement Act of 1989.
Graaskamp, J. A. "A Rational Approach to Feasibility Analysis." *Appraisal Journal* (October, 1972), 513–21.
Graaskamp, J. A. "Address by Dr. James A. Graaskamp to a meeting of Lambda Alpha on March 19, 1976a. Acceptance speech for membership of Lambda Alpha."
Graaskamp, J. A. "Critical Review of Appraisal and Feasibility Reports in Support of Capital Funding Decisions." Princeton MAI Conference, June 10, 1976b.
Graaskamp, J. A. "An Approach to Real Estate Finance Education by Analogy to Risk Management Principles," in *Essays in Honour of Richard U. Ratcliff and Paul F. Wendt* Vancouver: Urban Land Economics Division, Faculty of Commerce and Business Administration, University of British Columbia, September, 1976c.

Graaskamp, J. A. *The Appraisal of 25 N. Pinckney: A Demonstration Case for Contemporary Appraisal Methods.* Madison, WI: Landmark Research, 1978.

Graaskamp, J. A. "Contemporary Issues and Methods for Appraising Commercial Properties." Tempe, Arizona. Notes on a seminar to Arizona Chapter of the American Institute of Real Estate Appraisers. October 9th, 1985a.

Graaskamp, J. A. "Contemporary Issues and Methods for Appraising Commercial Properties." A seminar presentation to the Northwest Centre for Professional Education, St. Regis Sheraton, New York City, September 26–27, 1985b.

Graaskamp, J. A. "Institutional Constraints on, and Forces for, Evaluation of Appraisal Precepts and Practices." *The Real Estate Appraiser and Analyst* (Spring 1986).

Graaskamp, J. A. Real Estate 551. Madison: University of Wisconsin–Madison, Audio Tape 14.1, side B, 1987a.

Graaskamp, J. A. Footnote from the transcript of the presentation to Committee Hearings on H.R. 3675, "The Real Estate Appraisal Reform Act of 1987" (February 25, 1988a), 53–4.

Graaskamp, J. A. "In Support of H.R. 3675 to Organize and Consolidate Federal Matters Relating to Appraisals in Legislation to be Cited as Real Estate Reform Act of 1987." Written statement to the Committee on Government Operations, 100th Congress, First Session (February 25, 1988b).

Graaskamp, J. A. and Gene Dilmore. Unpublished manuscript of a book, labeled as Chapter 1, (ca. 1983).

Graaskamp, J. A. and G. Dilmore. "Introduction to the Appraisal Process." Unpublished manuscript, Chapter 1, pp. 7–11 (date unknown).

Graaskamp, J. A. "Impact of Changing Appraisal Regulation on the Developer." Milwaukee Chapter Organizational Meeting: National Association of Industrial and Office Parks. Speech notes (Sept 29, 1987b).

H.R. 3675. Real Estate Appraisal Reform Act of 1987 (November 20, 1987).

Kerch, Steve. "UW—Madison's Chief is a real power in the land" *Chicago Tribune* (November 15, 1987), 2H.

Kroll, Mark and Charles Smith. "Real Estate Development and the MBA Degree." *Journal of Real Estate Development* 3, (Winter 1988), 30–4.

Pearson, Thomas. "Education for Professionalism: A Common Body of Knowledge for Appraisers." *Appraisal Journal* 56, 4 (October 1988), 435–50.

Pilzer, P. Z. and R. Dietz. *Other Peoples Money: The Inside Story of the S&L Mess.* New York: Simon and Schuster, 1989.

Ratcliff, R. U. "A Restatement of Appraisal Theory." *Wisconsin Commerce Reports* 7: 1 (1963a).

Ratcliff, R. U. "A Restatement of Appraisal Theory." *Wisconsin Commerce Reports* 7: 1 (1963b), 1–14.

Ratcliff, R. U. *Valuation for Real Estate Decisions.* Santa Cruz, CA: Democrat Press, 1972.

Robbins, Michael L. "The Valuation of Large Scale Natural Landscapes Using Contemporary Appraisal Theory." *Appraisal Journal* 55: 2 (April, 1987).

Scott, M. "Changing Appraisal System Costly, Painful." *Seattle Daily Journal of Commerce* (3/18/88) 95, 64.
Real Estate Alumni surveys, 1982 and 1991.
Thair, Steven. "What's the Use?—Most Probable use Versus Highest and Best Use." *Appraisal Journal* 56: 2 (April 1988), 190–9.
US News and World Report (March 19, 1990).
Vickory, Frank A. "Regulating Real Estate Appraisers: The Role of Fraudulent and Incompetent Real Estate Appraisals in the S&L Crisis and the FIRREA Solution." *Real Estate Law Journal* 19: 3 (1990), 17.
Whipple, R. T. M. "Valuations: A Problem Solving Imperative." *New Zealand Valuers Journal* (June 1990), 14–24.

III MARKET ANALYSIS AND TRADE AREA DELINEATION

9 A FOUR-SQUARE DESIGN FOR RELATING THE TWO ESSENTIAL DIMENSIONS OF REAL ESTATE MARKET STUDIES

Dowell Myers and Kenneth Beck

Introduction

Real estate market analysis suffers from two major problems. One is the relative absence of usable data. The other is the relative lack of rigorous and defensible methods for analyzing the limited data that are available. In fact, these two problems are closely linked because the deficiency in methods both leads to underuse of the available data and also misdirects efforts at data collection. Sounder methods would help to reduce the problem of inadequate data.

For these underlying reasons, in recent years the quality of market studies in real estate has been widely criticized. Featherston (1986) laments the lack of attention to laws of supply and demand. Chapman

---

A previous version of this paper was presented at the annual meeting of the American Real Estate Society in Lake Tahoe, March 30, 1990. The authors acknowledge the helpful comments of the anonymous reviewers.

(1987) and Clark (1989) have called attention to the inadequacies of local demographic data that market analysts rely upon with so little scrutiny. Clapp (1987), among others, points to the excessive amount of "boiler plate," which he defines as all that data packaged in market reports that never enters materially into the analysis. Messner et al. (1977) note the underemphasis given the future in market and feasibility studies; all such studies should be forecasts for properties. Joining the criticisms by Clapp and Messner et al., Myers (1990a) criticizes the overemphasis on collection of current data that often substitutes for a forecast analysis pertinent to properties.

At the most basic level, it is clear that market studies suffer from inherently weak and indefensible logic. A teaching device often used by the late James Graaskamp was to have students diagram the analytical flow of feasibility studies drawn from respected industry sources. Forced to document the connections running through a report, invariably students would discover fuzzy portions, blank spots, and gaps requiring heroic assumptions and flying leaps. A reasonable observer might conclude that the excessive boiler plate and sheer weight of many market studies, together with the absence of a clear outline or analytical summary, is used often to disguise poor quality analysis and weak logic.

The present paper aims at the heart of the logic problem by offering a rigorous and defensible structure for analysis. We believe that sound logic requires the market study to address two essential problems that are inherently related: first, how to span the gap between current or historic market data and the future of the market; and second, how to define a linkage between the market and an individual property. From our observations of practice, the great majority of market studies have failed to adequately address these two fundamental problems; hence, the studies have been unable to relate a rational, coherent, and logically defensible analytical flow.

We will describe a four-square design for addressing the two interrelated problems essential to most market studies. The design is illustrated with regard to two apartment complexes proposed for acquisition in Austin, Texas. The specific model developed for this analysis employs a particular set of methods based on tabular scaling procedures introduced in Myers (1990b). These detailed methods will be only briefly described because our major emphasis is on the overall logic and structure of the four-square design. A number of alternative analytical procedures might serve well within the framework of the four-square design.

The Four-Square Design

The four-square design interacts the two fundamental aspects of market studies in a four-cell framework. This section describes the steps in the model and argues its preferability on logical grounds to the commonly employed procedures.

The Present–Future Problem

One key problem all market studies encounter is how to forecast a future outcome for a subject property when all of the market experience is in the present (or historical). Forecasting is essential because properties cannot be developed and brought to market overnight. Similarly, the present value of an existing property is based on an estimate of future returns. The problem is how to craft a future outcome from present data.

Lack of attention to forecasting has been identified as a major weakness of market and feasibility studies (Messner et al., 1977; Myers, 1990a). Analysts place excessive weight on collecting current information, perhaps in the vain hope that the answer can be looked up in a book or that it will somehow pop out if a large enough quantity of data is collected. At the very least, analysts may hope that a quantity of data will show they have done their homework. Clearly, however, ten pounds of current facts do not automatically yield an ounce of wisdom about the future.

The Macro–Micro Problem

The second key problem market studies must address is that most of our data are about the market, but we wish to analyze the prospects for a specific property. In some cases the proposed property does not even exist at present; in other cases the property exists, but all of the available market data and forecast information are marketwide. How do we relate this market wide data to the prospects for specific properties?

Appraisers address this problem by analyzing comparable properties deemed to be similar to the subject property. The recent history of these comparables is assumed to represent the subject property. The failing of this method is that it ignores the future by concentrating only on recent experience. Others seek to apply average market forecasts to all specific properties in a particular market area. The failing here is that this ignores the differential prospects facing specific properties.[1]

Solving the Two Problems in Combination

These two essential problems can be conceptualized as existing in a four-square framework that combines present–future and macro–micro dimensions, as portrayed in Figure 1. The challenge is that most of our data reside in the upper-left square, present macro, describing current and historical marketwide conditions. However, the goal of market studies is to reach the lower-right square, future micro, which describes the future prospects for a specific property.

Three parallel sets of data are required in each square. Supply data describe the characteristics of the subject property, comparables, and the market as a whole. (There is no need to forecast supply for the subject property itself.) Demand characteristics describe tenants in the subject or comparables, and in the market as a whole. The forecast of demand typi-

	PRESENT	FUTURE
MACRO (Market)	**Current & Historical:** Supply by Segment Demand Characteristics preferences income household types Absorption & Vacancies Rents & Value (cap rates)	**Market Forecasts:** Supply by Segment Demand employment growth population growth space needs Absorption & Vacancies Rents & Value (cap rates)
MICRO (Individual Properties)	**Subject Property and Comparables:** Unit Size & Quality Demand Characteristics preferences income type of tenant households Absorption & Vacancies Rents & Value (cap rates)	**Future Performance of Subject Property:** Demand Characteristics preferences income type of tenant households Absorption & Vacancies Rents & Value *GOAL*

Figure 1. Interrelating the Two Essential Dimensions of Market Studies.

cally reverts to different variables measuring growth in employment and population, and the projected space needs. Finally, a third set of variables joins supply and demand: absorption, vacancies, and market rents. The latter determines property value very closely through capitalization of gross income or net operating income (Mitchell and Bernes, 1990).

Every market study concocts some method for bridging the gaps defined in the four-square model. Most studies talk to some degree about issues related to all four squares, and relevant data may be presented for each square. However, the quantitative analysis that should tie together this information in an explicit model typically only utilizes data from one or two of the squares.

Some of the most common logical structures for relating the data are portrayed in Figure 2. The "appraiser's comparables" model takes in-

A. The Appraiser's Comparables Model

Appraisers estimate the value of a property based upon recent selling prices for a set of comparables. A direct connection is drawn between the recent experience and the near future, ignoring broader market trends and forecasts.

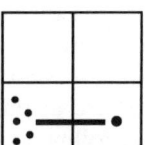

B. The Ideal Conditions Model

The analyst simply assumes that the property will operate with a given vacancy level and with given annual increases in rents. A method commonly employed in pro formas. No real data are used about current or forecasted conditions.

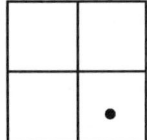

C. The Constant Conditions Model

Current market-wide conditions are assumed to apply to the subject property in the future. No forecast information is used

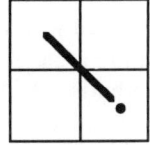

D. The Average Market Forecast Model

Average forecasts for the market as a whole are assumed to apply to the subject property. Information on segmentation or the current relation of the property to the market is not factored in.

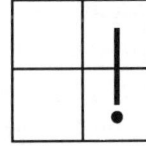

Figure 2. Common Logical Structures in Market Studies.

formation on recent sales for comparables and assesses the value of the subject property. This is a very limited form of forecast, as it fixes a present value as of a current date, but this value is assumed to reflect the future use expected to be derived from the property. In this model, no use is made of formal marketwide forecasts.

Another commonly employed model involves no analysis. The "ideal conditions" model simply assumes for the *pro forma* that the property will operate with a normal, expected vacancy and that it will experience a normal rate of annual rent increases. The "constant conditions" model is based on realistic market data, but assumes that current, average conditions in the market will hold constant and characterize the property in the future. No effort is made to factor in forecast information. The model simply leaps from the upper left to the lower right square. Finally, the "average market forecast" model takes information about expected market trends and applies these to the subject property. No information is factored in regarding the current relation of the property to the market (its relative vacancy rate, segmentation position, etc.).

These simple descriptions of the four common models focus on data that are actually tied into that model that yield the final result. Studies that follow any of the four procedures may well show additional information, and even discuss it, but often this is boiler plate that is not used in the quantitative model. Other logical procedures may well be used by different analysts. Each of these can likely be expressed as a sequence of steps between the four squares outlined here. What follows is the particular pathway recommended in this paper.

Six Steps in the Proposed Design

The pathway we recommend is outlined on Figure 3. This section focuses on the logic of the analytical flow. Later sections will describe the detailed methods used to implement the design and present a case illustration.

Step One: Identify the property to be analyzed, or identify properties that are similar to that proposed for construction. Virtually all market studies start with some idea of a target use. To make the study more relevant, this should be built into the model.

Step Two: Proceed immediately to collect available forecast information for the market. This is often the weak link in the chain, as the fewest resources are available, often in a very specific format. It is bet-

A FOUR SQUARE DESIGN

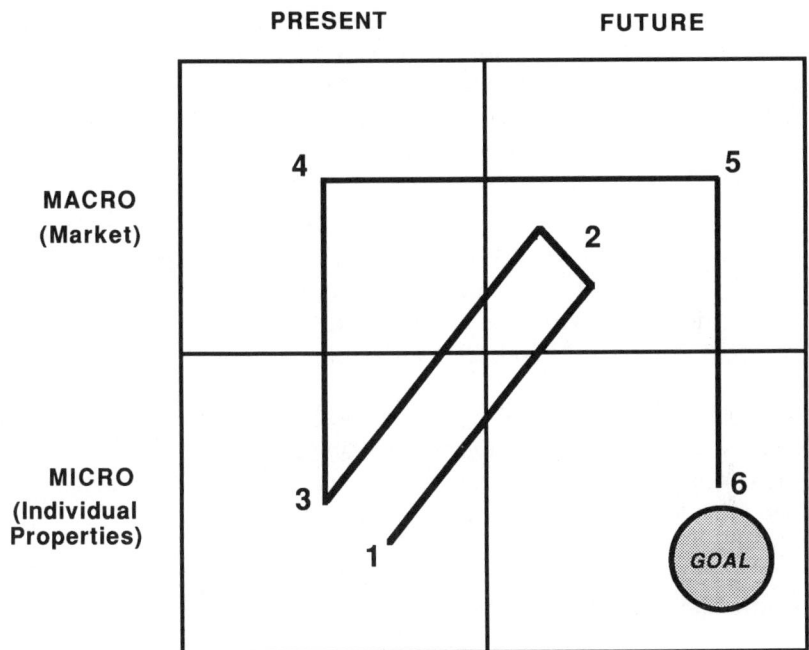

Figure 3. Recommended Four-Square Design for Linking the Two Essential Dimensions.

ter to build the whole analysis around the forecast data/method than to append the forecast task at the end after all data have been collected. This step should also consider how a forecast model will be structured with available data to link present and future conditions.

Step Three: Return to the subject property and measure it in terms that are compatible with the forecast data and model. For example, use the same categories and definitions as in the forecast information. The description and analysis of a currently observable property (or comparables) are far more adaptable than the forecast task, and so it should follow after we know the forecast constraints we must work within.

Step Four: Link the micro and macro levels in the present by relating the subject property (or comparable) to the market in which it competes. What are its capture rates for different segments of demand? How is it positioned?

Step Five: Project forward the market from the present to the future, using the previously identified forecast model. This should include both forecasted demand and supply. Implicitly this market forecast carries forward the subject property as well, and we will assume that its relative position holds constant, subject to the increases in demand or competing supply in each segment.

Step Six: Establish the implications of the forecasted market for the subject property. How will its previously established capture rates perform in the context of a changing array of competitors and a changing mix of demand? What are the implications for vacancies and tenant profiles? What is the implication for revenue streams?

The details of this model will be disclosed through an example that compares two apartment complexes in a single city. The model yields insights into how well each is likely to perform over time, suggesting which might be undervalued and which is the better investment.

Specific Methods Used in the Analysis

Before turning to the case illustration, it may prove helpful to preview some of the key steps in the methodology used for analysis and forecasting. There are three major sets of procedures: (1) scaling of tabular data in a "master matrix," (2) estimation of capture rates, and (3) forecasting future property conditions. A number of specific procedures might be used to carry out the logic of the four-square design. Although the methods we have selected make efficient use of available data for housing markets, we certainly do not claim that these are the only methods workable within the four-square framework. In particular, retail or office/industrial studies might require different specific methods.

The Master Matrix Strategy

We desire a segmented analysis for describing demand for the properties. The demographic method of segmentation (including an income dimension) has proven most useful in housing market studies. Although the most detailed studies have been carried out with national-level data, Myers (1987) shows how to bring this mode of analysis down to the level of the individual metropolitan area or county. The advantage of this segmentation strategy over popular alternatives is spelled out in Myers (1990b).

A master matrix of demand, classified by age, sex, marital status, income, and tenure can be defined from the most recently available Census data, 1980 in this case.[2] This matrix must then be updated to the present and forecasted to the future using available information. Following procedures outlined in Myers (1990b), we scale the matrix by new marginals describing population growth by age and sex. For example, each age row in the matrix is scaled up or down in proportion to the overall growth or shrinkage of that age group over the time period.

Adjustments for recent trends in owning/renting by each age group are made in a similar fashion. In addition, we adjust the master matrix for changes in income since 1980, taking account of both inflation and real income growth by age group. Further adjustments to the master matrix can be made for each available piece of information. The master matrix strategy is flexible enough to absorb increased levels of refinement should resources (data, time, or funds) permit. The default option is to assume that unadjusted dimensions have experienced no substantial change since the baseline period when the master matrix data were first collected.

Estimating Capture Rates

Capture rates for each tenant segment can be used to describe quantitatively a property's relative market position. The key assumption is that the differential attractiveness of a property is revealed by its relative capture of different tenant groups. Furthermore, we also assume that a property's capture rates today are the best evidence of tomorrow's market position, subject to new supply entering that niche.

Capture rates for each property may be calculated by comparing the number of tenants of each type with the total in the market. This calculation is carried out in a simple, yet elegant fashion by arraying the tenant profile of each property in the same categories as for the forecasted master matrix. We then simply divide each cell of the tenant matrix by the respective cell for the market (master) matrix. This yields a matrix of capture rates, by tenant characteristics, for the current year.

Market analysts have not made a practice of tracking capture rates over time. Time series data would yield more reliable estimates of future rates. Similarly, market analysts or property managers should closely monitor, and record, the annual fluctuation in turnover and residential mobility surrounding properties. This will provide needed information about trends in demand focused on specific properties.

Without these data, we propose an alternative strategy. Capture rates may be forecasted by forecasting how much new supply will be added to attract tenants of each type. Over time, the addition of new supply will progressively erode present capture rates, more in some categories than others. We will adjust the capture rates downward in each tenant segment according to the following formula:

$$C_{it_1} = C_{it_0} \times \frac{T_{it_0}}{T_{it_0} + T_{it_{0-1}}} \quad (1)$$

where C = capture rates, T = tenants, i = segments of demand, t_0 = current year, and t_1 = forecast year.

The effect of new construction is incorporated through the $T_{it_{0-1}}$ term. This construction forecast is drawn from sources outside this model. It is supposed to represent how many apartment units will likely be built, not necessarily how many units we think should be built. Total forecasted construction is then allocated to tenant segments according to recent patterns of occupancy of new construction. It is the relative increase of expected occupied units in each tenant segment that whittles away at the subject property's expected capture rate in each segment.

Forecasting Prospects for the Properties

The forecasted tenant profiles for each property are derived by multiplying the forecasted capture rates (by segment) for each property times the forecasted number of tenants in each segment of the master matrix. This yields an expected tenant profile for each property, expressed as the number of occupied units expected to hold tenants of different types. Note how the property is impacted by two forces. On the one hand, capture rates may fall significantly if new construction floods tenant segments targeted by the subject property. On the other hand, growth in tenant demand in particular segments might exceed the rate of supply increase, thus offsetting the lowered capture rates. However, if the character of market demand has shifted away from that targeted by the property, there will likely be fewer tenants in the property in the future. This negative shift can be absorbed as increased vacancies, or it could be offset by more aggressive marketing and a repositioning strategy employing increased amenities, lowered rents, or other strategies.

A property faced with dwindling demand in the future faces an uphill struggle against the odds, and this ought to be reflected in a loss of present value. Such a property will likely face declining revenues, due to increased vacancies or rent reductions, or increased expenses, due to more aggressive marketing, costs of installing amenities, etc. The purchase price of such a property should take account of its diminished future prospects, through a higher cap rate, but the forecast may not be known, and therefore not reflected in the current market valuation. Our method supplies an additional tool that may afford superior market insight.

Example of Two Apartment Complexes

The Texas housing market is beginning to show signs of recovery from the disasterous crash of the mid 1980s. The Austin market is particularly interesting for its strong long-term prospects. Unlike Houston, which is heavily based upon the oil industry, Austin has long relied on its stature as the capital of the state government and the home of the University of Texas. After 1980, Austin became widely regarded as the next Silicon Valley due to its capture of widely coveted research-and-development enterprises, such as MCC and Sematech. Unfortunately this recognition triggered an excessively optimistic boom in Austin immediately before the statewide crash. The sudden turnaround left Austin with one of the highest office and apartment vacancy rates in the nation. Data reported below show that permits for apartment construction plunged from just over 16,000 units in 1983 to an average of 438 units per year between 1987 and 1989.

Identifying the Subject Properties

Investors have been attracted back to the Austin market by the low prices being asked for existing projects and the absence of new construction. In the context of this market we wish to analyze the investment potential for two apartment complexes, hypothetical cases drawn from general data available for the market. Property A, offered at just over $7 million, has 280 units with an average size of 750 square feet, commanding rents of $0.50 per foot, and with a current vacancy rate of 12.1%. Property B, offered at $10.5 million, has 280 units of somewhat larger average size (950 square feet), commanding slightly higher rents of $0.55 per foot, and with a current vacancy rate of 8.2%. The asking price of each project is based on a cap rate of 10% applied to current net operating income. Which is the better long-term investment?

The four-square design provides an important means of shedding light on this question. Our methodology extracts information about the current tenant profile of each project and compares this to the projected future of the market. The end result is an assessment of the relative performance over time of each project.

Identifying Relevant Forecast Data

Once the properties are identified the four-square design calls for immediate search of available forecast data and methods. We have found only limited information for the Austin market: past trends in supply,[3] population forecast data by age and sex,[4] and a detailed matrix of housing consumer behavior for an earlier year.[5] Local information is lacking on other important trends since 1980, particularly with regard to income and tenure choice. For lack of any other data we make use of national data sources that identify trends in median income[6] and in homeownership rates by age[7] for the southern region of the nation. These data are not reported here for reasons of limited space.

We next selected a forecast methodology for updating the 1980 baseline matrix in correspondence to the information we have for 1989, and then forecasting this matrix to a future date that corresponds to the expected holding period for the properties. As described above, we utilize tabular scaling procedures to progressively adjust this master matrix of demand. The results of these procedures can then be used to help evaluate the subject properties.

Describing the Subject Properties

The importance of defining the forecast data so immediately is that we can now collect data for the subject properties that is consistent with the structure of the forecast data to be applied in a later step. The basic description of the two properties was revealed above; we now seek a more detailed description of their market position. Table 1 reports a tabulation of tenant characteristics of each property in 1989. The format of this tabulation is designed to correspond to that of the detailed master matrix that derives from the *Metropolitan Housing Characteristics* data for Austin (Tables A-3 and A-4). The only difference is that the household income has been tabulated in $10,000 dollar intervals, expressed in current (1989) dollars.

It is apparent that these two apartment projects are substantially different. Property A has most of its tenants under age 35, with relatively few married couples. The incomes of tenants in Property A are also generally lower than in Property B. The latter has somewhat older tenants and more married couples. The differences between the two properties are not extreme and reflect fairly typical tenant profiles, the one leaning toward characterization as a young-singles complex, and the other as an upscale rental complex. The larger size of apartments in Property B (950 square feet vs. 750 square feet) and the slightly higher rents per square foot ($0.55 vs. $0.50) are consistent with this difference in tenant profiles.

Segmentation Position of the Subject Properties

The next step is to define the properties' relation to the overall market. The most precise way of describing this relationship is to calculate the properties' capture rates of tenant demand in the market. The innovation here is that we calculate these capture rates separately for each tenant segment defined in the tenant profiles of Table 1. The tenant matrix is simply divided by the rental portion of the master matrix of market demand estimated for 1989.

Table 2 reports the estimated capture rates for the two properties. Property A has its highest capture of rental tenants in the age group under 25, for example, 0.77% of the market's unmarried male renters under age 25 with income between $20,000 and $29,999. In contrast, Property B has only a 0.22% capture in that segment, but instead exhibits higher capture rates in some of the older age groups and higher income segments.

Neighborhood submarkets are not explicity considered in this method. The necessary data are not available, but in any event the absence of a spatial submarket analysis is offset by the structure of the method. The capture rates proxy the effects of location. Properties near a university would capture a high share of young adults; those near low income areas would capture a high share of low income renters; and those in upscale neighborhoods would have higher capture rates of upscale renters. The neighborhood effects in these capture rates should be relatively stable, as the location of properties is fixed and the neighborhood demographics are unlikely to shift substantially in less than a decade. Of course, it would be

Table 1. Tenant Profiles

Household type	<$10,000	$10,000 to $19,999	$20,000 to $29,999	$30,000 to $39,999	$40,000 Plus	Total
A. Tenant profiles of subject property A						
Married						
Under 25	2	4	3	0	0	9
25–34	2	4	7	2	0	15
35–44	0	2	4	0	0	6
45–64	0	1	2	0	0	3
65 and over	0	0	0	0	0	0
Other male						
Under 25	6	18	14	8	5	51
25–34	3	16	20	12	6	57
35–44	0	4	7	2	0	13
45–64	0	0	2	1	0	3
65 and over	0	0	1	1	0	2
Other female						
Under 25	8	20	8	2	1	39
25–34	9	14	12	4	2	41
35–44	2	3	2	0	0	7
45–64	0	0	0	0	0	0
65 and over	0	0	0	0	0	0
Total	32	86	82	32	14	246

Total occupied units 246
Total available units in building 280
Vacant units 34
Vacancy rate 12.14%

B. Tenant profiles of subject property B

						Total
Married						
Under 25	0	2	5	8	0	15
25–34	0	3	8	18	15	44
35–44	0	0	8	12	17	37
45–64	0	1	2	4	2	9
65 and over	2	4	2	2	0	10
Other male						
Under 25	0	0	4	2	0	6
25–34	0	6	8	12	3	29
35–44	0	2	4	6	0	12
45–64	0	0	2	4	0	6
65 and over	0	0	1	1	0	2
Other female						
Under 25	2	4	6	2	0	14
25–34	0	5	7	11	3	26
35–44	2	1	8	12	5	28
45–64	1	2	3	2	0	8
65 and over	3	5	2	1	0	11
Total	10	35	70	97	45	257

Total occupied units 257
Total available units 280
Vacant units 23
Vacancy rate 8.21%

Source: Hypothetical cases derived by the authors.

Table 2. 1989 Capture Rates

Household type	<$10,000	$10,000 to $19,999	$20,000 to $29,999	$30,000 to $39,999	$40,000 Plus
A. 1989 capture rates by segment property A					
Married					
Under 25	0.20%	0.18%	0.15%	0.00%	0.00%
25–34	0.11%	0.09%	0.12%	0.04%	0.00%
35–44	0.00%	0.15%	0.17%	0.00%	0.00%
45–64	0.00%	0.09%	0.21%	0.00%	0.00%
65 and over	0.00%	0.00%	0.00%	0.00%	0.00%
Other male					
Under 25	0.11%	0.42%	0.77%	0.94%	0.78%
25–34	0.09%	0.31%	0.53%	0.47%	0.30%
35–44	0.00%	0.32%	0.51%	0.17%	0.00%
45–64	0.00%	0.00%	0.40%	0.25%	0.00%
65 and over	0.00%	0.00%	1.45%	1.16%	0.00%
Other female					
Under 25	0.15%	0.52%	0.60%	0.44%	0.41%
25–34	0.23%	0.21%	0.36%	0.28%	0.23%
35–44	0.11%	0.13%	0.15%	0.00%	0.00%
45–64	0.00%	0.00%	0.00%	0.00%	0.00%
65 and over	0.00%	0.00%	0.00%	0.00%	0.00%

B. 1989 capture rates by tenant segments property B

Married					
Under 25	0.00%	0.09%	0.25%	0.70%	0.00%
25–34	0.00%	0.06%	0.14%	0.40%	0.37%
35–44	0.00%	0.00%	0.34%	0.51%	0.53%
45–64	0.00%	0.09%	0.21%	0.39%	0.09%
65 and over	0.41%	0.83%	0.59%	0.86%	0.00%
Other male					
Under 25	0.00%	0.09%	0.22%	0.23%	0.00%
25–34	0.00%	0.12%	0.21%	0.47%	0.15%
35–44	0.00%	0.16%	0.29%	0.52%	0.00%
45–64	0.00%	0.00%	0.40%	1.00%	0.00%
65 and over	0.00%	0.00%	1.45%	1.16%	0.00%
Other female					
Under 25	0.04%	0.10%	0.45%	0.44%	0.00%
25–34	0.00%	0.08%	0.21%	0.77%	0.34%
35–44	0.11%	0.04%	0.59%	1.51%	0.96%
45–64	0.06%	0.12%	0.33%	0.41%	0.00%
65 and over	0.10%	0.40%	0.53%	0.73%	0.00%

Source: Derived by the authors.

Table 3. Historic and Projected Supply of New Rental Housing Units

A. *Historic Annual Supply*[1]

	1980–82	1983–84	1985	1986	1987	1988	1989	Total 1980–89	Average 1980–89
Historic annual supply of housing, buildings with 5 units or more[2]	4,157	12,623	7,997	5,308	900	275	8	52,206	5,221

B. *Projection of New Housing Supply 1990–1996*[3]

	1990	1991	1992	1993	1994	1995	1996	Total 1990–96	Average 1990–96
Low supply projection									
Projected new housing supply	160	320	480	640	800	960	1,120	4,480	640
Excess supply at beginning of year[4]	2,799	1,126	−386	−1,738	−2,930	−3,962	−4,835		
New renting households[5]	1,745	1,745	1,745	1,745	1,745	1,745	1,745	12,215	
Normal vacancy—5%	87	87	87	87	87	87	87	611	
Total new demand (new renting households + normal vacancy)	1,832	1,832	1,832	1,832	1,832	1,832	1,832	12,825	
Excess supply remaining at end of year	1,126	−386	−1,738	−2,930	−3,962	−4,835	−5,547		
Moderate supply projection									
Projected new housing supply	160	500	1,200	1,800	2,400	2,400	2,400	10,860	1,551
Excess supply at beginning of year[4]	2,799	1,126	−206	−838	−870	−302	265		

New renting households[5]	1,745	1,745	1,745	1,745	1,745	1,745	1,745	12,215
Normal vacancy—5%	87	87	87	87	87	87	87	611
Total new demand (new renting households + normal vacancy)	1,832	1,832	1,832	1,832	1,832	1,832	1,832	12,825
Excess supply remaining at end of year	1,126	−206	−838	−870	−302	265	833	

Source: U.S. Bureau of the Census, Current Construction Reports, Series C-40, 1980–89.

[1] Source: U.S. Bureau of the Census, Current Construction Reports, Series C-40, 1980–89.
[2] Number of units for which permits were issued is reduced by 10% to reflect uncompleted units between 1983 and 1988.
[3] Source: Derived by the authors.
[4] Based on 7.1% vacancy rate at beginning of 1990 and assumed normal vacancy of 5%.
[5] From population age projections.

wise to supplement our method with an examination of neighborhood trends using other methods.

Projecting the Market Forward

With the current market position of the properties established, we now proceed to forecast how the market will change overall. This involves projecting forward the master demand matrix, and it requires a forecast of supply as well. The importance of added supply is that it cuts into the properties' existing capture rates, more in some segments than others. We would prefer to utilize an outside forecast of new construction but could not locate one of sufficiently long term (7 years) for our market.

Accordingly, we have reviewed past trends in the Austin market and have developed two alternative supply forecasts. Table 3 summarizes the recent trend in building permits and projects annual increases in multifamily supply. Austin experienced a boom in multifamily construction during the 1980s, reaching a peak of 16,000 units in 1983, but new construction virtually vanished in recent years. Annual permits for 1989 were a mere eight units. The low construction alternative extends the recent experience of the market with a very modest rate of recovery, but this is judged unreasonable as supply falls over 5000 units short of projected demand by 1996. The moderate construction alternative assumes a rebound in construction after 1990. Locally based market analysts report an expectation that new construction will pick up in the coming year, in part because rising rents justify costs of new construction and in part because the vacancy rate has fallen to 7.1%.[8] We have assumed that construction will again overshoot the rate of new household formation by 1995, leaving a slight overhang at the end of the period.[9]

Our method requires distributing the total new supply by tenant segment. This may be accomplished by simply surveying a sample of new properties to see what are the characteristics of their occupants. We then would assume that future new construction is distributed in the same pattern. However, for lack of a new construction tenant survey, we have relied once again on Census data. Data from *Metropolitan Housing Characteristics* records tenants' demographic and income characteristics for residents in recently built structures. We have updated and projected that data with tabular scaling procedures similar to those described above. This matrix of expected characteristics for new construction tenants is then used to allocate the projected construction total into specific tenant segments.

The projected supply increase, distributed by tenant segment, is used to adjust the current capture rates, following the algorithm given in Equation 1. Any increase in supply to be occupied by a given tenant group will drive down the existing properties' capture rates for that group. Supply and demand can then be linked by multiplying the projected capture rates times the projected number of tenants (of each segment type) in the whole market. As previously described, this demand forecast by tenant segment is accomplished by scaling the detailed master matrix. These procedures can be summarized by tracing the calculations for one tenant segment, in this case unmarried male renters aged 25 to 34, with incomes between $20,000 and $29,999, and living in Property A. Table 4 summarizes the necessary steps. Beginning with twenty such tenants, this property has a 0.53% capture of all such households in the market. However, due to expected new construction, this capture rate will continue at only 0.945 of its present level. This yields a projected capture rate of 0.50%. When applied to the total tenants of this segment projected in the market for 1996, estimated at 3507, this yields an expected 17.46 tenants, for a loss of 2.54 tenants. Although this estimate might be rounded to a whole number, we leave it in decimal form to make clear the calculation.

Table 4. Tracing a Tenant Segment through the Four-Square Analysis

Segment: Unmarried males 25–34 years old, with incomes between $20,000 and $29,999, Property A

Property's 1989 tenants in this segment	20
1989 total renting households in this segment for entire market[1]	3,797
Property's 1989 capture rate of households in this segment[2]	0.53%
1996 capture rate adjustment factor[3]	0.945
Projected 1996 capture rate	0.50%
Projected 1996 households in this segment for entire market[6]	3,507
Property's projected 1996 capture of tenants in this segment	17.46
Projected change in tenants in this segment[5]	−2.54

Source: Derived by the authors.
[1] Estimated from population age projections in 1989 Master Matrix.
[2] Calculated by dividing property's 1989 tenants in this segment by tenants in this segment for entire market.
[3] Estimated from projected new housing supply, using Equation 1.
[4] Estimated from population age projections in 1996 Master Matrix.
[5] Projected 1996 tenants less 1989 tenants.

Table 5. Gainers and Losers

Household type	<$10,000	$10,000 to $19,999	$20,000 to $29,999	$30,000 to $39,999	$40,000 Plus
A. Property A gainers and losers					
Married					
Under 25	-0.07	-0.14	-0.09	0.00	0.00
25–34	-0.26	-0.51	-0.87	-0.25	0.00
35–44	0.00	0.45	0.91	0.00	0.00
45–64	0.00	0.42	0.85	0.00	0.00
65 and over	0.00	0.00	0.00	0.00	0.00
Other male					
Under 25	-0.22	-0.64	-0.43	-0.25	-0.51
25–34	-0.39	-2.08	-2.54	-1.52	-1.05
35–44	0.00	0.80	1.44	0.41	0.00
45–64	0.00	0.00	0.83	0.42	0.00
65 and over	0.00	0.00	0.09	0.09	0.00
Other female					
Under 25	-0.33	-0.81	-0.28	-0.07	-0.11
25–34	-1.16	-1.79	-1.50	-0.50	-0.36
35–44	0.49	0.73	0.50	0.00	0.00
45–64	0.00	0.00	0.00	0.00	0.00
65 and over	0.00	0.00	0.00	0.00	0.00

Total losses -10.31
Total available units in building 280
Projected vacant units 1996 44
Projected 1996 vacancy rate 15.83%

B. Property B gainers and losers

Married				
Under 25	0.00	−0.07	−0.16	−0.25	0.00
25–34	0.00	−0.38	−0.99	−2.24	−2.56
35–44	0.00	0.00	1.83	2.74	2.64
45–64	0.00	0.42	0.85	1.70	0.71
65 and over	0.11	0.22	0.12	0.12	0.00
Other male				
Under 25	0.00	0.00	−0.12	−0.06	0.00
25–34	0.00	−0.78	−1.01	−1.52	−0.53
35–44	0.00	0.40	0.82	1.23	0.00
45–64	0.00	0.00	0.83	1.66	0.00
65 and over	0.00	0.00	0.09	0.09	0.00
Other female				
Under 25	−0.08	−0.16	−0.21	−0.07	0.00
25–34	0.00	−0.64	−0.87	−1.37	−0.53
35–44	0.49	0.24	2.00	3.00	0.82
45–64	0.32	0.64	0.98	0.65	0.00
65 and over	0.17	0.29	0.12	0.06	0.00

Total losses: 11.75
Total available units in building: 280
Projected vacant units 1996: 11
Projected 1996 vacancy rate: 4.02%

Source: Derived by the authors

Forecasts for the Specific Properties

Finally, we calculate the implications of the forecasts for the subject properties. Given the marketwide forecasts, and given knowledge of the relationship between the subject properties and the market, we can calculate the likely futures for each property. Following the procedures outlined in Table 4, we can estimate the gains and losses in each tenant category. With calculations carried out in parallel on seventy-five different tenant segments, the fractional units can be cumulated into whole numbers of expected occupied units. Similarly, we assume that errors in estimation for individual tenant groups are offsetting. By chance one category may have begun with a greater number of tenants, while a neighboring category may have begun with a smaller number. These differences should average out between neighboring categories.

The sum total of gains and losses for each property is displayed in Table 5. The younger age groups are losing cases because the underlying demographics of the market are shifting toward older renters. However, only Property B is positioned to capture a large fraction of these older renters. In sum, Property A is likely to accumulate a growing number of vacancies, increased from 34 to 44 (from 12.1% to 15.8%), while Property B is likely to experience declining vacancies, from 23 to 14 (8.2% to 4.0%).

Managers of the two properties will face two very different scenarios. In the face of strong demand, Property B not only will enjoy fuller occupancy but also may be able to support higher annual rent increases. In contrast, Property A will face falling occupancy and there will certainly be resistance to raising rents. The manager of Property A must struggle to reposition the project. How much the property can be shifted toward more favorable tenant segments requires considerable study. Without knowing anything else about the property, the current tenant profile is the best gauge of the property's "natural position" in the market. The specific location of the property certainly cannot be changed, and it will prove difficult to expand the size of units or add the bathrooms expected by the growing numbers of more upscale renters. Other amenities might be added, but only at considerable expense. There is always the option of allowing the project to filter down, achieving fuller occupancy by lowering rents, and then reducing project expenses by avoiding any upgrading program and even cutting maintenance.

Which property is a better investment? We will compare the two properties under the conservative assumption that rents will increase at a constant 5% in both cases. Also, no allowance will be made for the greater repositioning expenses of Property A. In this analysis, the sole difference between the properties rests on their differential futures with regard to vacancies. Table 6 summarizes the relevant data.

It is assumed that both properties were purchased at the end of 1989 and would be held for seven years before sale. The sale price is assumed to be based on the 1996 net operating income, capped at 10% (as at purchase). Under these fixed assumptions Property A provides an all-equity IRR, before financing or taxes, of 12.92%, while Property B provides a return of 14.68%. This is a conservative comparison, because the difference in return on investment would be accentuated if the purchase were leveraged with a mortgage at an interest rate below the all-equity return. Regardless, the difference between the properties — 176 basis points — is a function of the increased vacancies projected for Property A and the decreased vacancies projected for Property B. In another view, the difference in revenue losses due to vacancies — approximately $100,000 in 1996 — when capped at 10% yields a loss of valuation for Property A of $1,000,000.

It is probably unwise to assume that Property A, with its growing vacancies, can sustain the same annual rent increases as Property B. As an alternative, the bottom panel of Table 6 assumes a 4% annual increase in rents for Property A. Under this assumption, the all-equity IRR falls to 12.04%, a drop of another 88 basis points below the already depressed rate of return for this property.

The alternatives facing the manager of Property A — lowering rents to increase occupancy or raising expenditures as part of a repositioning program — simply contribute to lower NOI in other ways, with consequent loss of valuation. In contrast, the manager of Property B may be able to raise rents even more quickly, given that occupancy is nearing its practical upper limit. This would improve still further the value at the time of sale and the return on investment.

Conclusions

Astute real estate analysts may have already perceived *intuitively* the relative advantages of upscale apartment complexes over young singles complexes. What we have offered in this paper is a *quantitative* method for reaching such judgements. With knowledge of the forecasts produced by our method, cap rates of present NOI should be adjusted up or down to reflect relative differences in future value. The absence of such perfect knowledge in the marketplace creates investment opportunity.

Table 6. Financial Projections

	1989	1990	1991	1992	1993	1994	1995	1996
A. Cash flow projections property A—5% annual rent incease								
Purchase price[1]	$7,290,000							
Projected vacancies[2]		34	36	37	39	41	42	44
Gross potential revenues[3]		$1,260,000	$1,323,000	$1,389,150	$1,458,608	$1,531,538	$1,608,115	$1,688,521
Less:								
Losses due to vacancies		$153,000	$168,525	$185,220	$203,163	$222,438	$243,132	$265,339
Operating expenses	30%	$378,000	$396,900	$416,745	$437,582	$459,461	$482,434	$506,556
Net operating income		$729,000	$757,575	$787,185	$817,862	$849,639	$882,549	$916,625
Proceeds of sale[4]								$8,707,941
Cash flows before financing	($7,290,000)	$729,000	$757,575	$787,185	$817,862	$849,639	$882,549	$9,624,567
Before tax all equity IRR Property A—5% annual rent increase	12.92%							
B. Cash flow projections property B—5% annual rent increase								
Purchase Price[1]	$10,847,100							
Projected Vacancies[2]		23	22	20	19	17	16	14
Gross potential revenues[3]		$1,755,600	$1,843,380	$1,935,549	$2,032,326	$2,133,943	$2,240,640	$2,352,672
Less:								
Losses due to vacancies		$144,210	$141,545	$138,254	$134,279	$129,561	$124,035	$117,634
Operating expenses	30%	$526,680	$553,014	$580,665	$609,698	$640,183	$672,192	$705,802
Net operating income		$1,084,710	$1,148,821	$1,216,631	$1,288,350	$1,364,199	$1,444,413	$1,529,237
Proceeds of sale[4]								$14,527,749
Cash flows before financing	($10,847,100)	$1,1084,710	$1,148,821	$1,216,631	$1,288,350	$1,364,199	$1,444,413	$16,056,986
Before tax all equity IRR Property B—5% annual rent increase	14.68%							

C. Cash flow projections property A—4% annual rent increase

Purchase Price[1] $7,290,000

	34	36	37	39	41	42	44
Projected Vacancies[2]							
Gross potential revenues[3]	$1,260,000	$1,310,400	$1,362,186	$1,417,329	$1,474,022	$1,532,983	$1,594,302
Less:							
Losses due to vacancies	$153,000	$166,920	$181,709	$197,414	$214,084	$231,772	250,533
Operating expenses 30%	$378,000	$393,120	$408,845	$425,199	$442,207	$459,895	$478,291
Net operating income	$729,000	$750,360	$772,262	$794,716	$817,731	$841,315	$865,478
Proceeds of sale[4]							$8,222,043
Cash flows before financing	($7,290,000)	$729,000	$750,360	$772,262	$794,716	$817,731	$841,315	$9,087,521

Before tax all equity IRR Property B—5% annual rent increase 12.04%

Source: Derived by the authors.

[1]For this analysis, it is assumed that the sale is at the end of 1989. For both properties the purchase price is based on the 1990 NOI, with a cap rate of 10%.

[2]1990 vacant units are from the tenant profiles (Table 1). 1996 vacant units are the total of 1990 vacancies plus gains or losses from Table 5. Vacancies are assumed to decline or increase uniformly over the seven years of this analysis.

[3]For Property A, average unit size is 750 s.f., with average rent of $0.50 per s.f. in 1990. For Property B, average unit size is 950 s.f., with an average rent of $0.55 per s.f. in 1990.

[4]The sale price is assumed to be the 1996 NOI capped at 10%, less 5% sales expenses.

The managers of the two properties examined here face very different odds in a competitive market. Using our vacancy projection method, guided by the underlying four-square design, investors would have a better means of gauging the prospective returns on the two alternative properties. The only special data our method requires are a simple survey of tenants that asks three questions: the age of the householder, marital status, and total household income. Alternatively, this information could be estimated from management records or another source.

This is but one illustration of how the four-square design can be employed to improve the logic and rigor of real estate market studies. All studies must come to grips with analytical problems on two essential dimensions: the gap between present and future, and the gap between the market and the specific property. With most of our information about the market in the present, how do we arrive at a conclusion for the future of a specific property?

The overall design objective behind the proposed method is to provide a parsimonious method for addressing the two essential dimensions that yields a standardized, quantified assessment of investment prospects. The method subsumes many factors in a streamlined fashion. The tenant profiles and capture rates encompass demand factors shaping a property's revenue stream. The capture rates also proxy the effects of neighborhood location and market position. This method is not intended to be exhaustive; there is a large amount of miscellaneous local information that deserves to be examined. Rather, the proposed four-square method should be viewed as an important analytic procedure to be added to the market analyst's tool kit.

The six-step pathway that we advocate has two steps that are especially significant. After identifying the subject property, analysts should proceed immediately to the question of forecast data and models. Too often these are appended at the end as an afterthought of the research design. Instead, from the beginning our model builds the whole analysis around the limited forecast data and models that are available. Thereby we integrate the future into the analysis of the present.

The second step that is especially noteworthy is the quantitative estimation of market position through the use of a matrix of segment-specific capture rates. Calculated in the present, and adjusted for expected increases in supply, these capture rates can then be applied to the future volume of the market expected to rest in each segment. Thereby we integrate the specific property into the market.

There are likely to be alternative specific methods for implementing the four-square design, and there may be an alternative sequence of steps that could be traced through the four squares, but there are few market studies that legitimately can avoid coming to terms with the two key dimensions forming the four-square framework. We wonder what other solutions there may be to this puzzle.

Notes

1. Malizia (1990) reports from his survey of major institutional investors and advisors that most are building and analyzing two different databases: one that contains specific information on each of the institution's investment properties, and a second that collects regional or marketwide data. Both are valuable, but the links between the two databases in actual analysis are as yet unclear.

2. The necessary 1980 Census data are reported for cities and metropolitan counties of at least 50,000 population in the series of printed reports, *Metropolitan Housing Characteristics*, or in summary files on computer tape (STF-5 series). Alternatively, users may prepare even more customized master matrices by accessing the Public Use Micro Samples (PUMS) data tapes, which report a 5% sample of all individual household records in each metropolitan area and state. The data from the 1990 Census will be released in similar form, except that the printed reports on *Metropolitan Housing Characteristics* have been eliminated. As partial compensation, these data will be included in STF-5 data files released on CD-ROM for use with microcomputers.

3. U.S. Bureau of the Census (19■■).
4. National Planning Association (1989).
5. U.S. Bureau of the Census (19■■): Tables A-3, A-4, and A-7.
6. U.S. Bureau of the Census (1988).
7. Joint Center for Housing Studies (1989).
8. Observations by Charles Heimsath, president of the Austin firm, Capitol Market Research, Inc. The vacancy rate is already surprisingly low, based on a survey of 60,000 multifamily units regularly conducted by Capitol Market Research.
9. More extensive research as to the most likely long-term forecast of construction is clearly warranted. Factors such as cited in Myers (19■■) clearly deserve to be incorporated. However, the recent history of the Austin market has been so volatile that there is little basis at this time for seeking such a precise long-term market forecast. Such a detailed effort may become warranted after another year of recovery. In the mean time, we feel the present forecast offers a degree of precision compatible with our degree of certainty about key forecast inputs.

References

Carn, Neil, Joseph Rabianski, Ronald Racster, and Maury Seldin. *Real Estate Market Analysis: Techniques and Applications*. Englewood Cliffs, NJ: Prentice Hall, 1988.

Chapman, John. "Cast a Critical Eye." *American Demographics* (February 1987), 30–3.

Clapp, John M. *Handbook for Real Estate Market Analysis*. Englewood Cliffs, NJ: Prentice Hall, 1987.
Clark, Dave. "Proprietary Demographic Projections are Unreliable." *Real Estate Review* (1989), 59–64.
Featherston, J. B. "Approaching Market Analysis in a New Economic Environment." *Journal of Real Estate Development* 1, 4 (Spring 1986), 5–10.
Joint Center for Housing Studies. *The State of the Nation's Housing: 1989*. Cambridge, MA: Joint Center for Housing Studies, Harvard University, 1990.
Malizia, Emil E. "Competition for Investment Spurs Innovative Real Estate Market Research." *Urban Land* (January 1990), 26–7.
Messner, Stephen D., Byrl N. Boyce, Harold G. Trimble, and Robert L. Ward. *Analyzing Real Estate Opportunities: Market and Feasibility Studies* Chicago: National Association of Realtors, 1977, Chap. 1.
Mitchell, Phillip S. and Gary L. Bernes. "An Analysis of Indicators of Multifamily Complex Values." Paper presented at the annual conference of the American Real Estate Society, North Lake Tahoe, California, 1990.
Myers, Dowell. "Extended Forecasts of Housing Demand in Metropolitan Areas." *The Appraisal Journal* 55 (April 1987), 266–78.
Myers, Dowell. "Systematic Biases in Housing Market Analysis," in *Research in Real Estate*, Vol. 3. Steven D. Kapplin and Arthur C. Schwartz, eds., 1990a.
Myers, Dowell. "The Contribution of Demographic Methods to Real Estate Market Analysis," in *Research in Real Estate*, Vol. 3, Steven D. Kapplin, and Arthur C. Schwartz, eds., 1990b.
National Planning Association. *U.S. Economic Growth: Regional Projections, 1984–2000*. Regional Economic Projections Series, Vol. 3. Washington, D.C.: National Planning Association, 1989.
U.S. Bureau of the Census. "Money Income and Poverty Status in the United States: 1988." *Current Population Reports*. Series P-60, No. 166. Washington, D.C.: U.S. Government Printing Office.
U.S. Bureau of the Census. *Current Construction Reports*. Series C-40. Washington, D.C.: U.S. Government Printing Office.
U.S. Bureau of the Census. *Metropolitan Housing Characteristics*. HC80-2-80. Washington, D.C.: U.S. Government Printing Office.

10 REFINING EMPIRICAL PROCEDURES FOR MARKET AREA DELINEATION

Kim Peterson*

Introduction

Market analysis plays a critical role in real estate valuation.[1] A critical first step in any market analysis is the delineation and characterization of a geographical area within which properties of the subject type are seen as competitive. Gravity models, regression, and the calculation of time–distance boundaries are methods often employed in the delineation process. For enterprises that draw from large geographic areas, however, the application of these methods may be problematic. In such cases the analyst typically resorts to an empirical procedure in which trade areas for the subject property and/or its competitors are mapped.

Most of these methods are based on customer-spotting procedures, such as in-store or automobile license plate surveys, raffles, or the collection of guest registration cards. Unfortunately, these approaches are limited in the information they can provide. The data generated describe only those customers who come to the facility or area, and say nothing about the population that is *not* represented. In many cases, this nonrepresented population is the one of greatest interest to the analyst, as it is

*Institute for Urban Land Economics Research, Inc., Madison, Wisconsin 53711

the one that may not be presently served. As such, it constitutes untapped potential and should be considered in the formulation of marketing strategy, or in the projection of future income streams available to the subject property.

In this paper, a case study approach is used to demonstrate that the customer-spotting procedure has serious weaknesses. Three general problems are identified. A recent spotting-based market study for marina and harbor development is used to investigate these problems, and a more comprehensive survey-based method is provided for comparison. Market delineation via the survey-based method is shown to produce more detailed and accurate results.

Background: The Market Analysis Problem

Civic leaders in Sheboygan, Wisconsin, a Lake Michigan coastal community, viewed harbor and marina development as a vehicle for revitalizing their downtown.[2] There were several slip-renting facilities already located in the harbor area, but it was questionable whether a significant new development could be supported, given the recent expansion of marina and harbor facilities in a neighboring coastal community to the north. Accordingly, the city hired a consultant who did a market study using a customer-spotting approach.

At about the same time, the State of Wisconsin commissioned a market study of Great Lakes marinas for the state as a whole. The study was needed to help evaluate requests for public assistance for marina and harbor development, and to provide data for community-specific plans. This study used a consumer survey-based approach and delineated a radically different market area for Sheboygan harbor. As a consequence, it projected a substantially different level of potential demand.

Customer Spotting

Description of Approach

In the customer-spotting or analog approach, a store or facility's primary trade area is conceived of as a contiguous geographic area from which the facility gets the majority of its patronage. Delineation procedures are numerous and well documented, but typically follow a multistep approach (Applebaum, 1966):

1. A representative sample of customers is interviewed in the store or facility of interest, and home addresses of these customers are plotted on a map.
2. This map is partitioned into a grid of quarter-mile squares, and the total number of spotted customers or weekly sales are calculated for each.[3]
3. A capture rate (or per-capita sales figure) is computed for each square; this rate is the ratio of customers to total population in the square.
4. A primary trade area is delineated by choosing a subset of these squares and cumulating the number of customers (or weekly sales) attributable to each. Selection begins with the squares nearest the subject facility and moves outward. Squares having the highest capture rates (or per-capita sales) are chosen first, with the further requirement that they be contiguous to squares already chosen.
5. The analyst stops choosing squares when an arbitrarily set percentage of the facility's total customer base or weekly sales has been attained; that is, when the total for selected squares equals the desired percentage of the facility's total, usually 60% to 70%.
6. Similarly, the secondary trade area is defined as the area adjoining the primary area that includes squares with the next highest ratios of customers to population (or per-capita sales), and from which the facility gets a stated amount of its sales (e.g., 15%, 20%, or 25%).
7. The tertiary area, when defined, contributes the remaining portion of the facility's trade.

Application

In lieu of spotting customers, the marina consultants used slip rental lists provided by the city's existing facilities. Counties were used in place of quarter-mile squares and results showed a highly localized pattern of patronage: approximately 94% of all current tenants were residents of Sheboygan County (see Table 1).

Assuming that this pattern was due to Sheboygan's older, modestly equipped facilities, and that a new marina would draw more customers from farther away, the consultants analyzed slip rental lists for two competitors located in coastal communities immediately to the north and south. These facilities offered more services than Sheboygan and were

Table 1. Market Area for Sheboygan Harbor (Based on Customer Spotting Approach)

County of origin	Boats in slips	Share of marina[1]	Total population[2]	Capture rate[3]
Sheboygan	77	.9390	489	.1575
Calumet	1	.0122	139	.0072
Ozaukee	1	.0122	461	.0022
Fond du Lac	1	.0122	447	.0022
Brown	1	.0122	1,303	.0008
Waukesha	1	.0122	2,756	.0004

Source: Calculations based on data provided in the consultants' report.

[1] Defined as boats in slips from each origin county divided by the total number of boats in the harbor (the column total, 82).

[2] Total number of boats at least 20 feet long in each county of origin as of December 31, 1986 (includes inboard, outboard and sail).

[3] Defined as boats of slips (column 1) divided by total population of boats (column 3). Table entries are arranged in descending order based on this characteristic.

similar to the kind of development being proposed. Results showed much larger trade areas for these competing facilities. Descriptions follow in Table 2. Counties of origin for marina tenants appear in descending order based on the size of capture rate, as specified in the customer-spotting approach.[4]

Problems

These listings highlight three fundamental weaknesses of the customer-spotting approach: conflicting information, incomplete specification of capture rates, and lack of representativeness.

Conflicting Information. The customer-spotting approach may produce conflicting indicators of a geographic area's importance to a facility, and the requirement that the trade area be contiguous may be inappropriate. For example, the counties contributing the second through fourth largest numbers of boats to the Manitowoc marina are neither contiguous nor highly ranked in terms of capture rates (i.e., the states of Illinois and Minnesota, and Milwaukee County). Only one of these areas is included in the facility's primary market (i.e., Minnesota). The Port Washington Marina provides a similar example: Waukesha County ranks fifth in terms

Table 2. Market Areas for Two Neighboring Marinas (Based on Customer-Spotting Approach)

County of origin	Boats in slips	Share of marina[1]	Total population[2]	Capture rate[3]
A. Manitowoc Marina				
Primary market[4]				
Manitowoc	72	.4045	392	.1837
Rock	7	.0393	462	.0152
Calumet	2	.0112	139	.0144
Columbia	4	.0225	306	.0131
Ozaukee	6	.0337	461	.0130
Minnesota (state)	15	.0843	1,768	.0085
Jefferson	2	.0112	258	.0078
Winnebago	7	.0393	1,192	.0059
Secondary market				
Illinois (state)	19	.1067	4,347	.0044
Fond du Lac	2	.0112	447	.0045
Sheboygan	2	.0112	489	.0041
Brown	9	.0506	3,108	.0029
Milwaukee	4	.0225	1,303	.0031
Dane	3	.0169	1,667	.0018
Waukesha	3	.0169	2,756	.0011
B. Port Washington Marina				
Primary market[4]				
Ozaukee	94	.5434	461	.2039
Washington	21	.1214	551	.0381
Secondary market				
Dodge	2	.0116	193	.0104
Jefferson	2	.0116	258	.0078
Milwaukee	15	.0867	3,108	.0048
Rock	2	.0116	462	.0043
Sheboygan	2	.0016	489	.0041
Illinois (state)	17	.0983	4,347	.0039
Dane	6	.0347	1,667	.0036
Waukesha	9	.0520	2,756	.0033

Source: Calculations based on data provided in the consultants' report.

[1] Defined as boats in slips from each county of origin divided by the total number of slips in the marina (the column total 178 in A, 173 in B; counties providing only one slip renter are included in this total but are not shown).

[2] Total number of boats at least 20 feet long in each county of origin as of December 31, 1986 (includes inboard, outboard and sail).

[3] Defined as boats in slips (column 1) divided by total population of boats (column 3). Table entries are arranged in descending order based on this characteristic.

[4] The primary market area is defined as including approximately 65% of the marina's slip rentals (64.6% in A, 66.48% in B). The secondary area includes the next 20% (20.2% A, 22% in B). By these standards Dane and Waukesha counties are part of these marinas' tertiary areas.

of current customers (nine boats in slips), third in terms of potential (2756 boats), but last on the basis of market capture rate.

Situations such as these can be confusing: Is a county or geographic area important because of the share of business it contributes, or because of the rate at which the facility captures its trade? If both features are equally important, how should conflicting ranks be resolved, and how should noncontiguous but important counties be assessed?

Incomplete Specification of Market Capture Rates. The question then follows how to use this information to determine if a new facility is warranted. For example, Illinois and Milwaukee boaters drive past Sheboygan to rent slips at the Manitowoc Marina. Because of Manitowoc's low market capture rates for these boaters, substantial residual demand is implied, but would these residuals be available to a new Sheboygan facility?

Unfortunately, this question cannot be adequately answered given the customer-spotting information the consultants gathered. Only the Sheboygan, Manitowoc, and Port Washington facilities were investigated, so it is impossible to know how many other competitors are drawing customers from these geographic areas, or the strength of this competition in terms of capture rates.

Lack of Representativeness. Even if all competitors had been identified, customer spotting may not have produced an accurate answer. This is because it promotes two types of bias. The first occurs because customers who live near a facility are generally over-represented, while customers living farther away may be under-represented. The second bias results from omission, as only the customers who actually patronize a facility are investigated; consumers who live near a facility but do not use it are lost to the analysis, and such nonresponse errors are hard to interpret.

In fact, lack of representativeness prevented the discovery of three segmentation variables that were critical to an accurate estimate of demand[5]:

1. The percentage of registered boats in each county that were inactive and therefore not potential customers.
2. The percentage of registered boats that are typically used on inland waters and therefore are not current candidates for Great Lakes slip space.
3. The percentage of boats in each area that are candidates for slip rental despite their smaller size.[6]

Table 3. Market Areas for Proposed Sheboygan Marina (Based on Customer-Spotting Approach)

County of origin	Boats 20'+[1]	Boats 26'+
Primary market		
Manitowoc	392	75
Ozaukee	461	163
Sheboygan	489	114
Secondary market		
Calumet	139	29
Fond du Lac	447	101
Milwaukee	3,108	939
Washington	551	86
Waukesha	2,756	554
Winnebago	1,192	285
Balance of market[2]		
Rest of Wisconsin	22,858	4,175
Illinois (state)	26,444	5,392
Minnesota (state)	31,913	6,631

Source: Taken from data provided in the consultants' report.
[1] Total registered boats in each area as of December 31, 1986 (includes inboard, outboard and sail). Boats in the 26'+ category are also included in this category.
[2] Illinois and Minnesota totals reflect all registered boats, not just those registered in Wisconsin.

Segmentation is critical to the accurate estimation of slip demand, and to demand forecasts for other land use types. Unfortunately, customer spotting may not provide accurate estimates of segmentation features, due in large part to its lack of representativeness.

Discussion. In the face of these considerable difficulties, the consultants retreated to what they felt were safe assumptions: They specified primary and secondary market areas for the proposed facility based in part on spotting data (mostly from the Manitowoc Marina) and in part on a drive-time or distance rule (not explained). This delineation is shown in Table 3. Note that the format differs substantially from that of Tables 1 and 2, reflecting the consultants' inability to calculate market capture rates either directly for the proposed facility or indirectly as residuals of the competition.

Failing to recognize the segmentation issues involved, the consultants then defined potential demand as the *total* population of boats at least 20 feet long in each county; applied expected growth rates; summed the resulting county increments to produce totals for the primary, secondary, and tertiary trade areas; and applied arbitrary 60%, 40%, and 25% capture rates.[7]

Consumer Survey

Description of Approach

The consumer survey approach to delineation gathers information from a representative sample of consumers and identifies the facilities they use. Because the sample is drawn to be representative of some larger population of interest, research findings can be generalized to that larger population base. The procedure comprises six steps (Churchill, 1987):

1. The population of elements about which the analyst wishes to make an inference is defined. In the present study the elements were boats.
2. A sampling frame is identified. This is a listing of the elements from which the actual sample can be drawn.
3. A sampling procedure is selected. This step depends largely on what the analyst can develop for a sampling frame (e.g., a simple random sample requires a complete and accurate list of population elements by name, registration number, or some other identification code).
4. Sample size is determined. This depends on the type of sample being drawn, the statistic being estimated (e.g., the proportion of boat owners who rent slips), the homogeneity of the population, and time, money, and personnel constraints.
5. A sample of elements is drawn according to the procedure selected and the size specified.
6. Data are collected from the designated elements. For market delineation work, these data are typically measures of activity (e.g., numbers of consumers patronizing facilities, shopping trips, or boat-days), and are arranged in a matrix where origins and destinations define rows and columns.

Application

Survey. The population of elements defined for the statewide survey consisted of those boats that would be most likely to need marina facilities along Wisconsin's Great Lakes coasts; these were boats at least 20 feet long (smaller boats are easily trailered). A current listing of all Wisconsin-registered boats provided an appropriate sampling frame, as it included all boats using Wisconsin waters at least 60 days during each year.[8]

Previous research showed that up to 73% of all Great Lakes boating activity is generated by boaters living within 60 miles of a Great Lakes coast (Peterson and Atwood, 1987; Stynes and Holocek, 1982), so sampling was limited to the 46 Wisconsin counties lying within 90 miles of either Lake Michigan or Lake Superior shores (the extra distance provided a sampling safeguard). All Wisconsin-registered Illinois and Minnesota boaters were included, as there were no county codes specified for out-of-state boat owners and therefore no way to restrict sampling on the basis of distance.

Boats were partitioned on the basis of size and a disproportionately smaller sample of large boats than of small boats was drawn. A boat length of 25 feet is the consensus upper limit for transporting via car trailer, so boats longer than this defined the "large boat" category. A smaller number of large boats was drawn to maximize sampling efficiency: The proportion of large boats kept in rented slips is typically much closer to 100% than is the proportion of small boats (this latter proportion was expected to be close to 50%), and so sampling precision and/or statistical confidence could be preserved with a smaller sample of large boats relative to small boats.[9]

A systematic random sampling procedure was used to draw 14 samples, one for each of the two boat size classes for each of seven geographic regions. These regions reflected a compromise opinion generated by a panel of Great Lakes boating experts (there was much disagreement), and included four regions located along Wisconsin's Lake Michigan coast, one bordering Lake Superior, and one each for the states of Illinois and Minnesota[10] (see Peterson and Atwood, 1988 for detail). Sampling was restricted to an overall limit of 2515 elements, as dictated by budget constraints.

The survey used three mailings (see Dillman, 1978), achieved an overall response rate of 82%, and was evenly distributed in terms of response rate across both region and boat size class.

Table 4. Origin-Destination Matrix[1]

County of origin	Ash	Bay	Brn	Dor	Dug	Irn	Ken	Kew	Man	Mar	Mil	Ocn	Oza	Rac	She
1. Ashland	1434	330	0	0	0	220	0	0	0	0	0	0	0	0	0
2. Bayfield	2286	4236	0	0	0	0	0	0	0	0	0	0	0	0	0
3. Brown	0	77	11492	16715	0	0	0	3661	473	783	45	1382	0	0	0
4. Burnett	0	312	0	0	0	0	0	0	0	0	0	0	0	0	0
5. Calumet	0	0	0	698	0	0	0	0	546	0	0	0	0	22	273
6. Columbia	0	0	31	496	0	0	0	0	0	0	0	0	0	0	1368
7. Dane	0	0	62	2433	0	0	0	0	0	0	31	0	190	0	93
8. Door	0	0	66	24799	0	0	0	538	45	178	0	0	0	0	0
9. Douglas	0	2420	0	176	7084	0	0	0	0	0	0	0	0	0	0
10. Fond du Lac	0	0	0	214	0	0	0	0	1075	0	13	0	130	0	2470
11. Kenosha	0	0	0	748	0	0	10503	0	0	0	0	0	0	3405	0
12. Kewaunee	0	0	0	352	0	0	0	3901	66	110	413	0	0	0	0
13. Lincoln	36	290	0	67	0	550	0	0	0	44	0	0	0	0	0
14. Manitowoc	0	0	0	1348	0	0	0	0	9178	0	0	52	0	0	689
15. Marathon	0	0	0	655	0	0	0	0	0	270	0	0	0	0	0
16. Marinette	0	0	0	1887	0	0	0	0	0	2340	0	88	0	0	0
17. Milwaukee	0	0	190	3470	0	0	0	0	324	380	46555	0	2024	2248	2665
18. Oconto	0	0	0	506	0	0	0	0	0	726	0	550	0	0	0
19. Oneida	0	360	0	330	0	0	0	0	0	0	0	0	0	0	0
20. Outagamie	0	0	746	6110	0	0	0	110	792	279	9	22	0	0	0
21. Ozaukee	190	0	0	3720	0	0	0	0	0	0	2158	0	11649	155	570
22. Portage	0	0	0	1239	0	0	0	0	0	0	0	0	0	0	0
23. Racine	0	0	0	182	0	0	2351	0	0	0	3039	0	18	22173	0
24. Rock	510	510	34	85	0	0	0	0	34	0	544	0	102	0	0

Destination counties

	County																
25.	Shawano	0	0	0	380	0	0	0	0	0	265	0	0	0	0	0	0
26.	Sheboygan	0	0	36	695	0	0	0	24	215	0	0	0	416	0	0	14465
27.	Vilas	0	96	0	0	0	0	0	0	0	0	0	0	0	0	0	0
28.	Walworth	0	170	0	189	0	0	154	9	85	0	0	43	9	1054	0	68
29.	Washington	0	0	0	0	0	0	0	0	0	0	0	791	3081	0	0	0
30.	Waukesha	0	798	304	2552	0	0	114	0	1912	0	0	13223	5974	2344	0	739
31.	Waupaca	0	0	0	0	0	0	0	0	27	0	0	0	0	0	0	0
32.	Winnebago	0	0	221	3227	0	0	0	505	355	0	0	13	0	0	0	260
33.	Illinois	0	0	0	9310	0	0	4942	0	252	168	0	1778	112	12992	0	70
34.	Minnesota	225	16350	0	1200	2370	450	0	0	150	0	0	450	0	0	0	0

[1] Entries are boat-days generated in origin counties and received in destination counties.

Analysis. The conceptual model used as a basis for analyzing these data was the functional region, which is defined as a grouping of areas or geographic entities having more interaction or connection with each other than with outside areas (Brown and Holmes, 1971). The variables used to define such regions are typically measures of interaction (e.g., trips or newspaper circulation).[11] For the present analysis this was the boat-day, defined as one day or part-day during which a boat was actually in water on the Great Lakes under power or sail.

Approximately 366,000 boat-days of activity were reported for 9288 Wisconsin-registered boats using Lakes Michigan and Superior during 1987.[12] Of these boat-days, 20,025 were for destination counties without Great Lakes shorelines or reflected other kinds of errors, and were omitted from further analysis. The remaining valid data are shown in the origin-destination matrix of Table 4.

This origin-destination matrix provides the basis for market area delineation, as it shows the overall pattern of Wisconsin Great Lakes boating activity. It follows that these interaction data are good indicators of the locus of demand for marina slips. Boaters who need space are likely to rent it where they recreate and/or at a convenient distance from their homes.

Analysis of this matrix suggests that the customer-spotting-based market is incorrectly delineated: Ozaukee and Manitowoc counties are included in the proposed facility's primary market (Table 3), yet these counties contribute only modestly to Sheboygan's boat-day activity totals (i.e., only 570 and 689 boat-days, respectively, as shown in the Sheboygan County (She) column of Table 4); in addition, two of the highest activity counties, Milwaukee and Fond du Lac, are given only secondary market status by the spotting approach, and the fourth most important county, Columbia, is not included at all.

In order to highlight these spotting weaknesses, Sheboygan County origin-destination data are isolated in Table 5. Total boat-days of activity generated by residents of each origin county are shown, and these data are then used to compute share of Sheboygan and capture rate figures. Origin counties are arranged in descending order based on capture rate, which in this case is defined as the percentage of an origin county's total boat-day activity that Sheboygan County claims.

Comparison of this ordering with that derived through customer spotting (Table 3) shows substantial differences, as discussed above. Perhaps more telling, however, are differences in the types of information the two tables provide. The consumer survey approach provides sufficient data to compute share of marina and capture rate figures for Sheboygan Coun-

Table 5. Market Areas for Proposed Sheboygan Marina (Based on Consumer Survey Approach)

County of origin	Boat-days in Sheboygan	Share of Sheboygan[1]	Total boat-days[2]	Capture Rate[3]
Sheboygan[4]	14,465	.6096	15,932	.9079
Columbia	1,368	.0576	1,895	.7219
Fond du Lac	2,470	.1041	3,902	.6330
Calumet	273	.0115	1,517	.1800
Manitowoc	689	.0290	11,267	.0612
Winnebago	260	.0110	4,581	.0568
Milwaukee	2,665	.1123	57,856	.0461
Walworth	68	.0029	1,772	.0384
Dane	93	.0039	2,809	.0331
Ozaukee	570	.0240	18,442	.0309
Waukesha	739	.0311	27,960	.0264
Illinois (state)	70	.0029	29,624	.0024

Source: Derived by author using consumer survey approach.

[1] Defined as boat-days in Sheboygan County generated by each origin county's residents (column 1) divided by total boat-days in Sheboygan County (column 1 total, or 23,730).

[2] Total boat-days generated by residents of each origin county.

[3] Defined as boat-days in Sheboygan (column 1) divided by total boat-days (column 3). Table entries are arranged in descending order based on this characteristic.

[4] A primary market defined according to the criteria specified in the customer-spotting approach would include only Sheboygan and Columbia counties (the total is 66.7% of county activity). The secondary market would include the next five counties (adding another 26.8%).

ty, whereas the customer-spotting procedure does not. In fact, because customer spotting must calculate the trade available to a proposed facility as a residual, it can never provide an accurate estimate of demand unless all relevant competitors can be identified and spotted. Obviously, this can be both expensive and time consuming, and as a consequence it is seldom done.

Extended Analysis

At this point an analyst might use survey-based capture rates to estimate slip renting potential—possibly with modifications based on features of the proposed facility and its competition.[13] Before doing this, however, boat populations would be segmented according to the following variables:

1. Percentage of inactive boats—Inactive boats are unlikely to require marina slip space, and these comprised approximately 7% of the total fleet.
2. Percentage of Great Lakes boats—This percentage varied from county to county, but was approximately 31% overall. The remaining boats were used primarily on inland waters.
3. Percentage of boats in the 20 through 25 foot class that were candidates for slip rental—Approximately 23% of the 24,024 owners of these boats rented space during 1987; 31% said they wanted to rent space. These percentages differed substantially for Great Lakes and inland waters boats.
4. Percentage of boats at least 26 feet long kept in slips—Approximately 68% of all boats in this class were kept in rented space; this percentage was much higher for Great Lakes boats (83.8%) than for those used on inland waters (46.3%).

In estimating slip-renting potential for the proposed Sheboygan marina, the analyst would be free to use these segmentation variables or any others he or she thought would produce an accurate estimate. These variables cannot be reliably estimated in the customer-spotting approach because there is no way to ensure their representativeness.

Discussion

This study compared the customer-spotting and consumer survey-based approaches to market delineation, and found the survey approach to be superior. By surveying a representative sample of potential customers in a geographic area that is large enough to capture relevant behavior patterns, the analyst can more accurately identify a market area.[14] This procedure also provides a better basis for understanding important segmentation features or of discovering those that may not have been known beforehand.

In addition to developing a more accurate estimate of market demand, the consumer survey approach provides a more complete picture of market supply. Survey respondents identify all relevant competitors, and so the analyst can compute capture rates for each geographic area, not just a subset. This means that the prospects for a new facility can be more accurately assessed, generally without going through a formal delineation process (i.e., without segregating geographic areas into arbitrary primary, secondary, and tertiary groupings).

In those circumstances where primary and secondary markets must be defined, these markets need not be contiguous. This means that the analyst is free to consider all relevant counties or geographic areas in the analysis, which adds considerably to the meaningfulness of the process.

Beyond resolving these basic shortcomings of the spotting approach, a consumer survey offers three additional benefits. The analyst can (1) identify the extent of dissatisfied demand—those current patrons of the subject and/or its competitors who may be attracted to a new or improved facility. (2) Define the level of potential move-up demand. In the present study this included boaters who presently trailer and launch their smaller craft, but were planning to buy larger boats that would need slip space. (3) Estimate induced demand—boaters who are not renting because of dissatisfaction with available facilities.

Finally, because a survey can be made representative of a larger population, it allows for the translation of census and other government-generated spending data into revenue potential, and serves as an appropriate basis for strategic marketing plans. Consumer activities can also be evaluated (e.g., sailing, fishing, cruising to a destination, etc.), and these have important implications from a public policy standpoint, especially with respect to community economic development.

The only features of this approach likely to discourage its use are time and money costs. This is unfortunate, as spending for market research is generally deficient. In fact, no American industry spends less on legitimate consumer research and product development than does the real estate industry. This failure to spend even 1% of project budgets on primary research about the intended consumer is one explanation for many business failures of real estate projects across the land (Graaskamp, 1980, p. 26).

Still, if costs pose significant problems there are remedies. To the extent that money costs are constraining, smaller samples can be used. There may be some sacrifice of accuracy or precision in estimating behaviors (e.g., in estimating the percentage of boaters who want to rent slip space), but the overall patterning of behavior should still be revealed. Computer-intensive statistical procedures may also prove helpful. Approaches that do not require assumptions of normality are now widely available (Diaconis and Efron, 1983; Efron and Gong, 1983), which means that the analyst can make inferences from small samples with greater confidence.

Neither should time costs discourage this approach. Although properly run mail surveys can take seven weeks or more to execute, telephone surveys can be run more quickly.[15] This is generally time well spent in any case. A significant level of nonresponse can render a survey useless, and thereby require that it be redone. Moreover, the analyst's ability to generalize from even a large sample depends upon the care with which it is obtained.

Notes

1. In fact, market analysis has been equated with appraisal: "Others before me have said that the appraiser is the interpreter of the market, and it is my intent to extend this verity only a little further: whatever the mechanism of interpretation, appraisal is market analysis and nothing more" (Ratcliff, 1975, p. 485).

2. Recent construction of a 921-slip marina and six-acre festival park in another Lake Michigan community (Racine, Wisconsin) led to the attraction of 50 new retailers and the addition of 100,000 square feet of first class office space in the central city. It also stimulated over $30 million in new private investment along the city's lakefront (Salvesen, 1988).

3. Any suitable geographic unit may be used so long as population levels can be determined and used to compute capture rates or per-capita sales.

4. Note that smaller geographic units would have afforded more precision in the analysis. Unfortunately, a census of registered boats for the state was available at only the county level. Wisconsin-registered Illinois and Minnesota boats had only a state level identifier.

5. The term *discovery* is used here because a more representative procedure would have alerted the analysts to these segmentation issues, whether or not they had considered them beforehand.

6. Boats in the 20 through 25 foot size class are more easily trailered than are larger boats, and are therefore less likely to compete for slip space. However, due to their large numbers, even small percentages constitute substantial demand (Peterson and Atwood, 1988).

7. These calculations are beyond the scope of this analysis and are not shown.

8. This was the best sampling frame available, but it did hold a potential for bias, as owners of multiple boats could be over-represented and nonregistered boats would be left out. By some estimates this latter group is substantial, especially in Wisconsin waters located near borders with Illinois and Minnesota.

9. The more variable a characteristic, the larger the sample needed to estimate it with any given level of precision or confidence. A value of 0.50 indicates maximum variability, since one-half of the population possesses the characteristic and one-half does not.

10. Results of the analysis showed that these regions were incorrectly specified in terms of both number and geographic extent.

11. Interaction or activity data have been used previously to study recreational boating markets (Ditton et al., 1975; Goodwin, 1982; Lentnek et al., 1969; Stynes and Holecek, 1982), transportation origin-destination zones (Goddard, 1970; Slater, 1976), interarea migration (Slater, 1976, 1984), and regionalization in the U.S. coal industry (Campbell et al., 1979; Elzinga and Hogarty, 1973, 1978; Solomon and Pyrdol, 1986).

12. These are weighted totals. Because of the survey's disproportionate sampling plan, which specified different numbers of boats from each geographic region and a larger number of small boats than of large boats, weights were developed to balance the sample by region and size class, making it representative of the total population of boats at least 20 feet long in the sampling frame.

13. A complete and careful analysis would obviously consider attractiveness features of the proposed facility and its competitors. These features were omitted from the present analysis in order to focus attention on the mechanics of the two delineation techniques.

14. Some have argued that customer spotting can be "fixed up" by surveying customers in the market area defined by the spotting procedure. This is not a safe or reliable option. If the market area has been misspecified (incorrectly delineated), a survey of the consumers living in it can do nothing to remedy this; consumers in areas that should have been specified, but were not, will not be reached. Such an approach also begs the question as to why a survey was not done in the first place.

15. See Dillman (1978) for an excellent step-by-step approach to conducting telephone and mail surveys. His reported average response rate for 48 mail surveys is 74%.

References

Applebaum, W. "Methods for Determining Store Trade Areas, Market Penetration, and Potential Sales." *Journal of Marketing Research* 3 (1966), 127–41.

Brown, L. A. and J. Holmes, "The Delimitation of Functional Regions, Nodal Regions, and Hierarchies by Functional Distance Approaches." *Journal of Regional Science* 11 (1971), 57–72.

Burnett, P. "The Dimensions of Alternatives in Spatial Choice Processes." *Geographical Analysis* 5 (1973), 181–204.

Campbell, T. C., M. Hwang, and S. Shahrokh. "Market Delineation in the Coal Industry." *The Review of Regional Studies* 9 (1979), 6–17.

Churchill, G. A., Jr. (1987), *Marketing Research.* New York: CBS College Publishing.

Diaconis, P. and B. Efron. "Computer-Intensive Methods in Statistics." *Scientific American* 48 (1983), 116–30.

Dillman, D. A. (1978), *Mail and Telephone Surveys: The Total Design Method.* New York: John Wiley & Sons.

Ditton, R. B., T. L. Goodale, and P. K. Johnsen. "A Cluster Analysis of Activity, Frequency, and Environment Variables to Identify Water-based Recreation Types." *Journal of Leisure Research* 7 (1975), 282–95.

Efron, B. and G. Gong. "A Leisurely Look at the Bootstrap, the Jackknife, and Cross-Validation." *The American Statistician*, 37 (1983), 36–48.

Elzinga, K. G. and T. F. Hogarty. "The Problem of Geographic Market Delineation in Antimerger Suits." *The Antitrust Bulletin* 18 (1973), 45–81.

Elzinga, K. G. and T. F. Hogarty. "The Problem of Geographical Market Delineation Revisited: The Case of Coal." *The Antitrust Bulletin* 23 (1978), 1–18.

Goddard, J. B. "Functional Regions Within the City Centre: A Study by Factor

Analysis of Taxi Flows in Central London." *Transactions of the Institute of British Geographers* 49 (1970), 161–82.
Golledge, R. G. "Conceptualizing the Market Decision Process." *Journal of Regional Science* 7 (Supplement, 1967), 239–58.
Golledge, R. G. and L. A. Brown. "Search, Learning, and the Market Decision Process." *Geografiska Annaler*, Series B., 49 (1967), 116–24.
Goodwin, R. F. (1982), *Recreational Boating in Washington's Coastal Zone: The Market for Moorage*. Seattle: Institute for Marine Studies, University of Washington.
Graaskamp, J. A. (1980), *Fundamentals of Real Estate Development*. Washington: The Urban Land Institute.
Lentnek, B., C. S. Van Doren, and J. R. Trail. "Spatial Behavior in Recreational Boating." *Journal of Leisure Research* 1 (1969), 103–24.
Peterson, K. and Atwood, P. D. (1988), *A Study of Market Demand for Marina Facilities Along Wisconsin's Great Lakes Coasts*. Madison: Recreation Resources Center, University of Wisconsin—Madison, 1988.
Peterson, K., A. Chesler, and G. Lamb. (1987), *Economic Benefits of Harbor Use in Oconto County—1986*. Madison: Recreation Resources Center, University of Wisconsin—Madison.
Ratcliff, R. U. "Appraisal *Is* Market Analysis." *The Appraisal Journal* (1975), 485–90.
Salvesen, D. "Coming About: Racine's New Harbor, Marina, and Festival Park." *Urban Land* (April 1988), 12–15.
Slater, P. B. "A Hierarchical Regionalization of Japanese Prefectures Using 1972 Interprefectural Migration Flows." *Regional Studies* 10 (1976), 123–32.
Slater, P. B. "Structuring N-Way Trip Distribution Matrices Using Standardization and Hierarchical Clustering Procedures." *Transportation Research* 11 (1977), 287–91.
Slater, P. B. "A Partial Hierarchical Regionalization of 3140 U.S. Counties on the Basis of 1965–1970 Intercounty Migration." *Environment and Planning A* 19 (1984), 545–50.
Solomon, B. D. and J. J. Pyrdol. "Delineating Coal Market Regions." *Economic Geography* 62 (1986), 109–24.
Stynes, D. L. and D. F. Holecek (1982), *Michigan Great Lakes Recreational Boating: A Synthesis of Current Information*. Ann Arbor, MI: Sea Grant Publications.

11 AN INVESTIGATION INTO THE COMPETITION BETWEEN THE DOWNTOWN SHOPPING AREA AND THE SUBURBAN SHOPPING MALL

Donald H. Bleich

Introduction

As cities grow, retail centers will relocate where they can serve the largest proportion of the market in the most efficient way. Since World War II, most cities have undergone suburbanization. This has put tremendous economic pressure on retail establishments to move out of the downtown centers to locations in suburbia that are closer to potential shoppers.[1] These changes in the spatial distribution of retail activity have left many cities with deteriorating downtowns and serious economic problems due to a loss of business, jobs, and income, and a lowered tax base.[2] In order to revitalize downtown shopping, decision makers in the public and private sectors must have a clear understanding of the mechanism through which consumer demand for retail centers is generated.

The purpose of this paper is twofold. First, a procedure will be illustrated for developing a probabilistic model, including attitudinal factors, which explains the process through which the consumer chooses between the downtown area and the suburban shopping mall. This model will then be compared to a Huff model that utilizes only travel time and assortment of goods.

Retail Shopping Models

One major set of models used to anticipate the access of retail centers assumes that the retail center behaves like a magnet, or gravity center, to which shoppers are attracted based upon the size and the access of the center.[3] The first of these models is Reilly's Law.

Reilly's Law

Reilly (1929) applied the Law of Gravity to estimate the relative drawing power between competing locations. Where Newton used mass, Reilly substituted population. Mathematically Reilly's Law can be stated as follows:

$$\frac{B_a}{B_b} = \left(\frac{P_a}{P_b}\right) \times \left(\frac{D_b}{D_a}\right)^2,$$

where B_a = proportion of trade attracted by city A; B_b = proportion of trade attracted by city B; B_a/B_b = attraction of city A relative to the attraction of city B (an index number); P_a = population of city A; P_b = population of city B; D_a = distance from intermediate town to city A; and D_b = distance from intermediate town to city B.

In words, Reilly's Law states that the relative drawing power of two competing spheres of dominance from intermediate areas is in direct proportion to the square of the distance from the intermediate areas to each sphere of influence. Using this model, the relative total retail sales of competing locations can be estimated.

Reilly's Law gained wide acceptance but it has several limitations. First, the calculation of breaking points between competing locations implies that a consumer will spend all expenditures at one location. Secondly, there is no differentiation between the type of goods being sold. Thirdly, Reilly assumes that we should always use the distance squared. Finally, there is very little theory or behavioral content underlying the ideas of the gravity model.

Huff Model

In order to overcome the shortcomings of Reilly's Law, Huff (1962) combined the choice axiom of Luce (1959) with the two principal constructs of Central Place Theory (Christaller, 1933; Losch, 1954), importance of center, and distance. The results are a probabilistic model at a disaggregate level utilizing a multiplicative utility function. Mathematically the model is

$$\Omega_H: P_{ij} = \frac{u_{ij}}{\sum_{j=1}^{n} u_{ij}} = \frac{S_j^{\lambda_s} T_{ij}^{\lambda_t}}{\sum_{j=1}^{n} S_j^{\lambda_s} T_{ij}^{\lambda_t}},$$

where U_{ij} = utility shopping center j to customer at i, P_{ij} = probability of a consumer at a given point i shopping at a given center j, S_j = size of shopping center, T_{ij} = the travel time involved in getting from location i to location j, λ_s, λ_t = parameter to be estimated empirically (s > 0, t < 0), and n = number of shopping centers.

Huff assumes that all shoppers have identical tastes. The square footage variable serves as a proxy for an assortment of merchandise. The larger the area, the wider the assortment of merchandise. In addition, Huff improves on Reilly's Law in the following ways. First, by using probability on the left side of the equation, it is no longer necessary to assume that a shopper will always shop at the same store. Secondly, by using the parameter λ_t, Huff eliminates the assumption that the disutility to the consumer is related to the distance squared. He found that the relationship is nonlinear and must be found empirically from the data. The inclusion of the parameter λ_s lets us consider the effect of the type of merchandise. Huff's equation indicates that λ_s must be derived from the data and can be expected to vary depending on the type of retail establishment being studied.

Methodology

The model to be implemented in this study is the multiplicative competitive interaction model (MCI), which is an extension of the Huff model.[4] This can be written mathematically as

$$\pi_{ij} = \frac{X_{ij1}^{\alpha_1} X_{ij2}^{\alpha_2} \ldots X_{ijk}^{\alpha_k}}{\sum_{j=1}^{m} (X_{ij1}^{\alpha_1} X_{ij2}^{\alpha_2} \ldots X_{ijk}^{\alpha_k})},$$

where π_{ij} = the probability that a consumer shops at alternative location j, X_{ijk} = k-th variable for location j for consumer i, and α_k = coefficient relating the importance of the k-th variable.

The basic advantage of this model over the linear additive model is that the multiplicative formulation allows it to incorporate interaction effects among explanatory variables. The estimation procedure to be used will be the logit model.

Detailed properties of the model can be found in Nakanishi and Cooper (1974). The basic advantage of this model over the linear additive model is that the multiplicative formulation allows it to incorporate interaction effects among explanatory variables. For example, if a shopping location is enclosed and has a high score for parking convenience, any interaction effect caused by being both is accounted for.

Two of the estimated procedures that can be used with the MCI model are the Nakanishi, Cooper, and Kassarjian (NCK) procedure and the logit model.[5] These two procedures are described below.

Nakanishi, Cooper, and Kassarjian Estimation Procedure

When using this estimation procedure it is best to use the simplified version, which is expressed as a dummy variable regression model.[6] This can be expressed mathematically as

$$\log p_{ij} = \sum_{i'=1}^{I} \alpha_{i'} D_{i'} + \sum_{h=1}^{H} \beta_h \log X_{hij} + e_{ij},$$

where $D_{i'}$ = a dummy variable that is equal to 1 if $i' = 1$ and 0 otherwise, $\alpha_{i'}$ = regression coefficient for $D_{i'}$, p_{ij} = probability individual i selects location j, X_{hij} = value of the h-th variable for location j for individual i, β_h = the parameter for the sensitivity of p_{ij} with respect to variable h, and e_{ij} = stochastic disturbance term.

Logit Model

A general transformation that produces a form linear in parameters for the model specified is the Logit Model. To implement this procedure, alternatives are expressed in a log ratio to some base alternative. Applying this to the extended Huff model, we get the following equation (see Appendix):

$$\ln(P_r/P_b) = \sum_{i=1}^{k} \beta_i [\ln z_i(x_r) - \ln z_i(x_b)],$$

where b = base alternative and r = feasible alternatives.

This estimation procedure was selected since it is better designed to handle the attitude variables, which are interval scale data.[7] Although the procedure is indifferent to which alternative is selected as the base, the downtown area was selected. Multiple regression analyses are then performed where the dependent variable is the log odds of patronizing a particular nonbase alternative rather than the downtown area.

Hypotheses

H1: The extended Huff model, which utilizes variables other than size and distance, will explain more of the variation in the consumer shopping decision process than the traditional Huff model.

$$H_1: \Omega_H \text{ vs. } \Omega_E$$

$$\Omega_E: P_{ij} = \frac{u_{ij}}{\sum u_{ij}} = \frac{S_j^{\lambda_s} T_{ij}^{\lambda_t} A_{ij1}^{\lambda_1} \ldots \ldots A_{ijm}^{\lambda_m}}{\sum S_j^{\lambda_s} T_{ij}^{\lambda_t} A_{ij1}^{\lambda_1} \ldots \ldots A_{ijm}^{\lambda_m}},$$

where U_{ij} = utility of shopping center j to consumer i, P_{ij} = probability of consumer i shopping at center j, S_j = size of shopping center j, T_{ij} = travel time for consumer i to get to shopping center j, $A_{ij1} \ldots A_{ijm}$ = additional attributes and factors of consumer i to shopping center j, and $\lambda_s, \lambda_t, \lambda_1, \ldots, \lambda_m$ = parameters to be estimated empirically ($\lambda_s > 0$, $\lambda_t > 0$, $\lambda_1 > 0$, $\lambda_m > 0$).

Experience with Central Place Theory, the gravity models, and the Huff Model indicates that size (assortment) and distance will be significant. The next set of hypotheses deal with the question of the significance of each attribute and factor proposed in the next sections as well as distance and size. If an attribute or factor has no effect on the consumer's decision, then we would expect its coefficient to be zero. Therefore, we will test the following hypotheses to determine which attributes and factors are significant.

$H_2 - H_n$: The model will perform better if attribute or factor i is included:

$$H_i: \beta_i = 0 \text{ vs. } \beta_i \neq 0,$$

where β_i is the regression coefficient for attribute/factor i.

Conceptual Framework for Consumer Choice Model

If the model specified in the last section is to truly explain the mechanism through which consumer demand for retail sales is generated, it must recognize the number and kinds of variables influencing choice behavior and how they will vary for different consumers, locations, and types of goods. This section of the paper will review the literature[8] to identify the important variables that must be considered in the development of the model.

The variables identified in the literature can be divided into three categories. These are attributes of the shopping location, consumer perceptions of how well the location will meet their shopping needs, and nonshopping factors. Below each construct is discussed and the rationale for including it is given.

Shopping Location Attributes

In this section we will identify the important attributes of the shopping location as reflected in the current literature. These attributes will have a direct effect upon how the location is perceived by the consumer.

Access Variables. The difficulties a consumer must overcome to travel to the retail location will impact strongly upon the decision process. The access variables will be the first to be discussed.

Distance. As described earlier, distance is one of the two constructs used in the Huff Model. Distance, however, can be measured in several ways, actual distance in miles, actual travel time, perceived distance in miles, and perceived travel time. There is empirical evidence (Cadwallader, 1975; Burnett, 1978; MacKay et al., 1975; Bach, 1981; Thompson, 1963; Brunerd and Mason, 1968) that perceived distance measured in time explains more variation in shopping location choice. Based on the conclusions from these studies, the subjective or perceived distance measured in time is used.

Although retailing has decreased, the downtown remains the center of other business activities. Thus, many people who have moved to the suburbs still travel each day to their office downtown. In addition, some retail shopping trips are made from the place of work rather than from home. To capture this effect, subjects are asked if they travel to each location from work. If the subject indicates that this is common, the perceived travel time from work is used in place of the distance from home.

Mode of Transportation. In addition to the distance a consumer must travel, the quality of the trip will be very important. In choosing a shopping location, the consumer will take into consideration performance, comfort, cost, and safety.⁹ The mode of transportation available to the consumer will, therefore, play a major role in selecting between downtown and suburban shopping.¹⁰

The mode of transportation may also be correlated with the importance of other attributes. Jonassen (1955) has shown that consumers are more likely to use public transportation for downtown shopping than for suburban shopping. In addition, he showed that this will vary from city to city. We can also expect the mode of transportation to have an important bearing on the importance of parking, since shoppers who use public transportation will not be as concerned with these factors as much as shoppers who use the automobile.

Parking. One of the advantages of shopping centers over downtown areas is the availability of convenient parking.¹¹ Convenient parking enables the consumer to reduce the time needed to shop. There is much empirical evidence (Timmermans, 1981; Bellenger et al., 1977; Bearden, 1977; Jonassen, 1955) to show that convenient parking plays a significant role in the shopping choice decision process.

In some situations it may be desirable to break down parking convenience into its components: the ability to find a parking space, the distance the shopper needs to walk to get to the stores, the safety in the parking lot, and the cost of parking. A location may be very convenient for one component but score very poorly on another. For example, the new regional centers offer free parking directly beneath the stores but many shoppers have expressed reservations about the safety of walking through an underground structure.

Use Mix. The type of goods sold at a retail center will have a large impact on total sales. The rest of this section will look at the use mix of the location. The important uses are identified and discussed.

Number of Women's Clothing Stores. Several studies (Thompson, 1971; Herrmann and Beik, 1968; Reynolds and Darden, 1972) have examined the motivations of shoppers who bypass the closest retail outlet for shopping further away. The results indicate that women's clothing was the item most often shopped for. Due to its ability to attract shoppers from long distances, the consumer's perceptions of the assortment of women's clothing will be measured.

Department Stores. Another important attribute of a shopping center is the number of department stores located at a center. The existence of at least two major department stores is considered mandatory for the success of a regional center. The department stores serve a dual purpose. In addition to selling their own goods, most of the stores in the center will rely on the department stores to attract shoppers.[12]

Number of Restaurants. One nonshopping motive for going to a shopping location is to have lunch with a friend. Eating may also be important if it is to be combined with a shopping trip. Downtown areas should be able to compete effectively with suburban centers. In addition to servicing the lunch crowds from the downtown office buildings, restaurants may attract shoppers from the suburbs.

Other Shopping Center Attributes. The remainder of this section will deal with the literature pertaining to the other shopping center attributes that may impact on the consumer.

Total Area and Total Retail Space. The second variable used extensively in the gravity models is size. This can be measured either as total area or total retail space. Size is assumed to be a surrogate for the overall assortment of goods.[13] Although it has been significant when used with a distance variable, there are reasons to suspect that the Huff Model puts an undue emphasis on the importance of retail center size as the determinant of drawing power.[14] The attitudinal variables to be added may prove to be better measures and may result in statistical insignificance of the size variable.

Promotions. Some of the shopping centers have an organized program of promotions managed by a director. The purpose of these promotions is to encourage shoppers to shop more frequently at the center. This variable has not been used elsewhere. However, it is reasonable to assume that consumers attending art shows and concerts will be likely to shop while they are there.

In addition, consumers attending promotions at a shopping location will become more familiar with the stores there and will be more likely to choose this location at a later time.

Advertising. In addition to promotions, such as art shows and concerts, shopping locations will rely on advertising in the media to attract shoppers. Deriving an actual measure of advertising is difficult. A review of local newspapers indicates that much of the relevant advertising is placed by the department stores that have stores located in several shopping locations. Since one ad is placed for all locations, it will be difficult to separate out. We can, however, get the subject's perceptions by asking how often they see ads for each location.

Another difficulty in measuring advertising is that it is not always clear which shopping and nonshopping factors are affected. For example, while one form of advertising may emphasize low prices, another may emphasize nonshopping factors, such as entertainment or special events. The effects of the different types of advertising will, therefore, be reflected in the individual factors.

Enclosed or Open. Today many regional shopping centers are built totally enclosed. In areas with a cold climate this serves both to protect shoppers from the weather and to create a pleasant atmosphere. This is, of course, one attribute a downtown area cannot match. It is possible, however, to enclose walkways and to build overpasses between the major stores.

Surrounding Neighborhood. Previous research has indicated that the type of neighborhood surrounding the shopping location will greatly affect the consumer's perceptions of the location center itself.

This is a major problem for downtown areas. In many cities, the downtown area is ether surrounded by or contains the poorer neighborhoods. If the empirical results indicate that this is a problem, downtown planners may decide to begin the revitalization process by eliminating or separating the slum areas from the downtown shopping areas.

Shopping Factors

During the location-choice decision process, the attributes of the location will be converted into consumer perceptions of how well the location will meet the consumer's shopping demands. As a source of goods, a retail location should offer the widest assortment of goods with the lowest expenditure of time and money. In this section, three shopping factors are discussed: assortment of goods, savings of time, and savings of money.

Overall Selection. A large number of consumer shopping trips are made under conditions of uncertainty. In this context, consumers will weigh the probability that their shopping demands will be met. The larger the selection of goods, the more likely it is that the trip will be successful.[15]

A study of Jonassen (1955) indicated that the overall selection was the attribute most often quoted by shoppers in deciding whether to shop downtown or in suburbia. Downtown areas were perceived as having a much larger selection of goods.

Savings of Time and Money. The location of many stores together can create an opportunity for consumers to do all their shopping in the least amount of time and money. This is an area where downtown areas can compete on an equal basis with shopping centers. Bellenger et al. (1977) and Singson (1975) have shown that this is an important consideration. Jonassen (1955) also showed that suburban and downtown shopping was perceived to be different on these two attributes. Downtown areas were perceived as having cheaper prices but requiring more time to shop.

Nonshopping Factors

In addition to meeting shopping needs, the consumer may also evaluate the location with regard to nonshopping factors.[16] In this section, three nonshopping factors are discussed. They are atmosphere, social amenities, and safety.

Atmosphere. Several studies (Bearden, 1977; Bellenger et al., 1977; Nakanishi, 1975) have found empirical support for the importance of atmosphere. To compete with the suburban shopping center, city officials will have to decide first on the importance and secondly on the type of atmosphere that is most effective.

Safety. In selecting amongst the alternatives, the safety of the shopping location will probably be significant. This safety component can be divided into two components, safety of the trip and safety at the shopping location.

To measure the effect of safety at the shopping location, subjects are asked if they feel safe walking around the shopping location. In addition to the effect of the mode of transportation, which is discussed above, the safety of the trip will also be effected by whether or not the consumer must pass through dangerous neighborhoods. This is a major problem for downtown areas. In most cities, the poorer neighborhoods are in close proximity to the downtown areas. Therefore, trips from the suburbs to the downtown area usually require the shopper to travel through the slums for part of the trip. If the empirical results indicate that this is a major factor, downtown planners may decide to build corridors to the downtown area that either bypass or shield the shopper from the slums. For each alternative location the subject is asked to evaluate the safety of the neighborhoods through which the subject must pass.

Nonshopping Amenities. The choice of one shopping location over another may be decided based upon the amenities that are available at the center other than shopping. Very often the shopping trip is combined with a social function, such as having lunch with a friend. Downtown areas can compete with shopping centers on this point. In addition to stores, the downtown areas of cities may include theaters, restaurants, cultural events, and museums.

An Empirical Application

In this section, the procedure for building a model to explain the competition between downtown areas and suburban shopping locations will be illustrated. The analysis is based on interviews with potential shoppers living on the west side of Los Angeles. The choice set will be selected, the data described, the methodology discussed, and the results analyzed.

The retail areas of both shopping centers and downtown areas are allocated amongst many types of goods. There is empirical evidence that each good must be treated separately in building the model.[17] To simplify the study, only clothing shopping trips were examined. Clothing was selected for three reasons. First, it has been identified as the major component of a regional shopping center and the good to which the most area is allocated.[18] Secondly, clothing has been identified in previous literature as a good for which shoppers are willing to travel long distances. Finally, both the downtown area of Los Angeles and the major suburban shopping centers have large clothing inventories.

Choice Set

Before administering the questionnaire, it was necessary to determine the choice set, the set of shopping location alternatives. This was complicated by the structure of the Los Angeles area. In addition to the central downtown area, Los Angeles has many unplanned shopping locations in the suburbs that have many of the characteristics of a downtown area. A distinguishing characteristic between a downtown area and a regional shopping center is that the latter is under single management, which can dictate the number, mix, and area allocation for each type of retail good. The management of regional shopping centers also has the ability to pressure individual stores to take actions, which these stores would not otherwise do, in order to increase the profits of the location as a whole. In an unplanned or downtown area, each individual store will act to maximize their own profits. For this reason, the four alternative locations consisted of the downtown area, two suburban regional shopping centers, and one unplanned suburban area. The shopping locations used and their characteristics are listed below.

Shopping area	Type	Location
Downtown Los Angeles	Unplanned	Central
Century Square Shopping Center	Regional center	Suburban
Santa Monica Place	Regional center	Suburban
Westwood	Unplanned	Suburban

Data

The sample on which the models in the study are tested consists of 45 female consumers residing on the west side of Los Angeles. The subjects as a whole were middle to upper middle class and highly educated. Nearly one half of the subjects earned at least $40,000 and 11% earned more than $100,000.

A questionnaire, designed to measure the reasons and frequency of shopping trips for clothing, was administered to each subject. For each individual four cases were generated, one for each location. Therefore the data set used for the study consisted of 180 cases.[19]

Respondents evaluated the four alternative shopping locations on fourteen characteristics[20] using a five-point scale.[21] In addition, the respondents were also asked their perceptions of how long, measured in minutes, it took to go from home and work to each location.[22] From this information four measures of access were computed. They are the perceived travel time to go from home to each location, the perceived travel time to go from work to each location, the shortest perceived travel time to either home or work, and a weighted average of perceived travel time to home and work based on the indicated relative frequency with which the individual traveled from work to each location.[23]

Several location variables are coded in binary form.[24] These variables were transformed using the index of distinctiveness measure as formulated in Nakanishi et al. (1974).[25] These indices of distinctiveness were then merged with the subject response data.

Another issue that had to be addressed was the use of the transportation mode variables. Due to the structure of Los Angeles and the tastes of the west side population, the private automobile is used for virtually all shopping trips. This lack of variation necessitated the omission of the transportation mode variables described earlier. It is anticipated that these variables will be significant in other applications and should therefore not be overlooked. The study did, however, include a question to measure the perceived safety of the trip with regard to the need to travel through high-crime neighborhoods.

Results

To compare the Huff Model with the Extended-Huff Model, two multiple regression analyses were performed. In the first regression analysis, the two variables stipulated by Huff, travel time, and assortment, were used to predict the probability of shopping at each center. The results are reported in Table 1. Both travel time and assortment were significant, explaining 27% of the variance.

For the Extended Huff Model, a multiple regression was performed using the variables described previously. The results indicate that there is much to be gained from introducing additional variables to the Huff Model. When additional variables were added to the Huff Model, the amount of variance explained rose from 27% to 52%.

To test if this difference is significant, a Chow test was applied and an F-value of 16.67 was computed. This is significant at the .01 level. We can therefore safely say that the Extended Huff Model is significantly better than the traditional Huff Model.

For the hypothesis pertaining to the significance of individual parameters, time savings, trip safety, getting more for your money, and the percent savings contribute most to the rejection of the Huff Model. The significance of the transportation variables could not be tested. All subjects indicated that they would use their automobile to go to each center. As a result there was no variation and all the transportation variables were omitted from the study.

Each model was also calibrated for each individual, in order to predict which shopping location would be chosen most often. Once again the extended model did better, predicting 77% correctly as compared to 68%

Table 1. Results: Dependent Variable: Probability of Selection[1]

	Coeff.	F-value	Sig. F	R^2
Huff Models				
Travel time[2]	−0.187	19.523	0.000	
Assortment[3]	0.341	27.369	0.000	
Intercept	1.023	478.878	0.000	.27
Extended Huff model				
Travel time[2]	−0.158	19.221	0.000	
Assortment[3]	0.199	10.409	0.001	
Time savings	0.265	27.478	0.000	
Trip safety	0.312	26.049	0.000	
Get more for my money	0.238	14.872	0.000	
Percent savings	−0.178	11.418	0.001	
Intercept	1.131	386.504	0.000	.52

[1] The probability of selection was derived from the questionnaire. The number of trips to each center was divided by the total number of trips for all centers.

[2] Travel time to the closest trip origin, home or work.

[3] The square footage allocated for clothing sales in the downtown area could not be found. Since Huff used areas as a surrogate for assortment, the assortment variable was used in its place.

Table 2. Proportion of Consumers Predicted Correctly

Huff Model	68%
Extended Huff Model	77%

for the Huff Model (Table 2). Given four shopping locations, a "blind prediction" would yield an average success rate of only 25%.

Conclusions

For policy purposes it is useful to observe that all the variables added to the Huff Model relate to shopping factors. The characteristics displayed by the subjects selected corresponds with the "economic" shopper discussed in Bellenger et al. (1977). A review of the demographics of the subjects also corresponds to the demographic patterns of the "economic" shopper—highly educated and lives in a house rather than an apartment. Any policy decision made based upon this study should be understood to apply to only one segment of the population. The results indicate that for, this segment, the most gain can be derived by improving the shopping factors.

With regard to the nonsignificance of the majority of the variables, there are several explanations. First, it is possible that the variable is not considered in the decision making process for the segment tested. Past empirical results indicate that this is probably true, in this case, for the variables that relate to recreational shopping. Another explanation for nonsignificance is the lack of variation. The transportation variables, and their subsequent omission from the study, are an extreme case of this. If shopper perceptions on one attribute are virtually equal for all centers then the attribute will not be significant in choosing between the centers, even though the attribute is important.

Notes

1. Muller (1983).
2. Black (1978).
3. These models, known as gravity models, are based upon Newton's Law of Universal Gravitation in physics. Gravitational pull of one object upon another is in direct proportion to size and inversely proportional to the square of the distance.
4. The Huff Model uses only two variables, distance and size (assortment). The MCI Model may have as many variables as is appropriate.
5. Gautschi (1981).
6. Nakanishi and Cooper (1982).
7. Gautschi (1981).
8. Nearly all of the empirical studies quoted in this section deal with the competition between similar retail outlets, such as supermarkets, department stores, and shopping centers, and do not include the downtown area. However, the significance of the variables in these studies gives insight into developing a model for the application discussed in this paper.
9. Gautschi (1981).
10. Jonassen (1955).
11. Jonassen (1955).
12. *Shopping Center Development Handbook*. Washington D.C.: Urban Land Institute.
13. Huff (1962).
14. Nakanishi and Yamanaka (1980); Bucklin (1967).
15. Huff (1962).
16. Bellinger et al. (1977).
17. Huff (1962), Nakanishi (1975).
18. *Los Angeles Shopping Center Directory*.
19. Although it is common practice to use an ordinary least squares procedure for such applications, there is theoretical evidence that only a generalized least squares procedure will produce (asymptotically) minimum variance estimators when you do not have independence between the cases. The validity of this theory will be tested in future empirical work.

20. Selection of these characteristics is based on the attributes and factors described earlier in the conceptualization of the problem.

21. Gautschi (1981).

22. The basis for using time, rather than distance measured in miles, is explained earlier in this paper.

23. The weighted average was computed by converting the five-point scale to a percentage (P) from 0% to 100%. This percentage was then multiplied by the travel time from work and added to the product of $1 - P$ times the travel time from home

$$\text{weighted average} = (P \times TW) + [(1 - P) \times TH],$$

where P = percentage of trips from work, TW = perceived travel time from work, and TH = perceived travel time from home.

24. Planned vs. unplanned, enclosed vs. open.

25. Nakanishi et al. (1974):

$$X = m/c \quad \text{if location i has attribute k}$$
$$= 1 - (c/m) \quad \text{otherwise,}$$

where c = number of locations that possess attribute k and m = total number of locations.

References

Bach. "The Problem of Aggregation and Distance for Analyses of Accessibility and Access Opportunity in Location-Allocation Models." *Environment and Planning A*. 13 (1981), 955–78.

Beardon. "Determinant Attributes of Store Patronage. Downtown Versus Outlying Shopping Centers." *Journal of Retailing* 53 2 (Summer 1977).

Bellenger, Robertson and Greenberg. "Shopping Center Patronage Motives." *Journal of Retailing* 47, 1 (Spring 1971).

Black. *The Changing Economic Role of Central Cities*. Washington. D.C.: ULI— The Urban Land Institute, 1978.

Brunner and Mason. "Influence of Driving Time on Shopping Center Preference." *Journal of Marketing* (April 1968).

Bucklin, Louis. "The Concept of Mass and Intra-urban Shopping." *Journal of Marketing* 31 (Oct. 1967), 37–42.

Burnett, P. "Time Cognition and Urban Travel Behavior." *Geog. Annlr* 60B (1978), 107–15.

Cadwallader, M. "A Behavioral Model of Consumer Spatial Decision Making." *Economic Geography* 51 (1975), 339–49.

Chow, Gregory C. "Tests of Equality Between Sets of Coefficients in Two Linear Regressions." *Econometrica* 51 (1960), 339–49.

Christaller, W. *Central Places in Southern Germany*, translated by C. W. Baskin. Englewood Cliffs, NJ: Prentice-Hall, 1966.

Gautschi. "Specification of Patronage Models for Retail Center Choice." *Journal of Marketing Research* 18 (May 1981), 162–74.

Herrmann, R. and L. Beik. "Shopping Movements Outside their Local Retail Area." *Journal of Marketing* (October 1968), 45–51.

Huff, David. *Determination of Intraurban Retail Trade Areas.* Los Angeles: Real Estate Research Program, University of California, Los Angeles, 1962.

Jonassen, C. T. *The Shopping Center Versus Downtown.* Columbus, OH: Bureau of Business Research, College of Commerce and Administration, The Ohio State University, 1955.

Los Angeles Shopping Center Directory, Los Angeles Times Marketing Research Department (September 1981).

Losch, A. *The Economics of Location*, translated by W. H. Woglom and F. Stolper. New Haven: Yale University Press, 1954.

Luce, R. D. *Individual Choice Behavior.* New York: John Wiley and Sons, 1959.

Moore and Mason. "A Research Note on Major Retail Center Patronage." *Journal of Marketing* (July 1969).

MacKay, Olsharsky, and Sentell. "Cognitive Maps and Spatial Behavior of Consumers." *Geogr Analysis* 7 (1975), 19–34.

Muller, Thomas. "Regional Malls. Their Growth and Impact." Paper prepared by the Western Regional Science Conference, Honolulu, Hawaii, February 1975.

Nakanishi. "Attitudinal Influence on Retail Patronage Behavior," in *Advances in Consumer Research*, Vol. III, Association for Consumer Research, 1975.

Nakanishi and Yamanaka. "Measurement of Drawing Power of Retail Centers: Regression Analysis." *Kwansei Gakuin University Annual Studies* 29 (December 1980).

Nakanishi, Cooper, and Kassarjian. "Voting for a Political Candidate Under Conditions of Minimal Information." *Journal of Consumer Research* 1 (September 1974).

Reilly, William J. *Methods for the Study of Retail Relationships.* Research Monograph No. 4, University of Texas Bulletin No. 2944. Austin: University of Texas Press, 1929.

Reynolds, F. and W. Darden. "Intermarket Patronage: A Psychographic Study of Consumer Outshoppers." *Journal of Marketing* (October 1972), 50–4.

Rich and Portis. "The Imageries of Department Stores." *Journal of Marketing* 28 (April 1964), 10–5.

Shopping Center Development Handbook. Washington, D.C.: ULI—Urban Land Institute, 1982.

Singson, Ricardo. "Multidimensional Scaling Analysis of Store Image and Shopping Behavior." *Journal of Retailing* 51 (Summer 1975), 38–52.

Thompson, Donald. "New Concept . . . Subjective Distance." *Journal of Retailing*, 47, 1 (Spring 1971).

Timmermans, H. J. P. "Multiattribute Shopping Models and Ridge Regression Analysis." *Environment and Planning A* 13 (1981), 43–56.

Appendix

$$P_{ij} = \frac{\prod_{k}^{K} Z_k(X_j)^{\beta_{kj}}}{\sum_{n=1}^{N} \prod_{k=1}^{K} Z_k(X_n)^{\beta_{kn}}}$$

For $b \neq j$:

$$\frac{P_{ij}}{P_{ib}} = \frac{\dfrac{\prod_{k}^{K} Z_k(X_j)^{\beta_{kj}}}{\sum_{n=1}^{N} \prod_{k=1}^{K} Z_k(X_n)^{\beta_{kn}}}}{\dfrac{\prod_{k}^{K} Z_k(X_b)^{\beta_{kb}}}{\sum_{n=1}^{N} \prod_{k=1}^{K} Z_k(X_n)^{\beta_{kn}}}}$$

$$= \frac{\prod_{k}^{K} Z_k(X_j)^{\beta_k}}{\prod_{k}^{K} Z_k(X_b)^{\beta_k}}$$

where $\beta_k = \beta_{kb} = \beta_{kj}$.

$$\ln(P_{ij}/P_{ib}) = \Sigma \beta_k [\ln Z_k(X_j) - \ln Z_k(X_b)],$$

where P_{ij} = probability that i^{th} individual chooses the jth alternative, $Z_k(X_b) = k^{th}$ scale function (attribute) on a vector of characteristics X, and β_{kj} = sensitivity parameter associated with k^{th} attribute on the characteristics measured on alternative j.

12 MULTIPLE STORE TRADE AREA RELATIONSHIPS AND LOGISTIC RESPONSE FUNCTION ESTIMATION

Craig E. Stanley

Introduction

During the past 20 years substantial progress has been made in linking Central Place Theory with Location Theory via spatial competition (Fujita et al., 1988). If Location Theory provides a means for evaluating alternative locations for industrial firms, then retail location theory must be concerned with the evaluation of spatial relationships at the local retail level. Until recently the theoretical support for retail location analysis, which should be derived from Central Place Theory, was almost uniformly lacking from retail locational analyses (Grigg, 1984). The literature has been characterized by a variety of ad hoc empirical procedures, making use of observable data for specific applications, but lacking the generality that linkage with Central Place Theory could provide.

This paper will briefly review the basic tenets of Central Place Theory and discuss well-known probabilistic modifications of Central Place Theory concepts. It will propose a probabilistic alternative and will test this alternative utilizing primary survey data and secondary socioeconomic data from eleven supermarkets in the city of Madison, Wisconsin. Differences between store trade areas will be shown to be related to basic Central Place Theory variables. Finally, estimates of store sales will be compared to observed sales and the implications for new sites will be discussed.

The Central Place Model

The underlying theory for the Central Place Model was first formulated by August Losch (1954) and Walter Christaller (1966) to explain the spatial arrangement of German villages. Refinements by Berry and Garrison (1958), Berry and Barnum (1962), Berry (1965, 1967), Boventer (1969), Curry (1967), and Dacey and Sen (1968) have led to the specification of the following set of basic assumptions as underlying the theory:

1. The market area is a flat, featureless plain.
2. Transportation cost and travel effort are equal in all directions.
3. Population distributions are even in all directions.
4. All consumers are uniform with respect to income, tastes, and preferences.
5. The product supplied is homogeneous with a fixed set of characteristics.
6. There are no restrictions on the entry or exit by other activities supplying the product.
7. Buyers and sellers possess perfect information.

Obviously restrictive, the model leads to a set of circular trade areas with a monopolistically competitive activity at the center. Overlapping circles and a hexagonal trade area pattern also exist to minimize the distance traveled by consumers to the activity from any point on the plain. The total quantity demanded of a good by consumers located at m distance from the store within a market area with radius r is given by Berry (1967) as follows:

$$D_i = S \int_0^{2\pi} [\int_0^{m=r} f(P_i + mt)m\,dm]\,d\theta, \qquad (1)$$

where D_i = total demand for good x at price P_i within the calculated market area, S = population density, m = distance from centroid location, t = transportation rate or effort required to reach the centroid, and π = a constant used in area calculations.

Subsequent additions to the theory have allowed for variation in population, density, transport costs, competition, intervening opportunity, income, and physical and psychological barriers. Regardless, the deterministic result depends on the Principle of Least Effort (Zipf, 1949) and always leads to elliptical or circular market areas, with the centroid retail location attracting 100% of the potential trade from adjacent zones.

The introduction of market area breakpoints was the prime contribution of Reilly's (1931) retail gravitation model, which also assigns varying levels of importance to the distance measure and recognizes the importance of variety in a shopping area by using center size as a proxy for variety of goods. The historical development of the model is contained in Rose (1987), with numerous advances such as Batty (1978). Most of the literature dealing with the Reilly model has dealt with mathematical refinements of the trade area break point, and extensions to multiple centers and mapping representations, as reviewed in O'Kelly and Miller (1989).

The basic elements of Central Place Theory have been incorporated into contributions that emphasize the role of choice under uncertainty and rely on the more generalized choice axiom developed by Luce (1959):

$$Pr(X; T) = v(x) / \sum_y v(y), \qquad (2)$$

where $Pr(x; T)$ indicates the probability of choosing alternative x from a set of T alternatives and is critically dependent upon the specification of $v(x)$, which represents alternatives chosen from a measurable discrete probability distribution function.

Well-known applications by Huff (1963, 1964) in predicting the spatial behavior of consumers utilize a specific form for $v(x)$ and $v(y)$:

$$v(j) = S_j / T_{ij}^\lambda. \qquad (3)$$

The Huff model of probable choice is then written as

$$P(C_{ij}) = \frac{S_j / T_{ij}^\lambda}{\sum_{j=1}^{n} (S_j / T_{ij}^\lambda)}, \qquad (4)$$

where $P(c_{ij})$ = the probability of a consumer at a given point of origin i traveling to a given shopping center j, S_j = the square footage of selling space devoted to the sale of a particular class of goods by shopping center j, T_{ij} = the travel time involved in getting from a consumers travel base i to a shopping center j, and λ = a parameter that is to be estimated empirically to reflect the effect of travel time on various kinds of shopping trips.

The Huff model implicitly assumes that consumers

1. Isolate a subset of "alternative shopping center choices" from a much larger set.
2. Calculate a positive measure of utility for each of these perceived alternatives.
3. Distribute their retail patronage spatially in a probabilistic manner.

Consumers are seen to discriminate imperfectly and to maximize the utility of a shopping center trip by choosing more than one exclusive alternative over time.

Although a great many variables may potentially affect the utility consumers attach to a given shopping center experience, the Huff model is limited to only two: shopping center size and travel time to the center. Recent improvements on the Huff model have allowed additional variables to enter the probability function. For instance, Okoruwa et al. (1988) incorporate mall-specific variables and demographic characteristics of shoppers within a Poisson probabilistic regression model to forecast patronization shares. The application does, however, require a Partitioned Newton–Raphson Algorithm to make the maximum likelihood procedure manageable as well as modification of the interview responses due to potential sample censoring biases arising from individual estimation of historical trip frequencies.

A major difficulty, however, with the Huff visitation probability estimates concerns the independence from irrelevant alternatives (IIA) property of the Luce choice system. As reviewed by O'Kelly and Miller (1989), the *relative* probability of visitation to any two centers will remain unchanged and independent of other available alternatives. In reality, a large number of similar alternative retailing centers could cause the ratio of any two visitation probabilities to vary. Consequently pairwise comparisons using the Huff method may lead to biased visitation probability estimates. A strong argument can be made for a full competing destinations model as described in this paper.

Another method has been suggested to derive estimates of frequency of visitation from residential origins to the retail store. Mackay (1973a) applied a binary filter and trend surface analysis to map the percentage of stops consumers make at individual retail stores. The sample observations were spatially clustered, as is the case with most retail store survey data. A systematic spacing scheme was adopted that allowed the specification of residential location by a coordinate system. Fitting of the map to the irregularly spaced data points was accomplished by a quadratic polynomial, which also resulted in substantial trend-surface residual autocorrelation. A binomially weighted smoothing function was adopted to reduce the autocorrelation, and this technique yielded a realistic and theoretically satisfying map of shopping patterns, characterized by regularly spaced rings surrounding the store. A number of disadvantages, however, may preclude widespread use of the method. First, as Mackay points out, there is substantial data loss using the binomially weighted filter. Second, there is no optimal filter or methodology for accumulating the data in regularly spaced intervals. Third, for the seven stores for which the percentage of stops was estimated, the coefficients of determination (R^2) varied from 59.7 to 89.8 percent using the adjusted filter, suggesting that other factors not in the model influence the dependent variable substantially.

Other work by Mackay (1973b) attempts to pattern the frequency of supermarket visits by determining the variance components or power spectra using spectral analysis. The data utilized were based on longitudinal surveys and non-trade-area-specific consumer characteristics, with certain stratifications providing significant results. These strata included low and high demand groups, families with children less than two years of age, professional and technical occupational groups vs. all others, and incomes less than $7500 or greater than $15,000. Shopping frequency was shown to be positively related to demand and disposable time, with power spectra significantly different for families with employed wives vs. those with wives who were not employed. As expected, most socioeconomic–demographic variables from the cross-sectional survey were not significantly related to the average number of shopping trips. Spectral analysis was useful in discriminating between ostensibly homogeneous groups on the basis of subtle differences in observed behavior.

A recent trend towards mapping of retail trade area visitation probabilities is well reviewed by O'Kelly and Miller (1989). They achieve a linking of the Reilly probability of visitation framework with the Applebaum method of estimating the proportion of a stores' sales from a particular area. Advocating a mapping approach to the location of a new center, they show that accumulating measures of demand under a probability surface is similar to the expected value methods, such as that utilized in this paper.

This paper will attempt to expand and improve the procedures utilized to date in the estimation of the probability of visitation at retail stores. The research reported is characterized by a number of features in common with previous work in the area:

1. The competing destinations model is adapted, using multiple centers of attraction (Fotheringham, 1987).
2. The ecological unit or analysis zone is the individual store trade area using the Mackay (1973a) definition.
3. Analysis is based on cross-sectional data gathered during one week's time by on-site stratified random sampling of food store customers as described by Applebaum (1966).
4. Survey data have been allocated to a system of one-quarter mile square rings for which secondary socioeconomic data are available. These rings form the within-trade area unit of observation similar to Applebaum (1966).

The major point of departure from previous work concerns the specification of the dependent variable—visitation rates—as categorical rather than continuous, taking on discrete values that vary with distance from the center as well as other variables that distinguish the population from which the sample is drawn.

The development of the procedure to be used in this study derives from work that specifies more rigorously the set-theoretical foundations of qualitative choice behavior. In conventional consumer analysis, it is often assumed that individuals in a population have a common behavioral rule when faced with alternatives of a continuous nature. In retail choice behavior, however, the individual is faced with qualitative or "lumpy" alternatives, and shifts in individual choice must result from a distribution of decision rules. McFadden (1974a, b) developed a general procedure for formulating models of population choice behavior from distributions of individual decision rules with emphasis on a particular case: the conditional logit analysis.

The logit function derives from work in the biological field by Berkson (1951, 1955), with extensive application in the statistics and economics literature. In store-choice behavior we posit that the probability of visitation at a store will vary systematically as distance increases from the store, not primarily because of distance itself, but because of the many independent factors associated with residence in a particular distance zone. Specifically, the odds in favor of visitation at a particular store is defined as the ratio $P/1 - P$, where P is the observed frequency. These odds, ranging from 0 to infinity, represent a monotonic transformation of P and unrealistically excludes negative values. However, if the odds are described as a log-linear function of distance, this obstacle is overcome. The basic estimating equation becomes

$$\ln\left(\frac{P_i}{1-P_i}\right) = \beta_0 + \beta_i \ln(x_i), \tag{5}$$

where x_i = the ith distance zone. In the current study of n_1 population in zone 1, n_2 in zone 2, etc., we replace the probability P_i, with the observed frequency of visitation for zone i. Estimation requires a weighted least squares procedure since the error variances are unequal. The approximate weights are calculated as

$$W_i = n_i P_i (1 - P_i). \tag{6}$$

Specific Application

This study will compare geographic shopping patterns for food purchases for eleven supermarkets in the city of Madison, Wisconsin. The purpose is to test the following hypotheses:

1. That the logit response function is able to generate statistically reliable estimates of the parameters for distance and other variables.
2. That the parameters for distance vary systematically and predictably between stores of different sizes and neighborhoods.
3. That the estimates of visitation, coupled with average expenditures based on income levels, yield reasonably accurate estimates of total sales for the survey week when compared to actual sales.

The Databases

The data utilized in this study are of two types. The first represents consumer primary data acquired through personal interviews. Important descriptive characteristics of this database are presented in Table 1. The survey measured 20 consumer characteristics, including income, employment, age, household characteristics, store loyalty, and frequency of visitation. Since one of the goals of the study is sales prediction, only the frequency of visitation from the trade area one-quarter mile rings and the distance to the store from each one-quarter mile ring group are utilized in this study.

The second database contains 41 variables selected from the census of population and housing for Madison. These variables were assigned to each one-quarter mile ring based on proportionate area representation

Table 1. Descriptive Summary: Madison Supermarket Survey

A. Primary Data

Store number	1	2	3	4	5	6	7	8	9	10	11	12
Store size (sq. ft)	16,400	13,500	38,000	15,000	24,000	15,000	15,000	6,000	9,000	6,000	25,000	10,000
Usage sample (nobs)	151	167	138	171	186	199	199	226	203	205	191	178
Refusal rate %	19	17	24	19	19	12	12	12	11	16	11	10
Contact rate %	1.6	3.3	1.6	3.6	1.7	2.3	2.3	5.5	3.9	4.6	2.0	2.0
Average sale ($)	9.64	6.28	16.82	6.94	12.03	11.59	11.59	5.40	6.91	7.00	12.31	5.78

B. Secondary Data (Census)

12 PRFEMPRI = Percentage of households with a female primary wage earner.
41 MSALES = Percent of males 14 years and older employed in a sales occupation.
33 EMPLOYED = Percent of males 16 years and older employed in the labor forces.
25 PR5059 = Percentage of structures built between 1950 and 1959.
25 PRHWF254 = Percentage of husband/wife families between 25 and 44 years of age.
11 PRCHILD = Percentage of households with children less than 18 years of age present.
35 MPRIV = Percent of males 16 years and older employed in the private sector.
24 PR1019 = Percentage of dwelling units with 10 to 19 units per structure.
34 UNEMP = Percent of males 16 years of age and older who are in the labor force and unemployed.
23 PRSINFAM = Percentage of single family dwelling units.
25 PARENTER = Percentage of renter-occupied dwelling units.
10 PRMLHEAD = Percentage of households with male head of household.
36 MSTATE = Percent of males 16 years and older employed in state government.
31 ELEM = Percentage of population three years of age and older enrolled in elementary school.

for each census tract and a population weight. A selected group of variables is described in Table 1. A measure of income was represented by seven variables, including average family, primary individual, male, and female incomes. None were significant in the equations that follow and the measure is not further discussed in this study.

Creating the Logit Transformation

The logit transformation requires a measure of probability of visitation divided by the probability of not visiting the store. For this empirical study the observed frequency of visitation is substituted. This procedure is described in Table 2 using data for a single store and seven rings for purposes of illustration. Table 2a requires the use of a customer-spotting procedure, similar to Applebaum (1966), but utilizing random sampling procedures with sample sizes based on prior knowledge of means and standard deviations for variables such as sales levels and income levels.

Estimating Procedure and Statistical Results

After linking the primary and secondary databases and completing the logit (Equation 5) and weighting transformation (Equation 6), weighted

Table 2A. Customer-Spotting Data (Example)

(X_i) Zone (miles)	Customers spotted	Drawing power	Weekly sales $	Zone Population	%
$0-\frac{1}{4}$	16	11%	$23,408	1,496	1%
$\frac{1}{4}-\frac{1}{2}$	8	5	10,640	4,198	2
$\frac{1}{2}-\frac{3}{4}$	15	10	21,297	10,362	6
$\frac{3}{4}-1$	29	19	40,341	9,033	5
$1-\frac{1}{2}$	17	11	23,408	16,018	10
$1\frac{1}{2}-2$	15	10	21,297	16,361	10
Beyond 2	43	28	59,583	59,583	36
Out of town (5 miles)	8	6	10,640	50,000	30
Totals	151	100%	212,797	167,051	100%

Table 2B. Creating the Logit Transformation (Example)

(1) (X_1) zone	Zone distance in miles to store	(2) Customers spotted	(3) Pop. zone	(2)/(3) Proportionate visitation (per capita visitation)	Ratio $\dfrac{P_i}{1-P_i}$	Logit transformation $Ln\left(\dfrac{P_1}{1-P_i}\right)$
.25	$0-\tfrac{1}{4}$	16	1,496	.0107	.0108	−4.5272
.50	$\tfrac{1}{4}-1$	8	4,198	.0019	.0019	−6.2611
.75	$\tfrac{1}{4}-\tfrac{3}{4}$	15	10,362	.0014	.0014	−6.5364
1.00	$\tfrac{3}{4}-1$	29	9,033	.0032	.0032	−5.7382
1.50	$1-1\tfrac{1}{2}$	17	16,018	.0011	.0011	−6.8472
2.00	$1\tfrac{1}{2}-2$	15	16,361	.0009	.0009	−6.9937
3.00	$2-3$	43	59,583	.0007	.0007	−7.2333
5.00	Out of town	8	50,000	.0002	.0002	−8.7402
		151	167,051			

least squares stepwise regression from the UCLA Biomedical Computer Programs (P2R) was used to test the hypotheses. The stepwise procedure was constrained as follows:

1. Criteria for entering variables was an F-to-enter level of at least 4.0.
2. Acceptable tolerance levels were set at .45, that is, no variable with a squared multiple correlation with all the other variables in the equation of greater than .55 were allowed to enter the equation.

The results of each equation for the eleven stores tested are displayed in Table 3. These results can be summarized as follows:

1. The sign of the distance variable is consistently negative, as expected based on Central Place (CP) Theory tenets. This implies a uniform negative slope and decreasing patronage as distance from the store increases.
2. The coefficient of the distance variable varies within a narrow range of 0.6 to 1.8. This suggests a stability in trade area characteristics as suggested by CP Theory. Additional analysis of these size relationships will follow in a later section.
3. The significance of the distance coefficient is quite similar regardless of the store, with only two exceptions (stores #2 and #4). T-values range from 3.7 to 8.0. This implies that the degree of variation about the regression line is on average quite similar for most stores.
4. A variety of census variables contribute additional explanatory power to the equations. No pattern is observed. A factor analysis completed on the 41 census variables could yield a set of factors and factor scores that, when introduced to the logit response equations, might enter consistently into all equations.
5. Coefficients of variation are quite good for all equations. Only two stores have an R_2 less than .80, and those two stores are across the street from each other, thus violating one of the assumptions of Central Place Theory that posits only a single activity at the center of a trade area.
6. Residuals analysis using graphic plots of the error vs. the predicted values indicate no hetereoscedastic pattern.

Table 3. Logistic Response Function Coefficients Derived from Weighted Least Squares Stepwise Regression—Eleven Suppermarkets, Madison, Wisconsin (Parenthetical Expression are t Values)

Variables/store #	1	2	3	4	5	7	8	9	10	11	12
Number of obs	24	18	20	18	18	23	18	19	115	18	18
Constant (log)	−5.5	−9.6	−6.7	−7.2	−6.4	−13.0	−4.6	−7.7	−2.1	−5.5	−8.3
Log of distance	−1.19	−1.4	−0.6	−2.1	−1.5	−1.8	−1.4	−1.7	−1.7	−0.9	−1.8
	(6.0)	(13.6)	(3.7)	(10.4)	(7.4)	(6.2)	(6.9)	(7.8)	(7.9)	(7.1)	(8.0)
PRFEMPRI	−18.7										
	(3.1)										
MSALES	21.5										
	(2.4)										
EMPLOYED		6.2									
		(2.7)									
PR5059			7.0								
			(4.7)								
PRHWF254				9.4							
				(5.8)							
PRCHILD					7.7						
					(2.7)						
MPRIV						15.8					
						(6.6)					
PR1019							23.5				−4.7
							(6.0)				(2.1)
UNEMP							66.1				
							(2.2)				

PRSINFAM								5.6			
								(5.2)			
PR RENTER									−5.0		
									(7.0)		
PRMLHEAD										6.8	
										(2.7)	
MSTATE										−5.6	
										(2.5)	
ELEM											17.6
											(7.1)
R^2 (Adj)	.77	.94	.73	.96	.83	.88	.93	.91	.96	.86	.96

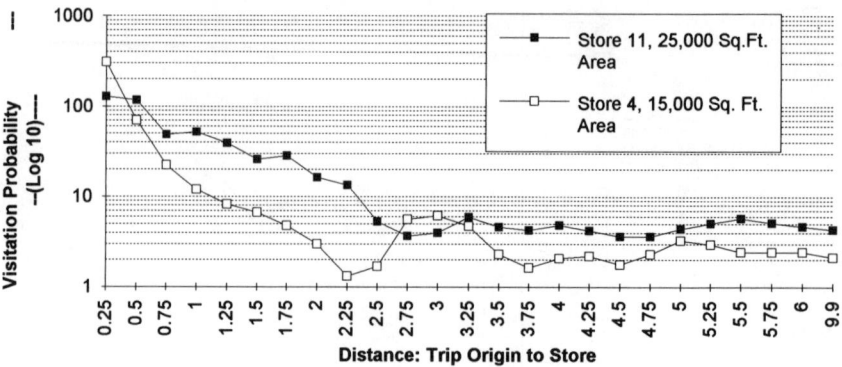

Figure 1. Predicted Visitation Probability for Two Madison Supermarkets.

Comparing Logit Coefficients

The logit coefficient is a single measure of the slope of the logistics curve (Figure 1). After retransformation, the predicted logit becomes the predicted frequency or probability of visitation. This probability varies markedly between stores. Two stores are presented for comparison in Table 4, one with 15,000 square feet and the other with 25,000 square feet of selling area.

These two logit functions can be graphed to illustrate the differences between the stores. Figure 1 depicts the spread of visitation probabilities and emphasizes the extent to which the larger store with a smaller slope parameter possesses a higher probability of visitation rate at every distance zone from the store (except the first, which is not shown on Figure 1).

The pattern of logit coefficients can be expected to vary with store size and distance, but much more is involved. Clearly, store image attributes not addressed in this study will have a large impact on the size of the logit coefficient. In addition, urban image attributes can be hypothesized to influence the size of the coefficient. To examine this relationship, the logit coefficient is hypothesized to be influenced by four directly measurable characteristics of the urban environment: distance to the central business district (CBD), store square foot size, population density within one mile of time store, and traffic density on the nearest arterial to the store. More formally,

Logit coefficient = f(DIS, CBD, STORSIZ, POPDEN, TRAFDN).

An adequate test of this hypothesis is not possible here because of the

Table 4. 1979 Estimated Probability of Visitation for two Madison Supermarkets by Distance from Trip Origin Ring to Store

Distance to store in miles	Probability of Visitation	
	Store #11 25,000 sq. ft.	Store #4 15,000 sq. ft.
0.25	127.523*	306.536*
0.50	117.307*	69.440
0.75	48.219	22.292
1.00	51.832	12.052
1.25	38.926	8.205
1.50	25.748	6.695
1.75	28.131	4.807
2.00	16.433	2.992
2.25	13.382	1.322
2.50	5.304	1.686
2.75	3.680	5.606
3.00	3.978	6.163
3.25	5.932	4.726
3.50	4.654	2.296
3.75	4.271	1.639
4.00	4.882	2.078
4.25	4.232	2.199
4.50	3.640	1.772
4.75	3.665	2.296
5.00	4.431	3.286
5.25	5.076	2.959
5.00	5.757	2.438
5.75	5.168	2.433
6.00	4.705	2.440
9.90	4.338	2.124

*Probabilities greater than 100% are caused by high visitation rates for certain groups not representative of the ring, that is, students from high school and workers from nearby offices purchasing lunch.

limited number of observations (eleven stores). However, an ordinary least squares test produced the following empirical result (t values in parentheses):

$$\text{Ln(Logit)} = .9619 - 0.389 \text{ STORSIZ} - 0.0665 \text{ POPDEN}$$
$$R^2 \text{ (adj.)} = .69 \quad (4.9) \quad\quad\quad (2.3) \quad\quad\quad\quad (7)$$
$$+ 0.016 \text{ TRAFDN}$$
$$(1.52)$$

All coefficients in the equation are significant at the 95% level, except TRAFDN at the 90% level. DIS CBD was not significant at any reasonable level. Subsequent work with a larger number of stores could better establish the significance of this equation.

Estimating Weekly Sales

The weighted least squares estimate of the logit coefficient can be used to measure how well the logit function performs in estimating the level of weekly sales activity at each of the eleven supermarkets. Predicted values for the logit ratio (dependent variable) are calculated and retransformed to obtain an estimate of the level of visitation (transactions). When total estimated transactions per week are multiplied by the average sale per transaction derived from the survey and store managers, an estimate of total weekly sales results that can be compared to actual weekly sales. These results are displayed in Table 5.

In general, the model estimates the weekly sales level with acceptable error. Only three stores have a percent error of greater than 10%. The store with the greatest error is sited on a major commuter arterial, but services a close-in population to a greater extent than would be expected because of competition with other nearby stores for suburban patrons.

Table 5. Estimated vs. Actual Weekly Store Sales Based on the Survey Average Sale Per Transaction

Store #	Store size	Predicted sales	Actual weekly sales*	Differences	Difference as % of actual
1	16,400	$123,447	$130,000	−$ 6,553	5.0%
2	13,500	40,799	38,448	+ 2,351	6.1
3	38,000	229,377	202,173	+ 27,204	13.5
4	15,000	32,667	32,808	− 141	0.4
5	24,000	157,549	132,421	+ 25,128	19.0
7	15,000	128,368	137,000	− 8,632	6.3
8	6,000	24,658	22,074	+ 2,584	11.7
9	8,000	37,681	35,707	+ 1,974	5.5
10	6,000	32,387	31,000	+ 1,387	4.5
11	25,000	123,153	115,419	+ 7,734	6.7
12	10,000	35,310	33,050	+ 2,260	6.8

*Source: Retail Trade Area Study.

It may be argued that knowledge of the average sale for a potential supermarket site is usually not known as it is in this example. The usefulness of the logit procedure in practical application depends not only on an accurate specification of the logit coefficient, but also on an estimate of average sale per transaction for a variety of supermarkets in order to translate visitation rates to estimates of sales revenue. However, standard average sale per transaction estimates can be obtained from a variety of industry sources. Average sale is highly correlated with store size, and a simple regression estimating average sale produces plausible values with a coefficient of determination of 83.8%. Using the predicted average sales levels leads to markedly increased error for three of the eleven stores displayed in Table 5. Average sale is a function of more than store size, and future work should attempt to determine those components of store image and urban image that are critical in determining average sale per transaction.

The procedure described previously presents a method for deriving the probability of visitation by zone for supermarkets using only the published census statistics and the well-documented properties of the logistics response function. To apply this procedure to a new area for other types of retail activities, the analyst should adhere to the following sequence of steps:

1. Acquire census statistics for all tracts or blocks within the SMSA and create a factor score matrix by one-quarter mile ring for the retail trade areas of interest.
2. Perform a customer-spotting analysis of a series of stores with widely disparate characteristics. Complete the logit regressions to derive the coefficients. A new store at any location within the SMSA can be expected to possess similar coefficients depending on its position relative to other stores, as indicated in Equation 7.
3. For a new store with planned square footage, possessing a known set of urban image attributes and store characteristics, the logit coefficient will be known. Solving the logit function for predicted transactions and multiplying by the average sale for a store of its type will yield an estimate of the potential revenue available to the store at maturity with a precision of $\pm 10\%$. Once the basic database is constructed, changes in store attributes, urban area characteristics, and other external variables can easily be integrated into the pattern of logit coefficients. New coefficients can be estimated quickly with a random sample survey of store patrons.

Summary and Conclusions

The primary tenets of Central Place Theory have been reviewed and incorporated within the context of a logistics response function to test the applicability of Central Place Theory within an intra-urban setting. The logit function was able to generate statistically reliable estimates of the parameters for distance and other variables. The logit coefficients were shown to vary systematically with store size and suggest that other urban image characteristics and store attributes could improve the strength of the relationship markedly. Using average expenditures from the surveyed stores, the level of expected sales was estimated with a high degree of precision, with some notable exceptions. Finally, a practical procedure for employing the logit response function within feasibility studies was detailed as a means of verifying and improving the estimation of potential retail sales associated with a new store location. As an adjunct to the market analysis component of feasibility analysis, the logistic response function is a valuable new procedure that will yield improved sales estimates and increased levels of confidence by establishing a common base for revenue projections with strong linkages to Central Place Theory.

References

Applebaum, William. "Methods for Determining Store Trade Areas, Market Penetration, and Potential Sales." *Journal of Marketing Research* 3 (May 1966), 127–41.

Batty, M. "Reilly's Challenge: New Laws of Retail Gravitation Which Define Systems of Central Places." *Environment and Planning* A10 (1978), 185–219.

Berkson, J. "Why I Prefer Logits to Probits." *Biometrics*, 7 (1951), 327–39.

Berkson, J. "Maximum Likelihood and Minimum Chi-Square Estimates of the Logistic Function." *Journal of American Statistical Association* 50 (1955), 130–62.

Berry, Brian J. L. "The Retail Component of the Urban Model." *Journal of the American Institute of Planners* 31, 2 (May 1965).

Berry, Brian J. L. *Geography of Market Centers and Retail Distribution*. Englewood Cliffs, NJ: Prentice-Hall, 1967, p. 61.

Berry, Brian J. L. and William Garrison. "A Note on Central Place Theory and the Range of a Good." *Economic Geography* 34 (November 1958), 304–11.

Berry, Brian J. L. and H. Gardiner Barnum. "Aggregate Relations and Elemental Components of Central Place Systems." *Journal of Regional Science* 4 (Summer 1962), 35–68.

Boventer, Edwin von. "Walter Christaller's Central Places and Peripheral Areas:

The Central Place Theory in Retrospect." *Journal of Regional Science* 9 (April 1969), 117–24.
Christaller, Walter. *Central Places in Southern Germany*, translated by Carlisle W. Baskin. Englewood Cliffs, NJ: Prentice-Hall, 1966.
Curry, Leslie. "Central Places in the Random Spatial Economy." *Journal of Regional Science* 7 (Winter 1967), 212–38.
Dacey, Michael F. and Ashish Sen. "Complete Characterization of the Central Place Hexagonal Lattice." *Journal of Regional Science* 8, (Winter 1968), 209–13.
Fotheringham, A. S. "Spatial Interaction and Spatial Choice." Paper presented to the Canadian Regional Science Association, Hamilton, Ontario, May 1987.
Fujita, Masahisa, Hideaki Ogawa, and Jacques-Francois Thisse. "A Spatial Competition Approach to Central Place Theory: Some Basic Principles." *Journal of Regional Science* 28, 4 (1988), 477–94.
Grigg, Trevor. "Parameters of the Retail Trade Model: A Utility Based Interpretation." *Urban Studies* 21 (1984), 73–9.
Huff, D. L. "A Probabilistic Analysis of Shopping Center Trade Areas." *Land Economics* (1963), 81–90.
Huff, D. L. "Defining and Estimating a Trading Area." *Journal of Marketing* 23 (1964), 34–8.
Losch, August. *The Economics of Location*, translated by William Woglom. New Haven: Yale University Press, 1954.
Luce, R. Duncan. *Individual Choice Behavior*. New York: John Wiley and Sons, 1959.
Mackay, D. B. "Measuring Shopping Patterns." *Geographical Analysis* (1973a), 329–37.
Mackay, David B. "A Spectral Analysis of the Frequency of Supermarket Visits." *Journal of Marketing Research*, 10 (February 1973b), 84–90.
McFadden, Daniel. "The Measurement of Urban Travel Demand." *Journal of Public Economics* 3 (1974a), 303–28.
McFadden, Daniel. "Conditional Logit Analysis of Qualitative Choice Behavior." In *Frontiers in Econometrics*, Pal Zarembka, ed. Academic Press, 1974b, pp. 105–43.
O'Kelly, M. E. and H. J. Miller. "A Synthesis of Some Market Area Delineation Models." *Growth and Change* (Summer 1989), 14–33.
Okoruwa, A. Ason, Joseph V. Terza, and Hugh O. Nourse. "Estimating Patronization Shares for Urban Retail Centers: An Extension of the Poisson Gravity Model." *Journal of Urban Economics* 24 (1988) 241–59.
Reilly, W. J. *The Law of Retail Gravitation*, New York, 1931.
Rose, G. "Reconstructing a Retail Trade Area: Tucker's General Store, 1850–1860." *The Professional Geographer* 39 (1987), 33–40.
Zipf, G. K. *Human Behavior and the Principle of Least Effort: An Introduction of Human Ecology*. Cambridge, MA: 1949.

IV PUBLIC POLICY ISSUES

13 TRANSFER OF OWNERSHIP RIGHTS VIA RENT CONTROL:
A Case Study of the Impact of Rent Control on Sales Prices of Mobile Houses Located in Twelve Selected Mobile Home Parks in Southern California, January 1983 to December, 1988

William N. Kinnard, Jr.

Background to the Analysis: The Research Problem

In California, all mobile home parks are subject to the California Mobile Home Residency Law (MHRL).[1] Among other things, MHRL specifies that existing tenants of mobile home parks may, after the effective date of MHRL, freely sell their mobile homes (commonly referred to as *coaches*), in place in the mobile home park, to a buyer of the seller-tenant's choosing. Such transactions are subject only to the park owner's acceptance of the buyer as a tenant within the mobile home park. The reasons why a mobile home park owner or the owner's managing agent may refuse to accept the buyer as an occupant and *de facto* tenant of the mobile home park are very limited and circumscribed.[2]

In effect, MHRL creates a tenancy of indefinite duration (rather than one of finite term) that may be readily transferred to another party of the tenant's choosing, subject to only minor constraints established by "reasonable" landlord acceptance or concurrence.

Thus, both the right of occupancy (use) and a substantial portion of the right of disposition (transfer) that are normally part of the Bundle of Rights possessed by the fee owner of the real estate are, for practical operating purposes, transferred to the tenant by MHRL. The tenant, in turn, has the legal authority to transfer them to a successor tenant, and so forth. The park owner (landlord) has thereby also lost the right of reversion at the end of the lease, because the lease (or occupancy) term is indefinite. These provisions of MHRL constitute a substantive transfer of real property rights from the landlord/fee owner to the tenant/occupant.

The Economic Transfer and Loss Argument

If the landlord were free to charge market rentals for the spaces in a mobile home park (commonly referred to as *pads*), the landlord would suffer no economic or financial damage. There would be no measurable market loss, even though part of the Bundle of Rights had actually been transferred from the landlord to the tenant through the operation of MHRL.

When rent control (also called *rent stabilization* in some California communities) is added, however, the landlord has experienced *both* a loss or involuntary transfer of part of the Bundle of Rights of park ownership, *and* a limitation on the revenues that can be generated from owning and operating a mobile home park. Since mobile home parks are investment properties, any effective decrease in revenues that the park owner is permitted to receive from pad rentals leads to a decrease in net operating income. This, in turn, means a corresponding decrease in the value of the property itself.

The Legal Argument and Associated Case Law

Therefore, MHRL in conjunction with rent control or rent stabilization produces an uncompensated transfer of ownership rights. Both MHRL and rent control have been held separately to be constitutional exercises of the police power by the California Supreme Court.[3] When the two are combined, however, there appears to be an uncompensated taking of both real property rights and the value of those rights from the landlord/ park owner, together with an involuntary transfer of those rights and their value from landlord to tenant. "The economic taking associated with mobile home rent controls is even more egregious [than that associated with apartment property rent controls]. Property rights are extracted from the landlord and conferred upon the tenant who may then personally monetize, alienate, and profit from the expropriated property right."[4]

In 1987, Judge Kozinski in the Ninth Appeals Circuit of Federal Court approached the constitutionality of mobile home rent control ordinances from a different, economic perspective. In the case of **Hall v. City of Santa Barbara**,[5] the court held that the constitutionality of the Santa Barbara ordinance rested upon certain unresolved factual issues. The case was remanded to District Court with an indication that "if it were shown the mobile home coach values increased *as a result of the rent control ordinance* [emphasis added], the court felt that the ordinance might constitute an unconstitutional taking."[6]

The factual issue raised by the court in the Ninth Circuit case of **Hall v. City of Santa Barbara** is the research issue addressed in this analysis and report.

Focus of the Research

Building on this background of legal direction and economic logic, the present research effort sought to identify whether observed, measurable value has been transferred from landlord to tenant in mobile home parks in California subject to rent control or rent stabilization. From the 105,600 mobile homes estimated to be subject to rent control or rent stabilization in California in 1987,[7] 168 sales in three rent-controlled parks in southern California were obtained. They were combined with 402 sales in nine non-rent-controlled parks, also in southern California. All parks and sales were located in Los Angeles and Santa Barbara Counties. The sales all occurred over the period January 1, 1983 through December 31, 1988.

The specific focus was on Los Amigos mobile home park in the City of Santa Barbara and Tahitian Terrace mobile home park in the City of Los Angeles. Los Amigos was subject to the Santa Barbara Rent Control Ordinance and was the park at issue in the **Hall v. Santa Barbara** case. Tahitian Terrace was subject to the Los Angeles Rent Stabilization Ordinance and was the park at issue in the **Azul Pacifico Inc. v. City of Los Angeles** case.[8]

The reason for focusing on Los Amigos in Santa Barbara and Tahitian Terrace in Los Angeles was that the owners of both had instituted separate suits in Federal District Court, seeking to upset their respective rent control/rent stabilization ordinances on federal constitutional grounds. They also sought compensatory damages for the period of the alleged takings, which for practical purposes encompassed the period January 1, 1983 through December 31, 1988.

The third rent-controlled mobile home park from which sales data were obtained was **Oak Forest in Westlake Village**. An action to upset the Westlake Village Rent Control Ordinance and to obtain compensatory damages was settled in September 1987. The settlement was approved in October 1987 by the Federal District Court judge presiding over the case.

Basically, this research undertaking sought to ascertain whether there was an identifiable and measurable premium paid for coaches in place in rent-controlled (or rent-stabilized) mobile home parks, as compared with prices paid for otherwise similar, competitive coaches in place in non-rent-controlled (or non-rent-stabilized) mobile home parks in the same general economic and regional market environment.

The Observed Market Phenomenon

Throughout southern California, mobile home coaches generally sold in place in mobile home parks for prices considerably in excess of the cost to acquire a new mobile home coach of similar size and make, transport it to the mobile home park, install it in place, and add standard improvements to both the pad area and the installed new mobile home. This premium or "placement value"[9] was observed in sales of coaches in both rent-controlled and non-rent-controlled parks over the entire period from January 1, 1983 through December 31, 1988.

In addition, mobile homes in place in mobile home parks also generally sold at prices substantially in excess of the calculated depreciated "values" of those mobile homes based on the Kelley Blue Book calculation method.[10] The Kelley Blue Book calculation method does *not* produce a market value estimate. Neither does it produce an indicator of likely or most probable selling price. Rather, it produces a consistently calculated depreciated cost new figure that serves effectively as a common denominator for purposes of comparative analysis. Installation cost, park amenities, pad amenities (view, added site improvements), age and condition of coach and other value-influencing factors are included in the Kelley Blue Book methodology.

Both appraisers in the three cases developed depreciated cost estimates for most (but not all) of the coaches in the sales sample, utilizing the Kelley Blue Book methodology. Their figures were remarkably similar, which made their analyses of the "margins" between recorded sales prices and Kelley Blue Book figures usable in their impact evaluations.

While the same Kelley Blue Book methodology applied consistently by the same analyst(s) produces a series of calculated figures that can be used appropriately and effectively to measure those "margins," this research study concentrated exclusively on a set of known and hypothesized influences on sales prices of mobile homes in place in mobile home parks. The Kelley Blue Book methodology is noted here solely because both appraisers whose data were used for this research analysis applied an analysis of "margins" that relied on Kelley Blue Book figures.

Nevertheless, the persistence of large "margins" for sales of mobile homes in place in mobile home parks in southern California raises the question of what causes these substantial differentials and how they can be measured properly.

The Likely Causative Factors

Explanations for the large price spreads or "margins" between market sales prices and installed cost new for mobile homes in place in mobile home parks are provided from many sources. They focus on three major sets of characteristics of the coaches themselves and of the mobile home park environments in which they operate.

General Characteristics

The Benefits of Being in Place in a Mobile home Park. This is especially important because of the artificially induced and maintained market shortage of available mobile home park spaces or "pads" in southern California.[11] Community land use policies generally have restricted the number and location of mobile home parks so that in practice access to any mobile home park as a tenant carries with it a premium or entry fee.

In a freely competitive, open market environment, this premium would be reflected primarily in higher rentals for the pads and generally received by (and retained by) the owner of the mobile home park. In an imperfect or artificially controlled market environment, a premium for entry into the park in the form of "key money" would be expected to be paid. This key money payment can be (and is in the Southern California market environment studied) reflected at least in part through higher prices paid for mobile homes (coaches) in place in a mobile home park.

Transportation and Installed Costs. Since cost new of a mobile home is commonly reported FOB the dealer's lot, the costs of transportation and installation must be added in making any comparisons with sales prices of mobile homes in place in a mobile home park. This figure is necessarily reflected in the sales prices of mobile homes in place.

Tenant Improvements. Almost invariably, mobile home owners make improvements to the exterior of the mobile home and to the pad area, as increments to the features of the mobile home and the pad area that are acquired by that pad tenant. These improvements take the form of skirting; steps, patios, and stoops; carports; "permanent" awnings; plantings; and the like. These items will also be reflected in the sales prices of "improved" mobile homes in place in mobile home parks.

Amenities of the Park Itself. Mobile home parks differ in the range and quality of park improvements available to tenants. These include such items as community or clubhouse facilities, swimming pools, landscaping, and others. These park amenities are reflected in both pad rentals (in the absence of rent control) and the prices paid for mobile homes in place in the mobile home park (as well as the margins of those sales prices over Kelley Blue Book calculated figures).

Specific Characteristics of Individual Mobile Homes, Mobile Home Parks, and Transactions. In addition to the general characteristics enumerated above, other identifiable and measurable differences have likely influences on the sales prices of mobile homes in place in mobile home parks in southern California. These items include the following.

Ocean View. It was anticipated (and borne out in nonsystematic interviews) that mobile homes would sell in place for higher prices if they were on a pad from which a view of the ocean exists than would otherwise be the case. In a noncontrolled, open and competitive rental market, such pads would also be expected to command higher monthly rentals.

Beach Access. Similarly, mobile homes in place in mobile home parks from which direct beach access is available, eliminating the necessity to cross the Pacific Coast Highway, would be expected to sell at higher prices. The pads in such mobile home parks would be expected to command higher monthly rentals in a noncontrolled, open and competitive market.

Size of Mobile Home (Coach). All things considered, size or living area in square feet is commonly the most important influence on price or rental of residential space. Experience indicates that mobile homes are no exception. Larger mobile homes would be expected to sell at higher prices (but lower prices per square foot).

Age of Mobile Home (Coach). Residential properties generally tend to sell for less as the structure ages. Mobile homes would be expected to follow that same general pattern.

Date of Sale. Changing market conditions tend to influence sales prices in open, competitive residential real estate markets. It would be expected that some influence of time would be felt on the sales prices of mobile homes in place in mobile home parks. However, the artificially controlled character of the market for mobile home pads, both as to supply and rentals, would likely reduce the impact of time or date of sale on those sales prices in southern California.

Community and Market Control Influences. The combined effect of the community in which the mobile home park is located and the existence or nonexistence of rent control/rent stabilization may be represented by specific factors in the market place.

Community. This includes the fact that there is or is not rent control/rent stabilization imposed on mobile home park pad rentals within the community in question, together with all other community amenities.

Rent Control. The existence of rent control may be identified as a separate variable for purposes of analysis.

The Research Hypothesis

In this market research analysis, it is hypothesized that there is a discernible, identifiable, and measurable impact on sales prices of mobile homes in place in mobile home parks in southern California associated with the existence of rent control or rent stabilization in the community. Moreover, sales prices of such coaches are hypothesized to be measurably and markedly higher than are prices of otherwise similar mobile homes in place in otherwise similar or competitive mobile home parks that are *not* subject to rent control or rent stabilization.

Data Used in the Analysis

To test the foregoing research hypotheses, sales transactions data for mobile homes in place in mobile home parks in Southern California were obtained for twelve mobile home parks in five different communities or political areas. These sales data were derived from appraisal reports and accompanying sales transaction tabulations produced by Robert L. Foreman, MAI and Robert M. Lea, MAI.[12]

The data represented a 100% sample of all reported sales of mobile home coaches in place in the twelve mobile home parks between January 1, 1983 and December 31, 1988. The original sales data were gathered and published in quarterly reports by the Berlin Research Corp. of San Luis Obispo, California. The Berlin reports include data on park address, community location, pad number within the park, sales price, date of sale, coach size (dimensions), coach model and manufacturer, year coach was built, and debt financing terms. Other data used in this study came from personal field inspection of each transferred coach and its site (pad).

A total of 570 sales transaction files was obtained and used. Many of the same sales transactions (77) were reported by Messrs. Foreman and Lea. In most cases, the pertinent sales transactions data were the same. In those few instances in which there were discrepancies or divergences, the information provided by Mr. Lea was used. There is no implication that one source was correct and that the other was incorrect. Rather, it was simply a convention adopted for the research analysis.

Mr. Foreman provided data on 476 sales in ten of the mobile home parks included in the study. Only Casa Grande and Rancho Adolpho, both in Santa Maria, were missing from the Foreman data. Mr. Lea provided data on 171 sales in all of the mobile home parks included in the study, except Oak Forest and The Summit.

Nine of the parks were in communities without rent control. Five of these were in Santa Maria (in Santa Barbara County), which has never had rent control, and in which the prospect of rent control is judged to be dim. These parks are all inland with no beach access and no ocean view. Santa Maria is a community with modest income levels.

The other four non-rent-controlled parks were in Los Angeles County. Rent control had previously existed for pad rentals of mobile home parks in Los Angeles County, prior to the time period covered by the study. There was also an informal but widely known and understood policy in Los Angeles County that rent control would likely be reimposed on any mobile home park owner who exceeded "reasonable limits" in pad rentals or "unreasonably" increased pad rentals.

Two of the Los Angeles County mobile home parks had both ocean view and beach access: Point Dume and Paradise Cove. They are in the affluent Malibu area. The other two Los Angeles County mobile home parks (Calabasas Village and The Summit) were both inland.

The three mobile home parks in communities with rent control or rent stabilization applicable to mobile home park pad rentals included:

Los Amigos in Santa Barbara (no ocean view
    or beach access: affluent community)

Oak Forest in Westlake Village (no ocean view
    or beach access; affluent community)

Tahitian Terrace in Los Angeles (ocean view but no
    direct beach access; Tahitian Terrace is on the east side of the
    Pacific Cost Highway; affluent neighborhood area)

All sales transactions data were confirmed by the appraiser(s) reporting each transaction. None was confirmed or inspected by the author. For purposes of this analysis, confirmation and verification by the appraisers were accepted as sufficient evidence.

Selected Data Set Characteristics

Of the 570 sales included in the total data set, 168 were in parks subject to rent control or rent stabilization: 35 in Los Amigos (Santa Barbara), 69 in Oak Forest (Westlake Village), and 64 in Tahitian Terrace (Los Angeles). The remaining 402 sales in parks not subject to rent control were distributed between 249 sales in Los Angeles County and 153 sales in Santa Maria. The sales dates ranged from January 1983 through December 1988.

While 150 sales were in parks with direct beach access (Paradise Cove and Point Dume), 189 sold mobile homes were on pads with an ocean view. Not all pads in Tahitian Terrace provide an Ocean view. The average age of the coach at the time of sale was 13 years. The average size of coach sold was slightly in excess of 1280 square feet. The average park density (coaches per acre of developed and usable land) was 4.70 pads per acre.

A summary of the characteristics of the twelve mobile home parks in the study sample is provided in Table 1. This shows, for example, the relatively large number of pads in the nine non-rent-controlled mobile

Table 1. Characteristics of Twelve Mobile Home Parks in Sample

Park name	Area	Number of spaces	Density	Rent control	Beach access	Ocean view
Casa Grande	SM	420	5,25	0	0	0
Casa del Rio	SM	185	4.73	0	0	0
La Maria	SM	152	7.92	0	0	0
Rancho Adolpho	SM	250	5.00	0	0	0
Trailerancho	SM	100	11.49	0	0	0
Calabasas	LA Cnty	211	4.28	0	0	0
Paradise Cove	LA Cnty	271	3.98	0	271	271
Point Dume	LA Cnty	297	3.31	0	297	297
The Summit	LA Cnty	203	5.46	0	0	0
Los Amigos	SB City	71	11.11	71	0	0
Oak Forest	WL Vill	162	1.40	162	0	0
Tahitian Terrace	LA City	158	5.70	158	0	91
Santa Maria	Total	1,107	5.12	0	0	0
L.A. County	Total	982	4.15	0	0	0
Rent control		391	4.90	391	0	91
Non-rent control		2,089	4.66	0	568	568
12-park total		2,480	4.17	391	568	659

SM = Santa Monica; LA = Los Angeles; SB = Santa Barbara; WL = Westlake.

home parks, as compared with the sizes of the rent-controlled parks. Although density (spaces per acre) varied rather substantially from one park to another, the averages for the rent-controlled and non-rent-controlled parks were quite close. As noted earlier, only two parks offered direct beach access (both in Los Angeles County), and only three had pads with an ocean view.

Table 2 provides a summary of the characteristics of the mobile home coach sales that constitute the sample of 570 sales transactions. Again, although there was noticeable variation from park to park, the average age and the average coach size in square feet was remarkably similar between rent-controlled and non-rent-controlled parks, as a group.

On the other hand, very noticeable differences by location and by rent control status are found when comparisons are made among average adjusted sales price, average adjusted sales price per square foot of living area of coach, and average adjusted margin. These differences will be explored in depth later. A preliminary examination of the data in Table 2

Table 2. Characteristics of Coach Sales in Twelve Mobile Home Parks

Park (area)	No. sales	Ave. adj. SP	Ave. adj. SPSF	Ave. adj. margin	Ave. coach age	Ave. coach size	Ave. date of sale
Casa Grands	21	$ 49,491	$ 36.37	NA	6	1,368	65
Casa del rio	39	43,188	35.23	$14,384	10	1,234	50
La Maria	39	34,567	31.64	9,401	15	1,107	44
Rancho Adolpho	19	89,431	59.41	NA	9	1,517	62
Trailerancho	35	26,607	28.82	8,576	12	943	42
Calabasas	47	69,744	46.68	21,391	16	1,501	34
Paradise Cove	50	90,915	88.12	65,131	14	1,079	42
Point Dume	100	83,367	61.80	48,321	14	1,354	52
The Summit	52	63,836	46.23	8,360	14	1,410	27
Los Amigos	35	64,332	72.54	44,259	14	898	37
Oak Forest	69	82,996	49.80	30,720	8	1,677	26
Tahitian Ter.	64	107,605	100.51	78,736	15	1,088	37
Santa Maria	153	43,807	36.01	10,941	11	1,189	50
L.A. County	249	78,232	60.98	38,268	14	1,338	41
Rent control	168	88,483	73.86	51,832	12	1,290	32
Non-rent Control	402	65,130	51.48	27,867	13	1,281	44
12-park total	570	72,013	58.07	37,057	13	1,284	41

SP = sale price; SPSF = sale price per square foot; NA = not applicable; Ave = average; Adj = adjusted.

suggests that inflation-adjusted sales prices, sales prices per square foot, and margins in rent-controlled parks were substantially in excess of those reported in non-rent-controlled parks. However, further and more refined comparisons are required between Tahitian Terrace, on the one hand, and Paradise Cove/Point Dume, on the other, for example.

It is quite apparent, moreover, that sales in Santa Maria exhibited much lower price levels, however measured, than did the parks in Los Angeles County. Even the parks in Los Angeles County need to be distinguished between those with beach access and ocean view, and those without such locational amenities.

Inflation-Adjusted Sales Prices

For purposes of comparability over time, all sales prices were adjusted via the Consumer Price Index to December 1988 price levels. Therefore, all sales prices used in the analysis were adjusted sales prices expressed in terms of December 1988 dollars.

Percentage Turnover Rates

Table 3 shows the turnover rates or percent of total spaces sold for each of the parks and for each of the communities covered by the sales data set. Since the sales data for each mobile home park represent all the sales reported for that park over the study period, these percentage sold figures represent a form of turnover rate. The annual rate is expressed as a simple straight-line proportion of the total six-year percentage.

It is quite clear from Table 3 that percentage turnover, both total and per year, is markedly higher in rent-controlled parks than in non-rent-controlled parks. The lowest turnover percentage or rate among the three rent-controlled parks (6.6%) was in Tahitian Terrace. This figure is still higher than the highest total or annual percentage turnover figure (5.8%) among all non-rent-controlled parks; that is, in Trailerancho Park in Santa Maria.

These data suggest strongly that there is substantially more effective demand for access to rent-controlled mobile home park spaces in southern California. This is apparent even when they do not offer ocean view or beach access amenities, which have been hypothesized to be substantial upward influences on in-place coach sales price.

Table 3. Percent Sold, by Park, by Area, and by Rent-Control Status: January 1983 to December 1988

Location	No. sold	No. spaces	Total percent	Annual S-L percent
Casa Grande	21	420	5.0%	0.8%
Casa del Rio	39	185	21.1	3.5
La Maria	39	152	25.7	4.3
Rancho Adolpho	19	250	7.6	1.3
Trailerancho	35	100	35.0	5.8
Santa Maria total	153	1,107	13.8	2.3
Calabasas Village	47	211	22.3	0.8
Paradise Cove	50	271	18.5	3.1
Point Dume	100	297	33.7	5.6
The Summit	52	203	25.6	4.3
Los Angeles County total	249	982	25.4	4.2
Los Amigos (S.B.)	35	71	49.3	8.2
Oak Forest	69	158	43.7	7.3
Tahitian Terrace	64	162	39.5	6.6
Rent control total	168	391	43.0	7.2
Non-rent control total	402	2,089	19.2	3.2
12-park total	570	2,480	23.0	3.8

The Research Design

The general framework of the research design was the application of the standard Hedonic Pricing Model in multiple linear regression analysis (MRA) format. This framework has proved particularly effective in other economic impact analyses of real estate market activity.

The specific issue to be addressed was, what influence (if any) does rent control or rent stabilization have on the inflation-adjusted sales prices of mobile homes in place, in comparison with the inflation-adjusted sales prices of otherwise similar, competitive mobile homes in noncontrolled parks in other jurisdictions? These other jurisdictions are communities in which rent control was absent over the entire period studied (Los Angeles County and Santa Maria).

The use of MRA allows for equal consideration (but not necessarily equal weight) to be given to all price-influencing factors for which data are available in each sales transaction file. Therefore, the model allows for measurement of the difference that the presence of rent control makes, taking into account all other factors that the appraisers whose data were employed agreed were significant, and that could be gathered. The model therefore permits isolation and separate measurement of the influence or impact on inflation-adjusted sales price associated with the existence or nonexistence of rent control in the community in which the mobile home park is located.

Standards for Comparison

The mobile home parks in Santa Maria are *not* subject to rent control or rent stabilization, and never have been. Moreover, they do *not* have an ocean view nor do they have beach access. As a result, sales in the five Santa Maria mobile home parks taken as a group are used as the norm or standard against which sales transactions in all the other mobile home parks, whether subject to rent control or not, are compared.

For technical reasons associated with the MRA modeling format, Santa Maria does not enter directly into the analytical Hedonic Pricing Model as an explicitly reported and measured variable. The data are all included in the analysis, but sales transaction data in all other locations are compared with those in the five Santa Maria mobile home parks taken as a group.

Further, within those communities for which variables are tested, Los Angeles County is taken as the specific exemplar of a non-rent-controlled environment. This is the case even though the potential for re-institution of rent control exists for mobile home parks in Los Angeles County.

Mechanical Procedures and Measures Employed

As noted above, the basic analytical framework for this research analysis is the Hedonic Pricing Model in the MRA format. In this quantitative procedure, the individual and joint effects of a series of variables whose values are known (independent variables) are measured simultaneously on the one transaction characteristic whose value or quantity is to be estimated (dependent variable). In this research analysis, the dependent variable is always some form of inflation-adjusted price.

Dependent Variables

Two different sets of MRA models were developed, each using three different dependent variables. All were based on inflation-adjusted sales prices expressed in December 1988 dollars or purchasing power. In the first set of models, the dependent variables are expressed in dollar amounts: adjusted sales price (ADJSP), adjusted sales price per square foot of living area (ADJSPSF), and the inflation adjusted margin between sales price and Kelley Blue Book calculated value (ADJMARG).

The second series of MRA models uses the *logarithms* of coach size and coach age as independent variables, with the same dependent variables. The titles, content, code names, and identification of dependent variables by model type are summarized in Table 4A.

Independent Variables

The independent variables whose values are known for each of the sales transactions used in the data set of 570 sales include the following:

Size of mobile home in square feet of living area*
Age of mobile home in years*
Date of sale (year and month)
Density of use of the mobile home park (pads per acre)
Ocean view (yes-no)
Beach access (yes-no)

Santa Maria location (yes-no)
Los Angeles county location (yes-no)
Los Angeles location (yes-no)
Santa Barbara location (yes-no)
Westlake Village location (yes-no)

Rent control/rent stabilization in effect (yes-no)

It should be noted that a Santa Maria location is *not* reported in any of the model runs on which Tables 5 and 6 are based The same is true for Appendix Tables A1 and A2. As noted earlier, this is because the Santa Maria location is the one against which all other locations are measured,

---

* Also logarithm of coach size and coach age

Table 4. Variables used in Regression Analysis of 570 Sales of Mobile Home Coaches in Twelve Mobile Home Parks in Southern California

Code	Title and Content	Type
A. Dependent Variables		
ADJSP	Sales price adjusted to December 1988 CPI	Continuous (dollars)
ADJSPSF	Sales price per square foot of mobile home living area, adjusted to December 1988 CPI	Continuous (dollars & cents)
ADJMARG	Difference between sales price and calculated Kelley Blue Book estimate, adjusted to December 1988 CPI	Continuous (dollars)
LOGADJSP	Logarithm of ADJSP	Continuous
LOGASPSF	Logarithm of ADJSPSF	Continuous
LOGAMARG	Logarithm of ADJMARG	Continuous
RCPADJSP	Reciprocal of ADJSP	Continuous
RCPASPSF	Reciprocal of ADJSPSF	Continuous
RCPAMARG	Reciprocal of ADJMARG	Continuous
B. Independent Variables		
LAC	Los Angeles County	Yes-no (1-0)
LA	Los Angeles City	Yes-no (1-0)
SB	Santa Barbara	Yes-no (1-0)
WL	Westlake Village	Yes-no (1-0)
RC	Rent control (or rent stabilization) in effect	Yes-no (1-0)
BA	Beach access (direct)	Yes-no (1-0)
OV	Ocean view	Yes-no (1-0)
DENS	Park density (number of spaces divided by acres of land area)	Continuous
DOS	Date of sale (number of months from January 1983 to sale date)	Discrete
AGE	Age of coach in years (difference between year of sale and year of manufacture)	Discrete
SIZE	Size of sold coach in square feet of living area	Continuous

Table 5. Comparative Results of Regression Models: In-Place Mobile Home Sales in Twelve Southern California Mobile Home Parks—January to December 1988

Statistic	Model 1	Model 2	Model 3	Model 4
A. Inflation-Adjusted Sales Price is Dependent Variable				
R^2 (adjusted)	.6439	.6439	.6202	.5972
F ratio	91.7	101.1	114.5	119.1
S.E.E.	$19,616	$19.580	$20,147	$20,711
Durbin–Watson	1.48	1.41	1.30	1.28
D.F.[a]	558	559	561	562
B. Inflation-Adjusted Sales Price per Square Foot is Dependent Variable				
R^2 (adjusted)	.6438	.6438	.5985	.5604
F ratio	91.7	101.1	104.5	102.3
S.E.E.	$15.76	$15.73	$16.64	$17.38
Durbin–Watson	1.29	1.29	1.19	1.15
D.F.[a]	558	559	561	562
C. Inflation-Adjusted Margin is Dependent Variable				
R^2 (adjusted)	.6551	.6551	.6056	.5986
F ratio	88.3	88.3	89.6	99.7
S.E.E.	$18,338	$18,338	$19,525	$19,655
Durbin–Watson	1.45	1.45	1.40	1.39
D.F.[b]	465	465	467	468

[a] n = 570.
[b] n = 476.

and in terms of which differences in dollar-adjusted sales prices are measured.

The title and content, code name, and type of independent variables are summarized in Table 4B.

Avoiding Double Counting of Impact (Multicollinearity)

Each of the three mobile home parks subject to rent control or rent stabilization is the only mobile home park reported for its community: Los Angeles, Santa Barbara, and Westlake Village. Further, beach access is directly associated with ocean view in two of the three mobile home parks with ocean view: Paradise Cove and Point Dume.

To avoid any double-counting hazard, which in MRA is referred to as

Table 6. Comparative Results of Model Runs by Coefficients and Significance Dependent Variable is Inflation-Adjusted Dollar Amount

Variable	Y = ADJSP coefficient	Y = ADJSPSF coefficient	Y = ADJHARG coefficient	
A. Model 1				
LAC	25082.70	17.32	NA	NA
	$(4.30)^2$	$(3.56)^2$		
LA	24810.58	14.43	NA	NA
	$(5.12)^2$	$(2.64)^2$		
SB	−3361.35	−3.43	NA	NA
	(−0.56)	(−0.63)		
WL	N/A	−24.30	NA	NA
		$(-3.95)^2$		
RC	40228.38	45.20	NA	NA
	$(10.21)^2$	$(10.05)^2$		
BA	4375.50	4.74	NA	NA
	(0.58)	(0.77)		
OV	23661.42	14.40	NA	NA
	$(5.07)^2$	$(3.71)^2$		
DENS	1414.88	−1.07	NA	NA
	$(2.52)^2$	$(-2.11)^1$		
DOS	1710.89	0.93	NA	NA
	$(2.58)^2$	(−1.72)		
AGE	−896.25	−0.57	NA	NA
	$(-4.52)^2$	$(-3.56)^2$		
SIZE	37.46	−0.02	NA	NA
	$(12.33)^2$	$(-7.50)^2$		
B. Model 2				
LAC	23510.51	21.72	14502.96	
	$(3.92)^2$	$(4.30)^2$	(1.33)	
RC	43763.94	41.18	34745.22	
	$(16.59)^2$	$(18.51)^2$	$(10.72)^2$	
BA	−18208.53	−15.59	−14288.45	
	$(-2.73)^2$	$(2.77)^2$	$(-1.24)^2$	
OV	44724.40	34.27	47881.38	
	$(14.90)^2$	$(13.54)^2$	$(11.51)^2$	
DENS	743.64	−0.22	2235.40	
	(1.74)	(−0.61)	$(4.45)^2$	
DOS	1972.41	1.74	2156.28	
	$(2.96)^2$	$(3.10)^2$	$(2.59)^2$	
AGE	−732.33	−0.40	78.69	
	$(-3.59)^2$	$(-2.37)^1$	(0.31)	
SIZE	33.51	−0.25	19.28	
	$(10.88)^2$	$(-9.50)^2$	$(5.40)^2$	

Table 6. (Cont.)

Variable	Y = ADJSP coefficient	Y = ADJSPSF coefficient	Y = ADJHARG coefficient
C. Model 3			
RC	41922.26	39.48	35300.24
	$(15.89)^2$	(17.68)	$(10.33)^2$
BA	3479.04	4.45	−2588.08
	(0.92)	(1.39)	(−0.46)
OV	43475.27	33.12	47507.25
	$(14.33)^2$	$(12.90)^2$	$(10.97)^2$
DENS	496.67	−0.45	864.20
	(1.16)	(−1.24)	(1.89)
DOS	2125.29	1.88	2872.05
	$(3.15)^2$	$(3.29)^2$	$(3.36)^2$
AGE	−636.99	−0.32	−365.11
	$(-3.10)^2$	(−1.84)	(−1.47)
SIZE	34.50	−0.02	25.91
	$(11.06)^2$	$(-9.20)^2$	$(7.56)^2$

Figures in parentheses are t-values.
[1] Significant at .05 level.
[2] Significant at .01 level.
NA = note available.

Multicollinearity, the cross-correlation of individual pairs of independent variables was tested with a correlation matrix. The results of that test are shown in Table 7, which indicates high but still acceptable partial correlation coefficients between ocean view and beach access. Regression model runs with beach access both included and excluded produced no significant differences in results.

The partial correlation coefficients between rent control and Los Angeles, Santa Barbara, and Westlake Village, in turn, were not so high as to negate their joint simultaneous use in the MRA models. Model 1 in Table 5 shows the incremental impact of rent control on each of the three dependent variables in the context of measuring the joint effects of all community effects except that of Santa Maria (the base).

Further, Model 2 shows the relative effect of rent control generally on sales prices of mobile homes in place in the three mobile home parks subject to rent control or rent stabilization, taken as a group. The results from Model 2 cannot differentiate among the effects of the different rent control or rent stabilization ordinances in Los Angeles, Santa Barbara, and Westlake Village. They simply compare the general effect of rent control on inflation-adjusted in-place sales prices in comparison with the

Table 7. Correlation Matrix

	ADJSPSF	LAC	LA	SB	WL
ADJSPSF	1.000000				
LAC	.189985	1.000000			
LA	.533262	−.343421	1.000000		
SB	.130251	−.209649	−.138820	1,000000	
WL	−.129402	−237668	−.157372	−.096072	1.000000
RC	.439298	−.493120	.462257	.425149	.481967
BEACCESS	.221949	.941035	−.323171	−.197287	−.223654
OCVIEW	.474156	.699105	.225739	−.257902	−.292369
DENSITY	−.142333	−.463935	.010115	.552746	−.453495
DOS	−.072379	.189744	−.026430	−.098732	−.387639
AGE	.227617	.193853	.122710	.105950	−.265794
SIZE	−.210516	.115467	−070077	−.268351	.406772
	RC	BEACCESS	OCVIEW	DENSITY	DOS
RC	1.000000				
BEACCESS	−.464043	1.000000			
OCVIEW	−.249679	.764969	1.000000		
DENSITY	.051749	−.450467	−.422691	1.000000	
DOS	−.415040	.155303	.177400	.008299	1.000000
AGE	.049988	.201170	.199421	.126382	.113638
SIZE	−.020805	.076899	.119332	−.504680	.039097
	AGE	SIZE			
AGE	1.000000				
SIZE	−.356148	1.000000			

effect of a Los Angeles County location (and implicitly a Santa Maria location) on adjusted in-place coach sales prices.

Finally, Model 3 shows the simple average effect of rent control or rent stabilization on inflation-adjusted sales prices in comparison with the effects of all other identified price-influencing factors in *all* mobile home parks within the data set that are *not* subject to rent control or rent stabilization. For analytical purposes, approximately equal emphasis is placed on the findings and results from the application of the different models.

Results and Findings

The application of the Hedonic Pricing Model to the data set of 570 sales produced the results summarized in Table 5 and 6. Appendix A shows the full MRA runs for each of the six models employed in the analysis, with adjusted sales price (ADJSP) as the dependent variable. The same independent variable were used in the several models with the other two dependent variables: ADJSPSF and ADJMARG. Two separate sets of models were run because age at sale (AGE) was missing from 122 sales files. The results were essentially the same, and the models including age at sale were used in Tables 5 and 6.

Summary Characteristics of Models

Table 5 shows the comparative results from different model runs, using adjusted dollar amounts as the dependent variable. It compares the R-squared (coefficient of multiple determination), F-ratio, standard error of the estimate, Durbin–Watson statistic, and degrees of freedom for each of three basic models applied to the three different dependent variables: ADJSP, ADJSPSF, and ADJMARG.

Whatever the dependent variable, Model 2 has a *higher* R-squared, a *lower* standard error of the estimate, but a *lower* Durbin–Watson score than does Model 1, Model 3 or Model 4. The F-ratio differences are for practical purposes trivial because of their very high levels to begin with.

The models have a reasonably high explanatory power, with R-squared generally in the .60 to .65 range. The ADJMARG models added nothing to the results of ADJSP and ADJSPSF models. Therefore, they were removed from further consideration in the analysis. In brief, it would appear that placing reliance on the results of Model 1 is justified, unless one wishes to measure the "typical" influence of rent control without reference to specific location.

Effects of Nonlinear Relationship Adjustments

The use of logarithmic independent variables produces virtually identical results, as Appendix Tables A4, A5, and A6 clearly show. In general, it can be said that some modest nonlinear model relationship is indicated by the Appendix tables. However, any gains in model robustness are judged to be offset by difficulties in interpretation and explanation to other users of the findings.

Values and Significance of Locational Variables

With ADJSP as the dependent variable, locational (community) variables are generally statistically significant at the .01 level. This means that community location does make a difference, both in comparison with Santa Maria and in comparisons between and among the other locations. All the coefficients are positive, which indicates that all the reported locations are, as far as the market is concerned, preferable to Santa Maria (and significantly so).

Much the same results are obtained when ADJSPSF or ADJMARG is the dependent variable. The difficulty with ADJMARG is that the Kelley Blue Book calculated "value" is an estimate made by an appraiser or other expert, rather than being an "objective" market fact. The same order of difference among locations appears in all three models, however. They confirm one another, and they support and substantiate one another. Given all of this, it would appear that greatest reliance can and should be placed on the results with ADJSP as the dependent variable.

Values and Significance of Nonlocation Variables

It must be remembered that the variables used throughout this analysis were those for which information could be obtained by Messrs. Foreman and Lea on a consistent, reliable basis. There is no claim that these are the only influences, or even the only major or significant influences, on adjusted sales prices of in-place coaches in mobile home parks in Southern California. They do, however, account for between 60% and 65% of the variance in the identified dependent variables.

Some of the independent variables other than those for location are both logical and *a priori* influences on sales prices, based on past observation and experience. Size (square feet of living area) and age at sale are always expected to be major and significant influences on sales price, although in opposite directions. The same considerations would appear to apply to date of sale, although much of the impact of changing market conditions with the passage of time may be partially obviated through the adjustment for inflation using the CPI.

Logic also suggests that the density of a mobile home park would influence sales price inversely; that is to say, the less densely developed a park is, the higher the price one might expect a purchaser to pay for an in-place coach in that park. Finally, both beach access and ocean view were included because of the great emphasis placed on visual or physical access to beaches and the ocean in Southern California.

Table 6 indicates that not all these expectations were fully borne out. Ocean view was a major positive influence on sales price and was statistically highly significant. Beach access, on the other hand, was not as significant, and in one instance was actually a *negative* figure! In point of fact, little reliance was placed on the results of Model 3 in the development of final conclusions and judgments.

Density proved to be nonsignificant, but *positive*. Date of sale was also positive. It was statistically significant when ADJSP was the dependent variable, but not always so for ADJSPSF (e.g., Model 1). Age of coach was both negative and statistically significant, except in Model 3 for ADJSPSF. Size, not surprisingly, was the most significant nonlocation influence on sales price; it ranked second in statistical significance to rent control in most of the models.

Generally speaking, the expectations based on prior experience and research were borne out with the results of the several models, as far as the major nonlocation independent variables were concerned.

Influence of Rent Control

No matter how it was measured, and no matter with what other locational variable(s) it was compared, rent control (including rent stabilization) proved to be a powerful and highly significant influence on the sales price of in-place mobile home coaches. Each of the communities with rent control (Los Angeles City, Santa Barbara, and West Lake Village) was represented by only one rent-controlled park in the study data set. Moreover, each of the three communities had rent control or rent stabilization in effect for all the mobile home parks within its borders.

The net influence of rent control as an independent variable on the inflation-adjusted sales price of in-place mobile home coaches was always positive, large, powerful, and robust. It was consistently a highly significant variable.

Implications and Conclusions

From the preceding analysis as well as the results presented in both the text tables and the Appendix tables, the following conclusions emerge:

1. Because rent control or rent stabilization regulations differ from one community to another, the impact of rent control or rent stabilization on coach prices in any given mobile home park included in the data set must be measured in the context of the community variable as well.

2. The first conclusion is borne out by the fact that the community variables are consistently statistically significant. They are also generally positive, relative to Santa Maria. The one exception is the measure for Santa Barbara.
3. One meaningful measure from Model 1 is the *difference* or *spread* over the Los Angeles County indicators. This compares inflation-adjusted sales prices or margins in Los Angeles, Santa Barbara, and Westlake Village with those in mobile home parks in Los Angeles County. The numerical differences measure the net market effect of the Los Angeles Rent Stabilization Ordinance, the Santa Barbara Rent Control Ordinance, or the Westlake Village Rent Control Ordinance on inflation-adjusted sales prices and inflation-adjusted margins.
4. The use of the Hedonic Pricing Model in MRA format takes into consideration all of the other factors influencing inflation-adjusted sales price or inflation-adjusted margin that were gathered and presented by the two appraisers from whom the sales transactions data were obtained. The inflation-adjusted sales price differentials or inflation-adjusted margin differentials between sales in rent-controlled parks and sales in the mobile home parks in Los Angeles County are nontrivial. Using the models with ADJSP as the dependent variable, the impact of rent control on ADJSP varies in a narrow range from $40,000 to $45,000.

   Similarly, strong and highly significant inflation-adjusted price per square foot differentials ($39.00 to $45.00 per square foot of coach living area) and margin differentials are associated with location in a park (and community) with rent control.
5. After all other available, measurable influences on inflation-adjusted sales price or inflation-adjusted margin are taken into consideration, the remaining effect or influence of rent control or rent stabilization on inflation-adjusted sales prices of in-place coaches in mobile home parks in southern California is large (nontrivial), highly significant (nonrandom), and meaningful. This is an average or "typical" figure based on *all* available market sales transactions data.

   It would therefore appear that rent control does "monetize" the rights transferred by the California MHRL and transfer substantial value from landlord to tenant.
6. The Research Hypotheses presented earlier have been substantiated by the findings based on the MRA analysis. There *is* "a dis-

cernible, identifiable and measurable impact" on inflation-adjusted sales prices of coaches in place in mobile home parks that is associated with the existence of rent control/rent stabilization in southern California over the 1983 to 1988 study period. It has also been demonstrated that these inflation-adjusted sales prices are "measurably and markedly higher" in rent-controlled/stabilized parks than in non-rent-controlled/stabilized parks.

Notes

1. California State Legislature, "Mobile Home Residency Law," *California Civil Code*, Chapter 2.5, Sections 798.1–799.6 (Stats. 1978, c.1031, p. 3178, 1, as amended).
2. Ibid., Article 7. "Transfer of Mobile home."
3. See, for example, Birkenfeld v. City of Berkeley, 17 Cal. 3d 129, 550 P. 2d 1001, 120 Cal. Rptr. 465 (1976).
4. Hirsch, Werner Z. and Joel G. Hirsch. "Legal-Economic Analysis of Rent Controls in a Mobile Home Context: Placement Values and Vacancy Decontrol." *UCLA Law Review*, 35 (1988), 399–466.
5. Hall v. City of Santa Barbara, 813 F. 2d 198 (9th Cir. 1987). It is interesting to note that none of the preceding constitutional cases concerning rent control "introduced evidence that the effect of the rent controls was to take wealth from the landlords and give it to the tenants, a subset of whom appropriated to themselves most of the benefits of the controls." Hirsch and Hirsch, op. cit., p. 451.
6. Hirsch and Hirsch, op. cit., p. 400.
7. Ibid., p. 411.
8. The Hall v. Santa Barbara case was settled after trial by a stipulation between the parties approved by Federal District Judge Lauglin B. Waters on March 21, 1990. It followed action taken by the Santa Barbara City Council to amend the Rent Control Ordinance by initiating Vacancy Decontrol on mobile home park pad rentals in the City. (U.S. District Court, Central District of California, Case No. 84-9506-LEW) Azul Pacifico v. City of Los Angeles was decided in favor of the plaintiff, also by Judge Waters, on May 31, 1990. Both vacancy decontrol and damages to the plaintiff were awarded. (U.S. District Court, Central District of California, Case No. 87-2287-LEW).
9. Ibid., p. 426ff.
10. For details of the *Kelley Blue Book, Manufactured Housing and Mobile Home Guide* calculation method, see Hirsch and Hirsch, op. cit., pp. 401 and 426. The Kelley Blue Book "value" calculations used in this research analysis were developed and provided by Robert L. Foreman, MAI, of Costa Mesa, California and by Robert M. Lea, MAI, of Los Angeles, California.
11. For example, the zoning ordinances of both the City of Los Angeles and the City of Santa Barbara do not currently permit any additional mobile home parks.
12. All of the data were developed in conjunction with the Hall (Los Amigos) and Tahitian Terrace cases. All the data were made public through court testimony and exhibits. Mr. Foreman and Mr. Lea prepared all the Kelley Blue Book calculations.

Selected References

Angell, Cynthia, Leonard Sahling, and Joseph G. Strubel. *The Real Estate Markets of the Los Angeles Basin*. Merrill Lynch Capital Markets, June 1989.

California State Legislature, *California Civil Code*, Chapter 2.5, Sections 798–799, "Mobile Home Residency Law," 1978 as amended.

California Department of Housing and Community Development, *Mobile Home Parks in California: A Survey of Mobile Home Park Owners Pursuant to SB 1835*, February 1986.

City of Los Angeles, *1984 Rental Housing Study*.

Clark, W. A. V. and Allen D. Heskin. "The Impact of Rent Control on Tenure Discounts and Residency Mobility." *Land Economics* (February 1982).

Clatanoff, Robert M. and Marc A. Levin. *An International Bibliography on Economics and Public Policy*. International Association of Assessing Officers, Bibliographic Series No. 11, December 1985.

Diskin, Barry A. and Joel B. Hayes. "Lender Reaction to Proposed Rent Controls in Florida Mobile Home Parks." *Journal of Property Management* (January/February 1984).

Diskin, Barry A., Karen E. Lahey, and V. Michael Lahey. "Manufactured Housing: An Alternative to Site-Built Homes." Paper Presented at the American Real Estate Society Annual Meeting, Washington, D.C., April 13–15, 1989.

Gregory, Tony A., et al. Plaintiffs and Respondents, v. City of San Juan Capistrano, Defendant and Appellant. Civ. 27114. 142 Cal. App 3d 72, Court of Appeal, Fourth District, Division 2, April 20, 1983.

Hall v. City of Santa Barbara, 813 F.2d 198 (9th Cir. 1986)

Hall v. City of Santa Barbara, 833 F.2d 1280 (9th Cir. 1988)

Hamilton, Rabinovitz, Szanton, and Alschuler, Inc., The Urban Institute. *The Los Angeles Rent Stabilization System: The Mobile Home Sector*, Rent Stabilization Division, Community Development Department, City of Los Angeles, May 1985.

Haynes, Joel B. and Barry A. Diskin. "Space Rental Perceptions and Problems in Mobile Home Parks: The Florida Experience." *The Appraisal Journal* (October 1985).

Hirsch, Werner Z. "An Inquiry into Effects of Mobile Home Park Rent Control." *Journal of Urban Economics* 24 (1988), 212–26.

Hirsch, Werner Z. and Joel G. Hirsch. "Legal-Economic Analysis of Rent Controls in a Mobile Home Context: Placement Values and Vacancy Decontrol." *UCLA Law Review* 35, (1988), 399–466.

Marks, Denton. "The Effect of Rent Control on the Price of Rental Housing: An Hedonic Approach." *Land Economics* 60, 1 (February 1984).

Moorhouse, John C. "Long-Term Rent Control and Tenant Subsidies." *Quarterly Review of Economics and Business* 27, 3 (Autumn 1987).

Muth, Richard F. "Redistribution of Income: Regulation in Housing." *Emory Law Journal* 32 Emory L.J. 691.

San Luis Obispo Planning Department. *Residential Land Use Economic Study: Expenditure/Revenue Comparison, Mobilehomes/Single Family/Multiple Family*. American Mobilehome Appraisal Co., 1985.

Shulman, David. "Real Estate Valuation Under Rent Control: The Case of Santa Monica." *AREUEA Journal* (1984).

Taylor, Gerald C. *Mobilehome Appraisal Guide*. American Mobilehome Appraisal Co., First Edition, 1971.

Appendix

Appendix Table 1: Model 1

Regression Analysis
STA570.MII: SUBSET: ST570.MII—STACEY DATABASE

Multiple Regression

Dependent Variable: ADJSP   Degrees of Freedom: 437

Ind Var	Coefficient	Std Error	Beta Coeff	t Statistic	Probability
LAC	25082.70846	5826.20572	.34160	4.30515	.00002
LA	24810.58560	4844.97486	.27683	5.12089	.00000
SB	−3361.35143	5956.29232	−.02590	−.56434	.57281
RC	40228.38511	3937.74912	.53857	10.21609	0.00000
BEACCESS	4375.50209	7439.82725	.05835	.58812	.55675
OCVIEW	23661.42964	4663.42049	.33729	5.07384	.00000
DENSITY	1414.88953	555.03296	.12055	2.54920	.01113
DOS	1710.89327	622.63329	.07717	2.58196	.01014
AGE	−896.25965	198.21497	−.13437	−4.52165	0.00007
SIZE	37.46918	3.03713	.40048	12.33702	4.4409e-16

Intercept: −156459.06510
F-Statistic: 112.97752
Standard Error: 18619.31589
Std Error (d.f.): 18809.63752

R 2: .72108
R: .84916
R (d.f.): .84578
Proportion Reduced: .00020
Cumulative Reduced: .72108

Analysis of Variance

	Sum of Squares	D.F.	Mean Squares	F Ratio	Probability
Regression	3.9167e+11	10	3.9167e+10	112.9775237	2.0593e-46
Residual	1.5150e+11	437	346678924.2		
Total	5.4317e+11	447			

Durbin-Watson: 1.516745209
Residual S.D./Dep Variable S.D.: .528125782   Residual S.D.: 18409.86810

Appendix Table 2: Model 2

Regression Analysis
STA570.MII: SUBSET: ST570.MII—STACEY DATABASE

Multiple Regression

Dependent Variable: ADJSP
Degrees of Freedom: 439

Ind Var	Coefficient	Std Error	Beta Coeff	t Statistic	Probability
LAC	23510.51206	5985.43354	.32019	3.92795	.00009
RC	43763.94329	2637.45443	.58590	16.59325	0.00000
BEACCESS	−18208.53689	6651.37862	−.24285	−2.73756	.00644
OCVIEW	44724.40993	3000.73571	.63754	14.90448	0.00000
DENSITY	743.64280	425.41086	.06336	1.74806	.08115
DOS	1972.41859	664.18482	.08897	2.96968	.00314
AGE	−732.33853	203.46178	−.10979	−3.59939	.00035
SIZE	33.51823	3.07924	.35825	10.88523	1.11026e-16

Intercept: −171023.9046
F-Statistic: 126.41807
Standard Error: 19352.25038
Std Error (d.f.): 19505.58130

R 2: .69731
R: .83505
R (d.f.): .83216
Proportion Reduced: .00210
Cumulative Reduced: .69731

Analysis of Variance

	Sum of Squares	D.F.	Mean Squares	F Ratio	Probability
Regression	3.7876e+11	8	4.7345e+10	126.41807	5.8348e-45
Residual	1.6441e+11	439	374509594.7		
Total	5.4317e+11	447			

Durbin-Watson: 1.44955
Residual S.D./Dep Variable S.D.: .55016   Residual S.D.: 19178.29404

Appendix Table 3: Model 3

Regression Analysis
STA570.MII: SUBSET: ST570.MII—STACEY DATABASE

Multiple Regression

Dependent Variable: ADJSP
Degrees of Freedom: 440

Ind Var	Coefficient	Std Error	Beta Coeff	t Statistic	Probability
LAC	41922.26013	2637.65691	.56125	15.89375	1.1102e-16
BEACCESS	3479.04076	3769.17980	.04640	.92302	.35650
OCVIEW	43475.27813	3032.36665	.61973	14.33708	5.5511e-16
DENSITY	497.67637	427.58189	.04231	1.16159	.24603
DOS	2125.29818	673.82730	.09586	3.15407	.00172
AGE	-636.99724	205.29427	-.09550	-3.10285	.00204
SIZE	34.50452	3.11890	.36879	11.06304	1.5543e-15

Intercept: -183005.6143
F-Statistic: 137.75626
Standard Error: 19666.99799
Std Error (d.f.): 19800.33510

R 2: .68667
R: .82865
R (d.f.): .82608
Proportion Reduced: .00060
Cumulative Reduced: .68667

Analysis of Variance

	Sum of Squares	D.F.	Mean Squares	F Ratio	Probability
Regression	3.7298e+11	7	5.3283e+10	137.75626	2.9100e-44
Residual	1.7019e+11	440	386790809.9		
Total	5.4317e+11	447			

Durbin-Watson: 1.391961982
Residual S.D./Dep Variable S.D.: .559754176   Residual S.D.: 19512.39819

Appendix Table 4: Model 1—With Logarithms of Age and Size

Regression Analysis
STA570.MII: SUBSET: ST570.MII—STACEY DATABASE

Multiple Regression

Dependent Variable: ADJSP

Ind Var	Coefficient	Std Error	Beta Coeff	t Statistic	Probability
LAC	19868.33078	6028.16358	.27059	3.29592	.00106
LA	9666.62313	6821.17954	.10785	1.41715	.15715
SB	−9037.35418	6671.98543	−.06965	−1.35452	.17626
WL	−20474.36481	7525.55478	−.17499	−2.72065	.00677
RC	47431.22515	5388.05464	.63500	8.80303	.00000
BEACCESS	−3022.06710	7611.86370	−.04030	−.39702	.69154
OCVIEW	28425.15084	4856.18981	.40519	5.85339	.00000
DENSITY	−10.17931	628.31496	−.00086	−.01620	.98708
LOGAGE	−15302.82138	3637.22282	−.11435	−4.20728	.00003
LOGSIZE	95432.05269	7448.29284	.40613	12.81261	4.4409e-16

Intercept: −237139.9690
F-Statistic: 109.1148768
Standard Error: 18853.16428
Std Error (d.f.): 19045.87624

Degrees of Freedom: 437

R^2: .71403
R: .84500
R (d.f.): .84152
Proportion Reduced: 1.7176e-07
Cumulative Reduced: .714033

Analysis of Variance

	Sum of Squares	D.F.	Mean Squares	F Ratio	Probability
Regression	3.8784e+11	10	3.8784e+10	109.11487	5.2044e-46
Residual	1.5533e+11	437	355441803.2		
Total	5.4317e+11	447			

Durbin-Watson: 1.599741358
Residual S.D./Dep Variable S.D.: .53475   Residual S.D.: 18641.08594

Appendix Table 5: Model 2—With Logarithms of Age and Size

Regression Analysis
STA570.MII: SUBSET: ST570.MII—STACEY DATABASE

Multiple Regression

Dependent Variable: ADJSP   Degrees of Freedom: 439

Ind Var	Coefficient	Std Error	Beta Coeff	t Statistic	Probability
LAC	22280.37239	5980.15686	.30344	3.72572	.00022
RC	43104.42876	2589.83020	.57707	16.64437	0.00000
BEACCESS	−17654.42145	6694.19958	−.23546	−2.63727	.00865
OCVIEW	43438.62167	3022.65790	.61921	14.37100	0.00000
DENSITY	424.99839	418.60551	.03621	1.01527	.31503
DOS	1667.12865	661.75052	.07520	2.51927	.01211
LOGAGE	−14551.34616	3759.36866	−.10873	−3.87069	.00012
LOGSIZE	83474.84012	7498.76726	.35524	11.13181	1.1102e-16

Intercept: −350544.0891
F-Statistic: 124.66607
Standard Error: 19446.44253
Std Error (d.f.): 19600.51975

R 2: .69435
R: .83328
R (d.f.): .83035
Proportion Reduced: .00071
Cumulative Reduced: .69435

Analysis of Variance

	Sum of Squares	D.F.	Mean Squares	F Ratio	Probability
Regression	3.7715e+11	8	4.7144e+10	124.66607	8.5087e-45
Residual	1.6601e+11	439	378164126.9		
Total	5.4317e+11	447			

Durbin-Watson: 1.50644
Residual S.D./Dep Variable S.D.: .55284   Residual S.D.: 19271.63950

Appendix Table 6: Model 3—With Logarithms of Age and Size

Regression Analysis
STA570.MII: SUBSET: ST570.MII—STACEY DATABASE

Multiple Regression

Dependent Variable: ADJSP   Degrees of Freedom: 440

Ind Var	Coefficient	Std Error	Beta Coeff	t Statistic	Probability
LAC	41576.30987	2594.20302	.55661	16.02662	0.00000
BEACCESS	3169.73985	3737.55533	.04227	.84808	.39685
OCVIEW	42273.92716	3050.13842	.60261	13.85967	4.4409e-16
DENSITY	205.23575	420.45132	.01748	.48813	.62569
DOS	1848.77512	669.54241	.08339	2.76125	.00599
LOGAGE	−13798.90485	3808.49177	−.10311	−3.62319	.00032
LOGSIZE	85083.54704	7595.11606	.36209	11.20240	.00000

Intercept: −368762.7953
F-Statistic: 136.49659
Standard Error: 19729.03581
Std Error (d.f.): 19862.79351

R 2: .68469
R: .82746
R (d.f.): .82486
Proportion Reduced: .00017
Cumulative Reduced: .68469

Analysis of Variance

	Sum of Squares	D.F.	Mean Squares	F Ratio	Probability
Regression	3.7190e+11	7	3.3129e+10	136.49659	3.7342e-44
Residual	1.7126e+11	440	389234853.8		
Total	5.4317e+11	447			

Durbin-Watson: 1.444751939
Residual S.D./Dep Variable S.D.: .56151   Residual S.D.: 19573.94834

14 INTERPRETING MONTE CARLO SIMULATION WITH GENERALIZED SENSITIVITY ANALYSIS:
The Case of Historic Rehabilitation*

George A. Overstreet, Jr. and Geoffrey M. Rubin

Introduction

Historic preservation is a vital component of the real estate sector because of its impact on business district revitalization, low-income housing, and architectural integrity. As a result, preservation has become a target of Congressional policy.[1] Unfortunately, the scope of Congressional control over rehabilitation is undetermined. Empirical data relating tax structure to rehabilitation activity is not available due to statistically sparse tax changes. The relationship between tax laws and rehabilitation is further obscured by the simultaneous change of many individual tax laws in the few tax code overhauls. Traditional empirical tests cannot provide crucial insight into Congressional influence over preservation.

Researchers commonly rely upon theoretical models when sparse empirical data hinder statistical research.[2] No model completely captures

---

*The authors would like to acknowledge the intellectual support of University of Virginia colleagues Bernard J. Cosby, Jr., Environmental Sciences, and David M. Maloney, McIntire School of Commerce. The financial support provided by the McIntire School of Commerce Center for Financial Services Studies and the Ramon W. Breeden, Sr. Research Professorship were greatly appreciated. The comments of two anonymous referees were also of great help. Any remaining errors in the paper are the sole responsibility of the authors.

system behavior, but even simple models can be used advantageously. Simulation models integrate hypothesized variable relationships into a series of equations that transform a vector of input values into an output vector. Although the modelling process itself can be instructive,[3] simulation models require interpretative analysis, loosely called *sensitivity analysis*.[4] Sensitivity techniques examine the effects of input variables on the output state. To date, the sensitivity techniques employed by real estate researchers have failed to properly identify implications of complex models.

Early financial sensitivity techniques studied the effects of a handful of predetermined variable changes on the output state. Input scenarios were selected by the researcher and the resulting output states were studied.[5] Selecting "best," "most likely," and "worst" case scenarios for each input variable is another popular method of analysis. These and similar methods are flawed. In general, there are no guidelines for the "best" or "worst" value per variable. Additionally, the probabilities of scenario occurrence are not explicitly stated. The most often cited defect in these techniques is the univariate treatment of variable perturbations.[6] The one-by-one variation of input values neglects potentially crucial multicollinearity among input elements. Researchers performing bivariate or multivariate changes in large models quickly run into the dual problems of incomplete sampling and staggering numbers of possible variable combinations.[7] Monte Carlo simulation, to be discussed in more detail, provides researchers an accessible method for studying multivariate relationships in large models.[8]

This paper introduces Generalized Sensitivity Analysis (GSA) to the real estate literature, a multiple variable sensitivity technique suitable for the analysis of Monte Carlo simulations. GSA has proven useful in the analysis and design of physical systems but has not yet been applied to financial systems such as real estate investment.[9] The dual goals of the paper are to (1) demonstrate how the power of Monte Carlo simulation can be harnessed with GSA and (2) identify the relationships between tax code components and rehabilitation development. GSA methodology is reviewed and the full modelling process—from model specification to Monte Carlo simulation to GSA—is applied to historic rehabilitation investment.

Historic Rehabilitation

The U.S. tax code grants investors in historically designated properties tax benefits not generally enjoyed by other real estate investors. Tax code

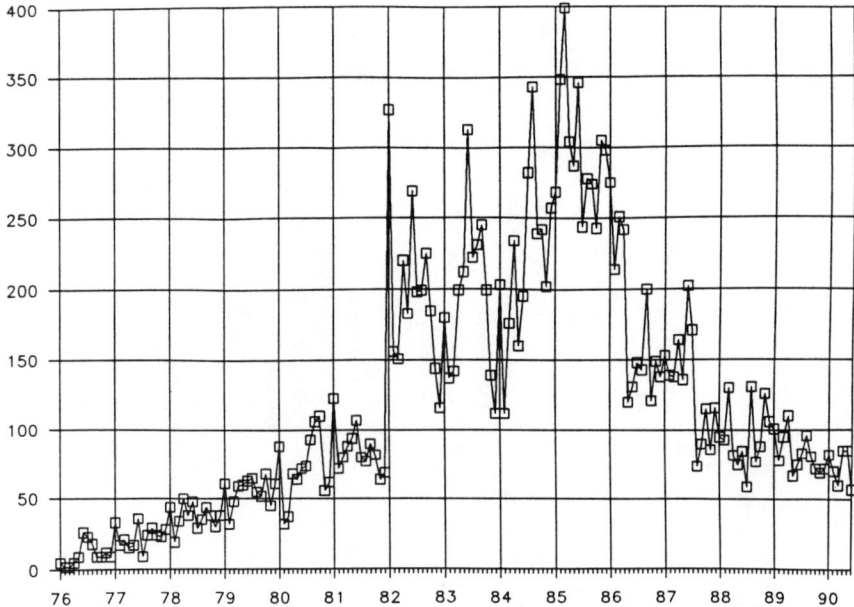

Figure 1. National Register Part I Applications.

modifications in 1976, 1978, and 1981 provided specific tax incentives to spur investment in historic rehabilitation projects. As illustrated in Figure 1, such activity grew slowly at first and exploded with the passage of the Economic Recovery Tax Act (ERTA) in 1981.[10] By the end of 1987, over 18,000 buildings, representing investments of $12 billion, had rehabilitation plans certified.[11]

To qualify for the rehabilitation tax credit (RTC), a structure must be listed in the National Register of Historic Places.[12] The demand for register listings should reflect investor demand for rehabilitation property. Inspection of Part 1 applications, placed with the U.S. Park Service as the first step of certification, confirms the influence of the tax code on rehabilitation (Figure 1). The Tax Reform Act (TRA) of 1986 removed incentives and discouraged many of the investors attracted by the ERTA laws.[13] A "Chow" test for the pre- and post-TRA periods confirms a drop in application quantity at the point of TRA legislation.[14] The shift suggests that one or more tax code changes impacted rehabilitation demand. Unfortunately, the subset of tax changes that most strongly impacted rehabilitation cannot be empirically identified because of the simultaneous change in factors (Table 1). The tax code has a theoretical effect on inves-

Table 1. Chronology of Historic Preservation Tax Incentives[1]

	Depreciation method for existing structure[2]	Depreciation method for rehabilitation expenditures	Credit for rehabilitation expenditure	Other restraints	Effective data
Pre-1976	Estimate life 125 DB or SL	Estimate life 125 DB or SL	None	Subject to depreciation recapture	N/A
1976					
Plan 1	Estimated life 125 DB or SL	60-month amortization SL	None	Subject to depreciation recapture and recapture of "excess amortization" on disposition	After 6/14/76
Plan 2	Estimated life 200 DB or 150 DB	Estimated life 200 DB or 150 DB	None	Subject to depreciation recapture	After 6/14/76
1978					
Plan 1	Estimated life 125 DB or SL	60-month amortization SL	None	Subject to depreciation recapture and recapture of "excess amortization" on disposition	After 6/14/76
Plan 2[3]	Estimate life SL	Estimate life SL	10%	Subject to RTC recapture	After 10/31/78
1981					
plan 1	15 years accelerated	60-month amortization SL	None	Subject to depreciation recapture and recapture of "excess amortization" on disposition	After 12/31/80
Plan 2[4]	15 years accelerated	15 years SL	10%	Subject to depreciation and RTC recapture	After 12/31/80

Year	Depreciation	Credit %	Provisions	Effective Date
1981	15 years accelerated	15 years SL	25%	Subject to depreciation and RTC recapture	After 12/31/81
1982	15 years accelerated	15 years SL	25%	Depreciable basis reduced by one-half of credit; subject to depreciation and RTC recapture	After 12/31/82
1984	18 years accelerated	18 years SL	25%	Depreciable basis reduced by one-half of credit subject to depreciation and RTC recapture	After 3/15/84
1985	19 years accelerated	19 years SL	25%	Depreciable basis reduced by one-half of credit subject to depreciation and RTC recapture	After 5/8/85
1986[5]	27.5 years, or 31.5 years SL	27.5 years, or 31.5 years SL	20%	Passive loss limitations depreciable basis reduced by full amount of credit subject ot RTC recapture	After 12/31/86

[1] The provisions summarized in this chart are the primary ones affecting the incentives intended to encourage investment in historic rehabilitation projects. Specifically, the relevant highlights of several tax laws are given: 1976, Tax Reform Act of 1976 (Pub. L. 94-455); 1978, Revenue Act of 1978 (Pub.L. 95-600); 1981, Economic Recovery Tax Act of 1981 (Pub.L. 97-34); 1982, Tax Equity and Fiscal Responsibility Act of 1982 (Pub.L. 97-248); 1984, Tax Reform Act of 1984 (Pub.L. 98-369); 1985, Simplification of Imputed Interest Rules (Publ.L. 99-121); and 1986, Tax Reform Act of 1986 (Pub.L. 99-514).

[2] Prior to 1981, accelerated methods of depreciation were available for residential rental real estates, while the straight-line method was required for nonresidential (i.e., commercial and industrial) realty.

[3] This option was not available for residential real property, but only for industrial or commercial realty.

[4] This option was not available for residential real property, but only for industrial or commercial realty.

[5] The shorter cost recovery period of 27.5 years applies to residential realty, while the longer 31.5 year recovery period applies to nonresidential or commercial realty.

tor return due to restrictions on write-offs and credits.[15] With GSA, one can attempt to identify the tax code changes most responsible for the drop in rehabilitation demand.

The Mechanics of Generalized Sensitivity Analysis[16]

GSA is a multifaceted sensitivity technique that incorporates characteristics from both univariate and multivariate analysis. GSA determines, in a multivariate sense, which of a host of input variables most heavily influence a given system. In essence, it is multiple variable sensitivity technique. Because it may be engineered to process simulated data, GSA can accommodate systems afflicted by poor empirical data. The diverse nature of the test enhances the robustness required of such analytical techniques.

GSA is perhaps most useful when strong theoretical relationships cannot be tested with empirical data. This situation is reflected in financial systems where simultaneous movements of many factors conceal the impact of individual factors on the real system. In these cases, empirical data must be complemented with theoretical assumptions to gain crucial insight into system mechanics. GSA assists the study of systems with solid theoretical foundations but poor evidentiary data.

Step One: Model Building

GSA analyzes a system of physical equations integrated into a single model. Models that systematically transform a vector of input parameters into an output vector can be studied. For ease of analysis, we consider a model composed of first-order ordinary differential equations. The system can be given in the form:

$$\dot{\mathbf{x}}(t) = f[\mathbf{x}(t), \mathbf{v}, \phi(t)], \tag{1}$$

where $\mathbf{v}$ is the vector of input parameters, $\phi(t)$ is the system of equations composing the model, and $\mathbf{x}(t)$ is the output state vector. $\phi(t)$ systematically transforms the input vector $\mathbf{v}$ into the output state vector. $\mathbf{v}$ should be comprised of all factors that have a hypothetical effect on the simulated system. $\phi(t)$ should best capture the hypothesized interaction between the individual variables $\mathbf{v}_i$ in the input vector. In this paper, the system and output vectors are time invariant, so writing ϕ and $\mathbf{x}$, respectively, will suffice.

From the state vector **x**, an observation vector **y** is defined. The observation vector is composed of elements that can be explicitly defined and evaluated. Whereas the elements of **x** may be unobservable, all y_i are perceptible in the system studied. Thus, a given model structure ϕ^* will define **y*** by transforming a particular input vector **v***. Every input vector **v*** and its observation vector **y*** make up a *scenario*, given a particular model structure. It is implicitly assumed that changes in the input vector **v*** *cause* changes in the observation vector **y***. The assumption of causality in the model facilitates later interpretation of input and output vector relationships. The most important assumption in this methodology is the authenticity of the model structure ϕ^*. GSA will only have intuitive significance if the model is relevant to the real system being studied.

Step Two: Monte Carlo Simulation

The above methodology is by no means an addition to the literature; models of this type are commonplace. The utility of GSA comes not from the structure of the model, but from the Monte Carlo simulation of input and output vectors. Whereas other models of this type constrain the elements of **v** to point estimates (or perhaps a discrete number of values), GSA assumes that individual elements of the input vector are realizations of random variables with known distributions. After a value is randomly selected for each input variable, the output vector is determined. Repeated iterations of this operation will cover many value combinations and reveal multicollinear tendencies. Thus

$$v_i^l \leq v_i^* \leq v_i^u \tag{2}$$

where v^l is the lower bound and v^u is the upper bound of parameter v_i. For example, the fate of the rehabilitation tax credit (RTC) in Congress may be uncertain, but it can be assumed that the rate will stay somewhere in the range of 0% to 50%. Instead of confining the RTC to a point estimate, the credit can be given a flexible range of possible realizations. If we assume that the *a priori* limits on the parameters form the range of a uniformly distributed random variable, each particular model will be characterized by an ensemble of scenarios, with each scenario anchored by a randomly generated value of **v***. Monte Carlo simulation can generate a large number of scenarios for further study.

Step Three: GSA Application

Behavior Specification. The ensemble of scenarios, consisting of different **v*** and corresponding values of **y***, is the heart of the GSA technique. This "generated database" supplies all of the information needed for a critical analysis of the system. Before analysis proceeds, an important transformation of the data is required. The scenarios are sorted into two different groups, based upon their particular values of **y***. The sorting algorithm can be based upon a number of rules, but, for purposes of simplicity and generality, our analysis utilizes a dichotomous sorting procedure. One typical algorithm sorts all scenarios with a particular y_i* higher than a certain minimum into a group defined as *behavior*, while scenarios with a value of y_i* below the minimum are placed into the *nonbehavior* group. Such a sorting technique can adequately analyze situations where threshold parameters exist. For example, assume an investor will only proceed with a project if the IRR is above a certain hurdle rate. An algorithm that sorts scenarios into groups having similar above- or below-hurdle rate returns helps to isolate the forces that underlie a worthy or unworthy project. In a narrow sense this method is analogous to discriminate function analysis.[17]

Univariate Sensitivity. Once the scenarios of the generated database have been sorted, GSA helps determine which input parameters are causing the output value of the model to fall under behavior or non-behavior. If an input parameter exhibits differing characteristics in the behavior and non-behavior groups, that parameter is likely influencing the value of the output vector at the predetermined algorithmic point of separation. Recalling that parameters are random variables with *a priori* distributions, cumulative distribution plots of the parameter under behavior and non-behavior will reveal any univariate sensitivity of the output to the parameter. Figure 2 illustrates how the difference between v_k in the behavior and nonbehavior groups is reflected in the respective distributions $F(v_k|B)$ and $F(v_k|NB)$. In this example v_k takes on lower values when it is part or a behavior scenario. The difference between the distributions $F(v_k|B)$ and $F(v_k|NB)$ suggests that the parameter v_k helps explain the difference between behavior and non behavior to some degree. An objective measure of parameter sensitivity via cumulative function separation is

$$d_{m,n} = \sup_{v_k} |S_n(v_k) - S_m(v_k)|, \tag{3}$$

where S_n and S_m are sample distribution functions of $F(v_k|B)$ and

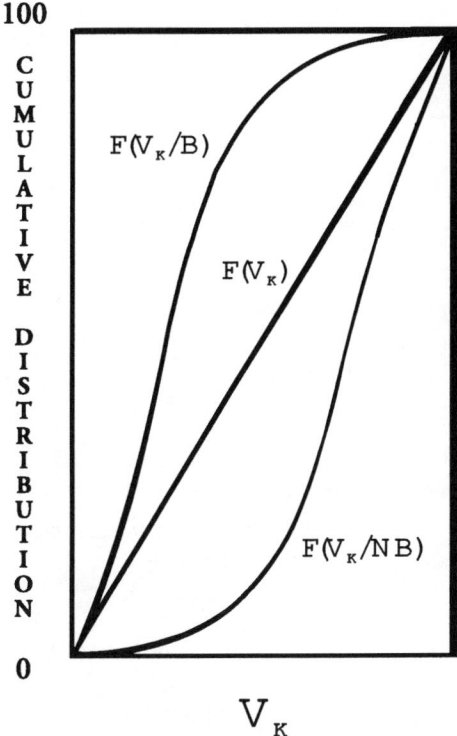

Figure 2. This figure shows the cumulative distribution of a hypothetical parameter over the entire sample [F(V_K)] and similar distributions for the variable in just the behavior [F(V_K) | B] and nonbehavior [F(V_K) | NB] groups. The difference between [F(V_K) | B] and [F(V_K) | NB] implies that the parameter V_K helps explain the occurrence of behavior.

$F(v_k|NB)$ for n behaviors and m nonbehaviors. $d_{m,n}$ is called the Kolmogorov–Smirnov two-sample test with known asymptotic and small sample distributions. v_k is normalized with zero mean and unity variance. $d_{m,n}$ represents the supremum of all vertical distances between the two curves, S_n and S_m, so large values of the statistic indicate that the parameter is important in determining behavior, while the converse is true for small values of $d_{m,n}$.[18] Notice that the statistic is sensitive to differences in both central tendency and distribution. The parameters of the input vector can thus be given a sensitivity ranking on the basis of the $d_{m,n}$ statistic. This test of univariate sensitivity, as we will see, is only one indicator of the influence a parameter has on the output vector.

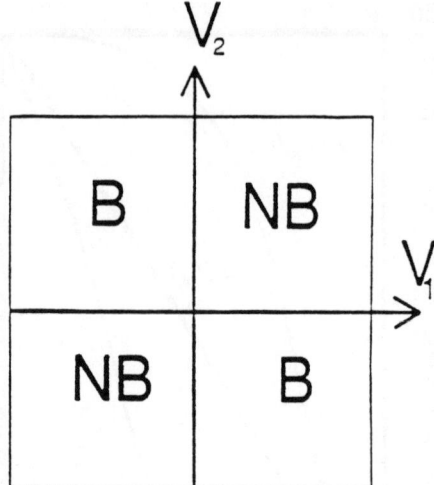

Figure 3. The distribution of these hypothetical variables (V_1 and V_2) shows no univariate separation but displays multicollinearity.

Multivariate Sensitivity. In addition to individual parameter influence, the interaction between parameters must be explored. It is possible, for example, that the first and second moments for a single parameter exhibit no impact on behavior determination. That parameter, however, may have a significant effect on the output state because of a strong correlation with other input parameters. For example, Figure 3 depicts a two-dimensional parameter space for which the cumulative distributions $F(v_1|B)$, $F(v_i|NB)$ and $F(v_2|B)$, $F(v_2|NB)$ are identical. Nevertheless, both parameters, when considered together, are important in determining the occurrence of behavior. A univariate test would misjudge the importance of these two variables to the system. In this case, covariance between the two parameters is crucial in assessing the sensitivity of the output vector.

One formal method for capturing the effects of parameter covariance is through the use of a principal components transformation. Importantly, principal components can examine the relationships between many input variables. In our two variable example, let **v** be the normalized parameter vector such that

$$E(\mathbf{vv}^T) = \mathbf{I} = P(B)E(\mathbf{M}_1\mathbf{M}_1^T) + P(B)\mathbf{m}_1\mathbf{m}_1^T \\ + P(NB)E(\mathbf{M}_2\mathbf{M}_2^T) + P(NB)\mathbf{m}_2\mathbf{m}_2^T, \quad (4)$$

where $P(B)$ = probability of obtaining behavior, $P(NB)$ = probability of not obtaining behavior, $\mathbf{v}_1$ = parameter vector associated with behavior, $\mathbf{v}_2$ = parameter vector associated with nonbehavior, $\mathbf{m}_1 = E\ (\mathbf{v}_1)$, $\mathbf{m}_2 = E(\mathbf{v}_2)$, $\mathbf{M}_1 = \mathbf{v}_1 - \mathbf{m}_1$, and $\mathbf{M}_2 = \mathbf{v}_2 - \mathbf{m}_2$.

If no separation was indicated by n of the distributions $F(\mathbf{v}_k)$ in the univariate analysis, then $m_{1k} = m_{2k} = 0$ for each of these distributions. When two parameters (say v_i and v_j) show no univariate indication of behavior but together have a distribution like that of Figure 3, the ij^{th} elements of $\mathbf{m}_1\mathbf{m}_1^T$ and $\mathbf{m}_2\mathbf{m}_2^T$ are zero and, according to Equation 4, the corresponding off-diagonal elements of the covariance matrices are such that

$$P(B)E(M_{1i}M_{1j}) = -P(NB)E(M_{2i}M_{2j}), \qquad (5)$$

where $i \neq j$. Thus, if a distribution does not show univariate separation but does show induced covariance, this covariance will be seen in the covariance matrices under B and NB. By inspecting these two matrices situations like that shown in Figure 3 can be assessed.

In the more general case we should observe some separation in both the univariate analysis and the parameter covariance matrix. When information on both mean and variance differences between parameters is important, then a principal components transformation of the covariance matrix of either the behavior or nonbehavior class defined with respect to the grand mean can be used to examine multivariate relationships.[19] Thus, Equation 4 can be written

$$E(\mathbf{vv}^T) = \mathbf{I} = P(B)E(\mathbf{v}_1\mathbf{v}_1^T) + P(NB)E(\mathbf{v}_2\mathbf{v}_2^T). \qquad (6)$$

If $\mathbf{T}$ is the matrix that diagonalizes the covariance matrix under behavior, $E(\mathbf{v}_1\mathbf{v}_1^T)$, then the same transformation must diagonalize the covariance matrix under $E(\mathbf{v}_2\mathbf{v}_2^T)$, the nonbehavior classification:

$$\mathbf{T}^T E(\mathbf{vv}^T)\mathbf{T} = \mathbf{I} = P(B)\mathbf{T}^T E(\mathbf{v}_1\mathbf{v}_1^T)\mathbf{T} + P(NB)\mathbf{T}^T E(\mathbf{v}_2\mathbf{v}_2^T)\mathbf{T}, \text{ or} \qquad (7)$$

$$\mathbf{I} = P(B)\Omega_1 + P(NB)\Omega_2, \qquad (8)$$

where Ω_1 and Ω_2 are diagonal matrices with the eigenvalues of the respective covariance matrices as the diagonal elements. The columns of the T matrix are eigenvectors of the covariance matrices, and the (normalized) components of those vectors are the direction cosines of the transformed axes relative to the original parameter axes. Thus, if the projections of the parameters onto a transformed axis are different for behavior and nonbehavior in terms of the $d_{m,n}$ statistic, that eigenvector helps explain the occurrence of behavior. The weights of individual eigenvalues in the eigenvector then indicate the multivariate importance of each parameter

$$T = \begin{bmatrix} .56 & -.09 & .17 & .42 \\ -.03 & -.33 & .01 & -.13 \\ -.11 & .28 & .03 & -.30 \\ -.21 & .21 & -.55 & -.10 \end{bmatrix}$$

Figure 4. The columns of the T matrix are eigenvectors of the new axes. The individual cells are parameter eigenvalues.

in explaining behavior. Graphically, Figure 4 shows a typical **T** matrix, the columns of which are eigenvectors whose significance is determined using the $d_{m,n}$ statistic.

GSA Mechanics: Summary

A priori analysis of mechanical models has long been accomplished with traditional univariate or bivariate sensitivity, in spite of substantial problems with this technique. Quade (1980) has shown that models incorporating point estimates fail to properly capture system variation.[20] Holling (1978) notes that parameter-by-parameter variation dangerously conceals multivariate influence.[21] Even more sophisticated Monte Carlo studies often utilize inferior statistical techniques. Ordinary least squares analysis falters because of univariance and the bias problems associated with classificatory analysis.[22] Traditional principal component analysis fails to capture the effect of different mean distributions in addition to central tendency variations.

Although the mechanics are quite different, the philosophies behind GSA and classical sensitivity analysis are quite similar. Monte Carlo sampling introduces little more uncertainty than systematic sampling. In our methodology, Monte Carlo sampling is simply a labor-saving device for assembling a set of diverse and independent input vectors. A wide range of input parameter combinations are required for a thorough check of multicollinearity. More traditional case scenarios do not provide as much coverage and, as mentioned earlier, can be quite cumbersome. The "generated database" assembled by Monte Carlo can be analyzed in a number of ways. We found that GSA provides more information on the variable relationships of our model than traditional statistical methods, such as ordinary least squares (OLS) regression, ridge regression, and principal components analysis. The methodology presented here requires no great leap of faith for those comfortable with traditional sensitivity analysis. Monte Carlo sampling replaces case scenarios and parameter-by-parameter changes, while GSA provides analytical insight usually supplied by OLS or visual inspection of graphs.

The limitations of GSA should also be pointed out. A systematic model must be formulated to represent the real system being analyzed. Construction and calibration of such a model is often difficult due to the inherent lack of empirical data, but this problem can be alleviated if a host of possible models is analyzed. GSA also requires an algorithm for the separation of generated data into behavior and nonbehavior groups. If a relevant point of division is not discernible, the results of analysis can be nonintuitive. A third limitation of GSA is the method of analytical interpretation. As with any statistical technique, a good deal of judgement and intuition must be used in deciphering the results of GSA.

The benefits of GSA far outweigh these limitations. The impact or nonimpact of a number of factors on a system can be reliably gauged, even when data are crude or sparse. Forecasting models that endogenize both changing parameters and structure can be formulated. Many types of behavioral and scoring models can be analyzed. With minor adaptations, the technique outlined here can be applied to a number of real estate and finance systems. The flexible and efficient approach to analyzing input/output systems makes GSA a valuable method for uncovering system behavior.

Application of GSA to a Historic Rehabilitation Project

As stated above, the GSA technique offers the most insight when (1) only sparse data exist, (2) the model being simulated has strong theoretical connections to the real system, and (3) the model inputs and outputs can be tangibly measured in the real system. These conditions are satisfied in the case of historic rehabilitation. The following sections demonstrate the application of GSA to an historic rehabilitation project. Following the algorithm of Table 2, a model is constructed, Monte Carlo simulation is performed, and GSA is run and interpreted.

Step One: Model Building

The first step to implementing GSA is construction of a model. The appendix contains a simplified version of the rehabilitation project *pro*

Table 2. Structure of Analysis

	Step 1	Step 2	Step 3
Methodology	Model building • v^* • y^*	Monte Carlo simulation	Statistical analysis • Behavior specification • Univariate analysis • Multivariate analysis
Application	Pro forma construction • Model equations • Input parameters • IRR	Simulated database	Statistical analysis • IRR hurdle rate determination • GSA statistics

Methodology and application of generalized sensitivity analysis.

forma income statement used as the model.[23] The *pro forma* systematically calculates an IRR—the output and observation vector for our analysis—by using the inputs and equations shown. The project is a tax sheltered investment with negative operating income. The structure of the *pro forma* was specified using field experience, due to a lack of empirical data. It was reviewed by four developers of such projects and found to be a realistic example of a marginal, tax-induced development. Model construction is the most controversial part of GSA and other sensitivity analyses. Without a credible link between model and real system, the results of analysis are thrown into considerable doubt.

Step Two: Monte Carlo Simulation

Specification of the input parameter vector is the first step of Monte Carlo simulation. We decided to model the impact of eleven parameters on the IRR of the project. Those parameters and their predetermined ranges are listed in Table 3. It should be emphasized that the parameter list could be greatly expanded for normal feasibility analysis. For example, financing and construction costs would form natural points of departure for such an analysis. Here, our emphasis is on tax-related variables. The parameters are loosely grouped into four classifications in Table 4. This provides a simplifying structure for the interpretation of results.

Table 3. *Pro Forma* Model

#	Parameter name	Description	Range
1	RTC	Rehab. tax credit as % of expenditures on rehab.	0–50%
2	RDB	Reduction of depreciable base as % of of expenditures	0–100%
3	Rate of appreciation	Annual rate of gross margin growth	0–7%
4	Normal tax rate	Investor's operating income tax rate	20–53%
5	Capital gains tax rate	Investor's capital gains tax rate	0–53%[1]
6	Rehab. deprec.— method	The method of depreciation used in writing off rehab. costs	S.line = 0 ACRS = 1
7	Rehab. deprec.— years	Number of years used in writing off rehab. costs	15–32
8	Building deprec.— method	The method of depreciation used in writing off cost of building	S.line = 0 ACRS = 1
9	Building deprec.— years	Number of years used in writing off cost of building	15–32
10	Passive activity rules	IRS rules that limit offset of passive losses on active gains	Yes = 0 No = 1
11	Exception	Dollar amount of passive losses that can offset active gains if passive activity rules are in force	0–20,000

This table lists the parameters of the *pro forma* model and their predetermined ranges.

[1] The capital gains tax rate was calculated in such a way that it is always less than or equal to the personal tax rate. The formula for capital gains tax rate is (RAND) * (personal income), where RAND is a random number between zero and one, and personal income is a rectangular random variable between 20% and 53%.

Recall that values for each variable are assigned from a predetermined, uniformly distributed range. In general, the parameter range should be large enough to include extreme, but credible, parameter values. Although the rehabilitation tax credit has never been as high as 50%, making the range that high gives the analyst an opportunity to see the potential effects of such a figure. In an area as uncertain as taxation law, it is important to allow for extensive future change. Specification of a large range does not severely affect analysis in the more realistic range, especially as the number of simulation runs is increased. The analyst can decide *ex post* what subrange is truly "realistic."

Table 4.

Economic Factors	Normal Income Tax Tax code factors
3. Appreciation rate	4. Normal tax rate
	5. Capital gains tax rate
Depreciation Tax Code Factors	Rehabilitation Tax Code Factors
2. RDB[1]	1. RTC
6. Rehab. deprec.—method	2. RDB[1]
7. Rehab. deprec.—years	10. Passive activity rules
8. Building deprec.—method	11. Exception
9. Building deprec.—years	

For analytical case, parameters are grouped into different categories. The nature of the parameters form the basis for classification.
[1] RDB (reduction of depreciable base as percent of rehabilitation costs) falls under both categories.

Parameter specification provides the necessary framework for Monte Carlo simulation. ϕ^*, the model structure, has been defined as the rehabilitation project *pro forma*. The dependent output vector we wish to study, y^* (or y_1^*, since it is a one variable vector), has been defined as the *pro forma* IRR. The input vector v has been defined as the eleven-dimensional set of parameters listed in Table 3. Monte Carlo iteration was performed by a computer program that defined a value for v^* by randomly selecting a value within the *a priori* range for each of the eleven parameters. The program then input the vector into the *pro forma* model and calculated a resultant IRR, or y^*. These steps were repeated 3364 times, with the values for v^* and y^* recorded each time. The resulting database, a segment of which is shown in Table 5, consists of a twelve-column, 3364-row matrix, where the first eleven columns hold randomly selected values of the input parameters and the twelfth column holds the resultant IRR. The frequency distribution of all IRR values is shown in Figure 5.

Step Three: GSA Application

Behavior Specification. The next step is to sort the scenarios of the generated database into behavior and nonbehavior, based upon some critical value of y_1^*. The algorithm implemented for this model was

Param. no.	1	2	3	4	5	6	7	8	9	10	11	IRR
Value	9%	73%	6.73%	49%	2%	0	26	1	16	1	12,470	19.79%
	3%	13%	4.32%	44%	17%	0	16	1	26	1	1,465	14.28%
	50%	52%	4.26%	27%	8%	0	28	1	15	0	9,959	15.56%
	18%	12%	4.33%	41%	34%	1	22	0	25	0	2,181	9.23%
	24%	34%	0.28%	28%	1%	1	19	0	30	0	18,395	8.41%
	28%	60%	2.20%	41%	2%	1	21	1	26	1	11,109	22.87%
	19%	54%	6.79%	48%	21%	0	22	0	25	1	18,725	21.04%
	38%	13%	3.47%	44%	2%	1	25	1	17	0	3,823	11.54%
	8%	38%	1.83%	31%	17%	1	28	0	30	1	17,083	7.09%
	43%	35%	0.01%	29%	22%	1	27	1	27	1	6,541	21.57%
	18%	56%	3.98%	23%	8%	0	27	1	19	0	16,869	13.99%
	27%	11%	6.72%	36%	8%	1	17	1	22	1	8,353	29.09%
	5%	99%	5.91%	28%	26%	0	16	0	26	0	10,275	12.99%
	35%	43%	0.52%	51%	29%	0	20	0	23	0	8,369	6.89%
	15%	34%	6.43%	34%	31%	1	21	0	22	0	11,054	14.53%
	29%	13%	6.94%	34%	20%	0	22	1	19	0	4,118	15.65%
	31%	40%	0.96%	27%	17%	1	21	0	17	0	8,549	8.57%
	11%	41%	5.00%	22%	19%	0	20	0	30	0	1,197	11.24%
	12%	27%	0.44%	41%	24%	1	20	1	19	0	2,961	3.91%
	37%	18%	0.61%	48%	26%	1	15	0	27	1	4,171	28.24%
	10%	33%	1.67%	52%	2%	1	27	0	26	1	1,878	11.95%
	48%	16%	2.38%	33%	10%	0	25	0	30	1	8,716	30.55%
	38%	6%	0.11%	23%	5%	0	29	1	19	1	18,042	17.73%
	40%	29%	4.87%	22%	11%	1	18	0	24	1	15,024	29.21%
	7%	46%	3.07%	48%	19%	1	21	0	19	1	8,379	11.24%
	48%	48%	0.30%	31%	10%	1	29	0	18	1	2,445	28.92%

Table 5 shows 26 of the 3364 lines of the generated database. The first 11 columns contain the randomly generated values of the parameters listed. The 12th column shows the resultant IRR of the parameter vector.

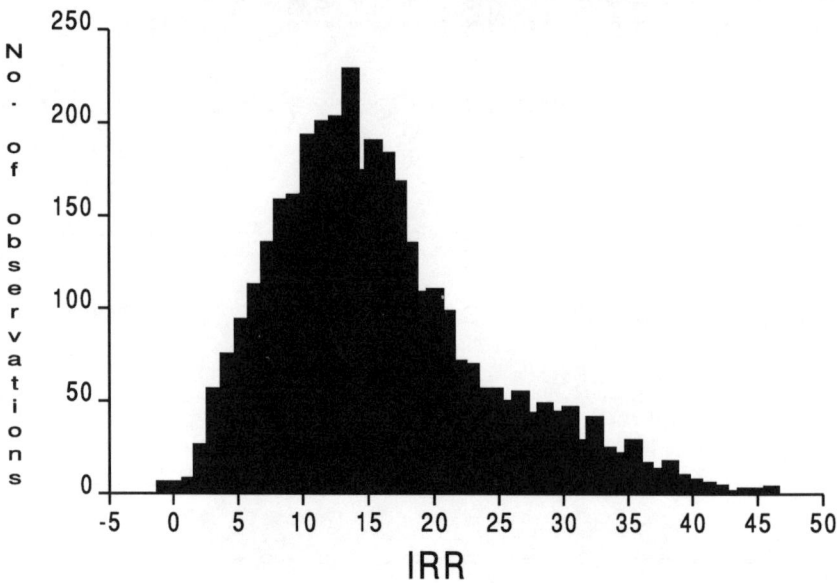

Figure 5. The IRR Frequency Distribution from the Generated Database.

$$\begin{aligned} &\text{If } y_1^* \geq \bar{y}, \text{ then } [v^*, y_1^*] \in B; \\ &\text{If } y_1^* < \bar{y}, \text{ then } [v^*, y_1^*] \in NB, \end{aligned} \quad (9)$$

where $y_1^* = $ IRR, $\bar{y} = $ *a priori* critical value of IRR, $[v^*, y_1^*] = $ specific realization of the parameter, vector and its resulting IRR (a scenario), B = set of scenarios defined as behavior, NB = set of scenarios defined as nonbehavior.

GSA was run three times on the simulated database, each with a different value for $\bar{y}$. The three values of $\bar{y}$ are 9.80%, 14.08%, and 19.81%, which correspond to the values that separate the IRR distribution into quartiles. These three values were selected so that parameter sensitivity could be explored across a wide range of conditions. GSA I, which uses a cut-off value of 9.80%, determines which parameters separate really poor projects (an IRR of less than 9.80%) from all others. GSA III, with its 19.81% cut-off, identifies the parameters that determine very high IRR values. GSA II, with a cut-off value of 14.08%, examines the basic differences between good and bad projects. Naturally, a number of other logical values for ȳ could have been selected.[24] For the purpose of this paper, though, the three different analyses should provide sufficient insight into the relative impact of parameters.

GSA Application: Results

Proper interpretation of GSA results, like interpretation of most analyses, requires a good deal of judgement. As noted by Spear and Hornberger (1983), the $d_{m,n}$ statistic should not be used as a criterion for hypothesis testing in the traditional sense, but rather as a useful index for ranking the importance of parameters.[25] For example, Figure 6 shows how the $d_{m,n}$ statistic can break down on dummy variable distributions. The abridged results of the three GSA runs are shown in Tables 6 through 8. The main table heading indicates the threshold IRR level used in the particular GSA. Parameters are listed in the first column (Table 3 contains

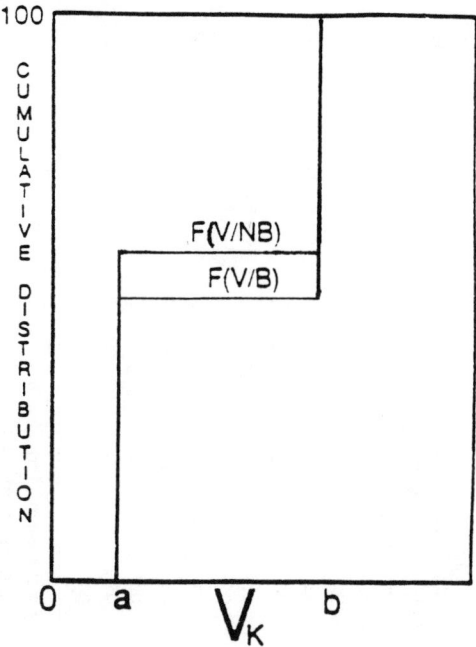

Figure 6. These Distributions have a Highly Significant $d_{m,n}$ Value Despite Being Nearly Identical. Dummy Variables are Prone to this Statistical Aberration.

Table 6. Abridged Statistical Results of GSAI ($\bar{y}$ = 9.80%)

Param. no.	Mean B[b]	Mean NB[c]	$d_{m,n}$[a]	Eigenvectors Behavior B1 .85[a]	Behavior B11 .29	Nonbehavior NB10 .79[d]	Nonbehavior NB2 .27	Nonbehavior NB11 .24
1	.80	−.27	.50	30.1%	−31.6%	30.8%	−31.7%	Y
2	−.04	.01	X	Y	Y	Y	Y	Y
3	.34	−.11	.21	11.4%	Y	11.8%	Y	Y
4	.04	−.01	X	Y	Y	Y	Y	−26.1%
5	−.18	.06	.13	−11.0%	Y	Y	Y	25.6%
6	.02	−.01	X	Y	Y	Y	Y	Y
7	−.01	.00	X	Y	Y	Y	Y	Y
8	−.01	.00	X	Y	Y	Y	Y	Y
9	−.03	.01	X	Y	Y	Y	Y	Y
10	.91	−.30	.60	30.1%	34.5%	31.3%	33.7%	−10.0%
11	.02	.01	X	Y	Y	Y	Y	Y

[a] $d_{m,n}$ statistics for the eigenvectors listed.
[b] Mean value for parameter in behavior group.
[c] Mean value for parameter in nonbehavior group.
[d] Eigenvalues computed as percent of total eigenvector variance explained. Sign denotes direction of eigenvalue.
X denotes value of less than .10; Y denotes value of less than 10%.
All eigenvectors with a $d_{m,n}$ statistic of greater than .20 are listed.

Table 7. Abridged Statistical Results of GSAII ($\bar{y} = 14.08\%$)

Param. no.	Mean		$d_{m,n}$	Eigenvectors			
				Behavior	Nonbehavior		
	B[b]	NB[c]		$B8$[a] .52[a]	$NB7$ .36[d]	$NB4$ .31	$NB8$ .30
1	.43	−.43	.40	Y	11.2%	12.7%	Y
2	−.03	.03	X	Y	−17.1%	Y	Y
3	.44	−.44	.40	29.4%	11.9%	−14.3%	26.9%
4	−.04	.04	X	Y	Y	Y	Y
5	−.19	.19	.17	Y	Y	Y	Y
6	.03	−.03	X	Y	Y	16.7%	19.0%
7	.01	−.01	X	Y	Y	Y	Y
8	−.01	.01	X	10.6%	Y	27.0%	Y
9	−.01	.01	X	Y	21.6%	Y	12.3%
10	.40	−.40	.40	16.7%	13.0%	−12.0%	Y
11	.11	−.11	.11	Y	Y	Y	Y

[a] $d_{m,n}$ statistics for the eigenvectors listed.
[b] Mean value for parameter in behavior group.
[c] Mean value for parameter in nonbehavior group.
[d] Eigenvalues computed as percent of total eigenvector variance explained. Sign denotes direction of eigenvalue. X denotes value of less than .10; Y denotes value of less than 10%.
All eigenvectors with a $d_{m,n}$ statistic of greater than .20 are listed.

Table 8. Abridged Statistical Results of GSAIII ($\bar{y} = 19.81\%$)

Param. no.	Mean		$d_{m,n}$[a]	Eigenvectors					
				Behavior			Nonbehavior		
	B[b]	NB[c]		B10 .72[d]	B11 .28		NB1 .52[d]	NB2 .27	NB3 .21
1	.19	−.57	.36	25.5%	Y		15.5%	Y	−22.8%
2	−.02	.05	X	Y	Y		Y	Y	Y
3	.29	−.88	.56	33.7%	−12.1%		15.5%	17.6%	Y
4	−.03	.08	X	Y	−29.7%		−20.2%	18.4%	−15.8%
5	−.09	.28	.15	Y	35.2%		−23.5%	19.5%	−14.7%
6	−.00	.00	X	Y	Y		Y	Y	Y
7	.01	−.02	X	Y	Y		Y	Y	Y
8	−.02	.07	X	Y	Y		Y	Y	Y
9	.00	−.00	X	Y	Y		Y	Y	Y
10	.15	−.45	.49	19.7%	Y		10.8%	15.7%	10.6%
11	.07	−.22	.16	Y	Y		Y	15.4%	15.1%

[a] $d_{m,n}$ statistics for the eigenvectors listed.
[b] Mean value for parameter in behavior group.
[c] Mean value for parameter in nonbehavior group.
[d] Eigenvalues computed as percent of total eigenvector variance explained. Sign denotes direction of eigenvalue.
X denotes value of less than .10; Y denotes value of less than 10%.
All eigenvectors with a $d_{m,n}$ statistic of greater than .20 are listed.

the number key). The next two columns contain the mean values of the parameter in the behavior and nonbehavior groups (the grand mean of each parameter is zero).

A difference in the mean of the behavior vs. nonbehavior group indicates univariate sensitivity of IRR to the parameter. The fourth column contains the $d_{m,n}$ statistic of the behavior and nonbehavior cumulative distribution functions. A high $d_{m,n}$ indicates differences in the cumulative distribution functions and implies univariate sensitivity of output to the parameter. The next group of columns contain the most important covariance matrix eigenvectors of the behavior group (as judged by the $d_{m,n}$ statistic of the eigenvector). The important non-behavior eigenvectors follow.[26]

For discussion purposes, eigenvectors are assigned a letter (B if from the behavior matrix or NB if from the nonbehavior matrix) and a number (1 through 11). The percentages listed in the eigenvector columns reflect the importance and direction of that parameter's eigenvalue, as determined by dividing the parameter eigenvalue by the sum total of absolute eigenvalues. Careful examination of these results reveals which of the parameters are most important in defining behavior.

In GSA I (Table 6; 9.80% hurdle rate), the most important parameters in determining behavior were the RTC (parameter 1) and passive activity rules (parameter 10), both of which are rehabilitation tax code factors. This is evidenced by both the very high univariate $d_{m,n}$ statistics and absolute eigenvalues for the most important eigenvectors (B1, B11, NB10, NB2). In the two most important eigenvectors, B1 and NB10, the eigenvalues for RTC and passive activity were both large and of the same sign. Thus, the occurrence of either behavior or nonbehavior can be largely attributed to the combination of a high RTC and the absence of passivity rules. The appreciation rate (parameter 3) is the next most important explanatory parameter. The univariate importance of the appreciation rate is seen in the $d_{m,n}$ statistic of .21, and high weight in eigenvectors B1 and NB10 implies positive correlation with RTC and passive activity rules. The normal tax code factors, income tax rate (parameter 4) and capital gains tax rate (parameter 5), explain less of the behavior occurrence. Depreciation factors for both the rehabilitation, method (parameter 6) and years (parameter 7) and building, method (parameter 8) and years (parameter 9), account for almost none of the difference between an IRR of less than or higher than 9.80%.

Behavior in GSA II (Table 7; 14.08% hurdle rate) is predominantly explained by economic (parameter 3) and rehabilitation tax code factors (parameter 1; parameter 2; parameter 10; parameter 11). Appreciation rate of the project is arguably the most important parameter, with a univariate $d_{m,n}$ of .40 and eigenvalues explaining more than 10% of the variation in each of the four important eigenvectors. RTC and passive activity rules are also important determinants of behavior, with similarly high $d_{m,n}$ statistics (.40) and high absolute eigenvalues in a number of eigenvectors. The appreciation rate and passive activity rules also have an important positive correlation. Unlike behavior determination in GSA I, depreciation tax code factors play an important role in behavior determination. Reduction of depreciable base (parameter 2), capital gains tax rate (parameter 5), and the method and number of years of building depreciation (parameter 8; parameter 9) show high eigenvalues in a number of eigenvectors. Normal income tax factors (parameter 4; parameter 5) lose almost all explanatory value, as evidenced by the low absolute eigenvalues and $d_{m,n}$ statistics.

GSA III (Table 8; 19.81% hurdle rate) shows yet another shuffling of important parameters. Normal income tax factors (parameter 4; parameter 5) and economic factors (parameter 3) are of primary importance in determining an IRR of 19.81%, while rehabilitation tax factors (parameter 1; parameter 2; parameter 10; parameter 11) are of slightly less importance in determining behavior. Again, the appreciation rate and rehabilitation tax factors have a high positive correlation. Depreciation tax code factors (parameter 6; parameter 7; parameter 8; parameter 9) exhibit almost no influence over behavior determination. As evidenced by their low univariate $d_{m,n}$ values, the normal tax code factors (parameter 4; parameter 5) are important in the multivariate sense only. In eigenvectors NB1, NB2, and NB3, normal and capital gains tax rate are of the same sign and of a direction that supports the high IRR when tax rates are low, a surprising result for a system constructed as a tax shelter. Eigenvector B10, the most significant eigenvector with a $d_{m,n}$ of .72, is explained not by normal income tax factors, but by economic and rehabilitation tax factors.

GSA Application: Summary

Table 9 summarizes the GSA findings. A number of conclusions can be drawn from these results. Project appreciation rate, a surrogate for economic factors not explicitly capitalized into other variables, is the single most significant indicator of success. High appreciation rates are almost always associated with high IRRs. Second, the availability of rehabilita-

Table 9. Relative Importance of Parameter Groups per GSAs I, II, and III

	Very unimportant	Unimportant	important	Very important
GSA I: $\bar{y} = 9.80\%$				
Rehab. factors				X
Normal tax factors		X		
Deprec. tax factors	X			
Economic factors			X	
GSA II: $\bar{y} = 14.08\%$				
Rehab. factors				X
Normal tax factors	X			
Deprec. tax factors			X	
Economic factors				X
GSA III: $\bar{y} = 19.81\%$				
Rehab. factors			X	
Normal tax factors				X
Deprec. tax factors	X			
Economic factors				X

Rehab. factors = parameters 1, 2, 10, 11; normal tax factors = parameters 4, 5; deprec. tax factors = parameters 2, 6, 7, 8, 9; economic factors = parameter 3.
See table 3 for description of parameters.

tion tax credits, as modified by passive activity rules, often determines whether a project has very low returns. In other words, favorable rehabilitation tax credits will not guarantee very high IRRs, but unfavorable rules are commonly associated with low IRRs. Third, depreciation tax rules may swing project IRR between 12% and 16%, but the occurrence of extreme IRR values is attributable to the other factors. Fourth, normal income tax rates play a significant role in determining the occurrence of very high IRRs. A combination of low ordinary income and low capital gains tax rates is essential to attaining a high IRR. Fifth, the rehabilitation tax rules and appreciation rate of the project, as seen by their high $d_{m,n}$ values, impact IRR in a univariate sense, that is, they act strongly upon IRR with or without special combinations of other parameters. Ordinary income tax rates and depreciation provisions, on the other hand, exert their influence on IRR in a multivariate fashion. Thus, these parameters cannot be examined independent of other parameter values.

A number of analytical conclusions can be drawn from these results.

First, Congress has limited power over the extent of rehabilitation activity. Project economics, as reflected in expected appreciation, is the most important factor in what has been traditionally considered a tax shelter. Second, unfavorable rehabilitation tax rules actuate low IRRs. Arguably, this condition exists today.[27] Third, Congressional manipulation of the depreciation tax codes will not influence rehabilitation projects to a great extent. Fourth, manipulation of capital gains and income tax rates will not greatly affect midrange rehabilitation projects. RTC and passive activity regulations are the most effective controls Congress has over rehabilitation investment. They will not, however, fully counteract project economics.

Conclusions

The effects of tax laws on historic rehabilitation were studied with the GSA technique. In this chapter historic rehabilitation has been reviewed, GSA methodology has been outlined, and an application of GSA to rehabilitation investment has been presented. The importance of economic factors constrains the ability of policy makers to manipulate historic preservation through the tax code. RTC and passive activity tax laws have strong univariate influence on rehabilitation feasibility but are of secondary importance to project economics.

The authors speculate that a pessimistic economic outlook may be depressing rehabilitation activity as much as the weak tax credits. The income tax and capital gains tax have a lesser, multivariate influence on rehabilitation returns. Depreciation tax rules are of minor importance to rehabilitation investment. There are also implications for the investor. Supply and demand for rehabilitated structures and their substitutes cannot be ignored, even within favorable tax environments. Thus, future changes in tax laws that are "grandfathered in" can affect present projects by discouraging future rehabilitation and depressing property values in historic districts.

The results of the GSA cannot be produced by traditional sensitivity techniques. Over 3000 different values for each parameter were considered, instead of the usual three. By examining 3364 different parameter combinations, a number of multicollinear tendencies that would have been overlooked by bivariate sensitivity were revealed. GSA not only identified the important parameters, it showed how those parameters interact.

The primary problem that GSA helps remedy is that of inferior data.

Applicable to *a priori* analysis of a wide variety of input-output systems, GSA offers researchers a systematic and dependable method for analyzing relationships among many variables. Certainly, GSA provides a much needed framework for analysis of Monte Carlo results. Real estate investment appears to be one of many potential systems suited to GSA application.

Notes

1. Historic preservation has been a stated national goal since passage of the National Historic Preservation Act of 1966. Tax advantages for historic rehabilitation were first made available by Congress in 1976, with subsequent revisions in 1981 and 1986. Jaffe (1988) discusses the roots of the historic preservation movement.
2. In the fields of finance and real estate, the *pro forma* statement exemplifies theoretical modelling of an empirically indeterminate system. A number of financial texts, including Brealey and Myers (1984), contain further explanation of the model building process.
3. The modeler is forced to consider the relevance of each relationship that is formulated as an equation. Brealey and Myers (1984) liken model building to spinach: "You may not like the taste, but it's good for you."
4. A thorough survey of simulation terminology is found in Kleijnen (1974).
5. Bible (1987), for example, constructs a *pro forma* income statement of a generic development project and incorporates pre- and post-1986 reform tax implications into his two input scenarios.
6. See, for example, Pyhrr et al. (1989) and Swartzman and Kaluzny (1987).
7. Even supposing that three values for each of ten parameters sufficiently covers all possible situations, 3^{10} or 59,049 simulation runs would be required to properly gauge multicollinearity. See Swartzman and Kaluzny (1987), pp. 220–223, for further discussion of problems with systematic sampling and incomplete sampling.
8. Hertz (1968) was a pioneer in the use of Monte Carlo simulation in capital budgeting. Thompson (1989) gives theoretical justification for Monte Carlo simulation and presents a case example.
9. See Hornberger, Cosby, and Galloway (1986), Hornberger and Spear (1980), Spear and Hornberger (1980), Spear and Hornberger (1983) as examples of GSA use in environmental sciences and Auslander, Spear, and Young (1982) as an example of GSA application to engineering.
10. P.L. 97-34.
11. Chittenden (1987).
12. Federal tax code 13.03 (Bible, 1987) states that "A certified historic structure is a depreciable building or structure that is either listed in the National Register or located in a registered historic district and certified by the Secretary of the Interior as being of historic significance to the district." Grunenwald and Kitchen (1987, 1988) provide a detailed account of the certification process.
13. P.L. 99-514. Although the RTC was retained at a lower rate, the effectiveness of the credit was reduced because of a number of TRA-related tax changes, such as passive activity limitations.
14. The TRA passed Senate Finance in April, 1986. The "Chow" test is a test for a shift

in parameters in a time series. Here, the dummy-variable approach formalized by Dufour (1980) is used. Regressing the data with a dummy for the 1986 tax change is highly significant (t-statistic = 11.71, p = .0000).

15. Due to space limitations, we cannot discuss the tax code in detail. See, for example, Higgins and Covell (1987) and Maloney (1989) for a complete explanation of how the tax code affects rehabilitation.

16. This section draws heavily upon the work of G. M. Hornberger and R. C. Spear. See Hornberger et al. (1986), Hornberger and Spear (1980), Spear and Hornberger (1980), and Spear and Hornberger (1983).

17. See Hornberger, Cosby, and Galloway (1986).

18. The Kolmogorov–Smirnov statistic has a tendency to break down as a dummy variable. Alternatives measures such as the Levy distance can be applied. See Huber (1981).

19. Fukunaga and Koontz (1970).

20. Quade (1980).

21. Holling (1978).

22. For a complete discussion, see Maddala (1983).

23. A more standard Lotus *pro forma* spreadsheet is available from the authors.

24. An optimal mechanism would advance the value of ȳ in increments approaching zero, thus exploring the entire range of output on a continuous basis. The authors are currently working on a program to accomplish this task.

25. Spear and Hornberger (1983).

26. In theory, these two principal component matrices should be of equal magnitude and opposite direction, but because of random behavior, they differ slightly. See Fukunaga and Koontz (1970).

27. Rypkema and Spatz (1987).

Appendix

The appendix contains the *pro forma* model used in analysis. A more standard Lotus version is available from the authors.

Parameters
(See Table 3 for full explanation of parameters)

p_1	RTC	p_7	Years rehab. deprec.
p_2	RDB	p_8	Method building deprec.
p_3	Rate of appreciation	p_9	Years building deprec.
p_4	Normal tax rate	p_{10}	passive activity rules
p_5	Capital gains rate	p_{11}	Exception
p_6	Method rehab. deprec.		

Constants
(Rounded to nearest '00)

k_1	General partner contribution:	$ 1,200
k_2	Note balance	337,000

k_3	Organization costs	8,000
k_4	Land purchase	65,000
k_5	Building purchase	100,000
k_6	Rehabilitation costs	270,000
k_7	Gross operating income (year i)	$29{,}600 \times (1.04)^i$
k_8	Interest expense (linear approx.)	$36{,}000 - 1{,}180 i \times (1.04)^{i-1}$
k_9	Loan payment	44,700
k_{10}	Amortization of organization costs	1,600

Other Assumptions

1. Investor has an adjusted gross income of $150,000 to $200,000.
2. The project is financed with a 15 year note at 10.5% APR.
3. The project is sold at the end of year 10.
4. General partner owns 1% of equity.

$$\text{IRR} = \left\{ \beta: \frac{CF_0}{1+\beta} + \frac{CF_1}{(1+\beta)^1} + \ldots + \frac{CF_{10}}{(1+\beta)^{10}} = 0 \right\} \quad (1)$$

$$CF_0 = k_1 + k_2 - k_3 - k_4 - k_5 - k_6 \quad (2)$$

$$CF_i = TS_i + NI_i + k_{10} + [DR_i] + [DB_i] + k_8 - K_9 \quad (3)$$
$i \in \{1,2,\ldots,9\}$

$$CF_{10} = TS_{10} + NI_{10} + k_{10} + [DR_{10}] - [DB_{10}]' + k_8 - k_9 + SP_{10} \quad (4)$$

If $p_{10} = 1$

$$TS_1 = (p_1 * k_6) * .99 \quad (5)$$
$$TS_i = 0$$
$i \in \{2,3,\ldots,10\}$

If $p_{10} = 0$ and $(p_1 * k_6) - \sum_{s=1}^{i-1} TS_6 > p_{11}$, $\quad (6)$
$$TS_i = p_{11}$$

If $p_{10} = 0$ and $p_{11} > (p_1 * k_6) - \sum_{s=1}^{i-1} TS_6 > 0$, $\quad (7)$

$$TS_i = (p_1 * k_6) - \sum_{s=1}^{i-1} TS_6$$

If $p_{10} = 0$ and $(p_1 * k_6) - \sum_{s=1}^{i-1} TS_s = 0$, $\quad (8)$
$$TS_i = 0$$

$$NI_i = [k_7 - k_8 - k_{10} - [DR_i] - [DB_i]] * (1 - p_4) \quad (9)$$
$i \in \{1,2,\ldots,10\}$

If $p_6 = 0$

$$DR_i = (1 - p_1 * p_2) * k_7/p_7 \qquad (10)$$

If $p_6 = 1$

$$DR_i \underset{i \in \{1,2,\ldots,10\}}{} = [[(1 - p_1 * p_2) * k_7] - \sum_{s=1}^{i-1} DR_s] * 1.75/p_7 \qquad (11)$$

If $p_8 = 0$

$$DB_i = k_5/p_9 \qquad (12)$$

If $p_8 = 1$ \hfill (13)

$$DB_i \underset{i \{1,2,\ldots,10\}}{} = [k_5 - \sum_{s=1}^{i-1} DB_s] * 1.75/p_9 \qquad (13)$$

$$SP_{10} = [[(k_4 + k_5 + k_6) * (1 + p_3)] - (p_5 * GS_{10})] * .99 \qquad (14)$$

$$GS_{10} = [(k_4 + k_5 + k_6) * (1 + p_3)] - [k_4 + k_5 + (1 - p_1 * p_2) * k_6] \qquad (15)$$
$$+ [\sum_{s=1}^{10} DR_s + \sum_{s=1}^{10} DB_s]$$

Explanation of Equations

1. The internal rate of return is the discount factor that equates cash flows to zero.
2. Cash flow in year zero is original inflows less outflows.
3. Cash flow in years one through nine are the tax shelter from the RTC, net income, and noncash expenses less interest payments.
4. Cash flow in year ten is the same as in years in two through nine, with the exception of proceeds from sale of the property.
5. If there are no passive activity rules, tax shelter from the RTC in year one is the amount of the rehabilitation tax credit, and zero in all other years. The limited partners own 99% of project and the tax credit.
6. If there are passive activity rules and the amount of unused rehabilitation tax credit is more than the exception, tax shelter from the RTC equals the exception.
7. If there are passive activity rules and the amount of unused rehabilitation tax credit is less than the exception (but greater than zero), tax shelter from the RTC equals the amount of unused rehabilitation tax credit.
8. If all of the rehabilitation tax credit has been used, there is no tax shelter from the RTC.

9. Net income is gross operating income less interest, amortization, and depreciation expense, taken at the relevant tax rate.
10. Yearly depreciation on rehabilitation expenses is the tax base multiplied by cost divided by years of depreciable life if the straight-line method is used.
11. If 175% declining balance is used, depreciation on the rehabilitation is the remaining tax base each year multiplied by 1.75 and divided by the number of depreciable years of life.
12. Straight-line depreciation of building expense is cost divided by the allowable number of years of depreciation.
13. 175% declining balance depreciation of building expense is remaining depreciable base multiplied by 1.75 and divided by years of depreciable life.
14. Sale proceeds are the appreciated original costs less gain on sale at the capital gains tax rate.
15. Gain on sale is appreciated original costs less original taxable costs plus all depreciation.

References

Auslander, D. M., R. C. Spear, and G. E. Young. "A Simulation-Based Approach to the Design of Control Systems With Uncertain Parameters." *Transactions of the ASME* 104 (March 1982), 20–6.

Bible, D. S. "Rehabilitation Tax Credits and Rate of Return on Real Estate Under Recent Tax Reform Measures." *The Journal of Real Estate Research* (Winter 1987), 55–61.

Brealey, R. and S. Myers. *Principles of Corporate Finance*. New York: McGraw-Hill, 1984, pp. 195–208.

Chittenden, B. *Tax Incentives for Rehabilitating Historic Buildings, Fiscal Year 1987 Analysis*, Preservation Assistance Division, National Park Service, U.S. Dept. of Interior, December 1987, pp. 1–25.

Dufour, J. "Dummy Variables and Predictive Tests for Structural Change." *Economic Letters* 6 (1980), 241–7.

Fukunaga, K. and W. Koontz. "Application of the Karhunen-Loeve Expansion to Feature Selection and Ordering." *IEEE Transactions on Computers* (April 1970), 311–7.

Grunenwald, D. C. and J. Kitchen. "Preserving America's Heritage: The Rehabilitation Tax Credit (Part I)." *Real Estate Accounting and Taxation* 2, 3 (Fall 1987), 5–14.

Grunenwald, D. C. and J. Kitchen. "Preserving America's Heritage: The Rehabilitation Tax Credit (Part II)." *Real Estate Accounting and Taxation* 2, 4 (Winter 1988), 23–32.

Hertz, D. "Investment Policies that Pay Off." *Harvard Business Review* 46 (1968), 96–108.

Higgins, W. J. and A. B. Covell. "Historic Rehabilitation and the Tax Reform Act of 1986." *Real Estate Finance Journal*, 3, 1 (Summer 1987), 44–51.

Holling, C. (ed.). *Adaptive Environmental Assessment and Management.* Chichester, England: Wiley, 1978, p. 105.

Hornberger, G. and R. Spear. "Eutrophication in Peel Inlet—I. The Problem-Defining Behavior and a Mathematical Model For the Phosphorous Scenario." *Water Research* (Fall 1980), 29–42.

Hornberger, G., B. Cosby, and J. Galloway. "Modeling the Effects of Acid Deposition: Uncertainty and Spatial Variability in Estimation of Long-Term Sulfate Dynamics in a Region." *Water Resources Research* (August 1986), 1293–302.

Huber, P. *Robust Statistics.* New York: Wiley, 1981.

Jaffe, A. J. "The Historic Preservation Movement: The Myths." *Real Estate Accounting and Taxation* 2, 4 (Winter 1988), 77–81.

Kleijnen, J. P. C. *Statistical Techniques in Simulation.* New York: Marcel Dekker, 1974, chap. 1.

Maddala, G. *Limited-Dependent and Qualitative Variables in Econometrics.* Cambridge: Cambridge University Press, 1983, chap. 2 and 4.

Maloney, D. M. "The Rehabilitation Tax Credit and Tax Avoidance Strategies." *Tax Ideas.* New York: Prentice Hall, 1989, pp. 17, 475–84.

Pyhrr, S. et al. *Real Estate Investment.* New York: Wiley, 1989, pp. 255–64.

Quade, E. "Pitfalls in Formulation and Modeling," in *Pitfalls of Analysis*, G. Majone and E. Quade, eds. Chichester, England: Wiley, 1980, pp. 32–3.

Rypkema, D. and I. Spatz. "The Tax Reform Act's Passive Activity Rules." *Urban Land* (October 1987), 7–11.

Spear, R. and G. Hornberger. "Eutrophication in Peel Inlet—II. Identification of Critical Uncertainties via Generalized Sensitivity Analysis." *Water Research* (Fall 1980), 43–9.

Spear, R. and G. Hornberger. "Control of DO Level in a River Under Uncertainty." *Water Resources Research* (October 1983), 1266–70.

Swartzman, G. and S. Kaluzny. *Ecological Simulation Primer.* New York: MacMillan, 1987, pp. 217–24.

Thompson, J. *Empirical Model Building.* New York: Wiley, 1989, chap. 3.

15 TOWARD SOCIALLY EFFICIENT BROKER BEHAVIOR IN FACTUAL REPRESENTATIONS

Donald R. Levi, Curtis D. Terflinger, and Samuel C. Webb

Introduction

It is often said that law deals primarily with equity while economics deals primarily with efficiency. Because the goals of equity and efficiency are evident in real estate brokerage liability cases, the interface between both equity and efficiency, and law and economics, is of important interdisciplinary interest to both practitioners and academicians. The purpose of this paper is to investigate (1) how state courts have made choices between equity and efficiency in selecting appropriate legal remedies and (2) the extent to which legal remedies employed in real estate brokerage misrepresentation cases are economically efficient, that is, efficient in satisfying the criterion that marginal social benefits and costs are equal.

This investigation is presented in three parts. First, recent trends in

---

*Donald R. Levi, Curtis D. Terflinger, and Samuel C. Webb, respectively, are Professors of Real Estate, Business Law, and Economics, Wichita State University. This paper benefitted from the helpful comments of two anonymous reviewers. Any deficiencies, of course, remain those of the authors.

real estate brokerage misrepresentation cases are summarized. Second, the principal misrepresentation legal remedies are analyzed from an economic efficiency standpoint. Finally, conclusions and policy implications are presented.

Trends in Brokerage Misrepresentation Liability Rules

Overview

While agency law and buyer-agency concepts have received much attention in recent years, the majority of brokerage liability cases do not involve agency principles but rather involve the applications of the law of factual misrepresentation to the buyer-broker context (Levi and Terflinger, 1988).[1] While the law of factual misrepresentation favors the buyer side of the real estate transaction, the legal principles have been relatively well settled for many years in non-real estate areas. A major result has been an increasing number of lawsuits filed against real estate professionals in recent times (Levi and Terflinger, 1988).

Factual misrepresentations may be fraudulent, negligent, or innocent. Fraudulent misrepresentations involve intentional deception and may lead to punitive as well as actual damages. While courts (and juries) freely assess liability for fraudulent misrepresentations, most recent cases have not involved fraud (Levi and Terflinger, 1988).

The most common factual misrepresentation is simply the result of negligence (Levi and Terflinger, 1988). A negligent misrepresentation is one that an ordinarily careful and prudent broker would not have made. Whether a factual misrepresentation was made, and whether it was made negligently, are questions of fact to be determined by a jury.

An innocent misrepresentation is one that involves no moral culpability (i.e., neither intentional deceit, as in fraud, nor breach of the duty of care, as where there is negligence). Yet, some courts [Alaska (Bevins, 1982); Wisconsin (Gauerke, 1983)] impose liability for innocent broker misrepresentations on the basis of strict liability. In the simplest analysis, since both the broker and the buyer are innocent, the strict liability rule assesses liability against the party who is more likely to know the critically important questions to ask (i.e., the "professional" broker rather than the "amateur" buyer).

Classifying the Negligence Cases

Brokerage cases based on negligent misrepresentations may be classified in many different ways. We divide them into two largely subjective categories: those that involve characteristics of unsuitability for the buyer's purposes and those that involve diminished value. Both may apply to any type of real property. In the unsuitability cases, buyers discovered following their purchases that their property was not suitable for their intended purposes. In contrast, in the diminished value cases the properties were suitable for the basic purpose of the purchase, but for various reasons were less valuable than anticipated. In the unsuitability cases, knowledge of the true facts likely would have led to decisions not to purchase. In contrast, in the diminished value cases enlightened buyers might well have purchased anyway but at a lower price.

Factual situations involving suitability for the buyer's purposes are many and varied. Actual cases in recent years include a variety of disputes and claims such as the unsuitability of former landfills for building (Easton, 1984; Pacific Northwest, 1988; Stanford, 1985); a gravel pit represented as having 80,000 cubic yards of gravel but containing only 6,000 cubic yards (Cousineau, 1980); a five-unit apartment project located in an area zoned single family (Craig, 1987); construction of a house prohibited because a zoning regulation requires additional frontage (O'Brien, 1982); land sold for subdivision that could not be legally subdivided (Andrepont, 1984); a property said to need only cosmetic repairs was condemned and destroyed under the housing code (Amato, 1982); buyers were informed of restaurant health code violations and told they could move in and continue the business, but were later shut down for operating illegally without a license (Gerrard Realty, 1983); a property represented as consisting of three parcels but actually containing only one, which did not front on a certain street (First Church, 1987); a buildable lot that failed a percolation test for a septic tank (Tennant, 1980); and boundary locations that were incorrect and had an 18 to 21 foot encroachment (Hoffman, 1989).

Unsuitability for the buyers' purposes also may involve legal interpretations of such issues as existing lease terms (Hagar, 1981); explanations of deed restrictions (Coats, 1978); representations of the seller's title based on quit-claim deeds (Duby, 1980); and the assignability and/or renewability of a lease (Turubull, 1985).

Recall that, in the diminished value cases, the buyer with knowledge of the true facts might have purchased anyway but at a lower price. Examples of this category include a four-plex represented as having off-street parking next door (in a situation where the city closed the street to parking, Matthews, 1987); a property on which a flood control easement existed, rendering it unusable for growing crops (McCurter, 1985); a resort property represented as containing 5.5 acres and 600 feet of river frontage but only containing 2.17 acres with 415 feet of frontage (Gauerke, 1983); a property described as 22.75 acres but only containing 6.9 acres (Dugan, 1980); properties were represented to be on a sewer line but in fact were served by a septic tank (Johnson 1986; Pacific Northwest, 1988); an irrigated farm that could no longer be irrigated because of geological limitations (Nordstrom, 1980); a building represented as recently reroofed but actually having a 25- to 30-year-old roof (Schmidt, 1957); a building represented as having 118,500 square feet of rentable area but later determined to have only 100,049 square feet rentable (Ambassador East, 1987).

A subset of the diminished value cases can be classified as investment decision cases. Yet they are unique in that they involve providing inaccurate information for a *pro forma* income statement. They include an estimated $5,136 effective gross income per month when $4,200 was later determined to be appropriate (Ford, 1974); and a projected net income of $12,000, which turned out to be only $3,700 (Pepper, 1975). Interestingly, our research has discovered no investment decision cases since 1975, which may suggest that recent educational efforts by the real estate brokerage industry may have improved the quality of investment analyses.

The negligent misrepresentation/nondisclosure cases appear to base liability in part on the status of the parties (Levi and Terflinger, 1988). Typically licensees, as professionals, are held to a higher standard of care than are less knowledgeable buyers. While still based on negligence, both state license laws and the Realtor Code of Ethics have been used as norms of conduct in recent cases (Hagar, 1981; Johnson, 1986; Menzel, 1985). This trend to liability based on status is consistent with the observed trend from buyer beware to seller beware, and even broker beware. Broker beware cases are those in which the broker is held liable but the seller is not, as where the seller is an innocent source of misinformation when he would not reasonably be expected to recognize the falsity of the misinformation. But it may be argued that the ordinarily careful broker, as a professional conduit, would have have checked the accuracy of the information before making a representation.[2,3]

The "Sophisticated Buyer" Defense

Experienced buyers can reasonably be expected to know the right questions to ask and where to obtain expert assistance. Thus, as the argument goes, sophisticated buyers should be held to a higher standard of care and their right to recovery could be lessened or eliminated by comparative or contributory negligence. This line of reasoning has been used to develop an argument that commercial brokers have less exposure to liability than residential brokers (Levi et al. 1989), but only two cases considering this issue have been found that held professional buyers to a higher standard of care (Ambassador East, 1987; Craig, 1987). For this reason, it appears that the sophisticated buyer defense has not been particularly helpful in minimizing broker liability.

Problem Properties

Properties with obvious problems present special challenges to brokers. A licensee who only assisted in the sale of a problem property gratuitously (charging no fee) was held not liable, but it was a close case (Walter, 1985). It is clear that brokers still have disclosure requirements when selling their own (problem) properties (Pritchard, 1986). An attorney handling the sale of a problem property was held to a lower standard of care than a broker (Heliotis, 1986). There appears be a trend toward brokers refusing to list problem properties because of uncertain liability exposure.

Economics of Misrepresentation

An Overview of Law and Economics

As previously noted, it is sometimes said that law deals with equity while economics deals with efficiency. Simply stated, this suggests that economics is concerned primarily with the size of the pie, while law, along with political science and fiscal policy, is concerned more with how the pie is sliced and distributed.

The two goals of efficiency and equity may or may not be in conflict, depending on the circumstances. If income redistribution costs are zero, no conflict exists from a Pareto optimality standpoint, because an increase in the size of the pie makes one or more party(ies) better off without making any other party worse off. But, when income redistribution costs are positive and significant, conflicts may arise between the goals of efficiency and equity.

The Coase theorem often is used as the starting point in legal-economic analysis (Coase, 1969).[4] This theorem holds that

> Regardless of the specific initial assignment of property rights, in market equilibrium the final outcomes will be efficient—provided that the initial legal assignment is well defined and that transactions involving exchange rights are costless (Hirschleifer, 1988).

But transaction costs in real estate cases are seldom close to zero. The seller, real estate broker, and buyer all may incur significant transaction costs in addition to damage awards when a dispute is fully litigated. Moreover, when an out-of-court settlement is negotiated, the buyer often accepts less than actual damages for at least two reasons. First, a pretrial settlement can benefit all parties by the avoidance of further transactions costs. Second, if the parties are risk averse, they may prefer a certain pretrial outcome to an uncertain jury determination of damages. Simply stated, risk averters typically will accept a certain sum of money smaller than the estimated value of the expected outcome.

Economic Efficiency of Legal Remedies

This section analyzes the efficiency of two different legal rules—negligence and strict liability—in brokerage misrepresentation cases. Recall that negligence involves seller or broker conduct contrary to that of a mythical ordinarily careful and prudent seller (or broker) under the same or similar circumstances. Strict liability implies that the seller or broker will be held liable for any misrepresentation without regard to negligence or other standards of conduct. For discussion purposes, we assume that the industry is perfectly competitive so that all private costs are fully reflected. Further we assume that any damage to the buyer is dependent on whether material property defects are fully and accurately disclosed. This suggests that the value of the negotiated transaction to the buyer is dependent on brokerage service quality.

Hypothetical data presented in Table 1 illustrate the case where the efficient solution to the problem of selling defective property is to disclose the property's true condition. By avoiding misrepresentation, the broker's cost per unit sold is greater (e.g., perhaps more time is required to negotiate a sale) by $500 ($6,500 to $6,000 from column 2), but damages

Table 1. An Analysis of the Efficiency of Negligence and Strict Liability Remedies for Misrepresentation

Behavior of broker (1)	Broker's cost/unit sold (2)	Buyer's damage/ unit bought (3)	Full cost of sale (4)	Broker's cost/unit under negligence (5) (4) − (3)	Broker's cost/unit under strict liability (6)
Misrepresent	$6,000	$1,000	$7,000	$7,000	$7,000
Do not misrepresent	$6,500	$ 100	$6,600	$6,500	$6,600

to the buyer are $900 less ($1,000 to $100 from column 3). This $400 differential is also reflected in column 4, which reflects the full cost of selling a home (cost to broker plus cost to buyer).

Note that, even though no-misrepresentation is the more efficient solution, it is still possible that an economically inefficient number of sales may occur in two instances—where some buyers value the brokerage service at either less-than or more-than its full cost.

To determine whether either negligence or strict liability provides an efficient solution to the liability problem, we first assume that brokers are liable only for negligent misrepresentation. Thus, when liability payments are included in total costs as shown in column 5, the brokers total costs are greater under misrepresentation than under no-misrepresentation ($7,000 vs. $6,500). Therefore, given a choice, the rational broker will not misrepresent.[5] Moreover, $6,500, being the more efficient cost, would be the long-run equilibrium price of brokerage services. However, the negligence liability rule is not socially efficient, because its application does not fully internalize all external costs to the broker. This is because the long-run equilibrium brokerage services price of $6,500 does not reflect the residual damages of $100 suffered by buyers when negligence is the liability rule and when negligent misrepresentation has occurred. Stated differently, buyers may be forced to bear some damages resulting from an innocent misrepresentation when courts utilize the liability rule of simple negligence.

In contrast, strict liability entails liability for *any* misrepresentation by the broker, even if innocent and non-negligent. Strict liability also encourages brokers not to misrepresent, because it results in a lower cost of brokerage services ($6,600 with no misrepresentation, $7,000 with misrepresentation, as shown in column 6 of Table 1). However, it also results in a socially efficient price for brokerage services, because all costs are fully reflected (internalized) in the long-run equilibrium price of $6,600. Thus, strict liability is a more socially efficient legal remedy than negligence because it fully internalizes all costs and serves as an even greater incentive to not misrepresent.

Note that our simplified analysis would need to be modified if the buyer can engage in conduct that would either reduce or enhance the damages suffered. However, if damages are determined by conditions existing on the date of closing (as often will be the case), no modification is required.

To illustrate a situation where our basic analysis of liability rules needs to be modified, consider the case of termite-infested structure represented to be free of termites. Likely the misrepresenting broker will be held responsible for structural damages occurring after closing up to the date they are (or should have been) discovered by the buyer. But if the buyer waits an unreasonable length of time before exterminating the termites, the buyer may be responsible for the structural damages incurred in the interim under the doctrine of contributory (or comparative) negligence. Since the rational buyer will choose not to incur this liability, the broker will bear all of the buyer's residual damages and a socially efficient legal remedy will still exist.

Conclusions

The major liability problem facing real estate licensees is factual misrepresentation and/or nondisclosure. Relatively few recent cases have involved fraud, the vast majority have involved negligence, and only the states of Alaska and Wisconsin were identified as holding real estate brokers strictly liable for innocent misrepresentations.

Strict liability was shown to be more economically efficient than the rule of negligence because it internalizes all costs to all parties. But both the negligence and strict liability legal standards provide economic incentives to licensees not to misrepresent material facts about property. The majority of state courts have adopted negligence, rather than strict liability, as the preferable legal standard of conduct to apply in real estate brokerage misrepresentation cases. This preference implicitly suggests that equitable considerations are of prime importance in most court systems and is consistent with the basic premise that courts generally are more concerned with equity than with economic efficiency.

Notes

1. The industry emphasis placed on buyer agency and "who the broker is working for" in recent years has led many to believe that the law of agency is critical in the resolution of *all* liability lawsuits. Clearly the law of agency creates legal duties of an agent to his principal, irrespective of whether the principal is the seller or the buyer. But, regardless of the existing agency relationship, a licensee still has disclosure duties to the buyer under the law of misrepresentation. Thus, it is important to recognize that the laws of agency and misrepresentation are separate legal concepts.

2. The amount of dollar damages granted in misrepresentation cases theoretically could be utilized to predict the expected value of misrepresentation claims. However, differences in factual circumstances surrounding each case would make this a difficult task. Furthermore, this task is made even more difficult by the fact that the amount of damages in some cases is not publicly reported. For example, a trial court judgment may be that of no liability, on appeal this case may be reversed and remanded for a new trial, and the parties may then either settle their dispute out of court or litigate again at the trial court level with no subsequent appeal. In either instance, the magnitude of the damage award will not be reported in the public records.

3. An interesting sidelight is the proliferation of liability disclaimer clauses being inserted in real estate sales contracts. Their inclusion may make it less likely that a buyer will initiate a lawsuit against a broker, simply because a buyer may read them, conclude that he has no recourse, and not consult his attorney. However, if a lawsuit is filed, the principal legal issue will likely be whether the broker negligently failed to disclose a material fact about the property to which he knew or should have known. Thus, the inclusion of liability disclaimer clauses may have little impact on the outcome of misrepresentation lawsuits in those instances where the buyer is not sophisticated with respect to his knowledge of real estate.

4. In his paper, Coase provides several practical examples in support of this theorem that the interested reader should review. For our immediate purpose of examining brokers' liability, we suggest the following example to illustrate the concept: Assume that the law holds brokers strictly liable for failure to tell potential buyers of hidden defects, say, lack of sewer hookups in a property for sale that would render it less valuable for its intended purpose as an apartment building site. If a broker fails to tell the buyer to whom he sells the property about the no-sewer-hookups problem, the broker becomes legally obligated to compensate the buyer for damages. The broker has an economic incentive to incur precautionary search costs in amounts up to the estimated damages to the buyer for which the broker will be held accountable. On the other hand, if the rule of law is buyer beware, the knowledgeable buyer would find it necessary to bear the sewer hookups search costs directly and to deduct these costs from the price he otherwise would have paid, exclusive of assuming risks for predictable defects in the suitability of the building site. Thus, if the market functions efficiently and there are no differences in costs of information search activities for either brokers or buyers, then the transaction can be consummated at the same net costs to the broker and the buyer. Furthermore, if brokers' search costs are less than those of buyers (as one would expect), then brokers could sell their services advantageously to buyers. Competition among brokers could reduce the price of such services to the point of eliminating economic (but not normal) profits.

5. In reality, the broker's choice to not misrepresent may be tempered by his perceived probability of being sued. This perception may well have increased in recent years because

of greater numbers of lawsuits being filed and because of greater understanding of liability risks for misrepresentation.

References

Amato v. Rathbun Realty, Inc., 98 N.M. 231, 647 P.2d 433 (1982).
Ambassador East Apartments, Investors v. Ambassador East Investments, 106 N.M. 534, 746 P.2d 163 (1987).
Andrepont v. Meeker, 158 Cal. App.3d 878, 204 Cal. Rptr 887 (1984).
Bevins v. Ballard, 655 P.2d 757 (1982).
Coase, Ronald, "The Problem of Social Cost." *Journal of Law and Economics* (October, 1969), 1–44.
Coats v. Uhlmann, 87 Mich. App. 385, 274 N.W.2d 792 (1978).
Cousineau v. Walker, 613 P.2d 608 (1980).
Craig v. ERA Mark Five Realtors, 509 N.E.2d 1144 (1987).
Duby v. Apple Town Realty, Inc., 417 A.2d 1 (1980).
Dugan v. Jones, 615 P.2d 1239 (1980).
Easton v. Staussburger, 152 Cal. App. 3d 90, 199 Cal. Rptr. 383 (1984).
First Church of the Open Bible v. Cline J. Dunton Realty, 19 Wash. App. 275, 574 P.2d 1211 (1978).
Ford v. Cournale, 36 Cal. App. 3d 172, 111 Cal. Rptr 334 (1974).
Gauerke v. Rozga, 112 Wis. 2d 271, 332 N.W.2d 804 (1983).
Gerrard Realty Corp. v. American States Insurance Co., 89 Wis.2d 130, 277 N.W.2d 863 (1979).
Hagar v. Mobley, 638 P.2d 127 (1981).
Heliotis v. Schuman, 181 Cal. App. 3d 646, 226 Cal. Rptr. 509 (1986).
Hirschleifer, Jack. *Price Theory and Applications*, 4th ed. Englewood Cliffs, NJ: Prentice Hall, 1988, p. 475.
Hoffman v. Connall, 108 Wash.2d 242 (1987).
Johnson v. Geer Real Estate Co., 239 Kan. 324, 720 P.2d 660 (1986).
Levi, Donald R. and Curtis D. Terflinger. "A Legal-Economic Analysis of Changing Liability Rules Affecting Real Estate Brokers and Appraisers." *Journal of Real Estate Research* 3, 2 (Summer 1988), 133–49.
Levi, Donald R., Curtis D. Terflinger, and Samuel C. Webb. "A Legal-Economic Analysis of Recent Development in Commercial Real Estate Brokerage Liability to Buyers." Paper presented at the annual meeting of the American Real Estate Society, Washington, D.C., April 1989.
Matthews v. Kincaid, 746 P.2d 470 (1987).
McCurter v. Older, 173 Cal. App. 3d 582, 219 Cal. Rptr. 104 (1985).
Menzel v. Morse, 362 N.W.2d 465 (1985).
Nordstrom v. Miller, 227 Kan. 59, 605 P.2d 545 (1980).
O'Brien v. Noble, 106 Ill. App. 3d 126, 435 N.E.2d 554 (1982).

Pacific Northwest Life Insurance Co. v. Turnbull, 51 Wash. App. 692, 754 P.2d 1262 (1988).
Pepper v. Underwood, 48 Cal. App. 3d 698, 122 Cal. Rptr 343 (1975).
Pritchard v. Rietz, i78 Cal. App. 3d. 465, 223 Cal. Rptr 734 (1986).
Rotello v. Scott, 95 Ill. App. 3d 248, 419 N.E.2d 1233 (1981).
Schmidt v. Millhauser, 212 Md. 585, 130 A.2d 572 (1957).
Stanford v. Owens, 332 S.E.2d 730 (1985).
Tennant v. Lawton, 26 Wash. App. 701, 615 P.2d 1305 (1980).
Turnbull v. LaRose, 702 P.2d 131 (1985).
Walter v. Moore, 700 P.2d 1219 (Wyo.) (1985).

16 THE PRICE OF OWNER-OCCUPIED HOUSING SERVICES: 1973–1989

David C. Ling

Introduction

There are two housing decisions for a household: whether to own or rent (the "tenure choice" decision) and how much housing to obtain, given that one owns or rents. Investigations of housing markets frequently begin by specifying a model that relates the tenure choice decision or the quantity demanded decision to some function of price, income, and a vector of demographic variables. Central, then, to these analyses is the accurate estimation of the expected price of owner-occupied housing services. It is widely recognized by economists, however, that housing is an investment as well as a consumption good, and thus the appropriate price term in these analyses is not the asset purchase price (or market value) but rather the periodic price or "user cost" of obtaining the housing services from the capital asset.[1] This economic cost or price should reflect the bor-

---

I would like to thank Dixie Blackley, James Follain, and Jack Harris for sharing their estimated expected inflation equations. Bill Lafayette provided data on several housing cost components, and Glenn Crellin made available the National Association of Realtors' housing affordability index.

rower's out-of-pocket expenses, state and federal tax savings, expected house price appreciation, and the opportunity cost of invested equity. The inherent difficulty in estimating this price term is that it is not directly observable. The primary purpose of this paper is to estimate the real price of owner-occupied housing services for a large distribution of income classes and household types for the period 1973–1989.

Housing affordability continues to be an important public policy issue as we enter the 1990s. A secondary purpose of this paper is to compare our estimated user costs to alternative measures of home ownership costs that focus on nominal house prices and mortgage interest rates as measures of affordability. We find, for example, that the widely cited index of affordability published by the National Association of Realtors (NAR) was *negatively* correlated with real user costs of housing capital during the 1980s. Thus, although housing affordability is certainly linked to nominal house prices and interest rates, there is a difference between the "cash cost" of home ownership and the real user cost, and the distinction continues to be crucial to the development of rational public housing policy.

The Importance of Disaggregating by Income Class and Household Type

Current tax law grants substantial tax subsidies to homeowners. The higher the tax rate of an individual, the larger the subsidy and the lower is the after-tax cost of owner-occupied housing. Disaggregating the calculations by household type as well as by income class is necessary because tax rate schedules differ by filing status and because of differences in expected mobility. For example, singles are likely to be more mobile, on average, and thus face transaction costs of buying and selling a home that are higher on an annual-equivalent basis. (Haurin, et al. 1988). In this paper households are distinguished by nineteen income classes and three household types: marrieds, singles, and household heads.[2]

The measurement of the price of owner-occupied housing services is further complicated because there are actually two "prices" of housing services that are relevant to the household: the *average* price, which influences the tenure choice decision; and the *marginal* price, which determines the quantity of housing services demanded, assuming the household chooses to own. The tenure choice price and the marginal price can differ significantly, especially for low and moderate income households, primarily depending upon the relationship between the amount of nonhousing itemized (Schedule A) deductions the household can claim and the size of the standard deduction.[3]

In calculating the price of housing services, past empirical analyses of housing markets generally ignore variations in housing costs attributable to differences in the size of the tax subsidy, assume all household deduct housing related expenses at the same marginal tax rate, or, at best, assign households to one of two or three marginal tax rates. Thus, the effect of taxes on the cost of owner-occupancy has been given little attention despite the fact that the tax subsidy, however measured, is known to be large and to vary significantly with income.[4] In addition, the difference between the tenure choice price of housing services and the quantity demanded price, as well as differences in annual-equivalent transaction costs by household type, are typically ignored.

The paper is structured in the following manner. First the general framework for computing the price or "user cost" of capital for owner-occupied housing is presented. Then the underlying data are discussed. Estimated tenure choice and marginal user costs from 1973 to 1989, and a comparison of these estimated user costs to alternative measures of housing affordability, are presented in the following section. The paper concludes with a summary and suggestions for future research. An extensive data appendix containing the various tax rate and user cost time series and other important variables is also provided.

The Conceptual Framework

Households will purchase sufficient housing so that the benefits of the (implicit) rental stream generated by the last dollar spent, plus the expected capital gains on that dollar, equal the cost of obtaining the rents and gains. Put another way, households will purchase sufficient housing such that the present value of all the after-tax cash flows, including the implicit rent, generated by the last dollar of house equals the equity (cash) the household supplied to obtain that dollar of house. The price of owner-occupied housing services is thus defined as the annual cost of using one unit of housing capital. The equilibrium user cost of a one dollar investment in owner-occupied housing (R) can be derived for an owning household in income group i, household type j, from the following expression:

$$(1-\delta) = \sum_{t=1}^{n} \frac{R(1+\pi-d)^t}{[1+i(e)]^t} \quad (1)$$

$$+ t_{ij}i(d)\sum \frac{L_{t-1}}{[1+i(e)]^t} - \sum \frac{PAY_t}{[1+i(e)]^t}$$

$$- [(1-t_{ij})PT + M]\sum \frac{(1+\pi-d)^t}{[1+i(e)]^t}$$

$$+ \frac{(1-B)(1+\pi-d)^N}{[1+i(e)]^N} - \frac{L_N}{[1+i(e)]^N}.$$

The assumptions are that gross nominal rents and prices are expected to grow at the rate $\pi - d$ (expected rent and price inflation less economic depreciation); the δ portion of the house is debt financed at the rate $i(d)$, where t_{ij}, is the tax rate of the ijth household, PAY is the fixed periodic mortgage payment, and L_t is the outstanding loan balance in period t. The annual property tax and maintenance rates are PT and M. The household expects to hold the house N years, at which time proportional selling costs equal to B will be incurred and the remaining loan balance, L_N, will be repaid. All cash flows are discounted at the rate $i(e)$; the after-tax, risk-adjusted, required rate of return on equity.

For the first dollar of house purchased, the right side of equation 1 exceeds the left because R, the marginal value of housing services, is initially high. However, R declines as more dollars of housing are purchased; eventually equality holds and the housing demand of the household is determined.

Solving equation 1 for R produces a complicated expression. A series of assumptions can transform the expression into a more familiar relationship that better illustrates the primary determinants of owner user costs. If the required after-tax return on equity equals the after-tax debt rate $[i(e) = (1 - t_{ij})i(d)]$, the expected holding period is infinite, and there are no transaction costs, then one obtains

$$R = [(1 - t_{ij})(i(d) + PT) + M + d - \pi]. \quad (2)$$

The right-hand side of Equation 2 is a simple user cost expression that reflects the current tax treatment of housing; no taxation of implicit rental income or capital gain income [neither term is multiplied by $(1 - t_{ij})$], and the deductibility of mortgage interest and property taxes.[5] As can be seen, the higher the tax rate at which housing related expenses are deducted, the lower is the user cost of owner-occupied housing.

The Underlying Data

This section describes the underlying data and assumptions used in the estimation of owner user costs from Equation 1. It begins with a discussion of the calculation of the two tax rates relevant to housing decisions. Next, the estimation of the expected inflation rate in house prices and implicit rental flows for each quarter is discussed. The treatment of debt and equity in the user cost model is then described, and a discussion of the remaining parameter assumptions concludes the section.

Marginal and Tenure Choice Tax Rates

Two tax rates are relevant to the housing decisions of households. For the quantity demanded decision, the appropriate tax variable is the tax savings due to a marginal dollar of housing related expenses. The tenure decision of households involves a comparison of the cost of obtaining housing (consumption) services from owner-occupied housing relative to the cost of obtaining the same services from rental housing; thus, the cost of obtaining the *average* dollar's worth of housing services, not the marginal dollar, is required. This requires that t_{ij} in Equation 1 be defined as the average tax rate at which housing related expenditures, including forgone interest on invested equity, are deducted. If the household's *nonhousing* itemized deductions are at least equal to the standard deduction, then the tenure choice tax rate will lie between the household's marginal tax rate as a renter and the household's marginal rate as an owner.[6]

Because the tax rates relevant to both the quantity demanded and the tenure choice decisions vary widely, households are distinguished by nineteen income classes and three household types: marrieds, singles, and household heads. The quarterly distributions of households into these 57 income/household-type cohorts come from the U.S. Bureau of the Census, *Current Population Reports*. Calculations for these 57 cohorts are performed for all 68 quarters. This is accomplished by including separate tax tables in the simulation model for each of the three household types for each of the relevant tax years. Midpoints of the income classes are used in the calculations. The calculations are meant to be representative of recent home buyers. Both married households and household heads are assumed to have one wage earner and two dependent children; single households have no dependents.[7] Separate calculations are performed for renting and owning households. The calculations also assume the following:

1. Households have average fringe benefits and nonhousing itemized deductions, including state and local income tax rates, of their household types and income classes (based on yearly *Statistics of Income Data*).
2. The dollar value of homes by income class are based on average house-value-to-income ratios from *Current Population Reports*.
3. Purchases are partially debt financed with constant payment mortgages with interest rates equal to those reported by the Federal Home Loan Bank Board (see Table A4).
4. Mortgage interest deductions of owning households are based on the FHLBB rates and initial loan-to-value ratios typical of the household's income class.[8]
5. States allow the same adjustments to AGI, and the same deductions from AGI to calculate state taxable income as does the federal government.

Estimated marginal and tenure choice tax rates are contained in Table A1. For each of the three household types, tax rates are first calculated for each of the nineteen income classes in each quarter. Weighted averages for each quarter are then computed for each household type where the weights are the percent of, say, total married households accounted for by each income class in that quarter. Overall weighted average tax rates in each quarter are based on the distribution of total households among the three household types. For comparison, calculations are also done each quarter for median income households, assuming they are married with two dependent children.

Figure 1 displays marginal tax rates by household type over the time period 1973–1989. As can be seen, married households have, on average, been in higher marginal tax brackets (*after* housing deductions) than similarly situated singles and household heads. Movement in these tax rates over time primarily reflects changes in statutory federal income tax rates and changes in mortgage interest rates. Marginal tax rates of married households climbed only slightly during the 1970s as increases in mortgage rates (and thus deductions) worked to offset increases in (nonindexed) statutory tax rates. The Economic Recovery Tax Act of 1981 (ERTA) reduced statutory and effective marginal rates beginning in 1982. As mortgage interest rates began to fall, marginal tax rates increased

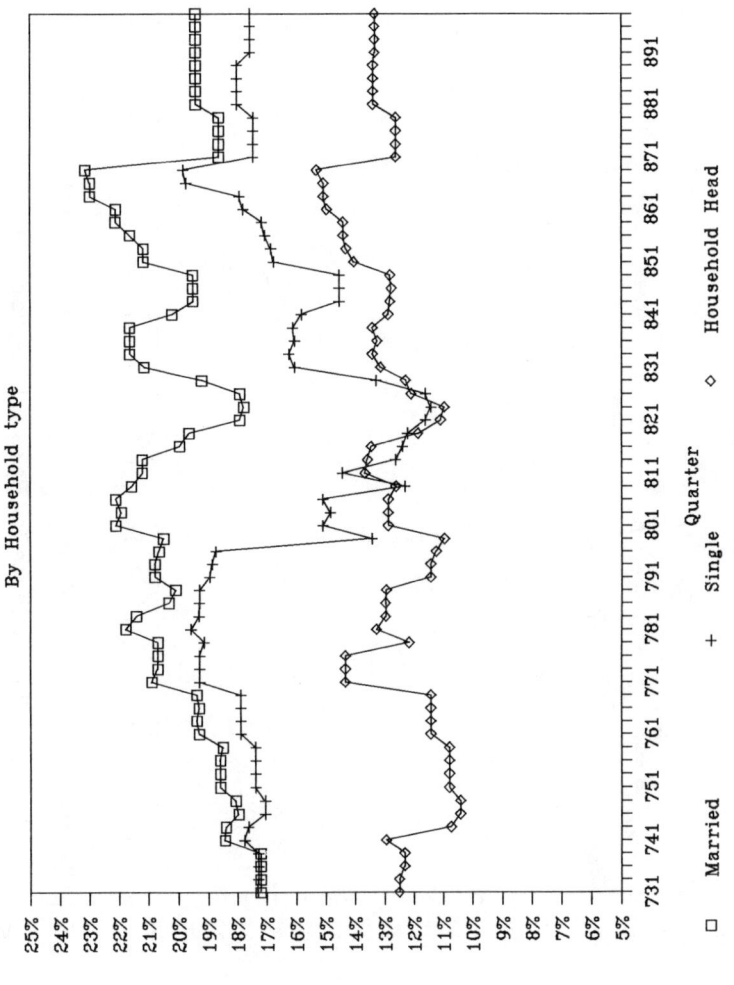

Figure 1. Margual Tax Rates of Owning HH's.

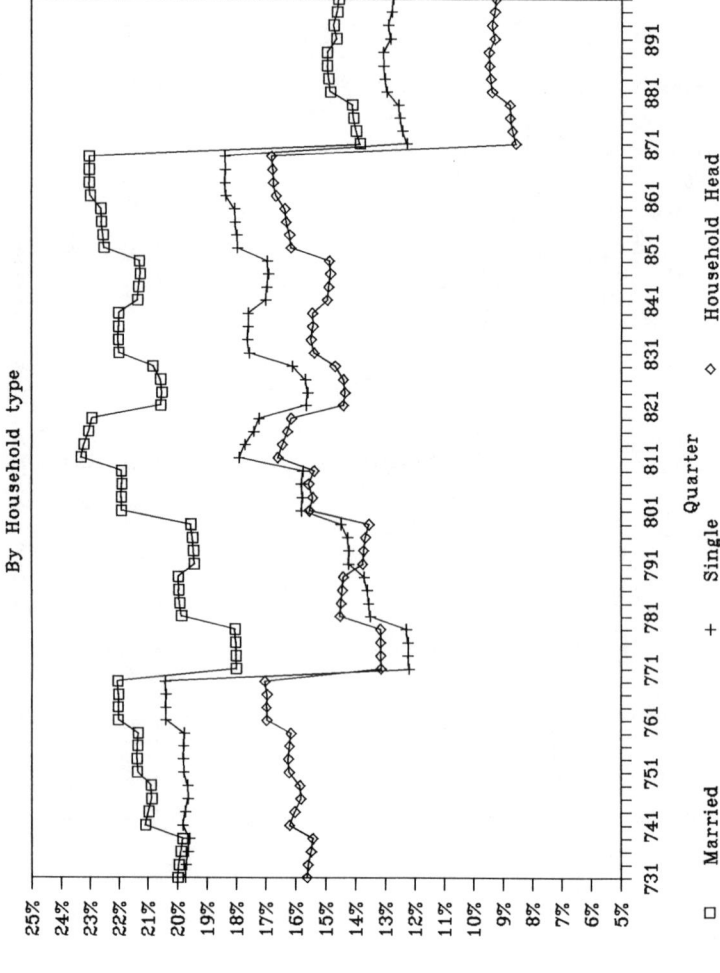

Figure 2. Tenure Choice Tax Rates by Household Type.

again to their pre-1982 levels, until they were slashed by the Tax Reform Act of 1986 (TRA).[9]

Figure 2 displays tenure choice tax rates by household type over the study period. These rates follow the same general pattern as do marginal tax rates, but with several important exceptions. First, the reductions in tenure choice tax rates brought about by the Tax Acts of 1976 and 1986 are much more pronounced than marginal rate reductions because these two Tax Acts also introduced large increases in household standard deductions. For example, the 1976 Act increased the standard deduction for married households to $3200 from $1000; the 1986 Act further raised the standard deduction to $5000 (in 1987). The 1986 Act also substantially reduced the number and size of nonhousing itemized deductions. These large increases in the standard deduction relative to nonhousing expenditures made it more likely that renting households would choose *not* to itemize. However, when converting from renter to owner status, these households would have to give up the standard deduction in order to itemize their housing related expenses. Thus, at least a portion of the household's housing deductions were wasted; that is, they did not reduce the household's taxable income below what it would be if the household were renting a comparable home. Put another way, it became more likely that low and moderate income households (that would not itemize as renters) were writing off at least a portion of their housing expenditures at a zero percent tax rate. Note also that, in the aggregate, the reduction in tenure choice tax rates caused by the 1981 Tax Act is relatively small, despite the significant reduction in statutory tax rates. This is because the 1981 Act did not increase standard deductions for nonitemizing households.

Figure 3 plots both marginal and tenure choice tax rates for our median income household. Before passage of the 1976 Tax Act, our median income household had sufficient nonhousing expenses to itemize as a renter, thus every dollar of mortgage interest and property tax expenses incurred by our median income household reduced taxable income by one dollar (relative to their taxable income as a renter). Thus their tenure choice tax rate was a weighted average of their marginal tax rate as a renter and the (declining) rates at which they deducted their housing related expenses. Since passage of the 1976 Act, our median income household has not itemized as a renter, thus at least a portion of the housing expenses of our median income household have been written off at a zero percent tax rate. Thus the tenure choice tax rate for this household has been below the marginal rate, with the largest differences immediately following the 1976 and the 1986 Tax Acts.[10]

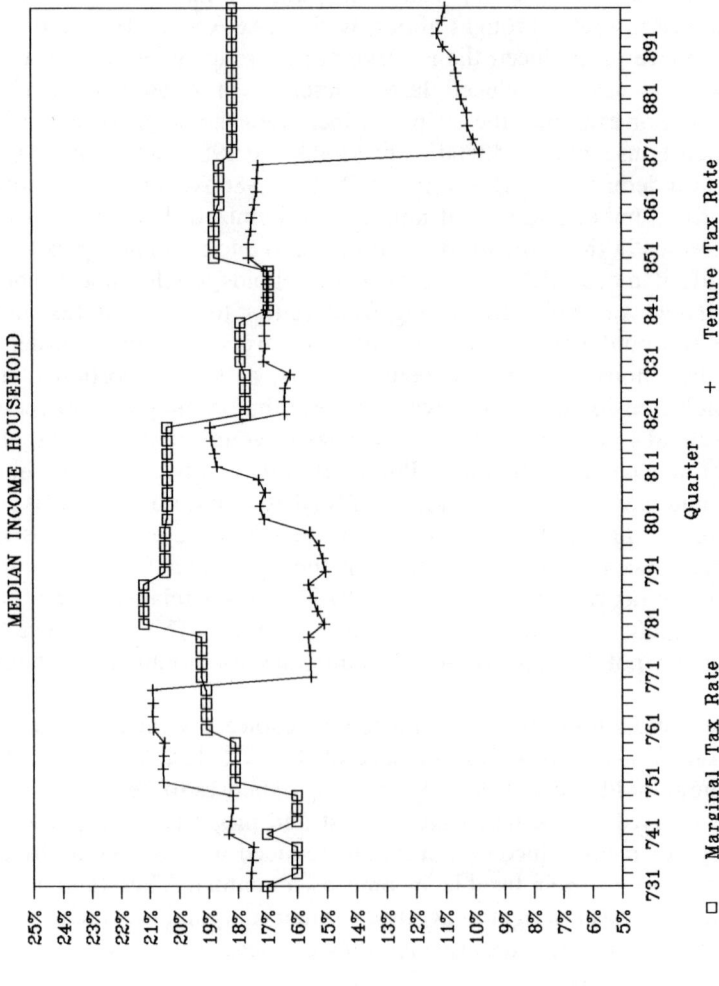

Figure 3. Marginal vs. Tenure Tax Rates for Median Income Household.

Expected Rent and House Price Inflation

Expected rates of inflation are not directly observable, and there is no agreement in the existing literature as to how they should be estimated.[11] We employ two procedures for estimating expected general and house price inflation. Our preferred or base-case estimate is based on recent work in progress by Blackley and Follain, who have estimated an adaptive expectations model of expected general inflation using quarterly data from 1964 through 1987. Separate models of the current inflation rate on lags of one to twelve quarters were tried. Blackley and Follain's preferred model is current inflation regressed on four lagged quarters. Blackley and Follain generate a predicted value for each quarter, and then calculate the mean of the predictions for the current and eleven lagged quarters. We use this mean predicted rate of inflation in each quarter as our measure of expected long-run general inflation. Expected rent and house price inflation is calculated as a weighted average of this measure of expected general inflation and the actual house price inflation over the last four quarters (as measured by the Census Bureau's constant quality house price index), where actual house price inflation is given a 10% weight.

Our second procedure for estimating expected inflation uses a technique described in detail by Hendershott and Hu (1981), and recently updated by Harris (1989). With this procedure expected (long run) general inflation rates are calculated as a distributed lag on current and past rates of change in the net of shelter CPI. The lagged weights were estimated by Harris (1989) from a regression explaining quarterly movements in the ten-year U.S. Treasury Bond rate. Expected rent and house price inflation is again calculated as a weighted average of expected general inflation (using Harris's lagged weights) and the actual rate of house price inflation over the last four quarters, where the latter again receives a 10% weight.

The net of shelter CPI inflation index and the constant-quality house price index are displayed in columns 1 and 2 of Table A2. The house price ratio (column 3) is an index of the rate of change in nominal house prices relative to the rate of change in prices generally (as measured by the net of shelter CPI). In calculating the house price ratio, the first quarter of 1973 is used as the base quarter; thus the real user cost of housing for each cohort equals the nominal user cost (or gross marginal product, R) in that quarter. In subsequent quarters, the real user cost equals the nominal user cost scaled up or down by the house price ratio.[12]

Column 4 of Table A2 contains Blackley and Follain's measure of

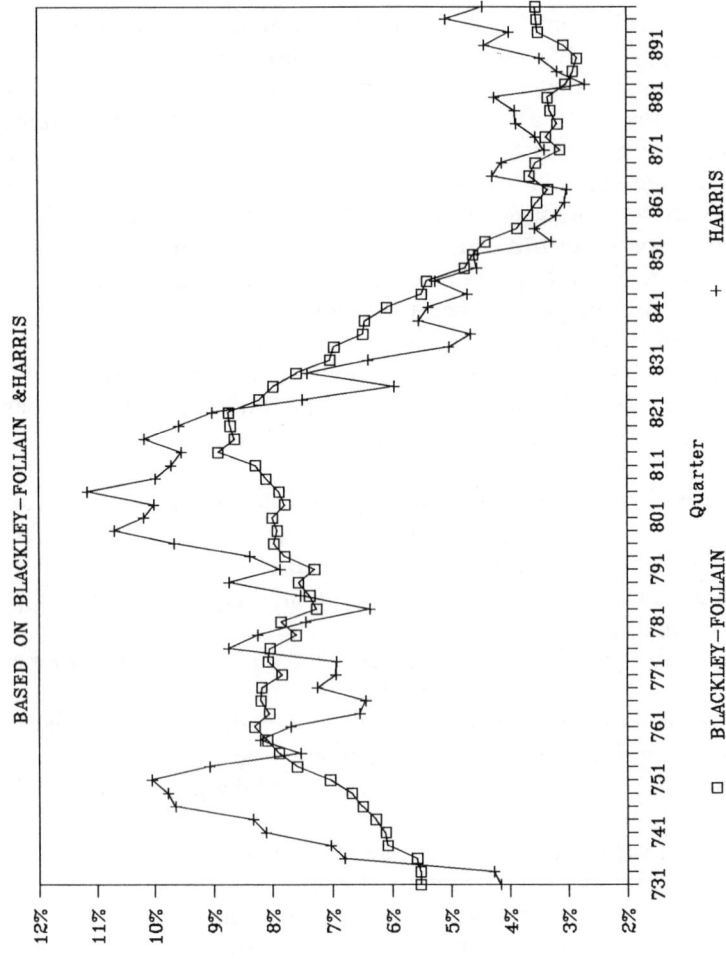

Figure 4. Expected House Price Inflation Based on Blackley–Follain & Harris.

expected general inflation, while column 5 contains our first measure of expected rent and house price appreciation (90% of column 4 plus 10% of the percentage increase in column 2 over the prior four quarters). Column 6 displays our second measure of expected general inflation and is derived from the lagged weights estimated by Harris (1989). Column 7 is our second weighted average measure of expected rent and house price appreciation (again using weights of 0.90 and 0.10).

Expected rent and house price appreciation under the two assumptions (columns 5 and 7) are displayed graphically in Figure 4. Both measures follow the same general trend; however, the adjusted Blackley and Follain measure is less volatile than the adjusted Harris measure. The adjusted Blackley and Follain measure is, effectively, an equally weighted moving average of expected general inflation over the current and previous eleven quarters. Although the adjusted Harris measure is based on a sixteen quarter lag, the weights on quarters one-three sum to 0.67, and the weight placed on the most recent quarter is 0.33. Thus our adjusted Harris measure of expected inflation places relatively more weight on recent rates of actual general inflation than does our adjusted Blackley and Follain measure. Although the method by which households form their long-run inflationary expectations is an open empirical issue, we choose the "smoother" Blackley and Follain measure as our "base-case" estimate of expected house price appreciation.

Required Rates of Return and the Treatment of Debt and Equity

Roughly, the price of owner-occupied housing services equals the household's out-of-pocket expenses, minus expected appreciation in rents and prices, *plus* the opportunity cost of invested equity. The specification of this opportunity cost is critical to the calculation of owner-occupied user costs. We employ an after-tax capital asset pricing model where the required after-tax equity return in Equation 1, $i(e)$, is equal to the after-tax debt rate $[(1 - t_{ij})i(d)]$ plus a risk premium that depends upon the market risk premium (MRP), the covariance of the returns on real estate and the market portfolio divided by the variance of the market portfolio (β), the loan-to-market value (δ), and the tax rate applied to the risk premium (tp_{ij}). When the debt has no default risk, the specification becomes

$$i(e) = (1 - t_{ij})i(d) + (1 - tp_{ij})(\beta/(1 - \delta))MRP. \qquad (3)$$

Equation 3 shows a clear dependence of the required equity return on financial leverage, tax rates, and before-tax interest rates.

Typically, researchers choose an initial δ and calculate the required equity rate, which is then applied to all future equity cash flows. There are two major problems with this approach. First, because the loan is amortizing and the property value is usually assumed to be inflating (at least in nominal terms), the loan-to-*market*-value ratio is decreasing over time. This implies that variability of equity returns is expected to decrease over time, thus so must the required equity return. Setting i(e) at a constant value over the expected N year holding period thus involves an internal consistency (Follain et al., 1987).

The second problem with the conventional approach is that the i(e) calculated from Equation 3, or in a similar fashion, is used to discount the cash flows that are invariant to the capital structure decision (the "equity" flows), as well as the cash flows associated with the debt financing. Because i(e), which includes a risk premium, will be greater than the after-tax cost of debt $[(1 - t_{ij})i(d)]$, this formulation imputes positive value to debt; that is, leverage is assumed to be a positive net present value "project,"[13] and calculated user costs are reduced the higher is the assumed loan-to-value ratio.[14]

To avoid imputing an incorrect value to the debt flows, the cost of capital approach is employed. Rather than explicitly including debt payments in the cash flows, all nondebt payments are discounted by the weighted average cost of capital,

$$\text{WACC} = \delta(1 - t_{ij})i(d) + (1 - \delta)i(e). \tag{4}$$

Substituting Equation 3 into Equation 4 produces

$$\text{WACC} = (1 - t_{ij})i(d) + (1 - tp_{ij})\beta \times \text{MRP}. \tag{4'}$$

Note that the weighted average cost of capital, and therefore owner user costs, are independent of the loan-to-value ratio.[15] In the simulations, we set i(d) equal to the treasury bond rate of maturity N plus one percentage point.[14] Based on Chan et al. (1990), we assume $\beta = 0.60$. Following Follain et al. (1987), MRP is set equal to 0.06 and tp_{ij}, is set equal to one-third the tax rate on ordinary income plus two-thirds the effective capital gain tax rate. To reflect the value of deferral, the effective capital gain tax rate is set equal to one-half the statutory rate.

Other Parameter Assumptions

To reflect differences in expected mobility and annual-equivalent transaction costs, we assume holding periods of 3, 5, and 7 years, respectively, for singles, household heads, and marrieds. Selling costs at the end of the holding period (B) are assumed to equal 6% of the resale price. Based on Malpezzi et al. (1987, Table 5, p. 384), real economic depreciation (d) is assumed to be 0.60% per year. Mortgage rates used in the tax rate calculations (column 2, Table A3) are from the Federal Home Loan Bank Board.

Estimates of maintenance and repair costs incurred by home owners come from LaFayette (1990) and are also listed in Table A3. These data are based upon a U.S. Census Bureau series that includes separate amounts for payments made to contractors for materials and labor, payments made by owners for materials needed for repairs and maintenance that they intend to perform themselves, and an estimate of the opportunity cost of time spent by owners in making such repairs. Estimated property tax rates also come from LaFayette (1990) and are effective tax rates derived by dividing total property tax payments by the aggregate value of owner-occupied housing.

The Price of Housing Services

Marginal user costs by household type, in the aggregate, and for the median income household are contained in Table A4; marginal user costs of owner-occupied housing capital (assuming Blackley and Follain expected general inflation) are plotted by household type in Figure 5. As expected, annual costs are lowest for married households both because of the higher marginal rates at which they deduct housing expenses and because of a longer expected tenure in the house (and therefore lower annual equivalent transaction costs).

Marginal user costs generally declined from 1973 to 1977, rose during the late 1970s, and finished the decade slightly above their 1973 levels. Increases in expected house price appreciation partially offset the rapid increase in nominal mortgage rates and house prices that occurred during the late 1970s. During the early 1980s, marginal user costs continued to increase as inflationary expectations waned and nominal mortgage rates increased (mortgage rates were still approximately 14% at the end of 1982). The sustained decline in nominal mortgage rates that began in late 1984 did push down real user costs into the 11% range for married households by the end of 1986, their approximate level at the end of 1989.

It is important to note that the real marginal cost of owner-occupied housing during the latter part of the 1980s was quite high relative to its seventeen year average, despite declines in mortgage rates from their re-

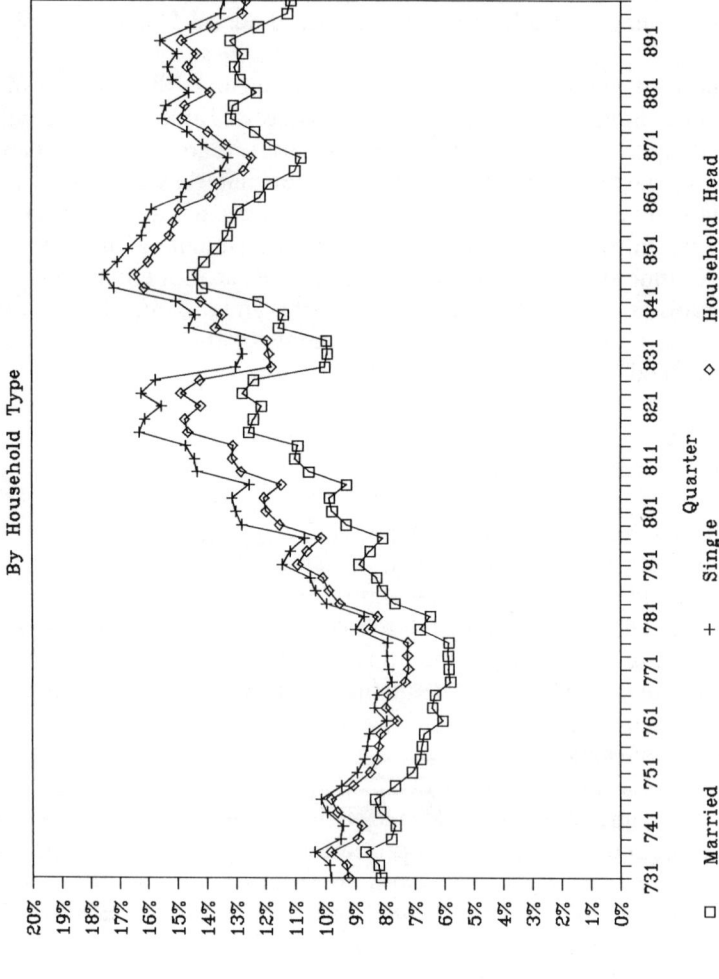

Figure 5. Marginal User Costs by Household Type.

cord highs in the early 1980s. Mortgage rates averaged 12.6% in 1978–1982. From 1985 to 1989 the average mortgage rate was 10.1%; a 2.5% decline. Yet the average aggregate user cost during 1985 to 1989 was 2.3% *higher* than the 1978–1982 user cost average (13.3% vs. 11.0%). Furthermore, the 10.1% average mortgage rate for 1985–1989 was 0.60% below the 10.7% average of the years 1973–1982; yet the average user cost in 1985–1989 was 4% greater than the 1973–1982 average (13.3% vs. 9.3%). Put another way, the average cost of an additional (or marginal) unit of housing capital in 1985–1989 was 43% greater than during the 1973–1982 period, despite the sixty basis point decline in average mortgage interest rates between the two periods. Clearly, factors other than the level of nominal mortgage rates, especially expected appreciation, are also important determinants of the true economic cost of owner-occupied housing capital.

Comparison of User Costs with Alternative Measures of Affordability

Housing affordability continues to be an important public policy issue. However, despite numerous articles in the early 1980s that questioned the validity of considering only house price and payment affordability as measures of housing costs, these affordability measures continue to be the focus of much of the public policy debate. This raises the question as to how well correlated these "cash cost" measures of affordability have been with the true economic cost of home ownership, as measured by the user cost of capital.

To address this issue, we compare our user cost of capital measures of housing prices with two cash based measures of housing affordability. The first measure we employ is the widely cited national composite index of housing affordability that is published monthly by the National Association of Realtors. We have also calculated a measure of the real cash cost of ownership equal to the sum of the nominal mortgage rate, the property tax rate, and the rate of maintenance expenditures (all from Table A3) times the house price ratio. The exclusion of transaction costs and economic depreciation biases this measure downward; ignoring tax savings and appreciation in rents and house values works in the opposite direction. This real, before-tax, cash cost measure of housing affordability, as well as the NAR index are contained in Table A3. To facilitate the comparison of changes in these indices over time with changes in our real user cost measures of housing prices, we designate the first quarter of 1973 as the "base" quarter for the analysis. These rescaled cost and affordability measures are contained in Table 1.[17]

The first two columns of Table 1 contain indices of our user cost calculations for our median income married household using estimates of expected general inflation from Harris and from Blackley and Follain. We use our estimated tenure choice user costs (not the marginal costs) in this analysis because we are interested in the average cost of home ownership, not the cost of acquiring the last unit of housing capital. Column 3 is an index of our cash cost measure of affordability; column 4 is the NAR index. Also included in Table 1 is an index of the constant quality house price series. Our base case user cost index and the NAR index are displayed graphically in Figure 6. The cash cost measure is shown below to be highly positively correlated with the NAR index and is therefore not included in Figure 6.

The real cash cost of home ownership rose steadily during the 1970s and accelerated to a peak in 1981. However, real user costs for the median income household actually declined from 1973 to 1976. User costs then increased sharply during the late 1970s, yet continued to lag cash costs until 1982. User costs continued to increase until late 1984, despite the precipitous decline in nominal mortgage rates that began in 1982 that had already begun to push down the affordability index. From the middle of 1984 to the middle of 1986, user costs and cash cost measures moved downward in unison as inflationary expectations stabilized and nominal mortgage rates continued to decline. Since 1986 the NAR index has remained relatively stable while the user cost index increased dramatically, primarily because of the sharp decline in tenure choice tax rates brought about by the passage of the 1986 Tax Act. From 1983 to 1989 the real economic cost of owner-occupied housing was greater, relative to its 1973 base, than the cash cost of home ownership.

To quantify the relationship between these various measures of housing costs over the study period, correlation coefficients for various time periods were calculated for the five indices reported in Table 1 and are contained in Table 2. Panel 1a displays results for the entire 1973–1989 time period. The correlation coefficient between our base-case real user costs and the cash and NAR index are 0.52 and 0.53, respectively. This positive relationship between cash and true economic costs was even stronger during the 1973–1980 subperiod (0.79 and 0.67, respectively).[18] However, during the 1981–1989 subperiod, measures of economic and cash costs displayed moderate to strong *negative* correlation. Furthermore, economic and cash cost measures of housing costs continued to display little or no correlation during the second half of the 1980s.

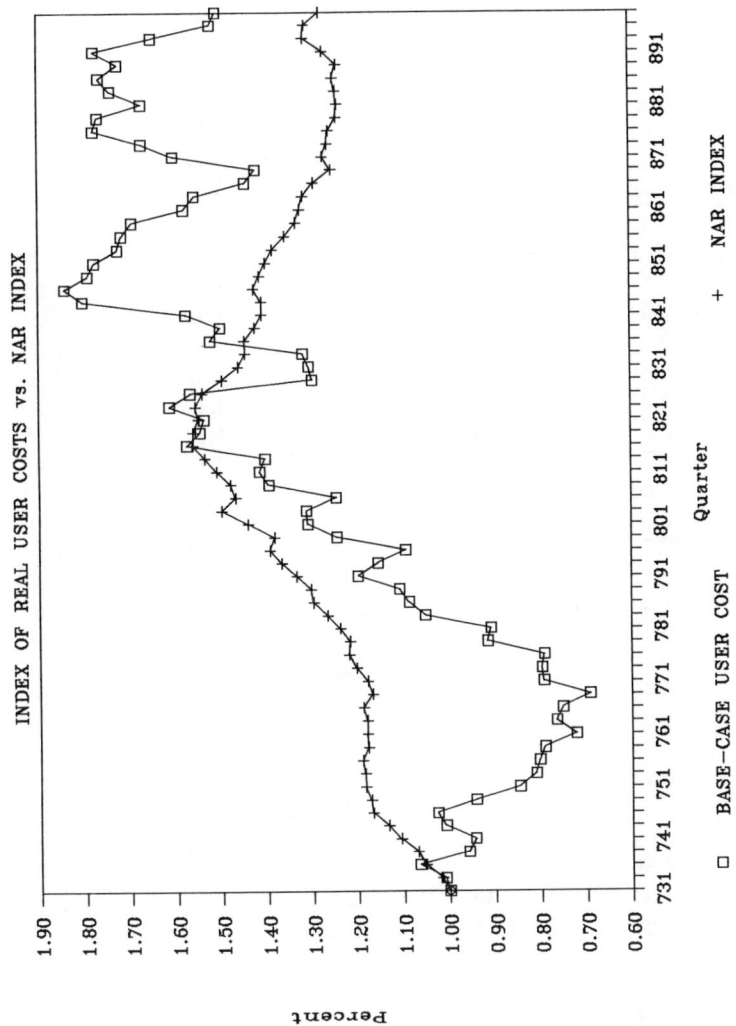

Figure 6. Housing Costs—Med Inc HH's Index of Real User Costs vs. NAR Index.

Table 1. Indices of Different Measures of Housing Affordability

Qtr	Harris-based user cost	Base-case user cost	Real cash cost	NAR adj index	Constant qlty house price
731	1.00	1.00	1.00	1.00	1.00
732	0.99	1.01	0.99	1.02	1.10
733	0.79	1.07	1.03	1.05	1.05
734	0.72	0.96	1.06	1.07	1.07
741	0.60	0.94	1.07	1.11	1.10
742	0.66	1.10	1.07	1.13	1.11
743	0.56	1.03	1.09	1.17	1.14
744	0.50	0.94	1.10	1.17	1.17
751	0.42	0.85	1.12	1.18	1.21
752	0.55	0.81	1.10	1.19	1.23
753	0.73	0.80	1.09	1.19	1.25
754	0.67	0.79	1.10	1.18	1.28
761	0.68	0.72	1.09	1.18	1.29
762	0.81	0.77	1.12	1.18	1.33
763	0.83	0.75	1.13	1.19	1.37
764	0.69	0.69	1.14	1.17	1.38
771	0.77	0.79	1.13	1.18	1.42
772	0.80	0.80	1.14	1.20	1.47
773	0.60	0.69	1.14	1.22	1.50
774	0.71	0.91	1.20	1.22	1.57
781	0.82	0.91	1.18	1.24	1.59
782	1.00	1.05	1.23	1.27	1.67
783	0.91	1.09	1.28	1.30	1.74
784	0.81	1.11	1.32	1.30	1.78
791	0.96	1.20	1.36	1.33	1.85
792	0.92	1.16	1.42	1.37	1.94
793	0.73	1.09	1.45	1.39	1.98
794	0.73	1.25	1.50	1.38	2.02
801	0.86	1.31	2.54	1.44	2.03
802	0.86	1.31	1.67	1.50	2.13
803	0.68	1.25	1.59	1.47	2.18
804	0.97	1.39	1.64	1.48	2.21
811	1.04	1.41	1.73	1.51	2.29
812	1.13	1.40	1.79	1.54	2.35
813	1.17	1.58	1.87	1.56	2.39
814	1.22	1.55	1.97	1.56	2.43
821	1.29	1.54	1.89	1.55	2.42
822	1.47	1.61	1.95	1.56	2.46
823	1.58	1.57	1.87	1.54	2.45
824	1.13	1.30	1.68	1.50	2.42
831	1.19	1.30	1.64	1.46	2.47

Table 1. (Cont.)

Qtr	Harris-based user cost	Base-case user cost	Real cash cost	NAR adj index	Constant qlty house price
832	1.36	1.32	1.54	1.44	2.48
833	1.52	1.52	1.57	1.45	2.55
834	1.39	1.50	1.53	1.42	2.54
841	1.43	1.58	1.51	1.41	2.55
842	1.64	1.80	1.52	1.41	2.62
843	1.60	1.84	1.56	1.43	2.63
844	1.56	1.79	1.58	1.41	2.66
851	1.53	1.78	1.54	1.40	2.69
852	1.61	1.73	1.49	1.38	2.67
853	1.51	1.72	1.42	1.36	2.69
854	1.51	1.69	1.40	1.33	2.70
861	1.41	1.58	1.37	1.32	2.72
862	1.37	1.56	1.37	1.32	2.80
863	1.16	1.44	1.36	1.29	2.79
864	1.15	1.42	1.28	1.25	2.72
871	1.34	1.60	1.25	1.27	2.82
872	1.41	1.67	1.26	1.26	2.85
873	1.44	1.78	1.27	1.26	2.89
874	1.45	1.77	1.21	1.24	2.84
881	1.33	1.67	1.21	1.24	2.86
882	1.53	1.74	1.19	1.24	2.85
883	1.48	1.77	1.18	1.25	2.85
884	1.41	1.73	1.17	1.24	2.84
891	1.37	1.78	1.35	1.27	2.94
892	1.36	1.65	1.26	1.31	2.90
893	1.13	1.52	1.27	1.31	2.95
894	1.19	1.51	1.25	1.28	2.96

The Harris-based user cost is based on the measure of expected inflation estimated by Harris (1989). The lagged weights were estimated from a regression explaining quarterly movements in the ten-year U.S. Treasury Bond rate. Expected rent and house price inflation is calculated as a weighted average of expected general inflation and the actual rate of house price inflation (using the constant quality house price index) over the previous four quarters where actual house price inflation receiver a 10% weight. The base-case user cost results are a weighted average using Blackley and Follain's estimates of expected general inflation and actual house price inflation over the previous four quarters, with the latter again receiving a 10% weight. Both user cost series are for married households with median income. The real cash cost equals the nominal mortgage rate plus property tax and maintenance expenditures as percentage of asset value times the house price ratio. The adjusted NAR index tracks movements in the actual NAR index since 731. For comparison, incease in the actual NAR index, which imply increases affordability, are reflected in decreases to our adjusted NAR index. The constant quality house price index simply reflects movements in the Bureau of Census, constant quality house price series.

Table 2. Correlation Coefficients Different Housing Cost Measures[1]

	Base-case user-cost	Harris user-cost	Real cash cost	NAR index
1a. 1973–1989				
Harris	0.91			
Cash	0.52	0.46		
NAR	0.53	0.47	0.97	
Price	0.92	0.85	0.52	0.58
1b. 1973–1980				
Harris	0.43			
Cash	0.79	0.30		
NAR	0.67	0.21	0.97	
Price	0.69	0.36	0.97	0.97
1a. 1981–1989				
Harris	0.75			
Cash	−0.36	−0.14		
NAR	−0.40	−0.15	0.98	
Price	0.51	0.20	0.91	−0.93
1d. 1985–1989				
Harris	0.83			
Cash	−0.02	0.31		
NAR	0.04	0.33	0.97	
Price	−0.02	−0.45	−0.74	−0.59

[1] See note to Table 1 for a description of variables.

Summary and Conclusions

Owner-occupied housing is an investment good as well as a consumption good, and thus the appropriate "price" term in most analyses is not the asset purchase price but rather the periodic price or "user cost" of obtaining the housing services from the capital asset. The inherent difficulty in estimating this price term is that it is not directly observable.

Empirical analyses of housing markets typically assume that all households deduct housing expenditures at the same (or, at best, at one of two or three) marginal tax rates. Such an assumption ignores variations in housing costs attributable to differences in the size of the tax subsidy, despite the fact that the subsidy is known to be large and to vary significantly with income. Differences in user costs by household types are also typically ignored.

The primary purpose of this paper is to calculate tax rates and user costs of owner-occupied housing services for nineteen income classes and three household types for the period 1973–1989. Calculations for these 57 income/household-type cohorts are performed for all 68 quarters. Tax rates and user costs relevant to both the buy-vs.-rent decision and to the quantity demanded decision are estimated.

These real user costs of housing capital are contrasted with measures of housing affordability that focus on house prices and nominal mortgage rates as measures of housing affordability. We find that the widely cited index of affordability published by the National Association of Realtors was strongly negatively correlated with the real economic cost of housing capital from 1980 to 1989. During the last five years of the decade, the NAR index displayed virtually no correlation with changes in the real user cost, despite much less volatility in inflation rates, interest rates, and house prices. Thus, although housing affordability is certainly linked to nominal house prices and interest rates, there is a difference between the "cash cost" of home ownership and the real user cost, and the distinction continues to be crucial to the development of rational public housing policy.

Although the user cost of capital model presented in this paper is internally consistent and relatively elaborate, several extensions would be worthwhile. Most importantly, a better developed model of the role of uncertainty in housing decisions is clearly called for. For example, the current version of the model does not take into account people's expectations on the future course of tax policy; nor does it allow for the expected holding period or the economic depreciation rate to vary with the tax structure. The effects of asset price uncertainty are also not explicitly considered. (Of course, similar problems are encountered when estimating the user cost of business capital). A model that assumes that investors maximize expected utility under some degree of risk aversion may provide results that vary from the essentially perfect certainty model presented here.

Notes

1. See, for example, Diamond (1980), Van Order and Villani (1982), Hendershott and Hu (1981), and Hendershott and Shilling (1982). Van Order and Villani derive a price index for the cost of housing services for homeowners utilizing the methodology of standard price theory. They thus show that the user cost of capital measure of home owner costs is theoretically relevant.

2. The quarterly distribution of households by income class and household type are available from the author upon request.

3. Diamond (1980) and Hendershott and Slemrod (1983) were the first to emphasize the importance of the distinction between marginal and average tax rates and user costs. Nonhousing itemized deductions have included excess medical expenditures, state and local sales and income taxes, charitable contributions, consumer interest other than home mortgage, and other miscellaneous expenses.

4. Follain and Ling (1991) discuss the housing tax subsidy in detail. They estimate the annual tax subsidy to owner-occupied housing to be $81.1 billion in 1988 dollars.

5. No tax rate is applied to the appreciation term (π) because of the ability of households to defer (rollover) the recognition of realized gains by purchasing a home of equal or greater value within 24 months, and because of the one-time, $125,000 ($62,500 for singles and household heads) capital gain exclusion for those over fifty-five years of age.

6. Note that if renting, the average and marginal costs are the same.

7. According to the 1986 *Statistics of Income*, married households claimed an average of 3.7 exemptions (excluding exemptions for old age and blindness). Household heads claimed an average of 2.7 exemptions. Figures for all earlier years were not significantly different. Thus the two-dependent assumption is, at least on average, appropriate.

8. The loan-to-value ratios for recent home buyers come from the Residential Finance Panel Survey conducted quarterly by the National Association of Realtors. The survey year used is 1988; it is assumed that leverage ratios were not significantly different in prior years. It should be emphasized that the calculations are not, in general, sensitive to this assumption. To see why, consider the case where the household's before-tax opportunity cost of equity invested in the house and the before-tax mortgage rate are both equal to, say, 10%. If the household finances an additional dollar of the acquisition with debt, a $0.10 tax deduction will be generated. However, if this dollar is invested at the 10% opportunity rate, the household will report an additional $0.10 in interest income; thus, taxable income would be unaffected. This assumes that every dollar of interest expense reduces taxable income by a dollar and that higher income households do not successfully arbitrage by purchasing tax-exempt securities with fully deductible debt.

9. Both ERTA and TRA phased-in the reduction in marginal tax rates over a period of several years. However, the tax rate used by households is the average rate at which they expect to deduct housing expenses over the projected holding period. Thus, in making housing decisions, it is assumed that households used the tax rate schedule that would be in existence after the phase-in period.

10. In the aggregate, tenure choice tax rates have also been less than marginal tax rates since the passage of the 1976 Tax Act. Before 1976, marginal tax rates were slightly higher than tenure rates.

11. There are survey data on expectations; for example, the Livingston Survey, but these data refer to expectations over short time horizons. We require inflationary expectations over an expected N year holding period.

12. The house price ratio tracks movements in the price of a constant quality house relative to movements in the CPI net of shelter. For example, the house price ratio in the first quarter of 1980 is equal to the change in the house price index from 731 to 801 divided by the change in the net of shelter CPI index over the same period, or (83.1/41.0)/(78.7/44.1) = 1.1357.

13. Leverage is a positive net present value project in the conventional model because the loan proceeds per dollar of house price (δ) exceed the present value of the after-tax mortgage payments, including the lump-sum payoff at the end of the N year holding period;

that is,

$$\delta + t_{ij}i(d)\sum\frac{L_{t-1}}{[1+i(e)]^t} - \sum\frac{PAY_t}{[1+i(e)]^t} - \frac{L_N}{[1+i(e)]^N} > 0.$$

14. Follain et al. (1987) point out that this inconsistency also leads to another error. When the required equity return is held constant, as loan-to-market value ratios fall, households are presumed to be moving further away from an "optimal" leverage ratio (using too much expensive equity and not enough cheap debt). Thus including the debt flows in the model with a time-invariant equity rate not only imputes false value to the debt flows, it also makes estimated user costs more sensitive to assumed holding periods than is actually the case.

15. Equation 1 and the specification of the discount rate in Equation 4 presume that households can purchase the optimal quantity of housing; that is, they are not liquidity (cash) constrained. For households that find the optimal quantity of housing unaffordable, the right side of Equation 1 is greater than the left, and the calculation of the equilibrium user cost is not meaningful. Explaining the housing decisions of these liquidity constrained households may therefore also require a measure of housing costs that focuses on initial affordability. An example of such an affordability measure of housing costs is developed later in the paper.

16. Hendershott and Ling (1986) argue that risk-free rate is more appropriate in the required rate of return calculation than is the commonly employed mortgage rate because the primary difference between the two is the price mortgage investors charge borrowers for the imbedded prepayment and default options. If the expected benefits of these options to the borrower equal the cost of the options, the owner user cost is not affected by their inclusion in the mortgage contract. However, as pointed out by one of the reviewers, treasury bond investors, unlike real estate investors, do not have to be concerned with liquidity. This bias is compounded by the fact that B is estimated using stock price data on REITs, which are considerably more liquid than direct investments in real estate. The one percentage point premium is added to adjust for this problem.

17. The NAR affordability index is a measure of median family income relative to the household income required to qualify for an 80% loan on the median priced existing single family home. Thus increases in the index imply increasing affordability. For comparison purposes, the NAR index was adjusted such that increases in the index imply decreasing affordability.

18. The cash and NAR index was not as positively correlated with our alternative user cost estimate based on the expected general inflation rates estimated by Harris (0.30 and 0.21, respectively). This is because the Harris-based measure gives more weight than our base case estimate to recent rates of actual inflation.

References

Chan, K. C., Patric H. Hendershott, and Anthony Sanders. "Risk and Return on Real Estate: Evidence From Equity REITs." The Ohio State University, Mimeo (December 1990).

Diamond, Douglas, "Taxes, Inflation, Speculation and the Cost of Homeownership: 1963–1978." *AREUEA Journal* (Fall 1980).

Federal Reserve Board, *Federal Reserve Bulletin*, various issues.

Follain, James R., and David C. Ling. "The Federal Tax Subsidy to Housing and the Reduced Value of the Mortgage Interest Deduction." *National Tax Journal*, (June 1991), 147–168.

Follain, James R., Patric H. Hendershott, and David C. Ling. "Understanding the Real Estate Provisions of Tax Reform: Motivation and Impact." *National Tax Journal* (September 1987), 363–72.

Harris, Jack C., "The Effect of Real Rates of Interest on Housing Prices." *The Journal of Real Estate Finance and Economics*, 2, 1 (February 1989), 47–60.

Haurin, Don, Patric H. Hendershott, and David C. Ling. "Home Ownership Rates of Married Couples: An Econometric Investigation." *Housing Finance Review*, 7, 2 (1988).

Hendershott, Patric H., and Joel Slemrod. "Taxes and the User Cost of Capital for Owner-Occupied Housing." *AREUEA Journal* (Winter 1983), 375–93.

Hendershott, Patric H., and James D. Shilling. "The Economics of Tenure Choice: 1955–1979," in *Research in Real Estate*, Vol. 1, C. F. Sirmans, ed. JAI Press, 1982, pp. 105–33.

Hendershott, Patric H, and Sheng C. Hu. "Inflation and Extraordinary Returns on Owner-Occupied Housing: Some Implications for Capital Allocation and Productivity Growth." *Journal of Macroeconomics* (Spring 1981), 177–203.

Hendershott, Patric H., and David C. Ling. "Likely Impacts of the Administration's Tax Proposals and H. R. 3838," in *Tax Reform and Real Estate*, James R. Follain, ed. Washington D.C.: The Urban Institute, 1986, pp. 87–112.

Lafayette, William C. "Measuring the Cost and Affordability of Housing With Applications to the Analysis of Housing Markets." University of North Texas, mimeo (March 1990).

U.S. Bureau of the Census. *Current Population Reports*, various issues.

Van Order, Robert and Kevin Villani. "Alternative Measures of Housing Costs," in *Research in Real Estate*, Vol. 1. C. F. Sirmans, ed. JAI Press, 1982, pp. 87–103.

Appendix

Table A1. Marginal and Tenure Choice Tax Rates

Qtr	Marginal tax rates					Tenure choice tax rates				
	Married	Single	Hse head	Wtd ave	Median	Married	Single	Hse head	Wtd ave	Median
731	0.1721	0.1731	0.1250	0.1652	0.1700	0.1998	0.1973	0.1561	0.1927	0.1756
732	0.1721	0.1729	0.1249	0.1651	0.1600	0.1994	0.1970	0.1557	0.1923	0.1755
733	0.1721	0.1729	0.1935	0.1755	0.1600	0.1986	0.1963	0.1547	0.1915	0.1750
734	0.2016	0.1729	0.1232	0.1840	0.1600	0.1981	0.1958	0.1542	0.1910	0.1747
741	0.1844	0.1776	0.1294	0.1754	0.1700	0.2108	0.1981	0.1619	0.2014	0.1832
742	0.1840	0.1763	0.1073	0.1719	0.1600	0.2097	0.1972	0.1601	0.2003	0.1825
743	0.1797	0.1706	0.1894	0.1791	0.1600	0.2087	0.1963	0.1581	0.1992	0.1817
744	0.2129	0.1706	0.1042	0.1891	0.1600	0.2089	0.1964	0.1584	0.1994	0.1817
751	0.1860	0.1738	0.1080	0.1731	0.1810	0.2136	0.1978	0.1620	0.2034	0.2053
752	0.1860	0.1738	0.1080	0.1731	0.1810	0.2137	0.1979	0.1623	0.2035	0.2055
753	0.1860	0.1738	0.1913	0.1840	0.1810	0.2135	0.1977	0.1619	0.2033	0.2053
754	0.2171	0.1738	0.1080	0.1933	0.1810	0.2133	0.1975	0.1614	0.2030	0.2051
761	0.1930	0.1789	0.1143	0.1802	0.1908	0.2202	0.2038	0.1696	0.2103	0.2088
762	0.1938	0.1789	0.1143	0.1807	0.1908	0.2202	0.2038	0.1697	0.2103	0.2089
763	0.1930	0.1789	0.2002	0.1906	0.1908	0.2201	0.2037	0.1694	0.2101	0.2088
764	0.2229	0.1789	0.1143	0.1995	0.1908	0.2205	0.2040	0.1702	0.2106	0.2090
771	0.2089	0.1929	0.1434	0.1970	0.1924	0.1800	0.1218	0.1314	0.1602	0.1552
772	0.2069	0.1929	0.1434	0.1957	0.1924	0.1801	0.1223	0.1315	0.1604	0.1554
773	0.2069	0.1929	0.1559	0.1973	0.1924	0.1802	0.1222	0.1315	0.1604	0.1555
774	0.2220	0.1915	0.1217	0.2023	0.1924	0.1805	0.1228	0.1315	0.1607	0.1559
781	0.2177	0.1958	0.1328	0.2013	0.2119	0.1985	0.1350	0.1452	0.1757	0.1508
782	0.2142	0.1932	0.1297	0.1980	0.2119	0.1991	0.1355	0.1447	0.1762	0.1530
783	0.2031	0.1930	0.1663	0.1958	0.2119	0.1994	0.1360	0.1443	0.1764	0.1546
784	0.2302	0.1930	0.1294	0.2079	0.2119	0.1995	0.1370	0.1439	0.1767	0.1560
791	0.2079	0.1896	0.1143	0.1910	0.2046	0.1942	0.1422	0.1374	0.1735	0.1503

Table A1. (Cont.)

Qtr	Marginal tax rates					Tenure choice tax rates				
	Married	Single	Hse head	Wtd ave	Median	Married	Single	Hse head	Wtd ave	Median
792	0.2079	0.1887	0.1143	0.1907	0.2046	0.1944	0.1421	0.1371	0.1736	0.1512
793	0.2064	0.1874	0.1658	0.1962	0.2046	0.1947	0.1426	0.1365	0.1738	0.1525
794	0.2225	0.1343	0.1095	0.1852	0.2046	0.1953	0.1448	0.1353	0.1746	0.1555
801	0.2210	0.1509	0.1287	0.1890	0.2038	0.2190	0.1580	0.1553	0.1936	0.1709
802	0.2191	0.1483	0.1287	0.1872	0.2038	0.2190	0.1576	0.1542	0.1933	0.1722
803	0.2210	0.1509	0.1858	0.1975	0.2038	0.2189	0.1580	0.1555	0.1936	0.1706
804	0.2343	0.1230	0.1260	0.1891	0.2038	0.2190	0.1574	0.1537	0.1932	0.1728
811	0.2120	0.1443	0.1365	0.1837	0.2038	0.2329	0.1790	0.1657	0.2095	0.1870
812	0.2120	0.1262	0.1357	0.1788	0.2038	0.2319	0.1770	0.1643	0.2081	0.1878
813	0.1994	0.1238	0.1814	0.1767	0.2038	0.2303	0.1741	0.1626	0.2062	0.1887
814	0.2342	0.1220	0.1184	0.1886	0.2038	0.2292	0.1724	0.1613	0.2049	0.1892
821	0.1791	0.1159	0.1108	0.1527	0.1772	0.2055	0.1565	0.1440	0.1839	0.1637
822	0.1776	0.1140	0.1095	0.1512	0.1772	0.2052	0.1560	0.1435	0.1835	0.1638
823	0.1791	0.1159	0.1568	0.1590	0.1772	0.2056	0.1567	0.1441	0.1840	0.1636
824	0.2171	0.1328	0.1227	0.1815	0.1772	0.2082	0.1611	0.1469	0.1871	0.1619
831	0.2114	0.1604	0.1312	0.1867	0.1789	0.2199	0.1756	0.1538	0.1990	0.1708
832	0.2163	0.1624	0.1341	0.1906	0.1789	0.2201	0.1762	0.1548	0.1994	0.1705
833	0.2163	0.1604	0.1659	0.1944	0.1789	0.2200	0.1759	0.1543	0.1992	0.1706
834	0.2233	0.1611	0.1341	0.1944	0.1789	0.2200	0.1760	0.1544	0.1992	0.1706
841	0.2019	0.1581	0.1287	0.1797	0.1692	0.2134	0.1700	0.1494	0.1925	0.1698
842	0.1949	0.1453	0.1280	0.1719	0.1692	0.2130	0.1697	0.1490	0.1922	0.1698
843	0.1949	0.1453	0.1584	0.1762	0.1692	0.2125	0.1691	0.1484	0.1916	0.1698
844	0.2101	0.1453	0.1280	0.1809	0.1692	0.2128	0.1695	0.1488	0.1920	0.1698
851	0.2116	0.1674	0.1402	0.1891	0.1877	0.2251	0.1797	0.1616	0.2034	0.1760
852	0.2116	0.1683	0.1428	0.1898	0.1877	0.2254	0.1799	0.1620	0.2037	0.1758

853	0.2162	0.1703	0.1720	0.1972	0.1877	0.2260	0.1805	0.1632	0.2044	0.1751
854	0.2285	0.1715	0.1438	0.2006	0.1877	0.2262	0.1807	0.1636	0.2046	0.1748
861	0.2209	0.1778	0.1493	0.1986	0.1860	0.2298	0.1836	0.1665	0.2078	0.1738
862	0.2296	0.1791	0.1504	0.2041	0.1860	0.2301	0.1839	0.1675	0.2082	0.1731
863	0.2296	0.1971	0.1831	0.2138	0.1860	0.2301	0.1838	0.1677	0.2082	0.1729
864	0.2432	0.1981	0.1528	0.2176	0.1860	0.2301	0.1839	0.1681	0.2083	0.1726
871	0.1862	0.1744	0.1259	0.1742	0.1814	0.1385	0.1227	0.0856	0.1264	0.0981
872	0.1862	0.1744	0.1259	0.1742	0.1814	0.1399	0.1242	0.0868	0.1278	0.1005
873	0.1862	0.1744	0.1356	0.1756	0.1814	0.1408	0.1251	0.0876	0.1287	0.1022
874	0.1923	0.1744	0.1259	0.1777	0.1814	0.1411	0.1255	0.0878	0.1290	0.1025
881	0.1939	0.1800	0.1337	0.1811	0.1814	0.1485	0.1294	0.0937	0.1351	0.1043
882	0.1939	0.1800	0.1337	0.1811	0.1814	0.1491	0.1301	0.0942	0.1357	0.1053
883	0.1939	0.1800	0.1432	0.1825	0.1814	0.1495	0.1306	0.0946	0.1361	0.1061
884	0.1995	0.1800	0.1337	0.1843	0.1814	0.1496	0.1307	0.0948	0.1362	0.1065
891	0.1939	0.1755	0.1332	0.1798	0.1814	0.1464	0.1282	0.0928	0.1334	0.1105
892	0.1939	0.1755	0.1332	0.1798	0.1814	0.1474	0.1290	0.0937	0.1343	0.1125
893	0.1939	0.1755	0.1432	0.1813	0.1814	0.1462	0.1277	0.0928	0.1331	0.1108
894	0.1939	0.1755	0.1332	0.1798	0.1814	0.1457	0.1273	0.0922	0.1326	0.1098

Table A2. Actual and Expected Inflation Rates

Qtr	(1) CPI net of shelter	(2) House price	(3) House price ratio	(4) Expected general inflation B.F.	(5) Expected house inflation adj. B.F.	(6) Expected general inflation Harris	(7) Expected house inflation adj. Harris
731	44.1	41.0	1.0000	0.0530	0.0552	0.0378	0.0415
732	45.4	41.4	0.9808	0.0522	0.0552	0.0384	0.0427
733	46.1	43.1	1.0056	0.0530	0.0558	0.0666	0.0680
734	47.4	43.9	0.9962	0.0552	0.0608	0.0658	0.0703
741	48.5	44.9	0.9958	0.0580	0.0611	0.0803	0.0812
742	50.1	45.7	0.9811	0.0592	0.0628	0.0820	0.0833
743	51.6	46.8	0.9756	0.0607	0.0650	0.0956	0.0965
744	53.2	47.9	0.9685	0.0647	0.0668	0.0990	0.0977
751	54.3	49.7	0.9845	0.0681	0.0704	0.1016	0.1005
752	55.0	50.4	0.9856	0.0724	0.0759	0.0889	0.0907
753	56.4	51.2	0.9764	0.0762	0.0789	0.0722	0.0752
754	57.3	52.4	0.9836	0.0794	0.0809	0.0808	0.0821
761	57.9	52.8	0.9809	0.0818	0.0830	0.0750	0.0769
762	58.5	54.6	1.0039	0.0825	0.0805	0.0658	0.0654
763	59.5	56.0	1.0123	0.0818	0.0820	0.0623	0.0644
764	60.2	56.4	1.0077	0.0805	0.0818	0.0701	0.0725
771	60.9	58.3	1.0297	0.0786	0.0784	0.0686	0.0694
772	62.5	60.4	1.0395	0.0781	0.0807	0.0654	0.0693
773	63.5	61.3	1.0383	0.0775	0.0804	0.0854	0.0875
774	64.0	64.5	1.0840	0.0739	0.0760	0.0811	0.0825
781	64.7	65.0	1.0806	0.0713	0.0785	0.0667	0.0744
782	66.2	68.4	1.1114	0.0679	0.0726	0.0580	0.0637

783	67.9	71.2	1.1279	0.0672	0.0737	0.0689	0.0752
784	68.9	73.1	1.1412	0.0660	0.0756	0.0792	0.0874
791	70.3	75.7	1.1582	0.0662	0.0729	0.0726	0.0787
792	72.5	79.7	1.1824	0.0682	0.0778	0.0749	0.0838
793	74.9	81.2	1.1661	0.0702	0.0797	0.0890	0.0966
794	76.6	82.8	1.1627	0.0723	0.0791	0.1033	0.1070
801	78.7	83.1	1.1357	0.0741	0.0800	0.0984	0.1019
802	81.6	87.5	1.1534	0.0756	0.0778	0.1003	0.1000
803	83.2	89.4	1.1558	0.0767	0.0788	0.1131	0.1116
804	85.3	90.7	1.1437	0.0788	0.0810	0.0996	0.0998
811	87.2	94.0	1.1595	0.0814	0.0828	0.0973	0.0971
812	89.8	96.2	1.1523	0.0845	0.0892	0.0914	0.0953
813	91.5	97.8	1.1497	0.0849	0.0864	0.1019	0.1017
814	93.1	99.5	1.1496	0.0863	0.0871	0.0959	0.0957
821	94.2	99.3	1.1338	0.0863	0.0874	0.0893	0.0901
822	94.6	100.9	1.1472	0.0850	0.0821	0.0769	0.0748
823	96.9	100.5	1.1156	0.0832	0.0798	0.0607	0.0595
824	97.9	99.3	1.0910	0.0812	0.0758	0.0792	0.0740
831	98.1	101.4	1.1118	0.0783	0.0703	0.0712	0.0639
832	98.9	101.7	1.1061	0.0750	0.0696	0.0535	0.0503
833	100.2	104.7	1.1239	0.0711	0.0648	0.0508	0.0465
834	101.2	104.0	1.1054	0.0670	0.0645	0.0569	0.0554
841	102.0	104.5	1.1020	0.0623	0.0608	0.0545	0.0538
842	103.2	107.3	1.1183	0.0576	0.0549	0.0490	0.0472
843	104.1	107.7	1.1128	0.0539	0.0540	0.0524	0.0526
844	105.2	108.9	1.1134	0.0497	0.0476	0.0474	0.0455
851	105.3	110.1	1.1246	0.0461	0.0462	0.0459	0.0460
852	106.6	109.4	1.1039	0.0430	0.0441	0.0305	0.0328
853	107.2	110.2	1.1057	0.0407	0.0386	0.0374	0.0356
854	107.9	110.8	1.1045	0.0383	0.0368	0.0329	0.0319

Table A2. (Cont.)

Qtr	(1) CPI net of shelter	(2) House price	(3) House price ratio	(4) Expected general inflation B.F.	(5) Expected house inflation adj. B.F.	(6) Expected general inflation Harris	(7) Expected house inflation adj. Harris
861	108.2	111.4	1.1074	0.0372	0.0352	0.0319	0.0304
862	107.3	114.9	1.1518	0.0357	0.0333	0.0321	0.0301
863	107.8	114.4	1.1415	0.0349	0.0364	0.0420	0.0428
864	108.4	111.6	1.1074	0.0351	0.0354	0.0415	0.0411
871	109.3	115.5	1.1366	0.0339	0.0312	0.0368	0.0339
872	110.8	116.9	1.1348	0.0333	0.0337	0.0353	0.0354
873	111.8	118.4	1.1391	0.0333	0.0317	0.0411	0.0387
874	113.2	116.3	1.1051	0.0327	0.0329	0.0393	0.0389
881	113.3	117.2	1.1126	0.0324	0.0334	0.0425	0.0425
882	114.7	116.8	1.0953	0.0321	0.0304	0.0285	0.0271
883	116.1	116.7	1.0812	0.0324	0.0291	0.0354	0.0318
884	117.9	116.4	1.0619	0.0331	0.0284	0.0402	0.0347
891	118.7	120.6	1.0928	0.0340	0.0307	0.0490	0.0442
892	121.0	119.0	1.0578	0.0357	0.0350	0.0412	0.0400
893	122.0	119.0	1.0492	0.0371	0.0353	0.0544	0.0508
894	123.1	119.0	1.0398	0.0372	0.0355	0.0473	0.0445

Table A3. T-Bond, Property Tax, and Maintenance Rates

Qtr	7-year T-Bond rate	Effective mortgage rates	Property tax rate	Maintenance and repair	Real B.T. cash cost	MAR index
731	0.0643	0.0770	0.0183	0.0114	0.1067	147.5
732	0.0671	0.0775	0.0183	0.0114	0.1051	145.1
733	0.0709	0.0799	0.0183	0.0114	0.1102	139.8
734	0.0671	0.0840	0.0183	0.0114	0.1133	137.2
741	0.0680	0.0859	0.0175	0.0114	0.1143	131.8
742	0.0781	0.0875	0.0175	0.0114	0.1142	127.8
743	0.0831	0.0908	0.0175	0.0114	0.1168	122.7
744	0.0772	0.0927	0.0175	0.0114	0.1178	122.2
751	0.0727	0.0917	0.0182	0.0114	0.1194	120.3
752	0.0761	0.0895	0.0182	0.0114	0.1174	120.2
753	0.0796	0.0891	0.0182	0.0114	0.1159	119.3
754	0.0803	0.0901	0.0182	0.0114	0.1177	121.3
761	0.0765	0.0895	0.0176	0.0118	0.1166	121.0
762	0.0762	0.0893	0.0176	0.0111	0.1192	121.0
763	0.0759	0.0902	0.0176	0.0112	0.1211	119.8
764	0.0697	0.0908	0.0176	0.0112	0.1211	122.8
771	0.0691	0.0900	0.0151	0.0112	0.1205	121.2
772	0.0714	0.0896	0.0151	0.0112	0.1212	117.3
773	0.0707	0.0902	0.0151	0.0119	0.1217	115.2
774	0.0736	0.0908	0.0151	0.0119	0.1277	115.5
781	0.0776	0.0920	0.0127	0.0118	0.1259	112.3
782	0.0812	0.0938	0.0127	0.0118	0.1315	108.3
783	0.0845	0.0967	0.0127	0.0118	0.1367	103.7
784	0.0876	0.0991	0.0127	0.0118	0.1410	102.9
791	0.0911	0.1020	0.0117	0.0116	0.1455	98.2
792	0.0913	0.1050	0.0117	0.0116	0.1516	93.4
793	0.0898	0.1090	0.0117	0.0116	0.1547	89.5
794	0.1027	0.1140	0.0117	0.0116	0.1596	91.0
801	0.1148	0.1210	0.0117	0.0116	0.1643	82.5
802	0.1107	0.1310	0.0117	0.0116	0.1782	73.8
803	0.1056	0.1240	0.0117	0.0116	0.1699	78.5
804	0.1229	0.1290	0.0117	0.0116	0.1750	76.9
811	0.1288	0.1360	0.0114	0.0113	0.1841	72.3
812	0.1366	0.1430	0.0114	0.0113	0.1910	68.4
813	0.1491	0.1510	0.0114	0.0113	0.1996	64.5
814	0.1474	0.1590	0.0114	0.0113	0.2097	64.6
821	0.1414	0.1540	0.0128	0.0114	0.2015	66.4
822	0.1400	0.1570	0.0128	0.0114	0.2080	65.4
823	0.1370	0.1550	0.0128	0.0114	0.1994	67.5

Table A3. (Cont.)

Qtr	7-year T-Bond rate	Effective mortgage rates	Property tax rate	Maintenance and repair	Real B.T. cash cost	MAR index
824	0.1101	0.1390	0.0128	0.0114	0.1788	74.1
831	0.1036	0.1340	0.0129	0.0113	0.1753	79.5
832	0.1045	0.1250	0.0129	0.0113	0.1648	81.9
833	0.1149	0.1250	0.0129	0.0113	0.1674	81.7
834	0.1148	0.1230	0.0129	0.0113	0.1632	85.1
841	0.1177	0.1220	0.0129	0.0113	0.1609	87.2
842	0.1284	0.1210	0.0129	0.0113	0.1625	87.3
843	0.1316	0.1250	0.0129	0.0113	0.1659	84.7
844	0.1190	0.1270	0.0129	0.0113	0.1682	86.6
851	0.1149	0.1210	0.0135	0.0116	0.1646	88.5
852	0.1105	0.1190	0.0135	0.0116	0.1595	90.8
853	0.1025	0.1120	0.0135	0.0116	0.1520	94.9
854	0.0982	0.1100	0.0135	0.0116	0.1493	98.6
861	0.0857	0.1070	0.0134	0.0116	0.1461	99.8
862	0.0758	0.1020	0.0134	0.0116	0.1464	100.9
863	0.0709	0.1020	0.0134	0.0116	0.1454	104.4
864	0.0713	0.0990	0.0134	0.0116	0.1370	110.2
871	0.0700	0.0930	0.0132	0.0117	0.1339	107.4
872	0.0789	0.0930	0.0132	0.0117	0.1342	109.0
873	0.0849	0.0940	0.0132	0.0117	0.1353	109.4
874	0.0898	0.0920	0.0132	0.0117	0.1295	112.0
881	0.0822	0.0910	0.0132	0.0114	0.1288	112.3
882	0.0869	0.0910	0.0132	0.0114	0.1267	111.8
883	0.0894	0.0920	0.0132	0.0114	0.1256	110.9
884	0.0879	0.0930	0.0132	0.0114	0.1250	112.4
891	0.0914	0.0980	0.0132	0.0114	0.1338	107.6
892	0.0904	0.1030	0.0132	0.0114	0.1346	101.4
893	0.0802	0.1030	0.0132	0.0114	0.1340	101.8
894	0.0803	0.1010	0.0132	0.0114	0.1305	106.5

Table A4. Prices of Owner-Occupied Housing Services

Qtr	Marginal user costs					Tenuer choice user costs				
	Married	Single	Hse head	Wtd ave	Median	Married	Single	Hse head	Wtd ave	Median
731	0.0814	0.0981	0.0922	0.0864	0.0817	0.0784	0.0954	0.0888	0.0834	0.0811
732	0.0821	0.0986	0.0929	0.0870	0.0835	0.0791	0.0959	0.0895	0.0840	0.0818
733	0.0866	0.1036	0.0981	0.0918	0.0881	0.0836	0.1009	0.0945	0.0887	0.0864
734	0.0779	0.0949	0.0891	0.0830	0.0794	0.0751	0.0923	0.0857	0.0802	0.0777
741	0.0764	0.0942	0.0878	0.0817	0.0779	0.0735	0.0919	0.0842	0.0788	0.0765
742	0.0816	0.0994	0.0960	0.0873	0.0844	0.0785	0.0969	0.0897	0.0839	0.0817
743	0.0834	0.1015	0.0980	0.0892	0.0858	0.0799	0.0984	0.0914	0.0854	0.0832
744	0.0765	0.0946	0.0907	0.0822	0.0789	0.0732	0.0916	0.0844	0.0786	0.0764
751	0.0708	0.0894	0.0850	0.0767	0.0714	0.0677	0.0866	0.0788	0.0733	0.0686
752	0.0681	0.0868	0.0826	0.0741	0.0687	0.0649	0.0839	0.0762	0.0705	0.0658
753	0.0674	0.0860	0.0820	0.0734	0.0679	0.0641	0.0831	0.0755	0.0698	0.0651
754	0.0666	0.0853	0.0813	0.0726	0.0671	0.0632	0.0825	0.0748	0.0689	0.0642
761	0.0606	0.0794	0.0757	0.0668	0.0607	0.0574	0.0765	0.0692	0.0632	0.0586
762	0.0641	0.0835	0.0797	0.0705	0.0643	0.0610	0.0806	0.0731	0.0670	0.0621
763	0.0631	0.0827	0.0787	0.0695	0.0631	0.0598	0.0797	0.0721	0.0659	0.0610
764	0.0580	0.0776	0.0732	0.0644	0.0582	0.0550	0.0747	0.0668	0.0610	0.0561
771	0.0585	0.0788	0.0720	0.0650	0.0601	0.0617	0.0869	0.0733	0.0691	0.0643
772	0.0588	0.0793	0.0724	0.0653	0.0603	0.0619	0.0875	0.0738	0.0694	0.0646
773	0.0585	0.0791	0.0721	0.0651	0.0600	0.0616	0.0872	0.0735	0.0691	0.0642
774	0.0682	0.0899	0.0853	0.0755	0.0697	0.0714	0.0984	0.0841	0.0794	0.0742
781	0.0647	0.0871	0.0824	0.0726	0.0661	0.0671	0.0947	0.0808	0.0758	0.0736
782	0.0765	0.0996	0.0951	0.0847	0.0774	0.0785	0.1073	0.0931	0.0876	0.0852
783	0.0808	0.1031	0.0986	0.0887	0.0803	0.0813	0.1109	0.0966	0.0907	0.0881
784	0.0827	0.1050	0.1007	0.0906	0.0818	0.0829	0.1131	0.0986	0.0925	0.0898
791	0.0886	0.1143	0.1090	0.0978	0.0893	0.0906	0.1213	0.1056	0.1004	0.0972

Table A4. (Cont.)

	Marginal user costs					Tenure choice user costs			
Qtr	Married	Single	Hse head	Wtd ave	Median	Married	Single	Hse head	Wtd ave	Median
792	0.0850	0.1115	0.1059	0.0945	0.0857	0.0871	0.1185	0.1025	0.0971	0.0937
793	0.0807	0.1068	0.1012	0.0900	0.0811	0.0824	0.1134	0.0977	0.0923	0.0887
794	0.0929	0.1280	0.1151	0.1048	0.0932	0.0945	0.1264	0.1110	0.1048	0.1010
801	0.0976	0.1300	0.1197	0.1093	0.1006	0.0980	0.1288	0.1152	0.1086	0.1062
802	0.0985	0.1314	0.1203	0.1103	0.1011	0.0985	0.1298	0.1160	0.1093	0.1064
803	0.0928	0.1254	0.1145	0.1045	0.0957	0.0932	0.1242	0.1102	0.1038	0.1011
804	0.1054	0.1432	0.1282	0.1187	0.1076	0.1048	0.1370	0.1232	0.1159	0.1131
811	0.1100	0.1440	0.1312	0.1220	0.1115	0.1061	0.1375	0.1257	0.1171	0.1147
812	0.1090	0.1471	0.1310	0.1222	0.1106	0.1051	0.1372	0.1254	0.1164	0.1137
813	0.1256	0.1629	0.1463	0.1384	0.1246	0.1192	0.1523	0.1404	0.1309	0.1278
814	0.1240	0.1610	0.1473	0.1370	0.1224	0.1172	0.1505	0.1384	0.1290	0.1254
821	0.1214	0.1553	0.1420	0.1333	0.1220	0.1161	0.1472	0.1354	0.1271	0.1247
822	0.1279	0.1622	0.1487	0.1400	0.1282	0.1224	0.1538	0.1418	0.1335	0.1309
823	0.1240	0.1573	0.1422	0.1355	0.1246	0.1189	0.1494	0.1377	0.1297	0.1272
824	0.1001	0.1302	0.1180	0.1106	0.1027	0.0976	0.1257	0.1141	0.1074	0.1052
831	0.0993	0.1279	0.1188	0.1096	0.1045	0.0980	0.1255	0.1153	0.1077	0.1058
832	0.0996	0.1286	0.1194	0.1101	0.1056	0.0990	0.1264	0.1162	0.1087	0.1069
833	0.1155	0.1460	0.1370	0.1266	0.1220	0.1149	0.1434	0.1333	0.1251	0.1235
834	0.1138	0.1439	0.1347	0.1247	0.1203	0.1132	0.1414	0.1313	0.1232	0.1217
841	0.1224	0.1505	0.1419	0.1328	0.1280	0.1205	0.1485	0.1384	0.1307	0.1279
842	0.1415	0.1717	0.1611	0.1525	0.1463	0.1382	0.1674	0.1572	0.1489	0.1462
843	0.1446	0.1750	0.1645	0.1557	0.1495	0.1413	0.1705	0.1606	0.1520	0.1494
844	0.1408	0.1706	0.1597	0.1516	0.1454	0.1377	0.1663	0.1561	0.1481	0.1453
851	0.1368	0.1667	0.1574	0.1480	0.1422	0.1345	0.1646	0.1537	0.1456	0.1442
852	0.1329	0.1620	0.1524	0.1437	0.1381	0.1307	0.1601	0.1492	0.1415	0.1400

853	0.1317	0.1609	0.1512	0.1426	0.1374	0.1302	0.1593	0.1482	0.1408	0.1393
854	0.1292	0.1587	0.1491	0.1402	0.1354	0.1284	0.1573	0.1461	0.1389	0.1374
861	0.1218	0.1485	0.1388	0.1317	0.1265	0.1206	0.1477	0.1364	0.1305	0.1282
862	0.1189	0.1470	0.1367	0.1293	0.1246	0.1189	0.1464	0.1345	0.1289	0.1263
863	0.1101	0.1354	0.1273	0.1197	0.1155	0.1101	0.1371	0.1251	0.1198	0.1171
864	0.1081	0.1328	0.1247	0.1174	0.1135	0.1082	0.1345	0.1229	0.1177	0.1152
871	0.1185	0.1414	0.1337	0.1271	0.1190	0.1247	0.1482	0.1390	0.1333	0.1300
872	0.1236	0.1466	0.1395	0.1323	0.1242	0.1301	0.1537	0.1450	0.1388	0.1356
873	0.1318	0.1551	0.1483	0.1407	0.1325	0.1386	0.1625	0.1539	0.1475	0.1442
874	0.1309	0.1537	0.1473	0.1396	0.1316	0.1377	0.1610	0.1529	0.1464	0.1434
881	0.1230	0.1459	0.1388	0.1318	0.1247	0.1294	0.1531	0.1445	0.1384	0.1356
882	0.1285	0.1513	0.1444	0.1373	0.1302	0.1350	0.1585	0.1502	0.1439	0.1412
883	0.1304	0.1530	0.1464	0.1392	0.1322	0.1369	0.1603	0.1521	0.1458	0.1432
884	0.1276	0.1499	0.1433	0.1362	0.1293	0.1339	0.1569	0.1488	0.1426	0.1399
891	0.1319	0.1556	0.1483	0.1410	0.1335	0.1390	0.1627	0.1543	0.1480	0.1441
892	0.1223	0.1453	0.1382	0.1312	0.1239	0.1290	0.1520	0.1438	0.1377	0.1337
893	0.1125	0.1352	0.1276	0.1212	0.1139	0.1188	0.1415	0.1329	0.1273	0.1233
894	0.1114	0.1340	0.1264	0.1200	0.1128	0.1177	0.1403	0.1317	0.1262	0.1222

17 THE MEASUREMENT OF EFFECTIVE RENT

Cynthia A. Kroll and Sam Taff

Issues in the Measurement of Rent

Rent levels are a key indicator of market conditions for speculative commercial or industrial markets. Theoretically, rent is a driving factor in determining how much space is added over time and how much of new and existing space is absorbed (Rosen, 1984, Shilling et al., 1987, Hekman, 1985). Practically, however, measurement of rent is not straightforward. A building owner's asking rent will differ from the initial level agreed to in a lease, and the initial level may be modified over the life of the lease by special provisions such as free rent allotments and rate increases over the term of the lease.

These details become quite important in analyzing a market that is changing rapidly. For example, a market with rapidly expanding stock and high vacancy rates may show increasing asking rents and even increases in the "contract" rents in new leases, while a more detailed look at lease provisions could indicate growing difficulties in attracting tenants. Unfortunately, brokers have only recently begun to report "effective" rents, and the measures used vary considerably among sources. This has made comparisons among and even within markets difficult.

This paper argues that the use of contract rent (the initial rent paid by the tenant), rather than effective rent in market analyses may produce a distorted understanding of the market. After reviewing the use of rent as a factor in the analysis of real estate markets, the paper describes the leasing processes that lead to the need for an effective rent calculation. The major elements of effective rent are then described and alternative measures are presented. These effective rent measures are applied to a set of lease agreements for industrial space in the Santa Clara County area between 1980 and 1987, and are compared descriptively and econometrically. The implications of alternative rent measures for understanding the Santa Clara County market and for market analysis more generally are discussed.

Definitions and Measures of Rent in Real Estate Literature

Rent has been used in a number of different papers examining nonresidential real estate markets. The type of rent measured and the sources of rent for empirical studies varies among these papers. Rents used may be an areawide average (e.g., for a city as a whole), the average rent paid per building, or the average among specific leases. Citywide averages may come from several sources. Rosen (1984) and Nelson (1980) use average rents as reported by commercial brokers. Brokers generally track either average *asking* rents for buildings on the market in that year or the average contract rent for leases signed that year. Shilling et al. (1987) use survey data published by the Building Owners and Managers Association (BOMA). The data are unweighted averages of rental cost per square foot for buildings responding to the BOMA survey, thus reflecting actual payments received for space under lease, regardless of the term of the lease or when the lease was written. Hekman (1985) argues that the BOMA data are biased by the small size of the sample. Instead, he uses data from The Office Network, *National Office Market Report*, which reports average rents for all office buildings by location.

Some authors concentrate on the limitations of all of these rental measures. Cannaday and Kang (1984) point out that most of the rental information sources described above report the actual contract rent received (regardless of when the lease was written) rather than the market rent that space could command if the building were on the market today. Their work develops a regression model to estimate a hedonic (market) rent from characteristics of the building, its location, and specific lease terms demanded by the owner. Brennan et al. (1984) demonstrate that the contract rent will vary with the lease structure, affected by such factors as the term of the lease, the number of months of rental abatement, and whether or not the lease includes CPI escalation.

Barnes (1986) directly addresses the effects of rental concessions on effective rents and the value of a building. Using a simple averaging technique to calculate effective rents, he argues that a concession such as free rent can have a "tremendous effect" on the appraised property value. Corgel and Rogers (1986) discuss some of the complexities of measuring effective rent, concentrating particularly on the need to include the time value of money in the calculation, through discounting later payments.

Both the Barnes and the Corgel and Rogers papers use hypothetical examples rather than actual rental agreements in their discussions. The analysis that follows uses actual rental agreements to highlight the complexities of the effective rent measure. Using over 900 lease agreements for Santa Clara County R&D space, the paper examines the degree to which the use of contract rents rather than effective rents in a market assessment gives a distorted picture of market conditions.

The Leasing Process

In a healthy, gradually expanding market, the leasing process may be quite standard, with little variation in the lease term, the type of escalators included over time, and the duration of rental abatements. In a rapidly changing market, however, leasing activity may become highly competitive, either from the point of view of the tenant or building owner, and lease terms may vary dramatically as tenants or building owners each try to reach "creative" rental agreements.

What goes into these "creative" lease agreements? In a market with growing demand and very low vacancy rates, the contract rent may hide a higher long-term value of the lease because many agreements include CPI or other escalation clauses. Markets with high vacancy rates and several years supply of space may find a far lower incidence of escalation clauses, while standard items may include rental abatements of up to 24 months and significantly higher tenant improvement allowances.

Considering contract rents alone may inadequately reflect changing market conditions over time. Consider, for example, the downtown San Francisco office market, which went from a vacancy level of below 1% in 1981 to 15% in 1986. This change led to a shift from lease agreements that included cost-of-living increases as a standard item to agreements with substantial rental abatement concessions.

Contract rents also may inadequately reflect the differences among markets or among niches within the same market. Owners with buildings in the periphery of a rapidly expanding and overbuilt industrial or office market may attract tenants through lease concessions while keeping the contract rent level closer to what they believe the space can command in the longer term.

In the most overbuilt markets, some of the significant leasing giveaways may not be reported or may be very difficult to classify. Despite this limitation, a significantly better measure of rent may be made by incorporating the major lease agreements into an effective rent calculation.

Deriving A Measure of Effective Rent from Lease Agreements

If the contract rent is defined as the initial dollar per square foot payment to be made by the tenant (after any initial period of rental abatement), then several factors are likely to affect the level of "effective" rent (the value landlords actually receive from the rental agreement). These factors include:

- Months of rental abatement (also called "free rent" — the period when the tenant actually pays no rent)
- Rent escalation over the course of the lease (either specified dollar amounts or tied to a price index)
- Total term of the lease (number of months)
- Tenant improvements (up-front payments by the landlord for improvements to the shell of the building)

Effective Rent (1) — Free Rent

The simplest (and most common) measure of effective rent is to average out the months of free rent over the total term of the lease, without adjusting for the time value of money. This is illustrated in Equation 1:

$$EF = \frac{1}{M} \times Rc \times (M - f). \qquad (1)$$

Here, Rc is the contract rent at the outset of the lease, M is the total number of months in the lease, and f is the number of months of free rent. (see, for example, Barnes, 1986).

Effective Rent (2) — Escalation

An expanded approach would take into account any escalation in rent paid over the term of the lease. Rent at time m is determined by the specific escalation requirements of the lease. These may be either a specified dollar amount of increase in particular months, or an increase at the rate of growth of the CPI (or some other price index), again set for particular months. In some leases, the increase may be tied to the CPI, but capped. For example, one Santa Clara County lease includes a CPI bump in the third year of the lease, capped at 8% annually. Before free rent is taken into account, a simple modification of average rent received, to adjust for cost of living increases would be

$$EB = \frac{1}{M} \times \sum_{m=1}^{m=M} R_m, \qquad (2a)$$

where Rm is the rent in month m, including all escalations, and M is as defined above.

Adjusting Equation 2a to account for free rent, gives an equation that accounts for both free rent and bumps:

$$EP = \frac{1}{M} \times (EB \times M - Rc), \qquad (2b)$$

where all variables are as defined above. In cases where rental abatements are offered later in the lease, after a cost escalator comes into effect, Equation 2b would need to be adjusted.

Effective Rent (3) — Adjusted to Present Discounted Value

Many commercial and industrial brokers who calculate effective rents rely on some version of Equations 1 or 2b. These equations adjust for periods when rent is below or above the contract rent. However, neither equation takes into account the timing of rental adjustments, which can have a significant effect on the value of the lease.

For example, consider three building owners, each of whom has agreed to a lease with a 60 month term. Owner A receives $0.60/month (per square foot) steadily for the full 5 years, Owner B receives no rent in the first 24 months and $1/month in the last 36 months of the lease, and Owner C receives no rent in the first 24 months, $0.80/month in next 12

Table 1. Comparison of Undiscounted Effective Rent and Present Value Estimates (60 Month Term, 8% Discount Rate)

Rent Estimates	Owner A ($0.60/mo./sq. ft.)	Owner B ($1.00/mo./sq. ft., 2 yrs free)	Owner C (2 yrs free, then yearly bumps $0.80/$1.00/$1.20)
Nominal rent	$0.60	$1.00	$0.80
Effective rent (undiscounted)	$0.60	$0.60	$0.60
Present discounted value of rental stream	$29.79	$27.47	$27.19

months, $1.00/month for months 37 through 48, and $1.20/month for the last 12 months of the lease. Using Equation 2b, all three landlords will have effective rents of $0.60, while contract rents range from $0.60 (Owner A) to $1.00 (Owner B). If the rents are discounted at an 8% discount rate, however, Owner A's rental stream will be worth 8.4% more than the rental stream received by Owner B and 9.6% more than for Owner C (Table 1).

A more complete view of effective rent, then, would be to calculate the present discount value of the stream of rents agreed to in the lease and to then translate this value into a constant stream of payments over the life of the lease. Equation 3a shows the calculation for the present discounted value of the stream of payments.

$$\text{PDV} = \left[\text{SUM}_{m=1}^{M} \frac{R_m}{(1 + i/12)^m} \right]. \quad (3a)$$

Here R, m, and M are defined as above, and i is the nominal interest rate at the time the lease was written. A nominal, rather than real, interest is used for these calculations to account for the effects of inflation.

An amortization equation is used to translate the discounted value of the rental stream back into an even set of monthly payments, as shown in Equation 3b.

$$\text{ED} = \text{PDV} \times \frac{r/12}{1 - \frac{1}{(1 + r/12)^m}}. \quad (3b)$$

In this equation, the real interest rate, r, is used to make comparisons among leases of different years consistent.

Effective Rent (4) — Tenant Improvements

In addition to analyzing the actual steam of rents received, it may be useful to add other costs or payments into the equation as well. A frequent factor modifying the value of a lease to a building owner (or to the tenant) is the amount spent on tenant improvements. The tenant improvement allowance, a one-time payment by the owner, can be added to the ED calculation to produce Equation 4:

$$ET = (PDV - TI) \times \frac{r/12}{1 - \frac{1}{(1 + r/12)^m}}, \quad (3b)$$

where variables are defined as above and TI is the dollar amount of tenant improvements provided per square foot at the outset of the lease.

Other Adjustments and Some Practical Limitations

If the purpose of the analysis is to compare lease rates over time, it would also be desirable to translate leases into constant dollars. This is a cumbersome process in Equations 1, 2a and 2b, requiring that each rental payment be adjusted to reflect changing price levels before the rental stream is averaged. In Equations 3a and 3b, the most appropriate approach would be to translate the present discounted value of the rental stream into constant dollars before making the amortization adjustment.

As one might expect, a number of other dilemmas also arise in trying to calculate the alternative effective rent measures outlined above using actual leasing records. The most significant come from circumstances in the leases that do not fit the standard process described above and from trying to choose appropriate interest rates. An example of a lease condition that is not easily incorporated into the equations discussed here is a preexisting tenant improvement that is taken over by the incoming tenant (it represents a value to the tenant but not a new cost to the owner).

The interest rate chosen for the present value calculation needs to reflect both the appropriate term of the lease and the fact that some risk is attached to the return (the tenant may be unable to fulfill the terms of the lease). For this study, treasury note rates are used matched to the terms of the lease (from 2 to 20 years) added to a risk factor calculated as the difference between the AAA corporate bond rate and the 7-year treasury note rate.[1]

The real interest rate may also change significantly over the period being studied, as it did with rapidly changing inflation levels in the first half of the 1980s. In addition, if the purpose of the calculation is to reflect the value as perceived by the building owner or tenants at the time of the transaction, then the expected real interest rate, rather than the actual rate as evident from hindsight, may be the most appropriate measure. For the amortization calculations done below, the real interest rate is calculated as the difference between the AAA corporate bond rate and the expected rate of inflation over the next 12 months, as reflected in the Livingston index.[2]

Effective Rent in Santa Clara Valley

Nowhere has effective rent more clearly become an issue than in the Santa Clara Valley in the 1980s. In this market, building activity continued strongly despite rapidly rising vacancies for several years. Contract rents also continued to rise during much of the building boom, even as many buildings stood empty. Thus, rent levels seemed to contradict other measures of market health. Reports from brokers indicated that, in many cases, the contract rent masked other important aspects of the lease agreement, with rental abatements and tenant improvement concessions cited as important elements in attracting firms to empty space. Thus, the measurement of effective rent in this market becomes very important as an indicator of the changing strength of market conditions.

The R&D Market in Santa Clara Valley

Santa Clara County and neighboring cities underwent a tremendous surge of industrial building activity in the 1980s. From December 1981 through December 1986 industrial stock increased by 84%. More than three fourths of the space added during this period was in the type of building classified as R&D (research and development; Kroll and Kimball ,1986).

As early as December 1982, vacancies in R&D space approached 20%. While this is far above average industrial or office vacancy rates, it is not necessarily a problem in rapidly growing markets. However, the Santa Clara County market on average through 1985 absorbed a net amount of about 4 million square feet of industrial space annually while adding space at more than twice this pace. The result was a vacancy rate of 36% by 1984. Building activity began to slow in 1985. The value of industrial

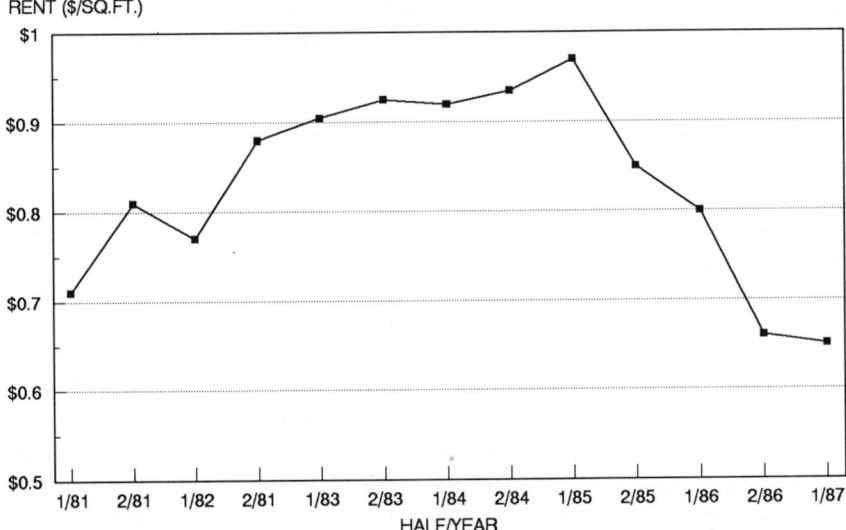

Figure 1. Average Research and Development Rents: Six Month Averages for January 1981 through June 1987.

permits dropped from a peak of $524 million in 1984 to only $122 million in 1986 (Security Pacific Bank, 1984, 1986), and vacancies dropped modestly to 32% by December 1986 (Kroll and Sturgeon, 1987). Further evidence that the market was changing was a yearly drop in the size of leases beginning in 1985 and a shift in the composition of tenants of leased space (Kroll, 1987).

Average contract rent continued to rise through mid 1985, and then dropped sharply over the next two years (Figure 1). Vacancy rates, however, indicate that problems in the market may well have preceded the mid 1985 period, when a recession hit the electronics industry. One means of addressing the discrepancies between rising rents and rising vacancy rates is to examine the difference between effective and contract rents.

The Database

Until recently, any tracking of rents in industrial markets focused on contract rents only. However, heavy leasing activity in the Santa Clara Valley and the complexity of leases being struck led a number of brokers to begin tracking the market in detail, keeping records of not only the contract rent agreed on but on such factors as rental abatements, cost of living bumps, and tenant improvement costs.

The analysis described here is based on rental agreements tracked by the San Jose office of Grubb and Ellis between 1981 and mid 1987. The Grubb and Ellis listing of lease agreements includes not only those leases in which the firm's own brokers were involved but all other lease agreements of which they were aware. This is neither a random sample of leases nor a complete listing of all lease agreements in the area. Comparison with information gathered by other brokers showed that while a great deal of overlap exists in the information, none are fully comprehensive over the time period covered. Nevertheless, the Grubb and Ellis listing provides a large sample of lease agreements over time.[3]

To make all leases as comparable as possible, only Grubb and Ellis records were used, and only triple-net leases were analyzed.[4] Leases for which only partial information was available on such factors as free rent, cost-of-living escalators, or tenant improvements were also excluded from the analysis.

Effective Rent Measures for Santa Clara Valley

There are several hypotheses on how an effective rent measure may clarify the changes in the R&D market. Two are examined closely in this analysis. The first is that, since many of the components in calculating effective rent are subject to negotiation, the effective rent may be more sensitive than the nominal rent in pointing to fundamental market changes. Thus, for example, effective rent may have peaked earlier than contract rents in Santa Clara Valley.

The second is that comparing contract rents among locations may mask some locational differences. Thus, effective rent may show a steeper (or shallower) rent gradient between peripheral and central areas in Santa Clara Valley than is indicated by contract rents. For the purposes of the location analyses, Santa Clara Valley is divided into five zones:

> Zone 1—the "service core," close to Stanford University, where R&D and high-tech linked financial and business services concentrate.
>
> Zone 2—the older "manufacturing core," where manufacturing headquarters concentrate, drawing R&D, services, and prototype production activity.

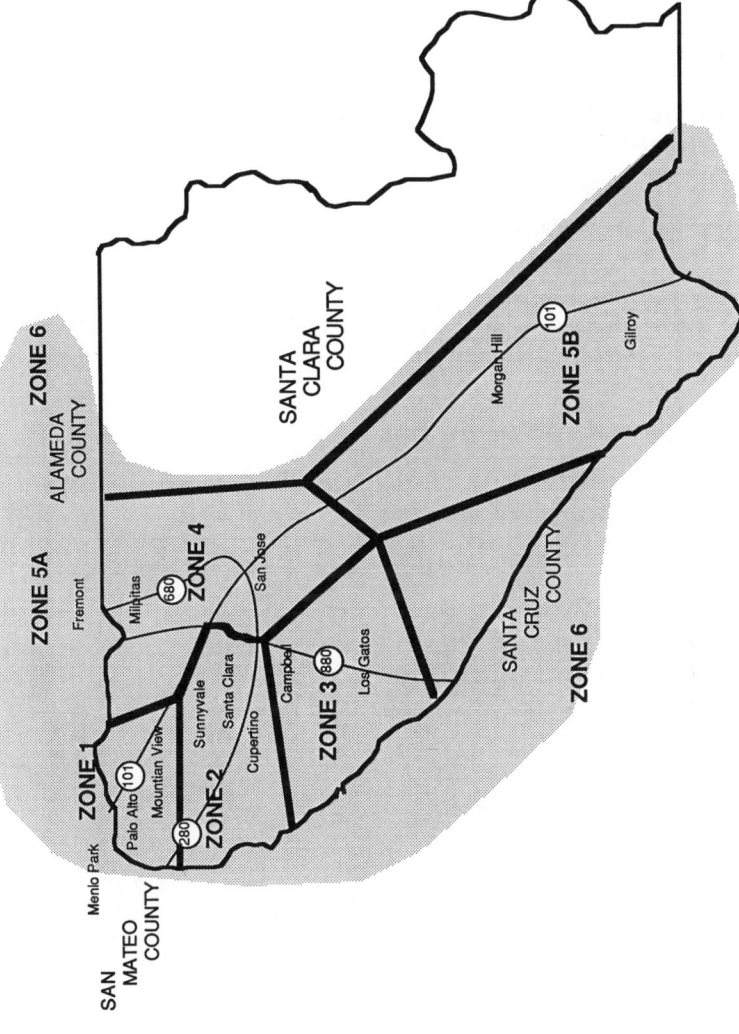

Figure 2. Zones of High Tech Activity in Santa Clara Valley.

Zone 3—the "new service center," where many non-high tech and smaller scale high-tech related services lease space.

Zone 4—the "new manufacturing center," with a combination of newer manufacturing headquarters and routine manufacturing operations.

Zone 5—the "peripheral manufacturing area," an area further from the central activity that has tried to capture spillover growth.

The zones are illustrated in Figure 2 and are described in more detail in Kroll and Kimball (1986).

Comparative Effective Rent Measures in Santa Clara Valley

Table 2 shows the major components of effective rent as analyzed for Santa Clara Valley. Differentials by year and place indicate that effective

Table 2. Lease Terms by Year and Zone

	Contract Rent	% of Leases with Bumps	Average Months Free Rent ($/sq. ft.)	Average TIs ($/sq. ft.)
Year				
1981	0.75	28.6	0.00	14.82
1982	0.87	40.5	0.40	12.49
1983	0.90	42.6	0.47	15.10
1984	0.94	57.7	1.63	12.18
1985	0.90	56.3	3.96	11.32
1986	0.73	34.6	5.65	12.06
1987	0.65	20.9	3.60	10.75
Zone				
1	0.94	47.8	1.80	9.52
2	0.85	40.4	2.35	9.35
3	0.76	38.5	4.73	11.48
4	0.82	41.6	4.24	14.40
5a	0.67	41.2	4.96	15.22
5b	0.91	50.0	2.20	18.80
Total N = 906	0.81	41.3	3.62	12.01

Source: Computations based on Grubb and Ellis lease records.

rent calculations are likely to show a different distribution of rents than is found with contract rent. For example, the percent of leases involving cost of living increases was much higher in earlier years than in later years (reflecting inflation expectations as well as changes in the marketplace), while the average period of rental abatement went from zero in 1981 to a peak of almost six months in 1986. Tenant improvement costs varied much less dramatically over time, but tended to be higher and less variable in earlier years.

All of these variations indicate that contract rent alone does not give a true reading of trends in the market. Identification of trends in factors such as free rent and cost-of-living escalation give further information on trends, but also do not give a clear indication of the net implications for the market if these trends move counter to the trends in contract rent. With an effective rent measure, the effects of each of these factors on income can be isolated and the net impacts calculated.

Free Rent and Escalation Components

Table 3 shows calculations of average rent per year, in current and constant dollars, accounting first for free rent (EF) and then for the addition of an escalation factor (EP). Contract rent, in both current and constant dollars, was highest in 1984. Using current dollar estimates, free rent left the peak at 1984, with a rental level little different from the contract rent. However, the drop off after 1984 is much steeper when free rent is considered. Adjusting for escalation as well gives a peak rent higher than the contract rent in 1984 ($0.96/sq. ft. as compared to $0.94) and a rent below the contract level in 1987 ($0.63 compared to a contract rent of $0.65).

Adjusting to constant dollars (1986 base) further changes the results. Contract rent continues to peak in 1984. However, average free rent is the same in 1983 and 1984, and rent adjusted for escalation as well peaked in 1983.

Locational differences using these two types of effective rent adjustments show little change from contract rent when analyzed in current dollars. When rents over time are adjusted for inflation, the ranking among locations remains unchanged. However, in zone 1, the most "prestigious," service oriented location, the EP calculation is $0.07 higher than the contract rent calculation, while in zone 5, a peripheral service and manufacturing location, the EP average is $0.03 below the contract rent. Thus, the spread among locations is much greater than contract rent figures would imply.

Table 3. Comparative Rent Measures Incorporating Free Rent and Escalation Factors (Average Rent, $/sq. ft. Monthly)

	Comparison A: Current $			Comparison B: Constant $		
	Contract rent	EF	EP	Contract rent	EF	EP
Year						
1981	0.75	0.75	0.77	1.00	1.00	1.03
1982	0.87	0.87	0.89	1.13	1.12	1.16
1983	0.90	0.90	0.94	1.15	1.15	1.20
1984	0.94	0.92	0.96	1.18	1.15	1.19
1985	0.90	0.83	0.91	1.09	1.02	1.11
1986	0.73	0.66	0.71	0.89	0.81	0.87
1987	0.65	0.60	0.63	0.77	0.72	0.75
Zone						
1	0.94	0.91	0.99	1.15	1.12	1.22
2	0.85	0.81	0.86	1.04	1.00	1.06
3	0.76	0.69	0.74	0.91	0.84	0.90
4	0.82	0.76	0.80	1.03	0.95	1.00
5	0.67	0.61	0.65	0.82	0.75	0.79
Total N = 906	0.81	0.76	0.80	0.99	0.93	0.99

Source: Computations based on Grubb & Ellis lease records.

Discounted Present Value and Tenant Improvements

Table 4 shows calculations taking into account the discounted value of rental streams, including both rental abatements and escalation. A second calculation subtracts the value of tenant improvements from the discounted value of the rental stream, before amortizing out payments.

Current dollar estimates show little change in the ranking of rental payments by year. However, some locational differences change sharply when tenant improvements are taken into account. For example, contract rents in zone 4 (where routine manufacturing concentrates) are close to those in zone 2 (the central agglomeration point for manufacturing headquarters) and are well above those in zone 3 (the new mixed-service area). When rents are discounted and tenant improvements taken into account, however, the ET rent in zone 4 is 28% below the zone 2 rent and 9% below zone 3 rent.

When adjusted for constant dollars, ED rents peak in 1983, while ET

Table 4. Comparative Rent Measures, Discounted and Adjusting for Tenant Improvement (Average Rent, $/sq. ft. Monthly)

	Comparison A: Current $			Comparison B: Constant $		
	Contract rent	ED	ET	Contract rent	ED	ET
Year						
1981	0.75	0.62	0.34	1.00	0.83	0.45
1982	0.87	0.76	0.51	1.13	1.00	0.66
1983	0.90	0.84	0.54	1.15	1.07	0.68
1984	0.94	0.83	0.59	1.18	1.03	0.73
1985	0.90	0.83	0.60	1.09	1.02	0.73
1986	0.73	0.67	0.44	0.89	0.81	0.54
1987	0.65	0.59	0.39	0.77	0.70	0.46
Zone						
1	0.94	0.89	0.71	1.15	1.09	0.86
2	0.85	0.78	0.60	1.04	0.96	0.73
3	0.76	0.69	0.47	0.91	0.83	0.58
4	0.82	0.73	0.43	1.03	0.90	0.54
5	0.67	0.57	0.28	0.82	0.70	0.35
Total N = 906	0.81	0.73	0.49	0.99	0.90	0.61

Source: Computations based on Grubb & Ellis lease records.

rents continue to peak in 1984. The peak rebound that is seen when tenant improvements are taken into account may reflect the fact that in later years tenants were taking over existing improvements, thus reducing the tenant improvement allowance required from the landlord.

The zonal differentiations continue to be much greater when rents are discounted and tenant improvements taken into account than they are with contract rents. Rents in zone 4, which are very close to zone 2 contract rents, are 6% below zone 2 rents when the discounted present value of the rental stream is taken into account and are 26% below zone 2 rents when tenant improvements are also considered. The differential between the lowest rent and highest rent zones is also much greater when a present value calculation and tenant improvements are considered. Zone 5 contract rents (in constant dollars) are 29% below zone 1 when measured by contract rents, 36% below zone 1 when discounted rents (ED) are used, and 59% below discounted rents minus tenant improvements (ET).

A Statistical comparison of Rent Measure

The descriptive tables of the preceeding section should give pause to market analysts trying to track changing trends. Clearly, contract rents do not tell the full story in evaluating the strength and direction of a market. Of further interest is the question of how much the use of contract rents distort statistical analyses of relationships in the market. One test of this is the comparison of regression models using contract rents and effective rent measures as dependent variables.

Table 5 compares the results of ten different linear models, one for each contract and effective rent measure, using first current dollar amounts and then constant dollar amounts.[5] The independent variables used include an employment growth measure (the ratio of average employment in the electronics industry in the most recent quarter to average employment one year previously), a supply measure (the percent of space vacant, by zone and year), and the square footage of the lease. Unfortunately, little information was available on the buildings, implying that there are certainly omitted variables.

The overall fit of the models is quite poor, with adjusted R-squares ranging from 0.10 to 0.20. This level is not surprising with a disaggregate analysis using approximately 900 observations but indicates that a complete market analysis requires more information on the characteristics of individual buildings. In all cases, the fit is slightly better for the constant dollar equation than for the current dollar equation.

The sensitivity of rent to the independent variables, as measured by elasticities, varies by the type of rent estimate used. Contract rent shows the lowest elasticities for all factors, while elasticities with respect to employment growth and vacancy rate are far higher for the estimate that includes tenant improvement allowances than for all other equations. The size of the lease is positively related to rent estimates that are not sensitive to the time value of money (contract rent, EF, and EP) but are completely insignificant for the time-adjusted rent estimates (ED and ET).

The results suggest that care should be used in interpreting models based on contract rent. The use of contract rent in this case underestimates sensitivity to key supply and demand factors, and may overestimate the importance of some other lease characteristics.

Implications for Market Analysis

This analysis has different implications depending on the use to which rent information is put. For analysts attempting to understand the current

Table 5. Analysis of Alternative Rent Measures

Dependent variable	Independent variables—estimated coefficient					Adjusted R-square	Estimated elasticities[1]		
	Electronics emp. growth	Vacancy rate by zone	Square feet leased		Constant		Electronics emp. growth	Vacancy rate by zone	Square feet leased
Contract rent									
Current $s	1.03419 (9.829)	−0.002827 (−4.651)	7.18828E-07 (2.140)		−0.151418 (−1.535)	0.116	1.262	−0.103	0.029
Constant $s	1.388173 (10.762)	−0.003511 (−4.711)	1.05810E-06 (2.569)		−0.304881 (−2.521)	0.137	1.377	−0.104	0.034
EF									
Current $s	1.25368 (12.474)	−0.003646 (−6.279)	9.08620E-07 (2.832)		−0.399768 (−4.242)	0.178	1.633	−0.141	0.039
Constant $s	1.652147 (13.346)	−0.004521 (−6.321)	1.28842E-06 (3.260)		−0.603548 (−5.200)	0.199	1.748	−0.142	0.045
EP									
Current $s	1.192572 (11.476)	−0.00365 (−6.079)	8.35448E-07 (2.518)		−0.288457 (−2.518)	0.155	1.458	−0.133	0.033
Constant $s	1.582299 (12.364)	−0.004508 (−6.096)	1.20195E-06 (2.942)		−0.472852 (−3.941)	0.176	1.573	−0.133	0.039
ED									
Current $s	1.010693 (9.504)	−0.003449 (−5.614)	−3.81002E-08 (−0.122)		−0.162345 (−1.628)	0.102	1.363	−0.138	NA
Constant $s	1.345874 (10.324)	−0.004244 (−5.634)	8.23354E-08 (0.198)		−0.305104 (−2.496)	0.117	1.477	−0.139	NA
ET									
Current $s	1.010148 (9.201)	−0.005952 (−9.383)	−4.75696E-07 (−1.357)		−0.306353 (−2.976)	0.131	2.000	−0.351	NA
Constant $s	1.31072 (9.776)	−0.007327 (−9.458)	4.94764E-07 (−1.156)		−0.447233 (−3.558)	0.139	2.110	−0.351	NA

[1] Estimated elasticities are calculated as the estimated coefficient divided by the ratio of the average for the dependent variable to the average for the independent variable.
NA = not applicable—estimated coefficient insignificant in equation.

direction of the market, the rent differentials calculated earlier are quite important.

These calculations show the degree to which contract rents may distort the understanding of trends in the market. First, contract rents made the market appear stronger than it actually was in 1984, with rents continuing to rise, despite growing vacancies. The addition of free rent alone, however, to the calculation, may exaggerate the weakness of the market in the other direction. A number of lease agreements show the owner trying to recoup rental give-aways in later years of the lease.

A second important point is that lease adjustments were not made evenly across all locations. More peripheral areas, with higher vacancies and greater competition for tenants, appear to have made far less advantageous deals for the landlord than the centrally located core of the market. Thus, when factors such as free rent, timing of payments, and tenant improvements are taken into account, differentials among areas may be far greater than they originally appeared.

For analysts attempting to understand the underlying factors affecting the market, the differential results of the econometric analysis suggest that some adjustments to contract rent are necessary. Where full information is not available to allow a complete calculation (ED or ET), it would at least be important to adjust for free rent and tenant improvement allowances, either in the estimate of rent or as additional independent variables. Contract rents will work best as an estimate of effective rent where the lease agreements are from a short time interval and for a homogeneous market area.

Information about free rent and cost of living bumps can illustrate any mismatches among contract rents and other costs over time or by location. The advantage of an effective rent calculation is that it gives a "net" assessment of the impacts of these different factors on the overall income from the lease.

Notes

1. Adding the AAA differential to the treasury note rate gives a time-sensitive interest rate that is somewhat higher than the very secure treasury note investment. We take this approach to reflect the fact that real estate was considered a higher yield but riskier investment.

2. The Livingston Index is available only at six month intervals. Because this index appears to change gradually, the intervening months are calculated through interpolation.

3. The listings from different brokerage firms differed significantly in the types of information provided. Some reported free rent as a lump sum payment, rather than by num-

ber of months. Others might note a "cost" escalator, without giving the actual level or index used. The Grubb and Ellis set was by far the most detailed in reporting lease conditions.

4. Most lease agreements were triple-net, that is, the tenant remained responsible for the operating costs of the property, such as utilities. Gross leases, in which all costs were included in the rental payment, were excluded from the analysis.

5. Ideally, we would like to estimate a system of equations as suggested in Rosen (1984). Data limitations make this impractical for the current study. The model suggested is a crude reduced for equation that resembles a hedonic price model without the variables that describe the building.

References

Barnes, Kenneth A. "Rental Concessions and Value." *Appraisal Journal* (April 1986), 167–76.

Brennan, Thomas P. Roger E. Cannaday, and Peter F. Colwell. "Office Rent in the Chicago CBD." *AREUEA Journal* 12 (Summer 1984), 243–60.

Cannaday, Roger E. and Han Bin Kang. "Estimation of Market Rent for Office Space." *The Real Estate Appraiser and Analyst* (Summer 1984), 67–72.

Corgel, John B. and Ronald C. Rogers. "Calculating Effective Rent for Leases with Landlord Concessions." *Real Estate Review* 16, 2 (Summer 1986), 59–61.

Hekman, John S. "Rental Price Ajustment and Investment in the Office Market." *AREUEA Journal* 13 (Winter 1985), 32–47.

Kroll, Cynthia A. "The Tenant Base for R&D Space: Responses in a Changing Market." Working Paper No. 87-122. Center For Real Estate and Urban Economics. University of California at Berkeley, January 1987.

Kroll, Cynthia A. and Linda M. Kimball. The Santa Clara Valley R&D Dilemma: The Real Estate Industry and High Tech Growth. Working Paper No. 87-122. Center For Real Estate and Urban Economics, University of California at Berkeley, October 1986.

Kroll, Cynthia A. and Timothy Sturgeon. "Issues in Measuring California's Industrial Building Activity." Quarterly Report. Center for Real Estate and Urban Economics. University of California at Berkeley, 1987, 2, pp. 1–4.

Nelson, Kristin. "San Francisco Office Space Inventory." Working Paper No. 80-20. Center for Real Estate and Urban Economics. University of California at Berkeley, November 1980.

Rosen, Kenneth T. "Toward a Model of the Office Building Sector." *AREUEA Journal* 12 (Summer 1984), 261–9.

Sears, Cecil E. "Has Excess Capital Caused Overbuilding?" *Urban Land* 45 (April 1986), 10–14.

Shilling, James D. C.F. Sirmans, and John B. Corgel. "Price Adjustment Process for Rental Office Space." *Journal of Urban Economics*. Forthcoming.

INDEX

AAA corporate bond rates, 469, 470
Absorption rates, 206, 222, 225, 226, 240, 263
Academic real estate, 133–141, *see also*, Real estate discipline
  curricular issues in, 137–138
  doctoral programs in, 137, 138
  external funding in, 137, 140
  industry gap and, 109–113
  lack of theoretical work in, 136–137
  political battles in, 137
Access variables, in retail shopp competition, 9, 312–314
Adaptive expectations model of inflation, 435
Adjusted purchase price, 174–175, *see also* Inflation-adjusted sales price
Advertising, 314–315
AFA, *see* American Finance Association
Aggregate regression, 178
Alaska, 420
Allocation method, 175
Alpine Lakes Management Act (ALMA), 151, 154, 172
Alpine Lakes Wilderness Area, *see* Wilderness appraisal
Alternative identification, 20, 22
Alternative methods to value, 95
Alternative use determination, 152–154, 155–157
Amelia Island Plantation, 228
Amenities, 9, 317, 352

Amenity dollars, 221–222
American Finance Association (AFA), 112–113
American Institute of Real Estate Appraisers, 242, 243, 250
American Real Estate and Urban Economics Association (AREUEA), 108, 112–113
American Real Estate Society (ARES), 3, 110, 112–113
American Society of Landscape Architects, 150
Amortization, 438, 469, 476
Analog approach, *see* Customer spotting
Analysis, in decision making, 21, 23
Andrews, Richard B., 149
Apartment complexes, 260, 269–283
Applied imagination, 212
Appraisal, 2, 5–7, 92, 190, 204, *see also* Appraisal reform; Mass appraisal; Wilderness appraisal
Appraisal of 25 N. Pinckney, The: A Demonstration Case for Contemporary Appraisal Methods (Graaskamp), 150, 244
Appraisal of Real Estate, 242, 243
Appraisal reform, 3, 7, 237–254
  areas of blame and, 245–247
  recommendations for, 247–248
  specific problems and, 243–245
Appraisal theory, 151, 155, 238
Appraiser's comparables model, 263–264

483

Appreciation
  in historic rehabilitation, 403, 404–406, 408
  of owner-occupied housing, 426, 439
Appreciation theory, 69, 72
A priori analysis, 387, 388, 392, 396, 398, 407
A priori information, 187, 188–196, 199–200
ARES, *see* American Real Estate Society
AREUEA, *see* American Real Estate and Urban Economics Association
Asking rents, 463, 464
Atlanta, Georgia, 224, 229, 231
Atmosphere, shopping, 316
Attribute-matching method, 175–176, 178
Austin, Texas (apartment complexes in), 260, 269–283
Australia, 243
Austrian classical economics, 71
Austrian marginalist theories, 69
Average market forecast model, 263, 264
Average price, 426
Azul Pacifico Inc. v. City of Los Angeles, 349

Babcock, F.M., 240, 241
Baltimore, Maryland, 217
Banks, 239, 245
Bargaining, 241
Barnard Report, 7, 245
Bayesian estimators, 192
Beach waterpark, 219
Berlin Research Corp., 354
Big Canyon residential development, 219
Binary filters, 328–329
Biomedical Computer Program, UCLA, 335
Birmingham, Alabama, 220
Bivariate sensitivity, 392
Black box effect, 51, 212, 213
Black Diamond Ranch, 219
Boiler plate, 260, 264
Bok, Derek, 126
BOMA, *see* Building Owners and Managers Association
Boston, Massachusetts, 230
Boston Harbor, 221, 226
Broker misrepresentation, *see* Misrepresentation

Builders/developers, 33, 53–54, 57, 140, 206
Building Owners and Managers Association (BOMA), 464
Bundle of Rights, 348
Bureau of Indian Affairs, 175
Business administration paradigms, 81–82
Business schools, 71–72
Business Week, 26

Calabasas Village mobile home park, 355
California, 221, *see also* Ownership transfer; specific areas of
Canada, 38, 243, *see also* specific areas of
Capital, 27, 56, 71, 79, 204
  changing access to, 35–39
  human, 71
  international flow of, 73, 74
  in spatial economics, 72
  weighted average cost of, 438
Capital asset pricing model, 107
Capital budget, 206
Capital costs, 211–212, 215
Capital formulation, 74
Capital gains, 427
Capital gains taxes
  historic rehabilitation and, 403, 404, 405, 406, 408
  owner-occupied housing and, 428–429, 438
Capitalization, 240, 248
Capital markets, 28, 29, 46–47, 49, 73
Capture rates
  consumer surveys and, 300
  customer spotting and, 291, 292, 294, 295, 302
  four-square design and, 8, 265, 266, 267–268, 271, 274–275, 278, 279, 286
Carnegie Foundation for the Advancement of Learning, 126, 127, 134
Casa Grande mobile home park, 354
Cascades shopping center, 214, 223
Cash-flow models, 51, 208, 211, 214, 215, 238, 240
Census statistics, 111, 333, 341, 435, 439
Centers of attraction, 330
Central Place Theory
  logistic response function estimation and, 9, 325–331, 335, 342
  retail shopping competition and, 308, 311

INDEX

Charlotte, North Carolina, 228
Chesterbrook office development, 221
Chicago, Illinois, 224
Choice sets, 317–318
Choice under uncertainty, *see* Uncertainty, choice under
Chow test, 319, 383
Cimmarron planned unit development, 214–215
Classical economics, 71
Coase theorem, 418
Cobb-Douglas production function, 119
Coefficient of multiple determination, 367
Coefficients of variation, 335
Coldspring phased housing development, 217–219
Columbia, Wisconsin, 300
Combined solutions, 214
Comingled funds, 38
Commercial property markets, 28, 29
Communism, demise of, 26
Comparable ranking, 176–177
Competing destinations model, 330
Competitive context, 21, 23
Competitive market theory, 79–80, 93–94, 110
Competitive prices, 239–240
Component diagrams, 214
Composite diagrams, 214
Composite solutions, 212
Computers, 21, 139
  cash-flow models and, 238
  financial analysis and, 139
  real estate decisions and, 21, 23, 48, 50–52, 55
Condemnation, 93
Conditional logit analysis, 330
Constant conditions model, 263, 264
Construction costs, 219
Construction debt, 211
Construction lenders, 204
Construction period equity investors, 204
Consumer choice models
  property rights and, 82
  retail shopping competition and, 9, 311–317
Consumer Price Index (CPI), 24, 359, 368, 435, 465, 467
Consumer profiles, 206

Consumer surveys, 8, 290, 296–304
  applications of, 297–301
  description of, 296
Contact diaries, 115, 116
Contextual fit, 222–223
Contract rents, 12, 463, 464–465, 466, 470, 471, 472, 475, 478, 480
Contributory negligence, 419
Coquitham regional shopping center, 219, 229–230
Cost approach, 158, 185, 200, 239–240
Cost efficiency, 216
Cost intensity, 215
Costs
  capital, 211–212, 215
  construction, 219
  hard, 211–212, 214, 215–216
  land, 211–212, 214
  mass appraisal and, 187–188
  price vs., 240
  replacement, 239–240
  soft, 211–212
  sunk, 114
  transaction, *see* Transaction costs
  transportation, 89, 90–91, 326, 352
  user, *see* User costs
Cost transfer, 215
CPI, *see* Consumer Price Index
Credit unions, 245
CRISP tapes, 110–111
Cultural Schemata, 227–228
Current Population Reports, 429, 430
Customer spotting, 8, 290–296, 302–303, 341
  applications of, 291–292
  description of, 290–291
  problems with, 292–295
Customer surveys, *see* Consumer surveys

Databases, 49, 50
  effective rent determined with, 471–472
  logistic response function estimation and, 331–333
  macro, 112
  micro, 112
  REUER and, 110–111, 112, 113
  wilderness appraisal and, 151, 155, 170–171
Data splitting, 185

Debt
  construction, 211
  mortgage, 206, 211
  owner-occupied housing and, 429, 437–438
  PHYS-FI model and, 211, 212, 215
Decision criteria, 20, 22
Decision formulation, 20, 22
Decision implementation, 19
Decisions, *see* Real estate decisions
Decision structure, 19
Decision systems, 46–47, 48
Deductive analysis, *see also* Inductive analysis
  PHYS-FI model and, 204, 206, 209, 210, 213, 232
  REUER and, 110, 117, 118–119, 120, 123, 124
Demand factors, 115, *see also* Supply factors
  consumer surveys and, 302, 303
  customer spotting and, 294, 295, 296
  four-square design and, 259, 262, 263, 266, 279, 282, 286
  historical perspective on, 24
  land use succession paradigms and, 90
  PHYS-FI model and, 206
  real estate decisions and, 42, 43, 58
  real estate process paradigms and, 79
  urban land economic land use paradigms and, 87
Demographic data, 46–47, 48–49
Denver, Colorado, 231
Department stores, 313–314
Depreciation, 404, 411, 439
Depreciation taxes, 405
Deregulation, 35, 39
Descriptive studies, 122–123
Design differentials, 213, 225–232
Design economy research, 209
Design with nature, 212
Detroit, Michigan, 226
Developers, *see* Builders/developers
Developmental emphasis, 30–31, 32
Diminished value, 415–416
Direct capitalization, 248
Distance
  in loglstic response function estimation, 330–331, 335, 338
  retail shopping competition and, 309, 312

Donaldson, Gordon, 141
Downtown shopping, *see* Retail shopping competition
Due diligence, 18, 52, 53, 54
Durbin-Watson statistic, 367

Eagle Bay condominium project, 227, 228
EBA, *see* Extreme bounds analysis
Ecological biology, 123–124
Ecological units, 330
Economic data, 46–47, 48–49
Economic/investment environment, 28, 29
Economic Recovery Tax Act (ERTA), 383 430
Economics
  classical, 71
  institutional, 69–70, 75–76, 77
  land, *see* Land economics
  of misrepresentation, 417–420
  neo-classical, 69, 71, 72, 75, 77
  real estate discipline and, 69–70
  REUER and, 107, 110
  spatial, 72–73, 84
  urban, 70, 72, 79, 107, 108, 114, 118
"Economics of Architecture and Urban Design" (Vandell), 203
Effective rent, 11–12, 463–480
  adjusted to present discounted value, 467–468, 476–477
  contract rents vs., 12, 463, 464–465, 466, 470, 471, 472, 475, 478, 480
  rent abatement and, 12, 463, 465, 466, 467, 470, 472, 475, 476, 480
  rent escalation and, 12, 466, 467, 475, 476
  tenant improvements and, 12, 466, 469, 470, 472, 475, 476–477, 480
Efficient market hypothesis (EMH), 107, 108, 110
  unexplained empirical results in, 113, 114–115
  value paradigms and, 92–93
Ellis, Harold, Jr., 73
Ellwood model, 95
Embarcadero Cove, 220
EMH, *see* Efficient market hypothesis
Eminent domain, 154
England, 243
Entrepreneurs, 18, 19, 32, 44–45, 71
Environment, 29, 212, 213, 216–221
  real estate, 27–33

INDEX 487

Environmental context, 20, 23
Environmental corridors, 212
Equilibrium, 77–78
Equity, 45
   owner-occupied housing and, 428, 429, 437–438
   PHYS-FI model and, 206, 211, 212, 215
   real estate development process and, 204
   sources of, 30–31, 32
ERTA, *see* Economic Recovery Tax Act
Euclidian distance model, 175, 176–177
Europe, 38
Extended Huff Model, 310, 311, 319
Extreme bounds analysis (EBA), 124–125

Factor analysis, 335
Fair market value, 154, 179
Falsification, theory of, 119
Fannie Mae, 245
FDIC, *see* Federal Deposit Insurance Corporation
Feasibility analysis, 5–7, 91, 238, 240 260
   forecasting deficiency in, 261
   logistic response function estimation and, 342
   market area delineation and, 8
   PHYS-FI model and, 204
   property rights and, 83
   risk management in, 80
Federal Deposit Insurance Corporation (FDIC), 245, 250
Federal Home Loan Bank Board (FHLBB), 247–248, 430, 439
Federal Housing Authority, 240, 245
Federal Savings and Loan Insurance Corporation, 250
FHLBB, *see* Federal Home Loan Bank Board
Fiduciary assest management, 34
Finance
   REUER and, 107, 110–111
   revolution in, 135–136
Finance theory, 73, 76
Financial analysis, 139
Financial control, 30–31, 32–33
Financial engineering, 35, 39
Financial Management Association (FMA), 112–113, 141
Financial management rate of return, 95
Financial theory paradigms, 83–84

FIRREA of 1989, 249
Florida, 220, 222, 224, 228, *see also* specific areas of
FMA, *see* Financial Management Association
Fond du Lac, Wisconsin, 300
Ford Commission, 134
Foreign investors, 25, 226
Foreman, Robert L., 350, 354, 368
Forest Service, U.S., 151, 161, 162, 171, 179
Formal theory, 69, 71
Form schemata, 230–232
Four-square design, 7–8, 259–287
   forecasting advantages of, 8, 261–265, 266, 268–269, 270, 278–279, 282–283
   steps used in, 264–266
F-ratio, 367
Fraudulent misrepresentation, 414
Freddie Mac, 245
Free rent, *see* Rent abatement
Friedman, Milton, 118, 119
Functional efficiency, 216
Fundamental analysis, 92
Fundamentals of Real Estate Development The, (ULI), 149

General equilibrium model, 85, 86
Generalized Sensitivity Analysis (GSA), 10, 382
   behavior specification in, 388, 396–399
   in historic rehabilitation, 393–407
   model building in, 386–387, 393–394
   Monte Carlo simulation in, *see* under Monte Carlo simulation
   multivariate sensitivity of, 390–392, 405, 406
   univariate sensitivity of, 388–389, 390, 391, 392, 403, 405
Genetic models, 89
Geographic information system (GIS), 152, 163, 165, 170, 171, 179
Geographic orientation, 33–34
Geographic scope, 30–31, 32
Geography journals, 115–116
Georgia, 220, *see also* specific areas of
GIS, *see* Geographic information system
Glass-box design theory, 212, 213
Goodness of fit, 183, 184, 189, 196
Gourmet Fair, 226–227

Graaskamp, James A., 1–3, 4, 15, 17, 27, 52, 53, 60, 133–134, 204, 216
  on appraisal, 5–7
  on appraisal reform, 237–254, *see also* Appraisal reform
  on appreciation theory, 72
  on economics, 69
  on feasibility analysis, 91, 238, 260
  on most fitting/most probable use models, 86, 87
  on property rights, 82
  on real estate process paradigms, 77, 78–80
  on REUER, 108–109, 112, 113, 120
  on risk management, 81
  on space-time to money-time equation, 75, 76
  on wilderness appraisal, 149–151
Graaskamp-Sharkawy multidisciplinary development planning model, 206–209
Gravity models, 8, 91, 289, 311, 327, *see also* Reilly's Law of Retail Gravitation
Great Depression, 24, 239
Great Lakes Regional Commission, 206
Grubb & Ellis, 73, 472
GSA, *see* Generalized Sensitivity Analysis
Gulf of Mexico, 230

Hall v. City of Santa Barbara, 349
Hard costs, 211–212, 214, 215–216
Hardware, *see* Computers
HASE, *see* Housing allowance supply experiment
Hawthorne study, 68–69
HBU concept, *see* Highest and Best Use concept
Hedonic pricing models, 115, 190, 359, 360, 366, 370
Hedonic regression, 107
Hedonic rent, 464
Highest and Best Use (HBU) concept, 85–86, 87, 179
Hilton Head, 230
Historic rehabilitation, 10, 381–411, *see also* Generalized sensitivity analysis
Home improvement, 184, *see also* Tenant improvements
Homer Hoyt Institute, 110, 113

Horseshoe Bend residential development, 220, 229
Housing affordability, 11, 441–42, 444–445, 447
Housing allowance supply experiment (HASE), 122
Housing characteristics, 183–184
Housing finance, 30–31, 33
Housing subsidies, 33
Huff Model, 327, 328
  extended, 310, 311, 319
  in retail shopping competition, 9, 307, 308–309, 311, 312, 314, 319, 320
Human capital, 71

IBM Tower, 231–232
Ideal concept, 214
Ideal conditions model, 263, 264
IDM, *see* Interactive Design/Marketing Model
Illinois, 292, 294, 297, *see also* specific areas of
IMSL Fortran subroutines, 187
Income capitalization approach, 158
Income taxes
  historic rehabilitation and, 403, 404, 405, 406
  owner-occupied housing services price and, 430
Inductive analysis, *see also* Deductive analysis
  PHYS-FI model and, 206, 208, 209, 210, 213, 215, 216, 232
  regional science and, 121
  REUER and, 117, 118–119, 120, 121
  urban land economics and, 120
Inequality-restricted least squares (IRLS) models, 6, 184–187, 200
  a priori information and, 188–196 out-of-sample performance and, 196–199
Inflation
  adaptive expectations model of, 435
  effective rent and, 468, 470
  four-square design and, 267
  historical perspective on, 24
  owner-occupied housing services price and, 11, 428, 429, 435–437, 439, 442, 447, 454–456
  paradigm transition and, 117–118

INDEX 489

real estate decisions and, 25, 32, 35
unemployment and, 119
Inflation-adjusted sales prices, 358, 359, 361, 364–366, 370, 371
Innocent misrepresentation, 414
Institutional economics, 69–70, 75–76, 77
Institutionalization, 34
Insurance companies, 35, 239, 249
Interactive Design/Marketing Model (IDM), 76, 77
Interest rates, *see also* Mortgage interest rates
   effective rent and, 470
   owner-occupied housing services price and, 11, 426, 437, 447
Internal rate of return (IRR), 240
   four-square design and, 283
   in historic rehabilitation, 388, 394, 396, 398, 399–403, 404, 405, 406, 410
   modified, 95
Intrinsic value, 92, 95
Investement/valuation technology, 46–47, 48
Investment analysis, 79, 80, 83, 204
Investors
   construction period equity, 204
   foreign, 25, 226
   long-term equity, 204
   real estate decisions and, 19, 35–39, 54
   risk management and, 81
IRLS models, *see* Inequality-restricted least squares models
IRR, *see* Internal rate of return
Itemized deductions, 433

Japan, 38

Kelley Blue Book calculation method, 350–351, 361, 368
Key money, 351
Kolmogorov-Smirnov two-sample test, 389
Kozinski, Judge, 349

Labor, 71
Lagged weights, 435, 437
Lake Ozark, Missouri, 225
La Mer condominium complex, 230
Land, 71, 79
Land costs, 211–212, 214

Land economics, 67, 69–70, 74, 75, 77, *see also* Urban land economics
   paradigms unique to, 85–96
   property rights and, 82
   risk management and, 81
Land market analysis, 87
Landmark Research, 244
Land use paradigms, 85
Land use succession paradigms, 89–90
Law of the Single Price, 119
Lea, Robert M., 350, 354, 368
Leases
   effective rent and, 12, 463, 464, 465–470, 469, 471, 472
   PHYS-FI model and, 214
Lecanto, California, 219
Lenders
   appraisal reform and, 239–241, 244, 245–246, 247–248
   construction, 204
   permanent, 204
   PHYS-FI model and, 206
Leopold, Aldo, 161
Levi's Plaza, 223
Liability rules, 414–417
   strict, 10–11, 414, 418–420
License laws, 416
Limited partnerships, 38, 52
Linear additive model, 309–310
Livingston index, 470
Loan-to-market-value ratio, 437, 438
Loan-to-value ratios, 33, 212, 240, 438
Location
   changing perspective on, 42–43, 45
   office market literature on, 116
   ownership transfer and, 367–368
   retail shopping competition and, 9, 312–315, 319–320
Location theory, 325
Logistic response function estimation, 9, 325–342
   logit coefficients in, 338–340, 341, 342
   logit transformation in, 333–335
   in supermarkets, *see* Supermarket shopping
Logit coefficients, 338–340, 341, 342
Logit model, 310–311
Logit transformations, 333–335
Longboat Key Club, 220

Long-term equity investors, 204
Los Amigos mobile home park, 349–350, 355
Los Angeles, California, 223
  ownership transfer in, 349–350, 354–355, 356, 358, 359, 360, 361, 363, 365, 366, 369
  retail shopping competition in, 317–320
Los Angeles Rent Stabilization Ordinance, 349, 370
Luce choice system, 308, 328
Lutherville, Maryland, 231

Macro databases, 112
Macro level, 86
  four-square design and, 7, 8, 261–264, 265
  real estate process paradigms in, 78–79
  spatial market structure paradigms in, 90
Madison, Wisconsin (supermarkets in), *see* Supermarket shopping
Maintenance rates, 441, 457–458
Malibu, California, 355
Manitowoc Marina, 292, 293, 294, 295, 300
Marginal price, 426–427
Marginal tax rates, 429–433, 446, 451–453
Marginal user costs, 442, 459–461
Marina harbor development, *see* Market area delineation
Mariner Sands planned recreational community, 222
Marketability analysis, 204, 206
Market absorption, *see* Absorption rates
Market analysis, 79, 289, 290
  effective rent and, 478–480
  forecasting deficiency in, 261
  four-square design for, *see* Four-square design
  land, 87
  mortgage, 72
  PHYS-FI model and, 204, 206
  problems in, 290
  property rights and, 83
  situs paradigms and, 88
Market analysis paradigms, 90–91
Market approach, 185, 200
Market area delineation, 8, 289–304, *see also* Consumer surveys; Customer spotting

Market choices, 82
Market Comp program, 172
Market force equalization, 173–174
Market risk premium, 437, 438
Market structure, 79–80
Market transactions, 172–173
Market value, 247
  fair, 154, 179
  Highest and Best Use concept and, 85–86
  of mobile homes, 350
  most probable price vs., 241–242, 250
  PHYS-FI model and, 212, 225
  user costs vs., 425
  wilderness appraisal and, 154, 179
Market value paradigms, 93–94
Marshall and Swift cost analysis, 248
Marshallian theory, 69, 239
Martin Luther King shopping center, 222
Mason, Ohio, 219
Mass appraisal, 6, 183–200, 242
  a priori information and, 187, 188–196, 199–200
  Monte Carlo simulation and, 6, 184, 186, 189, 191–196, 198
Master matrix strategy, 266–267, 270, 271, 278, 279
Matrix analysis, 210, 214, 215
MCI, *see* Multiplicative competitive interaction model
McMillan Place, 228
Means Home Improvement Cost Guide, 188
Mean squared error, 184
Memphis, Tennessee, 214
Merchantile Wharf, 230
Metropolitan Housing Characteristics, 270, 278
MFU model, *see* Most fitting use model
MHRL, *see* Mobile Home Residency Law
Micro databases, 112
Micro level, 86, 87
  four-square design and, 7, 8, 261–264, 265
  real estate process paradigms in, 78, 79
  situs paradigms in, 88
  space-time paradigms in, 76
  spatial market structure paradigms in, 90
Milwaukee, Wisconsin, 294, 300
Minimum yield, 149

INDEX

Minneapolis, Minnesota, 222, 228
Minnesota, 292, 297
Misrepresentation, 10–11, 413–420
  economics of, 417–420
  fraudulent, 414
  innocent, 414
  liability rules and, see Liability rules
  negligent, 10–11, 414, 415–416, 418–420
MKTCOMP program, 6, 175, 177, 241
MLS, see Multiple Listing Service
Mobile Home Residency Law (MHRL), 9–10, 347–348, 370
Mobile homes, 9–10, 347–379, see also Ownership transfer
  amenities of, 352
  benefits of, 351
  ocean view/beach access and, 352, 354, 355, 356, 358, 360, 361, 363, 365, 368–369
  tenant improvements to, 352
  turnover rates in, 358
Modified internal rate of return (IRR), 95
Money-time dimension, 4, 75–76, 80, 81, 82, 83, 84, 88
Monopolies, 80, 91, 114
  natural, 79–80
Monte Carlo simulation
  GSA and, 10, 382, 387, 392–393, 394–396
  mass appraisal and, 6, 184, 186, 189, 191–196, 198
Mortgage-backed securities, 24, 33, 245
Mortgage debt, 206, 211
Mortgage defaults, 119
Mortgage-equity analysis, 139
Mortgage interest rates
  four-square design and, 283
  owner-occupied housing services price and, 428, 430, 439–440, 442, 447
Mortgage market analysis, 72
Mortgage markets, 114, 115
Most fitting use (MFU) model, 86–87
Most probable buyer model, 154, 157–158, 242
Most probable price model, 94–95
  appraisal reform and, 7, 241–243, 250
  for mobile homes, 350
  in wilderness appraisal, 154, 158

Most probable use (MPU) model, 86–87
  appraisal reform and, 242
  in wilderness appraisal, 152–154, 157, 172–173
MRA, see Multiple regression analysis
Multicollinearity
  GSA and, 392, 406
  mass appraisal and, 183–184, 186, 188–190, 191, 200
  ownership transfer and, 363–366
Multiple Listing Book, 188
Multiple Listing Service (MLS), 111, 188, 189, 190, 197
Multiple regression analysis (MRA), 178
  ownership transfer and, 359–360, 361, 363–365, 366, 370
  of retail shopping competition, 311, 319
Multiplicative competitive interaction model (MCI), 309–310
Multivariate sensitivity, of GSA, 390–392, 405, 406

Nakanishi, Cooper, and Kassarjian (NCK) estimation procedure, 310
Naples, Florida, 226
National Association of Realtors (NAR), 11, 67, 108, 249–250, 426, 441, 442, 447
National Forest System, 162
National Office Market Report, 464
National Park Service, 175
National Register of Historic Places, 383
National Wildlife Services, 175
Natural monopolies, 79–80
NCK estimation procedure, see Nakanishi, Cooper, and Kassarjian estimation procedure
Negligent misrepresentation, 10–11, 414, 415–416, 418–420
Neighborhood life cycle, 89
Neo-classical economics, 69, 71, 72, 75, 77
Newport Beach, California, 219
New York, 227
Nondisclosure, 416

Oak Forest mobile home park, 350, 354, 355
Objectives, 20, 22
Ocala, Florida, 214

Office market literature, 108, 113, 115–116
Office Network, 464
Office space
 change in need for, 43–44, 48
 effective rent and, see Effective rent
 four-square design and, 269
Offshore investments, 38, 49
Oligopolistic models, 80, 91
OLS models, see Ordinary least squares models
One-factor perspective, 71
Operating income, 211, 213, 348
Opportunity assessment, 19–20
Opportunity initiation, 19
Opportunity sites, 215
Options pricing model, 107, 115
Opus 2 industrial/office park, 228
Ordinary least squares (OLS) models
 GSA vs., 392, 393
 mass appraisal and, 6, 184–186, 187, 188–199, 200
Organizational context, 20, 23
Organizational focus, 30–31, 32
Out-of-sample performance, 6, 183, 184, 185, 186, 187, 196–199, 200
Overbuilding, 24, 29, 466
Owner-occupied housing services price, 11, 425–461
 by income class and household type, 426–427
 maintenance rates in, 441, 4S7–458
Ownership transfer, 9–10, 347–379, see also Mobile homes
 data used in analysis of, 354–358
 dependent variables in, 360, 364–365, 367
 economic transfer and loss argument in, 348
 independent variables in, 360, 361–363, 367
 legal argument for, 348–349
 nonlinear relationship adjustments and, 367
 nonlocation variables in, 368–369
 research design for, 359–360

Packet of functions, 73–74
Pack River Management Company (PRMC), 151, 155, 161, 170, 173, 175

Paradigms, 74–96, 107–127
 business administration, 81–82
 defined, 107
 development of new, 120–126
 efficiency and exclusion in, 116–117
 financial theory, 83–84
 Highest and Best Use, see Highest and Best Use concept
 land use, 85
 land use succession, 89–90
 market analysis, 90–91
 market value, 93–94
 most fitting use, $_2$ 86–87
 most probable price, see Most probable price model
 most probable use, see Most probable use model
 property rights, 77, 82–83
 real estate process, 77–80, 81, 86, 88, 95
 risk management, 80–81, 82
 situs, 88, 90
 solvency, 95–96
 space-time, see Space-time paradigms
 spatial, 88–89
 spatial market structure, 90–91
 unique to real estate/land economics, 85–96
 urban land economic land use, 87
 urban structure, 88–89
 value, 91–93
Paradigm transition, 116, 117–118
Paradise Cove mobile home park, 355, 358
Pareto optimality, 417
Parking, 9, 313
Park Service, U.S., 383
Parkwood building, 229
Partial correlation coefficients, 365
Partial solutions, 212, 214
Partitioned Newton-Raphson Algorithm, 328
Partnerships, 38, 52
Passive activity regulations, 403, 404, 405, 406, 410
Pattern language, 212
Payback period, 240
Pension funds, 18, 25, 38, 49, 111–112
Pension Real Estate Association (PREA), 3
Perimeter Mall, 229–230

Permanent lenders, 204
Personal analytic tools, 46–47, 48
PGA National, 224
Philadelphia, Pennsylvania, 221
Phillips curve, 119
Phoenix, Arizona, 214–215
PHYS-FI model, 6–7, 203–232
  generating and grouping concepts in, 210, 215–216
  generating and grouping observations in, 210, 213–215
  grouping classes, categories, and concepts in, 210, 216
  trade-offs, defining classes of, 210–211
  trade-offs, identifying categories of, 210, 211–213
Placement value, 350
Plattage/plottage, 95
Point Dume mobile home park, 355, 358
Poisson probabilistic regression model, 328
Popper, Karl, 118, 119
Population density, 9, 44, 338
Porfolio theory, 55
Portfolio research, 111–112
Port Washington Marina, 292–294, 294
PREA, *see* Pension Real Estate Association
Presidential Towers, 224
Price, 240
  adjusted purchase, *see* Adjusted purchase price
  attribute-matching method in, 175–176, 178
  average, 426
  capital asset model of, 107
  competitive, 239–240
  cost vs., 240
  deductive vs. inductive models on, 118–119
  hedonic models of, 115, 190, 359, 360, 366, 370
  marginal, 426–427
  of mobile homes, 359–360
  most probable, *see* Most probable price model
  options model of, 107, 115
  of owner-occupied housing services, *see* Owner-occupied housing services price
  PHYS-FI model and, 206
  short-term transaction, 94
  tenure choice, 426–427
  value vs., 92
  wilderness appraisal and, 173–176
Principal component analysis, 392
Principle of Least Effort, 327
Prior information, *see* A priori information
PRMC, *see* Pack River Management Company
Probability analysis, 75–76, 80
Problem properties, 417
Productivity analysis, 76, 79, 83
Product mix, 224–225
Product synergy, 213, 221–225
Profit maximization, 78, 119, 149
Pro forma models, 393–394, 395, 396, 408
Project Reference Files, ULI, 210, 214, 216
Promotions, 314
Property markets, 46–47, 49
  commercial, 28, 29
Property rights paradigms, 77, 82–83
Property taxes, 428, 441
Public sector, 2, 54, 57, 78

Qualitative analysis, 21
Quality house price index, 435
Quality Pointscore, 241
Quantitative analysis, 21
Quantity demanded price, 427

Rancho Adolpho mobile home park, 354
Random sampling, 333
RARE, *see* Roadless Area Review and Evaluation
Ratcliff, Richard U., 2, 7, 69, 77, 120, 149, 239, 241, 242, 243, 250, 251
Rate of return
  financial management, 95
  internal, *see* Internal rate of return
  required, 428, 437–438
R&D space, 12, 465, 470–471, 472
Real estate and urban economics research (REUER), 107–127
  exclusivity of methodology in, 116–119
  industry-academia gap in, 109–113
  unexplained empirical results in, 113–116
Real estate appraisal, *see* Appraisal
Real Estate Appraisal Reform Act of 1987, 247
Real estate decisions, 15–60
  changing capital access and, 35–39

Real estate decisions (cont'd)
    historical context for, 23–27
    process and components of, 18
    real estate environment in, 27–33
    real estate markets and, 33–35
Real estate development process, 203, 204–206
Real estate discipline, 65–96, see also Academic real estate
    basis of, 72–74
    in business schools, 71–72
    issues in, 67–70
    paradigms in, 74–96
    philosophical basis of, 67–74
Real estate environment, 27–33
Real estate financial services, 28, 29
Real estate investment trusts, 38
Real estate market analysis, see Market analysis
Real estate markets, 33–35
Real estate process paradigms, 77–80, 81, 86, 88, 95
Real estate securitization, see Securitization
Real estate value, see Value
Realtor Code of Ethics, 416
Recessions, 24, 471
Refinancing, 212, 224
Regional science, 121
Regression analysis, see also Multiple regression analysis
    in market area delineation, 289
    in ownership transfer, 362, 363, 365, 374–379
Regulatory priority, 28, 29
Rehabilitation tax credit (RTC), 383, 387, 395, 403–404, 405, 406, 408, 410
Reilly's Law of Retail Gravitation, 9, 308, 309, see also Gravity models
Relational schemata, 228–230
Rent, 240
    asking, 463, 464
    contract, 12, 463, 464–465, 466, 470, 471, 472, 475, 478, 480
    definitions and measures of, 464–465
    effective, see Effective rent
    four-square design and, 263, 264, 268, 269, 278, 282, 283
    hedonic, 464

home ownership vs., 11, 425, 427, 428, 429, 430, 433, 435–437, 441, 447, 468, 469
    PHYS-FI model and, 211, 224
Rent abatement, 12, 463, 465, 466, 467, 470, 472, 475, 476, 480
Rent control, 9–10, 347–379, see also Ownership transfer
Rent escalation, 12, 466, 467, 475, 476
Rent theorists, 89, 90
Replacement costs, 239–240
Required rate of return, 428, 437–438
Residuals analysis, 335
Resource allocation, 82
Restaurants, 314
Retail shopping competition, 8–9, 307–324
    access variables in, 9, 312–314
    methodology used to explain, 309–311
    models used to describe, 308–309
    nonshopping factors in, 316–317
    safety and, 316–317
    selection and, 315–316
    time/money savings and, 316
REUER, see Real estate and urban economics research
Reversion, 224, 348
Rhetoric, 125–126
Risk management paradigms, 80–81, 82
Riverchase planned community, 220
Roadless Area Review and Evaluation (RARE), 162, 172
Rouse Company, 224
Rowes Wharf, 221, 226
R-41 regulation series, 7, 247–248
R-squared
    Central Place Theory and, 329
    effective rent and, 478
    logistic response function estimation and, 335
    mass appraisal and, 6, 183, 185, 186, 187, 189–190, 191, 192, 195, 196, 198, 200
    ownership transfer and, 367
RSVP cycles, 212
RTC, see Rehabilitation tax credit

Safety, retail shopping competition and, 316–317
Sales comparison approach
    alternatives to, 241

in wilderness appraisal, 151–152, 154, 158–161, 165, 174, 178
San Diego, California, 224
San Francisco, California, 223, 465
Santa Barbara, California, 349–350, 354, 355, 361, 363, 365, 369, 370
Santa Barbara Rent Control Ordinance, 370
Santa Clara, California, 12, 464, 465, 467, 470–477
Santa Maria, California, 354, 358, 359, 360, 361–363, 366, 368, 370
Sara Frances single-room-occupancy hotel, 224–225
Savings and loan industry, 25, 242, 245
Scaled bias, 191–192
Scaled mean absolute error, 6, 191–192, 194–195, 196, 200
Scaled standard error, 191–192, 196, 200
Scenic Quality System (SQS), 166, 167–170
Schematization, 212
Securitization, 34, 36, 38–39, 44
Segmentation
  customer spotting and, 295, 296, 302
  four-square design and, 266–267, 271, 278, 286
  PHYS-FI model and, 206
Seldin, Maury, 113
Sensitivity analysis, 382, 392, 406, *see also* Generalized Sensitivity Analysis
Service providers, 54, 57
Sheboygan Marina, 291–292, 294, 295, 300–301, 302
Sherway Gardens shopping center, 226–227
Short-term transaction price, 94
Shulman, David, 73
Signature quality, 223, 226, 231, 232
Sign tests, 195–196
Simulations, 124, *see also* Monte Carlo simulation
Simultaneous equation econometric models, 115
Site, 90–91
Situs paradigms, 88, 90
Size, 314, 327, 328, 338, 341
Social ecologists, 89
Society of Real Estate Appraisers, 250
Soft costs, 211–212

Solana Beach, California, 231
Solomon Brothers, 73
Solvency, 77, 149
  defined, 150
Solvency paradigms, 95–96
Sophisticated buyer defense, 417
Sophistications, 34
South America, 38
Soviet Union, 26
Space producers, 2, 78
Space-time paradigms, 4, 76–77, 81, 82, 84, 88
Space-time to money-time equations, 75–76, 80
Space use patterns, 16, 43–44
Space users, 2, 53, 56–57, 78
Spatial competition, 325
Spatial contact patterns, 115–116
Spatial economics, 72–73, 84
Spatial markets, 80, 81, 93, 115
Spatial market structure paradigms, 90–91
Spatial paradigms, 88–89
Spectral analysis, 329
Speculative building, 24, 25, 48
Spreadsheets, 48, 51
SQS, *see* Scenic Quality System
Standard deductions, 433
Standard error of estimate, 367, *see also* Scaled standard error
Statistical appraisal models, 190
Statistics of Income Data, 430
Stock Market Crash of 1929, 24
Stockton, California, 220
Stoney Brook residential complex, 231
Stoney Creek Villas, 230
Strict liability, 10–11, 414, 418–420
Strong inference models, 121–122, 123, 124
Suburban mall shopping, *see* Reta shopping competition
Summit mobile home park, 354, 355
Sum of squared errors, 185, 186–187
Sunk costs, 114
Supermarket shopping, 9, 325–326, 331–341, *see also* Logistic response function estimation
  visitation rates in, 329, 330, 331, 333, 338, 340
  weekly sales estimates in, 340–341

Supply factors, 115, *see also* Demand factors
 consumer surveys and, 302
 four-square design and, 259, 262, 263, 266, 268, 278–279, 286
 historical perspective on, 24
 land use succession paradigms and, 90
 real estate decisions and, 42, 48, 58
 real estate process paradigms and, 79
 urban land economic land use paradigms and, 87
Survey research, 109, 115, 116, *see also* Consumer surveys
Synectics, 212
Synthesis, 21, 23
Synthesis of misfits, 214
Synthesis of random facts, 214
Systematic design, 212
Systematic ranking, 214, 215
Systems thinking, 122–123

Tahitian Terrace mobile home park, 349–350, 355, 358
Tax Act of 1976, 433
Tax Act of 1981, 433
Tax Act of 1986, 433, 442
Taxes
 capital gains, *see* Capital gains taxes
 depreciation, 405
 historical perspective on, 24
 historic rehabilitation and, 10, 381–386, 394–395, 403–404, 405–406, 410
 income, *see* Income taxes
 marginal rates in, 429–433, 446, 451–453
 owner-occupied housing and, 11, 426–427, 437, 439, 447, 457–458
 property, 428, 441
 real estate decisions and, 29, 32, 35, 48, 54
 retail shopping competition and, 307
 tenure choice rates in, 429–433, 442, 451–453
Tax Reform Act (TRA) of 1981, 25
Tax Reform Act (TRA) of 1986, 383, 433
Technical innovation, 212
Tenant improvements
 effective rent and, 12, 466, 469, 470, 472, 475, 476–477, 480
 to mobile homes, 352

Tenants
 capture rates for, 267–268, 271
 four-square design profiles of, 267–268, 270–271, 272–273, 278–279, 282, 286
 space needs of, 53
Tenure choice decision, 425
Tenure choice price, 426–427
Tenure choice tax rates, 429–433, 442, 451–453
Tenure choice user costs, 442, 459–461
Thematic frameworks, 225–227
Thin markets, 114
Three-factor perspective, 71
Timber, 5–6, 151, 175
Time-distance boundaries, 289
Time-series analysis, 116, 125
Topographic fit, 216–219
Toronto, 226
TRA, *see* Tax Reform Act
Trailrancho Park, 358
Transaction costs, 114
 misrepresentation and, 418
 of owner-occupied housing services, 426, 427, 438, 439
 property rights paradigms and, 82
Transportation, 9, 42, 44, 312–313, 319
Transportation costs, 89, 90–91, 326, 352
Trapper's Alley, 226
Travel modeling, 9, 319, 327, 328
Treasury bond rates, 435, 438, 457–458, 469
Treetop Village, 225
Trend surface analysis, 328–329
Trophy properties, 38
T statistics, 196
Two-factor perspective, 71
Two-tiered markets, 38, 92

ULI, *see* Urban Land Institute
Uncertainty, choice under, 75–76, 83, 87, 93, 315, 327
Underground Atlanta shopping center, 224
Unemployment, 119
Unified field theory, 4, 95
Univariate sensitivity, of GSA, 388–389, 390, 391, 392, 403, 405
University and Technology Center, 222
University of Wisconsin, 2, 6, 109, 149, 151, 237–238, 243

INDEX

Urban economics, 70, 72, 79, 107, 108, 114, 117
Urban land economic land use paradigms, 87
Urban land economics, 1, 2, 70, 72, 73, 74, 77, 79
  business administration approach to, 81
  deductive vs. inductive models in, 119
  strengths and weaknesses of, 120–121
Urban Land Institute (ULI), 113, 149, 210, 214, 216
Urban structure paradigms, 88–89
Use mix, 313
User costs, 11, 425, 426, 446, 447
  alternate measures of affordability vs., 441–442
  marginal, 442, 459–461
  tenure choice, 442, 459–461
Utility theory, 6, 65–66, 204–206

Vacancy rates, 43, 54
  effective rent and, 463, 465, 470–471, 480
  four-square design on, 263, 264, 266, 268, 269, 270, 278, 282, 283, 286
  PHYS-FI model on, 211, 213, 214, 222, 228, 230
Valuation, 46–47, 48, 76, 158
  income capitalization approach to, 158
  in real estate process paradigms, 79
  sales comparison approach to, *see* Sales comparison approach
  in wilderness appraisal, 152–161
Value, 211, 212–213, *see also* Market value
  alternative methods to, 95
  appraisal and, 239–240
  cost approach to, 58, 185, 200, 239–240
  design differentials and, 213, 225–232
  diminished, 415–416
  environment and, 212, 213, 216–221
  historical perspective on, 239
  market approach to, 185, 200
  placement, 350
  price vs., 92
  product synergy and, 213, 221–225
  property rights and, 77
Value addivity, 95
Value paradigms, 91–93

Vancouver, Canada, 219, 229
Variety Class Assessment System (VCAS), 161, 162–163
Vector auto-regressive regression (VAR), 125
Venn diagrams, 70, 72, 82–83, 84
Veterans Administration loans, 245
View-It program, 171
Viewshed analysis, 165, 167, 170
Village Homes, 221–222
Visitor employed photography, 163, 167
Visual quality assessment, 162–163

Wall Street, 33, 39, 73, 238
Wall Street Journal, 26
WARS, *see* Wilderness Attribute Rating System
WAS, *see* Wilderness Attribute Score
Water context, 219–221
Watergrove apartment community, 214
Weak-form efficiency, 114
Weighted average cost of capital, 438
Weighted least squares stepwise regression, 335, 336–337, 340
WES, *see* Wilderness Evaluation System
Westlake Village, California, 350, 355, 361, 363, 365, 369, 370
Westlake Village Rent Control Ordinance, 370
Wilderness Act of 1964, 161–162, 172, 179
Wilderness and Scenic Beauty Evaluation, 179
Wilderness appraisal, 5–6, 149–179
  application of, 172–177
  natural integrity in, 162, 165
  primitive recreation opportunities in, 162, 165–167
  solitude opportunities in, 162, 165
  valuation in, 152–161
  visual quality assessment in, 162–163
Wilderness Attribute Rating System (WARS), 161, 162–163, 165, 170
Wilderness Attribute Score (WAS), 172, 174
Wilderness components, 161–163
  enhancement of, 163–172
Wilderness Evaluation System (WES), 163–165, 170–172, 174, 175, 178, 179
Wilderness Gulf Coast, 226

Wilshire Courtyard, 223
Wisconsin, 206, 420, *see also* specific areas of
Women's clothing stores, 313

World War II, 24

York Green office complex, 231